THE RISE AND FALL OF APARTHEID

D1596667

DATE DUE

GAYLORD	PRINTED IN U.S.A.

Reconsiderations in Southern African History

RICHARD ELPHICK, EDITOR

Milton Shain, *The Roots of Antisemitism in South Africa*

Timothy Keegan, *Colonial South Africa and the Origins of the Racial Order*

Ineke van Kessel, *"Beyond Our Wildest Dreams": The United Democratic Front and the Transformation of South Africa*

Benedict Carton, *Blood from Your Children: The Colonial Origins of Generational Conflict in South Africa*

Diana Wylie, *Starving on a Full Stomach: Hunger and the Triumph of Cultural Racism in Modern South Africa*

Jeff Guy, *The View across the River: Harriette Colenso and the Zulu Struggle against Imperialism*

John Edwin Mason, *Social Death and Resurrection: Slavery and Emancipation in South Africa*

Hermann Giliomee, *The Afrikaners: Biography of a People* (first and second editions)

Tim Couzens, *Murder at Morija: Faith, Mystery, and Tragedy on an African Mission*

Diana Wylie, *Art and Revolution: The Life and Death of Thami Mnyele, South African Artist*

David Welsh, *The Rise and Fall of Apartheid*

THE RISE AND FALL OF APARTHEID

David Welsh

UNIVERSITY OF VIRGINIA PRESS
CHARLOTTESVILLE

To the memory of Helen Suzman

Published jointly in 2009 in trade paperback by
Jonathan Ball Publishers (Pty) Ltd
PO Box 33977
Jeppestown, 2043
South Africa
and
University of Virginia Press
PO Box 400318
Charlottesville, VA 22904-4318
USA

ISBN 978-0-8139-3056-5

Cover design by Michiel Botha, Cape Town
Cover images by Africa Media Online
Text design by Triple M Design, Johannesburg
Map by Cartocom, Pretoria
Printed and bound by CTP Printers, Cape

Set in 10.75/13pt Sabon MT Std

Cataloging-in-Publication Data is available from the Library of Congress

Contents

Preface

South Africa's transition from a racial oligarchy to an inclusive democracy was one of the most remarkable processes of the late twentieth century. Few believed that it would occur as soon – and as relatively peacefully – as it did. The transition belied gloomy predictions of race war in which the white minority went into a laager and fought 'to the last drop of blood'.

This book examines the historical processes underlying the transition. That there were 'turning points', or seminal events, is undoubted. The Soweto Uprising of 1976 is an example. Perhaps a metaphor with greater explanatory force would be that of a river rising as a stream, fed along its course by tributaries, gathering force until it finally comes up against the dam wall. The wall has been steadily eroding as the power of the water mounts – and then? Does the wall break, or are the sluice gates opened to relieve the pressure? Did white South Africa crack, or did its leadership yield sufficiently and just in time to avert a revolution?

A note on terminology: Notoriously, labelling South Africa's diverse groups is a minefield, because much terminology is politically loaded. I have used 'Afrikaner' to denote people who, during the nineteenth century and before, were referred to as Dutch or Boers. 'Afrikaner' came into general usage only in the twentieth century. Similarly, the language of the Trekker republics in state and pulpit was High Dutch, although ordinary people spoke an earthy and vigorous mutation called Afrikaans, which replaced Dutch as an official language in 1925.

Following the practice maintained in contemporary South Africa, I use the terms African, Coloured, Indian and white to describe the components of the population. I have avoided altogether (except in quotations) the term 'non-white', which is widely deemed to be offensive. When referring collectively to the African, Coloured and Indian categories I use the term 'black', although I am aware many Coloured and Indian people do not like it. It seemed, however, to be the lesser of two evils.

I thank the following people who have helped me by providing information or criticising particular chapters:

Patrick Allitt, Ken Andrew, Breyten Breytenbach, Ebbe Dommisse, John Dugard, Colin Eglin, Hermann Giliomee, André Jaquet, Anthea Jeffery, Ronnie Kasrils, Derek Keys, Trevor Manuel, Johann Maree, Roelf Meyer, Ampie Muller, Michael Savage, Lawrence Schlemmer, James Selfe, Milton Shain, Jack Spence, Dave Steward, Richard Steyn, Stanley Uys, Chris van der Merwe, Van Zyl Slabbert, Francois Venter, Constand Viljoen, Carl von Hirschberg, Peter Wilkes, Oliver Williams, and Roger Williams.

Since this book is, in parts, controversial, it should be stressed that none of the listed people bears responsibility for my conclusions, with which some – perhaps many – will disagree. They are absolved from any complicity in errors, factual or ideological, that I may have made.

Warm thanks to Frances Perryer for meticulous editing of the manuscript.

My biggest debts of gratitude go to my wife, Virginia van der Vliet, who has been my frontline critic and main source of inspiration, and my daughter Catherine, who typed the seemingly interminable manuscript efficiently and cheerfully.

David Welsh
RONDEBOSCH, JANUARY 2009

Abbreviations

AAC	All Africa Convention
AB	Afrikaner Broederbond
AVF	Afrikaner Volksfront
AHI	Afrikaanse Handelsinstituut
ANC	African National Congress
ANCYL	ANC Youth League
AP	Afrikaner Party
Apla	Azanian People's Liberation Army
Assocom	Association of South African Chambers of Commerce
Azapo	Azanian People's Organisation
BC	Black Consciousness
BOSS	Bureau of State Security
CCB	Civil Co-operation Bureau
Codesa	Convention for a Democratic South Africa
Contralesa	Congress of Traditional Leaders of South Africa
Cosag	Concerned South Africans Group
Cosas	Congress of South African Students
Cosatu	Congress of South African Trade Unions
CP	Conservative Party
CPRC	Coloured Persons' Representative Council
CPSA	Communist Party of South Africa
Cradora	Cradock Residents' Association
DP	Democratic Party
EPG	Commonwealth Eminent Persons Group
FA	Freedom Alliance
FCI	Federated Chamber of Industries
Fosatu	Federation of South African Trade Unions

GNU	Government of National Unity
HNP	Herstigte Nasionale Party
ICU	Industrial and Commercial Workers' Union of South Africa
IEC	Independent Electoral Commission
IFP	Inkatha Freedom Party
JMC	Joint Management Centre
LP	Labour Party
Mawu	Metal and Allied Workers Union
MDM	Mass Democratic Movement
MK	Umkhonto we Sizwe
MPLA	Movimento Popular de Libertação de Angola
MPNP	Multiparty Negotiating Process
NAC	National Action Committee
Nactu	National Council of Trade Unions
NEC	ANC National Executive Committee
NGK	Nederduitse Gereformeede Kerk
O-B	Ossewa-Brandwag
NIS	National Intelligence Service
NNC	Native National Congress
NP	National Party
NPA	National Peace Accord
NUM	National Union of Mineworkers
Nusas	National Union of South African Students
PAC	Pan-Africanist Congress
PR	proportional representation
PWV	Pretoria-Witwatersrand-Vereeniging
RDP	Reconstruction and Development Programme
RSC	Regional Services Council
SABC	South African Broadcasting Corporation
Sabra	South African Bureau of Racial Affairs
Sactu	South African Congress of Trade Unions
SADF	South African Defence Force
SAP	South African Police
SAP	South African Party
SASM	South African Students Movement
SASO	South African Students Organisation
SCC	Special Cabinet Committee
SPR	States, Provinces and Regions
SSC	State Security Council
Swapo	South West Africa People's Organisation
TEC	Transitional Executive Council

TRC	Truth and Reconciliation Commission
UCM	University Christian Movement
UDF	United Democratic Front
Unita	União Nacional para a Independência Total de Angola
UP	United Party
Uwusa	United Workers of South Africa

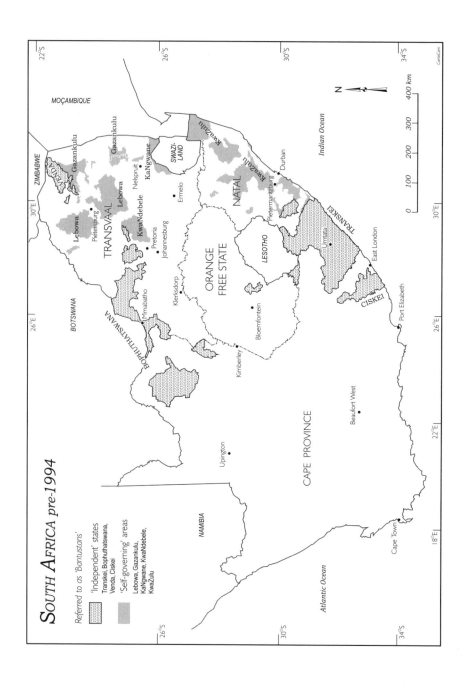

SOUTH AFRICA *pre-1994*

Referred to as 'Bantustans'

'Independent' states
Transkei, Bophuthatswana,
Venda, Ciskei

'Self-governing' areas
Lebowa, Gazankulu,
KaNgwane, KwaNdebele,
KwaZulu

MOÇAMBIQUE

ZIMBABWE

BOTSWANA

NAMIBIA

Atlantic Ocean

Indian Ocean

N

400 km

0 100 200 300

TRANSVAAL

VENDA

Gazankulu

Gazankulu

Lebowa

Lebowa

Lebowa

KwaNdebele

KaNgwane

SWAZI-
LAND

KwaZulu

KwaZulu

NATAL

LESOTHO

ORANGE
FREE STATE

BOPHUTHATSWANA

CAPE PROVINCE

TRANSKEI

CISKEI

Nelspruit

Ermelo

Pretoria

Johannesburg

Pietersburg

Klerksdorp

Mmabatho

Kimberley

Bloemfontein

Pietermaritzburg

Durban

Umtata

East London

Port Elizabeth

Beaufort West

Upington

Cape Town

18°E   22°E   26°E   30°E

22°S

26°S

30°S

34°S

CartoCom

CHAPTER I

Afrikaner Nationalism and the Coming of Apartheid

On Friday, 28 May 1948, South Africa awoke to astonishing election news: the National Party had clawed its way to power. In alliance with the small Afrikaner Party (AP), the NP had won the 26 May ballot by the narrowest of majorities: five seats – 79 seats for the NP–AP alliance compared to 65 for the defeated United Party (UP), six for its ally, the Labour Party (LP), and three 'Native Representatives' (elected on a separate voters' roll), who would certainly vote against the incoming government. 'Now we feel at home again in our own country,' proclaimed DF Malan, the NP leader and Prime Minister-elect.

The portents of this upset – only the second change of government via the ballot box since 1910 – had been visible for some time. Since 1939 the UP government, led by the Boer general JC Smuts, had been pre-occupied with the Second World War. It had won a comprehensive victory in the 'khaki' election of 1943, when Afrikaner nationalists were fighting viciously among themselves. But, beginning in 1944, signs appeared that the tide was turning against Smuts's party. The resignation of several MPs and supporters in protest against the UP's lack of a clearcut colour policy, and a series of by-election defeats or victories with much-reduced majorities, should have punctured the UP's complacency, but the assumption of invincibility continued. The illusion that Afrikaner nationalists would always squabble among themselves was widespread in UP circles, and with it the comforting corollary that this would thwart their political unity. It was a fatal misjudgement.

The underlying factor in the NP–AP victory in 1948 was the resurgence of Afrikaner unity. DF Malan, the 74-year-old patriarch who led the NP and now became Prime Minister, entitled his autobiography *Afrikaner Volk Unity and My Experiences on the Way to It* (translation).[1] As the title suggests, Afrikaner unity was not automatic, despite a substantial cultural commonality, a sense of racial identity, and, to some extent, a shared historical experience. Unity had to be forged, and it was no easy task.

The first stirrings of a sense of Afrikaner nationalism began in the last third of the nineteenth century as a response to the tightening grip of British imperialism. In a polemic published shortly after the outbreak of the Anglo-Boer War in 1899 Smuts, then state attorney of the Transvaal Republic, itemised with clinical detail and cold fury the injustices done by British 'capitalistic jingoism' to Afrikaners. Of the period after the discovery of gold on the Transvaal highveld in 1886, he wrote:

> [It] is characterised by the amalgamation of the old and well-known policy of fraud and violence with the new forces of Capitalism, which had developed so powerfully owing to the mineral riches of the South African Republic [the official name of the Transvaal]. Our existence as a people and as a State is now threatened by an unparalleled combination of forces. Arrayed against us we find numerical strength, the public opinion of the United Kingdom thirsting and shouting for blood and revenge, the world-wide and cosmopolitan power of Capitalism, and all the forces which underlie the lust of robbery and the spirit of plunder.[2]

This was strong stuff, and typical of the tone of the book. Famously and ironically Smuts made his peace with the British in the aftermath of the Anglo-Boer War (1899–1902) and became a strong protagonist of the Empire, earning for himself the sneering description 'handyman of the Empire'.

The war resulted in the comprehensive defeat of the Transvaal and its ally the Orange Free State. To expedite the ending of hostilities the British Army resorted to 'scorched earth' policies and to the internment of Boer women and children. In both republics the great majority of farmsteads were destroyed, and an estimated 28 000 women and children died in the concentration camps into which they were herded. These were the 'methods of barbarism' referred to by Sir Henry Campbell-Bannerman, the British Liberal leader, who became Prime Minister in 1905 and in 1906–7 granted self-government to the defeated republics, now British colonies.

The war and its aftermath was a huge stimulus to Afrikaner nationalism. Even in the Cape Colony, whose Afrikaner population was, on the whole, reasonably content under British rule, sympathy with the Boer republics was profound, though not sufficiently profound to provoke an uprising in support of their ethnic kin. Nevertheless, between 6 000 and 7 000 rebels defied British authorities and joined the Boer commandos, and 30 were executed.[3]

In the post-war period Lord Milner, High Commissioner for South Africa from 1897 to 1905 and the leading warmonger prior to 1899, determined to make South Africa 'British' by deliberate efforts to anglicise Afrikaners and by promoting the large-scale immigration of British to the Transvaal. Neither project succeeded, but the attempts increased bitterness among the Boers.

The war cast a long shadow over white politics. Even by 1948, 46 years after the Treaty of Vereeniging had concluded peace, many *oudstryders* (war veterans) were still alive; indeed, two – Smuts himself and NC Havenga, leader of the Afrikaner Party – were prominent politicians. Few Afrikaner families had been unaffected, whether directly or indirectly, by the war. PW Botha, who became an MP in 1948, recounted how his mother had been attacked by an armed black soldier on their Orange Free State farm. She managed to escape with her young sister and two toddlers, but the farmstead was destroyed.[4]

'Why should we fight Britain's wars?' was a question that struck a resonant chord in the minds of many republican Afrikaners in both 1914 and 1939 when South Africa fought alongside the Allies against Germany. In 1914 South Africa's entry into the First World War precipitated a rebellion among Afrikaners, including senior members of the Defence Force, who were protesting against participation in the war in general, and South Africa's occupation of German South West Africa (today Namibia) in particular. The outbreak of the Second World War in 1939 prompted even greater polarisation, which had direct effects on the outcome of the 1948 election.

The granting of self-government – in 1906 and 1907, respectively – to the Transvaal and the Orange River Colony (as it was now officially termed) paved the way for the political mobilisation of Afrikaners, and, in 1909, the unification of South Africa. Paradoxically, although the Anglo-Boer War had been the stimulus for unprecedented Afrikaner unity, its aftermath and the creation of a South Africa-wide parliamentary system also created the conditions for a divergence in Afrikaner political thinking that was to dominate white politics until at least the 1950s. An electoral political system had been established in which, as Smuts once observed, the fight was among Afrikaners over what attitude they should take to the English.[5] There were implications in this for colour policy.

The issue that presented itself to Afrikaner leaders in the immediate pre- and post-Union period can be stated crisply: should the white 'nation', made up of Boer and Brit, consist of 'one stream' or 'two streams'? The one-stream approach, also known as 'conciliation', was associated with Louis Botha, a Boer general who emerged as the leading Afrikaner politician after 1902 and became the unified South Africa's first Prime Minister in 1910. The 'two-stream' policy was identified with JBM Hertzog, also a Boer general, the principal Afrikaner leader in the Orange River Colony.

Conciliation, as propounded by Botha and his right-hand man Smuts, was never precisely defined, but it meant that enmity between Boer and Brit should be transcended in a spirit of mutual toleration and co-operation. Botha and Smuts 'believed that the wounds of war, as well as the passions which had caused the war, could best be healed by emphasising the things which the two sections of the European people held in common'. Hertzog, on the other hand, 'felt himself specially called to assert the rights of the section which had suffered defeat .... Why should Botha conciliate them? It was his business to fight them!'[6]

The issue turned principally on language rights: section 137 of the Union Constitution guaranteed equality of status to English and Dutch. Even before 1910 Hertzog had emerged as a champion of language equality by insisting on compulsory bilingualism in white schools. Botha and Smuts, while not unmindful of the rights of Afrikaners, were in a politically constrained position that was entirely different from Hertzog's: the white population of the Orange Free State was overwhelmingly Afrikaans; in the Transvaal the two white segments were roughly equal, and to gain power Het Volk, Botha's and Smuts's party, had to acquire the support of a significant percentage of English-speaking voters. Hertzog was cheered on by his constituency; Botha had to soft-pedal the language issue because the principle that was at the core of Hertzog's position, compulsory bilingualism, was unpopular among a large section of the English-speakers (this attitude continued after 1910).

For many English, 'Hertzogism' had replaced 'Krugerism' as the object of furious opposition. FV Engelenburg observed in his biography of Botha:

> The English-speaking section proceeded in the expectation that the subjugation of the Boer States, among other beneficial results, had also brought about unilingualism (English) for the whole of South Africa .... Every suspicion of compulsion led to hyper-indignation and strongly affected the political attitude of the man on the street.[7]

The attitudes of many English-speakers were typical of the imperial arrogance accompanying conquest. They riled Afrikaners and strengthened their resolve to win the peace and regain sovereign independence, even if they had lost the war.

Language was critical since it was the vehicle of Afrikaner nationalist aspirations and the emblem of their identity as a *volk*, but other issues were closely associated and were to constitute much of the stuff of Afrikaner politics for many decades. Hertzog's slogan, 'South Africa First', encapsulated many of the nationalists' grievances and aspirations. It meant that South Africa's interests should take precedence over those of the Empire, and, as a corollary, that South Africa should be governed by those 'imbued with the South African spirit' and not by those he contemptuously called 'foreign fortune-seekers', referring to English-speakers who, although living in South Africa, regarded Britain as 'home', showed greater loyalty to the Empire than to South Africa, and typically viewed Afrikaner rights with contempt.

Then there were questions of status: did South Africa have the right to secede from the Empire? And could South Africa renounce the King? In both cases Smuts's answer was an unequivocal no. Both he and Botha had accommodated themselves easily to the Empire. Indeed, Botha had been seduced by the charms of the metropole's pomp and circumstance, even donating the immensely valuable Cullinan diamond to King Edward VII in 1907 as a token of the Transvaal's loyalty to the Crown.

After 1910 Botha and Smuts found themselves increasingly in a bind: they needed the support of English voters, but Hertzog's strident advocacy of Afrikaner votes alienated them. After Hertzog had been dropped from the Cabinet in 1912 and set about forming the National Party in 1914, he was able to give free rein to his nationalist views, which were given a considerable fillip by South Africa's entry into the First World War, the suppression of the rebellion in 1914, and the foolish execution, at Smuts's behest, of Jopie Fourie, an army officer who had joined the rebels without resigning his commission.

At the NP's first trial of strength in the parliamentary elections of October 1915 it made deep inroads into Botha's and Smuts's South African Party (SAP), winning 27 seats compared to the SAP's 54, but attracting over 78 000 votes, compared with the SAP's 93 000. The SAP sustained major losses in the *platteland* (country areas) and was comprehensively beaten in Hertzog's stamping ground, the Orange Free State. The Unionist Party, unambiguously the party of the Empire connection and among the foremost critics of Hertzogism, substantially maintained its position, winning 40 seats and 48 000 votes.

An estimated 40 per cent of Afrikaner voters had supported the NP. The die in parliamentary politics had been cast: if a substantial majority of Afrikaners could be persuaded to vote for the NP, together with some (distinctly minority) support from English-speakers, then the NP could gain control of government. Hertzog, although never anti-English in the way that some of his successors were to be, recognised this. The Afrikaners' slight demographic edge over the English was growing, but there were two potential problems. First, large-scale immigration, mostly from Britain, could tip the scales against Afrikaner nationalists (exactly the same issue surfaced in the 1948 election). Second, and of even greater consequence, there was the possibility that the limited common voters' roll voting rights (supposedly) secured to African and Coloured males in the Cape in the compromise of Union could be enlarged, either by extension to the other provinces of the principle of the non-racial qualified franchise (a remote possibility), or by the rapid growth in the number of registered African and Coloured voters in the Cape. This, in turn, would mean the enlargement of a sizeable anti-NP voting bloc. Much of the first phase of the post-1948 period would be devoted to the elimination of the Coloured vote as a factor in 'white' politics.

The election in 1920 confirmed that the tide was flowing towards the NP and away from the SAP, now led by Smuts, Botha having died in 1919. Even with the support of the Unionists, Smuts's majority had shrunk to four. In a further election called in February 1921 the SAP, having absorbed the Unionists, gained a slight but only temporary reprieve. The Unionists, despite having muted their jingoistic image, had realised that as a purely English party they had no hope of winning power except in alliance with 'the moderate Dutch', as one of their members put it.

For Smuts, though, accepting the Unionists into the SAP fold, and giving three of their leading lights Cabinet portfolios in 1921, came at a price: confirmation for the Nationalists that he was a captive of Empire and its local acolytes. To this charge would be added in 1922 the additional one that he was also a captive of the 'geldmag' – literally 'the money-power', in the form of the mining houses whose attempts to lower costs by increasing the ratio of African to white mineworkers resulted in the general strike of 1922, whose suppression cost over 150 lives.

Since over 75 per cent of the white miners were Afrikaners, most of them with strong nationalist sympathies, it was hardly surprising that the strike led to a growing rapprochement between the NP and the English-led Labour Party, whose support-base nevertheless included a growing number of the rapidly urbanising Afrikaner working class. In April 1923 the rapprochement was transformed into a pact between Hertzog and FHP Creswell, leader of the LP, whereby common cause would be made against Smuts's SAP in the next election.

That election, in 1924, gave a comfortable victory to the NP–LP Pact and Hertzog was installed as Prime Minister, an office he would hold until September 1939. For the first time the NP decisively beat the SAP in terms of seats: 63 to 52; but SAP votes far exceeded those for the NP: 148 000 to 111 500. This reflected one of the anomalies of the single-member constituency 'first-past-the-post' electoral system agreed to at Union. The SAP could win by huge majorities in its urban strongholds, whereas the NP won more seats but with, on average, smaller majorities. The distortions were exacerbated, to the disadvantage of the SAP, by another feature of the system, also agreed to at Union, that rural constituencies – where the NP's strength lay – could be 'unloaded' (reducing the number of voters in a constituency) up to 15 per cent below the quota or average numerical size of constituencies per province, as determined by the Delimitation Commission.[8] Clearly the effect was to give over-representation to rural areas.

By the time of the following election in 1929, the LP had split, and although the NP won an outright majority over all other parties (and substantially increased the number of votes it won to over 141 000), the Pact was retained. The most significant feature of the election was the NP's resort to *swart gevaar* (black peril) electioneering tactics on an unprecedented scale.

Until the early 1920s there was a tacit agreement among the parties that colour policy ought to be kept out of party politics. Indeed, at the time of Union and for more than a decade afterwards, the agreement was underpinned by a substantial consensus across party lines that segregation was the appropriate policy towards Africans. One of the first major segregationist laws, the Natives Land Act of 1913, which prevented Africans from buying land outside certain 'scheduled' reserves, was passed with hardly a dissenting parliamentary voice. Likewise, there were few white politicians who challenged the basis of urban policy, namely that Africans who entered the cities and towns were 'temporary sojourners', and not part of the permanent urban population.

The 1929 election shattered the view that colour issues should be kept out of party politics, and suggested that the consensus on policy was, if not dead, then at least seriously ruptured. The election demonstrated also that *swart gevaar* electioneering was an effective tactic for winning votes. Over 80 per cent of all Afrikaner voters supported the NP.[9]

The background was Hertzog's decision in 1926 to begin seriously implementing political segregation by abolishing the right of qualified African males in the Cape Province to vote on the common voters' roll. The problem was that this right was contained in one of the two clauses (the other concerned language equality) 'entrenched' in the Union Constitution that could be amended only by a two-thirds majority of both the House of Assembly and the Senate sitting together – which the NP, despite significant support from SAP MPs, notably those from Natal, was unable to achieve. Hertzog would have to wait until 1936, when the landscape of parliamentary politics had changed dramatically, to attain his goal.

Hopes that the exponential growth of the NP was unstoppable after the 1929 election were to be dashed very soon. The Great Depression that began in 1929 hit South Africa with a vengeance, conditions being made worse by some of the worst droughts in living memory in the early 1930s. Economic decline was aggravated by Hertzog's and NC Havenga's (his trusted friend and Minister of Finance) refusal to follow Britain's example and leave the gold standard. It was less an economically motivated decision than a futile effort to demonstrate South Africa's financial independence, which nevertheless had to be abandoned in December 1932.

Rural distress among whites had assumed alarming proportions. The 'poor white' problem, already discernible in the late nineteenth century, immensely exacerbated by the Anglo-Boer War and festering throughout the early decades of Union, now became a crisis. (That African rural distress was of even greater proportions was predictably adjudged by white politicians to be a lesser concern.) A major investigation by the Carnegie Commission showed that of the white population, approximately 1.8 million in 1931, over 300 000 were 'very poor'. Since the great majority of poor whites were Afrikaners this meant that nearly one-third of all Afrikaners were afflicted by deepening poverty. Moreover, the Commission pointed out, these figures had been obtained in 1929/30 before the effects of the Depression were particularly noticeable.[10]

The political consequences of the economic situation were soon felt. From early 1930 into 1933 the NP and the faction of the LP that remained in the coalition suffered losses and reduced majorities in by-elections. It was evident that rank-and-file voters were becoming impatient with party political conflict which seemed only to worsen their economic plight.

Hertzog realised by early 1933 that the NP could not win the next election on its own. Smuts had suggested that the crisis demanded a 'national government' of the two major parties. Hertzog responded with initial caution, convincing himself that were Smuts's offer not acted upon he, Smuts, would be driven into the arms of the extreme jingoes like the Natal Devolutionists and Federalists, thus 'giving the Afrikaans language and Afrikanerdom an irreparable blow'.[11] Hertzog had also convinced himself, to the dismay of his more radical colleagues, that since the Balfour

Declaration of 1926, whereby the Imperial Conference declared the Dominions to be 'autonomous communities within the British Empire, equal in status, in no way subordinate the one to the other', the issue of South Africa's status had been satisfactorily resolved. Indeed, it was useful to South Africa to retain membership. Moreover, attaining a republic was not 'practical politics', and he angrily repudiated republican colleagues.[12]

During the protracted negotiations with Smuts for the formation of a coalition government, the mutterings about Hertzog's dilution of his nationalist principles increased. DF Malan, leader of the Cape NP and a minister in Hertzog's Cabinet since 1924, was deeply unhappy about these developments. Despite some wobbly moments, he acquiesced in the coalition agreement of 1933, but, under intense pressure from the influential pro-NP Cape Town newspaper *Die Burger* and its editor, Dr AL Geyer, Malan became the focus of NP opposition to the next stage of negotiations with Hertzog and Smuts, namely the fusion of the NP and the SAP into the United South African National Party, commonly known as the United Party.

The NP–SAP coalition had won a smashing victory in the 1933 election, winning 136 seats (plus two for the minuscule LP faction that supported coalition) out of 150. Even the breakaway of the Malanites or '*gesuiwerdes*' ('purified ones') over fusion in 1934 did little to dent the UP's huge majority: the 'purified' NP held only 27 seats countrywide, 20 of these being in the Cape, six in the Orange Free State, and one in the Transvaal (the latter being represented by JG Strijdom, 'the Lion of the North', who was to become one of the most formidable of the radical nationalists).

'*Skeuring*', the Afrikaans word for 'split', has a sharper connotation than its English translation, having been invested with profound emotional significance for Afrikaner nationalism. Piet Cillié, another formidable editor of *Die Burger*, writes of *skeuring* that it causes

> ... a shock, a wound, a trauma with enduring consequences. It becomes the signal for a cold civil war. No political struggle can be more bitter and malicious. It divides families, relatives, neighbours and communities. It activates old tensions and adversaries that were kept in check in the previous framework. It has the character of a stormy divorce in which commonly an evil heap of hidden dirt from the past is pushed to the surface.[13]

Out of this cauldron emerged a more rigid, uncompromising and ideologically driven form of Afrikaner nationalism. The doctrine of apartheid was to develop in this context.

*   *   *

It is necessary to stand back from the chronology of Afrikaner nationalism's rise and explore aspects of the Afrikaners' social and economic situation, some of which have been mentioned. After 1902 the Afrikaners of the defeated Trekker republics displayed many of the symptoms of a conquered people: impoverished, defeated, despairing, low in morale, and with a powerfully internalised inferiority complex. They were facing the possible obliteration of their identity by the overwhelming power of their conqueror's institutions and culture. For many the possibility of rebuilding farms was non-existent. Hence, the major demographic phenomenon (apart from lives lost during the war) was the trek to the towns. At the time of Union in 1910 only 25 per cent of Afrikaners were urban (living in towns with 5 000 or more inhabitants); by 1936 the percentage was 40, by 1948 approximately 65, and by 1960, 75. 'Back to the Land' strategies had little or no effect, despite widespread nostalgia among urban Afrikaners for the *platteland* (countryside).

The townward trek posed new challenges: few of the newly urbanised possessed skills appropriate to an industrialising society. Most of the bigger cities were English-dominated, and English was the language of commerce and industry. Moreover, many Afrikaner leaders portrayed the urban Afrikaners' plight as a deadly battle with blacks, who were also urbanising rapidly and who worked for far lower wages than those demanded for 'civilised labour' (the official term for poor whites who were given preferential treatment for work in the public service and private sector in accordance with a policy laid down in 1926).

In a speech commemorating the Battle of Blood River in 1838, when a small group of Voortrekkers defeated a Zulu army, DF Malan used emotive language to portray the urban Afrikaners' parlous situation:

> ... a no less disturbing fact [than the outnumbering of whites by blacks] is that at this new Blood River of our *volk* white and non-white meet in much closer contact with one another and in the grip of a much closer conflict than 100 years ago when the circle of tented wagons protected the laager and rifle and assegaai clattered against each other.[14]

Part of the struggle was the perceived threat of a breakdown of colour distinctions in the cosmopolitan environment of the city. A commission set up by the Nederduitse Gereformeerde Kerk, the biggest of the three Dutch Reformed Churches, echoed what was a frequent refrain among Nationalist politicians, cultural organisations and academics:

> Strict *racial apartheid* in the agrarian lifestyle stands opposed to the danger of *race-mixing* in the towns. The ingrained Boer tradition of blood-purity and a hatred of any social intercourse with non-whites was their means of self-preservation in the century that has passed. But urban poverty is a powerful means of eliminating the dividing line between white and black. In the slums all races live next to one another, sometimes in the same large building. And they work alongside one another in the same factory. Urban employers are people who are far less concerned with the maintenance of the dividing line of colour than the Afrikaner; they want the cheapest labour, regardless of colour or race; it is of little concern to them that the colour feeling of the Afrikaner is blunted in this way.[15]

Rapid social change, poverty, including the substantial economic inequality between Afrikaners and the English, and perceived threats to Afrikaner identity were the crucible from which the new, radical ('purified' in the Nationalists' terminology) Afrikaner nationalism emerged. The break from Hertzog, moreover, afforded the Nationalists the opportunity, which they gratefully seized, of engaging in the politics of ethnic outbidding: which party represented the 'true' soul of Afrikanerdom, and who was the 'real' leader of the *volk*? The new United Party's ambivalent attitude to the retention of symbols of the British connection and the question of a republic enabled the Nationalists to corner the market in making propaganda for the attainment of these goals.

How ethnic outbidding could affect issues of colour policy was demonstrated by the Nationalists' behaviour in 1936 when, at last, Hertzog, with his new-found colleagues, was able to muster the required two-thirds majority for the abolition of the Cape African franchise. While supporting the legislation, Malan proposed, by way of amendments, that Coloured voters, whose rights were unaffected by Hertzog's bill, should be given limited, separate representation, that there should be no representation of Africans whatever in Parliament, that the proposal for a (purely advisory) Natives Representative Council be abandoned, and that the bill providing for the 'release' of more land for the African reserves be rejected. It was classic *swart gevaar* politicking, and a model for the future. Especially after 1939, when Smuts had become Prime Minister and the fusion government had split on the issue of entry into war, when so-called 'native policy' appeared to be drifting aimlessly and the tempo of African urbanisation increased dramatically, the scope for the NP to indulge in *swart gevaar* politics widened, building up to a crescendo in the campaign preceding the 1948 election.

One of the 'historical paranoias' (the phrase is Piet Cillié's) of Afrikaner nationalism had long been the belief that the perfidious British would use the issue of black rights, and their violation by Afrikaners, as a stick with which to beat Afrikaners. In a speech to an NP Congress in 1938 Malan elaborated on this view:

> Imperialist interests of Empire in South Africa concern themselves with nothing more than retention of the British connection and domination of the 'British mind' and the British race, and it is for this reason that spoors of blood have been deeply impressed on the history of our *volk*. It was that interest, which from the inception gave the franchise to the native and the Coloured on an equal basis with the white man, not on merit or from principle – but with the specific purpose of using it as a counter-weight to the Boers' struggle for nationhood. That Imperial interest of Empire is still playing its role in South Africa. And as long as it is not defeated by the power of awakened and united Afrikanerdom, it will always, just as now, attempt to win the sympathy and support of the non-white races by tempting them with the idea of equality and by holding up to them segregation as a grievance. Friendship with the Imperialist in South Africa has always appeared to be hostility to white control and indifference to the survival of the white race.[16]

It was a telling message for a receptive audience, but it was hardly an accurate portrayal of imperial interests, whose indifference to black rights had nowhere been more graphically illustrated than in the neglect of them in the defeated Republics after 1902 (which even Milner came to regret), and the enactment of the racially discriminatory South Africa Act in 1909, which embodied the Union Constitution. Moreover, most of the strongest proponents of the Imperial connection among the South African English, especially those in Natal, held racial views that were as reactionary as those of their Nationalist counterparts.

The radical nationalism of the 1930s and 1940s incorporated the gains that Hertzog had made for Afrikaans and Afrikaners in the public service, as well as those relating to South Africa's status as a dominion in the Empire; but Malan and his party wished to go much further. If

Hertzog had satisfied himself that his attainments had been sufficient to move beyond the 'two-stream' approach, the NP denied this, adopting a more exclusive Afrikaner nationalism and pursuing the goal of reuniting Afrikaners with single-minded zeal. The strategy involved detaching '*smelters*' (those Afrikaners who had followed Hertzog into fusion) and '*Bloedsappe*' (literally 'blood-SAPs', meaning Afrikaners who had traditionally followed Botha and Smuts) from the UP and recruiting them for the NP cause.

The corollary of this strategy was the prevention of what was referred to as 'denationalisation', meaning the loss of Afrikaner identity, especially in the cosmopolitan cities, where being an Afrikaner – apart from any lack of skills – was a disadvantage in the Anglophone realm of business. It was of critical importance that working-class Afrikaners did not allow their consciousness as Afrikaners to be eclipsed by class-consciousness. A historian of Afrikaner nationalism, GD Scholtz, wrote that there were ominous portents of this phenomenon, and even that the first steps towards *rapprochement* and eventual assimilation with the black proletariat were evident. It was essential, therefore, that class differences among Afrikaners should not be allowed to jeopardise the unity of the group.[17]

The renewed and sharpened 'two-stream' approach of the NP had both strategic and organisational consequences. Strategically the belief was that the mobilisation and strengthening of Afrikaner power required the establishment of an exclusive Afrikaner bloc consisting of component spheres in which Afrikaner interests were at stake. Slabbert describes this process as 'the bureaucratisation of Afrikaner life', referring to the growth of organisations that controlled each sphere.[18] To some extent bureaucratisation had occurred prior to the 1930s, but the coming of the era of radical nationalism greatly extended its scale and scope.

Apart from the NP itself, the pre-eminent organisation was the Afrikaner Broederbond (AB) (literally the Afrikaner League of Brothers), founded in 1918 with the purpose of fostering unity and a national consciousness among Afrikaners and promoting all the interests of the Afrikaner nation. Membership was by invitation (after a rigorous character examination of the potential member) and open only to Protestant Afrikaner males. By the early 1920s the AB had become a secret organisation, the secrecy impressing upon members the gravity of their cause, and suggesting to non-members the AB's mystique and putative influence.

The aim of the AB was to be the 'axle around which all aspects of Afrikaner life revolved, or rather the authority above them that would co-ordinate with a view to unity of direction and purpose'. Individual members were expected to act like a 'yeast' in their respective environments.

AN Pelzer, the official historian of the AB at its fiftieth anniversary, maintained that its 'biggest and most effective activity' was its quiet influence. Furthermore, he claimed, hardly anything of significance had happened to Afrikaners over the past 50 years without the AB's involvement.[19]

For many years there has been debate about the extent of the AB's influence. Its critics have portrayed it not as an axle, but as a sinister spider sitting at the centre of its web. Both Hertzog and, subsequently, Smuts, attacked the AB for its propagation of Afrikaner domination and its alleged efforts to manipulate appointments in the public service, universities and schools, in the Afrikaans churches and elsewhere to ensure that 'right-minded' (*broers* or AB-approved) individuals occupied posts of key concern to the AB. Critics called this '*baantjies vir boeties*', meaning 'jobs for pals'.

Another aim of the AB was to prevent splits in Afrikaner unity, and to mend them when they occurred. In the case of fusion in 1934, when the 'purified' NP broke away, and again during the early 1940s when the NP's position as the political arm of Afrikaner nationalism came under serious challenge from the Ossewa-Brandwag (the 'Ox-Wagon Sentinel'), it proved to be ineffective. The emotional intensity generated by the splits was too great for even an influential body like the AB to ameliorate.

Two achievements of the AB in the 1930s and 1940s need particular mention: first, it was instrumental in creating an Afrikaner 'establishment', or what Slabbert has called 'a process of Afrikaner organisations interlocking with one another at the top or elite level ... [which] integrated leadership at the top of Afrikaner organisations'.[20] He was writing about the post-1948 period, when the 'establishment' played a major role in consolidating Afrikaner power; but the foundations were laid earlier. The Federasie van Afrikaanse Kultuurvereniginge (Federation of Afrikaans Cultural Associations), for example, was formed in 1929 by the AB – whose public face it became – and made a significant contribution to the promotion of Afrikaans and Afrikaans cultural societies countrywide.

The AB's second crucial achievement was to harness the services of the cream of Afrikaner intellectuals, most of whom had followed Malan and not Hertzog. School and university teachers, as well as clergy, were strongly represented in the AB's ranks: not only could they use their positions to influence the rising generation or their congregations, they also created an ethos in which ideas about 'nation', '*volk*', and apartheid could be shaped. It was no coincidence that of the first ten chairmen of the AB, between 1918 and 1968, five were university professors.[21]

Neither was it coincidence that so much of the burgeoning book and pamphlet literature on the colour question was written by academics, who were fashioning a more sharply etched ideology than had ever been the case with the traditional concept of segregation. Theologians assisted in the task by promoting the belief that the natural, God-given condition of humankind was its division into 'nations' with differing cultures, which should be kept apart. Perhaps the most influential of these writers was Geoff Cronjé, professor of sociology at the University of Pretoria, who produced a quartet comprising: *'n Tuiste vir die Nageslag* (1945) (A home for posterity), *Afrika sonder die Asiaat* (1946) (Africa without the Asian), *Regverdige Rasse-Apartheid* (1947) (Just racial apartheid), and *Voogdyskap en Apartheid* (1948) (Guardianship and apartheid). The first of these titles is dedicated to his wife and to 'all other Afrikaner mothers because they are the Protectors of the Blood-purity of the Boer nation'. WA de Klerk writes of the book's impact that it 'formed the subject of intense discussion within the Broederbond. In the cells (*afdelings*) Cronjé's facts, figures and arguments were thoroughly dissected, critically weighed and basically accepted'.[22]

If the AB was a secret driving force undergirding Afrikaner nationalism, the NP remained its public standard-bearer, claiming to speak on behalf of all Afrikaners even when in the 1930s and 1940s this was palpably untrue. Its support-base had apparently been eroded by the great split of 1934, and in the 1938 election Hertzog's UP won a thumping victory, with 111 seats to the NP's 27, and 447 535 votes to the NP's 247 582. Even the 'Lion of the North', JG Strijdom, retained his seat – the only Transvaal constituency won by the NP – by only 242 votes. It was evident that Hertzog's prestige remained high among many Afrikaners, while Smuts retained the loyalty of a faithful, if dwindling, number of *Bloedsappe*.

Two events, however, were to shatter the illusion of the UP's impregnability by giving an enormous fillip to the NP's brand of radical nationalism. 1938 was the centenary of the Great Trek, the large-scale exodus into the hinterland of Afrikaners escaping British rule and the principle of racial equality in the Cape Colony. The Voortrekkers were undoubtedly brave people who encountered many hardships and dangers, but essentially the Trek was a rolling frontier. Later generations of Afrikaners were to invest it with an aura of heroism, even, prematurely, proclaiming it to be a manifestation of Afrikaner nationalism.

The plan conceived by the organisers of the centenary celebration was that symbolic ox wagons from all parts of the country would converge on a hill outside Pretoria where the foundation stone of a monument to the Voortrekkers would be laid. The symbolic trek and the ceremony in Pretoria were, from the radical nationalists' point of view, a huge success:

in every village and town through which the wagons passed crowds assembled to greet them; and an estimated 250 000 – the biggest ever gathering in South Africa – attended the ceremony.

Alan Paton, later to win fame as a writer and a leading opponent of apartheid, but then in a phase of sympathy for Afrikaner nationalists, attended the proceedings, even growing a beard as was the fashion. The celebrations turned into a frenzy of anti-English feeling, captured by Paton's recounting of an incident in which a young Afrikaner asked him whether he had seen the crowd. When Paton answered that he had, he commented: 'Now we'll knock hell into the English.' Paton went home, and shed both his beard and his sympathy for the racial attitudes of Afrikaner nationalism.[23]

The celebrations were a seminal event in the renaissance of radical nationalism, playing into the hands of the NP and pushing Hertzog one step further into the wilderness. Schalk Pienaar, a reporter on *Die Burger* and later to become one of the outstanding journalists in the Afrikaans media, vividly (and with some exaggeration) described the symbolic trek as a '*volks*-demonstration', which had unlocked the Afrikaner's subconscious, releasing things of which he was unaware: 'The *volk* became powerfully aware of its existence and its will for life (*lewenswil*).'[24]

Less than a year later, in September 1939, Parliament's decision, by a narrow majority of 13, to enter the war on the side of the Allies compounded the radical nationalists' alienation. Hertzog had proposed neutrality, but Smuts was able to cobble together a bare majority for war. Hertzog resigned, but the Governor-General, Sir Patrick Duncan, declined to dissolve Parliament and hold new elections, and instead, invited Smuts to form a new government, which he did. It was anybody's guess what result an election might have produced: it would have been a close-run thing if Hertzog and his followers in the erstwhile Fusion party had made common cause with the NP. In the event, both the war decision and Duncan's action contributed massively to the radical nationalists' growth.

It was not, however, to be a tide that grew in strength and flowed without obstacle to the benefit of the NP. The war was to have paradoxical effects: on the one hand, nationalist sentiment swelled, but on the other hand, it led to yet another serious split in the nationalists' ranks that would, temporarily at least, delay the NP's ability to oust Smuts.

Attempts to re-unify Hertzog and his followers with Malan's NP failed, and in November 1940 Hertzog walked out of an NP congress in protest at the refusal of the Malanites to endorse his insistence that English and Afrikaners should have strictly equal rights. Most of his former followers, however, stayed with what was now called the Herenigde (Reunited) NP.

A remnant followed Hertzog's faithful lieutenant, NC Havenga, and later constituted themselves as the Afrikaner Party, which was to play a critical role in the 1948 election.

More serious than the final break with Hertzog was the rise of the Ossewa-Brandwag (O-B), a neo-fascist extra-parliamentary mass movement with an ostensibly independent para-military wing, Die Stormjaers, whose activities during the war years constituted a menacing fifth column. The O-B, whose supporters were reputed to number 400 000, captured the imagination of many Afrikaners, and threatened to eclipse the NP as Afrikaner nationalism's principal movement. Its ideology contained more than a tinge of support for the corporatist, even Nazi, state; but, notwithstanding UP criticisms to the contrary, relatively few Afrikaner nationalists fully embraced Nazism: apparent sympathy for the Axis cause and efforts to disrupt the domestic war effort by sabotage and spying on shipping movements owed more to the principle 'my enemy's enemy is my friend' than to support for Hitler – which, in any case, was dented after the German army had overrun the Low Countries, whose Flemish and Dutch populations were viewed as ethnic kinsfolk.

By 1943 it was evident that the tide of the World War had turned in favour of the Allies. The hopes of those nationalists who believed that an Axis victory would rid them of the British connection were dashed. Moreover the entry of Japan into the war had cooled the ardour of those wishing for defeat of the Allies. It was a propitious time for Smuts to call an election, which was held on 7 July 1943. The result was an overwhelming victory for Smuts, who won a huge majority of seats, 89 to 43, over the NP.

Circumstances had favoured Smuts: it was a classic 'khaki' election; the UP's main opponents were still feuding, and it was clear that thousands of Afrikaners, particularly O-B supporters, had heeded the O-B's call to boycott the elections. Another factor, impossible to quantify, was that thousands of soldiers' wives, who were dependent on a government allowance, voted for Smuts.[25] Since 70 per cent of the South African troops were Afrikaners (although volunteers, by no means all had joined up out of conviction – army pay and rations were preferable to unemployment), this must have significantly augmented the UP vote.

There was some consolation for Malan's NP: compared with 1938, when Hertzog was still Prime Minister, it had improved its share of the vote to 36 per cent of the total, while the UP's had dropped from 53,6 per cent to nearly 49 per cent. Moreover, the NP's hardcore support was virtually undiminished, its smaller rivals had been decimated, and there were signs that enthusiasm for the O-B was beginning to wane. An estimated

32 per cent of Afrikaners had voted for Smuts: it was possible that in more normal conditions of peace time this percentage would shrink; and, besides, Afrikaner numbers were increasing at a significantly faster rate than the English. The 1946 census showed that the percentage of Afrikaans-speaking whites in the total white population had increased from 55,9 in 1936 to 57,3 in 1946.[26] It would make sense for the NP to lower the voting age from 21 to 18 – which is what it did in 1958.

Smuts, by contrast, showed complacency: 'He called it a famous victory and believed it to be decisive for all time for his country's future.'[27] In five years' time this would be shown to have been an illusion. With much of Smuts's attention focused on the war, and thereafter on the creation of the United Nations Organisation, most of the administrative burden of running the country was left to Jan Hendrik Hofmeyr, Smuts's righthand man and by far the most efficient and intellectually acute member of what was a singularly lacklustre Cabinet. In Smuts's (frequent) absences abroad Hofmeyr acted as Prime Minister, and the general assumption was that he would be Smuts's successor (Smuts being 78 in 1948, and Hofmeyr 54). Hofmeyr's cautiously liberal views, however, were manna to the Nationalists, who would invoke him as the bogeyman in 1948.

With political mileage from anti-war sentiment being exhausted, Malan and his party turned to other issues. Foremost among these was colour: the NP's uncompromising policy of apartheid, a term that came into official NP terminology in 1944, found a soft target in the UP's ambiguous and vacillating commitment to segregation. No less amenable to exploitation by the NP were the evident differences of viewpoints in the UP. On the one hand, there was Hofmeyr and a small group of more liberally minded MPs who were elected in 1943; on the other, hardline conservatives with views on race that were hardly distinguishable from those of the Nationalists. The appointment of Piet van der Byl, a blimpish reactionary from the Western Cape with limited knowledge of Africans, as Minister of Native Affairs in 1943, symbolised the UP's seeming indifference to African affairs.

As usual, Smuts's attitude in these matters was one of studied ambiguity. The key issue in the debates among white politicians was the rate of the townward movement by Africans. As industry expanded during the war years the demand for African labour increased, and the pass laws which restricted African entry to the urban areas were suspended.

The result was that between 1936 and 1946 the number of urban Africans grew by 57 per cent. 'Swamping!' cried the Nationalists. Farmers, the NP's principal constituency, were being deprived of labour: urban work was better paid than farm work, and working conditions, although generally poor, were vastly superior to those on the farms.

The traditional segregationist policy that urban Africans were 'temporary sojourners' had become totally unrealistic as hundreds of thousands of Africans rooted themselves in the towns and cities, constituting a swelling proletariat. In a speech to the liberal South African Institute of Race Relations in 1942, Smuts addressed the issue, declaring that segregation had fallen on 'evil days'. It had tried to stop African urbanisation, but had failed: 'The process has been accelerated. You might as well try to sweep the ocean back with a broom.'[28] It was yet more manna to the Nationalist opposition – and a source of confusion to his hapless Minister of Native Affairs.

There were signs during the war years that the UP was moving, cautiously, towards recognising the need for reform of urban policy, and accepting the obvious social and economic fact of the permanence of African town-dwellers. The climax of this trend came on the eve of the 1948 election, with the publication of the Report of the Natives Laws (Fagan) Commission, which declared roundly that

> ... the idea of total segregation is utterly impracticable; secondly, that the movement from country to town has a background of economic necessity – that it may ... be guided and regulated, and may perhaps also be limited, but that it cannot be stopped or turned in the opposite direction, and thirdly, that in our urban areas there are not only Native migrant labourers, but there is also a settled, permanent Native population (para 28).

A message from Smuts, published in a propaganda pamphlet, *Election News* (1948), displayed the fundamental ambiguity of his stance: while remaining committed to segregation, the UP was 'determined to assist Natives to enter industry as semi-skilled and skilled workers'. Whites would retain the power to govern, but

> ... where the United Party differs from the Nationalist Party is that it does not arrogate to itself the power or the knowledge to lay down a policy for all time. It will do its best to lay a firm foundation for the future ... but cannot entail the future. Generations to come will decide their own policy, and it would be folly for us today to impede what will be their greater experience and riper judgement.

This was not a stirring call to the blood, and it was no match for the visceral appeal of a massive exercise in social engineering that was presented as a matter of life and death for whites in general, and Afrikaners in particular. If the scope of this social engineering remained unclear until 1947, what the NP was opposed to could be inferred with crystal clarity from parliamentary motions, proposed amendments to bills, resolutions at party congresses and speeches by politicians.

Apartheid was intended to shore up the supposedly eroding foundations of white domination: interracial contact on a basis of equality must be stopped; competition from blacks in the labour market must be prevented; African urbanisation must be frozen; subversion must be put down firmly, and the Communist Party be banned; the reasoned demands for lifting the colour bar that emanated from the Natives Representative Council were an intolerable affront to whites; and any possibility of trade union rights for Africans, or of racially mixed unions, was unthinkable.

The tenor of Nationalist thinking, especially in the Transvaal, where race relations were harsher, can be gauged from a comment made by JG Strijdom, a future Prime Minister, in 1939:

> The European had hitherto been able to maintain himself in South Africa because he was economically and culturally superior to the Native. If the Government went out of its way to civilize and uplift the Native in an unnatural manner, the White man would not be able to maintain his superiority.[29]

Another indication was provided by the NP magazine, *Die Kruithoring*, in 1945 in which exception was taken to an instruction from the Minister for Native Affairs that letters to educated Africans should use 'Dear Sir' and 'Yours faithfully':

> To order a white man to call a Kaffir 'Dear Sir' is a sin against the white race of South Africa. It is against all the holy traditions that our forefathers built up. We can no longer tolerate it! (translation)

Challenged to spell out precisely what apartheid implied, the NP responded by producing in March 1948 (at roughly the same time as the publication of the Fagan Report) its own *Report of the Colour-Question Commission*, chaired by Malan's Cape colleague, Paul Sauer. Whether this Report can be described as a 'blueprint' for apartheid, as Sauer's biographers claim, will be discussed below. What is true, however, is that practically every proposal in the Report was subsequently embodied in legislation.[30]

The Report begins by counterposing racial equalisation (*gelykstelling*) with apartheid. Equalisation is to be rejected out of hand because it 'must necessarily lead to the undermining and eventual destruction of the white race as an independent and ruling race'. Apartheid, on the other hand, had grown out of the historical experience of whites, and was based on Christian principles of justice and fairness: 'Any form of oppression is therefore rejected as wrong, damaging to the *volk* (*volkskadelik*), both whites and non-whites, and contrary to the policy of apartheid.' The essence of apartheid envisaged:

1. The maintenance of the white population of South Africa as a pure white race by the complete elimination of any miscegenation between white and non-white; its [the white population's] permanence as an independent political community and its further development on a Christian-national basis by the necessary protection in all spheres, and the drawing of a clear dividing line between white and non-white, thereby removing all possible causes of clashes of interest between white and non-white.

2. The maintenance of the indigenous non-white racial groups of South Africa as separate *volk*-communities (*volksgemeenskappe*) by combating all influences that undermine their respective identities, and the establishment of possibilities for them to develop separately, in a natural way, their own *volk*-character (*volksaard*), capabilities and calling, complemented and fertilised by Christian civilisation until becoming self-sufficient *volks*-units (*volkseenhede*).

3. The maintenance of the traditional trusteeship principle. The cultivation of national pride and self-respect by each group and the encouragement of mutual esteem and respect among the different race and racial groups in the country. (para A)

If a dividing line was to be drawn between black and white it did not imply the 'total separation' ('*algehele skeiding*') that some academic protagonists urged. Nimble semantic footwork was required to reconcile the utopianism of the academics with the cold realities of racial interdependence:

> As an eventual ideal and goal total apartheid between whites and natives is proposed, insofar as it is practically possible gradually to implement it, always with consideration being given to the country's needs and interests and with the necessary care to ensure that there was no disruption of the country's agriculture, industries and general interests. (para B7)

Thus was the circle squared. Cynics, however, might doubt the compatibility of para E12, which proclaimed that the reserves (later called 'homelands' or colloquially 'bantustans') were to be 'the fatherland of the Native ... a spiritual home ... the cradle of his personal and national ideals and aspirations'; and para E23, which recommended that 'every effort be made to curb the exodus of natives from [white-owned] farms'. Furthermore, an investigation must be launched into the possibilities of making it 'so attractive on the farms that it would show [the African] the great advantages that life on the farms offered compared with the cities and towns.'

Africans in the towns were to be regarded as 'temporary', a point of view that restated traditional policy; the number of so-called 'detribalised' Africans was to be frozen; efforts were to be made to restore 'tribal connections', thus anchoring the African once again in his 'volkseie' (literally, 'volks-own', referring to alleged unique ethnic attributes).

Henceforth the influx of Africans to urban areas would be strictly controlled, and as far as possible migrant labour would be used. Labour distribution and regulation would be in the hands of a Central Labour Bureau whose task it would be to ensure that the labour requirements of agriculture, industry, mining and the towns were met.

Again, the utopian vision of total separation was traded off against the realities of racial interdependence:

> The ideal to be aimed at is the gradual withdrawal of Natives from industries in the white areas, but it is realised that this is possible only over the course of many years. (para E45)

The limited degree of separate representation (by whites) of Africans in Parliament was to be abolished, and political institutions based around traditional leaders (so-called 'chiefs') were to be built up. In contrast to previous segregation policies, efforts were to be made to reinvigorate ethnic (so-called 'tribal') loyalties both in the reserves and in the urban areas.

Apart from its lyrical lucubrations about the bright future awaiting Africans in the reserves and other quasi-philosophical musings, the Sauer Report made nearly 30 concrete recommendations whose implementation would require legislation. The subject matter covered the full range of apartheid's toughest measures. Over the following decade virtually all were to be enacted. As a guide to what was to come, the Report was a useful indicator.

Unsurprisingly, the Report, in contrast to the Fagan Report, contained no statistical data; and it made no attempt to cost what was clearly going to be a massive project of social engineering. No single member of the five-man team appeared to have much or, indeed, any knowledge of economics – four were professional politicians and one was a cleric. It is hardly necessary to mention that no blacks were consulted in the course of drawing up the Report.

There has been debate in scholarly and other circles about whether the implementation of apartheid followed a 'blueprint'. Piet Cillié, for example, dismissed the notion that apartheid was a carefully worked out programme:

> A system? An ideology? A coherent blueprint? No, rather a pragmatic, tortuous process of consolidating a nationalist movement's leadership, of establishing the Afrikaner's right to self-determination, not primarily directed against a coloured force, but to prevent the return of the United Party. It [the UP], in turn, would try to ensure that the Nationalists would never get another chance. Revolt and coups would be the means left over for them.[31]

In more scholarly vein, Deborah Posel seeks to refute the view that the Afrikaner nationalist vanguard in the state had

> … [b]uilt the Apartheid edifice brick by brick, according to the dictates of a single, systematic long-term blueprint, the essence of which was already conceived in the minds of NP leaders on the eve of their election victory in 1948.[32]

Both Cillié's and Posel's arguments could have been strengthened by citing the ingenuous comment made by EG Jansen, the Minister of Native Affairs (and a former member of the Sauer Commission) in one of the earliest debates about apartheid after the NP–AP victory in May 1948, that 'the precise manner in which apartheid or separation is to be applied to [Africans] in industries, and in the urban areas, has still to be worked out' (*House of Assembly Debates*, 64, 16 August 1948, col. 609).

There remains some doubt about the validity of Cillié's and Posel's arguments: was the implementation of apartheid *really* as haphazard a process as Cillié suggests? And had the NP leaders not already conceived the essence of apartheid prior to the election? As mentioned above, a consistent line of attack was readily discernible in NP parliamentary activities and elsewhere, notably in newspapers like *Die Burger* and *Die Transvaler*, both of which played important roles in propagandising the NP cause.

No one who read *Die Transvaler* over the 10-year period up to 1948, when HF Verwoerd was editor, could have been under any illusion about what apartheid would involve. Verwoerd, who would be apartheid's master-builder, more than its architect, had decided, according to his biographer, even in the 1930s, what the principles of a successful party should be. Scholtz quotes Verwoerd as saying in 1936:

> By saying clearly well in advance what it is going to do, a party gains the support of people who will stand by it through thick and thin. Only in this way can a powerful government be built up. It cannot happen by means of a coming together [*samevoeging*] on an idealistic basis without a fully worked out policy.[33]

Verwoerd was (mercifully) atypical in his consistency and inflexibility, but others, mostly Transvalers, were hardly less so. As with Verwoerd, for them the essence of apartheid would be the shoring up of the supposedly eroding foundations of segregation, and the restoration to its full rigour of racial discrimination. It is hard not to suppose that hundreds of thousands of NP voters were principally concerned with putting up the barricades against racial equality, rather than with the lofty visions of separate freedoms proclaimed by the intellectual theorists of apartheid. The essence of apartheid, in JG Strijdom's words, was that 'in a bus I will not sit alongside a native'. Strijdom was also notable for propounding the doctrine of *baasskap* (mastership), by which he meant that:

> In every sphere the European must be master, the European must retain the right to rule the country and to keep it a white man's country.[34]

Why did the NP–AP coalition win the 1948 election? Answers have tended to focus on two issues: was it the appeal to Afrikaner unity? Or was it the 'black peril' electioneering under the slogan of apartheid? Schalk Pienaar dismisses the explanation in terms of apartheid as nonsense: 'what happened in 1948 was that the long dormant but growing Afrikaner nationalism reached its apogee'.[35]

It is misleading to see the result in 'either/or' terms. Essentially it was a fusion of both, brought together in defence of the perceived threat to Afrikaner identity and hegemony. Two pithy observations capture the dimensions of this fusion: At van Wyk, a historian, recalled the mood in 1947:

... the call from the platform and pulpit, in classroom and editor's office, was for the Afrikaner to be Christian, nationalist, anti-English and anti-black, all rolled into one. That, at any rate, was how it was broadly understood, if not openly advocated.[36]

Piet Cillié wrote:

The strategy of the Nationalist opposition was to win back the ex-Nationalist component of the United Party [the Hertzogites], and the weapons were Afrikaner rights, republicanism and the colour question, concerning which every sign of laxity or laissez-faire on the part of the authorities was mercilessly attacked.[37]

Another issue of importance, because it had implications for Afrikaner hegemony and identity, was immigration, which the Smuts government was encouraging, even to the extent of 50 000 immigrants per annum. Nearly 29 000 had arrived in 1947 and 35 631 in 1948, overwhelmingly of British origins: within two years of arrival they were eligible to vote. Should this rate of immigration be sustained, the Afrikaners' demographic edge over the English would be lost.[38] To the Nationalists it was obvious that Smuts's eagerness to attract immigrants had less to do with anticipated economic benefits than with an attempt to 'plough the Afrikaner under', as one of Smuts's ministers, Deneys Reitz, was alleged to have said.

As much as anything it was the ineptitude of the UP that lost it the election. Apart from irritating post-war shortages of food and housing, Smuts's studied indifference – or so his opponents claimed – to the question of Afrikaner rights, the 'Hofmeyr factor', and the British Royal Family's tour in 1947, at Smuts's invitation, played into the hands of his opponents. A series of by-election defeats or diminished majorities beginning in 1944 should have caused alarm bells to ring; but Smuts's preoccupation with the war and its aftermath meant that little was done to galvanise the UP into an effective fighting force. Complacency bred sclerosis.

The NP, on the other hand, had developed into a finely honed machine, a classic mobilisation party or liberation movement, of which Africa was to see many more. It was, as Malan said in 1941, 'no party political organisation in the ordinary sense of the word'. It embodied two basic ideas without which no Afrikaner volk would ever be possible: the idea of Nationalism and the idea of restored Afrikaner unity. The NP was, he said on a subsequent occasion, 'organised Afrikanerdom itself in the political sphere'.[39]

Comparing the two parties, Hancock remarks:

[The NP] had at their disposal a substantial force of paid organiz-
ers. Professionalism against amateurism; youth against age, attack
against defence – that, by and large, was the contrast between the
two parties.[40]

The small majority won by the NP–AP coalition meant that Malan's priority as Prime Minister was to consolidate the victory. For the UP the
shock of defeat gave way to the widespread view that Malan's victory was
a temporary aberration and that he would not be able to survive for long.
Although the UP and its Labour Party ally had won fewer seats than its
opponent, nevertheless it had decisively defeated it in terms of votes cast:
Heard has estimated that the UP–LP alliance won 53,3 per cent of the
total votes, while the NP–AP won only 39,4 per cent, the huge distortion
being caused principally by the vagaries of the plurality electoral system.
He estimates that on average the UP required 9 124 votes to win each seat,
compared with 5 683 for the NP–AP.[41]

In the postmortem that followed, many 'might-have-beens' were raised.
Ben Schoeman, a minister in Malan's Cabinet and thereafter until 1974,
believed that if the NP–AP had not won it would have remained in opposition for many years because the UP would have expanded the Coloured
and Indian vote, and quickly enfranchised immigrants from Britain, who
would continue to pour in if the UP were returned.[42]

If these were counterfactual speculations they nevertheless pointed to
action that the NP felt it must take over the next decade to insulate 'white'
politics from any direct black involvement. Qualified male Coloured persons were eligible to register as voters on the common roll in the Cape
Province – a right they had possessed since 1853 – and, even if their influence had been diluted by the extension of the franchise to white women in
1930 and the abolition of qualifications, apart from age, for white voters
in 1931, their votes were potentially decisive in 18 constituencies, where
Coloured voters constituted over 10 per cent of the total number of voters, and 37 seats where they constituted less than 10 per cent.

Moreover, only one-third of eligible Coloured males had, in fact, registered as voters, partly because registration was not compulsory for
Coloured people, whereas it was for whites – whose names, in any case,
unlike those of Coloured voters, had been automatically transferred to
the new voter rolls begun in 1946.[43]

Much of the first phase of apartheid dealt with the NP's efforts to abolish common roll voting rights for Coloured men; and, ironically, the political status of the Coloured people later became an ideological Achilles
heel for the NP that had serious consequences for party unity when,

belatedly, a way had to be found of politically reintegrating them without jeopardising NP control.

Another might-have-been arose out of the boycott by the Indian community of the provision for limited representation by whites – including three MPs in the House of Assembly – of qualified Indian men in Natal and Transvaal. The Asiatic Land Tenure and Indian Representation Act of 1946 had been Smuts's ambiguous way of responding to pressures from the Indian community, most of whom were resident in Natal, and from India itself, for the extension of civil rights to people of colour. The first part of the legislation, however, was a response to reactionary white pressure against alleged Indian 'penetration' of white residential areas. As a whole the legislation pleased no one, and the Indian community comprehensively boycotted the possible elections, which would certainly have returned three anti-NP MPs. The NP, whose platform included a proposal to repatriate Indians to Asia, repealed the legislation very shortly after coming to power.

Bernard Friedman, a liberal who won a UP seat in 1943, suggests that had Smuts accepted a recommendation by the Natives Representative Council in 1943 that the number of (white) MPs representing Cape Africans in the House of Assembly be raised from three to ten, he would have been spared the disaster of 1948. All ten would have been anti-NP.[44] Smuts, while not unsympathetic to the African cause, would not countenance even so moderate a move, fearing that the augmentation of support from the African representatives would be far outweighed by the loss of white support such a move would incur.

Democratising polities in nineteenth century Europe had often produced situations where ruling classes, or segments of ruling classes, had enfranchised new strata as a means of gaining new support. South Africa's situation was different. Where colour rather than class was the critical social distinction, even limited extensions of representation to blacks would evoke opposition from across the white political spectrum. The liberals in Smuts's caucus were pitifully few in number, and their spiritual leader, Hofmeyr, was if anything an electoral liability.

A might-have-been of the post-election period concerned the role played by NC Havenga's Afrikaner Party, whose winning of nine seats in 1948 gave the winning edge to the NP–AP alliance. The AP was essentially the remnant party of Hertzog's followers, which had also mopped up O-B supporters who had refused to vote for the NP. Malan had had to fight off strong opposition from Strijdom and others to the pact with Havenga, but finally had his way. By August of 1948 it was reported to Smuts that Havenga and some of his followers were deeply unhappy in the NP camp and, according to EG Malherbe, Smuts's Director of Military Intelligence during the War and thereafter Principal of Natal University College, that Havenga would rather co-operate with Smuts than Malan. Smuts was un-impressed with Malherbe's idea and sniffily dismissed Havenga and his colleagues as 'a lot of Fascists' – a reference to the AP's recruitment of O-B sympathisers.[45]

Whether the reports of Havenga's preparedness to strike a deal with Smuts were true is not known. If Havenga was uneasy about what the NP was prepared to do to abolish the Coloured common roll vote, he betrayed little or no sign of this publicly.

CHAPTER 2

The Black Experience:
A Prelude to Apartheid

By the end of the nineteenth century all of the African polities in what was to become the Union of South Africa had been brought under white control, either by conquest or, in some cases, by treaty. The frontiers of white settlement had rolled forward inexorably; even the most redoubtable of the indigenous chiefdoms could not indefinitely withstand the pressure of the guns and horses of the frontiersmen, or colonial and imperial troops.

Three interrelated issues dominated the black/white encounter: security, land and labour. Among Dutch and English farmers an insatiable land-hunger was accompanied by an equally insatiable demand for labour. As Lieutenant-Governor Scott of Natal wrote in 1858:

> It seems impossible for a body of white men to live in proximity to the coloured races, without adopting a conviction that as the dominant people, they have a right to command the services of the less civilised ... [1]

Independent or semi-autonomous chiefdoms were not only obstacles to the acquisition of land and labour, they were also potential rallying points for resistance to white rule. Reasons of security accordingly required that they be neutralised, even broken up; their chiefs sometimes deposed, deported or even imprisoned.

With the eventual defeat of the Zulu kingdom in 1879, the most powerful indigenous state in the region had been neutralised. The Bambatha Rebellion that broke out in Natal in 1906 and was harshly put down by the colonial authorities was the last revolt against white rule by an indigenous group. Henceforth, opposition to white rule would assume new forms.

Land had been a critical factor in the colonial encounter: it was an issue in all of the wars fought between 1779 and 1877 on the moving Cape frontier, and in the repeated skirmishes between the burghers of the Boer Republics and the indigenous people. Africans lost out in this contest for control of resources. A rueful Xhosa saying has it: 'At first we had the land and the white man had the Bible. Now we have the Bible and the white man has the land.' Land was alienated in various ways: by conquest in war, by confiscation after a rebellion, by merely staking out a farm which happened to have Africans already resident on it, and by concessions from chiefs who were either venal or unaware that whites' understanding of land grants was fundamentally different from theirs, which did not involve outright possession. In De Kiewiet's words, 'In the European mind ownership was more important than use; in the Bantu mind use was more important than ownership.'[2]

The extent to which land occupied by Africans was alienated is a matter of controversy: conservative white politicians consistently denied that any such alienation had occurred; some also denied that Africans had been in South Africa at the time of the original white settlement of 1652, claiming instead that the Dutch and Bantu-speaking Africans arrived in South Africa at approximately the same time. Both contentions are historical myths. The evidence suggests that Bantu-speaking people had settled in what became South Africa some 2 000 years ago; by the time of Van Riebeeck's arrival in 1652 much of the northern and eastern, summer rainfall area of South Africa had been long settled.

Modern historians, while prepared to acknowledge the fact of historical land alienation, have been reluctant to offer quantitative estimates of the scale on which it occurred. None, however, has successfully challenged WM Macmillan's estimate, made in 1930, that Africans were being required to live upon one-fifth of the land to which they had previously laid occupational claim.[3] (The allocation of land to Africans changed somewhat in 1936 – see below.)

Apart from the sacred and symbolic significance of land on which ancestors were buried, it was also the vital economic underpinning of traditional society. Alienation on so large a scale, combined with taxes that required men to go out to work as migrants, sounded the death-knell of self-sufficiency and the beginning of the incorporation of Africans into white-controlled society as a subordinate colour-caste. It was a major instrument of black disempowerment. It was not only self-sufficiency that ended; the ability of African peasant farmers to market surpluses to the growing towns also declined and was finally extinguished.

The land issue rumbled on through the twentieth century, and even under African National Congress rule from 1994 onwards African griev-ances about dispossession remain salient. Limited areas were set aside as 'reserves' for exclusive African occupation prior to 1909, but these were no more than residual or remnant areas. To a limited extent mounting pressure of population on land in the reserves was relieved by the ability of groups of Africans to club together to buy freehold land outside the reserves. By 1916 over one million morgen of land – or 2.12 million acres – were owned by Africans, either individually or collectively.[4] Others squat-ted on Crown Lands or lived as labour tenants on white-owned farms.

The inter-colonial South African Native Affairs Commission of 1903–5, chaired by Sir Godfrey Lagden, investigated land questions in some detail in the context of an examination of 'native policy' with a particular focus on the supposed labour shortage. Its findings concerning land purchase by Africans were a prelude to the first statutory instrument of territorial seg-regation, the Natives Land Act of 1913. The Lagden Commission warned against continuing to allow Africans to purchase land outside reserves:

> If this process goes on, while at the same time restrictions exclude Europeans from purchasing within Native areas, it is inevitable that at no very distant date the amount of land in Native occupation will be undesirably extended. Native wages and earnings are greater than they used to be, their wants are few, and their necessary ex-penses small. They will buy land at prices above its otherwise market value, as their habits and standard of living enable them to exist on land that it is impossible for Europeans to farm on a small scale. There will be many administrative and social difficulties created by the multiplication of a number of Native units scattered through-out a white population and owning the land of the country equally with them. Such a situation cannot fail to accentuate feelings of race prejudice and animosity, with unhappy results. It will be far more difficult to preserve the absolutely necessary political and social dis-tinctions if the growth of a mixed rural population of land-owners is not discouraged.[5]

The Commission recommended that legislation should prevent Africans from purchasing land outside certain areas (that is, the reserves), and that 'tribal, communal or collective possession or occupation' should not be permitted. Herein lay the germ of 'possessory' segregation, which the leg-islation of 1913 addressed: approximately seven per cent of South Africa's land surface was 'scheduled' as reserves. The same law sought to deal with squatting on white-owned farms and share-cropping agreements, and was applied with especial ferocity in the Orange Free State. 'Awaking on Friday morning, June 20 1913, the South African Native found himself, not actually a slave, but a pariah in the land of his birth.'[6]

The Natives Land Act was intended as an interim measure, pending a comprehensive settlement of the land issue. It was not until 1936, however, that further legislation was enacted, this time as part of Hertzog's 'solution' of the 'native problem'. The Native Trust and Land Act 'released' a further 7.25 million morgen from the provisions of the 1913 legislation. An official digest of legislation affecting Africans described the land situation succinctly:

> The grand total of seventeen and three-quarter million morgen [or 13.7 per cent of South Africa's land surface] will represent the extent of land that will either be owned by Natives or be held in trust for them. Great numbers of Natives will continue to reside on property outside of the Native areas as squatters or servants or in some other capacity but will not be able to enter into any agreement or transaction for the purchase, hire or other acquisition from a person other than a Native of any such land or any right thereto, interest therein, or servitude thereover except with the approval of the Governor-General. In such manner therefore will the rights of Natives in land be restricted so as to ensure attainment of the policy of territorial separation between Native and non-Native.[7]

The reserves, subsequently known as 'homelands' (and colloquially as 'bantustans'), were the ideological linchpin of segregation and thereafter of apartheid. They originated, however, not from a benign concern for the protection of threatened African land rights, but rather from the less benign consideration that access to land might inhibit the supply of labour. The mineral revolution of the last third of the nineteenth century and the beginnings of secondary industry meant that the demand for labour had reached new heights.

Denying access to land, and squeezing squatters and labour tenants were strategies to extract more labour. Prising Africans off the land did not, however, entail according them freedom of movement and the right to sell their labour in the best market. Another instrument of domination was the institution of the pass laws, which limited Africans' right to change employers at will or to move from place to place in search of better employment opportunities. Ostensibly the pass laws were supposed to prevent vagabondage, absconding from work and crime; in reality they served mainly to tie African workers to particular employers.

As industrialisation increased and population pressure on rural land caused more and more people, black and white, to seek a living in the towns, the pass laws acquired further functions – limiting the access of Africans to urban areas while serving as a mechanism for the bureaucratic allocation of labour to mining and agriculture, neither of which could compete with the wages paid in commerce or industry.[8] Under apartheid the scope of the pass laws, later known as influx control, was radically extended, enmeshing Africans ever more tightly in bureaucratic coils. No single institution of segregation cased more anger and irritation to Africans.

For many poor Afrikaners the townward trek was a traumatic experience in a hostile environment. It was the same for Africans, but with the critical difference that they were people with few rights, subjected to an all-encompassing inequality, and entering an environment that was not only hostile, but for many, dehumanising. These qualities are captured by the brutal recommendation of an official commission in 1922

> … that it should be a recognised principle of government that natives – men, women and children – should only be permitted within municipal areas in so far and for so long as their presence is demanded by the wants of the white population …. the masterless native in urban areas is a source of danger and a cause of degradation of both black and white.[9]

The official view of the urban African as a 'temporary sojourner' (a term that came into official usage) whose permanent home was in a reserve, was the basis of urban policy, and survived well into the apartheid era. It was another major instrument of domination whose corollary was the entrenchment of the migrant labour system. Smuts argued in 1929:

> While the native may come voluntarily out of his own area to work with a white employer, he will leave his wife and children behind in their native home … migration of the native family, of the females and children, to the farms and towns … should be prevented.[10]

The effects of these policies on the lives of Africans were devastating. In the reserves, overcrowding by both people and animals was exacting its toll. Quoting an African saying that 'Man begets, but land does not beget,' the Native Economic Commission of 1930–32 found that

> … we have now throughout the Reserves a state of affairs in which,

with few exceptions, the carrying capacity of the soil for both human beings and animals is definitely on the downgrade; a state of affairs which, unless soon remedied, will within one or at the outside two decades create ... an appalling problem of Native poverty.[11]

Harsh conditions in the reserves and, often, an eagerness to escape the drudgery and low wages of employment on white-owned farms were powerful push factors that accelerated African urbanisation. Between 1921 and 1936 the urban African population increased by 94.49 per cent, and between 1936 and 1946 by 57.16 per cent, bringing the percentage of the total African population that was urban to nearly 23 per cent (and, incidentally, totalling 1.794 million, which was approximately 75 000 more than the white urban population).[12]

Conditions in the urban African townships were harsh: local authorities were disinclined to spend generously on populations deemed 'temporary' by official policy and who, in any case, were not municipal voters. In 1942 an inter-departmental committee chaired by Douglas Smit, the Secretary for Native Affairs, investigated urban conditions, finding, among other things, an 'appalling amount of malnutrition', a 'high incidence of ill-health', and 'maladjustment arising from broken family ties'. The committee was 'impressed above all by the poverty of the Native community'.[13] Their report was a withering indictment of past neglect; it served in some measure to initiate a cautious measure of reform, which was extinguished in 1948.

Unlike poor blacks, poor whites possessed the vote, and could use it, as they did in 1924, to vote in a government that was actively concerned with promoting their interests. African and Coloured voting rights were confined to the Cape Province, in which a non-racial male franchise had survived since 1852, despite the imposition of tighter restrictions on potential African voters in 1887 and 1892. To register as a voter a male had to be 21 years old and had either to earn £50 per annum or own fixed property to the value of £75, and be able to sign his name and write his address and occupation.

On the eve of Union in 1909 nearly 15 per cent of Cape voters were other than white, including 6 637 (4.7 per cent) who were Africans.[14] None of the other prospective provinces accorded any voting rights to people of colour: the Transvaal and Orange Free State Constitutions had flatly excluded them, and even after the conclusion of the Anglo-Boer War in 1902 the British government as the colonial power had declined to insist on franchise rights for blacks. In Natal, Africans who sought to qualify as voters were required to complete a formidable obstacle race that involved acquiring exemption from African customary law – itself a difficult process – and thereafter, having been so exempted for seven years, resident in the Colony for 12 years, meeting the property qualifications and furnishing a certificate signed by three white voters who testified to the applicant's loyalty, the Lieutenant-Governor might, in his discretion, enfranchise the applicant. It was not surprising that by 1905 the voter rolls included the grand total of three Africans!

Indians, brought into Natal from 1860 onwards as indentured labour (together with so-called 'passenger Indians') were denied the franchise by legislation of 1896, which prevented the enfranchisement of 'Natives or descendants in the male line of Natives which have not hitherto possessed elective representative institutions ….'

Despite strong opposition from the Transvaal, Orange Free State and Natal, the Cape was allowed to retain its franchise arrangement, although it yielded up the previous (theoretical) right of persons of colour to become members of Parliament. Any hopes that Cape politicians might have entertained that the Cape franchise would be exported to the northern provinces were idle: from the inception of Union powerful voices were raised against common roll voting rights for blacks, more especially for Africans. Some measure of protection for the Cape franchise was afforded by 'entrenching' it, together with a clause guaranteeing equality of English and Dutch (later Afrikaans) in the Constitution: only a two-thirds majority of both houses of Parliament sitting together could amend it. The unified opposition of white South Africa to black political rights was enough to overcome the protection.

Opposition to effective voting rights for blacks reflected the historical paranoia to which reference has been made, although English-speaking conservatives, especially in Natal, were equally hostile to having any truck with a non-racial principle. The Anglo-Boer War had shown that large numbers of black people were hoping for a British victory in the (misplaced) expectation that a new Imperial order would liberate them from racial domination. Louis Botha, a Boer general and the Prime Minister of the united South Africa from 1910 to 1919, told a commission in 1903 that

> … the [British] military during the war spoiled the Kaffirs. They paid the Kaffir too much money. The Kaffir is a barbarian, but after being mixed up in the war, he now considers himself a sort of master in the country … . In one way they consider themselves better than [the Boers].[15]

Botha's language and the assumptions it expressed were typical of the times. There is, however, truth in his diagnosis that the dislocation of war had stirred up greater anti-Boer sentiment. Resentment of white rule was widespread. As early as 1851 Theophilus Shepstone spoke of 'the evident sympathy of colour that exists among the Black nations'.[16] It is plausible that as more and more indigenous societies were colonised, and their lands alienated, at least a sense of common plight developed.

Towards the end of the nineteenth century a new form of political activity among Africans of the Christian, educated class was emerging. Unlike the primary resistance of the indigenous societies, the new elite requested rights within the common society. André Odendaal's study of early black protest politics suggests continuity between the older and the newer politics:

> The strategies of the new class differed from the old tribal resistance strategies, but in seeking to protect African interests against expanding white domination, their aims were the same. By adopting a constitutional approach and seeking accommodation within the colonial systems, the educated Africans were merely displaying a different form of resistance.[17]

The colonial tributaries of the new protest flowed into a single stream: if Union in 1910 unified white politics, it also drew into existence a country-wide African organisation for the protection of their interests. Publication of the draft South African Act early in 1909 sparked a flurry of protest from Africans in all parts of the country. An ad hoc South African Native Convention assembled in Bloemfontein in March and placed on record 'its strong and emphatic protest' against the discriminatory clauses in the draft, and 'respectfully' pleaded for the extension of the Cape franchise to the prospective northern provinces.[18] A petition to the (British) House of Commons received a polite rebuff.

From 1910 onwards, organised black opinion had little option but to react defensively to the torrent of discriminatory legislation that poured forth from an all-white Parliament unfettered by any Imperial restraint. Certainly there were protests, but the essential theme of racial politics for the next 60 years or so would be that the South African state, with the support of the large majority of whites, could shrug off whatever challenge black opposition offered. The huge disparity in political resources virtually ensured that black political organisations could be little more than reactive – opportunities for seizing the initiative did not arise. Moreover, their weak bargaining position, reinforced perhaps by a degree of culturally prescribed respectfulness, lent to the African National Congress (ANC), for example, a restrained, dignified, and moderate style in supplicating government that would last into the 1940s. Unduly radical demands, it was believed, would make the white government even more intransigent in responding to African pleas for the amelioration of grievances.

The South African Native National Congress (the name was changed to African National Congress in 1925) was founded in Bloemfontein in 1912. The membership of the early NNC was rooted in the educated, Christian class, products of the mission schools who were the sole providers of education for Africans at that time. The formation of the Congress was largely attributable to the initiative of Pixley ka Seme, a lawyer with degrees from both Columbia and Oxford Universities. In a newspaper article written in 1911 Seme proposed a Congress of 'the dark races of this sub-continent' that would meet once or twice a year to take stock of the situation being experienced by Africans.

Optimistically, Seme anticipated that the Congress would be a channel for communication between government and the entire African population which would 'make it easier for the Union Government to deal with the Natives'. He also expressed hope that feuding and animosity among African ethnic clusters would be contained by the Congress:

> We are one people. These divisions, these jealousies, are the cause of all our woes and of all our backwardness and ignorance today.[19]

At the inaugural meeting in Bloemfontein an ethnically balanced team was assembled for the executive leadership. John L Dube, a Zulu clergyman who had established an excellent school at Ohlange, near Durban, and also edited a Zulu/English newspaper, was elected president in a deliberate move to avoid creating the impression of Xhosa dominance, an allegation that would crop up many times in the ANC's future history.[20]

The potential for Xhosa dominance derived from the far longer and deeper impact that missionaries and their schools had had on Cape Africans in comparison with those in the other provinces. The first school for Africans was opened in 1799 but it was not until the 1820s that missionary education began on a systematic basis on the eastern frontier. By 1905 the Cape Colony had over 60 000 African pupils in schools – or 4.2 per cent of the African population – which was more than twice that of the other three colonies combined.[21]

It was not until 1919 that the Congress produced a Constitution. It was an elaboration of what Seme had written in 1911. It included: the Congress was to be a watchdog for African interests; to serve as a means of educating white public representatives about 'the requirement and aspirations' of Africans; to educate Africans on their rights, duties and obligations to the state; to discourage ethnicity among Africans; and to agitate and advocate 'by just means' for the removal of the colour bar and for 'equitable representation' of Africans in Parliament and other representative bodies.

Nelson Mandela has often described the ANC as a 'broad church'. The embryo of this aggregative approach is contained among the 'objects' listed in the Constitution:

> To unite, absorb, consolidate and preserve under its aegis existing political and educational Associations, Vigilance Committees and other public and private bodies whose aims are the promotion and safeguarding of the interests of the aboriginal races.[22]

It was hardly a radical set of aims. Indeed, the entire document is suffused with a moralistic, even prim, tone bearing the stamp of the missionary education so many of the Congress's founding members had obtained. The essential moderation of the ANC was demonstrated by its views on the franchise. For more than three decades after its founding, the ANC favoured the extension of the Cape franchise system to the northern provinces, while, of course, fighting a rearguard action against Hertzog's legislation that destroyed it. By 1929 there were 15 780 African voters on the Cape common roll, constituting 7.5 per cent of the total Cape electorate and, so it was claimed, a decisive element in 12 or 13 eastern Cape seats, all held by Smuts's South African Party. In 1930 white women were enfranchised, lowering the percentage of African voters to 3.1 per cent; in 1931 a further dilution of the African vote occurred when educational and economic qualifications for white voters were abolished.[23]

It took from 1926 until 1936 for Hertzog to get his 'Native Bills' through Parliament with the required two-thirds majority of both Houses to amend an entrenched clause. Only 11 MPs voted against the legislation, demonstrating again that when white South Africans overcame their political divisions it was invariably at the expense of black rights.

The quid pro quo for the loss of the common roll franchise was three seats to be filled by white MPs, elected by Cape Africans, and four senators (again, white) to be elected by complex, indirect methods by Africans in Natal, Transvaal and Orange Free State, the Transkeian Territories, and the Cape Province excluding the Transkeian Territories. In addition, a Natives Representative Council (NRC) was created, consisting of (white) officials from the Native Affairs Department, four Africans nominated by the Governor-General and twelve elected African members. The Council was a purely advisory body, charged with considering proposed legislation affecting Africans, and any matter affecting Africans.

If the legislation was another serious setback to the cause of African rights, it served at least some indirect purpose by breathing life into African political organisation in general, and the ANC in particular. The 1920s and 1930s had overall been a bleak period for the ANC. It had participated in protests from time to time, but its organisation was poor, its finances were shaky, and it never attracted a mass membership. For much of the 1920s it was overshadowed by the Industrial and Commercial Workers' Union of South Africa, known simply as the ICU, led by a charismatic maverick named Clements Kadalie, who had been born in Nyasaland (today Malawi) and migrated to Cape Town in 1918.

Although the achievements of the ICU in the 1920s (after which it petered out in disarray) appear distinctly limited, it did at least pioneer new techniques of opposition in forming a mass movement – claiming, perhaps exaggeratedly, a membership of 100 000 in 1927 – and drawing in African and Coloured workers, both urban and rural. Wickens's study concludes:

> [The ICU] penetrated for the first time beneath the crust of the articulate and educated class and initiated the first genuinely popular movement among Blacks in South Africa. While it was the chief representative of Black opinion, the ICU explored what avenues were open to it, and if those turned out to be blind alleys, this does not mean that the exploring was not worth doing.[24]

Erratic and demagogic though his leadership may have been, Kadalie inspired his followers in a way that no other African leader had previously been able to do. He underlined exactly what the ANC lacked, notably during the period 1930–1937 when Seme was president. Quality of leadership, including the ability to inspire trust in one's followers and to take them into uncharted territory, would prove crucial factors when South Africa's transition reached its crucial phase in the 1990s.

The ANC was overshadowed yet again in mounting protest against the assault on the Cape franchise. The All Africa Convention (AAC), an umbrella body that included a wide variety of civic and political organisations, including the ANC, led the opposition. Its president, Professor DDT Jabavu, member of a famous Eastern Cape political family, had never been a member of the ANC, although, doubtless, he was in general agreement with its policies.

Predictably, the AAC's pleadings and its refusal to go beyond time-honoured, though demonstrably ineffective, methods of protest achieved nothing. The issue that now faced African politicians was whether to participate in the institutions set up by the 1936 legislation, namely the Natives Representative Council and the separate representation of Africans in Parliament. The question was: did you collaborate with devices designed to perpetuate your own oppression? Or did you acquiesce, and use whatever means were available to lobby government and air grievances? Initially the ANC chose acquiescence; younger members, increasingly radicalised – and not least by such patently racist legislation – wanted to boycott both the NRC and the election of MPs, but the older accommodationist stance prevailed. Albert Luthuli, who served briefly on the NRC in its dying phase, offered the following qualified defence of participation:

> There was this to be said …. At least the new body was elective, in a cumbersome way, and at least it was intended to represent *all* Africans. It was, perhaps, worth trying. At all events, here again was the appearance of an opportunity to make our voices heard. It can never be alleged that we turned aside from what means were open to us.[25]

Disillusionment with the NRC soon set in among its members and the African public. It was a 'toy telephone', in the words of one of its members. Some of the most distinguished African leaders of the day were members, and the quality of its debates compared favourably with those in the (white) Parliament. Frustration led to the NRC's adjournment *sine die* in 1946. It was finally abolished in 1951.

Much the same mixture of resignation and acquiescence lay behind the ANC's decision to participate in the election of (white) MPs to represent Africans. Margaret Ballinger was invited to stand by the Cape division of the ANC, and served with distinction from 1937 until 1960, whereupon legislation of 1959 terminating African representation came into effect. Most of the other MPs were either liberals or communists. Among the latter was Ray Alexander, whose parliamentary career must be among the briefest on record: she was elected on 21 April 1954 and six days thereafter was declared incapable of taking her seat in terms of the Suppression of Communism Act of 1950. The same legislation terminated the parliamentary careers of several other communists elected as African representatives.

The unlikely agent of the ANC's resuscitation from its moribund condition was Dr AB Xuma, a medical doctor, who returned to South Africa in 1927 after 12 years of study in the United States. Xuma, who was very much in the cautious tradition of the ANC's old guard, was elected president in 1940. He recognised that the ANC was in dire need of organisational reform if it was to have any hope of achieving its goals. Indeed, chronic financial problems, organisational incoherence and the absence of any paid full-time staff, including organisers, had consigned the ANC to ineffectiveness.

Mandela's comments on Xuma are acute:

> When he assumed the presidency, the ANC had 17s. 6d. in its trea-sury, and he … boosted the amount to £4000. He was admired by traditional leaders, had relationships with cabinet ministers and ex-uded a sense of security and confidence. But he also carried himself with an air of superciliousness that did not befit the leader of a mass organisation … . He enjoyed the relationships he had formed with the white establishment and did not want to jeopardize them with political action.[26]

For much of the first half of the twentieth century South Africa's racial system was broadly in alignment with a world of colonial empires and institutionalised racial discrimination, such as in the American South or in Australia's treatment of Aboriginals and its 'white Australia' policy. In the interwar years, the critique of imperialism grew. The Second World War was a war against a horrible form of racism, whose defeat provided an impetus for a far-reaching attack on racism in the postwar world. The war, moreover, weakened the foundations of colonial rule.

South Africa was unable to isolate itself from these consequences. Entry into the war had the perverse effect of providing a major stimu-lus to Afrikaner nationalism; for Africans the impact was indirect: the war against *herrenvolkism* prompted the signing in 1941 of the Atlantic Charter in which Winston Churchill and Franklin D Roosevelt spelled out the goals of the war, including Point 3, 'the right of all peoples to choose the form of government under which they will live'. Churchill was cha-grined to learn that Point 3 was being construed as applicable not only to 'nations of Europe now under the Nazi yoke', but to the Empire as well. Similarly Smuts and his Minister of Native Affairs, Deneys Reitz, while well aware of African grievances, declined to regard support for the Charter as implying readiness to extend democratic rights to all.

The ANC's response to the Charter was to issue in 1943 a carefully com-piled policy statement, entitled 'Africans' Claims in South Africa', which included a detailed analysis of the Atlantic Charter and a proposed bill of rights. It was the most far-reaching programme ever produced by the ANC and, in major respects, broke with the traditional accommodationist stance, by, for example, calling for the extension of the franchise to all adults, regardless of race, and demanding the abolition of 'all enactments which discriminate against the African on grounds of race and colour'.[27]

It was not only the contents but also the tone of 'Africans' Claims' that signalled the coming of a sea-change in the ANC's style: submissiveness, deference, the obsequious way of voicing demands had, apparently, vanished, reflecting the growing impatience of Africans.

Several factors were at work: large-scale urbanisation, facilitated by the suspension of the pass laws in all the major urban centres between 1942 and 1946; some evidence that the Smuts government was contemplating major reform – an overly optimistic belief fuelled by Smuts's remarks in 1942 about the failure of segregation; and the rise of a young, educated generation, impatient with the conservatism of their elders.

The war had a major impact on the economy, which, in turn, had implications for blacks. Apart from the massive townward movement, wartime conditions spurred diversification in the economy and a huge expansion of the manufacturing sector. This overall expansion, however, was hobbled by what would become a perennial problem: the shortage of skilled labour exacerbated by the absence of so many men on active service.

Hobart Houghton calculated that the industrial labour force grew by 53 per cent during the war years: of the increase of 125 000 persons, only 19 000 were white and the remainder black. Many of the latter, he noted, moved into skilled and semi-skilled positions previously occupied by whites: 'Had it not been for their contribution, South Africa could not both have expanded output and maintained its war effort.'[28] The biggest proletariat in Africa was being formed. The long-term consequences of this development were profound.

It was into this maelstrom of contending forces that the ANC's 'Young Turks' moved, making their presence felt, in Mandela's words, by forming a Youth League (ANCYL) 'as a way of lighting a fire under the leadership of the ANC'.[29] Xuma, as Mandela recounts, felt threatened by the prospect and sought to head off any thought of mass action. He finally acquiesced, however, and the ANCYL formally came into existence in 1944. It did, indeed, light a fire, shaping the future of the ANC's strategies and causing a questioning of the ANC's tradition of racial inclusivity as the desired goal for South Africa. Over time the radical 'Africanism' of the Youth Leaguers would lead to a change in the configuration of African political organisation.

Most of the moving spirits in the creation of the ANCYL were young graduates, several of them from Fort Hare (the South African Native College). Many would proceed to dominant positions in the ANC: Nelson Mandela, Oliver Tambo, Walter Sisulu and Duma Nokwe, for example. Robert Sobukwe was to become the founding president of the Pan-Africanist Congress (PAC) in 1959, after the breakaway of the 'Africanist' faction of the ANC in 1958. Another of Africanism's intellectual architects was AP Mda, president of the ANCYL from 1947 to 1949.

In what was a particularly bright firmament, the brightest star, which shone for a tragically short time (he died in 1947), was Anton Lembede, aged 30 at the time of the formation of the ANCYL. Coming from a poor background, Lembede managed by dint of hard work and intellectual brilliance to qualify as a lawyer and to earn a Master's degree in philosophy. More than anyone else he laid the intellectual foundations of Africanism, and injected into African political thought a perspective whose reverberations are still felt.

The fire that the ANCYL lit started with the publication of a Manifesto in March 1944. It was an uncompromising rejection of white supremacy that also threw down the gauntlet to the old guard leadership of the ANC, who were obliquely but unmistakeably excoriated as 'the privileged few' who 'imparted to the [African National] Congress character taints of reactionism and conservatism which made Congress a movement out of actual touch with the needs of the rank and file of our people'. This was strong stuff, but the Manifesto elected not to dwell on past shortcomings, but rather to point the way ahead for a rejuvenated Congress that would enable the African 'TO DETERMINE HIS FUTURE BY HIS OWN EFFORTS' (capitals in the original). A new chord had been struck.[30]

The implication was an assertion of African nationalism and the distinctiveness of African interests. The traditional ANC view had stressed interracial co-operation and identical white and black interests. The ANC had 'African' and 'National' in its title, but its general approach was devoid of the urgent sense of separate identity that generally characterises nationalisms. Lembede's approach was strikingly different:

Africans are Natives of Africa; they and Africa are one; their relation to Africa is superior to the relations of other sections of the population. This superiority of relation to Africa clearly places the Africans in a position of ascendancy and superiority over other sections of the South African population. Hence it is evidently wrong to place Africans on a footing of equality with other racial groups at present residing in Africa. Africans are fighting for Africa; but other sections

are fighting only for their rights to trade and extract as much wealth
as possible from Africa.[31]

(The snide, not to say racist, comment at the end of this quotation was
aimed at Indians as much as any other group. Another comment in the
same article, asserting that 'Indians have India as their motherland; they
are only here in Africa chiefly as traders', could have been written by any
white Natalian anti-Indian bigot.)

The ethnocentric tenor of Lembede's articles was reminiscent of
Afrikaner nationalism – and disturbed some of his fellow Youth Leaguers.
He was not averse to saying that African nationalism could learn lessons
about cohesiveness and discipline from Afrikaner nationalism; and he
quoted with approval the dictum of President Paul Kruger that 'Whoever
wishes to shape the future should not forget the past.' But, he insisted, the
goals of African and Afrikaner nationalism were irreconcilable.[32] Mda
used more robust language, deeming Afrikaner nationalism 'imperialistic
and neo-Fascist'. African nationalism, on the other hand, was 'the pure
Nationalism of an oppressed people', who did not hate whites, while hating white oppression and white domination.[33]

Nelson Mandela, who cut his political teeth in the ANCYL of the
1940s, was in those days far from being the apostle of racial tolerance
that served South Africa so well some 50 years later. He shared the anti-
Indian prejudice that was widespread among Africans and whites.[34]
Writing of his earlier attitudes, Mandela says, with admirable candour,
in his autobiography:

> I was sympathetic to the ultra-revolutionary stream of African na-
> tionalism. I was angry at the white man, not at racism. While I was
> not prepared to hurl the white man into the sea, I would have been
> perfectly happy if he had climbed aboard his steamships and left the
> continent of his own volition.[35]

The Youth Leaguers were vehemently anti-communist, communism being one of those 'foreign ideologies' that they rejected – South Africa's
conflict involved race, not class, as the Communist Party insisted. Many
of the Youth Leaguers were devout Christians – Lembede was a staunch
Catholic – and rejected the communists' materialist interpretation of
society. There was another reason that was to become a major issue of
contention in the 1950s: the belief that white and Indian communists, by
virtue of their generally better education and organisational experience,
would gravitate to leadership positions in joint ventures with Africans.[36]

Having performed several ideological somersaults since its inception in 1921, the Communist Party of South Africa (CPSA) in the early 1940s set its sights on the ANC, which it had previously regarded as an elitist petit-bourgeois organisation. Earlier ANC attitudes to communism are illustrated by the fate of James Gumede, who, as president of the ANC, returned from a visit to the Soviet Union in 1928 singing the praises of communism. He was voted out of the presidency in 1930 after the mobilisation of the anti-communist conservatives. Nevertheless, dual membership of the ANC and CPSA remained permissible, despite ANCYL efforts to end the practice.[37] By 1945 three prominent African communists, Moses Kotane, JB Marks and Dan Tloome, served on the ANC's National Executive Committee. All had backgrounds in the trade union movement, and all had impressive and forceful personalities that made an impact even on conservative anti-communist ANC members.

Unlike the ANC's old guard, the CPSA had no inhibitions about embarking on mass action. Between 1941 and 1943 it claimed that its membership increased fourfold. The Party's militants were active in the unions and in the townships; it could fairly claim to be the most militant force in the Johannesburg area during the 1940s. It was also the only political party that admitted members of all races, a fact that attracted to its ranks some idealistic young whites, the most famous of whom was Bram Fischer, scion of a leading Orange Free State family and a Rhodes Scholar.

The Party saw itself as a vanguard party of the working class. For tactical reasons it opted in 1941 to concentrate on building up national ethnic organisations – the (Coloured) African Peoples Organisation, the Indian Congresses and the ANC.[38] The Party's Central Committee resolved in 1944 that

> We must draw in thousands of the members of each racial and national group, provide them with Socialist education, and organise them for work among their own people. We must establish closer contact with Afrikaners, who are once again being plunged into disillusionment and dismay by the course that the war is taking, and by the failure of their leaders to find a solution for the national problems of the Afrikaner.[39]

The CPSA itself was fully multiracial, with a membership at the time of its banning in 1950 of between 2 000 and 3 000, mostly Africans.[40] Its emphasis on the organisation of each 'racial and national group' chimed with the approach of the ANC, which in practice accepted only African members, even though nothing in its Constitution prevented the enrolment of members of all races. The pattern of organisation by 'group' was subsequently to be consolidated by the 'Doctors' Pact' signed in March 1947 by Dr Xuma of the ANC, and Drs GM Naicker and YM Dadoo of the Natal Indian Congress and the Transvaal Indian Congress, respectively. The Pact provided for 'the fullest co-operation between the African and Indian peoples' in furtherance of efforts to secure equal rights. That Dadoo was a senior member of the CPSA and Naicker co-operated closely with Party members also strengthened the incipient alliance between the ANC and the CPSA, despite the ANCYL's opposition.

It was the miners' strike in 1946 that, more than any other single factor, promoted the alliance. The Party had been assiduous in trying to build up trade unions among African workers. (African trade unions, while not illegal, were not recognised for purposes of the statutory industrial conciliation system. Strikes by African workers, moreover, were illegal, and union organisers were commonly given a hard time by employers.) In 1941, largely under CPSA and Transvaal ANC auspices, the African Mineworkers' Union was formed, with JB Marks as chairman. Shamefully low wages, food shortages on the mines, safety issues and a punitive attitude by mine managements to the union combined to form a potent brew of grievances that resulted in a major strike in 1946 in which some 60 000 Africans participated.[41]

It was a seminal event in the evolution of white/African relations on the industrial front and in the development of what came to be known as the Congress Alliance. The brutal breaking of the strike led directly to the adjournment in protest of the Natives Representative Council. It also gave a fillip to the growing sense among many ANC members that the time for dignified, constitutional supplication to government had passed.

Many in the ANCYL, including Mandela, Oliver Tambo and, of course, Lembede, continued in their visceral mistrust of communists. Mandela's views circa 1946–7 are revealing:

> Even though I had befriended many white communists, I was wary of white influence in the ANC, and I opposed joint campaigns with the [Communist] party. I was concerned that the communists were intent on taking over our movement under the guise of joint action. I believed that it was an undiluted African nationalism, not Marxism or multi-racialism, that would liberate us. With a few of my colleagues in the [Youth] league, I even went so far as breaking up CP meetings by storming the stage, tearing up signs and capturing the microphone.[42]

Mandela's anti-communist views moderated gradually, as did those of Tambo and others, but by no means all Youth Leaguers. 'I found that African nationalists and African communists generally had far more to unite them than to divide them.' Friendships with individual non-African communists like Ruth First, Joe Slovo, Ismail Meer and Bram Fischer eroded his ethnocentric views; and the Soviet Union's support for colonial nationalist movements strengthened the appeal of Marxism.[43] In time Mandela became a sympathiser, even a fellow-traveller, and possibly, a member.

By 1949 the ANCYL had largely succeeded in becoming 'the brains-trust and power-station of the spirit of African nationalism'.[44] More than that, it had become the tail that wagged the ANC dog. With the assistance of the left, the ANCYL was able to push through its Programme of Action at the ANC's annual conference in December 1949, and also to depose Xuma, who had refused to support the Programme. Xuma's successor as ANC president-general was JS Moroka, a gentlemanly doctor from the rural Orange Free State (whose patients awaited his services in racially separate waiting rooms).

Moroka, who had not previously been an ANC activist, but had expressed his support for the Programme of Action, possibly did not know what he was letting himself in for. The Programme marked a new departure for the ANC: 'immediate and active boycott, strike, civil disobedience, non-co-operation', together with plans for a one-day national stoppage of work, crossed the border into illegality. The apartheid state would push the ANC far further across that border.

*   *   *

In 1948, on the eve of the coming of apartheid, South Africa was already a comprehensively racialised, segregated state. Apartheid would entrench and extend what were already established institutions, and apply them more ruthlessly. The segregation of the pre-1948 era served the interests of major sectors of white society, especially agriculture, mining and labour, in an ad hoc, even pragmatic or instrumental, way in comparison with what was to come. For all the continuity between the pre- and post-1948 eras, apartheid was yoked to an ideology of nationalism and religious particularism, and this made a difference to the zeal with which it was implemented.

The account of African political responses to the consolidation of white power has stressed how, in relation to the white-controlled state and its institutions, African political organisations were powerless: they were reactive because there were no alternatives. Even if white society was entirely dependent on black labour, law and practice (as implemented by employers and the state) ensured that potential countervailing labour power could not be successfully mobilised – and that when it was, as in the 1946 miners' strike, a combination of coercion and intimidation could neutralise it.

In spite of their evident powerlessness, it is incorrect to suppose that Africans submitted meekly or passively to subjugation and incorporation into colonial society. The steady and deliberate erosion of traditional African societies prompted adaptation to new cultural values, as well as to new economic necessities. As Absolom Vilakazi put it, disorganisation and disintegration are simultaneously accompanied by reorganisation and reintegration.[45]

The deprivation and discrimination that accompanied incorporation into white-ruled systems generated huge resentment, but also a widespread eagerness to learn new techniques (including the use of guns), to receive education and to convert to Christianity. By 1911, according to the *World Atlas of Christian Missions*, there were some 1.2 million Christian adherents of the mission denominations in South Africa, including Basutoland (now Lesotho) and Swaziland, with at least another 25 000 members of the independent African churches, often breakaways from the mainstream churches and commonly in reaction to paternalistic white control of those churches.

It was a creative response. Janet Hodgson's subtle study of Christian beginnings among the Xhosa shows that

> ... whereas the Xhosa became increasingly oppressed by white domination in their physical lives, spiritually they found a measure of liberation in that they were inspired to create new ways of expressing their Christian faith that resonated with the totality of their African experience.[46]

Racial domination rested not only on its political, economic, educational and social pillars, but also on what Steve Biko was to call 'colonisation of the mind'. Lembede was the first important leader to identify this phenomenon, calling it 'psychological enslavement' and a '*Ja-Baas*' ('Yes-Master'), submissive mentality:

> ... the African people have been told time and again that they are babies, that they are an inferior race, that they cannot achieve anything worthwhile by themselves or without a white man as their 'trustee'

or 'leader'. This insidious suggestion has poisoned their minds and has resulted in a pathological state of mind. Consequently the African has lost or is losing the sterling qualities of self-respect, self-confidence and self-reliance.[47]

There were parallels in the Afrikaner experience of conquest and incorporation into an imperial system, although Afrikaners never experienced the same degree of discrimination as Africans. In notes for a speech in 1912, Hertzog identified components of the syndrome of conquest among Afrikaners: apart from political and economic subordination, there was

> ... an exaggerated respect for the conqueror, his language, customs, morals, powers, rights, and everything that is foreign .... a continuous contempt for our countrymen and our language; a lack of faith in ourselves, our language and its durability, a low evaluation of our literature; a fear of being judged inadequate and ridiculed; a cowardly hypocrisy and imitativeness; and loss of the feeling of self- and national esteem.[48]

The psychological mechanism involved in the relationship between dominator and dominated has been differently described by authors such as Fanon and Mannoni. In a classic account of the internalisation of racism by dominated groups, Albert Memmi describes the consequences of the systematic dehumanisation of the colonised:

> Constantly confronted with this image of himself [as dehumanised], set forth and imposed on all institutions and in every human contact, how could the colonized help reacting to his portrait? It cannot leave him indifferent and remain a veneer which, like an insult, blows with the winds. He ends up recognizing it as one would a detested nickname which has become a familiar description. The accusation disturbs him and worries him even more because he admires and fears his powerful accuser. 'Is he not partially right?' he mutters. 'Are we not all a little guilty after all? Lazy, because we have so many idlers? Timid, because we let ourselves be oppressed.' Willfully created and spread by the colonizer, this mythical and degrading portrait ends up by being accepted and lived with to a certain extent by the colonized. It thus acquires a certain amount of reality and contributes to the true portrait of the colonized.[49]

Part of the Africans' vulnerability to the psychic impact of racial domination could be ascribed to the denigration of traditional culture that was inherent in the missionaries' efforts to convert and educate. Es'kia Mphahlele, a leading writer, speaks of the need 'to repair the damage that the missionaries ... have done to the African confidence by condemning his way of life as totally heathen and fit for firewood'.[50] Nelson Mandela, whose self-confidence seems to have been unaffected by the mission school experience, describes how a teacher – an African woman, as it happens – bestowed upon him the name 'Nelson', saying that thereafter it was the name by which he would be known at school. (It seems not to have been resented, although in recent times there has been a perceptible tendency for younger politicians to revert to using their African given names.)

Although Mandela's view of the mission school is more benign than Mphahlele's, his description of the denigration of traditional culture is similar:

> The education I received was a British education, in which British ideas, British culture and British institutions were automatically assumed to be superior. There was no such thing as African culture.[51]

Generalisations about loss of self-esteem, however, are dangerous. Different individuals and different groups probably reacted in varying ways to cultural and other domination, although Mphahlele's account of his reactions to whites while growing up in a location (as urban African areas were once called) outside Pretoria in the early 1930s was probably widely shared by Africans:

> We had to stay out of the white man's way on the sidewalks. Especially when a group of them, no matter how tender in age, walked abreast .... We lived in perpetual fear of the white man. He knew it and gloried in it .... We got to know the white man as an agent of fear and pain, before we had any idea of him as a human being.[52]

For many the ostensibly servile '*Ja-Baas*' mentality was a means of self-protection that concealed a raging resentment of white racism. In others, however, a deference that bordered on obsequiousness appears to have been genuine. Take, for example, the case of DDT Jabavu, a leading African intellectual whose role in the struggle against the attack on the Cape African franchise has been mentioned. In 1927 he made the following extraordinary statement to a parliamentary committee:

> We instinctively take off our hats to the white man even where we
> know he is distinctly inferior to us in educational and economic at-
> tainments …. I unconsciously say 'boss' to the white man who mends
> my fences, just because of my natural respect for the white colour
> which has behind it a history of 2000 years of development …[53]

Perhaps Jabavu was trying to ingratiate himself with a powerful committee in the interests of saving the Cape franchise; perhaps it reflected in
part his Mfengu background, the Mfengu being a widely regarded (even
today) by other Xhosa-speakers as lackeys of white administrations.

More plausible than these speculations is the generational dimension:
Jabavu was 42 years old in 1927, and deeply steeped in the non-confron-
tational style of Cape politics. The rising generation who established the
ANCYL in the 1940s would have been appalled by his remarks.

The generational factor in shaping African political attitudes is a significant variable. The Youth Leaguers of the 1940s, the 'Africanists' of
the late 1950s who formed the PAC, and the students who inspired the
Black Consciousness Movement of the late 1960s and 1970s each, in turn,
reflected the heightened impatience of a rising generation and, of course,
a changing world in which racism steadily became an ever more disrepu-
table doctrine. Its impact proved to be cumulative: herein lay one of the
profound forces that stormed apartheid's bastions.

CHAPTER 3

The Rise and Decline of Apartheid

In the 46 years of NP rule (1948–94) apartheid went through three over-lapping and imprecisely bounded phases: (1) from 1948 to 1959 the em-phasis was on entrenching NP power and extending discrimination; (2) from 1959 to 1966 a supposedly more 'positive' version, called 'separate development', was introduced in the hope that an increasingly hostile world would accept that preparing 'homelands' (bantustans) for self-gov-ernment was analogous to the decolonisation process occurring in Africa; and (3) from 1966 onwards apartheid began to erode at an ever-increasing pace and the previous relative solidarity of Afrikaner nationalism started to break up.

This chapter does not purport to provide a history of apartheid, but rather a thematic overview of the principal issues of the era. Obviously policy did not unfold in a political vacuum: it was (feebly) challenged by a parliamentary opposition, the United Party, that was fatally compro-mised by its own commitment to white control. In later years a spirited liberal opposition developed, based initially on the Liberal Party (founded in 1953) and then on the Progressive Party (founded in 1959) and its suc-cessive incarnations. Neither, however, was capable of electorally defeat-ing the NP.

The main challenge to the NP came eventually from the black extra-parliamentary opposition, which went through phases that broadly cor-relate with those of the NP.

* * *

Much of the first phase of NP rule, corresponding to the terms of office as Prime Minister of DF Malan (1948–54) and JG Strijdom (1954–8), was devoted to reducing its electoral vulnerability: after a long struggle the Coloured common roll voting rights were abolished in 1956, the limited parliamentary representation accorded to Indians in 1946 (elections for which were boycotted) was abolished in 1948, six seats for whites (all of them easily won by the NP) were given to South West Africa in 1949, and in 1958 the voting age for whites was reduced from 21 to 18, to the benefit of the NP.

The abolition of the Coloured vote caused a constitutional crisis, and also demonstrated the lengths to which the NP would go in the interests of self-preservation. It became a matter of urgency for the NP to do this when, in the 1949 elections for the Provincial Councils, the United Party won back the Western Cape constituencies of Paarl and Bredasdorp from the NP. Although there was no evidence to show that the NP's losses were attributable to increased registration of Coloured voters, the NP interpreted the setback as the writing on the wall for its narrow parliamentary majority. Its efforts in 1951 to enact legislation that would eliminate the Coloured vote were temporarily thwarted by the Appellate Division of the Supreme Court's decision that the legislation was unconstitutional since it had not been passed with the required two-thirds majority of both Houses sitting together as prescribed by the Constitution. There were suggestions that the obstinate judges be dismissed, but Malan refused. Means scarcely less reprehensible would be adopted to enable the NP to get its way.

It took until 1956 for the law, the Separate Representation of Voters Act, to be enacted, and then only by enlarging the Senate with NP-supporting Senators who thereupon provided the required two-thirds majority. At the same time the Appellate Division was 'packed' with five additional judges who could be relied upon to accept the validity of the legislation, thereby avoiding another embarrassing setback to the government.

Why was it deemed necessary to go to such extraordinary lengths effectively to disenfranchise a group that was culturally and biologically so close to the Afrikaners themselves? Some Nationalists were troubled by the morality of the legislation and the means whereby it was eventually validated; a few Afrikaner professors dared to protest at the disregard of constitutional norms – and suffered condemnation from their institutions in consequence.

Apart from the perceived immediate political threat there was, according to the newspaper *Die Burger* (the Cape NP's mouthpiece), a wider issue:

> ... in a political system where the struggle for power was waged

between two White groupings with sharply different views of the
past as well as the future of South Africa, the dragging in of a growing political 'Brown power' [Coloured voting power] necessarily had
to have the most serious implications. When the constitutional position allows a White party to compensate for its decline among the
Whites by the registration and mobilization of Brown votes, it must
expect its opponents to want to change that position at any price.[1]

In place of their common roll voting rights Coloured voters in the Cape
were accorded four (white) representatives in the House of Assembly.

*   *   *

In significant respects the linchpin of the apartheid system was the
Population Registration Act of 1950, which in principle sought to classify
every South African according to 'race'. Introducing the legislation, the
Minister of the Interior provided the underlying rationale:

> The determination of a person's race is of the greatest importance
> in the enforcement of any existing or future laws in connection with
> separate residential areas ...[2]

For the great majority 'racial' classification was unproblematic, however
reprehensible the principle. But for a minority in the Coloured category
and for those who 'passed' as white, the problems could be severe. The
intention was that the system should be as inflexible as possible, and be
based upon appearance, general acceptance and repute. Descent was later
added as a further criterion.

Given the extent of miscegenation over 300 years of history, however, it
proved impossible to make 'determinations' with any degree of rigour or
consistency. Numerous amendments to the law testified to the elusiveness
of individuals' 'race' – and the absurdity and cruelty of attempting to
determine it.[3] F van Zyl Slabbert, an MP from 1974 until 1986, dealt with
many cases of applications to change 'group'. His vivid descriptions of
the arbitrariness of 're-classification' procedures led him to conclude:

> The Population Registration Act is the generic act structuring racial
> privilege over a wide range of activities of which sexual intercourse
> and marriage across the colour lines happen to be the sensational
> exceptions. It is in the competition for jobs, land, schools, houses,
> that the real sense of racial deprivation and discrimination is kept

alive, and a source of explosive political, economic and social conflict as well. Nothing competes with the Population Registration Act
in drawing the racial lines of this conflict.[4]

As cruel in its consequences, though for many more people, the Group
Areas Act of 1950 was another fundamental pillar of apartheid. It sub-
sumed all previous legislation, notably the ad hoc attempts of previous
governments to curb so-called Indian 'penetration', by providing for the
comprehensive residential and business segregation of the different colour
groups in every city, town and village. It was, claimed the Minister of the
Interior,

> ... designed to eliminate friction between the races in the Union be-
> cause we believe, and believe strongly, that points of contact – all
> unnecessary points of contact – between the races must be avoided.
> If you reduce the number of points of contact to the minimum, you
> reduce the possibility of friction. Contact brings about friction, and
> friction brings about heat, and may cause a conflagration.[5]

The Minister's claim about reducing contact to reduce friction was the
stock defence of segregation; but this was not the only reason for the
legislation. Alan Paton, who had extensive knowledge of the effect of the
Group Areas Act in his native Natal, witnessed the devastating impact it
had on many Indian communities. He wrote:

> Another strand in the Group Areas rope was pure unadulterated
> anti-Indian hatred, an anger at the success of Indian shopkeepers,
> and a contempt for their way of life. Another was greed, a desire
> to get hold of the property of Indian people, and particularly those
> Indian areas which had been surrounded by the growing white towns
> and cities, and so had become unbelievably valuable. This applied
> also to the property of coloured people, particularly in the Cape ...[6]

Despite assurances that the procedures for proclaiming group areas would
ensure that no group's interests were jeopardised, the Act operated in a
highly discriminatory way. The statistics tell their own story: between the
inception of the legislation and 31 August 1984, 83 691 Coloured, 40 067
Indian and 2 418 white families had been removed.[7]

The number of Africans removed was smaller, largely because separate townships for Africans had been statutorily required since 1923, and
partly because many urban African freehold areas, of which Sophiatown

in Johannesburg was the most famous, were abolished in terms of other legislation. As Minister of Native Affairs, Dr HF Verwoerd laid down elaborate plans in 1952 for the siting of new urban townships, whose effect was to ensure that Africans continued to be consigned to the periphery of towns.[8]

The obsession with separation extended to virtually every sphere of society, including public facilities, restaurants, transport, beaches and even learned societies; 'mixed' sport was prohibited; blood given by donors was racially separated, and the dead were buried in racially segregated cemeteries. Many of these manifestations of separation were colloquially termed 'petty' apartheid, although there was nothing petty about the monstrous indignities that it inflicted on its targets. In the late 1970s and 1980s, when questions began to be raised in Nationalist circles about the necessity for, and wisdom of, 'petty apartheid', ultra-rightwingers insisted on its retention. There was a perverse truth in their contention that this was necessary to ensure that race consciousness should not be blunted. 'Whites Only' signs, moreover, were a constant reminder to blacks of their subordinate position.

One of apartheid's chief aims was the elimination of competition between black and white, invariably to the benefit of whites. Since the labour market was the principal arena of such competition it was logical that additional steps would need to be taken to protect white workers – the more so because it was precisely this class whose support had given the NP the vital breakthrough on the Witwatersrand in 1948.

The principle of reserving better-paid jobs was nothing new. The mining industry had long since pioneered the principle; and, of course, all civil service posts, except for menial ones, were de facto the preserve of whites. The exclusion of blacks had been compounded and aggravated by the introduction in 1924 of the 'civilised labour' policy, in terms of which national, provincial and local governments were expected to replace black menial employees with poor white ones.

Formal and informal exclusions meshed with other devices that entrenched black subordination in employment, including the non-recognition of black unions, the prohibition of the right to strike, and 'closed shop' agreements that gave a veto to white unions, which ensured that only whites would be employed in better-paid, skilled posts. Masters and Servants Laws dating from the nineteenth century were ostensibly intended to provide protection for both categories, but in practice their enforcement was heavily biased in favour of employers, and commonly served to tie black workers down to a particular 'Master'.

As noted above, the years of the Second World War had seen the rapid

growth of secondary industry and, in the absence of many whites on military service, the job colour bar was significantly breached, especially in
the manufacturing sector. Accusations that the white worker was in mor-
tal danger of 'unfair' competition from 'lower standards of living' were
part of the Nationalists' argument that segregation was breaking down,
with the UP's connivance.

Two laws enacted in this first phase of apartheid deserve mention. First,
the Bantu Building Workers Act of 1951 permitted Africans to perform
skilled building work in the African townships (at lower wage rates than
their white counterparts), but prohibited them from doing so outside
African areas. This was not a concession but a response to the chronic
shortage of accommodation that had arisen as industry developed.

Secondly, and more far-reaching in its scope, was the introduction of
'job reservation' in terms of an amendment to the Industrial Conciliation
Act in 1956. This empowered the Minister of Labour to reserve particular
categories of work for a specific racial category. It also outlawed racially
mixed trade unions. A Department of Labour pamphlet published in
1960 claimed that the purpose of job reservation was as 'a precautionary
measure against inter-racial competition and a positive measure to ensure
the orderly co-existence of the different races.'

The measure was also intended to protect 'the traditional spheres of
Coloured employment' against African competition, especially in the
Western Cape. It dovetailed with an administrative effort, the so-called
Eiselen line of 1955, strictly to control the influx of Africans into the
Western Cape.

* * *

The core of apartheid was the attempt to thwart, neutralise or abort the
African urbanisation that – from the segregationists' point of view – had
begun to assume such alarming proportions. What kind of separation
would be feasible unless tough measures were taken to stem the tide? EG
Jansen, the Minister of Native Affairs, appeared not to have a clue about
how to proceed. In response to opposition questions about the conclusions of the Fagan Report, he artlessly responded:

> On the whole I think we are prepared to accept the findings of fact,
> but we are not prepared to accept all the conclusions and the reme-
> dies recommended in that report …. I am not satisfied that the move
> to the urban areas is entirely natural.[9]

This and other signs of helplessness on Jansen's part dismayed the hard-liners, who began agitating for his removal. Jansen's most notable acts as Minister were to appoint two commissions of considerable importance – one, an inquiry into African education that would pave the way for the most destructive component of apartheid, and the other, an inquiry into the rehabilitation and potential carrying capacity of the African reserves that would pose damning questions about the feasibility of apartheid.

The second commission produced its report, *Socio-economic Development of the Bantu Areas within the Union of South Africa (U.G. 61/1955)*, in 1955. Its chairman, Professor FR Tomlinson, was an agronomist, and, predictably, its other members were white, most of them close to the Afrikaner nationalist establishment. HF Verwoerd, who succeeded Jansen as Minister of Native Affairs late in 1950, was opposed to the commission's very existence, believing that his and his officials' knowledge of the reserves was sufficient to render its endeavours superfluous.

As Minister, Verwoerd had immediately sought to make his mark on policy implementation. He was not one to be wracked by self-doubt. A journalist who asked him whether his huge responsibilities for policy caused him sleeplessness reported the answer: 'Oh, for sure, he sleeps well, he answered spontaneously, and then he added, "See, a person doesn't really have the worry of doubt about whether you are perhaps wrong."'[10]

Shortly after his appointment he intimated to Cabinet that he proposed introducing legislation to impose a complete ban on Africans in the Witwatersrand, particularly in the Johannesburg area. He was immediately attacked by Ben Schoeman, then Minister of Labour, who pointed out that such legislation 'would have a fatal effect on the country's economic growth'. Other ministers supported Schoeman, and Verwoerd was forced to back off.[11]

A few years later, in 1956, Schoeman and Verwoerd were involved in another Cabinet skirmish, caused by Verwoerd's decision not to permit any African workers to enter the Western Cape, this having been declared a 'Coloured labour preference area'. Schoeman called this a 'stupid proposal', and, now as Minister of Transport, insisted, to Verwoerd's fury, that he would continue to employ Africans on the Railways.

This row had been preceded by another argument at an informal policy discussion. Verwoerd had acknowledged that total territorial separation ('*algehele gebiedskeiding*') was impracticable, but that it should be held up to 'our people' as an ideal to be striven for – it would encourage them to support government policy even more strongly. Schoeman was having none of this, saying it was 'blatant fraud' to put forward a policy that he knew could never be realised. The dispute, in which Schoeman admitted using 'crude language', had to be settled by the Prime Minister, JG Strijdom.[12]

Verwoerd's arrogance and ruthlessness were illustrated by his attitude to the Tomlinson Commission and its chairman. Apart from rejecting its principal recommendations, that white capital should be permitted to invest in the reserves, that individual tenure should replace communal land tenure, and that £104 million should be spent on development over the next decade, he launched personal attacks on Tomlinson – a scrupulously honest person – even accusing him of embezzling Commission funds. He pressured two departmental officials who served on the Commission to retract their support for certain recommendations and instead to sign a minority report (which Tomlinson believed to have been formulated by Verwoerd himself). Moreover, Tomlinson was ordered to refrain from public comment on the Report, and his career advancement in the public service was blocked.[13]

The main significance of the Tomlinson Report lay in demographic projections that cast considerable doubt on the feasibility of apartheid. Indeed, population growth among Africans would become a raging torrent that contributed massively to apartheid's downfall. The report posited two projections of population growth and accepted the second or higher one as more realistic. This yielded the following breakdown for the year 2000: 4.58 million whites, 21.36 million Africans, 3.9 million Coloureds, and 1.38 million Indians. It left open the possibility that the white population's size might be augmented to 6.15 million by immigration.

For the apartheid government the problem was the daunting one that even on the Commission's (over-optimistic) projection of the likely carrying capacity of the reserves – namely that they would accommodate 70 per cent of the entire African population by the year 2000 – some 6.5 million would remain in the 'white' areas, outnumbering the white population, whose numbers in any case were most unlikely to reach 6.15 million, and in fact fell far short.

Verwoerd did not appear fazed by the bad news, whose impact he sought to mitigate by making claims that were simultaneously facile and bogus. First, of the 6.5 million Africans in 'white' areas, four million would be in the rural areas (mostly on white-owned farms) 'where the problem of apartheid presents no difficulty to us and where apartheid is maintained locally'. This meant simply that in the caste-like conditions of the *platteland* (countryside) there was no question of equality because the colour bar was rigidly enforced.

Secondly, the 6.5 million 'will have their anchor in their homeland ...'. This was an early manifestation of the chimerical hope, fundamental to apartheid, that Africans could be induced to channel their political aspirations into their 'homelands', regardless of where they happened to live and work at any given time. Verwoerd elaborated:

> They will be like the Italians who go to France to take up employment there. They remain Italians and they remain anchored in their homeland; that is where they seek their rights; they do not expect and ask for rights in the other place.[14]

Verwoerd was deluding himself: African migrants in the 'white' areas could hardly be expected to be as pliant as Italian and other Gastarbeiter in Western Europe were supposed to be. The history of their incorporation into the South African economy was not a matter of choice, as Verwoerd claimed. It was the consequence of the deliberate and systematic undermining of the self-sufficiency of pre-colonial indigenous societies so as to provide labour for farming and industry. African claims to a share in the wealth of a common society built in no small measure by their labour were entirely justified.

Thirdly, regarding the 6.5 million Africans in the 'white' areas, Verwoerd claimed that 'the assumption is unfounded that the same persons will always be domiciled here permanently'. He predicted that Africans who worked in the 'white' areas and who obtained knowledge and skill while doing so would 'use it in their own areas'. In other words, as far as possible the African labour force would be migrant workers. Moreover, Verwoerd accepted without reservation the principle of so-called 'border industries', tentatively proposed by the Sauer Commission and accepted as policy. Africans employed in such (white-owned) industries located near to reserve borders would commute on a daily or weekly basis.[15]

Subsequent to the debates about the Tomlinson Commission, Verwoerd conjured up the notion that by the year 1978, a veritable *annus mirabilis*, the number of Africans in the 'white' areas would begin to decrease. How exactly this piece of demographic legerdemain was arrived at remains unclear. It was obliquely repudiated by his successor, BJ Vorster, but not before Verwoerd had rebuked his Minister of Bantu Administration and Development (as the Native Affairs portfolio had been renamed), MDC de Wet Nel, for letting slip in Parliament that the date 1978 should not be taken too literally.[16]

The main instrument for limiting the flow of Africans to the 'white' urban areas was the pass system, now called 'influx control'. In one form or another pass laws had had a long history as a means of control and as a source of anger for Africans who were caught in their web. As a system they were even more comprehensive and vexatious than the internal passports required of individuals wishing to change localities in the former Soviet Union. As Michael Savage observed in a comprehensive analysis of South Africa's pass laws, they were used

> ... to balance two apparently contradictory white needs: an 'exclusionary' need to obtain political security by controlling and policing the number of Africans in 'white' areas, and an 'inclusionary' need to ensure a supply of cheap labour within these areas.[17]

In 1952 Verwoerd radically tightened up the existing pass law system. With further, increasingly restrictive, amendments in 1955 and 1957, the legislation provided that no African might remain for more than 72 hours in a proclaimed urban area unless he or she:

(a) had continuously resided there since birth; or
(b) had worked there continuously for one employer for 10 years, or had been there continuously and lawfully for 15 years and had thereafter continued to reside there, and was not employed outside the area, and while in the area had not been sentenced to a fine exceeding £50 or to imprisonment for a period exceeding six months; or
(c) was the wife, unmarried daughter, or son under 18 years of age of an African falling into classes (a) or (b), and ordinarily resided with him; or
(d) had been granted a permit to remain, by an employment officer in the case of workseekers, or otherwise by the local authority.

This was the notorious Section 10 of the Native (Urban Areas) Act of 1945. Draconian as the provisions were, the 'rights' they afforded people were even further limited by subsequent amendments.

In terms of other legislation enacted in 1952, the various passes that Africans were required to carry were coordinated into a single document, and the principle was adopted that women, too, should carry reference books, as passes were now officially termed. The issuing of reference books to women began in 1956, and from 1963 they were subjected to the full force of influx control.

The brutal character of urban policy could be inferred from an official circular issued in 1967:

> It is accepted government policy that the Bantu are only temporarily resident in the European areas of the Republic, for as long as they offer their labour there. As soon as they become, for some reason or

other, no longer fit for work or superfluous in the labour market they are expected to return to their country of origin or the territory of the national unit [bantustan] where they fit in ethnically if they were not born or bred in the Homeland .... It must be stressed here that no stone is to be left unturned to achieve the settlement in the homelands of non-productive Bantu presently residing in the European areas.[18]

It was in the very nature of influx control that it could only be enforced by the institutionalised and continual harassment of Africans by police and other officials to check that they were 'lawfully' in particular areas. The consequence was prosecutions on a large scale: Savage's calculations indicate that between 1946 and 1964/5 a total of 6.5 million were prosecuted for pass law offences.[19]

Helen Suzman, who waged a lone (and lonely) parliamentary battle against the very principle of influx control, said in 1964, regarding a further amendment that reduced the scope of Section 10 rights:

> One can only say that in the last analysis, because these laws apply only to Black men – laws which nobody would dare to impose upon White men in this country – the only conclusion one can reach is that the government does not consider the Black man as a human being. It does not regard him as a person with the normal aspirations of a human being to have a secure family life .... It ignored all the fundamental concepts of human dignity. It strips the African of every basic pretension that he has to being a human being, to being a free human being in the country of his birth, and it reduces him to the level of a chattel ...[20]

Policy was deliberately designed to make the cities and towns as unattractive as possible, and to prevent the development of stable communities. Apart from the continuous vexation of pass law enforcement, night-curfews and other regulations, the effort to 'freeze' the urbanised (meaning here 'town-rooted') African population took other forms as well, including:

- limitations on the scope of African traders, who were, in any case, confined to African townships;
- the phasing out of sub-economic (subsidised) housing after 1958;
- the abolition in 1968 of the right of urban Africans to lease property on a 30-year leasehold agreement;
- the requirement that 'nie-plekgebonde' (literally 'not locality-bound') institutions in 'white' areas, including certain types of

hospital, old-age homes, and homes for the blind and deaf, must be transferred to the 'homelands';
- the limitation after 1959 on the expansion of secondary and technical schools for Africans in the 'white' areas;
- from 1968 onwards the supply of urban housing for Africans was drastically reduced, being replaced by the construction of barrack-like hostels for single migrants; and
- from 1954 onwards a policy directive required that township houses be allocated strictly according to ethnic group.[21]

The last point reflects another dimension of apartheid, that Africans should 'develop along their own lines'. The principle had been enunciated during the pre-1948 era by Smuts and others, but apartheid would elevate it to a new importance. For reasons that were transparently obvious, apartheid sought to emphasise 'tribal' identities at the expense of a national African identity. Verwoerd spelled out the motivation with characteristic candour:

> … it is clear that the key to the true progress of the Bantu community as a whole and to the avoidance of a struggle for equality in a joint territory or in common political living areas lies in the recognition of the tribal system as the springboard from which the Bantu in a natural way, by enlisting the help of the dynamic elements in it, can increasingly rise to a higher level of culture and self-government on a foundation suitable to his own inherent character.[22]

It was Verwoerd's view, moreover, that many of the 'so-called urbanized natives still have their roots in the native areas and have their tribal ties'.

The linchpin of 'cultural apartheid' was the attempt to restore the position of chiefs by means of the Bantu Authorities Act of 1951, which made chiefs the fulcrum of political development in the bantustans. It was proclaimed as 'the restoration of the natural Native democracy'. In traditional African political systems chiefly power was circumscribed by various popular checks, including the possibility that an alienated segment could hive off; but in the overpopulated reserves this was no longer possible. In any case, chiefly power was rigorously limited by the central government, which did not hesitate to depose chiefs who were alleged to be 'troublemakers'.

Verwoerd's view of the African's 'inherent character' had profound policy implications for education. The Commission on Native Education, 1949–1951, chaired by Dr WWM Eiselen, one of apartheid's ideological progenitors and later Secretary for Native Affairs, laid the ideological basis and the administrative framework for the Bantu Education Act of 1953. The legislation accepted the Commission's recommendation that control of African education be removed from the provincial governments and given to the central government, and that missionary bodies, who were responsible for the great majority of schools, should cede control to government.

The ideological aims of the new dispensation were frankly stated by Verwoerd in a speech in 1954 that was still being quoted decades later by angry protesters. Beneath the crudities of the speech lay two of his fundamental premises. First, that policy should be 'an organically related system', which it had not previously been. Education, in other words, should not be out of alignment with the overall aims of apartheid. Second, Verwoerd bitterly resented past educational policy for turning Africans into 'black Englishmen':

> It is in the interest of the Bantu that he be educated in his own circle.
> He must not become a black Englishman in order to be used against
> the Afrikaner.[23]

In particular, the Anglican church was singled out as a prime offender in this respect. Verwoerd's view was typical of that Afrikaner paranoia that regarded the attempts of the perfidious English to use black votes and the power of cultural assimilation as weapons against Afrikaner hegemony. Bizarre as Verwoerd's views may have sounded, Mandela's school experience suggests that there was some truth in the contention that the missionaries were intolerant of African traditionalism; though whether they had an underlying political agenda is doubtful.

The tenor of Verwoerd's notorious and oft-quoted speech in 1954 can be gauged from a quotation:

> It is the policy of my department that education should have its roots
> entirely in the Native areas and in the Native environment and Native
> community. There Bantu education must be able to give itself complete expression and there it will have to perform its real service. The
> Bantu must be guided to serve his own community in all respects.
> There is no place for him in the European community above the level
> of certain forms of labour. Within his own community, however, all
> doors are open. For that reason it is of no avail for him to receive a
> training which has as its aim absorption in the European community
> while he cannot and will not be absorbed there. Up till now he has
> been subjected to a school system which drew him away from his

own community and partially misled him by showing him the green
pastures of the European but still did not allow him to graze there.[24]

It was not realised at the time, and certainly not by Verwoerd and his colleagues, that dragon's teeth were being sowed by the new system. There
were vehement protests after its introduction in 1954, but the apartheid
juggernaut ploughed relentlessly on, destroying in the process the possibilities of a good education for a generation of African youngsters. It
was not as if African education prior to 1954 was all that good: it suffered
serious deficiencies of funding, facilities and high-quality teachers, but at
least it was not underpinned by an ideology that sought to emphasise the
'otherness' of Africans.

In 1959, after delays caused by legal issues, the apartheid principle
was extended to universities: henceforth 'white' universities could no
longer invoke their autonomy to admit qualified students of all colours.
In practice this mostly affected the universities of Cape Town and the
Witwatersrand, which accepted black students while maintaining 'social segregation' in sporting and other social activities. The University
of Natal, Durban, admitted black students, but they were mostly taught
in separate classes in a separate venue. Its medical school admitted only
blacks. Rhodes University admitted only the occasional black student at
the post-graduate level, although between 1951 and 1959 Fort Hare had
been an affiliated institution. None of the Afrikaans-medium universities
admitted blacks.

Henceforth no 'white' university could admit black students, except by
official permit, granted only if the course(s) that an applicant wished to
study were not offered by the new university colleges that were established
for blacks in terms of complementary legislation that excluded them from
'white' universities. The new institutions, predictably, were structured along
'ethnic' lines. Those for Africans were: the University College of the North,
serving the Tswana, Sotho, Venda, Tsonga and Transvaal Ndebele groups;
and the University College of Zululand, serving the Zulu; Fort Hare was
taken over and now became a University College for the Xhosa. All three
African institutions were situated in isolated rural areas, far from urban centres. Each was expected to develop a special focus on the culture and development of the groups for which they catered. For the Coloured 'group', the
University College of the Western Cape was established near Cape Town, and
for Indians the University College of Durban-Westville, near Durban.

In each case the new colleges were under the tight control of the relevant Minister, who appointed the rectors and council members, and over-
saw appointments and dismissals of staff. Student activities were carefully

controlled. The councils and senates were to be exclusively white, and, insultingly, 'advisory' councils and senates were established for blacks. The rectors were apartheid supporters, while the teaching and administrative staff were preponderantly Afrikaans-speakers. In many cases the lecturers were either former schoolteachers or young graduates from the Afrikaans-medium universities. More dragon's teeth had been sown: in time, each of the 'tribal' or 'bush' colleges, as they were derisively called, would become focal points of militant opposition.

Brief mention must be made of three aspects of Bantu Education. First, it was Verwoerd's view that Africans themselves should carry an increasing amount of the cost of expanding their own education. The basic components of funding for African education comprised an annual payment of R13 million from general revenue, which was fixed (and remained so until 1972), plus four-fifths of the general tax paid by Africans. The consequence was a striking discrepancy in the annual per capita expenditure on white and African pupils: in 1953 the figure for whites was R127.84; for Africans R17.08; in 1969–70 the respective figures were: R282.00 and R16.97, the latter differential meaning a ratio of 16 to 1 in the spending on a white pupil *vis à vis* an African pupil.[25]

Second, with the assumption of control by the central government, Afrikaans assumed a new prominence, the role of English being correspondingly reduced. Ken Hartshorne, a former education official who subsequently became one of Bantu Education's sternest critics, wrote:

> In a very short time Afrikaans became the dominant language in black education, especially at the levels of management, control and administration, and teacher training.[26]

Furthermore, a new policy was adopted whereby from 1956 onwards the medium of instruction in primary schools should be the mother-tongue (an indigenous African language), while both English and Afrikaans were to be taught as subjects. By 1959 the Standard 6 public examination was to be written in an indigenous language, instead of English.[27] The intention was that mother-tongue instruction was gradually to be extended to all standards.

The language policy was laid down in spite of previous Afrikaner nationalist opposition to dual-medium (English and Afrikaans) instruction in white schools. Educationalists with long experience considered it indefensible, its motivation being purely political, a manifestation of Verwoerd's eagerness to stop the schools' producing 'black Englishmen', and, perhaps, the desire of Afrikaans publishers to exploit a potentially lucrative market in Afrikaans textbooks for African schools. Bantu Education, and within it the issue of medium, became the foremost single grievance among Africans, for the majority of whom ensuring that their children received a decent education – and with it, the hope of upward occupational mobility – was a prime aspiration. The dragon's teeth would demonstrate their ferocity in 1976 when Soweto students rose up in protest.

❊   ❊   ❊

By the late 1950s the basic framework of apartheid had been established, thanks in no small measure to Verwoerd's ideological zeal and imperviousness to criticism. The NP was riding the crest of a wave. In the 1958 election it had increased its majority over the UP to 50 seats and, for the first time, exceeded the UP in the number of votes actually cast for it. The UP, moreover, was beginning a long process of decline. In 1959, tired of the Party's shilly-shallying on racial matters, 12 of its ablest MPs, including the indefatigable Helen Suzman, resigned and thereafter formed the liberal Progressive Party.

Verwoerd, no doubt encouraged by all of these developments and totally in control of the NP and the wider Afrikaner nationalism, decided to reach for the highest attainment, a republic. With the additional votes created by a lowered voting age, he won a narrow victory in a referendum held in 1960. This victory, his apparent omniscience as a leader, and his miraculous survival of an assassination attempt on 9 April 1960, all contributed to virtual deification by his supporters, now including a growing number of English-speakers.

However dogmatic and inflexible Verwoerd may have been, he was anything but stupid; nor was he incapable of reading the writing on the wall. The independence of Ghana in 1957 was a portent of things to come; Harold Macmillan's 'Wind of Change' speech, delivered in the South African Parliament on 3 February 1960, infuriated Verwoerd, but it is likely that he had already understood the basic message, that South Africa's racial policies were unacceptable in the modern world.

It was with such thoughts in mind that Verwoerd initiated the second phase of apartheid, henceforth to be termed 'separate development'. If the first phase had been pre-eminently concerned with shoring up the supposedly eroding dam wall of white control, the new phase purported to advance African ethnic 'nations' to self-determination in their 'homelands'. In a revealing speech delivered in 1965 Verwoerd explained why the change of emphasis was necessary:

We would rather have seen the old position, but in the circumstances of the post-war world that was obviously not possible … . Years ago the position prevailed where nobody doubted the White man's supremacy. The old British colonial policy itself was one of White supremacy over other states, and particularly the Black states. We had this policy in South Africa under Generals Botha and Smuts, and even thereafter. The position was always that the White man ruled and expected the Bantu always to regard him as his guardian. For obvious reasons I said that we all wished that all these post-Second World War changes had not come about, because then surely the world would have been very comfortable for us … . But … in the light of the new spirit and the pressures exerted and the forces which arose after the Second World War it is clear that no country could continue as it did in past years. The old traditional policy of the White man as the ruler over the Bantu, who had no rights at all, could not continue.[28]

This was a comprehensive, if grudging, repudiation of previous doctrines of *baasskap* ('mastership') espoused, among others, by his predecessor as Prime Minister, JG Strijdom. It also raised new questions: was what was being offered to Africans anything more than the shadow of freedom, since *baasskap* was being firmly maintained in the 'white' areas? And what if the discrepancy between (pseudo-) freedom being offered in the homelands and the kind of freedom that Africans were demanding became too great?

The statutory basis for homeland evolution was laid down by the Promotion of Bantu Self-Government Act of 1959. It also abolished the limited parliamentary representation of Africans that had survived since 1936 (and, incidentally, got rid of one of Verwoerd's most formidable critics, Margaret Ballinger). To allow the continuation of such representation was, in Verwoerd's view, a symbolic affront to the direction of his new policy. The premise of the legislation stated:

Whereas the Bantu peoples of the Union of South Africa do not constitute a homogeneous people, but form separate national units on the basis of language and culture…

The law identified eight such ethnic national units, the first statute ever to make these distinctions. It provided also for an extension of the Bantu Authorities Act of 1951 and vested additional powers, duties and functions in territorial authorities for each homeland, territorial authorities being the apex of the hybrid system of chiefly rule envisaged by Verwoerd as the 'restoration of natural native democracy'. Commissioners-General were to be appointed to represent the South African government in the homelands. Furthermore, each territorial authority was empowered to appoint representatives or 'ambassadors' to 'their' people in the urban areas.

In speaking to the proposed legislation Verwoerd was at his patronising worst: 'We must guide these people and teach them to govern properly and to assume responsibility.' It was quite wrong, he declared, that Africans would have no rights in the 'white' area: 'They will even have the right, while they are in the White area, to take part in the government of their Bantu homeland ....'

He reiterated an earlier view, even more frankly, that urban Africans would not be permanent residents of the white areas, and, moreover, that they would be 'interchangeable':

> Large numbers of them will come and work and live here for a number of years as family units but will then be interchangeable. They will remain anchored in their homelands, and as they find uses and rewards in the developing Bantu areas for the skills they have acquired in the White area in the meantime, they will return to the Bantu areas and reap the benefit of their knowledge there. Those who will then have to seek work elsewhere again, will find employment here. In this way the Bantu, even if some of them remain in the White area for years, will nevertheless remain a changing group of workers' families.

Contradicting previous official statements, Verwoerd now also acknowledged that: 'If it is within the power of the Bantu, and if the territories in which he now lives can develop to full independence, it will develop in that way.' On the question of the possible ceding of more land to the bantustans, Verwoerd was inflexible:

> ... each group, White or Black, always inhabits the area which it has occupied. If this argument [that it was immoral for 80 per cent of the population to have only 13 per cent of the land] has any validity, then it means that those who are numerically in the minority in any part of the world would continually have to surrender land to their neighbours who, in proportion to their numbers, have less.[29]

As with so much of Verwoerd's reasoning, the logic was impeccable, but the premise was faulty, ignoring both history and context. A huge castle in the sky was being built. Relatively few Africans would wish to occupy it.

A further development in the evolution of homelands occurred in 1970 when legislation provided that every African was to be a citizen of a homeland, regardless of whether a person lived in a particular homeland, or even had any knowledge of the homeland in question. For purposes of dealings with foreign states, however, citizens of homelands remained South African citizens. With the coming of 'independence' – Transkei in 1976, Bophuthatswana in 1977, Venda in 1979, and Ciskei in 1981 – citizens of these bantustans lost their South African citizenship. Over eight million people were affected. Dr CP Mulder, the Minister of Plural Relations and Development (as the Department of Bantu Administration and Development had been renamed), said in 1978:

> If our policy is taken to its logical conclusion as far as black [African] people are concerned there will not be one black man with South African citizenship ... . Every black man in South Africa will eventually be accommodated in some independent new state in this honourable way and there will no longer be an obligation on this parliament to accommodate those people politically.[30]

Independence for the bantustans weakened already precarious Section 10 rights. If Mulder's prediction was realised, within two or three generations, all Africans in the 'white' areas would be 'foreigners', devoid of rights and vulnerable to deportation if they were infirm or if their labour was not required.[31]

Hope that Verwoerd's 'new vision' could be translated into viable, credible and legitimate (in the eyes of their putative citizens) states was chimerical. The homelands were fragmented, poor and dependent; serving as huge labour dormitories for 'white' South Africa – and, of course, as a standing pretext for denying political rights to Africans in a shared society, as well as dumping grounds for those deemed surplus to requirements.

Fragmentation was the legacy of the nineteenth-century practice of breaking up large contiguous areas occupied by African societies. This could be seen most egregiously in the KwaZulu homeland in Natal which consisted of 29 separate blocks of land. Ciskei and Bophuthatswana were hardly more credible as putative independent states. In total the nine homelands were made up by 91 discrete blocks. The description of the homelands as a 'horseshoe' around the perimeter of South Africa was misleading: rather they resembled the spots on a Dalmatian dog.

In addition to the homelands, so-called 'black spots' and 'poorly situated' pieces of homeland (that jutted into 'white' areas) had to be eliminated. 'Black spots' were areas of land bought by African communities prior to the land legislation of 1913. Like their urban counterparts, they were anomalies in apartheid's grand design, and therefore had to be removed, the owners being granted compensatory land in a homeland. The number of such 'black spots' ran into hundreds. The detailed survey by the Surplus People Project calculated that there were 383 'black spots' in Natal alone, although this definition included land owned by churches and mission stations and leased to individual Africans.[32] According to official figures the number of Africans resettled from 'black spots' between 1970 and 1979 was 240 555.[33]

These removals were but one component of the massive displacement of people that occurred as a consequence of apartheid's social engineering. The Surplus People Project estimated in 1983 that three-and-a-half million people, some 10 per cent of the entire population, had been subject to forced removal. Apart from those mentioned above, there were removals of tenants from white-owned farms, urban relocations, removals in terms of the Group Areas Act, evictions from urban areas in terms of influx control, and yet other categories.

In 1955 the Tomlinson Commission had recognised that the fragmentation of the reserves had resulted in 'scattering and consequent incoherence' of ethnically related African groups. It proposed far-reaching consolidation, which became official policy and was actively pursued as the homeland policy developed. 'Final' consolidation proposals were presented to Parliament in May 1975, but even had it been possible to implement them only three homelands (including minuscule QwaQwa) would have consisted of a single bloc of territory. Altogether the ten homelands would have been made up of 35 blocs, including ten for KwaZulu, three each for Transkei and Gazankulu, and six each for Bophuthatswana and Lebowa.[34]

Criticism that 'national states' (as official terminology now described them) which were still fragmented could not become independent, evoked the spurious response that there were several states made up of discrete blocs: Alaska and Hawaii in relation to the United States of America, and Greece, which apart from its mainland, possessed over 3 000 islands![35] These were hardly compelling precedents.

Even these proposals proved impossible to implement. By 1981 the entire project was effectively abandoned, the chairman of the Central Consolidation Committee telling Parliament that 'if we wanted to carry out consolidation on a geographic basis, then we could possibly have succeeded 40 years ago but today it is no longer possible.'[36]

*   *   *

Notwithstanding the post-1959 emphasis on homelands, the towns and cities of 'white' South Africa continued to be the main focus of conflict. Mention has been made of the basic tenets of urban policy and the harshness with which it impacted on the lives of ordinary people. The killing of 69 Africans by police at Sharpeville on 21 March 1960 arose out of a protest against the pass laws. Apart from heightening international condemnation of South Africa's racial policies, the episode and serious protests elsewhere gave some Nationalists cause to ponder where Verwoerd's obsessive drive was leading the country.

A mere three weeks after Sharpeville Verwoerd was shot at point-blank range by a would-be assassin. Miraculously he survived, but during his recuperation the senior minister Paul Sauer (of Sauer Commission fame) acted as Prime Minister and took it upon himself to call for major policy changes in a speech in his constituency. Sauer, who had expressed misgivings about policy even before Sharpeville, began boldly by declaring that 'the old book of South African history was closed'. Now, he continued, the entire basis of racial policy would have to be reconsidered with seriousness and honesty. He called for a new spirit of trust between the races and major changes in how policy was implemented (but he was careful to qualify this recommendation by specifying that no deviation from declared policy would be involved). Africans, he said, must be given hope for a contented existence 'and not feel that they are continually being oppressed'.

In particular Sauer called for major changes in the enforcement of the pass laws, which were one of the main causes of friction, as well as being the trigger for Sharpeville; the prohibition on the sale of liquor should be lifted; contact between peace-loving urban African leaders should be strengthened; serious attention should be given to raising African wages; and large-scale development of the homelands should be undertaken.[37]

Sauer's suggestions seemed small beer, especially since he had completely ducked the crucial issue of political rights; but with Verwoerd at the helm and in the tense circumstances prevailing, they were explosive. Before delivering the speech Sauer had shown it to Dr Eben Dönges, leader of the Cape NP, who responded: 'I agree with you, but I will not say so.' Ben Schoeman also expressed agreement, but warned Sauer that Verwoerd would be displeased. That even powerful and senior ministers evinced such fear of incurring Verwoerd's wrath was a telling comment on the atmosphere prevailing in the Cabinet.

Verwoerd, who had not been informed about Sauer's speech prior to its delivery, was, indeed, much displeased, making it clear to Sauer that major policy statements were to remain his prerogative. His wife recorded in her diary even before Sauer's speech that:

> He wanted to end the situation by drastically limiting the number of [urban] Bantu. Industrialists will kick against this but it must force them to the border industries. 'If I cannot save our country, I would rather resign. I will *never* be party to the destruction of our *volk* by abandoning our policy.'[38]

Sharpeville was a seminal event that went to the heart of apartheid. Despite warnings even from pro-NP newspapers that the future of the country depended critically on the treatment of urban Africans, Verwoerd made it clear that no policy changes were intended and that 'the black masses of South Africa … are orderly' and 'faithful to the government of the country'. The disturbances were caused by a 'few troublemakers'.[39]

Nothing came of Sauer's proposals, except for the removal in 1961 of the ban on Africans buying liquor. The pass laws, which had been suspended during the turmoil after Sharpeville, were reinstated and enforced with full rigour. It was even announced that as from 1 December 1960 it would be compulsory for African women to carry passes (officially termed 'reference books').

Sharpeville was undoubtedly a crisis, but there was never any serious danger that the ensuing countrywide disturbances could escalate into an uprising that threatened the state. The imposition of a state of emergency, the detention of over 11 500 people of all races, and the banning of the ANC and the Pan-Africanist Congress ensured that the state's grip was not loosened. A further consequence was the substantial enlargement of the security branch of the police and the beginning of special training of police officers in the use of Sten guns and Browning machine guns aimed at countering the potential escalation of violence.[40] The change from what he called the 'bumbling ineptitude' of the security police in the 1950s was noted by Joe Slovo, a leading figure in the (banned) South African Communist Party. Torture, solitary confinement, indefinite detention without trial, and deaths in detention were to become commonplace.[41]

By mid-April of 1960 protests had largely petered out. Verwoerd had satisfied himself that the mailed fist was the only way to deal with the 'few troublemakers' – and the whites who allegedly encouraged them. The appointment of BJ Vorster (a former leading light in the O-B and a wartime internee) as Minister of Justice marked another critical development in the resort to draconian security legislation that was vital to the enforcement of apartheid. On being appointed, Vorster had said to Verwoerd that 'you could not fight communism with the Queensberry Rules'. Verwoerd agreed, saying, according to Vorster, 'that he would leave me free to do what I had to do – within reason'.[42] Vorster claimed that South Africa was 'on the verge of revolution', an opinion shared by the security police; he predicted that the crisis of threats to state security would materialise in 1963.[43]

The legal system was a major pillar of the racial hierarchy. The criminal law was the major instrument for the enforcement of apartheid. Judges, who were appointed from among senior advocates by the executive (in practice, the Minister of Justice), were, generally speaking, conditioned by the environment in which they lived and worked. Although formally independent, some were susceptible to (white) community and political pressure, although neither form was applied directly. What John Dugard described as the judges' 'major inarticulate premise' operated to ensure that they saw it as their duty to uphold law and order, which was invariably interpreted as supporting the status quo.[44] George Bizos, a leading advocate and prominent defence counsel in many political trials, cites as an example the presiding judge in the Rivonia trial (see chapter 4), who asked one of the defendants 'how do you know that the ordinary-Bantu-about-town wants the vote?' It indicated the different worlds in which the judge and the accused lived. Bizos commented that the judge's views 'were those of the vast majority of his fellow Afrikaners, namely that the relationship between white and black should be that of master and servant, and that was the end of the matter'.[45] (Many English-speakers, including some judges, shared the same outlook.)

Judicial bias was seldom overtly expressed, and, moreover, different judges manifested it to differing degrees. The small numbers of liberal judges were aware of the danger and consciously resisted it, but their numbers declined and, in several cases, they were overlooked for promotion to the highest posts in the judiciary, including that of Chief Justice. The character of the courts changed in the 1960s and 1970s: after 1948 a concerted effort was made to reduce the overwhelmingly English orientation of the Supreme Court by appointing Afrikaner judges, including many political appointees, most of whom could be relied upon to accept as legitimate the state's methods of upholding 'law and order'.

The Treason Trial, which lasted from 1956 to 1961, was a landmark: all 156 accused were eventually acquitted of charges that revolved around the Freedom Charter's (see chapter 4) allegedly being a blueprint for the revolutionary creation of a Marxist-Leninist system. The defence, which included some of the finest legal minds, tore the state's case to shreds, leaving the three judges, none of whom could be described as liberal, in no doubt that the prosecution had failed in its task. Bizos comments that the Treason Trial 'was the last of the political trials in which some of the normal legal procedural safeguards to ensure a fair trial were observed. In its wake, the rules were changed and acquittals made even more difficult.'[46]

The changed character of the courts in the 1960s and after reflected the changing composition of the judiciary, as well as the state's arming itself with increasingly authoritarian and arbitrary powers that excluded judicial review. Executive-mindedness became dominant, and the law became the principal instrument for the enforcement of policies that rode rough-shod over civil liberties. It became common practice for political trials to be assigned to conservative judges, even those on the Appellate Division, often political appointees, who could usually be relied upon to be sympathetic to the prosecution's case. The converse of the appointment of conservative judges was the non-appointment of liberally minded advocates, whose skills and accomplishments would otherwise have qualified them for a seat on the bench. It was not until the late 1970s and 1980s that a few liberals were appointed (among others, John Didcott and Richard Goldstone).

An exception to the principle of not appointing liberals to the bench was the appointment of Judge Michael Corbett to the Appellate Division of the Supreme Court in 1974 (after serving as an acting judge for a few years). Corbett's distinction as a jurist and a legal scholar had made it difficult to overlook his claim to the position. His liberal convictions and staunch advocacy of human rights were widely known – and mistrusted by the Nationalists and conservative fellow-judges. When Pierre Rabie, the archetypically executive-minded Chief Justice, reached retirement age in 1986, Corbett was his logical successor. But PW Botha was reluctant to appoint him, and asked Rabie to stay on, which he did until 1989, by which time the case for Corbett's appointment was irresistible, even for Nationalists whose suspicions remained. (With the approval of FW de Klerk and Nelson Mandela, he remained Chief Justice after reaching retirement age in 1993.)

Some advocates who were of undoubted judicial calibre declined appointment because they would be obliged to enforce laws that they found abhorrent; and several declined because they would be required to impose the death penalty, which offended their abolitionist convictions. (Others declined for the more mundane reason that a successful advocate's practice was more lucrative than being a judge.)

The executive-mindedness of the courts was characterised by 'an overweening and pliant willingness to acquiesce in the most stringent and unjust executive action'.[47] The clearest evidence for this contention is to be found in the courts' treatment of cases involving persons detained without trial. The scope and duration of such detention was steadily increased during the 1960s: legislation enacted in 1963, the so-called 'Sabotage Act', greatly extended executive power beyond that provided for in already tough security laws. Apart from a definition that went far beyond any conventional understanding of the notion of sabotage, provision was made for savage penalties, equivalent to those for treason (which might incur the death penalty) and carrying a minimum of five years' imprisonment. The power to ban allegedly subversive organisations was widened, and the Minister of Justice was empowered to place persons deemed a threat to the state under house arrest. Power was also given to commissioned police officers to detain persons for up to 90 days if they were suspected of committing various political offences or of possessing information about such offences. Detainees were required to answer questions to the satisfaction of the police; but should the police not be satisfied, detention could be extended for another and, conceivably, yet another 90-day period.

Detention without trial, without access to lawyers, friends or family, put a detained person wholly at the mercy of security police interrogators. Further legislation in 1965 extended the period of possible detention to 180 days, and in 1967, in terms of the Terrorism Act, the possibility of indefinite detention was introduced. It was, to quote the anodyne words of the official history of the police, 'a very handy legal lever' for the police, who were entitled to act, according to Vorster (who became Prime Minister in 1966), 'as if the country were in a state of war'.[48]

The absence of any effective safeguards and the abandonment of the ancient principle of *habeas corpus* opened the way for abuse, mostly by way of systematic and institutionalised torture. By 1990, 73 detainees had died in custody, including Steve Biko, the Black Consciousness leader, who died a miserable death at the hands of security police interrogators in 1977. According to the Truth and Reconciliation Commission established in 1995, which provided graphic evidence of some of the methods used, over 2 900 people reported 5 002 instances of torture, most commonly beating, but including over 2 000 cases of being forced into painful postures, electric shocks, suffocation or mental torture.[49]

In a challenge to the Minister of Police in 1982, Helen Suzman received a categorical assurance that torture was not used, to which, in turn, she responded by citing evidence to the contrary, and pointing out that none of the policemen involved in torture had been disciplined – 'in fact some of them have even been promoted'.[50]

Apart from the evidence of informers who had penetrated opposition movements, legal and underground, much of the evidence used in political trials was extracted under duress from detainees. In democratic states in which the rule of law was maintained such evidence would not have been admissible in the courts. The South African courts, including the Appellate Division of the Supreme Court (the highest court), for the most part accepted evidence beaten (often literally) out of detainees, prompting Anthony S Mathews, a leading academic lawyer, to write that a court

> ... deceives itself in believing that it can evaluate the evidence of a detainee subjected to prolonged isolation by the usual methods of assessment. The trauma experienced by detainees who are interrogated in isolation makes a reliance on the witness's demeanour, and on general impressions of him, extremely dangerous.

Mathews argued that the courts should have adopted as a basic rule that credibility be denied to the evidence of detainees who had been held for anything but a short period, during which their interrogation had not been excessively severe: '[The courts'] failure to react decisively against detainee evidence has been a lost opportunity to render full justice in security trials.'[51]

The Supreme Court emerged from the apartheid era with its reputation severely tarnished, redeemed only by the few judges with strong commitments to civil liberties. The TRC predictably gave the Court a roasting:

> Part of the reason for the longevity of apartheid was the superficial adherence to 'rule by law' by the National Party (NP), whose leaders craved the aura that 'the law' bestowed on their harsh injustice .... In the intervening thirty years [after the constitutional crisis of the mid-1950s and the changed personnel of the judiciary], ... the courts and the organised legal profession generally and subconsciously or unwittingly connived in the legislative and executive pursuit of injustice .... Perhaps the most common form of subservience can be captured in the maxim *qui facet consentire* (silence gives consent).[52]

It was true that the principle of parliamentary sovereignty meant that Parliament could make or unmake any law and that judges were obliged to enforce duly enacted legislation. Moreover, much of the security legislation providing for detention without trial or 'banning' under the Suppression of Communism Act precluded judicial intervention. In spite of the judiciary's failures, apartheid justice could not be compared with that dispensed under communism or Nazism. Raymond Tucker, a liberal

attorney who acted for many accused of political offences, took umbrage
at this comparison, while unreservedly declaring apartheid evil: would
Nazism or communism have permitted any form of opposition or other
forms of freedom?

> More importantly, though, would they have allowed even the sugges-
> tion of a fair trial for those they considered enemies of the state? If
> in no other way, the apartheid state distinguished itself from those
> totally repressive regimes by the maintenance of a justice system
> (however flawed) that permitted committed lawyers to appear before
> judges (frequently politically tainted but not always evil) to defend
> their clients in a Treason Trial, a Rivonia Trial, a Pretoria Twelve
> Trial, a Delmas Trial.
>   Not all the trials were fair, especially those in the rural areas ....
> The dice were always loaded in favour of the state. But the fact is that
> many people accused of politically motivated activities were acquit-
> ted either initially or on appeal.[53]

Tucker himself was one of a small band of lawyers who took on political
cases, thereby earning the opprobrium of the authorities, including some
judges, and even some of their professional colleagues. It was their commitment, with the assistance of ingenious ways of channelling foreign
funds to local attorneys, that ensured that the accused in major political
trials were defended by some of the best lawyers.

During the apartheid era South Africa became notorious for its extensive use of the death penalty: between 1949 and 1968 an average of 76
persons were hanged annually; between 1969 and 1987 the figure rose to
96.[54] There were good grounds for believing that the death penalty was
imposed in a racially selective way. It is, however, difficult, if not impossible, to extract from statistics on executions those persons who received
the death penalty for politically motivated offences. This was so partly
because the state declined to distinguish political offences from non-
political ones (although it did, in practice, make such a distinction for
imprisoned political offenders who, unlike other prisoners, were invariably denied remission of sentence).

Amnesty International found in 1978 that no executions for overtly
political offences had occurred since the 1960s, and advanced as a possible reason that judges had sometimes refrained from imposing the death
penalty for political reasons.[55] There was some plausibility in this explanation: many judges, and the ministers who could recommend commuta-
tion, were aware of the bitterness that the execution of Afrikaner political

offenders had caused in the past: 44 Cape 'rebels' who had sided with the Boer forces in the Anglo-Boer War had been executed by the British authorities, while the execution of Jopie Fourie, the army officer who joined the rebellion in 1914, was a major fillip for Afrikaner nationalism, Fourie being immediately elevated to the status of martyr. Smuts learned a valuable lesson, and, as Prime Minister during the Second World War, commuted the death sentences imposed on pro-Nazi Afrikaners convicted of treason and other serious offences. All were released from prison when the Nationalists came to power in 1948. No such amnesty or remission of sentence was granted to black political prisoners during the apartheid era. According to a plaque in the Apartheid Museum in Johannesburg, however, 131 persons (whose names are listed) were executed for political offences between 1948 and 1990. By February 1990, when State President FW de Klerk suspended the death penalty, 79 persons were awaiting execution for political offences.[56]

By 1965 the authorities were congratulating themselves on apparently having averted the revolution that Vorster had predicted. Several thousand people had been arrested, and many convicted, for furthering the aims of the banned ANC and PAC; an uprising in Pondoland, principally a revolt against Bantu Authorities, had been put down; Poqo had been broken up and many of its members imprisoned; and, most important of all, the leadership of Umkhonto we Sizwe (the Spear of the Nation), the ANC's underground guerrilla organisation, had been arrested in July 1963. Nine of the ten accused, including Nelson Mandela, were found guilty of planning to overthrow the government by violent revolution, and seven were sentenced to life imprisonment. In other cases more Umkhonto members were convicted and given lengthy sentences. It was unsurprising that after these breakthroughs the official history of the police could report that '1965 was one of the quietest years the South African police had experienced in decades'.[57] The respite, however, proved to be short-lived.

The increasingly authoritarian nature of the apartheid state involved not only a crackdown on opponents and the subversion of the rule of law. Government grew more centralised as uncooperative or recalcitrant local authorities, controlled by opposition councils, were forced into line.

Traditionally, urban African affairs had been the responsibility of local governments, but Verwoerd began steadily to erode whatever discretionary powers they once possessed. He made it clear that 'local authorities are the agents of the state with respect to the execution of [racial] policy.' Local authority managers of 'Non-European Affairs' had to be licensed by the central government, and their primary function was to see that their town councils 'know exactly what the state's policy is and how it is

applicable to the activities of their town'.[58] Legislation in the 1950s and
after gave the Native Affairs Department of the central government powers to oversee, and, if necessary, intervene in municipalities' administration of African affairs.

Cape Town and Johannesburg, both controlled by anti-Nationalist
councils, clashed with the central government on several issues relating to
policies to whose implementation they were opposed. Mostly these concerned African administration, but also the Group Areas Act, which required 'racial zoning' that effectively reconfigured towns and cities. WJP
Carr, the humane manager of Johannesburg's Non-European Affairs
Department from 1952 until 1969, was appalled by the impact of apartheid on people and communities. Of Verwoerd's era, both as Minister of
Native Affairs and as Prime Minister, he wrote that it was

> ... probably the most difficult phase in African administration, in
> Johannesburg in particular, but also throughout South Africa. There
> was no evidence of compassion on his part for African people, suf-
> fering under conditions of poverty, bad housing and the weight of in-
> numerable oppressive laws, the infringement of one of which brought
> serious retribution .... This lack of compassion characterised his
> entire administration, with few exceptions. Every situation was met
> with another law, always repressive and often punitive. I cannot think
> of one instance where the lot of ordinary African people was eased
> or made more comfortable by the actions of the Verwoerd adminis-
> tration. An illustration of this was the instruction we received that
> nothing should be done to create conditions of 'luxury' in Soweto
> which would act as a counter-pull to the ... policy to repatriate as
> many as possible of the urban Africans to the homelands. We also re-
> ceived instructions forbidding any white official from shaking hands
> with an African, or addressing him as 'Mr' and 'Dear Sir' in corre-
> spondence. The correct form was to be 'Mna' (a form of address in
> Sesotho).[59]

The temper of the times, described by Carr, was illustrated by many ab-
surdities, laughable if they were not so insulting. Perhaps the most absurd
of all, in a very competitive field, was the decision by the Oudtshoorn
Municipality, an extremely reactionary body, to blast a separate entrance
for 'non-whites' into the Cango Caves, one of the scenic wonders of the
country!

Beginning in 1952 with an abortive proposal to extend the principle
of Bantu Authorities to urban areas, various attempts were made to link

urban Africans with their supposed homelands. In 1959 legislation provided for the appointment of chiefs' 'ambassadors' to the urban areas. This, too, was rejected, as was the principle of requiring the 'ethnic grouping' of township residents. Equally unsuccessful were efforts to establish Urban Bantu Councils in 1961: most members of these councils were to be elected, but some were to be nominated by officially recognised urban representatives. The legislation permitted the Councils to be granted certain executive powers. The new system was almost universally opposed by urban Africans, and the nickname 'Useless Boys' Clubs' soon gained wide currency. The message was clear: large majorities were not going to be inveigled into making apartheid work by participating in essentially powerless institutions.

*　　*　　*

Verwoerd's assassination on the floor of the House of Assembly on 6 September 1966 ended an era, though it was by no means an end to apartheid. He had stifled any debate in his party on where racial policy was heading, and any hardy soul, whether in the party or in the wider Afrikaner nationalist movement, who stuck his neck out by questioning Verwoerd's judgement was likely (metaphorically speaking) to have his head chopped off. In 1966 he was at the pinnacle of his power, facing minimal opposition from the white electorate (indeed, the elections of March 1966 had seen unprecedented support for the NP by English-speakers) and the extra-parliamentary forces.

Nearly 30 years after Verwoerd's death, Anton Rupert's biographer, Ebbe Dommisse, revealed a remarkable story told to him by Rupert: in 1995 the elderly and frail former chief whip of the NP, Koos Potgieter, who had served under Verwoerd's premiership, asked Rupert to visit him. Potgieter claimed that two days before his death Verwoerd had told him that the policy of apartheid was impracticable and could not be implemented. In response to Potgieter's question, why did he then not change it, Verwoerd replied that this was not politically feasible at the time: 'You can't turn the car around too sharply, it will capsize.'[60] By all accounts Potgieter was an honest man, unlikely to have fabricated the story. Although the puzzle cannot be solved, it seems inherently unlikely that Verwoerd would have, or could have, changed to a more liberal approach.

While Verwoerd's death caused shockwaves among Nationalists, dismay was mingled with a sense of relief. A leading Nationalist newspaperman, Schalk Pienaar, who had clashed with Verwoerd in the past, quoted a friend asking how much longer South Africa could have endured him.

Pienaar himself wrote that Verwoerd had engendered a false sense of security among whites:

> In the fermentation and eddying [*gistinge en malinge*] of our time so many South Africans became lazy under Verwoerd. Some stopped thinking about colour issues. Others allayed their doubts in the belief: He knows; leave it to him.[61]

According to a Dutch Reformed clergyman, Nico Smith, who heard him say it, Verwoerd was determined to entrench apartheid so deeply that whatever government came to power afterwards would find it impossible to undo what had been done.[62] Not only did he create a false sense of security, he entrenched myths about apartheid's viability that made his successors' task of dismantling it more difficult. His ideological heirs came dangerously close to being able to stage a counter-revolution when the time for apartheid's final abandonment arrived.

Just as Verwoerd had used his prominence as Minister for Native Affairs as a springboard for the premiership, so Vorster used the Justice portfolio and his responsibility for security to become Prime Minister. Vorster was cast in a different mould from Verwoerd. While possessed of a certain native cunning as a political infighter, he had none of Verwoerd's intellectual qualities. He was primarily a party manager, a fixer, and more of a pragmatist, who came into high office with little knowledge of how the big departments of state worked. Inevitably, the iron grip that Verwoerd had maintained and his close supervision of ministries gave way to looser control under which individual ministers enjoyed greater freedom of action.

Verwoerd's demise resembled a spring thaw in some respects: the hardline conservatives, who had muttered *sotto voce* about the dangers of independent homelands, now became more vocal, heralding the *verkrampte* (reactionary) versus *verligte* (enlightened) feud that was to rumble on for years. Even Vorster, despite his complete acceptance of the basic apartheid order, came under *verkrampte* fire for what were really minor adjustments to existing policy. The infighting grew intense, fanned by Afrikaans newspapers that were eager to expose the *verkramptes'* scheming to infiltrate all Afrikaner institutions with a view to controlling them.

Vorster was emotionally drained by the struggle, and had to be dissuaded from resigning in August 1967.[63] He regained his composure and finessed the four MPs who broke away in 1969 by holding an election early in 1970 in which their party, the Herstigte Nasionale Party (HNP) – the 'Reconstituted National Party', declining to use the English version– was trounced. Despite a thumping victory, Vorster was aware that the defectors of 1969 were the merest tip of a large *verkrampte* iceberg, whose spiritual leader, Andries Treurnicht, had declined to defect only for tactical reasons.

Vorster's biographer, John D'Oliveira, wrote that in lengthy discussions with him Vorster 'consistently evaded serious discussion of the future, like a chess player determined not to reveal his moves to anybody'.[64] Unlike Verwoerd, he had no faith in the *annus mirabilis* of 1978, and he would not spell out what the political future of the Coloured people might be, deeming this to be a problem for which 'our children after us will have to find a solution'.[65] Apparently, Vorster had reached the same conclusion as Verwoerd: that apartheid was unworkable – or so he told Ian Smith, the Prime Minister of Rhodesia.[66] But he was not the man to engage in a radical revision of policy, for which he had neither the vision nor the courage. He would continue to tread water, publicly proclaiming his commitment to apartheid.

Vorster did not persecute and hound opposition from within his own ranks with the same vindictiveness as Verwoerd. He tolerated more freedom of discussion inside the NP, and the intensity of the *verligte–verkrampte* battle significantly unfroze the debate within Afrikaner civil society. While it is true, as their critics have argued, that the *verligtes* were hardly daring in their thinking, they were nevertheless symptomatic of changes occurring among Afrikaners. The crude racism of the HNP offended many, especially those among a rising generation who were better educated, more affluent, and more secure in, and less obsessive about their Afrikaner identity than their elders. Increasingly, traditional conceptions of Afrikaner nationalism became restraints against which they chafed. In short, as Afrikaners became a more middle-class group, the psycho-social impact of *embourgeoisement* accompanied the process. The tight interlocking of the Afrikaner nationalist bureaucracy was beginning to loosen.

Although Vorster's commitment to the basic tenets of apartheid was not in doubt, and its human costs continued to be exacted, he deconsecrated apartheid in one significant respect: Dirk Richard, a prominent Afrikaner journalist, quoted him as saying to a group of NP MPs shortly after his election as Prime Minister:

> No, chaps, you have all got it wrong. The cardinal principle of the NP is the retention, maintenance and immortalisation of Afrikaner identity within a white sovereign state. Apartheid and separate development is merely a method of bringing this about and making it permanent. If there are other better methods of achieving this end, then we must find those methods and get on with it.[67]

This seemingly innocuous comment deeply offended Jaap Marais, a leading figure in the breakaway *verkrampte* HNP in 1969. It appeared to presage a pragmatic approach that would violate the principles that Verwoerd had sought to cast in iron. Vorster did, in fact, make minor adjustments that in themselves were trifling, but led to a huge uproar in the NP. There were four issues:

1. Sports policy, where he reversed Verwoerd's decision of 1965 to disallow a touring New Zealand rugby team to include Maori players. The New Zealand selectors could, and did, include whom they wished for the 1970 tour. For *verkramptes* this was the thin end of the integrationist wedge: what might happen in off-the-field socialising?

2. Immigration policy, where, in order to boost the size of the white population, whites were to be encouraged to emigrate to South Africa. The policy had actually started in Verwoerd's time, but *verkrampte* criticism that over time Afrikaners would no longer be a majority of the white population sharpened after it became known that in 1966 over 48 000 immigrants had entered the country, 97 per cent of whom would associate with the English-speaking section, according to *verkrampte* projections.

3. Co-operation with English-speakers, who would be welcomed into the NP if they subscribed to its principles. For the *verkramptes*, however, it meant the inevitable dilution and downfall of Afrikaans culture. The culture of the English, moreover, was sated with liberal values; the Afrikaners' Calvinist values made them the only people who could be entrusted with ruling South Africa.

4. The arrival in South Africa of African diplomats from elsewhere in the continent as a consequence of Vorster's 'outward policy', whereby he sought to establish diplomatic links with other African states. The prospect of African diplomats enjoying equal status with their non-African colleagues and their South African hosts, and exempted from petty apartheid rules, horrified the *verkramptes*: it would erode the established pattern of race relations and become 'the starting point from which the very foundation of the apartheid policy would be attacked'.[68]

There was a perverse logic to the thin-end-of-the-wedge arguments advanced by the HNP and its *verkrampte* allies who were entrenching themselves in the network of Afrikaner institutions: once 'adjustments' began to be made to what had previously been regarded as inviolable principles, where was the line to be drawn? The question became even more pressing as sports policy slowly and painfully developed to permit multiracial sports under tortuously specific circumstances, and as petty apartheid regulations began equally slowly and painfully to be abolished. Whatever political gain Vorster may have achieved in the changed sports policy was wiped out in 1968 when he declined to allow the England cricket team due to tour South Africa to include Basil D'Oliveira, a Coloured ex-South African then in exile. Vorster believed that his inclusion had a political motive behind it. His foolish and petulant action resulted not only in the cancellation of the tour by the English cricket authorities but also the termination of cricketing ties with the rest of the world.

Treurnicht advanced a more sophisticated response to the view presented by some Nationalists that once 'grand apartheid' (the establishment of independent bantustans) had been achieved, the need for petty apartheid would fall away:

> If petty apartheid lapses completely, then grand apartheid is senseless, superfluous and unnecessary, because if white and non-white are acceptable to one another at all levels of everyday life and they mix everywhere without reservation, then it is senseless to force them to live in separate states or residential areas.[69]

Quite so. Treurnicht's argument could be rebutted only by the counter-argument that *all* apartheid, grand or petty, was intrinsically wrong and should be abolished. Obviously, no Nationalist was prepared to make so radical a case, least of all Vorster, who despite his limited pragmatism (and despite his comment to Ian Smith) remained firmly rooted in the apartheid paradigm.

Vorster had been unnerved by the ferocity of the disputes and the vehemence of the *verkrampte* criticism levelled against him. He was unsure of himself, and, above all, desperately anxious not to go down in history as the NP leader on whose watch the Party had split. By calling an early election in 1970 he had succeeded in his aim of demolishing the HNP before it had had time to put itself on a proper electoral footing: it was heavily defeated in each of the 78 constituencies it contested, all but three of its candidates losing their deposits.

Vorster was aware, though, that the *verkrampte* threat remained: even inside his own party perhaps as many as 25 per cent of its MPs were at least sympathetic to *verkrampte* causes, but declined to hazard jumping ship, thereby possibly endangering career prospects and/or pensions. Like Treurnicht, these closet sympathisers thought it prudent to remain within the NP fold and prevent any slippage to the left, or, even better, in due course to gain control of the party. Treurnicht himself entered Parliament in 1971 as the MP for the rural Transvaal constituency of Waterberg, located in the heart of Afrikaner ultra-conservatism. In 1972 his prestige and influence were greatly augmented by his election as chairman of the Broederbond, which, ironically, was then engaged in flushing out members who were HNP supporters.

Whatever his limitations, Vorster's political antennae were acute when it came to assessing moods and trends among his own people. (Of black feelings he knew nothing.) A year after his elevation to the leadership, Vorster told a newspaper:

> I never saw it as my task to push forward policy, either in Parliament or outside. A person can never become a good leader unless he is also a good follower. No leader chooses himself. He is pushed forward by his own people to fill that position.[70]

It would be wrong to suppose that Vorster was brimful of suppressed reformist zeal. His inscrutability and refusal to discuss future possibilities reflected his reluctance to go out on a limb ahead of his support base, as well as his essential lack of vision. He was *par excellence* the party manager whose preoccupation was preserving unity.

Opinion surveys conducted in the late 1960s demonstrated the immense conservatism of whites. In a survey of white positional elite attitudes conducted in 1968–9 HW van der Merwe and his associates found that

> ... about two-thirds of the respondents favour some form of rigid segregation (separation legally enforced without exception). The other third of the elites do not favour rigid segregation in any sphere, though only 12 percent advocate no legal segregation at all.[71]

Heribert Adam's 1966–7 survey of attitudes among the power elite (officials, parliamentarians and entrepreneurs) showed similar findings. The response to questions that probed beliefs about biologically determined race distinctions included 74 per cent affirming a difference between whites and Africans in 'skull formation and brain structure', and 80 per cent claiming a difference in 'hereditary character predispositions'; 73 per cent agreed with the statement that the 'Bantu is a child who needs centuries', and 91 per cent believed that 'Democracy is not practicable'. It was also found that there was virtual unanimity that white rule could be secured in the long run. A mere nine per cent believed that black nationalism inside South Africa posed the greatest threat to South Africa, 73 per cent claiming that 'international communism' was the biggest threat.[72]

*   *   *

Developments elsewhere in Africa contributed to the apparent intractability of white attitudes. The 'wind of change' was indeed blowing through Africa, as Harold Macmillan warned the South African Parliament in 1960, but a decade later the poor survival rate of post-colonial democratic systems, their proneness to military coups and the widespread predilection for one-party states were grist to the apartheid propagandists' mill, supposedly confirming the view that universal franchise in a unitary South Africa was unthinkable. Authoritarian tyrants like Nkrumah of Ghana and monsters like Idi Amin of Uganda were cited as further evidence that democracy could not work in Africa. The disruptive effect of ethnicity – so-called 'tribalism' – was seized upon to confirm the wisdom of the Nationalists' efforts to impose ethnic separation on Africans.

The illegal declaration of independence by Ian Smith's Rhodesian Front in 1965 had a considerable impact on South African whites, whose sympathies were overwhelmingly with their Rhodesian counterparts. Although Verwoerd, followed by Vorster, declined formally to recognise the rebel colony, both refused to cooperate with the sanctions imposed by the British government, thereby giving Rhodesia a critically important lifeline, and enabling South Africa to prop up an important component of its *cordon sanitaire*.

In such circumstances, hardline rightwing attitudes flourished: making concessions would put the country on the slippery slope to 'integration'. As has been observed, the intensity of the *verkrampte* attack on even the smallest concession had shaken Vorster, so much so that he became paralysed and incapable of any policy innovation. Schalk Pienaar's biographer, reflecting Pienaar's own gloomy views, writes:

> He [Vorster] simply trod water and amidst the relative political calm between 1970 and 1974 let things go their own way. The NP had no goal. There was a total lack of urgency. Vorster's fear of division in his party undermined the possibility of firm and effective leadership. Ironically, his inertia, in fact, exacerbated the tension and division inside the NP. Notwithstanding Vorster's image of vigour, there was a leadership vacuum in South Africa.[73]

Pienaar, a journalist and later an editor of major Afrikaans newspapers, fought fierce battles to expose the *verkramptes*' activities. In his autobiography he related how he told Vorster, shortly after he became Prime Minister, that Albert Hertzog and Jaap Marais were busy undermining him and his party. Vorster replied that he knew nothing about this.[74] He would soon learn that it was true.

Vorster's style was to let individual ministers manage their respective portfolios virtually undisturbed – which was in sharp contrast to Verwoerd's tight control. The Department of Bantu Administration and Development, a huge *imperium in imperio* that controlled the lives of Africans, was entrusted to MC Botha, a wooden reactionary and an ideological clone of Verwoerd. Many of the personnel held similar views, making the Department a veritable *verkrampte* redoubt, from which no innovative or ameliorative policy shifts could be expected.

As part of a wider process of the centralisation of state power, legislation in 1971 removed the remaining powers of local authorities (already much reduced) to control urban African administration, and vested them in Administration Boards answerable only to the Minister and chaired by persons of known pro-apartheid sympathies. Ostensibly the rationale for the change was to provide greater uniformity in the implementation of policy, but in reality the purpose was to exclude local authorities that were controlled by opposition councils, such as Johannesburg, Cape Town and Durban (the three biggest cities in the country). The Boards, which covered both urban and rural areas, were supposed to be financially self-supporting, which inevitably meant that they were chronically short of money.

Even into the 1970s official policy was based on the old principle that urban Africans were 'temporary sojourners', present in the 'white' areas 'to sell their labour and for nothing else', as MC Botha put it in August 1976. This was the core of apartheid: the attempt to abort the urbanisation revolution among Africans and to institutionalise their insecurity in the towns. The implications for urban Africans, of whom some 60 per cent and more regarded themselves as 'town-rooted', were severe.

The Boards, together with the police, were the cutting edge of apartheid. They were bureaucratic leviathans, required to implement, unquestioningly and inflexibly, a harsh policy that took little or no account of its impact on the lives of the people under their control. A senior official, JC de Villiers, of the West Rand Administration Board (WRAB), which was responsible for Soweto and other Johannesburg townships, gave telling evidence to the Cillié Commission that was set up to examine the Soweto Uprising of 1976 (see chapter six). Referring to WRAB, he described the entire system as 'clumsy and cumbersome': even to build a hall in a township required ministerial approval; urban administration had become 'troublesome' (*lastig*) to the central government, which was now preoccupied with homeland issues. He cited the question of family housing, which was a burning issue for a majority of Sowetans: between 1968 and 1975 the Department of Bantu Administration and Development became 'obsessed' with building family housing in the homelands, and conversely putting emphasis on single accommodation in urban areas.

The Department acknowledged that its priority had switched to the homelands, but denied that the provision of family housing in the 'white' areas had been prohibited: requests for such housing, though, were much more strictly vetted than previously – which, De Villiers pointed out, had led to a chronic shortage and considerable frustration.

Even though the Prime Minister himself had announced a relaxation of the policy and the reinstatement of a home-ownership scheme, it took a year before Boards were finally authorised to begin implementing it. But there was a catch: a homeland 'certificate of citizenship' had to be obtained by an applicant before approval could be granted. Another catch was that the scheme granted only right of occupation for a 30-year period, although this might be extended for up to another 30 years – in other words, there was no question of freehold ownership. (In the aftermath of the Soweto Uprising of 1976 the hugely unpopular certificate of citizenship requirement was dropped.)

De Villiers concluded that official red tape and the 'passive and at times negative role of the Department ... made a gigantic contribution to the build-up of an "anti-climate"' in which the spark of the language-medium issue could unleash such destructiveness (see chapter six).[75] In evidence given subsequently during a court case, De Villiers was asked by the judge whether the policy of 'not making things easy' for urban Africans to encourage them to return to the homelands was stated policy or just an inference. De Villiers replied:

> I cannot produce documents for you, but it was said by politicians in the Department, the political heads, and I think the circular letters also testified that this was the broad approach.[76]

Coming from someone with insider knowledge of the administration, De Villiers's evidence was devastating. To add to the Department's discomfiture, it was largely accepted by the Cillié Commission.

Vorster's apparent paralysis left him seemingly unmoved or unaware of the mounting crisis. It was obvious that separate development was not working, since the number of Africans in the 'white' areas was increasing, and the magical year 1978, by when the flow should begin to reverse itself towards the homelands, looked even more of an illusion than before. Vorster sought to fend off this criticism with the tortuous argument that numbers were not the only issue:

> Numbers are not the most important factor, nor can they ever be ...
> for the simple reason that one can have separate development with
> a million people in one's midst, whereas one can have integration
> with a hundred thousand people in one's midst. It simply depends on
> what one's approach is.[77]

Vorster's approach was vintage Verwoerd: provided racial inequality in the 'white' area was maintained, integration could be prevented.
Strenuous efforts, however, would continue to be made to limit African
numbers outside the homelands. The pass laws were enforced with full
rigour throughout the Vorster era even though their effectiveness was declining, as the proportion of Africans whose presence in the 'white' area
was technically illegal continued to rise.

Vorster showed no sign of recognising that his government was sinking
more deeply into a morass of self-deception. His speeches emphasised his
commitment to the main principles of separate development. Moreover,
he took a hard line on the question of land: no more land additional to
the 13.7 per cent of the country allocated by past legislation would be
granted to homelands. He fully subscribed to the historical myth that
African land had not been alienated in the nineteenth century. Thank
God, he said, that 'the black man retained his land in South Africa'.[78]

It was during Vorster's premiership that separate development began
to bear what was supposed to be its finest fruit: independent bantustans –
Transkei in 1976, Bophuthatswana in 1977, followed, in PW Botha's time, by
Venda in 1979 and Ciskei in 1981. If Vorster hoped that these developments
would be a vindication of apartheid, he was sadly disappointed. None of
the new states was recognised, except, of course, by South Africa and by
one another. Even Malawi, the only African state to establish diplomatic
relations with South Africa, declined to recognise them. Whatever credibility
South Africa might have hoped to gain was comprehensively outweighed by
depriving citizens of the new states of South African citizenship, whether
they lived in 'white' South Africa or in their putative bantustan. In 1970 less
than half of the African population actually lived in the homelands, and 52
per cent were in the 'white' areas.[79]

Vorster stuck firmly to the old belief that Africans could exercise political rights only in 'their' homelands, regardless of where they lived. In an
interview in 1976 he said:

> The urban Black, when it comes to exercising his political rights,
> will exercise them in his own state. They have the vote and urban
> Blacks have made themselves eligible for election to the parliaments

of the various Black states. Urban Blacks have served in the Cabinet of Black states and in one case the leader of a Black Homeland is an urban Black.[80]

The homeland led by an urban African was QwaQwa, which was hardly a persuasive example, since it was minuscule, fewer than 2 per cent of its citizens actually living within its boundaries, and over 80 per cent of its GNP being generated outside the homeland by migrants and commuters.

In another interview Vorster rehashed the same argument to a sceptical American journalist, who thereupon posed the following (rhetorical) question:

> As I understand your parallel, Sir, it would be similar to saying that if a man came from the State of Louisiana and lived all his life and reared his family in New York, his children could only exercise their rights in Louisiana because that was their homeland. Is that the kind of state you really want for your country?

Vorster's lame response was that this had always been the position 'and nobody seemed to find fault with it'.[81] It was stark evidence of Vorster's ignorance of African views. His assumptions about African politics were refracted through an apartheid prism, which denied the reality of African nationalism and scorned the claims of its modern political leadership. His paranoid views on communism caused him to regard all domestic nationalist organisations as communist-inspired.

*   *   *

As its critics had long argued, apartheid was bound to fail, even on its own terms, and certainly by any broader criterion of justice. To suppose that pseudo-independence for bantustans, superimposed on what a Cabinet minister had called 'one umbrella of a South African economy', could produce an outcome that satisfied African aspirations or any notion of equity was a delusion.

In 1974 Professor FR Tomlinson, chairman of the Tomlinson Commission, bemoaned the failure of government fully to implement his recommendations. In the 1950s, when the Report was published, government could have spurred great enthusiasm, idealism and support among whites; but, he continued, it seemed as though the authorities underestimated the will of the people to accept huge challenges, while the white population overestimated the authorities' efforts and remained preoccupied with making themselves rich. 'White South Africa must beware lest one day future generations do not reproach them.'[82] PW Botha, Vorster's successor, made the same lament in 1985: 'We failed to accept [the Tomlinson Report], and today we are paying the price for that.'[83]

How much idealism and preparedness to make sacrifices there was available to tap, however, is a moot point. Even Verwoerd had had to contend with subterranean rumblings among rightwingers in the NP that 'too much was being spent' on Africans. Another question is whether, even if fully implemented, Tomlinson's recommendations would have 'solved' the racial problem. The answer is almost certainly not. Even accepting the Commission's projections of African population growth – which were too low – Africans would still have outnumbered whites in the 'white' areas. The most one could say is that allowing white capital into the reserves and moving away from communal to individual land tenure *might* have slowed the pace of rural impoverishment.

The 1960s were a decade in which the South African economy grew at an annual average rate of 5.5 per cent, and gross fixed domestic investment averaged over 20 per cent of GDP. This occurred in spite of the Sharpeville killings in 1960: it seemed to confirm De Kiewiet's famous dictum that 'South Africa has advanced politically by disasters and economically by windfalls'. The argument advanced by neo-Marxists that the high growth rate, coinciding with a period of increased repression, demonstrated the functionality of apartheid to capitalism, is difficult to sustain. It was a period of high growth throughout the world economy, which created spinoffs for South Africa. Moreover, by the end of the decade the restrictions imposed by apartheid were beginning to affect growth, notably by limiting the development of skills among Africans and by restricting the ability of enterprises to expand their operations in the 'white' areas.

The structure of the economy was changing as the contribution of agriculture and mining to GDP continued to decline, while that of manufacturing and services continued to rise. These trends would have a significant impact on employment patterns and, hence, on African bargaining power, economically and politically.

Hard data about the extent of African unemployment in the 1960s and 1970s are difficult to obtain. An official estimate put the figure as of March 1971 at 86 721 (including over 26 000 in the Transkei alone) who were registered as work-seekers or unemployed. Almost certainly the figure was an underestimate. In 1976, in the middle of an economic downturn, an official estimate put the number of economically active Africans living in the 'white' areas registered as unemployed at 118 500, but this, too, was an underestimate since many Africans avoided official channels for job-seekers and, indeed, illegally (in the technical sense) entered the urban areas. Other estimates varied from 600 000 to two million.

The inescapable truth was that the economy was dependent on African labour: in 1970, 69 per cent of the total labour force were Africans, and the projections suggested that this figure would increase. A semi-official report published in 1976 provided statistical evidence to show that there was a relative decline in the number of unskilled African workers and an increase in skilled employment; it noted that there had been a significant increase of African employees in professional, technical and related occupations, of which teaching was the most important.[84]

In an effort to restrict the scale of integration in the 'white' areas, policy switched to decentralisation in the early 1960s. As early as 1950 industrialists were warned against establishing labour-intensive enterprises, requiring large numbers of African workers, in existing industrial complexes. Instead, they were asked to locate such enterprises near homelands. By 1960 so-called 'border industries' had crystallised as a concept: they were to be established in the 'white' areas but close to a homeland border. Despite concessions offered to industrialists, progress was extremely slow, and by 1967 the most successful border industries had been established close to pre-existing industrial complexes in Durban, Pretoria, East London and Pietermaritzburg, cities which abutted homelands.

The slow progress caused the government to adopt tougher measures: in December 1966 it announced plans to reduce African labour complements by 5 per cent per annum, beginning in the Western Cape, but in principle applicable to the entire country. Legislation enacted in 1967 gave the state power to control the establishment or extension of factories in particular areas, the purpose clearly being to limit the increase of African workers in the 'white' areas. The responsible minister made it clear that when such increases were envisaged, permission would not be granted, and the enterprise in question would be required to locate, or relocate in the case of expansion, to a border area.

In explaining the policy, MC Botha said that between 1928 and 1967 the ratio of Africans to whites in all industries had risen from 1.01:1 to 2.2:1. By restricting the expansion of labour-intensive industries in existing complexes it was hoped to achieve a ratio of one white worker to less than one African worker. In the border industries, however, 'the ratio of Bantu workers to white workers ... can be unrestricted'.[85] Moreover, significantly lower wages could be paid.

None of these initiatives had much success in creating jobs or in deflecting the flow of Africans away from the existing metropolitan conurbations. Nor did sustainable enterprises materialise as a result of the decision, adopted by legislation in 1968, to allow white entrepreneurs to establish themselves in the homelands on an agency basis. Despite increasingly generous concessions to entrepreneurs, few were attracted to the border areas (except where they abutted existing industrial complexes) or to the homelands. Raymond Ackerman, a leading businessman, declined to participate on grounds that the entire border industry concept was 'immoral':

> Profits generated from border industries stayed of course in South Africa. I thought this system was wrong because it exploited people living in the homelands and benefited no one other than the owners of border industries, able to employ cheap labour.[86]

The legislation aimed at reducing the ratio of African to white workers in the 'white' areas also failed to achieve its goals in any substantial sense. Although a handful of employers were prosecuted for contravening the restrictions placed on the employment of Africans, the general pattern was the wholesale granting of exemptions, which obviously undermined the aims of the legislation. In 1977, for example, over 90 per cent of applications for exemption were granted.

A comparable fate awaited 'job reservation': as the economy grew the shortage of skilled labour, overwhelmingly the preserve of whites, became increasingly acute, and many employers resorted to the illegal placement of black workers. Another factor resulted from the increasing embourgeoisement of whites, fewer and fewer of whom were entering traditional blue-collar occupations. By 1977, according to official figures quoted by the Minister of Labour, SP Botha, there were considerable shortages of whites in professional occupations (9 000), clerical jobs (4 000), transport and communications (8 000) and artisans (9 000). (In the same speech he noted that the number of economically active Africans had risen from 4.3 million in 1960 to 6.3 million in 1978.[87]) According to another minister, PJG Koornhof, speaking in 1979, between 30 000 and 40 000 more 'nonwhite' skilled workers were required annually.[88]

The implications were clear: economic necessity required that job reservation determinations be lifted, albeit by means of an ad hoc and gradual process. In 1979 SP Botha told Parliament that of the 28 determinations imposed over the years, three had lapsed, 20 had been phased out, and only three remained. Job reservation was not a principle, he said, the principle being 'the meaningful protection of workers groups or interests', and this was now being achieved in a different way.[89] In practice, what happened was that white trade unions' approval was sought prior to the breaching or lifting of the determination, and white workers were often thereafter elevated into more highly paid jobs. By the late 1970s fewer than three per cent of the labour force were affected by the job colour bar, although this figure concealed the denial of adequate training facilities for Africans, which, of course, limited their ability to acquire more skills.

In the mining industry, however, statutory job colour bars survived until 1990, principally because the (white) Mine Workers' Union was a stronghold of extreme rightwing opinion, indeed, almost a wholly-owned subsidiary of the HNP. As early as the 1960s, however, evidence existed of a shortage of skilled workers on the mines, and an ad hoc process of exemptions from racial restrictions began. In its detailed examination of the labour situation in the industry, the Wiehahn Commission found that mining was 'heavily affected' by the skill shortage, largely because the industry enjoyed 'a low occupational priority among [white] school-leavers and job seekers'. It acknowledged that white workers had fears – possibly with some historical justification – that mining houses would try to replace white workers with African workers, but

> ... there can also be no doubt that Blacks are the only resource available for satisfying long-term skilled manpower needs and that furthermore the frustration of Black career ambitions could pose as much of a threat to industrial peace as the prospect of a 'White backlash'.⁹⁰

*   *   *

Difficult questions arose for Vorster in pondering the political future of the Coloured people, a minority numbering 2.3 million and constituting 9.3 per cent of the total population (1974 figures). Nearly 90 per cent lived in the Cape Province, the biggest concentrations being in the south-western section. They were also highly urbanised. Culturally and biologically they were akin to Afrikaners. As the great Afrikaans poet and dramatist NP van Wyk Louw put it: 'The brown people [*bruinmense*, i.e. Coloured] are our people, they belong with us.'⁹¹ They were not an ethnic group in any sense; rather, they were a residual category, the result of over 300 years of racial mixing. The official Nationalist designation that they were 'n-volk-in-wording (a-people-in-the-making) was a nonsense.

Qualified Coloured males had lost their common roll voting rights in 1956, and even the separate representation of Coloured voters by four white MPs was abolished in 1970. Coloured voting rights had been progressively whittled away for no reason other than that most voted for opposition parties and were regarded by the Nationalists as an anti-Afrikaner force that sided with English-speaking whites. The question in the 1970s was: since a 'homeland' for Coloured people had been ruled out by the NP, how could effective political rights be accorded to them? Direct representation of Coloured voters by Coloured MPs was unacceptable in Nationalist thinking, although in correspondence in 1960 with the Australian Prime Minister, Robert Menzies, Verwoerd did concede that 'it is one of the possible alternatives for the future'.[92] It was hard to reconcile this seeming flexibility with his ferocious repudiation of some Cape Nationalists, journalists, academics and clergy who advocated direct representation.

Characteristically, Vorster ducked the issue, declaring that 'the final word [on the political future of the Coloured people] will not be spoken by me and my generation, but by our children'.[93] How much, if any, say in the determination of their future Coloured people themselves would have was a question that was ignored. Vorster was also aware that there were divisions in his party on the issue: many *verligtes* were troubled by the alienation among Coloureds and wanted them to be accorded more rights, especially political rights. This invited the criticism from their left – the so-called '*oorbeligtes*' (the 'over-enlightened ones') – that it was inconsistent to plead for greater rights for Coloureds while appearing to overlook the situation of Africans, who possessed even fewer rights. On the other hand, the *verkramptes* were implacably opposed to any concessions being made, especially granting direct representation in Parliament. Many, in fact, favoured the establishment of a Coloured 'homeland', which was a preposterous idea, since, in spite of the localised segregation enforced by the Group Areas Act, the Coloured people lived in close proximity to whites in every town and village, and on every farm, in the Cape.

Even though proponents of a higher status for Coloureds were probably a minority in the NP caucus, Vorster had no stomach for a bruising conflict in the party: accordingly, in 1973 he appointed a commission to investigate all aspects of Coloured life, including the effectiveness or otherwise of the political machinery, the Coloured Persons' Representative Council (CPRC), established in 1968. The membership of the commission, chaired by Professor Erika Theron (of Stellenbosch University), broke new ground by including four Coloured persons.

The commission's report, published in 1976, was a comprehensive analysis of the position of Coloured people in society. The sections dealing with constitutional and political issues were a devastating critique of official policy, so-called 'parallel development'. Implicit in the analysis was the finding that 'white' and 'Coloured' spheres of interest or jurisdiction were so intertwined that they could not effectively be separated. The commission found that in the six-year period of the CPRC that it examined, only three laws had been enacted, most of the Council's activities being devoted to debating motions – the large majority of which concerned matters over which it had no jurisdiction. It found also that the 'overwhelming and effective majority of the Coloured population were opposed to the existing dispensation'.

The majority report, rejected by seven rightwing commissioners who had opposed every liberalising recommendation, advocated direct Coloured representation on all levels of authority and decision-making, including direct representation in Parliament. To achieve this, the existing Westminster-based constitutional system would have to be changed to accommodate 'the unique requirements of South Africa's plural population structure'.[94]

In its response the government declared its willingness wholly or partly to accept many of the recommendations concerning developmental issues, but it flatly rejected direct representation of Coloured people in Parliament, provincial councils or local authorities. Neither was it prepared to accept repeal of the Mixed Marriages or Immorality Acts (clause 16 of the latter made sexual relations between white and black a criminal offence). Repeal, according to government, would break down 'the recognition and development of the identity of the various population groups'.

Subsequently, however, Vorster declared that the solution to the problem of finding a *modus vivendi* for whites, Coloureds and Indians might be found in a Cabinet council 'at which consultation with regard to common problems could take place at the highest level between the leaders of these population groups'.[95] Initially, little came of this idea, largely because the Labour Party, the biggest party in the CPRC, declined to attend the first meeting in September 1976, as well as subsequent meetings. It was, nevertheless, the germ of proposals that were to dominate the constitutional debate among whites over the next few years, and result in such internal wrangling that the NP would split in 1982.

*   *   *

In another area, labour relations, Vorster perhaps unwittingly initiated a process that would result in apartheid's first major reform, the recognition of African trade unions – but only after he had stepped down as Prime Minister and, thereafter, as State President. The precipitant was a series of strikes in the Durban area in early 1973, involving over 67 000 African workers. Despite the usual suspicions of subversive forces lurking behind the strikes, voiced by Nationalist politicians, there was no hard evidence to suggest that they were anything but a response to appallingly low wages. Vorster surprised everyone by taking a calm, even humane, view, telling Parliament that

> ... in the past there have been too many employers who saw only the mote in the Government's eye and failed completely to see the beam in their own. Now I am looking past all party affiliations and past all employers, and experience tells me this, that employers, whoever they may be, should not only see in their workers a unit producing for them so many hours of service a day; they should also see them as human beings with souls.[96]

Vorster's sentiments, however, did not immediately herald a new dawn in industrial relations. During 1974 there were over 370 stoppages, involving 57 000 African workers; in 1975 there were 119 strikes by African workers, 75 per cent related to wage demands.[97] Legislative provision for alternatives to trade unions, and even the allowing of a carefully circumscribed right to strike (previously illegal), made little difference to the fundamental structural conflict.

Trade unions for Africans were not illegal, but the principal legislation governing industrial conciliation excluded African workers from the definition of 'employee', and only employee representatives were permitted to participate in the statutory bargaining process. Traditionally strike action met with heavy-handed reaction from both employers and the police. In the great mining strike of 1946, which involved 60 000 African miners, strikers were forced down the shafts, often at bayonet point. It was not uncommon for striking workers to be fired, sometimes resulting in their being expelled from the urban area ('endorsed out') and replaced by fresh recruits. Even if trade union activity was not illegal, those who sought to organise black workers led a dangerous existence: Helen Suzman told Parliament in 1979 that since 1952, 159 trade union officials had been banned under the Suppression of Communism Act.[98]

The 1973 strikes sounded the death-knell of the old order in industrial relations. RM Godsell (an executive of the giant Anglo American Corporation) noted that many employers reacted sympathetically, and wage increases of 20–25 per cent were often granted.[99] A survey of employer attitudes conducted between July and September 1973 found that out of 255 firms in all of the major industrial centres 71 per cent were prepared to negotiate with African trade unions, although 88 per cent would have preferred to negotiate with works committees elected by workers in individual enterprises.[100] Harry Oppenheimer, chairman of Anglo

American, added his influential voice, saying it was in the interest of management to negotiate with the unions. The Association of Chambers of Commerce also called for the granting of registered trade union rights to African workers.[101]

Another factor had also come into play: multinational corporations, especially American ones, had found themselves under increasing pressure from domestic lobbies to bring their labour relations into line with more acceptable international norms. As the Wiehahn Commission noted in 1979, the events of 1973 'brought the position of the Black worker and his organisation under the focus of international attention ....'[102]

Underlying the calls for change was a growing awareness that the heavy-handed methods of the past, such as firing strikers and recruiting replacements, were subject to diminishing returns. Increasingly Africans had to be appointed to more skilled positions, a trend that would accelerate. The African worker was no longer necessarily 'an interchangeable unit of labour', who could be fired at the whim of an employer. This was the beginning of a momentous development, a major tributary swelling the river as it approached the dam wall.

Eventually government responded. No doubt with some prodding from SP Botha, who became Minister of Labour in January 1976, it appointed, in mid-1977, a Commission of Inquiry into Labour Legislation under the chairmanship of an academic labour lawyer, Professor NE Wiehahn. The debates and legislative consequences arising out of the Commission's six-part report, published in 1979–80, are considered below.

*   *   *

Vorster stepped down as Prime Minister in September 1978. His last three years in office had been tumultuous ones of crisis, scandal, and deepening involvement in the Angolan civil war that had begun in the chaotic aftermath of the country's independence in 1975. Moreover, the end-game in Rhodesia was approaching fast, requiring Vorster to make difficult decisions: continued support for the illegal regime was not compatible with what he hoped to achieve, namely *détente* with the states of Africa on the basis of 'mutual understanding' and the acceptance by those states of South Africa's sovereign right to determine its own policies.

The Soweto Uprising of 1976 was sparked by an official requirement that certain subjects in African schools in the 'white' areas be taught in Afrikaans. The language issue demonstrated the perverse way in which relations between the two white linguistic groups had repercussions on racial policy. Afrikaner nationalists had long resented the dominance of English in African education: not only did it create, in Verwoerd's words, 'black Englishmen', but it also tilted the entire cultural environment of the country towards English. (If Afrikaans were more widely used there could also be lucrative spin-offs for publishers of Afrikaans textbooks.)

The Afrikaner Broederbond had considered the issue in 1968 and concluded that while vernacular languages were to be primary, the second language in African schools must be Afrikaans. It quoted figures to show that most of the whites (officials, farmers, police and so on) with whom Africans came into contact were Afrikaans-speaking – 'Let the Bantu understand in all circumstances that Afrikaans is the language of *most* whites and also the *most important* whites.'[103]

Although the uprising fell far short of toppling the state, it was nevertheless a major crisis for Vorster's government. The ineptitude of Dr AP Treurnicht, the Deputy Minister of Bantu Administration and Development, and the senior minister in charge of the Department, MC Botha, are recounted in the following chapter; but, since the Cabinet operated on the principle of collective responsibility, Vorster had to bear overall responsibility. What happened in Soweto and elsewhere was an indictment of official policy.

Treurnicht's ascent of the hierarchy of Afrikaner nationalism had been rapid: an ordained clergyman, a former provincial rugby player, a newspaper editor and a member of the Broederbond were roles that stamped him for higher things. Becoming chairman of the Broederbond in 1972 was a major advance. His orotund, if florid, speeches pushed all the right emotional buttons among Nationalist audiences and gained him considerable grassroots support in the Transvaal. Vorster, who was aware of Treurnicht's *verkrampte* views, nevertheless appointed him as a deputy minister in January 1976. Perhaps he regarded the appointment as a way of reining in Treurnicht's propensities. Vorster's views on Cabinet appointments reflected his reactive, even 'hands-off', style of leadership:

> Basically, it is not for a Prime Minister to pull somebody up, it is up to his contemporaries to thrust him forward. If you see that his contemporaries have thrust a man up, if you see that his contemporaries listen to him with some respect in the caucus and in Parliament, then you must keep your eyes on him.[104]

In contrast to Verwoerd's style, Vorster's was very much that of the 'chairman of the board'.[105] One of his ministers, Frank Waring, said:

> Soon after he took over he made it clear to the cabinet that he was
> relying on his ministers. Each minister would have the responsibility
> of looking after his own portfolio. Vorster would not hand down
> decisions, he would listen to his ministers, question them, make sug-
> gestions … never give orders.[106]

These comments go some way towards explaining Treurnicht's rise, and
the extraordinary failure to anticipate the crisis that was building up in
Soweto early in 1976, though Vorster's (misplaced) trust in his ministers
in no way exculpates him.

Treurnicht was unrepentant about the uprising. Not only did he retain
his post as Deputy Minister of Bantu Administration and Development
for the remainder of Vorster's premiership and beyond, but he was able to
rely on Vorster's protection against the criticisms directed at him – even
from within the broad Nationalist camp, notably the Afrikaans press.
Treurnicht was suave, but also crafty and sly. FW de Klerk, who was a
Cabinet colleague, writes:

> It was tragic that in his final years Mr Vorster had allowed himself
> to be misused by his former political enemies in the person of Dr
> Treurnicht and his followers, who had undermined and attacked him
> behind his back during the time of his premiership.[107]

In 1982 Treurnicht and his followers broke away to form the ultra-rightwing Conservative Party (CP), committed to the restoration of apartheid
in its full rigour. How that potentially dangerous backlash, which could
have threatened the NP, was fended off is one of the remarkable features
of the transition.

The Soweto Uprising was a seminal event in the decline of apartheid. It
occurred at a time when international isolation and pressure for economic
sanctions were increasing. Apart from insisting that there was no revolutionary situation at hand and suggesting that the uprising had been timed
to sabotage his forthcoming visit to Germany,[108] Vorster remained silent
for nearly ten weeks after the initial outbreak of violence. Gerald Shaw
wrote that Vorster, as was his wont in times of crisis, 'is waiting until he
is sure of the drift of public opinion, particularly among Nationalists,
before he shows his hand'.[109]

Treurnicht was adamant that in the 'white' areas it was the government's right to determine the language dispensation; moreover, he asked,

since there was no compulsory education for Africans, why were pupils sent to school if that dispensation did not suit them? He continued, with hypocritical piousness:

> No-one knew better than the Afrikaner about someone else's language being forced on him .... We have never applied the policy relentlessly [onverbiddelik].[110]

Other ministers blamed whites, communists and agitators. Jimmy Kruger, the Minister of Police (and a subsequent defector to the Conservative Party) rejected the criticism that water cannon or rubber bullets might have been used: water cannon would be ineffective in Soweto because there were too few water points and the pressure was too low. Rubber bullets would not work because 'the moment people in a riot situation know that you have rubber bullets it means, in effect, that you also have rubber guns'. Rioters, he continued, should get out of the way when a policeman picks up a gun.[111]

The crude harshness of these comments contrasted with the agonised soul-searching elsewhere in the Afrikaner nationalist establishment. The Afrikaans Sunday newspaper *Rapport* asked: 'What Afrikaner wants to fight with Blacks because they do not wish to use his language? We don't want blood on our language.'[112] *Die Burger*, the most influential of the Afrikaans dailies, noted that Afrikaans-speakers would have mixed feelings 'in the light of their own insistence that their children not be taught through the medium of another language'.[113] For some the inflexible application of the language policy evoked historical memories of the imperial proconsul Lord Milner's attempts to ram English down the throats of children in the defeated Boer republics after 1902; and there could only be chagrin when the famous lament uttered by President Steyn of the Orange Free State Republic, 'the language of the conqueror in the mouths of the conquered is the language of slaves', was flung back at Afrikaners by critics of the policy.

In the same vein, Schalk Pienaar, the most vigorous of the Afrikaans editors who sought to flush out the *verkramptes*, caused a stir by denying that the youngsters involved in the Soweto Uprising were 'terrorists', 'because they were just as inspired by idealism as were Afrikaners in the past'.[114] His invoking of a parallel with Afrikaner history raised an awkward moral issue: Afrikaner nationalism was the oldest nationalist movement on the African continent, as Harold Macmillan had observed in 1960; it had been forged in an anti-imperial struggle, yet, as Piet Cillié, editor of *Die Burger*, pointed out, 'we rejected domination of ourselves, but we do not find domination of other peoples by ourselves as objectionable (*verwerplik*)'.[115] Verwoerd had changed the basis of policy legitimation: *baasskap* (overlordship) had become 'separate development' or 'multinationalism', and, in theory, homelands were being led to independence in a way similar to that whereby African colonies had become independent; but the policy was palpably not working.

Contrary to the popular belief that all Afrikaners were heartless racists with little or no moral sensitivity, many especially in elite educated circles were deeply concerned. The famous words of NP van Wyk Louw, written in 1952, retained their resonance: 'I would rather go down than continue to exist in injustice.'[116] The argument is not that Afrikaner nationalism was undergoing a moral renaissance – many whites in both language communities were unmoved by such moral considerations, and remained determined not to budge whatever the moral implications of their intransigence – rather, it is that years of political control and increased prosperity had heightened the internal diversity of the movement.

According to JL Sadie's calculations, between 1960 and 1980 the number of Afrikaners with a Standard 10 (the final year of the school system) had more than doubled; and those with post-school qualifications had increased by nearly 250 per cent; moreover, those in agriculture and blue-collar occupations had declined: by 1980 fewer than one-third of Afrikaners were classified as working class.[117] Class divisions had always existed in the Afrikaner community, but consciousness of them had increased, partly as a consequence of the HNP's deliberate appeal to poorer people's resentments.

Theodor Hanf and his associates found in their surveys in 1974 and 1977 that better-educated whites were about twice as open to change as the less-educated. This was especially so among better-educated Afrikaners, even though the Afrikaner ethnic group as a whole did not change in outlook to any remarkable extent. There were also signs of a more pragmatic view among NP politicians, especially regarding the gradual abolition of petty apartheid and job reservation. In 1974, 25 per cent thought that African migrant labourers should be sent back to the homelands; in 1977 none supported this view. In what the authors define as the 'inner circle', which included individuals from outside the Cabinet, pragmatic views had gained ground, but there were no takers for the rejection of separate development and its replacement by a multiracial polity. By 1977 the Soweto Uprising had left its mark: levels of fear had increased significantly since 1974, 85 per cent of NP supporters declaring themselves ready to 'fight to maintain South Africa as it is'.[118] Nevertheless, as the authors pointed out, debate had been started about the future.

The official hardline continued: the sketchy minutes of a Cabinet meeting held on 10 August 1976 show concern that the basic danger was growing Black Consciousness and the inability of the authorities to prevent incidents. It was agreed that the Black Consciousness Movement 'must be broken' and that the police 'should perhaps act a bit more drastically and firmly (*hardhandig*) which would cause more deaths'.[119]

It would not, however, be until October 1977, by which time the violence had substantially declined, that Vorster acted decisively by banning 18 mostly BC-orientated organisations. In the previous month Steve Biko, the foremost BC leader, had been murdered by the security police in horrifying circumstances. As if the murder were not bad enough – and embarrassing to Vorster – Kruger's remark, shortly after Biko's death, that '*Dit laat my koud*' ('It leaves me cold'), created shockwaves of disgust, not least among his colleagues. Kruger is said to have offered his resignation to Vorster, who declined to accept it. (He remained in office until mid-1979, when he was dropped by Vorster's successor, PW Botha.)

Vorster's paralysis and lack of vision continued. He could not fail to understand the massive significance of the black protest, but neither could he see a way out of the morass. Eventually he appears to have decided to proceed with minor tinkerings while perpetuating the main pillars of apartheid. In November 1976 a Broederbond circular reported Vorster's thoughts at a secret meeting of its executive:

> The Executive was riveted by the declaration of faith with which the Prime Minister recently concluded a frank discussion. He stressed with great determination that his profound analysis of the recent trying months and weeks had convinced him anew that there is no way to handle race relations but the way of separate development. He added that the greatest legacy of Dr Verwoerd was his vision of separate homelands which could be developed to full independence. Without the homeland policy ... we would now have been in the same position as Rhodesia. He called on the [Broederbond] to take stock and throw everything into the battle to maintain and promote this policy.[120]

Vorster's last three years in office until he stepped down, under duress, in September 1978 were stressful ones that took a toll on his health. He left office in humiliating circumstances that forced him to quit as State President (then only a ceremonial office) less than a year later. Although he had won an overwhelming victory in the election held in November 1977, obtaining a majority of 100 seats out of 165, it turned out to be a pyrrhic victory. What was to become the 'Information Scandal' was already upon him, and in the months following the election it would destroy him.

The scandal arose out of the unorthodox activities of the Information Department and its energetic, maverick Secretary, Eschel Rhoodie. Rhoodie's activities centred on seeking to improve South Africa's image in the West. A survey commissioned by the Department in the early 1970s had shown that in the 15 countries investigated, apartheid was the word most commonly associated in people's minds with South Africa. It made South Africa the most unpopular state bar Idi Amin's Uganda, even more unpopular than the People's Republic of China and the USSR. Rhoodie and his colleagues took the view that South Africa 'had to buy, bribe or bluff its way into the hearts and minds of the world'. It meant secret projects, deception and spending a lot of money. If South Africa could not get a good press abroad, then, said Rhoodie, 'it should buy the right opinions'. At a meeting in February 1974, Vorster gave his approval to Rhoodie and the Minister of Information, Connie Mulder, to proceed with covert propaganda.[121]

It all went horribly wrong. Attempts to buy foreign newspapers, notably the *Washington Times*, and South African Associated Newspapers, which published opposition newspapers, including the *Rand Daily Mail*, came to nothing. Then it was decided to put up money through a front-man, Louis Luyt, a successful businessman, to publish an English-language daily, *The Citizen*, that would be an ostensibly independent conservative counterweight to the liberal English-medium dailies. Vorster is said to have connived at this ruse. It had long been a Nationalist aspiration to have such a newspaper, partly at least because it might be an antidote to the *Rand Daily Mail*, which it was believed fed poisonous lies about apartheid to its growing African readership.

Enterprising journalists soon discovered that *The Citizen* was inflating its circulation figures by simply dumping up to 30 000 copies a day and then including this number in the circulation figure.[122] Luyt soon fell out with Rhoodie and withdrew from the operation, saying years later that his involvement was 'the most stupid move I ever made'.[123] In a short time the full story of the government's role was uncovered, and, thanks to the investigative reporting of several English-language newspapers, the astonishing dimensions of the Information Department's activities began to emerge.

It was not only the newspapers, however: crucial evidence was provided by anonymous informants, a Pretoria advocate, Retief van Rooyen, who was also a friend of Vorster's; a courageous judge, Anton Mostert, who made public the evidence he had gathered about the misuse of taxpayers' money in the course of an investigation of exchange control violations; and the Auditor-General, Gerald Barrie, who was the first official to draw attention to the Information Department's misuse of funds.

Vorster had resigned as Prime Minister on 27 September 1978, shortly before the torrent of news about the scandal began to appear in the press. He cited ill-health as the reason, but nevertheless made himself available for election (by Parliament) to the State Presidency, the previous incumbent having died in August. While Vorster was in poor health, much of it probably attributable to the stress of knowing that the scandal would soon break, uncertainty remains about whether he was jumping before he was pushed. There is little doubt that he was deeply implicated in covert activities right from their inceptions, and his attempts to deny this enraged Rhoodie and Mulder. At all events Vorster's reputation was badly tarnished by the (Erasmus) Commission that was set up by his successor to investigate the affair. (It was alleged that the Commission's report was altered by PW Botha prior to publication.) He was thereafter forced to resign as State President in June 1979 and died shortly thereafter, a deeply embittered man.

Mulder had long been regarded as Vorster's most likely heir. As leader of the NP in the Transvaal, he had a strong base in the province that was the NP's centre of political gravity. His reputation, too, had been tarnished, resulting in withdrawal of support for his candidacy by key elements in the NP caucus. He nevertheless came within six votes of PW Botha in the first round of voting, but in the second round Botha won 98 votes to Mulder's 74.[124] Mulder was forced to resign from the NP early in 1979 when his assertion to Parliament on 10 May 1978 that neither his Department nor the government had funded *The Citizen* was exposed as a lie.

Approximately R80 million of taxpayers' money had been wasted by the Department of Information. No discernible improvement in South Africa's image had occurred as a result of its activities. For Vorster it was a comeuppance: his managerial style had allowed abuses of ministerial power which might have been prevented in a more tightly controlled Cabinet.

The most important consequence of the scandal, however, was the impact that it had on many NP supporters. Although in its history Afrikanerdom had been fractious, one of the characteristics of its internal political culture had been respect, perhaps exaggerated respect, for leaders. Leaders, not only in politics but throughout civil society, tended to remain in office for long periods. Moreover, they were expected to be, and invariably were, beyond reproach in the conduct of their public and private lives, at least as far as corruption and dishonesty were concerned. In an angry article Willem de Klerk, editor of *Die Transvaler* and brother of FW de Klerk, wrote of the Information Scandal that lies were told in important meetings, in private conversations, in statements; lies were told to the press. People were taken for fools, and in the process were allowed to make themselves ridiculous:

> We are credulous, we willingly let authority-figures go their way 'because they know best'. We rely heavily on the arbitrary powers of the man at the helm. We neither dispute nor cross-examine. And just look at where a few men have landed us – authority-figures whom we virtually idolised.[125]

Similar sentiments were widespread, especially among the intelligentsia and other elites. It is impossible to state precisely what the political impact of the scandal was – apart, obviously, from PW Botha's becoming Prime Minister. It seems reasonable to suppose, though, that it contributed to the growth of cynicism about politicians and to a further decline in the cohesiveness of the Afrikaner nationalist movement. It has been stressed throughout that Afrikaner nationalism was never monolithic. It did, however, reach an apogee of internal solidarity under Verwoerd, whose excommunication of dissenters or doubters was swift and ruthless. Vorster's times were the locust years of apartheid and of Afrikaner nationalism.

On the face of it, Vorster's changes to the apartheid system seem small beer: ad hoc lifting of the job colour bar; convoluted changes to sports policy that secured limited desegregation by invoking the fiction of 'multi-nationalism', meaning that each 'national group' had to play sport separately, but they could play against one another in 'multinational' events. Similarly, higher class hotels and restaurants might acquire 'multinational' status and admit people of all races. An elaborate (and ultimately unworkable) system of permits for mixed gatherings, events and venues was initiated; and a cautious start was made in weeding out 'unnecessary' discriminatory rules.

Critics derided these changes as 'cosmetic', but in fact each was a symbolic beachhead won against the entrenched ranks of *verkramptes*, who regarded each change, however trifling, as setting a precedent and creating cumulative momentum for further change. The process was aptly described as 'significant insignificant change'.[126]

Some significant changes occurred more opaquely: if the core of apartheid was the assertion that Africans could not exercise political rights in the 'white' areas, indeed that they were 'temporary sojourners', how could this be squared with the decision in 1977 that Africans could henceforth acquire their own homes in urban areas on a 99-year leasehold basis; and that they could inherit, sell or mortgage these properties (though they could not own them in freehold: that, said Vorster inscrutably, 'is in conflict with the policy of the NP')? Another change rescinded an earlier regulation that prevented urban Africans from owning more than one business. The *annus mirabilis*, 1978, was clearly a non-event.

Other changes included the dropping of the previous requirement that Bantu Education be funded from the taxes paid by Africans; in future revenue would come from the state's consolidated revenue fund. Furthermore, the Verwoerdian view that the expansion of secondary and technical education should take place in the homelands was relaxed.[127] Indeed, after 1970 other objectionable features of the system, including the so-called 'tribalistic' element in the syllabi, were dropped. The impact of the reforms, however, was negated by the dogmatic insistence on the use of Afrikaans as the medium of instruction in certain subjects. The events that began in Soweto in June 1976 prompted further reforms: a commitment, in principle, to phasing in compulsory education for Africans; salary parity for teachers of all races with equal qualifications; improved facilities in African schools; and, more generally, a commitment in principle to maintain the same educational standards for all groups, including curricula, syllabi and the same matriculation examination.[128] Too little, too late! Bantu Education remained seriously dysfunctional, a condition that would survive into the new, post-1994 South Africa, blighting the chances of creating a more equal society.

The locust years of Vorster saw the steady erosion of the élan that had inspired so many apartheid supporters: policy was degenerating into a holding operation interspersed with periods of crisis management. This would continue into the turbulent 1980s, when the state faced unprecedented militancy and mass mobilisation.

* * *

The flip-side of declining élan and weakening solidarity was a resurrection of *volkskritiek*, a concept that originated with Van Wyk Louw, meaning criticism of the *volk* by one of its members, knowing that 'he is indissolubly bound in love and fate and guilt to the *volk* he is daring to criticise'.[129] The reference was mainly to critics who still regarded themselves as Afrikaner nationalists and chose to wage their battles *binne die raamwerk* (literally 'within the framework'). Others, whose numbers grew significantly in the 1970s and 1980s, were Afrikaners who had either never supported the NP, or had previously, but thereafter had left or been expelled. The latter category included some of the leading Afrikaner intellectuals and writers.

Debates between those who sought reform from *binne die raamwerk* and those who had abandoned the faith, or had never subscribed to it, became increasingly acrimonious. And the many reactionaries, inside and outside the NP, continued their efforts to white-ant Afrikaner institutions and to block even the most modest reforms. Especially after the Soweto Uprising a sense of *fin de siècle* was widespread, and the urgency of decisive action to end the rudderless drift of Vorster's government became greater. It was into this maelstrom of forces contending for the leadership of Afrikaner nationalism that PW Botha stepped in 1978. In some respects he was to become South Africa's Gorbachev: pulling down some of the main pillars of the apartheid order, but unable to free himself completely from the ideological paradigm of the past.

CHAPTER 4

The Decline and Rise of
the Black Opposition

For nearly three decades after 1948 the black opposition struggled against overwhelming odds. As the NP consolidated its power and tightened its grip on society, black organisations were forced onto the defensive. Increasingly draconian security legislation limited the political space in which they could operate. The Suppression of Communism Act of 1950, for instance, apart from outlawing the CPSA, gave the Minister of Justice power to 'ban' individuals, requiring them to withdraw from organisations and in other ways curbing their freedom, thereby limiting their ability to organise and mobilise. Since banning orders were imposed in the sole discretion of the Minister, and could not be challenged in court, the Act became a handy instrument of repression.

Despite the reactive posture it was forced to adopt, the ANC did its best to resist the spate of discriminatory laws. Its backbone had been stiffened by the ANCYL and the rise to positions of influence of tough-minded young men, including Nelson Mandela, Walter Sisulu and Oliver Tambo, who were determined to break with the traditional elitist and non-confrontational stance of the ANC. The 1949 Programme of Action, engineered by the ANCYL, was an intimation of more militant strategies.

In 1952, the ANC, in collaboration with the Natal and Transvaal Indian Congresses, organised a Defiance Campaign. Passive resistance on the Gandhian model was to target unjust laws by deliberately entering segregated 'whites only' facilities, ignoring the curfew regulations applying to Africans, and entering African 'locations' without permits. Volunteers were selected, instructed to avoid violence, to decline bail and serve time in prison instead of paying fines.

The Campaign was launched on 26 June 1952 and petered out in November of that year, but not before 8 500 volunteers had participated and been arrested. Riots in Port Elizabeth, Johannesburg, Kimberley and East London in October and November had led to 40 deaths, whereupon the ANC called the Campaign off, while insisting that the violence had been caused by *agents provocateurs*, and that none had emanated from volunteers.

Describing the government's reaction, Chief Albert Luthuli, who became President-General of the ANC in 1952, observed:

> Behind the thousands arrested there were more, many more. The challenge of non-violence was more than they could meet. It robbed them of the initiative. On the other hand, violence by Africans would restore this initiative to them – they would then be able to bring out the guns and the other techniques of intimidation and present themselves as restorers of order.[1]

This was an acute insight: preventing initiatives taken by African organisations, or nipping them in the bud, was a useful technique of control. The laws targeted by the Defiance Campaign were, of course, not repealed; instead government armed itself with more formidable powers and imposed banning orders on many of the organisers. Undoubtedly the violence accompanying the Campaign and the government's strong-arm reaction helped the NP to boost its majority to a comfortable 31 seats in the 1953 election.

In one respect the Defiance Campaign was a failure: the government increased its intransigence; but in another it had shown that the spirit of opposition had not been cowed. As Mandela wrote, prior to the Campaign,

> ... the ANC was more talk than action. We had no paid organizers, no staff and a membership that did little more than pay lip-service to our cause. As a result of the campaign, our membership swelled to 100 000 [from less than 7 000]. The ANC emerged as a truly mass-based organization with an impressive corps of experienced activists who had braved the police, courts and jails. The stigma usually associated with imprisonment had been removed. This was a significant achievement, for fear of prison is a tremendous hindrance to a liberation struggle.[2]

On the other hand, the Campaign aggravated problems in the emerging alliance between the ANC and non-African organisations, notably the South African Indian Congress and white communists and other radicals who formed the South African Congress of Democrats in 1952. Anti-Indian feeling was rife in African communities, whose stereotype of Indians, like that of whites, was of a rich, exploitative group of merchants. Severe conflict between Africans and Indians in Durban in January 1949 left 142 dead, including 87 Africans and 50 Indians. It was sparked by a rumour that an Indian shopkeeper had cuffed an African youth; but the spark would not have ignited a conflagration had the material not been combustible.

There was cooperation between ANC and Natal Indian Congress leaders in trying to douse the flames, but it was a case of elite cooperation that did not percolate through the two communities. Mutual suspicion continued to characterise relations between the groups.

Many whites cheered on the Africans, but whether there was 'racist incitement from the cabinet level downwards,' as Ismail Meer alleges,[3] could not be proven. Since official policy was that Indians were to be repatriated, it is possible that the NP government was not unduly dismayed at the riots.

The Defiance Campaign strengthened the elite pact; but many of the Youth Leaguers in the ANC opposed the involvement of Indians in the Campaign, as well as the emerging Congress Alliance that included the South African Indian Congress. Mandela had become President of the ANCYL in 1951 and shared the 'Africanist' views that Africans must go it alone and shun cooperation with non-Africans. As late as 1950 he accused Walter Sisulu of selling out to Indians and even of being a 'traitor' for supporting joint African–Indian action. His views on communism and Indians softened, however, as the weight of common repression bore down on all groups that were not white.[4] For a small hard-core of Africanists no such softening was conceivable: Africans were oppressed in unique ways, and the most appropriate weapon with which to fight was a 'pure' African nationalism.

Achieving unity of the black groups was anything but an automatic process. All three groups suffered grievously in the face of racial discrimination, but Africans were the worst afflicted, and consequently found themselves at the bottom of the racial hierarchy, with Coloureds and Indians constituting intermediate categories.

In spite of the obstacles, formation of the Congress Alliance proceeded incrementally, with the inclusion of the (white) Congress of Democrats and the South African Coloured People's Organisation in 1953, and the South African Congress of Trade Unions in 1955. The activities of the Alliance were coordinated by a National Consultative Committee comprising representatives of each Alliance component.

Being illegal, the underground CPSA could not formally join the Alliance, but since it allowed dual membership with other organisations many individual communists were also members of one or other Alliance partner. On the eve of its banning, the CPSA had laid down the ideological and strategic line: national organisations (such as the ANC) must be transformed into a revolutionary party of workers, peasants, intellectuals and petty bourgeoisie, in alliance with 'class conscious European workers and intellectuals'. The Communist Party, which was, before and after its dissolution, fully inter-racial, would remain separate, while setting the pace for developing among workers of all races 'a positive class consciousness' against capitalism and for socialism.[5] In embryo this was the 'two-stage' theory of revolution: a 'national democratic revolution' to establish 'bourgeois' democracy, to be followed by a socialist revolution.

During the 1950s CPSA individuals came to exert considerable influence in the ANC and its allies. The 'two-stage' theory of revolution was incorporated into ANC thinking, as was the view that South Africa represented a case of 'colonialism of a special type' in which 'race' masked the real source of conflict, class. Apart from its theoretical and organisational contribution to the ANC – which was considerable – the CPSA's emphasis on the primacy of class and the readiness of many of its leading members to identify fully with the cause of black liberation helped to prevent the mainstream of the ANC from espousing a narrow, chauvinistic understanding of the struggle. Individual friendships, for example, between Mandela and Joe Slovo and Ismail Meer, both members of the CPSA, eroded Mandela's suspicion and his earlier reluctance to cooperate with non-Africans.

The link between the ANC and the CPSA became so close as to warrant the description of symbiotic. This had two important consequences: first, it fuelled the resentments of the Africanists in the ANC who objected to the influence of non-Africans and to communism as a 'foreign' ideology; secondly, it was grist to the NP's mill: like all rightwing governments the NP thumped an anti-communist drum and extracted considerable propaganda value from the 'communist threat'.

Both of these factors came into play in the mid-1950s: the acceptance of the Freedom Charter in 1955 (ratified by the ANC in 1956), and the commencement of the Treason Trial in 1956, in which 156 members of the Congress Alliance were charged with high treason, a charge that arose principally out the state's view that the Freedom Charter was a blueprint for a Marxist-Leninist state.

The Freedom Charter had its origins in an impeccably non-communist source, namely Professor ZK Matthews, Cape leader of the ANC and the country's most distinguished African scholar, who suggested in 1953 that the time was ripe for the ANC to draft a charter for a future democratic South Africa. In a memorandum to the ANC's National Executive he elaborated his proposal:

> The main task of the Congress [of the People] will be to draw up a 'Freedom Charter' for all peoples and groups in South Africa. From such a Congress ought to come a Declaration which will inspire all the peoples of South Africa with fresh hope for the future, which will turn the minds of the people away from the sterile and negative struggles of the past and the present and to a positive programme of freedom in our lifetime. Such a Charter properly conceived as a mirror of the future South African Society can galvanise the people of South Africa into action and make them go over into the offensive against the reactionary forces at work in this country, instead of being perpetually on the defensive, fighting rearguard actions all the time.[6]

Matthews's idea eventually came to fruition in June 1955 at Kliptown (near Johannesburg). In spite of harassment by the security police, nearly 3 000 delegates from all parts of the country, plus spectators, deliberated on the draft Charter, said to have been compiled from 'thousands of bits of paper' containing demands submitted by organisations and individuals. The organisers had issued a general invitation for delegates to attend the Congress and had canvassed opinion as widely as their organisational capacity permitted. How wide the canvassing was, and to what extent the Charter actually reflected what was contained in the 'bits of paper', cannot be known since Rusty Bernstein, who drafted the Charter, has acknowledged that they were stuffed into a trunk that was thereafter 'lost for ever'.[7]

Preparatory work for the Congress of the People, at which the Freedom Charter was to be adopted, had been carried out under the aegis of a National Action Committee (NAC), consisting of eight representatives from each of the organisations making up the Congress Alliance, namely, the ANC, the South African Indian Congress, the (white) Congress of Democrats, and the South African Coloured People's Organisation. In the month preceding the event, the NAC complained that 'not enough demands were flowing in'; and after the event it was highly self-critical:

> The core of the leadership of the campaign was immobilised as a result of government bans …. The people must be shown that there is

> a direct connection between the more long term aims of the Freedom
> Charter and their struggles and immediate threats. Your NAC and
> the four sponsoring organisations at no stage managed successfully
> to link the [Congress of the People] with the day-to-day struggles of
> the people … . Only a negligible number of local committees were
> set up. Our failure to do so resulted in the Congress of the People not
> being as representative as it might otherwise have been.[8]

How wide the consultation process actually was has generated controversy. Claims that the message about the Congress was taken to industrial
areas and communities, including the most remote rural areas, have to
be viewed sceptically, even while acknowledging limitations imposed by
security police harassment.

Equally controversial is the extent to which the actual wording of the
Freedom Charter reflected a distillation of the (missing) 'bits of paper'
submitted by the people, rather than the views of a small group of activists about what the people *ought* to wish. In a revealing comment, Ben
Turok, one of the moving spirits behind the organisation, observes that
an earlier draft of the Economic Clause (Clause 4) of the Charter 'would
not adequately reflect my own understanding of what the congress was
supposed to achieve'. Accordingly, he drafted an amendment, calling for
the commanding heights of the economy to be placed in public ownership.[9] Even more revealing of pre-packaging of popular demands was the
instruction given by a regional committee of the Congress of the People to
volunteers who would do the actual canvassing of opinion:

> It is essential for each and every volunteer to attend these lectures [on
> the significance of the campaign] where they will be trained to under-
> stand, analyse and correctly assess the local and national situations
> … so that they will be able to give the correct lead to the people.[10]

Fine and Davis conclude that while the Congress of the People was an
imaginative and mobilising event, it presented 'an already established political programme rather than … an echo of the voice of the people'.[11] It
was difficult to pinpoint where the Freedom Charter was placed on the
ideological spectrum: there was something in it for every ideological position within the broad alliance camp. The 'Africanists' in the ANC, however, had serious objections to its generous multiracialism as well as to the
prominent organisational role played by non-African leftwingers.

The Freedom Charter caused controversy not only in the ANC but also
in other bodies. The Liberal Party, led by Alan Paton, initially accepted

the invitation to be a co-sponsor of the Congress of the People, but subsequently had second thoughts, especially in view of the close involvement of and manipulation by the Congress of Democrats and the South African Indian Congress, whom they regarded as little more than communist front organisations. Whether to participate became a controversial issue, but in the end it was decided not to, a decision which strained relationships between the Party and the ANC.[12]

The Charter itself was accepted virtually unanimously, literally moments before the Congress of the People was forcibly closed by the police. It was a poetically written document. Its preamble declared that 'South Africa belongs to all who live in it, black and white, and that no government can justly claim authority unless it is based on the will of the people'. It went on to proclaim that there shall be 'equal status in the bodies of the state, in the courts and in the schools for all national groups and races'. All racial discrimination was to be outlawed and civil liberties were to be secured to all citizens.

The controversial clauses were contained in a section entitled 'The People Shall Share In The Country's Wealth!', which included proposals that 'the mineral wealth beneath the soil, the banks and monopoly industry shall be transferred to the ownership of the people as a whole', while 'all other industries and trades shall be controlled to assist the well-being of the people'. The next section declared that all racial restrictions on land ownership were to be abolished, 'and all the land re-divided amongst those who work on it'.

Much of the Charter was laudably democratic in tone, but the economic clauses cited above were immediately deemed 'socialist' by its critics, who included the state. In an article written in 1956 Mandela denied the charge; while acknowledging that the Charter demanded nationalisation of banks, mines and the land – which would strike 'a fatal blow' at the interests that controlled them – he insisted that their break-up and democratisation would 'open up fresh fields for the development of a prosperous Non-European bourgeois class'.[13]

The state's response was not long in coming: in December 1956, 156 persons – 105 Africans, 21 Indians, 23 whites and 7 Coloureds, all members of the Congress Alliance – were arrested and charged with treason. Among the accused was virtually the entire leadership of the ANC, including Luthuli, Matthews, Tambo, Mandela and Sisulu. The core of the charge was that the ANC and its allies sought by violent means to overthrow the state and replace it with a communist system. The case dragged on through the preparatory hearing and thereafter to the Supreme Court. Along the way charges were dropped against many of the accused, leaving only 30, who were finally acquitted in March 1961. The Court's verdict was that there was no proof that the ANC was committed to the violent overthrow of the state or that the Freedom Charter envisaged the establishment of a communist state.

It had been a costly and embarrassing experience for the state. If it had been intended as a 'show trial' it had backfired badly. Nor had the state reckoned with the fair-mindedness of even conservative judges. With characteristic magnanimity Mandela praised the three judges who 'rose above their prejudices, their education and their background', while emphasising that he did not regard the acquittal as a vindication of the legal system or evidence that a black man could get a fair trial in a white man's court.[14] At least, though, the case suggested that show trials in South Africa did not inevitably result in mass convictions followed by executions, as was regularly the case in Stalin's Soviet Union.

The trial had a major disruptive effect on the lives of the accused and their families; but, perversely from the state's point of view, its effect was to weld an unprecedented unity among the accused, which several have described. Forced together for long periods, the previously dispersed Congress leadership could now hold what Mandela described as 'the largest and longest unbanned meeting of the Congress Alliance in years'.[15] Rusty Bernstein, one of the accused, argued that the real significance of the trial was

> ... its political fallout, which provided the conditions for a new-style Congress movement and so set the agenda for the next three decades of South African political struggle .... [The trial] had given rise to an extraordinary fraternity which became the bedrock from which the modern Congress was sprung. That close fraternal spirit was the core which held together the enduring unity of the liberation movement for the next forty years, and kept it free of the factionalism and strife which destroyed so many movements in so many other countries.[16]

This assessment, while substantially true, ignores the impact of the multiracial Congress Alliance on the increasingly alienated 'Africanist' wing of the ANC that would break away in 1958 to form the Pan-Africanist Congress in 1959. How the racially inclusive Congress Alliance was, over time, to eclipse the narrow racial chauvinism of the PAC is an important part of the story of the transition.

The Africanists, as has been noted, were the rump of the ANC Youth League, which had been largely responsible for driving the Programme of Action through the ANC's conference in 1949. Throughout the 1950s the

Africanists accused the ANC leadership of having betrayed the core principle of the Programme by collaborating with non-Africans in the Congress Alliance. To some extent the accusation was true: the Programme was more militantly nationalist than any previous ANC declaration; it spoke of the African people's right of self-determination, of bringing the people together 'under the banner of African nationalism', and it focused specifically on African grievances. At the same time, however, nothing in the Programme precluded cooperation with non-Africans. In any case, as Luthuli subsequently observed, while he was prepared to concede the logic of the Africanist argument, 'this is no longer 1949'; that it was 'unnecessarily doctrinaire to cling to an outlook which may have been appropriate then'.[17]

The Africanists advanced the arguments put forward by Lembede: the sense of inferiority inculcated by generations of white domination had to be eradicated; Africans must go it alone because multiracial cooperation, in whatever form it took, would inevitably result in non-Africans gravitating to controlling positions, just as white and Indian communists were exerting an undue influence, out of all proportion to their numbers, in the governing councils of the Congress Alliance. This, in turn, would reinforce Africans' sense of inferiority. Communism continued to be seen as an alien ideology. Instead, Africans must organise for self-reliance, and to instil pride in themselves by invoking the history of resistance to white rule by some of the major chiefdoms of the nineteenth century, and emphasising the large-scale alienation of land that accompanied the expansion of white rule.

Land was a major issue for the Africanists and the emergent PAC. Thus TT Letlaka, writing in the cyclostyled journal *The Africanist* in December 1956:

> After fierce wars in defence of their fatherland the Africans were conquered and dispossessed of their land by European Imperialists. The African people to all intents and purposes were rendered homeless in the land of their birth. They could no longer own but were merely herded into small reserves where a few held small plots of land with the grace of the white rulers .... The entire African nation was converted into a vast reservoir of cheap labour for the insatiable European-owned farms, mines and secondary industries. The immediate goal of the African Liberation Struggle, therefore, is clear and unequivocal. It is an uncompromising reversal of this unhealthy state of affairs .... The struggle for national emancipation, and the regaining of all things that were lost as a result of White conquest of

Africa, is the cornerstone of Africa's struggle for liberation.[18]

Given their claim to all the land, the Africanists were incensed by the Freedom Charter's declaration that South Africa 'belongs to all who live in it, black and white' and that 'all national groups shall have equal rights'. Africa was for the Africans, and minorities of non-African origins would not be recognised as eligible for any specific protection, as the Charter appeared to imply. In theory, the PAC allowed, in Robert Mangaliso Sobukwe's words, that 'everybody who owes his only loyalty to Africa and accepts the democratic rule of an African majority [will be] regarded as an African.' Sobukwe, who became leader of the PAC, was not personally anti-white; nor, according to his close friend and biographer, Benjamin Pogrund, were other leading figures in the PAC.[19] But the subtleties of Sobukwe's account of who might qualify as an African were lost on relatively unsophisticated audiences whose resentment of white racism was deep. Sisulu denounced PAC thinking as a 'crude appeal to African racialism', which contrasted with the ANC's refusal to respond to racial oppression with 'a blind and irrational "anti-Whiteism".'[20]

Nevertheless, the ANC had reason to worry about the potential appeal of anti-white racism. On the whole, the PAC's activists and its prospective support-base were younger than their ANC counterparts, and many were recent immigrants from, and maintained links with, the decaying rural society in which land was a highly emotive and symbolic issue. As had occurred in the 1940s and was to recur in the 1970s, the generational issue was also significant. Discussing the 1950s, Lewis Nkosi, a young writer, spoke of his generation's refusal to forgive the 'indecent readiness with which our immediate elders were prepared to believe that after this history of war and pillage white people meant well by us'.[21]

As a classic flanking organisation whose strategy involved racial outbidding, the PAC had to maintain the momentum generated by its dramatic breakaway from the ANC. This meant wresting the initiative from the ANC and preparing for militant action against apartheid. Sobukwe struck this note in an address in August 1959. The decks were being cleared for action, he said:

> The African people ... are awake! They are waiting, waiting eagerly and expectantly, waiting for the call, the call to battle, to battle for the reconquest of the continent of Afrika [sic] ....[22]

Although Sobukwe was not specific about what action the PAC would take, in hindsight it can be seen that the decks were being cleared for a major protest against the pass laws that would have tragic consequences at Sharpeville (near Vereeniging) and Langa (near Cape Town) in March 1960. It would be a milestone in the conflict.

The pass laws, whose rigour had greatly increased in the 1950s, including being extended to women, were a ready-made goad to African protest. Passes symbolised African subordination, and no single institution in apartheid's armoury caused more anger to urban communities. In 1958 nearly 400 000 people were convicted of offences under the pass laws and related control measures.[23] This equalled nearly 20 per cent of the total African population of the main metropolitan areas in which the great majority of pass law arrests occurred.

At its conference in December 1959 the ANC planned for a series of demonstrations to counter the official celebration of the fiftieth anniversary of the unification of South Africa in 1910. These were to include an anti-pass protest on 31 March 1960, which would also commemorate previous anti-pass struggles dating back to 1913. The protest would culminate on 26 June 'with a great bonfire of passes'.

The PAC was invited to join the protests, but declined, opting instead to stage its own anti-pass protest on 21 March. The exigencies of the time made it essential for the PAC not to allow itself to be overshadowed by the older organisation. To steal a march on the ANC was, in Mandela's words, 'a blatant case of opportunism … motivated more by a desire to eclipse the ANC than to defeat the enemy'.[24]

The PAC's plan was simple: on Monday, 21 March people would leave their passes at home, go to the nearest police station and seek arrest. If the police declined to arrest them, they should return home and try again later. On being arrested, the rule would be 'no bail, no defence, no fine'. No violence would be allowed – and Sobukwe even addressed a letter to the Commissioner of Police asking him to instruct the police to 're-frain from actions that may lead to violence'. Shortly before the campaign Sobukwe addressed instructions to PAC supporters, urging them to observe 'ABSOLUTE NON-VIOLENCE' and explaining that the principal aim of the campaign was

> … to get ourselves arrested, get our women remaining at home. This means that nobody will be going to work. Industry will come to a standstill and the government will be forced to accept our terms. And once we score that victory, there will be nothing else we will not be able to tackle.[25]

Indeed, the PAC belief was that South Africa would be liberated by 1963 and that a (Pan-African) United States of Africa would thereafter be established. These hopes grievously underestimated the power and the ruthlessness of the state.

The events at Sharpeville and, subsequently, at Langa have been described elsewhere, and no detailed recounting is required. Sixty-nine people were shot dead at Sharpeville when the police opened fire on a crowd variously estimated to have been as low as 3 000 and as high as 25 000 (including many children); the police estimate was over 20 000.[26] There are equally disparate assessments of the mood of the crowd: some described it as 'perfectly amiable', whereas the police considered it 'extremely militant'. The approximately 200 police inside the police station, which was surrounded by protesters, included a number of young reservists who had been hastily mobilised as reinforcements. The police had had virtually no training or experience in crowd control, let alone riot control. There was, according to Frankel, 'a deep sense of dread … a veritable psychosis of fear'.[27] Their jumpiness was heightened by shouts of 'Cato Manor' from the crowd, referring to the brutal killing of nine policemen in the Durban township of Cato Manor two months earlier.

As the fatal moment, 1.35 pm, drew nearer, a futile effort was made by Colonel Att Spengler of the security police to negotiate with PAC or community leaders in the crowd, a procedure that had successfully defused tense situations in other townships. The fuse was lit when one Geelbooi, a petty criminal who had been harshly interrogated by the police some months before, arrived on the scene, drunk, and on seeing the man he took to be his interrogator, fired two shots into the air with a pistol. Unfortunately this episode coincided virtually to the second with a scuffle involving Spengler who, according to the police account, had opened the gate of the fence surrounding the police station to admit an African who said 'that he wished to surrender'. The shots fired by Geelbooi and the stones being thrown, combined with Spengler's fall, evidently panicked the police, who, without any order having been given by the officer in command, opened fire on the crowd and continued firing for some 20 seconds until ordered to cease.[28] Allegedly, 52 of those killed were shot in the back.

In Langa and other African townships near Cape Town the PAC had enjoyed some success in attracting support, partly because of the ineffectiveness of the ANC in the area and partly because of the unique ferocity with which the pass laws were enforced in the Western Cape. On the morning of 21 March crowds gathered in Langa and other African townships to offer themselves for arrest, but the police declined to do so and forcibly prevented a march to the Langa police station, whereupon

Philip Kgosana, a 23-year-old student at the University of Cape Town, who was regional secretary of the PAC, urged them to disperse but not to go to work. He called for a demonstration for 5 pm that day. Kgosana, a charismatic figure, was a remarkable young man who idolised Sobukwe. He was to play a major role in the unfolding drama in Cape Town.[29]

The evening meeting in Langa, which was attended by an estimated 10 000 people, ended in disaster. Three were killed, after (inaudible) demands for the crowd to disperse proved fruitless.[30] Disturbances also occurred at other places on the Cape Peninsula and in the Western Cape. The strike by African workers was now firmly under way despite police efforts to force them to go to work.

On 25 March the ANC called for a day of mourning on 28 March, and was supported in this by the PAC. It turned out to be the biggest strike thus far in the history of the country. On 26 March Luthuli publicly burned his pass, partly, no doubt, as Peter Brown of the Liberal Party observed, in an attempt to recapture the initiative which the PAC had seized from the ANC.[31] In Cape Town the Divisional Commissioner of Police of the Western Cape, Colonel IPS Terblanche, announced that no pass law arrests would be made, and on the following day, the (national) Commissioner of Police, Major-General CI Rademeyer, suspended the pass laws country-wide. Some had high hopes that this was the end of a hated system, but it was reimposed on 7 April.

The state was not about to relinquish one of its main techniques of control. Indeed, on 30 March a State of Emergency was declared, giving the authorities powers to ban meetings and to detain people. By the end of August, when the State of Emergency was lifted, 11 503 had been detained.[32] Furthermore, the Unlawful Organisations Act was rushed through Parliament, with support of the official opposition United Party (though not of the breakaway Progressive Party), and came into effect on 1 April: both the ANC and the PAC were banned.

Major drama occurred in Cape Town on 30 March, even though it seemed that the steam had gone out of protest. The strikes continued, however. Kgosana describes the massive march on the centre of Cape Town as having originated in police raids on Langa that were conducted with great ferocity:

> ... a massive police raid was launched very early that morning [in Langa]. The violence was more brutal than on any other day since March 21. The police smashed doors, kicked and beat up workers with sticks and rubber truncheons. It was a really savage affair. In the Zones [single quarters for male migrant labourers], some strikers

regrouped and attacked the police with sticks and stones. At the end of the duel, about 50 strikers had been severely wounded, more than 10 with broken arms. In the wake of the savagery, the leadership made a snap decision to organise another massive invasion of the city, but this time on parliament buildings … where we would have a final showdown with the white rulers of South Africa.[33]

The Langa marchers were augmented by others, and a mile-long column numbering an estimated 30 000 walked through the white suburb of Mowbray and up to the arterial De Waal Drive that skirts the mountain before descending into the city. The crowd was disciplined, unarmed and silent, although the noise of 30 000 pairs of marching feet created an eerie sound that unnerved whites who heard it.

Terblanche, an archetypical 'good cop', realised that 'even the smallest spark could result in the greatest bloodbath in the history of South Africa'.[34] Undoubtedly he was aware of the recent massacre at Sharpeville. He and two other officers, all unarmed, went out to parley with Kgosana, who had led half of the marchers into the city, but to the police headquarters and not to Parliament. What had happened was that Eulalie Stott, a member of the Liberal Party and the Black Sash, had telephoned Sir de Villiers Graaff, then leader of the parliamentary opposition, to tell him about the impending danger. Graaff, in turn, said that the army was present in force around Parliament and would certainly open fire if the marchers approached.

Stott raced off by car to warn Kgosana of what might happen. Kgosana, on hearing this, changed tactics and diverted half of the marchers to police headquarters, saying that it was unwise to force a way to Parliament 'because an opportunity would have been presented to the racists to shoot'.[35] The situation nevertheless remained extremely tense and highly inflammable. At his meeting with Terblanche, Kgosana demanded an interview with the Minister of Justice, Frans Erasmus, a hardliner devoid of both humanity and commonsense, and the release of detained PAC leaders, as well as an end to the police brutality that had prompted the march.

Terblanche responded that he was not in a position to release the detainees, but he undertook to arrange a meeting with Erasmus if Kgosana would lead his followers out of the city. Kgosana then told the marchers that an interview with the Minister had been promised and that they should now go back to the townships – which they did. The control that Kgosana was able to exercise over his followers is one of the remarkable aspects of the episode.

At the height of the drama a telephone conversation between Erasmus and Terblanche took place. According to the official police history, Erasmus ordered Terblanche to defuse the situation, but without recourse to violence. The exact nature of the conversation remained a secret until Terblanche's death in 1988: far from Erasmus's having instructed him to avoid violence, he had told him to use force to disperse the marchers and if necessary to shoot into the crowd if his orders were not immediately obeyed. Subsequently, Terblanche was given a dressing down by Erasmus for having disobeyed orders. He was also treated as an outcast by many of his colleagues, who took their cue from Erasmus.

Even worse, when Kgosana returned to the city later, together with the three PAC officials, expecting to meet Erasmus for the promised interview, all were arrested. Erasmus had not had the slightest intention of granting the interview: Kgosana was told (not by Terblanche) that 'the Minister was not interested in seeing us'.[36]

Different fates awaited the principal actors in the drama: Kgosana spent months in detention before going into exile and disappearing from the public eye. He returned to South Africa in 1990, but whatever promise he had shown as a political leader was not realised. Erasmus, whose foolishness had nearly cost South Africa dear, was dropped from the cabinet in 1961 and packed off to Italy as ambassador. Whether having made a hash of a previous portfolio, Defence, and thereafter nearly having caused havoc in Cape Town had anything to do with the termination of his political career is not known.

Terblanche's future promotion was blocked, apparently at Erasmus's behest, which he described as 'one of the tragedies of my life': he should have reached the rank of brigadier, but remained a colonel until his retirement. He consistently refused to speak publicly about what had transpired between him and Erasmus, fearing that there might be repercussions on his family. He wrote a full account and attached it to his will for release to Roger Williams of the *Cape Times*, whose reports form the basis of the foregoing paragraphs. (As a belated recognition of the injustice done to him, the rank of brigadier was conferred on him in 1987, at the age of 84.)

Urban protest petered out as the State of Emergency took its toll. Sobukwe and other PAC leaders were charged with incitement, Sobukwe being sentenced to three years' imprisonment; Kgosana, who had been detained for four months, was charged with the same offence but estreated bail and fled the country. Perversely, it was a sign of the government's wariness of Sobukwe's potential as an inspirational leader that on completion of his sentence in 1963 special legislation, commonly known as the 'Sobukwe clause', was enacted whereby Sobukwe continued to be detained but now on Robben Island, seven miles off the coast of Cape Town. He was not grouped with other prisoners, but was housed separately and given special 'privileges' denied other prisoners. He remained there until May 1969, when he was moved under strict banning orders to Kimberley, where he died in 1978. It was a sad end for a bright star that had shone for a tragically brief time.

*   *   *

During the tense times of March and April 1960 some believed that the revolution was at hand. Sharpeville and Langa, international condemnation, a massive outflow of capital, the failed assassination attempt on Verwoerd on 9 April, the temporary suspension of the pass laws, and evidence of doubts about policy in NP circles, combined to suggest that the government was in trouble. The wobble, however, was of strictly limited duration. With Verwoerd back at the helm, and a hardline new Minister of Justice, BJ Vorster, appointed in August 1961, the state unleashed ferocious new powers to combat opposition.

In organisational terms the ANC could never have been described as strong, but with the muscle lent to it by the SACP it was in a better position than the PAC to make the transition to operating underground. With Sobukwe incarcerated and Kgosana in exile, the PAC lacked credible leaders whose names were widely known in African townships. Potlako Leballo, the national secretary, served a two-year sentence after Sharpeville, whereafter he fled to Basutoland (now Lesotho) and became acting leader of the PAC. He was given to wild, rash statements, in contrast to Sobukwe's calm and rational approach, claiming exaggeratedly that a terrorist offshoot called Poqo (Xhosa for 'alone') had 150 000 members and that the aim of liberating Azania, as South Africa was called in PAC terminology, by 1963 was still the goal.

Poqo's stronghold was in the Western Cape, particularly among Transkeian migrants bitterly resentful of the ferocity with which influx control was enforced in the area. Its terrorism targeted whites virtually indiscriminately. During 1962 and early 1963, eight whites were brutally murdered, together with an unknown number of Africans who had refused to cooperate with the campaign. The police managed to infiltrate Poqo, and by mid-1963, according to official figures, 3 246 members had been arrested, of whom 124 were convicted of murder.[37] Effectively Poqo had been neutralised. By September 1966, 1 310 were serving sentences for political offences.[38] It was the beginning of a decade with an even bleaker outlook than that with which the previous one had begun.

The question whether the time for non-violent methods of opposition had passed now came to the fore in the Congress Alliance. Mandela, Walter Sisulu and other leading ANC figures (though not Luthuli) had no doubts. At the time of Sharpeville Mandela was aware that ANC supporters were becoming impatient with passive forms of struggle. The killings in March 1960 and the relatively unsuccessful national stay-at-home strike in May 1961 tipped the balance. 'I felt let down and disappointed by the reaction,' he said, concluding that the era of non-violent methods was over. Not long thereafter Mandela told a secret meeting of the ANC's National Executive in Durban that the repressive actions of the state had left no alternative to violence:

> I said it was wrong and immoral to subject our people to armed attacks by the state without offering them some kind of alternative. I mentioned again that people on their own had taken up arms. Violence would begin whether we initiated it or not. Would it not be better to guide this violence ourselves ...?[39]

Luthuli's moral commitment to non-violence, underlined by his winning the Nobel Peace Prize in 1961, was a potential stumbling block, although he was under no illusions about the state's determination to stamp out opposition with violence and repression. In 1952 he made a speech that included the famous words 'who will deny that thirty years of my life have been spent knocking in vain, patiently, moderately and modestly at a closed and barred door?'[40] In his autobiography, published a decade later, he wrote pessimistically of the tragedy that most whites were opposed to peaceful evolution: 'It is this ... which rules out the possibility of bargaining and compromise.'[41] Ultimately he acquiesced in the decision to establish Umkhonto we Sizwe (the Spear of the Nation), commonly termed MK. His suggestion that MK should be an autonomous body, linked to and under the overall control of the ANC, was accepted.[42] In theory, this left some legal space open to components of the Congress Alliance that had not been banned, while not implicating members of the ANC who disapproved of, or were unaware of, the change in strategy. Joe Slovo, who was to be the SACP's leader on MK's High Command, explained the decision:

> In general, if the issue [of forming MK] had been placed before the ANC leadership as a whole some of them would undoubtedly have rejected the steps which were already being planned. These steps required the utmost secrecy which would have been undermined by a

more generalised debate. In addition, the ANC's underground life was barely a year old and the process of creating effective underground structures was still far from complete. It seemed likely that an open acknowledgement by the ANC that MK was its military wing would encourage a more concentrated assault on structures which still needed more time to mature in the new conditions.[43]

The stratagem of putting space between the ANC and MK did not work. It was blown out of the water in 1962 when Robert Resha, an ANC representative in East Africa, publicly declared MK to be the ANC's military wing. It was an unauthorised statement, but it was not repudiated.

The international context was important in the switch to violence: the Viet Minh's stunning defeat of the French army at Dien Bien Phu in 1954; Castro's revolution in Cuba in 1959, and the brutal war in Algeria that finally ended in 1962 all contributed to a climate of opinion in ANC and SACP circles that guerrilla war was a viable option. South Africa's terrain and the surrounding *cordon sanitaire* of territories that were still under colonial rule were not considered to be fatal obstacles: after all, had Mao Zedong not likened the guerrilla among the people to a fish swimming in a pond? Even if South Africa lacked jungles MK could be confident of securing safe refuges among millions of Africans. Romantic views of what guerrilla war might achieve abounded. Ronnie Kasrils, a young white communist recruit, on leaving for military training in the Soviet Union in October 1963, believed that he would return as part of a victorious revolutionary army 'in a couple of years at the most'.[44] Slovo commented ruefully 'how utterly unreal our expectations were'.[45]

MK began its operations on 16 December 1961, a day sacred to Afrikaners because it commemorated a victory by the Voortrekkers over the Zulu leader Dingane in 1838. The actions, amateurish though they may have been, required considerable bravery, but the blasts in Durban, Port Elizabeth and Johannesburg achieved only limited damage – according to the police account – and spurred Vorster into promoting the 'Sabotage Act' in 1963, which equated the crime of sabotage with high treason, and, accordingly, made it punishable by death.

In a flyer that was distributed on 16 December MK announced itself with the message 'submit or fight':

> We of Umkhonto We Sizwe have always sought – as the liberation movement has sought – to achieve liberation, without bloodshed and civil clash. We do so still. We hope – even at this late hour – that our first actions will awaken everyone to a realization of the disastrous

situation to which the Nationalist policy is leading. We hope that we
will bring the Government and its supporters to their senses before
it is too late ....[46]

MK's strategy was to target government buildings and installations, taking care not to involve loss of life; but thereafter operations would be
ratcheted up to revolutionary violence. Sabotage, it was recognised, might
have value as propaganda, but it could not cause revolutionary change.[47]
Sabotage operations nevertheless continued into 1963, by which time, according to the police, over 200 blasts had occurred.

Operation Mayibuye was the strategic plan, drawn up in 1963, whereby
MK proposed the transition to guerrilla warfare. Hundreds of MK recruits would go abroad for military training, thereafter returning to four
rural areas to be joined by thousands of local recruits. Attacks would
be launched on strategic targets, complemented by urban sabotage and
mobilisation for protest, including a national anti-pass campaign. By
mid-1963, 300 people had been sent abroad for training.[48] The plan was
accepted by the High Command, although it evoked strong opposition in
the SACP's Central Committee.[49]

In the meantime the SACP had acquired a small farm, named Lilliesleaf,
in Rivonia, about ten miles north of Johannesburg. It was intended as a
safe house for the Party's Central Committee but it soon became the nerve-
centre of MK. Lilliesleaf's seclusion and the assumption that the security
police would not be able to find out about it soon bred a fatally casual
attitude to security. Rusty Bernstein wrote candidly of these failings:

> Things which need not have been done there, were, because it was
> easy and available. Things that should never have been kept there,
> were; and people who should not have known of its existence were
> taken there .... Unconsciously, MK was turning our safe house into
> a place of peril.[50]

It would be purely a matter of time before the police rumbled to Lilliesleaf's
real function. Various rumours have purported to tell how the leak occurred, but the police account is plausible: a tip-off was given to the police
by an informer who claimed to know the whereabouts of Walter Sisulu,
a member of the High Command, and the underground headquarters of
the ANC and the SACP. The informer, possibly someone who had been
broken in detention, led the police to Lilliesleaf, and they then kept it under surveillance for several days.

Enquiries at neighbouring properties yielded the information that

Lilliesleaf 'was visited by a steady stream of well-dressed black men'. On the afternoon of 11 July 1963 the security police swooped and arrested 17 people, including several members of the High Command. Others, not at Lilliesleaf at the time, were picked up later. The illusion of security had led to carelessness with incriminating documents: even a copy of Operation Mayibuye was discovered. It included a list of the explosives required for the campaign.

Two of the principals were not among those arrested at Lilliesleaf. It was Joe Slovo's good fortune to have been sent abroad a month before; Nelson Mandela was already imprisoned, after a conviction for incitement. He had gone underground and evaded the police for 17 months before being arrested on 5 August. He eventually stood trial in October 1963 with nine other accused. They were charged with acts of sabotage preparatory to mass revolutionary action and other offences. After a trial lasting 86 days eight of the accused were convicted and sentenced to life imprisonment; one, Rusty Bernstein, was acquitted, and another, Bob Hepple, had the charges against him withdrawn because he had agreed to be a state witness (he fled the country before having to give evidence).[51]

Conventionally, life imprisonment meant 15 years, but Vorster announced in February 1963 that for political offences the customary remission of sentence applicable to common criminals would not apply. It was a fair bet that the life sentences handed down in the Rivonia trial would literally mean life imprisonment.

The trial, which had ripped the heart out of MK, marked the end of an era in resistance politics, and the beginning of a new era in law enforcement. The prosecutor, Dr Percy Yutar, was an arrogant and bigoted man, evidently anxious to curry favour with the Nationalist government. Subject to the constraints of the legal system, he intended the case to be a 'show trial', in which the wickedness of the accused would be demonstrated to the entire country. The judge, Quartus de Wet, although deeply conservative and steeped in white prejudice, nevertheless retained some sense of judicial propriety. It was feared that he would impose the death penalty, as the law permitted. He chose not to, since, he said, the accused had been charged with sabotage and not high treason. Whether he had been impressed with the human calibre of the accused, and whether he was sensitive to the potential political fall-out of executions, remain open questions.

The accused knew exactly how high the stakes were. Mandela, however, was undaunted, and insisted on seizing the opportunity to place on record his fundamental beliefs and the reasons for creating MK. It was the most powerful speech of his life, and ensured his place in the worldwide pantheon of political prisoners. It ended on a note that captured the high drama of the trial:

> During my lifetime I have dedicated myself to this struggle of the African people. I have fought against White domination, and I have fought against Black domination. I have cherished the ideal of a democratic and free society in which all persons live together in harmony and with equal opportunities. It is an ideal which I hope to live for and to achieve. But if needs be, it is an ideal for which I am prepared to die.[52]

More MK operatives were arrested in 1963 and 1964: three were sentenced to death and executed for having ordered the killing of a witness who might have incriminated them. Five other trials of MK members were held in 1964, resulting in the conviction of 33 persons, all of whom received long sentences.

Another sabotage movement, the African Resistance Movement, had also become active in the early 1960s. It consisted mainly of young whites, most of them members of the Liberal Party, acting in contravention of the Party's strict adherence to non-violence. One of them, John Harris, was convicted of murder for placing a bomb in the concourse of Johannesburg Railway Station, resulting in the death of an elderly woman. Despite appeals for clemency that included a detailed account of Afrikaner nationalists' insurrectionary activities, and the loss of life caused by them during the Second World War, Harris was executed. Some members of the ARM managed to flee the country, but others were convicted and sentenced to imprisonment.

Draconian new legislation and more brutal methods of interrogation by the security police had made underground activity immeasurably more difficult. Detention without trial and the denial of access to lawyers or the right of *habeas corpus* gave interrogators virtually free rein to torture suspects. Rusty Bernstein wrote ruefully:

> We had not been prepared for institutionalised torture. Our codes of conduct were based on our mutual determination to take the consequences of silence regardless of the penalties. They had served us well for years – but they could not survive the new combination of sleep deprivation and physical torture.[53]

Detainees subjected to such pressure were liable to crack, and thereafter say anything to satisfy their interrogators and be freed from torture.

Howard Barrell, writing in 1990, calculates that some 241 detainees became state witnesses and gave evidence against former colleagues.[54] In the
Rivonia trial and thereafter few courts were prepared to reject the credibility of evidence extracted from detainees under torture or mental duress.[55] The defence in the Rivonia trial sought to discredit highly damaging evidence given against the accused by former detainees. Judge de Wet,
however, peremptorily ruled out the admissibility of expert testimony on
the effect of solitary confinement on the credibility of a detainee's evidence. 'No doctor, he said, was needed to tell him what weight should be
attached to the evidence of witnesses.'[56]

Underground organisations also had to cope with a new danger, the
more skilful use of informers by the security police. Previously, even
banned people were able to move around relatively easily, which, according to Brian Bunting of the SACP, 'lulled them into a false sense, not
so much of the effectiveness of their own security as of the impotence
of the Government and the police'.[57] By the early 1960s a false sense
of security was liable to be fatal. The SACP had prided itself on the
tight security it had maintained since 1953. That changed in 1963 when
a plausible police spy, Gerard Ludi, after a few years on the fringes,
was invited to join a cell – of which Bram Fischer happened also to
be a member. Ironically, Fischer warned the cell, in Ludi's presence, of
police attempts at infiltration and urged members 'to take special care
to recognise and isolate these people as soon as they come near us'.
(Subsequently Ludi gave damning evidence against Fischer and 13 others accused of furthering the aims of communism.[58]) Infiltration by spies
or informers, constant surveillance, bugging of offices and houses, tap-
ping of telephones and the interception of post became commonplace.
Banning orders that provided for house arrest contributed further to the
difficulty of underground work.

In the aftermath of the Rivonia and other trials in the 1960s, overt black
political protest or resistance dwindled. In the laconic words of the SA
Institute of Race Relations Survey for 1966: 'Most of the prominent leaders of the past are in exile, or in prison, or have been subjected to strict
banning orders.'[59] The state did not relax its vigilance, although no doubt
many white politicians claimed that the peacefulness vindicated their
belief that the removal from society of 'agitators' and other subversives
would demonstrate that the great majority of blacks were content with
their lot. It was a profound misreading of black attitudes to suppose that
sullen acquiescence equalled contentment. If anything, the apparent quiescence was the lull before the storm. Powerful forces were building up to
launch further challenges to white supremacy in the following decade.

In spite of severe setbacks, the internal ANC was not comprehensively eliminated, as the authorities hoped. By 1968, over 2 000 persons had been convicted of political offences, many for furthering the aims of a banned organisation. Raymond Suttner, himself a member of the underground ANC, argues that ANC activities continued in a 'highly secretive and unobtrusive' way. ANC veterans, including those released from prison, and the wives of imprisoned men were critical in keeping a rudimentary organisation in place.[60]

Segregated black university colleges had been in existence for a decade by 1970 and were producing their own reaction to white racism; MK might have been down, but it was not out – by as early as 1965, 800 trainees were abroad,[61] and in 1967 a detachment had fought, unsuccessfully, alongside Zimbabwean counterparts in the Rhodesian bush. Meanwhile, the government's 'homeland' programme was being implemented, bringing onto the scene a new kind of African political actor, the compliant bantustan functionary.

In terms of legislation enacted in 1959, eight homelands or bantustans were identified, and two more were subsequently added. By 1981, four (Transkei, Bophuthatswana, Venda and Ciskei) were nominally 'independent', though universally unrecognised as sovereign states, other than by one another and South Africa itself. The others were at various stages along the road to 'self-government'.

The decisions to opt for independence could hardly be described as expressing the will of the inhabitants of these putative states. The closest approximation was an attitude survey held among Ciskeians on the eve of its independence in 1981: it found that a clear majority of the (Xhosa) inhabitants, either resident in Ciskei or in an urban area, opposed independence.[62] The results, part of a report commissioned by the Ciskei government, did not deter Chief Lennox Sebe, the head of that government, from taking independence, though not before he had staged a referendum in which 99 per cent supported it, in a 59.5 per cent poll. The figure of 99 per cent support sounded suspicious. Many, no doubt, lacked confidence in the secrecy of the ballot and feared retribution if they voted against independence.

In spite of the widespread unpopularity of the homeland concept and the (varying) degrees of popular hostility to the respective leaderships, a new factor was introduced into black politics. The aims of the bantustan policy were transparent: to divert African political aspirations into the (harmless) channels offered by heavily dependent satraps that would continue to supply labour to the 'white' areas; and to 'retribalise' African politics by ensuring that power in each so-called 'national unit' was vested in the hands of a malleable chief, of whom Paramount Chief Kaiser Matanzima of Transkei was the prototype.

Notwithstanding these Machiavellian motives, the development of the bantustans had *some* advantages for *some* of their inhabitants. The leaderships commanded unprecedented patronage that benefited the coteries that surrounded them; civil services, armies and police forces had to be staffed, and, over time, huge, bloated and corrupt bureaucracies developed. None was likely to develop into a prosperous, democratic state. On the positive side there were some benefits with a wider spread that even Mandela acknowledged: educational systems could break out of the hated Bantu Education system; there were possibilities of upward occupational mobility that were denied to Africans in the white-controlled areas; and, in a general way, the absence of racial discrimination in the territories (including not having to carry a pass, except on entering 'white' South Africa) was a source of some relief, however limited.[63] Corrupt, authoritarian and prone to *coups d'état*, the bantustans were classic banana republics, in which Joseph Conrad's *Heart of Darkness* met Evelyn Waugh's *Black Mischief.*

Not all of the bantustan leaders, however, were as malleable as the government wished. Mangosuthu Gatsha Buthelezi, who became Chief Minister of KwaZulu, was a case in point. As a young chief he played a cat-and-mouse game with the authorities in refusing to accept Bantu Authorities, the linchpin of the homeland system of governance, declaring that he could not do so until his people gave their consent. The consequence of this 'insubordination' was years of pressure and harassment in the late 1950s and 1960s. Buthelezi, a former Fort Hare student and a descendant of the Zulu king, Cetshwayo, was a well-educated man, deeply steeped in Zulu traditions but also a devout Christian. He regarded himself as an ANC supporter, in that strand of the ANC represented by his friend and mentor, Luthuli. He was one of the few traditional leaders able to straddle modern and traditionalist politics.

Friendship with Mandela, Oliver Tambo and other ANC leaders went back many years, to the time of the formation of the ANC Youth League. Mandela never repudiated the friendship, saying of buthelezi that he had regarded him then 'as one of the movement's upcoming young leaders'.[64]

The ANC was under no illusions about the aim of bantustans, namely to undercut support for national opposition movements, but it looked at them with an eye to the possibilities of using them as bases of support. There had been vigorous resistance to official policies in several homelands in the 1950s and early 1960s, notably in Zeerust and Sekhukhuneland, as well as in Pondoland. Indeed, MK's original plans sought to use the rural areas for developing guerrilla warfare.[65]

Mandela's attitude to bantustans was more nuanced and pragmatic than simply outright rejection. He hated the concept on which the policy was based, but he raised some awkward questions for his colleagues who damned all homeland functionaries as 'collaborators' and would have nothing to do with them. He wrote: 'Though I abhorred the Bantustan system, I felt the ANC should use both the system and those within it as a platform for our policies'.[66] Even before his imprisonment he had opposed boycotting the elections to be held in Transkei in 1963, suggesting instead that the ANC should throw its weight behind the opposition to Matanzima with a view to building a mass organisation in the territory. His proposals led to a serious clash in 1969 with his fellow-prisoner, Govan Mbeki.[67]

In an essay written on Robben Island in 1976 he maintained that rather than branding bantustan functionaries as 'sellouts', the better strategy was to reason with them, and at least try to neutralise them. Mandela feared that, apart from dividing the liberation movement, bantustans would fragment the country and encourage 'regionalism and clannishness'. Prompted by the concerns expressed by pro-government security experts in an Afrikaans newspaper, he enquired whether the Transkei might not be considered as a forward base for guerrilla operations.[68] His fellow-prisoner, Walter Sisulu, broadly concurred, insisting that it would be a mistake 'to see in every man and woman who works within these apartheid institutions an enemy of the revolution'.[69]

Oliver Tambo, the acting President of the ANC since Luthuli's death in 1967, held similar views, hoping that 'mass democratic organisations' could be created in the bantustans. It was in this context, he continued, that regular contact was maintained with Buthelezi, in the hope that as a former ANCYL member who had taken up his position in the KwaZulu bantustan after consultation with the ANC, he would use the legal opportunities provided by the bantustan policy 'to participate in the mass mobilisation of our people on the correct basis of the orientation of the masses to focus on the struggle for a united and non-racial South Africa'.[70] Out of these consultations Inkatha was born in 1975; its official colours, black, green and gold, were identical to those of the ANC.

According to Buthelezi's biographer, in a discussion in 1971, Tambo warned him that 'he was rocking the boat too much' and that he should be less visible and less outspoken, occasionally even attacking the ANC. It was advice that Buthelezi declined to follow.[71]

Buthelezi filled the political vacuum created by the decimation of the

ANC, PAC and MK, and remained an important player in national politics. Even after his popularity as a national leader had weakened and he had fallen out with the ANC in the late 1970s, he retained a significant power-base in KwaZulu that could not be ignored.

*   *   *

The 1960s and early 1970s were a bleak period for the ANC and its allies. With much of its leadership imprisoned it fell to Oliver Tambo to begin the slow process of building up an organisation in exile. Similarly, the SACP's internal structures had been smashed by the mid-1960s; nine of the 17 members of the Central Committee were in exile, and others were in prison.[72]

The formation of MK and the readiness of the Soviet Union to provide funding and training strengthened the role of the SACP: organisationally and ideologically the ANC was drawn into a closer relationship. Slovo's claim that SACP involvement in the ANC's external mission, which included direction of MK, was 'negligible' has to be viewed with some scepticism.[73] As the main conduit for Soviet assistance to the ANC, the SACP's leverage in the ANC was bound to be considerable. The importance of this assistance was such that Irina Filatova, a leading Russian Africanist scholar, could argue, correctly, that without Soviet assistance 'the ANC as we know it would not have existed and South African history would have been very different.'[74]

The role of communists in the ANC had long been a contentious issue. It might have alienated the Africanists, but the support of communists was welcomed by the mainstream leadership, including non-communists. Luthuli, for example, the last of the liberal Christian leaders, rejected communism as 'a mixture of a false theory of society linked on to a false "religion",' but he was nevertheless prepared to cooperate with communists:

> The [African National] Congress stand is this: our primary concern is liberation, and we are not going to be sidetracked by ideological clashes and witch hunts. Nobody in Congress may use the organisation to further any aims but those of Congress. When I co-operate with Communists in Congress affairs I am not co-operating with Communism. We leave our differing political theories on one side until the day of liberation, and in the meantime we are co-operating in a defined area, in the cause of liberation.[75]

A stock ANC response to hostile questions about its cooperation with communists was to cite the Allies' cooperation with the Soviet Union to defeat Nazi Germany during the Second World War. Others parried the question by asking the questioner how one could be sure that it was not a case of the ANC's manipulating the communists rather than the other way around.

In an address in 1981 Tambo, a non-communist, said of the ANC–SACP relationship that 'we are a powerful force because our organisations are mutually reinforcing'. He rejected accusations that the SACP influenced the ANC; rather, the two organisations influenced each other: 'The ANC is quite capable of influencing, and is liable to be influenced by, others.'[76]

How realistic Tambo's and others' accounts of the relationship were remains a controversial topic. Dual membership made the boundary between the separate identities permeable and hence, blurred; in MK, although under the ANC's direction, it was clear that SACP members were preponderant in the leadership. Its soldiers, moreover, many of whom had received their training in the Soviet Union, received lectures on Marxism-Leninism in the military camps. In some cases, notably those delivered by Jack Simons, a former professor at the University of Cape Town, they were of high quality and considerable analytical rigour.[77]

Estimating the number of SACP members on the ANC's National Executive Committee (NEC) was (and is) a guessing game, usually played by those hostile to or suspicious of the relationship. Accuracy was impossible because SACP members who were also ANC members did not generally reveal their SACP affiliation. Entry of non-African SACP members into the ANC became possible as a result of a decision at the ANC's Consultative Conference in Morogoro (Tanzania) in 1969, but membership of the NEC by non-Africans was permitted only in 1985, after the Kabwe (Zambia) conference.

In practice, the earlier restrictions on the membership of non-Africans made little difference to the close relationship between the two organisations or to the influence that the SACP was able to exert on the ANC. Partly this was attributable to the common 'anti-imperialist' stance: it did not require much persuasion to convince non-communist members of the ANC of the case against imperialism and, in general, of the alleged complicity of the Western powers in shoring up the surviving bastions of colonial or white rule in southern Africa. Many, probably most, ANC members also shared the SACP's hostile view of capitalism, as well as the belief that segregation and apartheid had been generated by capitalism. Given the extreme degree of inequality and the extent of exploitation in South Africa, their receptivity to such ideas was understandable.

Moreover, this receptivity was heightened by the prevailing view in much of newly independent Africa that some form of socialism was the best way forward: its disastrous consequences could not have been foreseen.

Although the ANC was careful not to identify itself as a socialist movement, most of its leading figures believed that South Africa, when liberated, would eventually adopt socialism, once the 'bourgeois' forms of the national democratic revolution had run their course. Writing in his prison cell in 1976, Mandela argued that 'no serious-minded freedom fighter' would deny that the ideas of Marx and Engels 'are a blueprint of the most advanced social order in world history, that have led to an unprecedented reconstruction of society and to the removal of all kinds of oppression for a third of mankind'.[78] Mandela's rose-coloured view of Marxist-Leninist states derived largely from their support of liberation movements. During the Rivonia trial he had denied being a member of the SACP, but Gavin Evans, a security operative in the SACP during the 1980s, quotes a 'trusted party member', who was also a key member of the ANC's National Executive Committee and an underground colleague of Mandela's, as saying that Mandela had, in fact, joined the SACP after the banning of the ANC in 1960 'partly because it was seen as useful in winning the trust of the Soviets and their clients'.[79]

An important factor in cementing the links between the ANC and the SACP was the selfless commitment of many individual communists to the cause of black liberation. Prominent African communists in the ANC, such as JB Marks, Moses Kotane and Dan Tloome, earned their spurs as hardworking and dedicated people. Non-Africans such as Ahmed Kathrada, Reg September, Bram Fischer and Joe Slovo also demonstrated total identification with the cause, and, in the process, helped to break down anti-Indian and anti-white attitudes that were widespread in ANC circles and in wider African communities.

Many communists were 'true believers' whose faith in the inevitable triumph of 'scientific socialism' provided a carapace that shielded them from fear or doubt. Their evangelical zeal was reminiscent of European missionaries who went, undaunted, to the 'dark continent' in the eighteenth and nineteenth centuries in the full knowledge of the high risk they ran of succumbing to disease or being killed by unreceptive and hostile targets for conversion. Gillian Slovo's descriptions of her parents, Joe Slovo and Ruth First, capture elements of distinctive personality traits: '... they were so optimistic. It must have seemed to them that they were cresting a wave that would never break;' they were drawn into the underground, 'heading deeper into a secret world where excitement and danger were to run side by side. It was a cosy, in-bred universe they occupied'; and '... my parents lived with constant danger. It seemed to suit them both.'[80]

Nothing can detract from the dedication and fearlessness that many individual communists displayed, and which cost some dearly. First, for example, was killed in Mozambique in 1982 by a letter bomb sent by the 'dirty tricks' department of the South African security authorities. Others spent long periods in jail or in exile. Few, however, questioned the monstrous dictatorships that ruled in the Soviet Union and all other Marxist-Leninist states. Nor could they accept that there was any parallel between Western imperialism and the relationship between the Soviet Union and its Warsaw Pact satellites, or, indeed, the relationship between the Soviet Union's Russian core and the republics that collectively made up the USSR. Even the invasions of Hungary in 1956 and Czechoslovakia in 1968 and other deplorable manifestations of Soviet *force majeure* were accepted as necessary measures to ward off the threat from 'reactionary, anti-socialist forces in the country, based on remnants of the former exploiting classes and supported by international imperialism' (the SACP's comment on the Czechoslovakian crisis).[81] Individual SACP members who voiced criticism were liable to censure. Ruth First, who had carved for herself an academic career of distinction, retained a critical independence of mind and was saved from expulsion from the Party only by Joe Slovo's intervention.[82]

The guessing game about the extent of SACP influence on the ANC gained fresh impetus after the Kabwe conference in 1985 when the ANC's National Executive Committee was opened to all races, and five non-Africans, all SACP members, were elected to it. Of the 30 members of the NEC possibly as many as half were known or suspected SACP members; Ellis and Sechaba claim that the figure was 22; while Davis, unable to provide a precise figure, quotes the stock response offered by ANC leaders that SACP representation 'gives party members significant but by no means controlling influence'.[83]

It is apparent that SACP members who were also involved in the ANC caucused before meetings. Most were intelligent, skilled in debate and efficient – conforming closely to the Leninist model of 'professional revolutionaries'. They were also ruthless, seeing themselves as a 'vanguard force within the national liberation movement'. Shubin quotes an internal SACP document which hints that the skills of the 'professional revolutionaries' could be used in highly manipulative ways (though, predictably, this was always vehemently denied by the SACP):

> Experience has shown that the Party can fulfil its vanguard role without 'being at the head' of the movement in the physical or public sense. Our leadership must rather depend on the correctness of our

political line, on our ability to win non-Party comrades to supporting our line, and on our cohesiveness as an organisation.[84]

Breyten Breytenbach, an Afrikaans poet with strong leftwing but non-
communist sympathies (and thus hardly a dupe of the South African government), offered an altogether more robust account of SACP influence:

> The SACP actually has the nerve centres of the liberation movement
> in its control .... The SACP has in its hands the secretariat of the
> ANC, the financial structure of the ANC, the control over the armed
> wing of the ANC ....[85]

Breytenbach himself lived in Paris with his Vietnamese wife (her being
a 'non-white' made it impossible for them to live in South Africa) but
retained a passionate interest in South Africa. He was a key figure in the
establishment of Okhela, a non-communist group of white militants
who hoped to provide underground support to the liberation movement.
Breytenbach returned to South Africa in 1975 in disguise to identify potential activists. Even before his departure he was betrayed by an informer,
believed by some (though Breytenbach himself cannot categorically confirm this) to have been an SACP member, so that from his arrival his movements were monitored by the security police, who subsequently arrested
him and charged him with terrorism, resulting in his spending seven years
in prison.

*   *   *

The bleak years for the ANC continued into the 1970s, despite its patient
work at building up an exile organisation, lobbying governments and international forums, and Tambo's efforts at preserving unity – which stood
in sharp contrast to the PAC's seemingly inherent fractiousness. Building
underground structures inside South Africa was even more difficult than
exile activity. Much of the ANC's potential support-base had been cowed
by the ferocity of the state's crackdown in the 1960s. Ordinary people
might have sympathies for the liberation movement, but they were also
aware that their communities were riddled with informers whose testimony could land them in gaol, even on the flimsiest of evidence.

   In making the decision to form MK, the ANC and the SACP had
stressed that armed struggle was only one prong of a multi-pronged strategy. In a report adopted in 1969, *Strategy and Tactics of the South African
Revolution*, the ANC insisted that revolutionary struggle could succeed

in the long run only if it attracted mass support that 'has to be won in all-round political mobilisation which must accompany the military activities'.[86] In practice, little occurred on the ground, and the powerful stirring of popular sentiment that began the early 1970s owed far more to the rise of the new forces of Black Consciousness and the independent labour movement than to the ANC.

MK was also hamstrung by other powerful constraints. Botswana, Lesotho and Swaziland, the independent former British High Commission territories, were economic hostages to South Africa and could not afford to offer bases to MK. South West Africa (now Namibia) was under South African control; Rhodesia (now Zimbabwe), the rebel British colony, was under white control; and Angola and Mozambique were still Portuguese colonies. Entry routes were difficult – and a proposed sea-landing had to be abandoned. The few who did manage to infiltrate South Africa found no reception facilities to provide safe havens or local information. By 1973 MK 'had not fired a single shot on South African soil'.[87]

Understandably, morale among the several hundred soldiers in MK camps sagged. They were bored and eager to return to South Africa and fight. To allay their discontent many were sent for retraining, referred to as the 'sharpening of the spear'. This evoked the tart response that there was a danger that the ANC might continue sharpening the spear 'until there was no spear left!'[88]

The circumstances of exile are inevitably tough and, in the absence of discernable progress, dispiriting. For soldiers in MK camps it was even worse: life was Spartan and operational duties were dangerous.

After the unsuccessful Wankie campaign in 1967, which was a joint operation with the Zimbabwean African People's Union aimed at toppling the illegal Rhodesian regime, matters blew up. The campaign had started with high hopes: Rhodesia was an important part of South Africa's *cordon sanitaire* and, moreover, Chris Hani, an MK commissar, sought to open a 'Ho Chi Minh' trail into South Africa. Little was achieved, and there were even (false) rumours that it had been a suicide mission intended to result in the elimination of disaffected MK soldiers.

That there was disaffection was true, and it boiled over when, after their return, Hani and others submitted a memorandum that made scathing criticism of the ANC leadership. It spoke of the 'frightening depth reached by the rot in the ANC and the disintegration of MK accompanying this rot'. The exile leadership was accused of 'careerism'; they had become 'professional politicians' instead of 'professional revolutionaries', and were divorced from the realities on the ground in South Africa. Further allegations were made of nepotism: 'virtually all the sons and daughters of the leaders had been sent to universities in Europe', which was assumed to mean that they were being groomed for leadership positions in the ANC.

Predictably the leadership did not take kindly to the accusations, especially since there was more than a grain of truth in them. Hani and his co-signatories were charged with violating military discipline, and came within a hair's breadth of being executed.[89] Instead, they were suspended and subsequently reinstated. Hani's memorandum was nevertheless a wake-up call for many in the leadership. O'Malley writes of the exile community that 'inertia was the preferred modus operandi' and that they 'grew comfortable in exile'.[90] There were, however, extenuating circumstances: the late 1960s and early 1970s were hard times for revolutionaries, whether externally or internally based.

CHAPTER 5

The Soweto Uprising and
its Consequences

In answer to the question, 'What is the single most important moment in South African history?', we believe it was the instant the first
shot was fired on 16 June 1976, because it effectively killed the dream
of grand apartheid. The traumatic death throes would last for many
more years, but the beast was mortally wounded.[1]

Hyperbole? Dramatically expressed perhaps, but containing the essential
truth that South Africa was never the same again after the uprising began
in Soweto and spread to many parts of the country, petering out during
1977 but leaving in its wake a combustible mix of rage and determination. It was the beginning of the end of apartheid. A new spirit galvanised
blacks, and even in the face of fierce repression by the powerful state, resistance would gradually force the leaders of the apartheid government to
recognise that suppression of its opponents was no longer a viable long-
term strategy.

By the late 1960s the state was congratulating itself on the supposed
eradication of black opposition, but there was to be no let-up in vigilance.
In 1968 the Deputy Minister of Police, SL Muller, warned that

> ... the spirit of Communism has not been completely eradicated .... .
> The ANC is not dead, and another flare-up is entirely possible. At
> the moment there is peace in South Africa but I cannot give the as-
> surance that this will always be the case.[2]

The security police confirmed the warning. Indeed, the state's anti-communist paranoia had been heightened by the arrest in July 1967 of a Soviet

spy, one Yuriy N Loginov of the KGB. It appeared to confirm the long-held belief that communists were behind all manifestations of protest and unrest: the Russian bear was eager to get its claws on South Africa's mineral wealth.

In spite of the apparent acquiescence of blacks, the calm on the surface belied a 'sullen resentment of white privilege, coupled with a certain apathy and an overwhelming sense of the inevitability of white power'.[3] Citing Lawrence Schlemmer, the South African Institute of Race Relations warned that the country was drawing closer to mass unrest. In an analysis, Schlemmer described the 'political incapacity' of blacks as one of the foundations of apartheid. By this he meant the ability of repression, police informers and other coercive measures to perpetuate black quiescence. Theoretically, 'concerted action by all Blacks, say on the labour front, could destroy the present system almost immediately by crippling the economy'. In his extensive experience of polling, Schlemmer had concluded that less-educated Africans 'still have the ethos of a conquered people'. Moreover, blacks as a whole lacked coherence because of internal status divisions and, of course, concerted attempts by government to force Africans into separate ethnic categories.[4]

Though there was little overt political activity among Africans from 1968 until 1972, there were warnings of 'explosive discontent' building up among urban Africans.[5] Two factors were making their presence felt: one was the growth of labour militancy, and the second was the rediscovery and elaboration of a radical strand of black political thought and its underpinning by an organisational network. Both were to have momentous consequences.

Black Consciousness was not an entirely new phenomenon. The 'Africanism' propounded by Anton Lembede and the ANC Youth Leaguers in the 1940s, and the ideas of the 'Africanists' in the ANC in the 1950s, prior to their breakaway in 1958, were partial precedents. The late 1960s, moreover, were a time of ideological ferment in various parts of the world: many African colonies obtained independence during the decade, student protest was widespread even in developed countries, and in the United States 'Black Power' took off, both as a strategy and as an affirmation of black dignity. A heady brew was in the making.

The pre-eminent figure in BC was Steve Biko, who was born in the Eastern Cape in 1946 and died at the hands of the security police in 1977. Biko was born into a poor family, his father having died when Steve was four, and he and his siblings were raised by his mother, a domestic worker. By dint of intelligence and hard work he was able to matriculate and proceed, in 1966, to the University of Natal medical school (which admitted only blacks). His increasing involvement in student politics caused him to neglect his studies and he was excluded from the University in 1971, by which time BC had begun to make its mark. Biko was a handsome, articulate young man with a magnetic personality who was able to hold his audiences spellbound.

BC has been the subject of several good analyses that make it superfluous to do more than briefly describe it. Its organisational embodiment arose out of the experiences of black students in multiracial student organisations, the University Christian Movement (UCM) and the National Union of South African Students (Nusas). The UCM, established in 1967, and Nusas, founded in 1924, were, apart from some churches, virtually the only organisations in which students of all colours could meet on a basis of formal equality.

Many black students, however, chafed against white control of both organisations, which reinforced a sense of inadequacy and inferiority among blacks. White students, moreover, however strong their (rhetorical) commitment to the principle of non-racialism, were, according to their black critics, from the dominant and privileged group, and thus incapable of fully empathising with the plight of blacks, while being able to retreat when necessary into the stronghold of racial privilege, or to emigrate.

The decision to withdraw from Nusas in 1969, and to form the South African Students Organisation (SASO), was nevertheless hotly contested by a number of black students, who valued the link with even a predominantly white body. The critique of racially mixed organisations was widened to incorporate a blistering attack on white liberals. Steve Biko, the main figure in the emerging idea of BC and its embodiment in SASO, said in 1971:

> The [white] liberals set about their business with the utmost efficiency. They made it a political dogma that all groups opposing the *status quo* must *necessarily* be non-racial in structure. They maintained that if you stood for a principle of non-racialism you could not in any way adopt what they described as racialist policies. They even defined to the Black people what the latter should fight for. With this sort of influence behind them, most Black leaders tended to rely too much on the advice of liberals.[6]

Blacks, in the BC view, had to separate from multiracial bodies, organise on their own, and insist upon exclusively black initiatives. As a kind of consolation, Biko urged white liberals to realise 'that the place for their fight for justice is within their white society'.[7]

It was not only white liberals who were attacked by Biko: the ANC and its partners in the Congress Alliance, including the (white) Congress of Democrats and the multiracial SACP, also violated the principle of black exclusivity. This stricture, however, was seldom voiced in BC circles since SASO was anxious not to take sides either against the ANC or the PAC, and Biko himself (coming from a family background that was PAC in orientation) expressed the hope that the older movements and BC could join together to form one liberation group. He also acknowledged that Mandela, Sobukwe, Ahmed Kathrada and MD Naidoo 'will always have a place of honour in our minds as true leaders of the people'.[8]

In BC terminology 'blacks' were defined as those 'who are by law or tradition politically, economically and socially discriminated against as a unit in the struggle towards the realisation of their aspirations'. 'Non-white' was rejected since it was an insult to be defined as the negative of something else, but it was retained as a pejorative term for 'collaborators' and others labouring under the delusion that whites were superior:

> If one's aspiration is whiteness but his pigmentation makes attainment of this impossible, then that person is a non-white. Any man who calls a white man 'Baas' [master], any man who serves in the police force or Security Branch is *ipso facto* a non-white. Black people – real black people – are those who can manage to hold their heads high in defiance rather than willingly surrender their souls to the white man.[9]

'Black', in other words, referred less to pigmentation than to a common status, as well as a mental attitude. Indeed, BC, even as it developed, was more a state of mind than a coherent ideology, although strategic options for political action could readily be derived from it. Moreover, being principally a state of mind made communicating the essential tenets of BC to a wider audience easier.

Unlike the Youth Leaguers of the 1940s and the Africanists of the 1950s, who had displayed a pronounced anti-Indian streak, BC included as 'blacks' both Coloured and Indian people. In spite of the invidious status distinctions among the dominated groups, and the fact that apartheid's restrictions weighed less heavily on them, Coloureds and Indians were grievously discriminated against and thus fell within BC's definition of 'black'. There was some resistance by Africans to their inclusion in the formative days of BC, but it was overcome. There was even stronger resistance to being classified as blacks from more conservative Coloured and Indian people.

The fundamental theme of BC was the need for blacks to overcome the internalised sense of inferiority and the acquiescence in subordination that centuries of racial domination had instilled in black people. This was the phenomenon, described in various ways by writers such as Fanon and Memmi, that BC termed 'colonisation of the mind'. Colonised minds had to be liberated before apartheid could be effectively challenged. In a powerful passage Biko wrote:

> All in all the black man has become a shell, a shadow of man, completely defeated, drowning in his own misery, a slave, an ox bearing the yoke of oppression with sheepish timidity .... The first step therefore is to make the black man come to himself; to pump back life into his empty shell; to infuse him with pride and dignity, to remind him of his complicity in the crime of allowing himself to be misused and therefore letting evil reign supreme in the country of his birth.[10]

BC, whatever its critics averred, was an idea whose time had arrived. The question is: *why* did it arrive when it did? Few of the SASO members who conceived BC had been alive in 1948, but many, even if only about 10 years old, would have been aware of the Sharpeville episode in 1960 and the outrage that it caused among African communities. The names of Mandela, Sobukwe and others remained well known, despite their incarceration. The older generation, however, had been cowed by the state's apparently invincible power and its ruthless exercise.

The late 1960s were the highwater mark of student protest worldwide. Black South African students were aware of this, which must have aggravated their own sense of powerlessness. The black university colleges created after 1959 (including Fort Hare) were mediocre institutions whose students were kept on a tight rein by apartheid-minded authorities. Biko noted the failure of these universities to produce graduates 'who could give some kind of lead to the Black community'. Mostly, he said, students went to acquire degrees and thereafter they melted into the professional elite 'that was not well motivated within our society'. SASO's founders believed that graduates should plough back into the community part of what they had learned, but this could happen 'only if there is a guiding student organisation which operates on Black campuses'.[11]

On the face of it, BC's rejection of association with whites appeared to be the mirror-image of white racism. Mandela, for example, considered the BC movement's exclusivist philosophy to be 'racialistic' because it 'blindly bundles a section of the progressive forces with the enemy'.[12] The SACP, while acknowledging the powerful inspirational and 'conscientising' force of BC, nevertheless condemned it as lacking in 'scientific social analysis' because by proclaiming colour as its sole foundation it obscured the economic and class basis of racism. It also violated the interracial basis on which the Congress Alliance was premised.[13]

Biko would have none of this:

> [T]hough whites are our problem, it is still other whites who want to tell us how to deal with that problem. They do so by dragging all sorts of red herrings across our paths. They tell us that the situation is a class struggle rather than a racial one. Let them go to van Tonder [a common Afrikaans surname] in the Free State and tell him this.[14]

Apart from its effect in liberating blacks from the 'colonisation of the mind' syndrome of subservience and a sense of inferiority, BC sought also to mobilise black group power as a counterweight to white group power. It was the identical strategy advocated by exponents of 'Black Power' in the United States. In explaining this, Biko invoked Hegel's account of how a synthesis was reached:

> That since the thesis is a white racism there can only be one valid antithesis i.e. a solid black unity to counterbalance the scale. If South Africa is to be a land where black and white live together in harmony without fear of group exploitation, it is only when their two opposites have interplayed and produced a viable synthesis of ideas and a *modus vivendi*. We can never wage any struggle without offering a strong counterpoint to the white races that permeate our society so effectively.[15]

But how could mobilisation around colour avoid becoming racist? Sophisticated BC thinkers deflected this question ingenuously: Bennie Khoapa, for example, argued that black integration had to precede black and white integration because 'blacks must unite before they can separate and must separate before they can unite'. History, he wrote, had charged BC 'with the cruel responsibility of going to the very gate of racism in order to destroy racism – to the gate not further'.[16] Whether black leaders would be able to stem the tide of anti-white racism they had unleashed was a moot issue.

A corollary of BC's refusal to acquiesce in white initiatives or to be inveigled into apartheid's pseudo-representative institutions for blacks was the outright rejection of participation in bantustans or comparable bodies for Coloureds and Indians. These institutions, wrote Mamphela

Ramphele, 'are designed to cheat the black man into participating in his own oppression because of built-in safeguards that make it impossible for any person using them to liberate himself'.[17] So strong was the hostility to participating in apartheid institutions that Temba Sono, the president of SASO, was drummed out of the organisation in 1972 for suggesting that it was wrong to shun people such as Buthelezi. Biko excoriated Sono for very dangerous thoughts, deeming Buthelezi to be 'the one man who has led the entire world to believe in the bantustan philosophy'.[18] It was a milestone in Buthelezi's deteriorating relationship with young radicals.

The episode involving Sono raised an awkward issue: if bantustans and the like were apartheid institutions that should be boycotted, did not consistency require that other apartheid institutions like the university colleges for blacks also be boycotted? Sono's ill-fated address had pointed out that attendance at these institutions contradicted the boycott principle and compromised students who were vehemently opposed to apartheid and the principle of segregated university colleges. It was a difficult question: attempts by the ANC to organise a boycott of schools after the imposition of Bantu Education in the 1950s had failed because the huge majority of African parents preferred their children to receive some education, however bad, rather than none at all. Similarly, given the difficulty of gaining admission to the 'white' universities, the choice boiled down to attending one of the so-called 'tribal' colleges or foregoing higher education altogether – unless one undertook the arduous task of obtaining a degree by correspondence through the University of South Africa, which, in 1972, had a higher enrolment of African students (3 341) than all the other institutions combined. Principle, then, had to be traded off against necessity in a situation of tightly constrained choice.

It was predictable that the five black universities would become strongholds of protest. The three African universities, designated for particular ethnic groups, were located in relatively isolated rural areas inside homelands. Their student numbers had grown appreciably: by 1970 Fort Hare had 610, the North 810, and Zululand 591.[19] For purposes of political mobilisation critical mass in numbers was being reached. Tight controls over student activity and the heavy preponderance of pro-apartheid rectors and lecturers were ready-made targets for protest. Similar conditions prevailed at the (Indian) University of Durban-Westville and the (Coloured) University of the Western Cape.

Initially SASO avoided a confrontational style, and concentrated instead on building an organisational infrastructure. Ironically, it was indirectly helped by university authorities and the government who mistook SASO's attacks on the white-led Nusas as evidence of the emergence among blacks of a new philosophy of separateness that could be aligned with separate development. Nothing could have been further from the truth, but the breathing space that this Marcusean repressive tolerance afforded enabled SASO to entrench itself on the black campuses, including theological colleges, and become the dominant force in black student politics.

BC did not confine itself to student activism. It sought a broader reach into black communities by means of literacy campaigns, health projects, building schools and clinics, especially in impoverished rural areas. Music, theatre and poetry also became infused with the BC spirit. Among churches, both the traditional denominations and the myriad African Independent Churches, the message of Black Theology spread quickly. Efforts were also made, though only with limited success, to move into the field of black trade unionism.

During 1972 the relative peacefulness of the campuses was shattered. Protest had been simmering in previous years but a speech delivered by Onkgopotse Tiro at a University of the North graduation ceremony in April 1972 brought student discontent to a head. Tiro, a former president of the student representative council and a SASO activist, used the occasion to lambaste the university authorities for the apartheid measures practised on the campus (including segregated seating at the ceremony) and the entire system of segregated education. Tiro was promptly expelled, and much of the student body, followed by those on other campuses, began a boycott of lectures.[20] It was the biggest country-wide protest ever staged by black students – and a portent of things to come.

Various estimates of SASO's membership at this time were made. In 1973 the estimated number was 6 000, although the number of committed activists among them was smaller. SASO publications, notably its *Newsletter*, and those of other BC organisations were widely read by students and others in black communities, and fostered an intellectual and ideological ferment that had not been known for decades.

BC's influence spread into black schools, which was a critical development. A number of teachers who had been trained on black campuses returned to schools and spread the BC message. This was to be a significant factor in Soweto in 1976. Another scheme was providing intensive training programmes for high school pupils and youth groups, which, in turn, led to the formation of a network of youth organisations throughout the country. An organisation for high school students, the South African Students Movement (SASM), was to play an important role in the events of 1976. Mamphela Ramphele, a medical doctor who was a key SASO activist (and Biko's lover), says of the youth who were involved in these leadership training programmes that they 'spearheaded' the 1976 revolt.[21]

In July 1973 the government's (predictable) heavy-handed response to student protest came: eight SASO leaders, including Biko, and eight Nusas leaders, including its president, were served with crippling banning orders in terms of the Suppression of Communism Act that prohibited them from entering educational institutions or being quoted, as well as the usual restrictions on attending gatherings. Most of the replacements for the banned SASO leaders were soon also banned. It was apparent that, apart from the rising temperature of student protest, the wave of strikes that began in the Durban area early in 1973 had convinced the government that 'subversion' was on the increase, and had to be dealt with severely.

*　　*　　*

In a tribute to Biko, commemorating the twenty-fifth anniversary of his death, Mandela described him as the spark that lit a veldfire across South Africa.[22] This was true enough: BC, in the short time of its existence, had indeed infused young blacks with a new determination not to submit any longer to the humiliations inflicted on their elders. In her (insider's) assessment of BC, Ramphele writes:

> Black Consciousness managed to attain unprecedented success in empowering activists in its ranks at all levels. Most of these individuals attained total psychological liberation and realised the meaning of being active agents in history. The impact of this success also had a multiplier effect on the wider black community. Nothing succeeds like success.[23]

How exactly the mechanism of psychological liberation – or the lighting of a veldfire – worked is an intriguing question. Young people, still unencumbered by family and other responsibilities, were less likely to be intimidated by their powerful adversary, and more optimistic about the possibilities that accompanied, collectively, a heightened sense of self-esteem and personal efficacy. It was a more complex process than having the scales removed from one's eyes, although this undoubtedly occurred. BC was able to tear down old visions of 'reality', acquiesced in by an older generation, and open up new vistas of what was attainable.

Biko insisted that 'we must remove completely from our vocabulary the concept of fear', but not replace it with a devil-may-care recklessness. Resistance, and taking the initiative, required cool heads and carefully considered strategies. Others warned of the disempowering impact of exploiting victim status and its accompaniment, the 'culture of entitlement'.[24] All of this was summed up in the BC slogan 'Black man, you are on your own.'

*   *   *

By the mid-1970s, it was evident that discontent was increasing in Soweto. As the biggest African township in the country, adjacent to the biggest city, Soweto was the hub of African politics. What happened there was liable to have repercussions throughout black townships in South Africa. In a sombre editorial, *The Star* (Johannesburg) warned that Soweto was 'pregnant with menace'.[25] Its population had grown rapidly: in 1976 the official estimate was nearly 650 000, but this was widely considered to be less than half of the actual number. The population was also young, probably over 50 per cent being under the age of 21.

Much of Soweto was a gigantic slum. The official view that urban Africans were 'temporary sojourners' had drastically limited the supply of housing, so that by 1975, according to figures cited by Helen Suzman, over 17 000 families, or approximately 86 000 people, were on waiting lists.[26] In turn, this meant overcrowding, with an average of up to 14 occupants in each house. Only one in three houses had electricity. Poverty was also deepening: a Markinor survey in 1975 showed that the number of people worse off than previously had risen from 18 per cent in 1973 to 41 per cent. A survey by the Johannesburg Chamber of Commerce published in 1976 estimated that the monthly budget for a family of five in Soweto had risen by 75 per cent since 1970. As South Africa's GDP dipped in the mid-1970s, unemployment became serious: a survey conducted in September 1977 showed that Johannesburg Africans – a large proportion of them being of the younger age group – had an unemployment rate of nearly 20 per cent.[27]

In these circumstances it was hardly surprising that crime was a serious community issue: in the year July 1978–June 1979, 877 murders, 1 180 rapes, 7 462 assaults and 3 802 robberies were reported. Fewer than half of these led to prosecutions; in the case of murder the figure was approximately 20 per cent. Non-existent or poor street lighting made victims easy prey for criminals.[28] Soweto, moreover, was grossly underpoliced, having only six police stations and a ratio of one policeman for every 1 000 inhabitants.[29]

In addition life was made even more vexatious by the myriad statutory offences in which people were mired, and insecurity was heightened by the deprivation of South African citizenship and its substitution by citizenship of a bantustan. According to a survey in 1978 over 25 per cent of Sowetans were 'foreigners', mostly citizens of Transkei and Bophuthatswana.[30] Nevertheless, over 95 per cent of respondents to a survey had lived in Soweto for at least 20 years.[31]

Further aggravation of difficult living conditions had begun in 1971 when, as part of a process of centralising state control over African affairs, the central government had removed urban administration from the hands of local authorities and vested it in regional Administration Boards that were answerable only to the Minister of Bantu Administration and Development. Most of their senior officials were political appointees like Manie Mulder, who became chairman of the West Rand Administration Board, under which Soweto fell, despite his having no experience of African administration, let alone knowledge of Johannesburg's African population. The Boards were required to be financially self-supporting, which meant heavy reliance on profits from the sale of liquor and traditional beer (over which they had a monopoly), rents (which were not subsidised), and a levy on employers, accounting for, respectively, 20.75 per cent, 48.06 per cent and 22.59 per cent of the WRAB's entire income for 1976-7.[32] Even this was insufficient, resulting in periodic squeezes on residents to pay higher rentals.

The entire staff of the WRAB, apart from menial posts, was white, most of them supportive of the apartheid government and beneficiaries of its patronage. Sam Moss, a prominent opposition politician in Johannesburg, described the WRAB as an extension of government, riddled with *verkramptes* who would never fight the central government for additional development funding: 'The Board is constituted to carry out policy and those in top posts will never buck the Government because they owe their positions to it.'[33] The Board carried on into 1976, serenely ignorant of the brewing storm. Little more than a month before the uprising began Manie Mulder was quoted as saying:

> The broad masses of Soweto are perfectly content, perfectly happy. Black-white relationships at present are as healthy as can be. There is no danger whatever of a blow-up in Soweto.[34]

It was a monumental misjudgement; but Mulder was not alone in his failure to read the signs.

Effective political channels for Soweto's inhabitants did not exist; nor, inherently, could they, given the premise of official policy that Africans must exercise their political rights in the bantustans. In 1968 an Urban

Bantu Council was established in Soweto, but it was given very few powers and, consequently, cut little ice with the inhabitants whose principal demand was for direct representation on the Johannesburg City Council. Percentage polls in elections declined steadily: 32 per cent in 1968, 21 per cent in 1971, and 14 per cent in 1974, when only 12 000 out of a potential 84 000-strong electorate voted.[35] Its lack of credibility earned it the title 'Useless Boys Club'.

The explosion that occurred on 16 June 1976 might have been averted if the many warning signs had been heeded. That the fuse was an educational issue was no coincidence, although there are grounds for believing that other grievances were so widespread and generated so much community anger that any one among several might sooner or later have caused an outburst.

The NP had long demanded that Afrikaans enjoy equal status with English in African schools once pupils had passed through the earlier standards in which the mother tongue (an indigenous language) was the medium of instruction. The rationale for this policy was that the South African Constitution stipulated equality between English and Afrikaans; subsequently, Nationalists would argue that it was the state's right to determine the language dispensation in African schools in the 'white' areas (i.e. outside the bantustans) since it was the white taxpayers' government that provided the school buildings, gave subsidies and paid the teachers. This reasoning was specious since the Constitution's supposed requirements had never applied to the media of instruction in schools for non-African pupils. Indeed, one of the NP's long-standing aims had been to ensure that the education of Afrikaner pupils, from kindergarten to university, was through the exclusive medium of Afrikaans. Clearly, the envisaged medium dispensation for African schools was based on political and not educational grounds.

The shortage of African teachers able to teach in Afrikaans, however, necessitated the flexible implementation of dual-medium instruction. In practice, most schools opted to use English. Meanwhile, bantustan administrations, once they acquired control of education, nearly all opted for the exclusive use of English from Standard Three onwards. From about August 1974, according to Hartshorne, 'a doctrinaire line' began to replace previous flexibility.[36] It was now laid down by the Department of Bantu Education that in all schools under its control (those in the 'white' areas), English and Afrikaans should be used on an equal basis from Standard Five onwards. Permission to deviate from this instruction had to be given by the Department. From 1975 Social Studies and Mathematics were to be taught in Afrikaans, science and practical subjects in English, and

Religious Education, Music and Physical Education in the vernacular.

The directive flew in the face of what every representative African teacher body demanded. For example, the African Teachers' Association of South Africa recommended that in all subjects, except Afrikaans, the mother tongue, and religious instruction, English should be the medium of instruction from Standard Three onwards up to Senior Certificate, the final year of schooling. English, the Association said, was an international language and the lingua franca of many African peoples (which is precisely why the Department wanted its influence diluted). Moreover, African pupils would be more burdened than they already were if two European languages were used as media for different subjects. The Department, however, refused to budge.[37] Young Africans, also, had made known their feelings about the medium issue: a survey of Soweto African matriculation pupils' parents' attitudes published in 1972 showed that 88.5 per cent of the respondents preferred that their children be educated through the medium of English. The same survey found that 96.5 per cent considered themselves 'proud' to be a black person – which may have been an early indication of the influence of BC.[38]

School boards, representing parents, were peremptorily told by the Department that their belief that they could decide what medium their schools would use was mistaken: 'This is completely [geheel en al] wrong. [The medium issue] is a professional matter and no school board has any say in it.'[39] Kane-Berman estimates that at least 18 Soweto school board members were dismissed from their posts by the Department in what amounted to a purge of those opposed to the new policy.[40] The dismissals obviously contributed to the mounting tension in the first half of 1976.

In theory, schools could apply for exemption from the 50:50 rule, principally on grounds that teachers able to teach in Afrikaans were not available, or that textbooks in a particular language were unavailable. In practice hardly any exemptions were granted. Even the judicial commission of inquiry headed by the conservative Judge PM Cillié that investigated the uprising was scathingly critical of the bureaucratic ineptitude surrounding the question of exemptions, the conditions for which were never satisfactorily explained to school boards or parents. Nor were the reasons for refusals provided, which heightened suspicions.[41]

A serious complicating factor was the rapid rise in pupil numbers, which was a critically important factor in heightening pupil frustration. Country-wide, the number of Africans attending secondary schools increased from 178 959 in 1974 to 252 515 in 1975, and to 389 046 in 1976, according to figures cited in the Cillié Report. The Bantu Education Department, beginning to retreat from its earlier policy of not expanding secondary education facilities for Africans in the 'white' areas, had increased the number of high schools in Soweto from 19 in 1972 to 38 in 1975, but, according to WRAB, there remained a backlog of approximately 800 classrooms for all standards, equivalent to some 30 schools.[42]

To complicate matters further, in 1975 African schools were brought into line with schools for other groups by reducing the 13-year structure to 12 years, with secondary classes now beginning in Standard Five. The disappearance of the old Standard Six, and the examinations that pupils had to pass before being admitted to the next standard meant that the great majority could proceed to what was now called Form 1. In 1976, no fewer than 257 505 enrolled in Form 1, whose facilities in Soweto could accommodate only 38 000.[43] Form 1 classes had physically to remain in primary school buildings, mostly having to be taught by primary school teachers. In Soweto this meant that the number of schools which had to enforce the new language policy, even if only in one class, jumped from 39 to 160,[44] thereby expanding the range of angry pupils.

Educational inequality was pervasive; apart from palpably poorer facilities in comparison with those enjoyed by white schools (and to a lesser extent by Coloured and Indian schools), the teacher:pupil ratio (countrywide) in 1975 was 1:20 in white schools, compared with 1:54 in African schools; and per capita expenditure from public funds was R605 for white pupils and R39.53 for Africans.[45] The disparity in teacher qualifications was equally marked: only a little over 10 per cent of African teachers possessed professional teaching qualifications with a university degree or a matriculation certificate.[46] Hartshorne wrote:

> Pupils found themselves in large classes, often in temporary accommodation at a distance from the main school building, under teachers who were dealing with secondary school work for the first time, and at the same time trying to cope with a strict application of the dual medium rule. Conditions were ripe for revolt, and the language issue added to the numbers explosion was to prove a powerful mix.[47]

It was hardly surprising that what began as a protest against the use of Afrikaans broadened to encompass the entire system of Bantu education and then to the whole apartheid policy.

Simmering tensions began to reach boiling point in the early months of 1976. By May, pupils at various schools had gone on strike; on several occasions police investigating incidents were stoned and on one occasion an African Afrikaans teacher was stabbed with a screwdriver. A number of headmasters, school board members and teachers who were sympathetic to the protest were dismissed, while those prepared to implement the new dispensation were given a rough time by their pupils.

The Department acted with a stony indifference. The police, apart from trying to investigate cases of violence, said that they were powerless to act against striking schoolchildren because school education for Africans was not compulsory and therefore staying away from school involved no offence.

On 25 May the SA Institute of Race Relations sent a telegram to René de Villiers, an MP who was also an executive committee member of the Institute, asking him to discuss the serious crisis developing in Soweto with the deputy minister responsible for Bantu Education, Dr Andries Treurnicht. Treurnicht, incredibly, responded that he was not aware of any real problem, but that he would make enquiries. Shortly thereafter he sent a note to De Villiers, saying, in effect, that the situation was under control.

The appointment of Treurnicht – a hardline *verkrampte*, due to become leader of the breakaway Conservative Party in 1982 – to so sensitive a post was a monumental blunder by Vorster. A subsequent telegram sent by the Institute on 11 June expressed alarm at the deteriorating situation and received, via De Villiers, the bland reply from Treurnicht that he 'had reason to believe that the matter [the language issue] would be amicably settled'.

Equally dire warnings, of course, had been voiced by various organisations in Soweto itself. The UBC, despite its lack of credibility, had tried to negotiate a settlement with the authorities but, like attempts by other bodies, it had been brushed aside. However, one of its members, Leonard Mosala, had presciently warned on 14 June that the Afrikaans issue 'could result in another Sharpeville'.[48]

No less amazing than what the Cillié Report described as the 'inflexible implementation of the policy and the underestimation of the resistance' on the part of the education authorities, was the extent to which the police remained ignorant of the protest planned for 16 June. According to the Report

> ... clear signs of developing unrest in the last few weeks before the sixteenth [of June] were ignored. There had been gatherings where threatened danger was discussed and knowledgeable persons expressed genuine fear; there were episodes of violent opposition that bore testimony to the build-up of tension; there were public warnings from speakers and writers of coming insurrection. Because the police did not realise the importance of these portents, there was

apparently no further or sufficient investigation. They were unaware not only of the insurrection that would occur but also when it would happen; and consequently on the day they were unprepared in terms of manpower, equipment and state of mind [*gemoedsgesteldheid*]. It is difficult to understand how a group of young people could prepare for three days for a demonstration of 15 000 or more pupils from all over Soweto, and that the police could only receive incomplete reports about this on the day before the demonstration was to happen .... The Commission is of the opinion that the police themselves were in large measure responsible for their lack of knowledge of what was planned and therefore for their own lack of preparedness.[49]

How spontaneous was the uprising – and, indeed, was it actually planned as an uprising? The BC message had certainly spread in Soweto. Apart from BC stalwarts like Tiro, Aubrey Mokoena and others who had been teaching in schools with sympathetic headmasters, the 'junior' branch of SASO, the South African Students' Movement (SASM), had been active among pupils, with the encouragement of SASO. The regional president of SASM was a 19-year-old pupil, Tsietsi Mashinini, who had been taught by Tiro and had become steeped in BC ideas.

Mashinini was a young man of high intelligence and forceful personality. He and his siblings had been born to hardworking Soweto parents who encouraged them in their schoolwork. At high school Tsietsi was soon drawn to BC and to the clubs organised by SASM. BC's emphasis on black pride and self-reliance 'fitted well with Tsietsi's loathing of whites'.[50] His leadership qualities made it virtually inevitable that he would become the principal figure in the demonstration against the new medium of instruction and thereafter, the police's most wanted activist.

Organisation was hasty: plans were publicised by word-of-mouth, incredibly, right under the noses of the security police, who were reputed to have many informers in Soweto. At a critical meeting called by SASM leaders on 13 June, attended by some 400 pupils, Mashinini called for a mass demonstration on 16 June in a fiery speech that swayed the many doubters who feared the consequences of the inevitable harsh reaction by the police. The protest march was to be non-violent, he insisted, which would ensure that the dire consequences feared by the doubters would not happen. The proposal to march was accepted unanimously, and an action committee consisting of two delegates from each school was formed. Over the next two days the delegates visited high and junior secondary schools to inform pupils of the proposed march:

> Draw up placards in secret ... . Don't tell your parents. During the
> march, remain disciplined. Follow the instructions of your school
> leaders. Above all, do not be afraid.[51]

Marchers were to be instructed to avoid violence, to remain disciplined
and not to provoke the police.

Recruiting pupils to join the march continued up to the very morning
of 16 June. In a collection of personal experiences, a high school pupil
recounts how the mobilisers approached his class:

> What I can tell you for sure was that there was no negotiations, be-
> cause if there was any negotiations we would have expected to be
> formally addressed [and told] that is what is happening, and this is
> the reason you must join the other guys ... . These guys just came in
> and went: 'Out, out, out, out, out', and 'Amandla!' [Strength] ... .
> Honestly I didn't understand why [we] should be forced to march.
> And I didn't even understand where we were going. I didn't grasp the
> objective of the march.

A pupil at another high school recounted that similarly robust methods
were employed during an examination. An activist shouted: 'If you don't
join us, you are against us.'[52] The class duly joined. That there was initial ambivalence about the march is undoubted; but what happened on
the fateful morning and during the subsequent police action contributed
massively to the dramatic politicisation of a generation, complementing
the veldfire lit by BC.

The plan was for marchers from the various schools to converge in
a massed column and then to proceed to Orlando Stadium for a protest meeting. Estimates of the size of the column vary from 10 000 to
15 000; equally varied are assessments of the collective attitude of the
marchers: some accounts speak of a peaceable, good-humoured mood;
the Cillié Report acknowledges that many 'walked and sang or chatted
and did not make themselves guilty of disorderly behaviour'; but it also
cites several instances of vehicles being stoned, in one case a government
official narrowly escaping serious injury. It is clear from the evidence
cited by the Commission and other sources that the protesters were excited and that if provoked, many might have abandoned their peaceable
intentions. The Commission appeared to accept the evidence given by
a reporter from *The World* (a newspaper with an African readership)
who cited a student telling the marchers that the organisers were aware
that police vehicles were following the march 'but that it was a peaceful

demonstration and that the police must not be provoked'.[53]

In the event, it mattered little what all or most of the demonstrators intended: a tragic confrontation occurred and set in motion a chain of events that changed the course of South Africa's history. The fatal confrontation took place in Vilakazi Street near Orlando West High School. A small detachment of police, 48-strong, under the command of Colonel Johannes Kleingeld, encountered the first wave of protesters, numbering initially at least 6 000 but increasing as further marchers arrived. As the Cillié Report notes, virtually every incident and aspect of what happened was (and is) controversial: who was responsible for the first resort to violence?

Judge Cillié had not been noted as a critic of police behaviour in trials where he had been the presiding judge. Indeed, a former colleague at the Johannesburg Bar observed that he had never been known to disbelieve the word of a senior police officer;[54] and the official who led evidence before the Commission was no less than Percy Yutar, who had appeared for the state in the Treason and Rivonia trials. Despite this background and some strictures on the police for their failure to obtain information about the planned march, the Cillié Report was implicitly critical of police bungling on the morning of 16 June. First, the Report noted that Kleingeld had been unable to give an 'audible and effective' order to the crowd to disperse, as the law concerning illegal gatherings required, since no one had thought to bring a loud-hailer. Secondly, tear-gas canisters proved ineffective because only one of possibly ten canisters actually exploded, presumably because of defects in their manufacture or their age. According to the Report, the crowd did not disperse 'probably' because they and their 'opstokers' (inciters) were now convinced that the police were not well armed and could be driven from the scene.[55]

The Report was, however, a whitewash of police behaviour in Soweto and elsewhere in the country where clashes occurred. HW van der Merwe, a scrupulously honest Quaker academic, who was Director of the Centre for Intergroup Studies at the University of Cape Town, wrote of his experiences as a witness before the Commission, that the Judge was 'openly dismissive' of his submission, before he had even read it!

> All of us who supported the Centre's dossier became aware of the Commission's reluctance to accept viewpoints which did not fit its preconceived ideas. Cillié and the state attorney, Percy Yutar, continually challenged the Centre's evidence while that of the police went unchallenged.[56]

Of the confrontations on 16 June the Report says:

> The Commission cannot fail to mention that the small group of po-
> lice officers did their best to preserve the peace and to restore it. In
> spite of their shortage of personnel, equipment and preparation they
> were not panic-stricken.

To some extent this finding is contradicted by another finding that while
Colonel Kleingeld had fired warning shots above the demonstrators, 'several members of the unit fired in desperation, without any order having
been given'.[57] The truth remains elusive.

To what extent the lives of the 48 policemen (40 of whom, incidentally,
were black) were endangered is unclear. Parleying with the leaders of the
march, who had repeatedly warned against provocation of the police and
insisted that there be no violence, might have defused a potentially dangerous situation – as had happened in Cape Town in March 1960. But it
was not to be, and the entire character of the situation changed when the
first shots were fired. A young African pupil, who was an eye-witness,
recollects:

> This gunshot suddenly [sic], and we were down. I was 600 metres from
> there ... I don't know what happened, and we just picked up stones.
> And I've never seen so many stones coming. It was a huge crowd –
> those police could not stand there, they would have been killed ....
> There was a lot of shooting that happened at that time after the first
> shot was fired, because [the police] were stoned, they could not have
> [lasted] for longer because they could have been killed.[58]

At the end of the day 15 people had been killed, including two schoolchildren shot in the initial confrontation. Soweto residents insist that many of
the dead had been shot in the back, suggesting that, as at Sharpeville, they
had been fleeing. Pictures of the dying 13 year-old Hector Pieterson being
carried away from the scene were soon flashed around the world. (Among
the later fatalities was Melville Edelstein, a humane social worker for
WRAB, whose survey was cited above.) The journalist Harry Mashabela's
account describes what happened in vivid language:

> Bang, a shot rang out; then another and yet another. In rapid suc-
> cession. The throng broke up with pupils fleeing in all directions: to
> the rugged ridge behind the two schools, into alleyways, side streets
> and into homes. Some collapsed in their tracks as they fled, some ran
> on. Some, apparently petrified, remained in the middle of the street.
> The police paid no attention to them .... It seemed everybody was

terribly shaken, but much more so the pupils themselves. They were baffled, sullen, grim. They had not, it seemed, expected it.[59]

Mashabela's account is corroborated by Murphy Morobe, a student leader (and subsequently a prominent ANC politician):

> We were inadequately prepared to deal with the situation once those shots were fired. The only thing on our minds was to disperse everyone as soon as possible. We went back to the area to try to do that, but it was difficult. The first question people asked us was, 'If you say we must go away, where must we go to? If these policemen come into Soweto, where must we go because this is where we stay'. We were entirely out of our depth in terms of what to do.[60]

No attempt will be made here to trace the course of events that ravaged the country for the remainder of 1976 and continued into 1977. According to the Cillié Report, 575 people were killed in the period covered by its investigation, namely 16 June 1976 to 28 February 1977. Another 111 were killed in 1977.[61] Many township residents believed that the figure of 575 was a deliberate undercount, but no authoritative higher figure could be produced. In addition to the fatalities, extensive damage was inflicted on property, especially buildings belonging to the authorities and thus symbolising white control. In Soweto, for instance, many WRAB buildings, including beerhalls, were damaged or destroyed. There was also a widespread anti-white feeling. Albertina Sisulu, wife of the imprisoned ANC leader Walter Sisulu, was particularly distressed by the killing of Melville Edelstein, whom she liked and admired: 'Children were impossible in those days. You could not say anything to defend a white person.'[62]

Sympathy demonstrations, school boycotts and other protests were widespread over the country in the aftermath of the Soweto clash. Apart from Cape Town, where serious confrontations occurred, there was also violence in the townships around Pretoria, Port Elizabeth and East London. Townships on the East Rand and West Rand, as well as Alexandra (which is part of greater Johannesburg), saw extensive violence. Clashes, sometimes resulting in fatalities, occurred in nearly 60 other towns and villages in all four provinces and in several bantustans, although few occurred in Natal, where, according to Kane-Berman, the townships around Durban remained relatively peaceful because of greater police restraint.[63] Buthelezi's hostile view of school protests no doubt also exerted a restraining influence.

The anger in many black communities was greatly increased by the murder of Steve Biko by security policemen on 12 September 1977 and the banning a month later of 18 organisations, mostly with BC orientations. By September 1977, 2 430 persons had been tried and convicted; and by 30 November at least 65 BC leaders and organisers were still in detention.[64] Clearly, the state was unrepentant, hoping perhaps that it could re-establish the quiescence of the post-Sharpeville period.

But the mood among blacks had changed – permanently – and that was why the country was never the same again. Njabulo Nkonyane, 14 years old in 1976, recalled the impact many years later:

> Like any 14-year-old, we were naïve but the situation forced us to mature much faster than we would have, facing bullets every day of your life, teargas just about all the time. I remember we used to joke that if we have not smelled or seen teargas for a week, something was wrong – breathing clean air for two days. Things like that made one mature very quickly. We started reading books, we got politicised almost overnight …. We decided then we would never go back to school, we would boycott Bantu Education henceforth … .[65]

Bantu Education had turned full circle: it had been imposed to align African education with apartheid's political aims; now, the youngsters of Soweto and elsewhere had grabbed the initiative by politicising education for their own ends, namely, ensuring that henceforth schools would be 'sites of struggle'. It meant the serious dislocation or even collapse of secondary education for Africans over wide areas of the country, as boycotts, resistance to school discipline and the breakdown of what was called the 'culture of learning' entrenched themselves as elements of new forms of opposition.

The change of mood had several dimensions. In an interview with a British television network Mashinini said:

> What the people, especially the White people, should realise is that the student today is not saying that people must be free, but that the people will be free. I believe the time is near when people will be free.[66]

His anti-white views were clearly expressed:

> The system has done so many things and so much harm to my people that the people are no longer interested in having equal rights with the white people of South Africa. They want the tables to be turned

so the white man can get a taste of his own medicine and feel what it is like to be oppressed.[67]

Another dimension was the changed relationship between pupils and their elders, which was all the more striking since one of African society's main characteristics had traditionally been deference to the older generation. Indeed, what occurred was an important benchmark of the extent to which traditional values had been shattered. Nimrod Mkele, a prominent African psychologist, lamented that adults had very little to do with what was going on:

> The kids say we are irrelevant, that we have been talking to the authorities since 1912 but with no result …. You'd be amazed to hear 12-year-olds saying: 'Daddy, on Monday, Tuesday and Wednesday, you are staying away from work. Just to ensure that you do, will you please see to it that your car stays in the yard' …. No teacher or principal dares order the students around any more.[68]

The Cillié Report drew attention to the inability of parents to discipline their children, citing evidence that in many cases both parents worked and could not exercise control over their children during daytime; and, because schooling was not compulsory, they did not know whether their children were actually attending school. The Report quoted an investigation which showed that 95 per cent of the children detained during the unrest did not have fathers at home or came from family homes where the father and mother were estranged from each other. Often, the Report noted, parents were far less educated than their children, making them apprehensive about confrontation with them. The Commission appeared to accept evidence that the father of a household was commonly treated in humiliating ways by police, officials and whites in the presence of his children, which also diminished his authority.[69]

To some extent the generational gap was bridged by action taken by parents on behalf of the children. The most notable example was the formation a few days after 16 June of the Black Parents' Association, an umbrella organisation that sought to act as a conduit between the pupils and the authorities. Its chairman was Manas Buthelezi, a Lutheran clergyman; other prominent members were Ntatho Motlana, a medical practitioner in Soweto, and Winnie Mandela, wife of the jailed ANC leader. Motlana described the BPA's aims in the following terms:

> As parents we could not allow a situation in which our children were

dying. I mean, they died by their thousands; we believe the figures given by the government were way off the mark. And, therefore, we could not allow that kind of thing to happen .... We had to be seen to be involved with our children in the ongoing struggle. And we decided ... to form a committee which could talk to the children, talk to the authorities, form a bridge between the warring factions, which were the police, the state and the children.[70]

Subsequently other branches of the BPA were formed in Pretoria and on the Witwatersrand, as well as in the Cape and Natal. Victims and their families were given financial assistance, including the cost of funerals. The government, deeply suspicious of the BPA, gave it short shrift. When some student leaders sought the BPA's assistance in an attempt to negotiate with the authorities, the Minister of Justice and Police replied that if the BPA could prove its legitimacy by stopping the rioting he would accept a memorandum from them and thereafter consider a meeting. The Minister, Jimmy Kruger, was probably the most callous and inflexible of all apartheid-era ministers, in what was a very competitive field. Predictably, the BPA's initiative got nowhere, and in due course several of its members were detained. It was banned in October 1977.

* * *

The initial aim of the protest, the lifting of the Afrikaans-medium requirement, widened as the conflict intensified to encompass demands for the abolition of the entire Bantu Education system, as well as apartheid. Even the Cillié Report could find no evidence that pupils had any intention of eventually overthrowing the government by violent means; nor, despite its suspicions, could it find conclusive evidence of ANC involvement in the planning and execution of violence, even if the ANC supported the pupils' activities as a step that would assist it in furthering the revolutionary struggle.[71]

ANC involvement, such as it was, was confined to individuals, notably Winnie Mandela, whose role both during the pre-16 June period and in the aftermath is reckoned to have been substantial. As the conflict progressed other ANC-aligned individuals were consulted. It is also probable that ANC operatives were involved in making arrangements for the reception of the (at least) 4 000 youngsters who fled the country, many of whom were absorbed into ANC camps elsewhere in Africa.

The ANC appears to have been caught unawares by the uprising. Many of the exiles, particularly SACP members, were sceptical of BC, but there was more to it than ideological differences: the ANC feared that the BC Movement might eclipse the ANC as a political organisation or become a parallel movement enjoying the same legitimacy as the ANC.[72]

On Robben Island Mandela and his colleagues were heartened by the uprising which signified a renaissance of resistance and mass protest that had been extinguished in the 1960s. Young activists who had been convicted for participation in the uprising now joined their elders on the Island. Mandela was startled by their brashness and aggressiveness, but declined to confront them in debate. Instead, he wisely sought to engage them in discussion, recalling his own younger days as an 'Africanist', when he, too, strongly asserted ethnic pride and racial self-confidence, as well as rejecting co-operation with non-Africans:

> But just as we had outgrown our [Africanist] outlook, I was confident that these young men would transcend some of the strictures of Black Consciousness. While I was encouraged by their militancy, I thought that their philosophy, in its concentration on blackness, was sectarian, and represented an intermediate view that was not fully mature. I saw my role as an elder statesman who might help them on to the more inclusive ideas of the Congress Movement. I knew also that these young men would eventually become frustrated because Black Consciousness offered no programme of action, no outlet for their protest.[73]

The ability of the ANC to co-opt and absorb the majority of BC supporters inside and outside the country was of decisive importance; conversely, the PAC's seemingly inherent factionalism denied it the opportunity of recruiting large numbers of activist new members. As Mandela had implied, BC was closer to the PAC's Africanist philosophy than to the ANC's, although SASO's Policy Manifesto, adopted in 1971, resembled the Freedom Charter in at least one notable respect by declaring that 'South Africa is a country in which both black and white live and shall continue to live together.'[74]

Recalling the Soweto Uprising in a report to the ANC's Consultative Conference in Zambia in 1985, Oliver Tambo acknowledged that it had been a 'historic watershed':

> Within a short period of time, it propelled into the forefront of our struggle millions of young people, thus immeasurably expanding the active forces of the revolution and inspiring other sections of our people into activity … . [This] resulted in the accelerated expansion

of our movement both inside and outside the country. That process
… resulted in increasing the relative proportion of youth and students within our ranks. It brought into our ranks comrades many of
whom had had very little contact with the ANC, if any. It put at the
immediate disposal of our movement militant cadres who were ready
and yearning to carry out even the most difficult missions ….[75]

Tambo acknowledged that in the bleak years of 1976–7 the ANC was still
in too weak a position to take advantage of the new situation created by
the uprising: there were very few active ANC units in the country (50 formal units, comprising some 200 people[76]); there was no military presence
to speak of; and communication links between the ANC in exile and the
masses inside the country were 'too slow and weak'.[77]

In the same report Tambo claimed that by 1976 Biko and his colleagues
had decided that the ANC was the leader of the revolutionary movement.
Attempts in 1976 and 1977 to arrange meetings between representatives
of the BC Movement and the ANC failed. Tambo's claim is not corroborated, at least in such unambiguous terms, by any of the writings by or
about Biko, but it is unlikely that he would have misled his audience on so
critical an issue. Biko's own comments, however, suggest a consistent refusal to side with one or other of the liberation organisations: both were
important. He hoped for unification:

> I personally would like to see fewer groups. I would like to see groups
> like ANC, PAC and the Black Consciousness Movement deciding to
> form one liberation group. It is only, I think, when black people are
> so dedicated and so united in their cause that we can effect the great-
> est results.[78]

Many of the youngsters involved in the Soweto Uprising had little or no
knowledge of the liberation movements' histories. If anything the BC
Movement had overshadowed both the ANC and the PAC, and some
of the young Soweto activists had tended to be dismissive of both. On
Robben Island Mandela and his ANC colleagues recognised the potential
of these fiery young BC men, but decided not to recruit them, sensing that
this would alienate both them and the other parties:

> Our policy was to be friendly, to take an interest, to compliment
> them on their achievements, but not to proselytize … . I wanted these
> young men to see that the ANC was a great tent that could accom-
> modate many different views.

A key figure in the shift of allegiance to the ANC by BC men on the Island was an intelligent and personable man called Patrick 'Terror' Lekota, 'Terror' being a nickname acquired from his skills at soccer, and not from any violent propensities. Lekota, who had been a full-time SASO organiser, spent six years in prison, from 1976 to 1982, for the 'crime' of organising public rallies to celebrate the independence of Mozambique. Mandela was aware that Lekota did not share the general BC view on racial exclusiveness and that he was edging towards the ANC. Mandela discouraged his joining the ANC group, but Lekota declined to heed his advice and publicly announced his change of allegiance. For this he was assaulted by some erstwhile BC colleagues. ANC people, in the interests of avoiding further tension, advised him not to lodge a complaint, to which he agreed. Mandela writes:

> After that incident, the floodgates seemed to open and dozens of BCM men decided to join the ANC, including some of those who had planned the attack on Terror. Terror rose to the top of the ANC hierarchy in the general section [of the prison], and was soon teaching ANC policies to other prisoners.[79]

Lekota displayed his commitment to the ANC in a series of letters to his daughter, Tjhabi, written from prison, declaring that by virtue of its history the ANC was 'our natural political home'.[80] After his release he threw himself into participation in the United Democratic Front (UDF), facing further charges in the Delmas Treason Trial. The UDF would become a major mass movement in the 1980s.

✼ ✼ ✼

Tambo's analysis of the limitations of the Soweto Uprising was substantially correct in pointing out that it could not be sustained because it lacked organisation and overall political direction to channel the pupils' anger. Despite three relatively successful work stoppages in Johannesburg and Cape Town in August and September 1976 (and an unsuccessful one in November), the gulf between students and workers had not been bridged, even though many workers were also parents.[81] The strikes were demonstrations of sympathy and solidarity, rather than independent displays of worker muscle. Moreover, it was risky for workers to participate in stayaways, particularly in tough economic times when such participation led to loss of wages and, possibly, dismissal.

Student calls for stayaways aggravated the division between town-dwellers and migrants, many of whom lived in hostels and saw their spells in town as temporary, their aim being to earn money and return to their rural homes. Most of the migrants were poorly educated and, their families being in the homelands, little involved with the crisis in the schools; moreover, dismissal could mean forced repatriation to a homeland. For the most part, relations between townspeople and migrants had been peaceful until 1976, although tensions arose when migrants were accused of being a 'menace' to the women of the settled urban communities. The migrants also resented being regarded as simple, uncouth yokels by townspeople, viewing with distaste the townspeople's urban lifestyles and the crime that was so widespread. Especially regrettable, in their view, was the uppitiness of the young, and their disrespect for their elders. There were also suggestions by townspeople that migrants were competitors for jobs in an increasingly tough labour market. This was especially so in the African townships in Cape Town, where, because the region was deemed a Coloured Labour Preference area, influx control was applied with especial ferocity, and rights to be in the urban area were precarious.

The latent fissure between townspeople and migrants offered the authorities an opportunity to drive a wedge between the two groups. Evidence of police efforts to orchestrate a migrant backlash against the students' efforts to organise stayaways was considerable, although denied by the police and, predictably, dismissed by the Cillié Commission. It was in the Cape Town townships, notably Nyanga, that the conflict spilled over into large-scale bloodletting. The migrants refused to participate in a stayaway called for 6 and 7 December 1976, and rejected the student demand that Christmas was not to be celebrated with the customary festivity, meaning principally that shebeens (illicit pubs or 'speakeasies') and liquor be boycotted.

Unlike Soweto, where, after consultations with the hostel dwellers, many were persuaded to join the stayaway of 13–15 September, the conflict in Cape Town seemed unbridgeable. The Cillié Report, despite its disingenuous whitewashing of police tactics, was at least correct in describing the violence in Nyanga over the Christmas period as worse than anywhere else:

> It was indeed a total war because man, woman and child participated and attacked, defended or took revenge with everything at their disposal. Nobody, and nothing, was overlooked; compatriots of both sexes and all ages were injured or killed, and houses and other property were destroyed by fire.[82]

Thirty-six people were killed over the Christmas weekend, 17 on 26 December alone. Clergy in the area drew up a memorandum detailing the activities of the police and alleging their connivance with the migrants' attacks on townspeople. The evidence was dismissed by the Cillié Commission. The memorandum and a follow-up document that contained eye-witness accounts of events in Nyanga and the role of the police were banned. HW van der Merwe's submission to the Commission is worth quoting:

> Our evidence suggested reasons for the inflammatory effect of the riot squad on events. In the first place, their behaviour did not match the golden rule of keeping order with a minimum of force. They did not wear protective helmets and, often, they raced into crowds of bystanders in undisciplined pursuit of individuals whom they had targeted. Judging by their language, many recruits came from environments where racist views prevailed. As they were without identification numbers, it was virtually impossible for victims of police brutality to identify the culprits.[83]

Hostilities between townspeople and migrants gradually petered out, but underlying tensions remained. Many of the hostel-dwellers on the Witwatersrand were Zulu, which suggested an ethnic dimension to the conflict – although in Cape Town virtually all of the combatants were Xhosa-speakers. Negative stereotypes of alleged Zulu propensities have a long history among Africans, dating back to well before the apartheid era. Frieda Matthews (wife of ZK Matthews), for example, says of Natal in 1924 that all she knew about it was that 'it was inhabited by Zulus, whom we had all been taught were cruel and treacherous'.[84]

Anthropological evidence in the 1960s and 1970s suggested that the salience of ethnicity among Soweto Africans was declining, and that inter-ethnic marriage or cohabitation was common; but it was also found that 'a sharp dichotomy' between migrants and townspeople had replaced the former gradual transition between them.[85] The predominance of Zulu among the migrants and the growing rejection of homeland leaders by townspeople found a combined focus in the 1980s, when conflict between migrants and townspeople recurred, in the hostility to Chief Mangosuthu Buthelezi and the Inkatha movement that he had established in 1975.

One consequence of the Soweto Uprising was the dramatic hardening of popular opposition to homelands and bodies such as the UBC, which was effectively drummed out of business by student pressure; thereafter it was suspended by WRAB. Efforts by homeland leaders, notably Buthelezi, to mediate between protestors and the authorities were in vain.

Symbolic of the new intensity of opposition was the burning down of
the Bophuthatswana Legislative Assembly by students on 9 August 1976.
The popular view was that all of these government-created bodies were
snares designed to make Africans responsible for their own oppression.
In the case of the UBC, resentment focused on the allegation that it had
collaborated with WRAB in proposing rent increases.

Another consequence of the uprising was a rapid growth among young
militants of the view that 'armed struggle' was not only necessary but inevitable if apartheid were to be destroyed. Theodor Hanf and his associates
found that more than 25 per cent of their African respondents believed that
no change was possible without violence. This group, most strongly represented in Soweto, comprised students, more urbanised, better-educated and
in the upper-income strata. Nevertheless, the survey also found that a clear
majority still believed in the possibility of peaceful change:

> ... even among the urban black population, in political terms the
> best informed and most involved section of black South Africa,
> there is a clear majority in favour of non-violent change. However,
> the black political leadership groups fear that this situation could
> quickly change, and their fears are confirmed by the empirical data:
> disillusionment increases with the degree of urbanization, and hopes
> of peaceful change decrease. The readiness for conflict is growing,
> especially among urban black youth.[86]

The most important consequence of the uprising was that it breathed
new life into the ANC, which, while not moribund, was certainly dispir-
ited. Many of the youngsters who fled across the border were angry and
brutalised. Ronnie Kasrils, a senior operative in MK, writes that

> ... recruitment into the ranks of MK, which had been at a trickle
> in the previous years, began speeding up and was soon a torrent.
> Youngsters were leaving South Africa in droves, heading for the
> neighbouring states in search of the ANC, with the single wish: 'To
> learn how to shoot, to get a gun and get back home to *moer* [finish]
> the Boers.'[87]

By the end of 1978 MK had gained an estimated 3 000 new recruits.
Guerrilla attacks had begun again and the ANC claimed to have established underground organisation in nearly all parts of the country.[88] A
new phase of armed struggle had begun.

*   *   *

Amid the tumult an important victory was won by the Soweto students: on 6 July 1976 MC Botha, the Minister of Bantu Administration and Development, announced the withdrawal of the dual-medium requirement, saying that henceforth school principals would be able to choose the medium of instruction, provided that extra tuition in the language not chosen would be offered. For the government to back down under pressure was a rare phenomenon. Pupil power had made its mark.

In a shrewd comment on the uprising the writer and academic Njabulo Ndebele noted the new relations of power that had emerged:

> Clearly, the structural position of the oppressed now was such that they could no longer be cowed into a submission reminiscent of the fifties. The inevitable growth and consolidation of this new power would definitely lead to new general perceptions of what was possible. While previously the range of what was possible had been severely limited by the condition of powerlessness, now the newly found power could extend that range considerably in all kinds of directions. Suddenly, the possibilities became immense.[89]

Morale and hope are important components of any political struggle, and they were widely diffused in the aftermath of the uprising. Young blacks were now hopeful that liberation would happen in their lifetimes. Moreover, a powerful ally in the form of the independent black trade union movement had been growing steadily in the 1970s, and it would become an even more powerful force for change in the 1980s. The uprising was not the end of apartheid; but unmistakably it was the beginning of the end.

CHAPTER 6

Fissures and Fractures in Afrikaner Nationalism

In terms of cohesiveness Afrikaner nationalism reached its zenith in the 1960s under Verwoerd's premiership: all of its component spheres were locked into a bureaucracy, headed by the NP, that co-ordinated and controlled their activities. With the growing diversification of Afrikaner interests and the steady embourgeoisement of Afrikaners, cohesion became more difficult to maintain. It is a theme of this book that a weakening of the resolve to maintain apartheid was a significant factor in opening the way for the negotiated transition. The ties that bound Afrikaner nationalism together began to loosen. It had never been a monolithic movement; in the 1970s and 1980s especially, significant segments signalled their concern about the morality of persisting with a palpably failing policy – and, moreover, the danger it posed for the country.

Contrary to the widely assumed belief that a common sense of threat promotes solidarity, or even a laager mentality, the internal divisions among white South Africans, especially Afrikaners, grew sharper as the pressures on apartheid mounted. Among blacks the trend was in the opposition direction, with one significant exception. The mass movement of the 1980s, which was crucial to the ending of apartheid, broadly acknowledged that the ANC was the leading force in the liberation struggle, and accepted the Freedom Charter's provisions as aims with which it identified. The exception was Inkatha, whose leader, Mangosuthu Buthelezi, fell out with the ANC in the late 1970s, thereby rupturing the earlier tacit alliance.

The demise of Verwoerd in 1966 and Vorster's less vindictive attitude to Afrikaner critics, together with the increasingly visible failure of apartheid, created space for more vigorous debate about policy. The changed circumstances of the Afrikaner community also promoted this process:

by 1980 Afrikaners were highly urbanised, better educated than previous generations, more widely travelled, and more sceptical of the pronouncements of political and clerical leaders. *Volksfeeste* (*volk* festivals commemorating episodes in history) generated decreasing enthusiasm. Popular fervour for nationalist causes could no longer be whipped up as it had been in 1948 or with the coming of the Republic in 1961 and the celebration of its fifth anniversary in 1966. Hard-nosed technocrats were coming to the fore, who measured success less by devotion to old pieties and more by rational and universal criteria. Demographers in particular drew attention to the rapidly growing population imbalance: between 1970 and 1980, the African population grew at 3 per cent per annum, nearly double the rate for whites. Few of the individuals or institutions caught up in those processes, however, contemplated the abandonment of white control or the abolition of residential or educational segregation, despite the limited admission of blacks to English-medium private schools. Much the same was true of most English-speakers.

The Afrikaans press illustrates these developments. The earlier generations of pro-NP editors were mostly party men before they were journalists. DF Malan was a staunchly Nationalist clergyman and politician when he became editor of *Die Burger* in 1915. HF Verwoerd was a university professor before becoming editor of *Die Transvaler* in 1937. Neither was a success as an editor. Although there were other examples of non-journalists assuming editorial positions in more recent times (Treurnicht's becoming editor of *Hoofstad* in 1968 is a case in point), the trend was increasingly for journalistic skills to be the criterion for advancement. Most of the senior journalists were university graduates. This did not mean, however, that non-Nationalists were likely to become editors of newspapers owned by the big Afrikaans publishing houses. Commitment to the Nationalist cause did not necessarily entail poor journalistic quality: *Die Burger*, for example, provided excellent news coverage throughout the apartheid era.

Although never mere party organs, the Afrikaans press arose as institutions of the wider Afrikaner nationalist movement, which in practice imposed some limits on their freedom to criticise the NP. Cabinet ministers, moreover, sat on the boards of two big publishing houses, Nasionale Pers and Perskor, until 1978, which was a further deterrent to overly robust criticism. The close relationship between party and press, described by Schalk Pienaar as *onafhanklikheid-in-gebondenheid* (independence-in-commitment)[1], did not preclude occasional skirmishes or expressions of disapproval from politicians. Willem de Klerk, editor of *Die Transvaler*, for example, tells how in November 1976 he was rebuked by Vorster for publishing a cartoon depicting Treurnicht sitting back-to-front on a horse, pulling its tail, suggesting Treurnicht's resistance to change; and Pienaar clashed regularly with politicians.

More than anything else it was the *verligte/verkrampte* conflict that gave the Afrikaans press its head, enabling it to prise out greater autonomy. Not only did more *verligte* editors like Pienaar and De Klerk loathe the views of the *verkramptes*, but the Afrikaans reading public was riveted by the regular exposés of their intrigues, which were also good for circulation figures. Flushing out *verkramptes* and exposing their reactionary attitudes gave *verligte* editors the opportunity to promote their own views – but only within limits. Press and party were mutually dependent. As Pienaar put it:

> Neither of the two sides can afford a split. The newspaper must always keep a foot in the door of the establishment, otherwise it becomes powerless, as every person outside the establishment is powerless, except if he seeks revolution. Equally the establishment cannot afford a war against a newspaper without taking the broad Afrikaner public with it … . There is only one formula for all Afrikaner institutions: independence in commitment, friendship in tension.[2]

Willem de Klerk's comments pointed to a similar conclusion: 'The Afrikaans newspapers will be able to retain their influence as change-agents only if they can project themselves as being indubitably rooted in the Afrikaans community and in service of the Afrikaner's retention of his self-determination.'[3]

Newspapers, especially in a society with sharp conflicts and high levels of partisanship, could not afford to run too far ahead, politically, of their readers and advertisers. The closure of the *Rand Daily Mail*, which ceased publication in 1985, was widely interpreted as the fate that awaited those doing so, although inept management had as much, if not more, to do with its demise than the crusading liberalism and extensive coverage of black politics that had won it international renown – and a black readership that outnumbered whites by three to one.

Hennie van Deventer, editor of *Die Volksblad* (a Bloemfontein daily), is probably correct in claiming that it was primarily the Afrikaans newspapers 'who won Afrikaans-speakers' hearts and minds for reform'.[4] He was referring to reforms introduced by PW Botha, Prime Minister from 1978 to 1983 and State President thereafter until 1989. The reforms advocated were cautious, within the paradigm associated with Botha's programme of *eieseggenskap* and *medeseggenskap* (loosely translated as 'control of own [group] affairs' and 'joint control of common affairs' for whites, Coloureds and Indians; but including acceptance of the permanence of urban Africans and recognition that homelands were insufficient as channels for their political rights). The critical question looming up, however, concerned the ANC: was it realistic to suppose that a durable accommodation could be reached without involving the ANC? Whatever their private convictions may have been, hardly an editor or columnist dared to advocate talking to the ANC, thereby risking the fearsome wrath of PW Botha. The one exception was Piet Muller, a senior journalist on *Beeld* (Johannesburg) who, in 1984, visited the ANC in exile in Lusaka.

*   *   *

Further ferment occurred among Afrikaner writers and intellectuals. The opening salvo in what became a conflict between politicians and avant-garde writers was fired in 1966 when Verwoerd, obliquely but unmistakably, criticised NP van Wyk Louw's play, *Die Pluimsaad Waai Ver*, which had been commissioned by government to mark the fifth anniversary of the Republic. It is a powerful play, set during the Anglo-Boer War when the overwhelming British forces were inexorably wearing down the Boers' resistance. The Boers are depicted in all their colours: the stout heart of Marthinus Steyn, President of the Orange Free State, the bravery of some Boer soldiers, the cowardice and treachery of others, the anti-war Boers and *hensoppers* ('hands-uppers', those who gave up the fight), differences between the Free Staters and the Transvalers, and the loyalty of Ruiter, Steyn's Coloured servant.

Verwoerd had wanted a monochromatic picture of a 'heroic nation', a writer who 'in accordance with the fixed pattern of paying homage to his own people, could push aside what is carnal and ugly and see the spiritual, the beauty and the greatness … and sing their praises.'[5] No doubt he also recognised that the sympathetic portrait of Ruiter was a reflection of Louw's views that the Coloured people were 'our people, belong with us', a sentiment that Verwoerd did not share, his nationalism being race-based, while Louw's was culture-based, and did not preclude the incorporation of Afrikaans-speakers who were not white.

The controversy caused by Verwoerd's remarks lasted for several months. Louw asked the rhetorical question: 'May a national poet not illuminate his *volk*'s weaknesses, even its times of downfall? Not only *may* he; he *must*.' He went on to raise a wider issue, asserting that there was a small but active group trying to bring Afrikaans literature to heel. 'They want to recreate the whole great national literature in their own image'.[6]

This was a reference to the *verkramptes* whose cultural commissars were vigilant in hunting down deviations from what Verwoerd had implied was the desirable norm.

The 'fixed pattern' to which Verwoerd referred equated 'good' writing with 'patriotic' writing that expressed the needs and aspirations of the *volk*. Louw and a few other writers had drawn attention to the potential gap between Christian values and nationalist aspirations; and Louw had repeatedly warned against making nationalism an absolute value at the expense of Christian or human values. In the 1960s and after, the tension between traditional or 'patriotic' values and Christian values was increasing. CN van der Merwe writes:

> As long as the Afrikaner was the underdog, Christianity and nationalism could to some extent be reconciled, because Christian morality demands charity toward those in need, and at this stage the Afrikaners found themselves to be in need. But, later on, when the Afrikaner got what he wanted … then the tension between Christianity and nationalism grew and became almost unbearable.[7]

The adoption of new, experimental styles of writing and the questioning or outright rejection of traditional values found expression in *Die Sestigers* (literally 'the Sixty-ers'), a young group of Afrikaans writers that included Coloured dramatist and poet Adam Small, André Brink, Etienne Leroux and Breyten Breytenbach, the latter succeeding Louw (who died in 1970) as the uncrowned but undoubted Poet Laureate of Afrikaans. Although the *Sestigers* were not a cohesive school of writers or people with similar political outlooks (few, if any, for instance, shared Breytenbach's radical leftwing views), their break with 'the fixed pattern' and the hostility of the old literary establishment towards them imposed a sense of common plight. They were unified by opposition to censorship and stifling community pressures. They broke taboos, notably by the inclusion of titillating sex scenes, attacked religious and political prejudices and in doing so influenced thousands of especially younger Afrikaners.

The turning point was Verwoerd's attack on Louw, and his implicit belief that writers could no longer be trusted to act as praise-singers for the nation. When Breytenbach was arrested, convicted and imprisoned in 1975 (see chapter 4), it was widely interpreted by the literary old guard and the NP establishment as proof that writers had become 'traitors', stabbing the *volk* in the back. Hence the need for censorship 'out of fear that the writer's freedom would impair the authorities' control over their *volk*'.[8] A television documentary on censorship screened in 2005 argued that censorship of Afrikaner writers was not so much about protecting the *volk*'s morals, as preventing Afrikaners from discovering that there was a world outside apartheid: censorship was the watchdog that kept all thought inside apartheid's wall.[9]

In 1974 a document compiled by TT Cloete, a retired professor of Afrikaans literature and a cultural vigilante, was circulated to members of the Broederbond and to the security police. It accused modern Afrikaans writers of deprecating Afrikaans, Christians and whites, of trying to bring down the system by violence, and of inciting youth. The writers, said Cloete, had become a 'power-group' (*magsgroep*) who had succeeded in exerting pressure or influence to the extent that they gained control of literary criticism in the journals and newspapers, thereby creating a climate of admiration for themselves. The charges were absurd, but JC Kannemeyer, who had unearthed the document, speculated plausibly that it had been the source of much of the hostility in the 1970s between the government and writers, and had led to the censorship of some of their work.[10] It was hardly coincidence that a volume of protest poetry by Breytenbach and Brink's novel *Kennis van die Aand* were banned in 1974.

An equally serious restriction of writers' freedom occurred in 1977 when Leroux's acclaimed novel *Magersfontein, O Magersfontein* was banned. Drama followed in 1979 when the Akademie vir Wetenskap en Kuns (Academy for Science and Art), the Afrikaans equivalent of a Royal Society, awarded the Hertzog Prize, the highest accolade for Afrikaans literature, to Leroux for the novel. Despite a vigorous rearguard action by the cultural commissars to have the award rescinded, the Akademie stood firm. It was a sign of changing times.

Not long afterwards, the personnel of the censorship bureaucracy changed, and a somewhat more liberal attitude prevailed. Looking back over the dark period, Koos Human (whose publishing house had published both Brink's and Leroux's books) described the climate in which writers and publishers had to work as one of 'megalomania, banality, oppression and lies'.[11]

Political writing by blacks and many books critical of apartheid by foreign authors had regularly been banned prior to 1974; and the writing of persons restricted under the Suppression of Communism Act were automatically banned; but these were the first Afrikaans writings to suffer this fate. Brink observed later that 'for Afrikaans writers there is reserved a special form of viciousness ... for its own [Afrikaner] people who transgress rules.'[12] The battle against censorship continued well into the 1980s. During 1975 a group of Afrikaans authors formed the Afrikaans Writers

Guild to oppose censorship; in 1978 it decided to stop petitioning the
Minister of Justice, Jimmy Kruger, to unban works by listed communists
because 'the person who is left cold by the death of a human being [Biko],
won't feel much for the life of a book'.[13]

It is impossible to measure the influence exerted by these writers on the
broad Afrikaner community, but they surely played some part in opening
cracks in what had previously been a well-integrated structure of ideological unity. To situate the change within the theme of this section – the
transition from particularism to universalism – they were writers who
happened to write in Afrikaans, whereas much of the earlier writing was
by avowedly Afrikaner writers, working within the 'fixed pattern'. Special
reference must be made to Elsa Joubert's novel *Die Swerfjare van Poppie
Nongena*, published in 1978. The book is a socio-economic biography of
an African woman, Poppie, who is caught up in the merciless bureaucratic
controls exerted by the pass laws as she tries to hold her family together
in Cape Town. Eventually she is forced out and 'resettled' in the impoverished Ciskei 'homeland'. The book was one of the best-selling novels ever
published in Afrikaans. JJ Degenaar, a courageous liberal who taught political philosophy at Stellenbosch University, considered it an important
contribution to the political awakening of the Afrikaners:

> She has made it impossible for us to state apologetically in future:
> 'But we never knew what the real situation was and that our laws had
> such a violent effect on people's lives.'[14]

An improbable agent of change was Pieter-Dirk Uys, an openly gay co-
median who invented an alter ego, Evita Bezuidenhout, married to a fic-
tional former minister in Verwoerd's Cabinet. Evita was an extravagant,
over-the-top take-off of her prototype, Evita Peron. Uys's satire was clever
and sharp, with hilarious imitations of prominent politicians, notably
PW Botha, whose appearance and demeanour lent themselves to mimicry.
One might suppose that homophobic South Africa would not tolerate a
drag-act, especially one that mercilessly made fun of leading politicians:
'Criticising the government was one thing our "free speech" allowed
within reason, but making fun of them was something else,' Uys writes.

Remarkably, Uys's shows were popular, even among those being lam-
pooned, and he became something of a national institution.

> The laughter that welcomed us into the laager of 1981 was shocking.
> We expected to be arrested. Instead we were sold out! It must have
> come at the right time. The people needed the relief of humour to

counter the burden of fear …. Some came to laugh at themselves. Others were relieved to spurt forth the contempt they felt for their leaders. Even some of the leaders themselves were seen to laugh and applaud. Maybe it proved that … there wasn't anybody out there who blindly believed that apartheid was a sacred gift from God.[15]

It is impossible to gauge how effective attacking racism with humour was in changing beliefs and perceptions. Nevertheless, that Uys could get away with it suggested a more relaxed environment, at least for whites. It is doubtful whether Verwoerd or Vorster would have tolerated anything of the kind.

Dissent among other intellectuals, notably academics, was confined to hardly more than a handful of individuals until the 1980s.[16] In an early model the Afrikaans university was seen as a *volks* university, rooted in the culture of a particular group and serving its particular needs (*volksgebonde*). The five Afrikaans universities, Stellenbosch, Rand Afrikaans, Orange Free State, Pretoria and Potchefstroom, had been powerful sources of Afrikaner nationalism. (Effectively, the University of Port Elizabeth, founded in 1964, was another Afrikaans university despite offering tuition in Afrikaans and English, since it was under strong Nationalist control.) Stellenbosch, where five of South Africa's seven Prime Ministers had been educated, was widely known was 'the cradle of Afrikaner nationalism'. Academics were prominent in the Broederbond, on government-appointed commissions, and as informal advisors to government. They had also been instrumental in fleshing out the apartheid programme.

The academic in an Afrikaans university was in a different structural position from the writer, who enjoyed at least a formal independence. Despite their supposed commitment to collegiality, universities, both Afrikaans- and English-medium, were hierarchical institutions whose senior staff wielded considerable power. Although it is difficult to name a single clear-cut case of a tenured academic in an Afrikaans university who was dismissed for voicing dissent against apartheid, there were other ways of penalising dissenters, notably by blocking promotion (usually on the head of department's recommendation), social ostracism and marginalisation in the community. Moreover, there is evidence to suggest that, at least in some institutions, candidates for posts in 'sensitive' disciplines, such as History or Political Science, were carefully screened (even by the security police in one known instance) for ideological conformity prior to appointment.

The 13 Pretoria-based Afrikaner academics, all NP supporters, who protested in 1955 against the removal of Coloured voters from the common roll, were 'beaten into the ground' (*tot in die grond afgetakel*) for daring to criticise government.[17] The Prime Minister, JG Strijdom, referred to them as 'the pitiful thirteen', and they became the target of a concerted smear campaign and even threats of violence.[18]

The next serious clash between politicians and academics occurred in 1961 when a purge, orchestrated by Verwoerd, removed several Stellenbosch professors from the South African Bureau of Racial Affairs (Sabra), a Broederbond-inspired think-tank that was supposed to undertake objective research into race relations. The leader of the Stellenbosch group was Nic Olivier, and their 'sin' had been to produce a report on the status of the Coloureds that was highly critical of existing policies, advocating that they be accorded direct parliamentary representation by Coloured MPs on a 'group' basis. This was anathema to Verwoerd: Olivier and his colleagues had to go, and be replaced by more reliable ideological clones – with the consequence that Sabra lost any capacity for genuinely independent research and, over time, shifted steadily towards the ultra-right of the NP, its headquarters having been moved to the more ideologically rigid environment of Pretoria.

It was not until 1971 that some Afrikaner academics ventured to reject official policy on the Coloured people, and to advocate 'full citizenship' and 'political integration': a total of 140, most of them from Stellenbosch, signed declarations to this effect; furthermore, a conference attended by some 80 people, held in the Cape village of Grabouw, addressed the economic problems of the Coloured community and called for 'the democratic redress of their situation'.[19] The hostile reaction from the Afrikaans press (especially in the Transvaal), from colleagues and the NP might have led one to suppose that they were advocating a revolutionary overthrow of the state, rather than mild reforms that ignored the even more serious plight of Africans in the apartheid system. Vorster took the lead in attacking the declarations as the 'uncooked' product of people with 'too much time on their hands'.[20] A part of the response was a declaration signed by nearly 1 500 academics, mostly from Afrikaans institutions, expressing support for apartheid. Throwing aside any pretence at institutional neutrality, AN Pelzer, the vice-rector of Pretoria University, requested all signatories to make practical contributions to the implementation of the policy.[21]

A few hardy souls braved the wrath of government and their universities by continuing to protest. The doyen of this group was JJ Degenaar of Stellenbosch University, an erudite, gentle and unassuming philosopher whose Socratic methods of teaching influenced many of his students, so much so that the Theological Faculty diverted its students away from his classes. Apart from a discussion group that he initiated in 1966, Degenaar wrote books, articles and dozens of letters to *Die Burger*, most of which it published. Describing himself as a 'moral-critical Afrikaner', Degenaar was critical of the *verligtes*' pretensions, describing them as an obstacle to change because what they advocated was not fundamental change, but only change that did not upset the balance of power.[22] Among his principal critics were *verligte* Stellenbosch colleagues. He noted ruefully in 1979 that he had been accused of conducting a 'hunt on the Afrikaner' and of causing the 'emotional paralysis' of the Afrikaner. Younger colleagues such as André du Toit and Hermann Giliomee, as well as the classicist André Hugo, kept the flag of dissent fluttering, although in time all three would transfer to the University of Cape Town.

Another source of academic dissent was the Potchefstroom University for Christian Higher Education, a stronghold of the Doppers, as the Gereformeerde Kerk, the smallest of the three Afrikaans churches, was colloquially known. It had developed a reputation for extreme nationalism and theological conservatism in the 1930s and 1940s, but in the 1970s some of its leading Calvinist professors became highly critical of apartheid's failure to live up to its moral pretensions. Even earlier, in 1958–9, one of the University's best-known professors, LJ du Plessis, a founder-member of the Broederbond, had criticised the way in which apartheid was being implemented. He was expelled from the NP in 1959. Two other professors, JH Coetzee and DW Kruger, also criticised the gap between apartheid's ideal and the reality of its implementation. Both Du Plessis and Coetzee contended that the government should be talking to the ANC, not tribal chiefs (whom Du Plessis had described as *huurlinge* – hirelings).

The University's Council was displeased with the stir that the professors had caused, especially with the forum – articles in the *Sunday Times* (Johannesburg) – in which Coetzee's and Kruger's comments had been published. In a statement, it upheld the academic freedom of staff ('due consideration being given to the University's principles') to express their personal views 'but expects that in future this freedom will be used carefully and in a dignified manner'.[23]

Coetzee was nothing if not careful and dignified. A Nationalist and Broederbond member of long standing, as well as a good scholar, he cleaved to the simple view that what was morally wrong could not be politically right. At the same time he believed firmly in trying to reform from within:

It is my conviction, strengthened by experience, that Afrikaners

staying with their people have had far more success in changing attitudes than those who have estranged themselves from the flock.[24]

He was the dominant figure in the Potchefstroom-based Afrikaans
Calvinist Movement and its journal *Woord en Daad*, which began publication in 1960. Irving Hexham writes that

> ... the authors of *Woord en Daad* considered themselves the true
> conscience of Afrikanerdom untainted by liberalism or by the perni-
> cious influence of English evangelicalism. They saw themselves as
> speaking from within the Afrikaner community to recall it to the
> Word of God ... .[25]

Sharp though it often was, the criticism levelled in *Woord en Daad* at
apartheid's failures fell within the ambit of Van Wyk Louw's notion of
volkskritiek. By the late 1970s the criticism had been ratcheted up a few
notches: at a conference of the Afrikaans Calvinist Movement in 1976,
Coetzee called the homeland policy 'a caricature'; and the conference
came close to accepting a motion that the Movement could no longer
support the homeland policy unless the homelands were 'meaningfully
consolidated into materially and spiritually (*geestelik*) viable father-
lands'. Tjaart van der Walt, a rising star in the Potchefstroom academic
firmament who subsequently became Rector, made the telling point that
Afrikaners would certainly not have accepted from the 'Englishman' –
a reference to the post-war situation after 1902 – a 'patchwork-quilt'
(*lappies-kombers*) homeland: 'How then can we expect the black peoples
to accept with gratitude something like that from the Afrikaner?' The
conference decided to continue making the public aware of situations of
injustice and to consider reform in accordance with the biblical demands
of love and justice. 'It is axiomatic that we must first be Christians, and
then Afrikaners, and not the other way around.'[26]

Tolerance, however, had its limits: during 1978 Johan van der Vyver, a
bright young professor in the Law Faculty, made himself unpopular by writing in the *Sunday Times* that the state's security methods 'amount to nothing less than executive anarchy and, as such, they have become a disgrace
to Western civilisation'. In the light of Biko's killing and Jimmy Kruger's
brutal remark, it was fair comment, but the Nationalist and Potchefstroom
establishments were infuriated, and Van der Vyver was called to account
by the Rector. He was also attacked by Louis le Grange, a Cabinet minister
who was also a member of the University Council, for having 'consorted
with the enemy'.[27] He subsequently resigned from the University.

The influence of the Potchefstroom Doppers is hard to gauge. Although the Gereformeerde Kerk is the smallest of the three Afrikaans churches, numbering about 4 per cent of Afrikaners, the Doppers are widely regarded as high-achievers, and they were said to occupy well above 4 per cent of elite positions in the Afrikaner community, including the public service. (One such Dopper was a young lawyer named FW de Klerk, who was steadily climbing the political ladder in the 1970s.)

It is difficult to gainsay the conclusion of Pierre Hugo's detailed analysis of Afrikaner academics during the apartheid era, namely that they were one of the principal institutional supporters of the policy. He acknowledged the role of the (few) dissenters and also that from the mid-1980s onwards, greater numbers took a more critical stance:

> But earlier, when it had mattered, Afrikaner academics, in the main, either as vocal supporters or in silent acquiescence, effectively had functioned as the intellectual handmaidens of apartheid. A multi-faceted syndrome of 'tribal instincts', conformist conditioning, societal reward, ideological conviction and a natural human tendency to avoid controversy help to account for this outcome.

In line with these strictures, Hugo noted the paucity of research publications that were critical of apartheid:

> Afrikaner academics cannot ... point to a significant body of literature that would affirm their allegiance to the 'politics of truth' by way of their critiques of official racial policies during the high tide of apartheid.[28]

It is no invidious comparison to contrast this performance with that of the English-medium universities, whose scholars produced a steady stream of research that was explicitly or implicitly critical of apartheid and the historical foundations of the unequal society.

Despite acquiescence and complicity in apartheid, there were stirrings beneath the surface. By the late 1970s most of the Afrikaans universities were beginning to admit small numbers of black students. Especially in the aftermath of the Soweto Uprising, consciences were increasingly troubled. In an editorial, *Die Burger* wrote that an important part of the Afrikaner nationalist intellectual world was undergoing intensive soul-searching which here and there went over to self-reproach: 'Policy is being tested against principles and conscience and found wanting.' It acknowledged that the grand vision of the early 1960s 'had been only incompletely realised, to put it mildly'.[29] Many intellectuals agreed with this, but most opted to operate 'within the framework'. Here and there, though, a new urgency had crept into *verligte* utterances, but they nevertheless continued to attack the likes of Degenaar and his fellow-dissenters with vigour. They urged various reforms, while insisting that overall white control be maintained.

To what extent the isolation of academics (including English-speakers) affected Afrikaner academics is hard to say. There were excellent scholars scattered around the Afrikaans universities; many wrote in English (because this was the main international language of science) and attended conferences abroad, sometimes being accorded a frosty reception.

By the late 1970s what the historian FA van Jaarsveld described as a 'cold war' between politicians and dissident academics was entrenched: 'only when academics slavishly go along with "the policy" and bless it with praise (*saligprys*), justify it and defend it do they grow in stature'.[30] Van Jaarsveld was a scholar in the traditional nationalist mould who nevertheless sought to debunk historical myths about the nationalist movement's origins and symbols. He was also moving in a *verligte* direction. In March 1979 he discovered that such activities could be dangerous: a group of rightwing thugs led by one Eugene Terre'Blanche broke up a lecture he was delivering and tarred and feathered him. It was one of the earliest public demonstrations by a neo-Nazi group calling itself the Afrikaner Weerstandsbeweging (Afrikaner Resistance Movement), established in 1973. Terre'Blanche was to become a significant demagogue in the 1980s. Threats against Van Jaarsveld and other dissident Afrikaners continued, and attempts were made to break up NP meetings.

*   *   *

Reference has already been made to the critical role played by the Dutch Reformed churches in the development of Afrikaner nationalism. Their legitimation of apartheid remained important to the political leadership, which is why it went to considerable lengths to ensure that the churches, especially the Nederduitse Gereformeede Kerk (NGK), which was the biggest of the three, remained in alignment with policy. As in most of the institutions of the Afrikaner nationalist movement, there had always been individual dissenters. Leading theologians such as BB Keet of Stellenbosch and Ben Marais, both with impeccable church credentials, rejected arguments that sought to give apartheid a biblical foundation. Such arguments had played into the hands of the NP: if apartheid were scripturally enjoined then it was sinful not to support it.

In December 1960 a major clash loomed when delegates from the NGK synods of the Transvaal and the Cape (the NGK was then a loose federation of provincial synods) participated in a World Council of Churches consultation at Cottesloe, a residence on the campus of the University of the Witwatersrand, Johannesburg. The consultation also involved the other main Protestant denominations who, with varying degrees of stridency, opposed apartheid. Several politically contentious (as far as whites were concerned) resolutions were adopted, including:

- there are no scriptural grounds for a prohibition of mixed marriages;
- the migrant labour system had a destabilising effect on African family life, which disrupted community life;
- wages paid to blacks were so low that the great majority were forced to live below the poverty line;
- job reservation should be replaced by a fairer system;
- the right to possess land wherever one was domiciled and to participate in the governing of one's country was part of the dignity of the adult person, and for that reason a policy that permanently denied this principle could not be justified;
- there could be no objection in principle to direct parliamentary representation of Coloured people;
- the danger of nationalism was that its drive for self-determination could jeopardise the interests of others, and make the interests of a people an absolute value that took the place of God.

The delegates from the Hervormde Kerk, the most conservative of the three Afrikaans churches (its Constitution stipulated that only whites could be members) rejected the consultation *in toto*, and reaffirmed its commitment to separate development. The NGK delegates, however, supported the declarations, subject to some qualifications, notably that participation in government by Africans referred to those Africans living in declared 'white' areas who had no other homeland.[31]

The fat was now in the fire: a storm of protest broke out in the press and church newspapers; many church councils passed condemnatory resolutions; and leading NGK men, including AP Treurnicht, then editor of *Die Kerkbode*, the NGK's newspaper, voiced strong criticism. Worse was to follow, when Verwoerd himself joined the fray, declaring in his New Year message for 1961 that the World Council of Churches was meddling in South Africa's internal affairs, and, moreover, that the NGK delegates were merely a group of individuals who did not speak for the Church:

'The voice of the Churches must still be heard, and particularly at their Synods at which members as well as clergy will be represented.'[32] As with most issues, Verwoerd had definite views on the respective roles of church and state. In 1959 he told the Gereformeerde Kerk that

> ... although there are points of contact between [church and state], the functions of these two bodies are nevertheless different. Each acts along its own lines and has its own duty to fulfil. They must understand one another. They must adapt themselves to one another. They must appreciate one another.[33]

Stripped of circumlocution, this meant that policy issues were to be decided by government, and government alone, and that no outside 'meddling' would be tolerated.

The threat to the churches implicit in Verwoerd's words was not an idle one: he recognised that their continuing support was vital, and that dangerous heresies committed by leading churchmen must be snuffed out immediately and vigorously lest their corrosive influence spread, with dangerous implications for Afrikaner nationalist solidarity. Probably at Verwoerd's behest, the Broederbond went into action, sending a circular letter to all its branches, asking them to reject the Cottesloe resolutions.[34] Predictably, all four provincial synods of the NGK repudiated them, even though they were substantially similar to what the Cape synod had proposed in a memorandum submitted to the consultation.

The witch-hunt that succeeded Cottesloe and whipped the NGK churches into line ensured that they would remain pillars of support for apartheid. Individuals and small groups of clergy and laymen, including the Potchefstroom Doppers, might occasionally express dissident sentiments, but the institutional church would shift its position only at a glacial pace. For one of the Transvaal NGK's most prominent dominees (ministers), Beyers Naudé, Cottesloe and its aftermath spelled the end of the road. Naudé, a man of great charm, was also a powerful preacher and immensely popular with his congregation. He was clearly destined for high office in the church. Already deeply troubled by political developments and his church's support for apartheid, Naudé refused to repudiate any of the Cottesloe decisions. His decision to establish an interdenominational Afrikaans newsletter, *Pro Veritate*, and, subsequently, the interracial Christian Institute, both intended to stimulate debate about racial issues in the light of Scripture, sealed his fate. Despite having been elected as moderator of the Southern Transvaal Synod of the NGK in March 1963 (probably a strategy to induce him to stay within the fold), Naudé refused to resign as editor of *Pro Veritate*. Accordingly, he was defrocked as a dominee.

Further problems beset Naudé shortly thereafter. He had resigned from the Broederbond, of which he had been a member since 1940, because its doctrines reflected an interpretation of the Scriptures to which he could not subscribe.[35] To help his friend and fellow-dissident, Albert Geyser, an academic theologian who was a member of the Hervormde Kerk, Naudé lent him Broederbond documents, which Geyser photocopied and subsequently passed on to a journalist. Geyser was facing a trumped-up heresy charge, the real issue being his church's strong disapproval of his mildly liberal political views. The serial publication of Broederbond documents in the *Sunday Times* (during 1963) led to a national uproar and huge consternation in the Broederbond, whose members were required to swear an oath of secrecy on joining. With the assistance of the Security Police, the leak was soon traced to Naudé, who readily acknowledged that he had loaned the documents to Geyser, but that he had not been aware that Geyser had copied them and given them to a journalist.

Naudé subsequently apologised to the Broederbond, but it was too late: the violation of the oath aggravated his status as a marked man and made it immeasurably more difficult to persuade dominees and other church members openly to support the Christian Institute. Naudé had believed that there were as many as 400 'troubled' dominees in the NGK who could be won over to rejecting the church's pro-apartheid beliefs. It was a wildly over-optimistic estimate, since ultimately Naudé and his colleagues were supported by perhaps two dozen. The Christian Institute was never able to gain a significant foothold in the church. It moved steadily in a more radical direction and was finally banned by the state in 1977. Naudé himself and four senior colleagues were also banned, and in Naudé's case the banning order lasted for seven years.

Naudé's situation provided an early manifestation of the perennial question facing dissenters: should one try to influence policy from inside or outside the institution? In a discussion with his brother-in-law, FE O'Brien Geldenhuys, also a senior NG dominee and one of the delegates to Cottesloe, Naudé expressed the hope that he would retain his status as a dominee and continue to influence the church via the Christian Institute. Geldenhuys responded that this was wishful thinking, and predicted, accurately, that the church would find this unacceptable. For his part, Geldenhuys said that he would try to create from within the structure of the church 'a favourable climate for the spirit of the Cottesloe resolutions'. Twenty years later he ruefully acknowledged that he had not succeeded in any significant respect in moving the church from its support for apartheid in church and state. He asked himself: 'Who was right – Bey[ers] or I?' There was no easy answer.

In an obituary, Naudé was quoted as saying:

> What really annoyed the leaders of Afrikaner nationalism when I broke ranks was that I was every bit as much a white Afrikaner as they were …. I reminded them of that side of Afrikanerdom which they have never been able to tame. It is an Afrikaner willingness to cross frontiers, relating to their own experience of exploitation, struggle and poverty.[36]

For dominees, especially young ones, the perils of overt dissidence were considerable: an estimated 60 per cent of dominees and, in many congregations, some of the *ouderlinge* (elders) as well, were members of the Broederbond, and could be relied upon to keep a watchful eye out for doctrinal deviations. Alienating a congregation could have serious consequences, especially since it would thereafter be more difficult to receive a call (an invitation to become their dominee) from another congregation. As in all spheres of the nationalist movement, the potential weight of institutional disapproval exerted a strong deterrent effect. Conformity was the safer option.

After years of paralysis in the aftermath of Cottesloe, and abortive efforts to produce a statement on race relations that commanded general agreement, the NGK eventually, in 1974, published *Ras, Volk en Nasie*. The report was notable for its ambiguities, which reflected differences of opinion in the church that had become manifest after Cottesloe. It was, according to an academic theologian, Johann Kinghorn, the result of a long process of gestation: 'A theology which had been born about four decades before, reached maturity here. In [*Ras, Volk en Nasie*] the apartheid ideology found its *classic* expression.'[37] The NGK had convinced itself that apartheid could be scripturally justified, but that its implementation should be subject to the ethical injunction to love one's neighbour. Little in the document, however, showed any awareness of the misery that apartheid was causing to black people. A section of the report, while in draft form, had dealt with the position of urban Africans, but it was scrapped 'because it moved onto political territory'. Nevertheless, mixed marriages were condemned not only as 'undesirable' but also as 'impermissible' – that is, unscriptural.[38]

The report was a damp squib, but its support for apartheid dismayed some of the rising generation of theologians and, through them, their students. It also widened the alienation of the 'daughter' (subsequently called 'sister') churches, as the missionary branches of the NGK were known. From the late 1970s onwards the (white) NGK would be subjected to a barrage of criticism from the daughter churches, essentially demanding that the church repudiate apartheid. In 1982 the NG Sendingkerk (for Coloured people) reiterated earlier resolutions and declared 'with the deepest sorrow' that it could not but accuse the NGK of 'theological heresy and idolatry' because of its declared support for apartheid.[39]

The impasse which apartheid had entered, and the continuing injustice that marked its implementation, prompted criticism of the NGK establishment from within. This was not an unprecedented phenomenon: in 1960 senior theologians from the three Afrikaans churches had produced a collection of essays that were critical of theological justifications of apartheid. This was entitled *Delayed Action*, and the contributors were mainly older critics, including BB Keet, Ben Marais and Adriaan van Selms.[40] Although publication of the book caused a stir, it had little apparent impact on the respective church establishments, although, given the scholarly eminence of its authors, it is very likely that it sowed seeds of doubt among some of the younger theologians and clergy. When the old guards of church establishments retired or died, more propitious times for theological renewal might come.

In 1981, a group consisting mostly of theological professors produced *Storm-kompas*, a collection of spirited essays that posed some tough questions for the NGK. The book concluded with 44 propositions concerning the NGK in the current context. Proposition 35 read:

> It is time that the NGK says clearly that the apartheid policy has borne many bitter fruits, in spite of the good intentions of the authorities to try to let the population groups develop separately. Therefore the church ought to state clearly that the Christian cannot support this policy unreservedly.

Severe criticism of the Broederbond was expressed in proposition 40:

> Because so powerful an instrument of opinion forming as the Afrikaner-Broederbond's activities occur in secret, the free formation of public opinion is constrained. Fear of jeopardising future career prospects discourages its members from openly and impartially questioning the political and social system in South Africa ....

Moreover, the close links between members and officials of the Afrikaans churches and the Broederbond, and the links between the Broederbond and the NP and government, caused serious damage to the credibility of the churches.[41]

Equally strong criticism was voiced in 1982 when 123 dominees and *gelegitimeerdes* (those qualified as clergy but not yet actually ministering to a congregation) signed an open letter to the NGK that was published in the church's newspaper, *Die Kerkbode*. In numerical terms this was much the biggest expression of discontent yet by members of the (white) NGK. Unity of the church, the signatories wrote, allowed for diversity of language and culture within the church; but unity was primary and diversity was secondary – the implication being that the church had reversed this order. The letter went on to state that a system that elevated irreconcilability (*onversoenbaarheid*) to a principle of society and estranged the different sections of the population from one another, was unacceptable. It was proposed that all people who regarded South Africa as their fatherland 'should be involved in working out a new social system'.[42]

In the same year, 1982, the isolation of the NGK increased when the World Alliance of Reformed Churches suspended both the NGK and the NHK from membership on grounds that they sought to justify apartheid by misuse of scriptures and the Reformed creed. The NGK synod was shocked by this decision, and many of the delegates pressed for a complete withdrawal from the Alliance, but were unable to secure the required two-thirds majority. The instigator of the suspension was a young (Coloured) NG Sendingkerk dominee named Allan Boesak, who was to be one of the leading figures in black protest politics in the 1980s. To the chagrin of many NGK members, he was unanimously elected as President of the Alliance.

In 1986, the General Synod of the NGK moved significantly, if cautiously, to distance itself from apartheid by agreeing to a new statement entitled *Church and Society*, which replaced all previous statements on racial affairs. As the most conservative of the spheres that collectively constituted the Afrikaner nationalist movement, the church was aligning itself with other spheres that had already set the pace. PW Botha's government had made significant shifts away from apartheid; and the Broederbond, now under reformist control, was reconnoitring new fields for reform. The split in the NP in 1982 and the formation of the Conservative Party thereafter had affected every institution in Afrikaner society, including the churches. In the NGK, the battle between conservatives and reformers had raged for over two decades; with its acceptance in 1986 of the policy document *Church and Society*, many of the conservatives broke away to form the Afrikaanse Protestantse Kerk. Many Afrikaners, dismayed by the split in the NP, had pinned their hopes in the church as the last redoubt of *volkseenheid* (Afrikaner unity). These were now dashed.[43] The new church attracted nearly 40 000 members, including some from the other Afrikaans churches, and about 100 dominees from the NGK.[44]

The key findings of *Church and Society* were:[45]

- '… the conviction has grown over time that forced division and separation of peoples cannot be derived from the Bible as a prescription. The attempt to justify such a prescription … must be acknowledged as an error and rejected.'
- 'The NGK is convinced that the working of apartheid as a political and social system that does injustice to people and unjustifiably advantages one group above another cannot be accepted on Christian ethical grounds, because it conflicts with the principles of love of one's neighbour and justice and inevitably injures the human dignity of all involved.'
- 'The suffering of people, with which the church commiserates, must not be ascribed only to apartheid, but to a variety of factors of social, political and economic realities … . In so far as the church and its members were involved in this, it confesses this with humility and remorse.'
- 'The Scriptures do not forbid racially mixed marriages. The church, however, in its pastoral work must warn against social circumstances, life- and world-views [*lewens- en wêreldbeskoulike*], cultural, socio-economic and other similar differences and factors that can cause serious tensions. Where such marriages do occur, they must be pastorally assisted in all facets of marriage.'
- The church declared unequivocally that it was not its calling to prescribe any political policy to the authorities: 'The church preaches only that the demands of love, justice and human dignity must be embodied in society. Consequently it will continue to test every existing or proposed model against [these demands].'
- Racism was condemned in unprecedentedly strong terms as 'a grievous sin which no person or church may defend or practice'.

The vexed question of whether black members of the sister churches might attend services of the (white) NGK was resolved succinctly with the statement that membership of the NGK was open. Consideration of whether church unity of the 'sisters' was desirable was fudged, and the question of a single church structure, although not ruled out, was deferred, pending discussions among the different member-churches 'in the light of the demands of Scripture and the present realities'.[46]

In an analysis of the NGK's grappling with apartheid, JA Loubser, a reformist dominee, expressed criticism of fuzzy aspects of *Church and Society*, but nevertheless concluded that viewed from within the church 'it was a giant theological leap, a paradigm shift'.[47] To what extent the findings were taken to heart by rank-and-file church members is a matter of debate – just as there could be legitimate doubts about the extent to which the unequivocal denunciations of apartheid by the English-language denominations elicited agreement from their white congregants. The important issue, however, was that one of the principal pillars of Afrikaner nationalism had jettisoned what Loubser called 'the Apartheid Bible'.

Another dimension of change in the church, noted in the early 1970s, was the growing refusal of younger people and those in the higher socio-economic bracket to obey the churches' rules about Sabbath observance, which included not reading papers, playing sport or gardening. Surveys conducted among NGK members by Cornie Alant revealed that substantially more respondents who were younger, better educated or more affluent than other categories reserved the right to disagree with the dominee's sermon. Majorities, moreover, did not consider it a sin to vote for a party that was not specifically Afrikaans in orientation, or for a white to marry a 'non-white' if it were legal. Alant concluded that for many, continued membership of the church served as more of a symbol of group identity than as a mandatory set of rules and beliefs.[48] Secularisation was under way.

*   *   *

The rise of an Afrikaner business elite after 1948 further contributed to the loosening of the ties that held Afrikaner nationalism together. The business sphere had developed under the aegis of the movement, and originally it had relied upon Afrikaner sentiment and the mobilisation of Afrikaner capital as its driving force. In the divided context of South Africa, Afrikaner business was originally as much a political phenomenon as an economic venture. The first editorial of *De Burger* in 1915, written by the editor, DF Malan, proclaimed, '*De Burger* is a child of pain and hope. It was born of the weeping of our *volk*.' Sanlam, which became a giant financial conglomerate, similarly proclaimed its nationalist roots when it was founded in 1919: 'Born out of the Afrikaner people to serve the Afrikaner people.' The chairman's address in 1921 contained an appeal to Afrikaner sentiment:

> SANLAM is a genuine Afrikaner people's institution in the widest sense of the word. As Afrikaners you will naturally give preference

to an Afrikaans concern. I would just remind policy-holders that we are busy providing young Afrikaners with employment and training in the insurance business … . If we [Afrikaners] wish to become economically self-reliant, then we must support our own institutions.[49]

Sentiment, however, proved insufficient to sustain a take-off, and efforts by Afrikaner leaders to exhort Afrikaners to 'buy Afrikaans' and to raise their economic consciousness were of only limited success.[50] Success required dynamic entrepreneurs and, especially after 1945, numbers of them rose to the fore. Slowly but surely the Afrikaner share of the private sector (excluding agriculture, where Afrikaners had long been dominant) grew. Sadie's calculations show that between 1948–9 and 1975 the contribution to the private sector by Afrikaner-controlled businesses doubled from 9.6 per cent to 20.8 per cent, with significant advances being recorded in mining, manufacturing and construction, the professions and finance.

For most Afrikaner businesspeople the historic links with Afrikaner nationalism inhibited their criticism of the NP. Writing in 1962, Heinz Hartmann said that 'the Afrikaner in business generally wavers between identification with economic goals and Nationalist policies. Unhappily, these two commitments tend to exclude each other.'[51] That assessment remained substantially true throughout much of the apartheid era. In an economy that was subject to a high degree of dirigisme, with state approval necessary on a variety of issues, the Afrikaner businessman would inevitably be reluctant to express criticism of policy, especially in public. If criticisms (often requests for modifications in the implementation of, for example, labour policy) were made, they were invariably made privately. Since Afrikaner business had relatively easy access to ministers and civil servants, issues could be taken up discreetly. The Broederbond, moreover, served as a convenient channel of communication between the economic and political elites.

Muted criticism of policy was voiced from time to time in *Volkshandel*, the organ of the Afrikaanse Handelsinstituut (AHI) (effectively, the Afrikaans Chamber of Commerce); but invariably overall support for apartheid was stressed. In 1971 the vice-president of the AHI was quoted as saying:

The Instituut in principle underwrites government policy, but we will always reserve the right to discuss matters with the authorities when we feel the business community may be harmed by a certain policy. We prefer not to do this in public.[52]

The major figure in the post-1948 Afrikaner economic renaissance was Anton Rupert, whose Rembrandt Group grew out of a cigarette-manufacturing company into a major international conglomerate. In his younger days at the University of Pretoria, a stronghold of Afrikaner nationalism, Rupert held fairly conventional Nationalist views. By the late 1940s, however, his attitudes had changed: after listening to a debate between Judge HA Fagan (of Fagan Report fame) and Professor AC Cilliers, he concluded that Fagan was right and that there would be no salvation in racial separation. He propounded a philosophy of 'partnership' or co-operation between white and black on the basis of common interests. Rupert had discovered early in his career that a 'focus on an exclusively Afrikaans clientele narrowed their market considerably. An appeal to sentiment was not a winning recipe ...'.[53]

His first significant clash was, predictably enough, with Verwoerd, whose views on economics were primitive and who believed that businessmen should keep their noses out of politics. In 1959 Rupert had decided to open a tobacco factory in Paarl in partnership with Coloured people. Having been informed as a courtesy, Verwoerd demanded to know if there would be Coloured directors and whether whites would have to work under Coloureds. When Rupert affirmed that this would be so, Verwoerd immediately threatened to close down the factory.

Clashes on other issues followed: Rupert opposed the refusal to allow white capital into the homelands; after Sharpeville in 1960 he pleaded, unsuccessfully, with Verwoerd to grant property rights to urban Africans; he defended Harold Macmillan's right to criticise apartheid, which he had done in the 'Wind of Change' speech in 1960; he opposed South Africa's leaving the Commonwealth; he opposed excessive state control of the economy; and in 1961 he declared that the Afrikaners' 'third trek' had to be away from discrimination towards participation in freedom by all population groups. In 1985 he said in a press interview:

> Apartheid is dead, but the corpse stinks and must be buried and not embalmed. If you have to leap from cliff to cliff across an abyss you can't do so step by step.[54]

Like other Afrikaner businesspeople – and the great majority of their English-speaking counterparts – Rupert avoided party politics and public involvement in political controversy. He saw no need for an organisation like the Broederbond and allowed his membership to lapse. Neither he nor any of his companies gave money to the NP or, indeed, to any other party. He described himself as a 'liberal Cape Afrikaner', who rejected 'one-person-one-vote'. Instead, he favoured a Swiss-style canton system, with maximum devolution of authority.[55] Although his public pronouncements after the 1976 uprising reflected greater urgency, he declined an invitation to accompany a small delegation of businessmen led by Gavin Relly, chairman of the Anglo American Corporation, who met an ANC group led by Oliver Tambo in Zambia in 1985. He said subsequently that he had no objections to the meeting, which, he warned, could be counterproductive 'if it is not realized and acknowledged that differences do exist'. He objected also to 'the dogma of violence', which was presumably a reference to the ANC's guerrilla campaign.[56]

Criticism of official policy was voiced by Andreas Wassenaar, the chairman of Sanlam, whose book *Assault on Private Enterprise*, published in 1977, was a scathing attack on government overspending and the bureaucratic shackling of the private sector. It was not popular with the authorities, even though neither this book nor his other publications discussed apartheid. Wassenaar's view was that the state, by establishing state-controlled corporations like the Industrial Development Corporation, entered into direct competition with the private sector.[57] Many in the private sector shared this belief. Louis Luyt's autobiography contains several references to bureaucratic obstructiveness and the refusal of Afrikaner institutions to lend money to his burgeoning business. He wrote:

> I sometimes wonder what might have been if I had become one of the select few in the Broederbond. Would I have received better, even preferential treatment from the national government? Would there have been a willingness to make certain concessions or to hand me a parachute? Or might I have been better off by not being an Afrikaner at all? After all, I had seen Oppenheimer and other English-speaking South Africans receive special treatment as well. Perhaps it was my stubborn refusal to kowtow and my impudence in challenging officialdom that caused the backlash. Who knows?

Luyt's was a classic rags-to-riches story: born into a poor white family, he built a substantial group out of his original fertiliser factory, Triomf. He was a daring and innovative entrepreneur whose success was a living refutation of the widespread belief – among Afrikaners themselves – that Afrikaners had no talent for commerce and industry. His brashness and fierce independence carried over into his role as a rugby administrator, in which capacity he became a staunch opponent of government interference in sport (an opposition that he maintained after 1994, when a preponderantly ANC government was in power). Long before any other

Afrikaner businessman was prepared to do so, he was advocating the release of Mandela. In an interview in 1985 he was quoted as saying that 'for far too long businessmen have not said what they have felt because they have feared reprisals from Government. Now he is prepared to stand up and be counted. "The black vote must come," he says.' In 1987 he announced a formal break with the NP, and not long thereafter he became the first Afrikaner businessman to hold talks with the ANC.[58]

That few Afrikaner businessmen were prepared to raise their heads above the parapet and criticise government by no means implied that the business sphere of Afrikaner nationalism was monolithic. There were sharp rivalries between the more *verligte* 'Southern' group that included some giants like Sanlam, Rembrandt, Trust Bank and Nasionale Pers, and more conservative 'Northern' businesses. The disputes, however, were not about political issues. In general, small business was more conservative, and, especially in the northern provinces, more susceptible to the siren calls of the *verkramptes*, who continued to harp on about the corrupting influence of the '*Geldmag*' (money power). How English and Jewish capitalists had engineered the Anglo-Boer War and thereafter enmeshed Afrikaners in a web of exploitation was a prominent theme in traditional Afrikaner nationalism. It was still being propounded by the HNP in the 1970s, its eccentric leader, Albert Hertzog, maintaining that the '*Geldmag*' was intent on gaining control of government and *volk*.

This was conspiratorial nonsense. The only grain of truth in the ravings of the ultra-right was that increasing numbers of Afrikaner businesspeople, especially in the larger enterprises, were becoming concerned at the direction in which apartheid was leading the country. Another factor was the recognition not only that Afrikaner sentiment was not a sufficient basis for sustainable profitability but also that the Afrikaner nationalist tag was a handicap in seeking to expand business across colour lines. Business, in other words, was bursting out of the seams of nationalism. Writing in 1984, Willem de Klerk said:

> In Afrikaner business circles political conservatism is definitely on the decline. The current generation of businesspeople are the frontrunners of reform. This is a significant fact in the light of the shift in occupational status in the Afrikaans community. The businesspeople, and together with them the professions, have edged out teachers and clergy as 'people of note'. They have accordingly grown even more in status and authority. They have become important pace-setters.[59]

The rise of Afrikaner big business – and the corresponding decline in the economic importance of agriculture – did not, however, mean that the business lobby was now the dominant influence in the NP or that agricultural lobbies had become unimportant, even though agriculture's contribution to GDP had slipped below 4 per cent by 1994, and only 4.7 per cent of Afrikaners were employed in agriculture by 1991, compared with 41.2 per cent in 1936. Conversely, 66.2 per cent of Afrikaners were employed in white-collar jobs by 1991, compared with 27.5 per cent in 1936.[60] What, then, *was* the dominant influence in or on the NP? An attempt to answer this question is made below.

In a presentation to the Truth and Reconciliation Commission in October 1997, the AHI sought to explain its *raison d'être* and the views that it had upheld. In answer to the question whether apartheid benefited the business community it said:

> Apartheid caused South Africa to be much poorer than the country and its people could otherwise have been. Lost and unused human potential, wasted resources, people and capital that left the country, growth that did not take place and job opportunities that were not created: these and many other examples are indications of how much poorer we are – not to mention the influence of apartheid on the moral standards of our society. A poorer community means simply fewer business opportunities. The business sector did not benefit from this. Indeed the business sector could have created considerably more welfare than if apartheid had not been enforced – on the assumption that the transition would have occurred peacefully.

The presentation acknowledged, however, that apartheid had disadvantaged the African business sector in various ways: prohibitions on the ownership of land prevented land being used as a means of building up capital; restrictions on commercial and trading activity inhibited 'latent entrepreneurship, potential abilities and hidden talents'; while job reservation denied Africans access to skills.

In conclusion, the AHI acknowledged its 'big mistakes', including its support for apartheid: 'As a business organization we should have realized much earlier that moral and economic realities totally contradicted even the most rose-coloured interpretations of separate development.'[61]

* * *

Much of the received view of the Broederbond portrays it as a sinister spider spinning its web around the activities of the Afrikaner nationalist movement. That it was influential across the board in Afrikaner society and that it exerted pressure to get 'right-minded' people into important posts can hardly be denied; but it was never in a position to dictate to the Nationalist government, even though all six Prime Ministers/State Presidents and the great majority of Cabinet ministers between 1948 and 1994 were members. By the mid-1980s it had a membership of approximately 13 000, most of them occupying elite positions nationally or locally.

Apart from promoting Afrikaner interests in all fields, the Broederbond's principal role was two-fold: to co-ordinate the activities of the different spheres that constituted the Afrikaner nationalist movement; and to preserve the unity of Afrikaner nationalism. Not surprisingly, the internal activities of the Broederbond mirrored the divisions and rivalries in the Afrikaner community. It proved impossible to fulfil the unifying role in times of high tension in Afrikaner ranks, such as in 1933–4 when the old NP split or in the 1940s when the NP and the O-B fought for possession of the movement. The Broederbond was to prove incapable of preserving unity when the HNP was formed in 1969, after several years of infighting inside the Broederbond as well. Under pressure from Vorster most known HNP supporters were purged, although Piet Meyer, chairman of the *Uitvoerende Raad* (Executive Council) since 1960 and an ultra-conservative, retained his post until 1972, to be succeeded by Andries Treurnicht, another ultra-conservative. Under these auspices, it was unlikely that the Broederbond would transform itself into a force for reform, especially since many *verkramptes* who had opted not to join the HNP remained within its ranks.

In 1974 Treurnicht was succeeded by Gerrit Viljoen, the Rector of the Rand Afrikaans University and an intellectual of considerable stature. During his six-year chairmanship fresh winds began to blow in the Broederbond. While there could be no doubting his commitment to the nationalist cause and, at least in the earlier period of his chairmanship, his support for separate development, Viljoen warned against elevating nationalism above Christian values: Afrikaner nationalism, he said, was a nationalism that was 'qualified' by Christianity. Moreover, he declined to regard separate development as an ideology or a dogma: it was merely a method of ensuring the survival of Afrikaner identity 'as it was seen within a certain period and in the circumstances of the time, which may ... change.'[62] It had continually to be tested against its usefulness in attaining this goal.

Circumstances *did* change, and so did Viljoen's views, leading him over time to look for alternatives to apartheid. In the aftermath of the

Soweto Uprising, his sense of urgency increased: discriminatory legislation, especially when it benefited whites at the expense of other groups,
'in reality, will eventually create for us more dangers and problems than it
solves'.[63] According to Willem de Klerk, a colleague on the Broederbond's
Executive Council, Viljoen's role during his chairmanship was to act as a
'warning prophet in the inner circles of Afrikanerdom that things would
have to change and in what direction they would have to change'. He also
lifted the Broederbond out of its role as a 'lap-dog' (*skoothondjie*) of the
NP's bosses and gave it significant standing as a player of equal status in
politics. Under his leadership the Broederbond acquired the profile of an
agent of change:

> The general impression among the public was and is that the
> Broederbond was a brake on the process of political change. The
> opposite is true. The AB helped to release the brakes. As an or-
> ganisation of influence it made a gigantic contribution to making
> Afrikaners ripe for the turning point in 1990.[64]

Under Viljoen's leadership, the Broederbond became primarily a think-
tank. Its influence derived from

> ... the moulding and sharpening of its members' views. The AB
> is a place of thought (*dinkplek*) where people pool their resources
> to think through the affairs of the day .... And all of the thought-
> material (*dinkmateriaal*) is distributed among one another and dis-
> cussed. Meetings are arranged and influence is exerted on authorities
> and powers in society with the composite results of the thought-
> material.[65]

It was a two-way process: government, through its Broederbond members
and in formal discussions, explained its problems and options, and received
feedback and advice from Broederbond members. In turn, Broederbond
members could explain policy in their various communities.

The scale of the changes contemplated by Viljoen's reformism at this
stage – and, indeed, by the great majority of *verligtes* – should not be
exaggerated. He was a long way off accepting that South Africa should
be an undivided society whose preponderantly African population would
inevitably have a concomitantly preponderant share of power. It was still
widely believed in the white community that its leaders could call the tune
in determining the scope and pace of change. By 1980 apartheid may have
been pronounced dead by some Afrikaner leaders; but neo-apartheid, in

which whites would still exercise de facto control, had arisen to take its place. In 1980 Viljoen joined Botha's cabinet as Minister for National Education. He would become a key lieutenant of Botha's successor, FW de Klerk.

Viljoen had had to contend with a significant *verkrampte* presence inside the Broederbond. His successor, Professor Carel Boshoff, a Pretoria theologian and Verwoerd's son-in-law, was in this category. A man of great personal decency, Boshoff eschewed the crude racism expressed by many of the ultra-rightwingers, but nevertheless cleaved strongly to the core apartheid concept of geographical and political 'self-determination'. Ever since the purge engineered by Verwoerd in 1961, Sabra (of which he was also chairman) had moved to the right, and had become little more than a rightwing think-tank.

Boshoff, who had been a member for 27 years, believed passionately that, in spite of political divisions among Afrikaners, the Broederbond 'should embody the higher and deeper unity of the Afrikaner *volk*'. It was a vain hope, and when the Broederbond came out in support of neo-apartheid's first constitutional innovation, the Tricameral Parliament, established in 1983, which Sabra opposed, he felt obliged to resign as Broederbond chairman in July 1983, and not long thereafter as a member. Boshoff had a legitimate point: by endorsing the new Constitution, the Broederbond had acted contrary to its own rules, which forbade taking a stance on political issues that divided its members. Many conservative fellow-members followed him out of the Broederbond.

Boshoff was succeeded by Pieter de Lange, an educationalist, who, like Viljoen before him, was the Rector of the Rand Afrikaans University. According to his own account, De Lange had seized 'every opportunity' to oppose apartheid 'ever since I heard Verwoerd for the first time'.[66] On becoming chairman of the Broederbond, he said that 'he would do everything in his power to promote talks with all black leaders as equals within the limits set by the university'. He would not mind meeting Nelson Mandela 'but it will be difficult to meet him in prison'.[67] In 1979, when this statement was reported, the NP establishment would have viewed it as rank heresy.

De Lange was as good as his word: meetings with African and Coloured leaders, mainly those who worked 'inside the system', had begun in 1978, but the big step towards making contact with the ANC did not occur until 1986 when he secretly met Thabo Mbeki in New York. Mbeki was then the ANC's Director of Information and Secretary for Presidential Affairs. (Unfortunately, the story that De Lange introduced himself to Mbeki by saying, 'the name's Bond, *Broeder* Bond', is apocryphal!) Although the meeting was cordial – both men possessed an abundance of charm and intelligence – the Broederbond's reaction was one of sceptical wariness. An official document published by the Afrikanerbond (the name-change occurred in 1994) in 1997 noted that

> ... the AB was fully aware of the ANC's strategic thinking regarding negotiation as an instrument in its liberation struggle. The AB realized that the ANC simply saw this as another opportunity to establish a Black takeover and knew that any negotiation strategy with the ANC had to take this into account.[68]

Nevertheless the meeting broke the ice and, despite PW Botha's visceral mistrust of the ANC, it signalled that influential sectors of the Afrikaner establishment were beginning to grasp the nettle: that no settlement would be possible without the ANC's involvement. Meetings with the ANC by private individuals or groups still attracted Botha's wrath – a formidable force – but the era of stealthy emissaries from the establishment to the ANC, including the imprisoned Mandela, had begun.

For much of the late 1970s and into the 1980s the Broederbond concerned itself with alternative constitutional models. By 1977 it had concluded that the Coloured and Indian minorities needed political incorporation within the 'white' areas and that the 'Westminster' system had to be modified. It produced proposals for different representative bodies to handle 'own affairs' ('*eiesake*') or matters specific to the affairs of each group, while provision would also be made for an interlinking system for joint decisions on 'common affairs' or matters affecting all three groups. As the Broederbond acknowledged, 'the focus was still on the survival of White sovereignty'. Much the same proposals were floated by the NP in the 1977 parliamentary elections, but were not acted upon, pending further consideration.

Further deliberations continued, with the Broederbond having been largely freed of its *verkrampte* incubus in 1982 after the breakaway from the NP of Treurnicht and his followers and the formation of the Conservative Party. In 1985 the Broederbond produced a document which emphasised that only a constitutional model acceptable to *all* groups had any chance of success, a condition which, if taken at face-value, marked a breakthrough.

An even more significant breakthrough occurred in 1986 with the publication *Basiese Staatkundige Voorwaardes vir die Voortbestaan van die Afrikaner* (Basic political conditions for the survival of the Afrikaner). It marked the Broederbond's final break with apartheid. The key points are

quoted from the summary contained in the document published by the
Afrikanerbond in 1997:

- An entrenched white government is no longer acceptable. The status quo cannot be sustained.
- Abolishing statutory discriminatory measures is a condition for
  survival. This does not entail 'yielding under pressure'. It is a condition for just survival.
- All citizens must be afforded effective participation in the legislative
  and political processes.
- Participation by all, and consequently also power sharing, should
  be of such a nature that it prevents domination of one group by
  another. The rights and aspirations of groups need to be satisfied
  and protected.
- Devolution of power to limit government interference to a minimum.

These proposals were intensively debated, and the Executive Council approved the document in November 1986. When asked to respond, 89 per
cent of branches and 86 per cent of individual members indicated their
agreement with the general trend. It was clear that the Broederbond favoured a negotiated settlement. Members agreed that there could be no
guarantees that the proposals were workable:

> We have to think in terms of probabilities, calculated risks. The big-
> gest risk we could take was to avoid risks altogether. If Afrikaners could
> not reach a negotiated settlement, it was inevitable that they would face
> structures forced on them without having had any say in the matter.[69]

Several issues arise: 1986 was a time of tumult in the streets of towns and
cities; guerrilla attacks had increased in number, sophistication and daring;
and the screws of sanctions were being tightened. The economy, moreover,
was in poor shape, registering minus 1.2 per cent growth of GDP in 1985
and zero in 1986. The Broederbond statement appeared to imply that a
revolution was in the making: what else could the comment about having
'structures forced on them' mean? Secondly, the proposals resembled in important respects those put forward by the NP in 1991. This was not because
the Broederbond dictated to the government, as conspiracy theorists were
wont to argue; rather, the resemblance reflected the extent of interpenetra-
tion and cross-fertilisation between the two organisations.

Thirdly, despite the disavowal of apartheid, the gap between the proposals and the ANC's constitutional thinking as it was to crystallise was wide.
'Power-sharing', federalism and reference to the 'rights and aspirations of

groups' would have been construed by the ANC as manifestations of neo-apartheid thinking that were inimical to their quest for hegemony in a unitary system in which groups, however configured, would have no role as prescribed political entities. Apartheid was based squarely on the compulsory group membership of individuals, the 'groups' being designated by the Population Registration Act. The assumption that these groups would be the building blocks of any new Constitution was widely accepted in Afrikaner circles.

*   *   *

The brief description of developments inside the spheres of the nationalist movement shows a community that increasingly reflected the ferment in the wider society. By the early 1970s Afrikaners were a preponderantly urban people, and the relatively closed community life of the *platteland* (countryside) had largely broken down. 'Poor whiteism' had all but disappeared; white unemployment was minimal, and a thrusting bourgeoisie was making its mark in the private sector as well as in the state-owned enterprises. By 1970 Afrikaner per capita incomes were in a ratio of nearly 70:100 in comparison with those of English-speaking whites – a substantial change from the figure of 47.8:100 in 1946.[70] Afrikaners were better educated and more widely travelled than previous generations; and much of the Afrikaner 'inferiority complex' had gone. Hostility to the English-speakers, which was strong in the aftermath of the Anglo-Boer War and continued in the 1950s, had abated. Perhaps as many as 25 per cent of English-speakers had supported the NP in the 1966 election, although that percentage would fluctuate up and down in the future. Although no exact figures are available, Afrikaner hostility to *ondertrouery* (marriage to an English-speaker) was decreasing, and 'mixed' marriages, though still relatively few, were increasing.

In an article written to mark the twenty-fifth anniversary of the NP's coming to power in 1948, Schalk Pienaar remarked that the Afrikaner, conscious of his own power, especially after the attainment of the Republic in 1961, 'had become a much more relaxed person in his relations with people of another language' (referring here to English-speakers). Much the same was true of attitudes to blacks: 'Much more than before, there is a readiness to accept them as fellow-beings and to accommodate them in the South African system.'[71] Most blacks would have viewed this statement with scepticism; but there was some truth in Pienaar's view: it was widely recognised – and Verwoerd had laid the basis for this – that white domination in perpetuity could not be justified.

There was also a rising feeling, reflected in the accounts of developments in the spheres of Afrikaner nationalism, of guilt and growing recognition of the moral costs of apartheid. NP van Wyk Louw's dictum, that it was better to go under than continue to live in injustice, haunted an increasing number of troubled souls. Another factor was deepening this introspection: the rise of the ultra-rightwing, including the establishment of Treurnicht's Conservative Party in 1982, held up a mirror to more modern-minded Nationalists of what the NP had stood for in the not-so-distant past – and they did not like what they saw. The crude racism of the HNP, AWB and other groups in the mushrooming ultra-right embarrassed and repelled them, thereby lending urgency to the quest for a more equitable system.

* * *

By the mid- to late-1980s there were signs that some younger Afrikaners were staging their own rebellion against their elders. It assumed various forms: rock music with a decidedly anti-establishment bent; alternative journalism, principally in the form of the weekly *Vrye Weekblad*, founded by the mercurial Max du Preez; and a more generalised protest against the Border War in Namibia/Angola. Other younger people took up the anti-apartheid cudgels through sober analysis.

While by no means all of those who turned against apartheid were in the younger age cohort, generational differences undoubtedly played a role in widening divisions within the Afrikaner community. Those born after 1948 – and, more particularly, after 1960 – enjoyed life-chances that were far superior to those of their parents and, even more, their grandparents. Folk memories of the Anglo-Boer War had faded; the depressed 1930s and the poor white problem had been overcome. By the 1980s some 60 per cent of Afrikaner school-leavers went on to university or other higher education, with every prospect of obtaining a well-remunerated job after graduation.

But the shadow of violence, and even the prospect of civil war, hung over the younger generation's chances of a comfortable and peaceful life. There was another factor that troubled many: guilt at recognition of the hardship and injustices that apartheid inflicted on blacks. As observed by the (young) editors of a book, significantly subtitled *Young Afrikaners Speak* (translation), this generation especially had the responsibility of acknowledging the untenability of apartheid, but also of giving form to the vision of an apartheid-free South Africa: this was the responsibility of all South Africans who were concerned at the growing polarisation and violence, but the greatest responsibility lay with the post-1948 generation of Afrikaners:

> This generation undoubtedly derived the most advantage from the inequalities and privileges that apartheid brought, although their share in the formulation and institutionalisation of apartheid was limited.

In words reminiscent of conclusions reached by the Broederbond in 1986, the editors asserted there was an increasing realisation that 'the perpetuation of the status quo was a greater threat to white interests than changing it would be'.[72]

Conscription of white males at 18 years of age had been introduced in 1967 and thereafter incrementally increased from nine months to two years in 1977. Some 600 000 had undergone military training by the early 1990s. The Border War, involving conflict in northern Namibia and Angola, was deemed necessary by the state to halt communist (Cuban troops and Soviet advisors) penetration and to prevent Swapo (the major Namibian liberation movement) from establishing an armed presence in Namibia. The war was unpopular among many *troepies*, as the young conscripts were colloquially known: army life was tough, and, for the minority who were involved in actual combat, dangerous.

It is impossible to be precise about the breakdown of attitudes towards the war: for many it was no doubt a hardship that had to be endured because it was one's patriotic duty. Others, however, hated their involvement in a conflict caused by a system they regarded as unjust. This was especially so when conscripts were deployed in townships during the turbulent 1980s. For many, military duty was a traumatic experience from which they returned *bosbevok* (literally 'bush-fucked'), suffering post-traumatic stress syndrome.

The Anglo-Boer War had produced an entire genre of writing that described the heroic deeds of the Boer forces. The literature of the Border War reflected an entirely different reaction: the War was a consequence of apartheid, and none of the significant Afrikaans writers supported it. Their sympathies were reserved for its victims, including the traumatised *troepies* who returned to their communities with severe emotional burdens.[73]

If opposition to the war was diffuse and muted, *Vrye Weekblad*'s opposition to apartheid and all its works was direct and uninhibited. Its first issue was published in November 1988. It survived official harassment, defamation suits, prosecution in terms of security legislation, and a virtual boycott by potential advertisers until, in February 1994, losing a costly defamation case brought by a police general forced its closure. It had been a short, action-packed existence that had inflicted some body-blows on the apartheid establishment, notably by its exposure of the practitioners of dirty tricks. Sales never exceeded 25 000. With only minimal advertising, it was kept afloat by foreign donors. Du Preez ruefully records that nearly half the money spent on *Vrye Weekblad* went towards legal expenses.[74]

To what extent *Vrye Weekblad*'s hard-hitting message penetrated the Afrikaner community is impossible to assess: its sales were low, but the readership consisted mostly of well-educated, younger Afrikaners. That its investigative journalism forced the authorities onto the defensive – as their aggressive responses sometimes showed – is hardly deniable.

In terms of mass appeal, the rock music of Johannes Kerkorrel, Koos Kombuis and Bernoldus Niemand (all stage names) went further than the manifestations of youthful revolt cited above. They represented a break with traditional *Boeremusiek* (literally 'Boers' music') whose origins stretched back into the nineteenth century, and with the schmaltz of much popular contemporary Afrikaner music. Collectively, the musicians were known as *Voëlvry* and, with the Gereformeerde Blues Band, they toured the country to huge acclaim during 1989. With exuberant hyperbole, Kombuis claimed:

> The National Party fell after the Tour. Well, not immediately. But it was only a matter of time. The biggest power-base of the Party, its grip on Afrikaner youth, was whittled away. We were not the biggest, cruellest, angriest resistance to the regime – the Struggle of the ANC and the UDF and the struggling and fighting of thousands of activists was in total more than our modest contribution – but I still believe that the Voëlvry tour was the death blow.[75]

Voëlvry's racy lyrics attacked and satirised pillars of the traditional Afrikaner establishment, including politicians (notably PW Botha), the churches, the SABC, the army and some of the most hallowed symbols of Afrikaner culture. It was not only political protest, but also a demand for liberation from what they regarded as the stifling pressure for conformism exerted by Afrikaner institutions.

How deep was Voëlvry's impact? Albert Grundlingh concludes an important analysis on a note of judicious ambivalence:

> 'Voëlvry' did rock the boat, but more gently than often assumed.
> It was mainly a white middle class movement which in the eighties

sought to redefine elements of Afrikaner ethnicity without fully re-jecting it. Although the movement was largely restricted to the white community and its proselytising effects were uneven, it was a brave stand to take at the time.[76]

The various manifestations of a rejection of the old order reflected a de-gree of ferment among younger Afrikaners. None of those who partici-pated repudiated their Afrikaner backgrounds or the use of Afrikaans. Indeed, Max du Preez, among the most radical of the rebels, prided him-self on rescuing Afrikaans from the straitjacketed standardised form and restoring the vigorous, earthy version spoken by ordinary people. In the last issue of *Vrye Weekblad* he wrote:

> If there is one thing we're proud of, it is the favour we did to the Afrikaans language by de-stigmatising it, but also making it looser and more sexy. We were part of the movement to hijack Afrikaans back to where it belongs: the ordinary people who speak it.[77]

CHAPTER 7

The Turbulent Eighties

PW Botha became Prime Minister on 28 September 1978 at the age of 62, after the NP caucus had voted by 98 votes to 74 (for Connie Mulder) to elect him as *hoofleier* (leader-in-chief). Botha had spent his entire adult life in the service of the NP, having become a party organiser in 1936 (in which capacity he developed expertise in disrupting opposition meetings) and an MP in 1948. By 1978 he was the sole survivor of the crop of Nationalists who had entered Parliament in 1948. His rise in the NP was rapid: between 1948 and 1958 he was Chief Secretary of the Cape NP; in 1958 he was appointed a deputy minister; in 1961 he entered the Cabinet as Minister of Housing, thereafter occupying several other portfolios until in 1966 he was appointed Minister of Defence, a post that he held until October 1980. He was elected Cape leader of the NP in 1966, a position of power in the federal structure of the party as a whole. As a minister Botha was efficient and vigorous, with a firm grasp of administrative detail. He had been elected Prime Minister as a consequence of Connie Mulder's involvement in the Information Scandal. But Botha's performance as a hawkish Minister of Defence in times when South Africa, in the official view, was the target of a 'total onslaught', created the platform from which he could grasp the leadership.

Botha was an unlikely reformer. During his years as a minister he gave no overt signs of dissent from the prevailing orthodoxy, although he disliked the term 'apartheid' and avoided using it. He bemoaned the failure to implement the proposals of the Tomlinson Commission and criticised 'petty' apartheid regulations – some of which he proceeded to abolish after 1978. Few opponents of the NP, black or white, expected much of Botha; but in July 1979 during the so-called 'adapt or die' speech, he struck a reformist note, declaring that politics could not be based on hate but only on love for one's fellow-beings:

> Do not ask me to say that I stand for a Christian nationalism and then come and tell me that I must neglect the interests of the black man and the brown man, because then I shall not be a Christian and I shall not be a Nationalist.[1]

Botha's reformism was bounded by a commitment to separate development; if he were to modify policy it would be in accordance with NP principles. Fundamental to his thinking was that South Africa was 'a country of minorities', each of which was to be accorded recognition. 'Groups' had to be the building blocks of any new system:

> South Africa's biggest problem is not its racial problem, but its minority problem. The white nation consists of minority groups: the Afrikaans-speakers, the English-speakers, the Portuguese-speakers, the Greek-speakers and other minority groups. Each of the black [African] peoples is also a minority group. The Xhosa are a minority group in relation to the rest of South Africa's population, the Zulu are also such a group, as are the Sotho and the Venda. Among the Coloured population there are the Malays, who constitute a small minority group, and the ordinary Cape Coloureds. There are also the South African Indians. Each of them is a minority group, and each has its own traditions, its own ideals and interests.[2]

Botha's obsession with groups never wavered. It was disingenuous, but it created a framework within which neo-apartheid could evolve. It would also remain a stumbling block to any potential agreement with the ANC on constitutional issues. His dogmatic belief in the compulsory group affiliation of people placed obvious limits on his being able to envisage or accept leaders or movements that had arisen outside or above these group boundaries and, moreover, were implacably opposed to Botha's belief.

Pressed on this issue by interviewers in 1986, Botha refused to budge from his view that 'the black man himself does not look at himself as being part of a big black majority'. There were different African groups, each with its own leadership who could participate in negotiations. But, asked the interviewers, could these groups be represented as one black mass if they chose to? Botha's reply was unconvincing:

> But they won't be, they *won't* prefer to have it that way. Bishop Tutu

will tell you that they … wish to have it that way, but he is *not* a representative of *all* of the Black people in South Africa. Chief Buthelezi tells me that *he will not* recognise Bishop Tutu as a leader.

Botha could not bring himself to recognise that the ANC might command majority support among Africans. In his view the ANC consisted of two groups, one communist and the other nationalist, mainly Xhosa. He acknowledged that it was difficult to determine how much support the ANC actually enjoyed, but he did not believe that it was more than that enjoyed by Buthelezi's Inkatha.[3] Strategy was aimed at driving a wedge between the ANC and the SACP, which, given the symbiotic nature of the relationship between them, was unlikely to succeed.

While Botha was no closet liberal, some of his reforms tore down significant institutional and ideological pillars of apartheid; others, notably the Tricameral Constitution, sought to shore up apartheid by pragmatic adjustments – but failed calamitously and produced unintended consequences that actually eroded it.

His first major reform was the enactment of legislation in 1979 that granted African trade unions statutory recognition and enabled them to participate in the industrial conciliation machinery. This stemmed from the Wiehahn Commission's recommendation that the law governing industrial relations be deracialised. On the subject of trade union rights for Africans the Commission concluded that the risks in not granting such rights were greater than the risks involved in doing so. It said, in response to conservative fears, that they are

> … not only unlikely to materialize, but in fact pose a far lesser threat than would the continued denial of elementary rights and the perpetuation of the existing uncontrolled situation of proliferation.[4]

The government accepted most of the recommendations of the Commission, but the bill embodying them stipulated that only workers (of all races) who had permanent jobs and were permanent residents could qualify for trade union membership. As Helen Suzman noted during the parliamentary debate, the exclusion of migrants and so-called 'frontier commuters' (workers from the 'independent' bantustans who had lost their South African citizenship) meant the denial of trade union rights to over two million workers, including 80 per cent of the labour force in the manufacturing sector. Effectively, she continued, trade union rights would be confined to Africans who were entitled to permanent residence in urban areas under the influx control legislation – the so-called

'Section 10-ers' – who numbered 1.4 million people.[5] The exclusion of these categories was part of a deliberate strategy to differentiate between permanently urbanised people, 'insiders', and the rest, most of them rural people whose deteriorating economic condition would inevitably cause many to seek permanent work in the towns. Also excluded from the legislation's purview were domestic workers and farm labourers, arguably the two occupations most in need of the protection afforded by unions.

The underlying intention of the legislation was two-fold: to bring some order to the potential chaos that a proliferation of unregistered unions might bring to the industrial relations front; and secondly, to impose some measure of control on the burgeoning union movement, while heading off any possibility that some unions would seek affiliation with foreign unions which were deeply hostile to apartheid. In addressing these questions, the Minister of Labour, SP Botha, said that existing African unions were not subject to any legal requirements and therefore found themselves in a more favourable position than registered unions. There was, for example, no control over their funds, which were often channelled in directions that had nothing to do with conditions of service. He defended another clause in the legislation which prevented employer organisations and trade unions from participating in political activities, including supporting parties or candidates: 'The Republic is too vulnerable today to allow an intermingling of labour relations and politics.'[6]

To what extent the government recognised that the legislation would have, in SP Botha's words, 'far-reaching implications for this country' is unknown. The alacrity with which the bulk of Wiehahn's recommendations were accepted suggests that the Cabinet agreed that the controls contained in the legislation would bring order to a troublesome field. PW Botha, who knew little or nothing about industrial relations, allowed his Minister free rein – and also to take flak from rightwing sources that objected to the recognition of African unions and to the abolition of 'job reservation' that was included in the legislation.

Wiehahn and his family faced serious security threats in the aftermath of publication of the Commission's Report. His obituary quotes him as having said that the workplace 'was the right place to light the fuse to implode apartheid', and that the recommendations to abolish job reservation and other restrictions were a prime cause of the subsequent breakaway of the Conservative Party.[7]

Another reason for PW Botha's 'benign neglect'[8] was his interest in reducing the state's involvement in labour relations by leaving negotiations and disputes to employers and the unions to resolve, or, failing that, to the Industrial Court that was also set up in terms of the legislation. In an essay published in 1983 Wiehahn argued that prior to 1979 the state had intervened extensively in labour relations as a peace-keeper and peace-restorer, with the consequence that negotiating skills remained 'undeveloped' at the company or plant level. After 1979, however, state intervention declined: 'It has now shed its policing function and henceforth will no longer be responsible for the restoration and maintenance of industrial peace.'[9] The restraint did not apply, however, when security or political issues impinged on union activities. It was widely believed by unionists that employers colluded with the state in enforcing security legislation, a belief that is suggested by the detention of at least 108 trade union officials, including several in Ciskei, between 1981 and 1984.[10]

The new dispensation was viewed with initial suspicion by the emergent unions who scented a ruse to inveigle them into registration for purposes of tighter control. This had indeed been one of the legislation's aims. In two critical attempts the official strategy failed: the government soon acknowledged that it made no sense to differentiate between permanent residents and migrants in determining eligibility for union membership – and the Minister used his powers to waive the restriction. It also proved to be an idle hope that unions could be kept out of politics: black unions would become a major component of the black opposition.

The liberalisation of the labour laws was an acknowledgement of reality: even before 1979 the emergent unions had demonstrated their durability. Their recognition, however, created an anomaly insofar as the overall reform programme was concerned, because there were other areas where reality needed acknowledgement. Nowhere was this more evident than in the question of the status of urban Africans.

One of apartheid's principal aims – if not *the* principal one – was to abort the urbanisation revolution among Africans by deeming urban Africans to be 'temporary sojourners'. Hard demographic reality had undermined the population projections used by Verwoerd; the *annus mirabilis* of 1978 had come and gone, but the growth of the urban African population in the 'white' areas had continued, limited partly by the statistical trick of excluding residents of townships that abutted 'white' areas and were socio-economically part of urban conurbations, but technically were located in a homeland. For example, the big African township of Mdantsane was part of the Ciskei homeland; effectively it was a satellite town of East London.

Despite its general ineffectiveness influx control did have some effect in curbing the townward flow of rural people. A committee of the President's Council accepted estimates by Charles Simkins in 1985 that were influx control to be lifted, between 1.5 and 3 million more people would enter the prescribed areas by the year 2000. Most, according to Simkins, would be dependants of people already in the area. The Committee found that about 60 per cent of the growth of the African population in these areas derived from natural increase and 40 per cent from in-migration.[11] Many in the urban African population were 'illegals', who had simply ignored the influx control regulations. Quite possibly 50 per cent and more of the African population of the bigger metropoles were technically 'illegals'. This was hardly surprising: an economist, Jan de Lange, calculated that it was economically rational to move from a homeland to Johannesburg even if it meant varying lengths of time spent in prison for influx control offences: thus, a worker coming from Lebowa homeland to Johannesburg improved his living standard by an estimated 255 per cent even if he spent three months in prison; by 170 per cent if he spent six months in prison; and by 85 per cent if he spent nine months in prison.[12] A consequence of illegal entry was the mushrooming of squatter settlements around many cities and towns. When asked by the President's Council Committee whether influx control was working, a senior official in the Western Cape replied that if it was working 'there would not be 202 000 illegal squatters at Crossroads' (on the periphery of Cape Town).[13] Many squatters were the dependants of migrant workers, who had been unable to gain lawful entry to a prescribed area.

Statistical legerdemain continued to dominate Nationalist thinking. In 1981 Piet Koornhof, Minister of Co-operation and Development (formerly the Department of Bantu Administration and Development), was quoted as saying:

If Gazankulu, Lebowa, QwaQwa and KwaNdebele [homelands] become independent [in addition to the already 'independent' TBVC states] it means that there will be 13.5 million completely independent Blacks. Then only about 6.25 million Black citizens of KwaZulu and KaNgwane will remain under the control of the South African Parliament. These 6.25 million Blacks will be fewer than the sum total of 7.8 million Whites, Coloureds and Asians in South Africa.[14]

Government continued to tinker with urban policy. As noted, the decision to allow 99-year leases to qualified urban Africans in 1978 was de facto acknowledgement that they could no longer be considered 'temporary sojourners'; but, as the ferocity with which enforcement of influx control continued into the 1980s showed, it was still considered to be a vital part of the state's armoury against 'swamping': between 1980 and 1985 an annual average of over 200 000 Africans were arrested under the pass laws.

The President's Council Committee noted the deleterious effects this had on victims: their human dignity was degraded, and their contempt for the law and the agencies that enforced it was increased. Moreover, convictions had little deterrent effect.[15]

Attempts to modify the pass laws had been recommended by the Riekert Commission in 1979 and the Grosskopf Committee in 1981, but neither advocated grasping the nettle and abolishing influx control in its entirety. Some reforms afforded greater mobility to qualified people, but only within the context of the strategy to drive a wedge between urban 'insiders' and 'outsiders'. Enforcement of influx control now focused on the limitation of entry to prescribed areas to those who had employment and accommodation. Employers who employed 'illegals' faced severe fines for doing so. This device, too, was doomed to fail, and legislation drafted by Koornhof's department that sought to strengthen the barricades against 'outsiders' was never enacted.

During 1984 violence flared up again, and an estimated 175 people were killed, most of them between September and December.[16] It was the beginning of a new cycle of protest and resistance that would last into 1987. This was the context in which PW Botha finally did grasp the nettle and abolish influx control in 1986. It was clear from the President's Council Committee Report and a mountain of other evidence that the pass laws were not working and that they were the biggest single cause of grievance among Africans. Since an important component of the state's strategy was 'winning-hearts-and-minds' (WHAM), the pass laws had to go. The President's Council Committee, which contained a majority of Nationalists, had prepared the way:

> It is neither possible nor feasible to retain control and remove only its discriminatory elements. Influx control is discriminatory *per se* in that it applies only to Blacks and not to the other population groups in South Africa. To make influx control applicable to all population groups ... is not feasible, politically or otherwise and also in practice unnecessary, because Whites, Asians and Coloureds are already to a large extent urbanized.

The Committee found also that attempts to limit access to the urban areas to those who had approved housing and work would not succeed, and were liable to create 'a great many new problems' if applied.[17]

In a White Paper the government accepted most of the Committee's recommendations, agreeing that the arguments for the abolition of influx control far outweighed those supporting its retention:

The Government has ... accepted the permanence of Black [African] people in the RSA and has decided that all South African citizens should enjoy equal political rights, with the protection of minority rights and the retention of the option of independence for those communities which might prefer it, in an undivided RSA, within which government institutions already exist at various levels – and could still develop. The Government therefore states emphatically that influx control can no longer serve any constitutional objective.[18]

In 1986 legislation abolished influx control. The Minister of Constitutional Development and Planning, Chris Heunis, under whose portfolio 'African administration' now fell, declared that 'freedom of movement is granted to all South Africans for the first time in history'. There were no more legal barriers to urbanisation: the notorious 'Section 10' was being repealed. Heunis noted that between 1960 and 1970, a time of apartheid's most rigorous enforcement, there had been a 42 per cent increase in urbanisation. He acknowledged that 'in the long run the drawing power of the metropolises still remains greater than all the ways and means we have used to reduce it'.[19]

The change was more than an admission of defeat; it was, as a senior NP MP put it, 'finally burying apartheid'.[20] This was an exaggeration, of course, but the central plank of apartheid and its segregationist predecessors had been removed. Erstwhile 'temporary sojourners' could now acquire property in freehold, albeit in segregated areas.

Another significant reform was the repeal in 1985 of legislation prohibiting mixed marriages and sexual relations across the colour line. Section 16 of the latter legislation, the Immorality Act, had long been contentious: between 1974 and 1983, 2 055 persons had been prosecuted, and 1 712 convicted, often resulting in heartbreak and, in a few cases, suicide.[21] It was also discriminatory since 'immorality', defined as having sexual relations outside of wedlock, was an offence only if the persons involved were of different colours. The provision also opened up possibilities for voyeurism, snooping and blackmail.

As early as 1979 Botha had intimated his distaste for the legislation, declaring that while mixed marriages and immorality were undesirable, he was unaware of any biblical grounds for deeming mixed marriages sinful. In the following years, the views of churches were sought, and, like Botha, none could establish biblical authority for the legislation, although most considered such marriages 'undesirable'. Both laws were considered by parliamentary committees, but the eventual conclusion was that neither could be 'improved', leaving repeal as the only option.

Botha himself said in 1984 that the laws had created embarrassment for the country (especially when prominent whites were charged under the Immorality Act), and that 'a nation that required laws to maintain itself was not worth maintaining'.[22] Both the Mixed Marriages Act and section 16 of the Immorality Act were repealed in 1985. During the parliamentary debate Helen Suzman, who had long campaigned for the repeal of section 16, noted that repeal of the Mixed Marriages Act and section 16 of the Immorality Act made little difference to the social fabric: 'Citizens did not leap across the colour line in their thousands into one another's beds, either within or outside matrimonial bonds, after the repeal of these two grotesque examples of apartheid.'[23]

Most black leaders pooh-poohed the significance of these reforms, which did not affect the balance of political power, but for the Nationalists, apart from sparing the government some embarrassment, they were symbolically significant as pillars of apartheid ideology. Moreover, how could the Group Areas Act, which prescribed separate residential areas, accommodate mixed couples and their offspring? The Act would have to be modified. In practice, black people were already technically breaking the law by moving into previously white areas in all of the major cities, creating so-called 'grey areas', although breaches of the law could result in prosecution.

Botha would not countenance repeal of the Group Areas Act: 'own' residential areas and schooling were fundamental to his notion of 'groups' and the rights supposedly associated with them. He was, however, prepared to make the law more flexible, and he accepted a recommendation by the President's Council that provision be made for specific open residential areas in which people of all races could live, provided that those who placed a high premium on an 'own community life' (racially exclusive residential areas) were also catered for.

Similarly, state schools were to remain racially segregated, but private schools, many of them run under church auspices, were permitted to enrol pupils of all races. By early 1988, 14 543 black children (and 92 682 white children) were attending private schools.[24] Official permission, however, was routinely denied to black children seeking to attend state schools, in spite of requests from a few governing bodies to allow their enrolment.

Segregation at the tertiary level was fraying at the edges. Despite the application of apartheid to universities in 1959, small numbers of black students had been granted permits to register for courses that were not offered at the black institutions. By 1983, 14 per cent of the students at the four 'white' English-medium universities were black; even the 'white' Afrikaans-medium universities had begun to admit blacks in minuscule numbers that did not exceed 1 per cent. The earlier 'ethnic' stipulations governing admission to the black institutions were also giving way, if only slowly. The University of the Western Cape, for instance, originally designated as an exclusively Coloured institution, had a handful of non-Coloured students, including 58 whites.[25]

No doubt fearing that it would be unable to control the process of desegregation, the government enacted legislation in 1983 to empower the Minister of National Education to impose quotas that would regulate the entry of students to universities established for other groups. Within the limitations established by the quotas, individual universities could control their own admissions policy, thus obviating the cumbersome permit system. The legislation was totally unacceptable to its principal targets, the four 'white' English-medium universities, who argued that they were now being required to do the government's dirty work in enforcing racial quotas. Their sustained protest and the embarrassment, nationally and internationally, that the legislation was causing the government led in stages to the government's undertaking not to enforce it. Admissions were now in the discretion of individual institutions: an important component of university autonomy had been regained.

Desegregation of facilities, amenities, transport, hotels and cinemas proceeded slowly and messily, with significant regional variation. Where the ultra-right Conservative Party controlled local authorities, facilities under municipal control remained segregated, sometimes resulting in consumer boycotts by angry blacks that cost white businesses substantial declines in turnover. It was a powerful new weapon in the hands of the black opposition that reflected the significant rise in black consumer power. The Conservative Party and other ultra-rightwing organisations such as the AWB were readily able to fan the flames of racism, and even to incite white thugs to use strong-arm methods on blacks who dared to 'invade' what they regarded as exclusively white amenities. The widespread violence in the townships in the mid-1980s, and the increase in guerrilla attacks by MK, heightened the climate of fear among whites, and made them even more resistant to change.

Desegregation was an emotive issue for both blacks and whites – for opposite reasons – just as it had been in America's Deep South. It was not only the opening of beaches or cinemas that attracted resistance: 'tortoises', as a minister famously called obstructive bureaucrats, in the public sector often did their best to impede, thwart or frustrate reform initiatives. In 1988, over 30 per cent of economically active whites were employed in the public sector (which included central, provincial and local governments and other state-controlled bodies). Persuading many to implement even modest reform measures was going to be difficult; acceptance of fundamental change, involving a re-ordering of power relations in the entire society, looked impossible.

*   *   *

Not all of Botha's reforms were 'cosmetic', as his critics claimed. Some removed pillars of the apartheid order and destroyed much of its ideological sub-structure. The centre-piece of his administration's reform programme, the Tricameral Parliament of 1983, however, was a disastrous failure that actually hastened the end of apartheid.

It had proved difficult for the NP to remove Coloured voters from the common voters' roll in the 1950s; it was going to prove even more difficult to grant them equal political status. Proposals for a system of three separately elected parliaments, one each for whites, Coloureds and Indians, had surfaced during the 1977 election campaign. They were the brainchild of an NP committee chaired by Botha, then Minister of Defence and leader of the Cape NP. They were regarded as an alternative to the Theron Commission's recommendations for direct Coloured representation in Parliament. The election campaign's principal focus, however, was a jingoistic attack on alleged foreign (mostly American) meddling in South Africa, so that the constitutional proposals tended to be crowded out. They were nevertheless endorsed by the NP caucus and the four NP provincial congresses in 1979. Thereafter they wound their way through a tortuous and sometimes acrimonious process of refinement inside the NP, as well as in the President's Council, an advisory appointed body established in 1981.

The constitutional proposals were eventually presented to Parliament in August 1983 and rushed through. Botha announced that a referendum among white voters would be held on 2 November 1983: voters would be asked the simple question whether they approved the implementation of the legislation embodying the new Constitution. There was one significant difference between the proposals unveiled in 1977 and those of 1983: the latter provided for three separate chambers of a single parliament, whereas the former had proposed three separate parliaments. It was a difference that partly explained the rejection of the 1983 Constitution by Treurnicht and his supporters (see below).

The new Constitution was premised on what Botha regarded as the fundamental difference between 'discrimination' and 'differentiation': discrimination occurred when injustice was done by one group to another; differentiation was merely the drawing of distinctions. 'Hurtful, unnecessary' discrimination had to go, but differentiation, as provided for in the 'healthy power-sharing' contained in the Constitution, was fundamental for white survival and self-determination.[26] It was difficult to grasp Botha's argument since the Population Registration Act, providing for racial classification, and the Group Areas Act, together with the total exclusion of Africans from participation, were the very foundation of the Constitution. In fact, the Constitution amounted to the constitutionalisation of apartheid. FW de Klerk acknowledged that 'the baggage of our apartheid history' and the emphasis on race rather than on culture and language prevented the Constitution's acceptance as a genuine attempt at cultural self-determination, which was widely accepted as legitimate in other multicultural societies.[27]

In terms of the Constitution the membership of the three houses reflected the numerical proportions among the population categories. Thus:

House of Assembly (whites): 178
House of Representatives (Coloured): 80
House of Delegates (Indian): 40

In each case small numbers of MPs were nominated by the executive State President or indirectly elected by the MPs who had won their seats in parliamentary elections. The size of the Houses could not be altered other than by a constitutional amendment requiring the assent of a majority of the members of each House.

The State President, who was vested with substantial executive powers, was elected by an electoral college consisting of MPs elected by majority vote of each House. The members of the electoral college reflected the respective sizes of each House, thus ensuring that the 50 members elected by the House of Assembly had an overall majority over the total of 38 members elected by the other Houses.

The critical distinction that underpinned the Constitution was that between 'own' and 'general' affairs. 'Own' was a direct translation from the Afrikaans *eie*, and in this context it meant 'group-specific'. The Constitution defined 'own affairs' as matters 'which specially or differentially affect a population group in relation to the maintenance of its identity and the upholding and furtherance of its way of life, culture, traditions and customs'. Matters that affected all three groups were 'general affairs'. The State President was empowered to decide, in cases of doubt, into which category particular matters fell. 'Own affairs' included social welfare, education, art, culture and recreation, health, community development, local government, and aspects of agriculture and water supply. Funding for the legislative programmes of the respective Houses came from transfers from the State Revenue Account by means of a general law – which, in practice, meant that the House of Assembly had control of the purse-strings.

The operating principle of the system was that 'own affairs' legislation could be enacted by the House concerned, whereas 'general affairs' legislation required approval by all three Houses. Should there be disagreement among the Houses and different versions of a bill enacted, a deadlock-breaking mechanism was invoked. The President's Council was carefully constructed to ensure that the members designated by majority vote of each House (35) and appointed by the State President (25) would give the NP-dominated House of Assembly the effective final say. In the event of disagreement among the Houses on legislation, the Council was empowered to decide which version of a bill should be presented to the State President to sign into law. The mechanism was used on several occasions.

Critics described the system as 'sham consociationalism'. Even a number of Nationalist MPs were sceptical about the chances of its successful operation. F van Zyl Slabbert, then leader of the Progressive Federal Party, recounts how, in 1984, a senior Nationalist MP reproached him for alleged delaying tactics in a debate on proposed Rules and Orders for the operation of the new Parliament. Slabbert explained why his Party's amendments were important, whereupon the Nationalist shrugged resignedly, saying, 'In any case, the bloody thing is not going to work.'[28] It was probably not an atypical view.

Acceptance of the proposals by the NP had dramatic consequences for the solidarity of Afrikaner nationalism, as well as for the mobilisation of black opposition. Treurnicht and his fellow-*verkramptes* were deeply unhappy about the supposed power-sharing, but bided their time before showing overt opposition. An opportunity arose unexpectedly in February 1982: Jan Grobler, chief information officer of the NP, wrote an article in *Nat 80's* describing current policy initiatives. In outlining the proposed accommodation of the Indian and Coloured groups, he concluded that 'it was only logical that there could not be more than one government in the same country', and therefore they had to share in the decision-making process. Treurnicht, who was then Minister of Statistics and of State Administration – both minor portfolios – and leader of the NP in the Transvaal, wrote a note to Grobler, objecting to the 'wholly unacceptable thought' that Coloured and Indian ministers would co-rule over him and fellow-whites.

In reply, Grobler disputed Treurnicht's interpretation, but added a postscript:

Doctor, I would also like very much to know your view on the idea that at any price we have got to associate the Coloureds as a bloc of 2.5 million with whites, in order to broaden our own power-base and not to surrender them to a 'black power' situation.[29]

This was an artless confirmation of what the Nationalists had strenuously denied, namely that the principal aim of the new system was what Slabbert called 'co-optive domination' of these non-African minorities as a means of shoring up white rule.[30]

When details of the dispute became public, it was immediately apparent that a major row was in the offing. Treurnicht, who had no stomach for confrontations, did not realise how serious it was. He had written the letter without informing Botha, probably to place his objections on record for use in future debates. It is also likely that as Transvaal leader – the second most powerful position in the NP – he reckoned that he was in a good position to succeed Botha, and thereby take control of the entire NP. Botha, on the other hand, disliked Treurnicht and his sly methods; in De Klerk's view, he was in a fighting mood (not unusual for him) and had decided that Treurnicht must go.[31]

Despite attempts to paper over the cracks, matters came to an explosive head at a caucus meeting on 24 February 1982. After heated debate, Fanie Botha, the Minister of Manpower, proposed a motion of full confidence in PW Botha and his right to interpret party policy. One hundred MPs supported the motion, 22 opposed it, and one abstained. The dissidents, who included another minister, Ferdi Hartzenberg, were given eight days to reconsider their position or face expulsion.

Treurnicht now craftily switched the battlefield to his Transvaal stronghold, in which he believed he enjoyed majority support – 20 of the 22 dissidents were Transvaal MPs. His stratagems, however, were finessed by De Klerk and others, who persuaded Treurnicht to convene an Executive Council meeting for 26 February. Unknown to Treurnicht, Botha was in Pretoria on that day, and De Klerk and his colleagues secretly invited him to attend as national leader. 'It took the wind right out of the sails of Treurnicht and his supporters.' Eventually, when matters came to a vote, they were trounced by 172 votes to 36, and Treurnicht's leadership was finished. Shortly after, De Klerk was unanimously elected as Transvaal leader, his springboard for the succession to Botha.[32]

Hostilities commenced almost immediately: the Conservative Party was formed on 20 March at a boisterous rally in Pretoria attended by some 7 000 people. Treurnicht had lost the battle inside the NP, but it seemed that the racist politics of the CP gave it huge growth potential in times of recession and (from 1984) militant black opposition. The split was far more serious than the breakaway of the HNP in 1969: that was a mere *afskilfering* (flaking), and the rough, crude style of the HNP put off many who otherwise were sympathetic to its resolute advocacy of white domination. With the suave Treurnicht as leader, the CP was a far more formidable threat, and the effects of the split were apparent everywhere in Afrikaner society, from the Broederbond down to church councils and school boards in local communities. There was also a widespread sense that rightwingers 'eventually always triumphed in Afrikaner politics', although this had not invariably been so in Afrikaner history.[33]

The 1977 election had put the NP in what seemed an impregnable position, with 134 seats out of 164 – the biggest parliamentary victory recorded since 1910; all 58 HNP candidates were heavily defeated. In 1981, despite losing a few seats, the NP retained a commanding majority, with 131 seats out of 165. There were, however, some disquieting indications of rightwing advances: the HNP, while not winning a single seat, significantly increased the number of votes cast for it, from some 30 000 in 1977 to nearly 200 000, or from 3.3 per cent of the vote to 14.1 per cent. Moreover, Connie Mulder's National Conservative Party, which had positioned itself to the right of the NP (and would later be absorbed by the CP), won 2.5 per cent of the vote. It was also true that *verkramptes*, who had busily been white-anting the NP and other Afrikaner institutions, had strengthened their presence in the ranks of the NP MPs, an estimated 20 being sympathetic to Treurnicht's views.

The split of 1982 was perhaps the unavoidable consequence of the growing diversification of Afrikaner society. Urbanisation, growing secularisation, greater educational opportunities, and widespread but unevenly distributed prosperity had all contributed to increasing internal diversity, to the point where a single party could no longer accommodate all Afrikaner interests. Moreover, since the time of Verwoerd and the coming of the Republic in 1961, détente had been sought with English-speaking whites – with some electoral success: since the 1966 election an estimated 25 per cent of English-speakers had regularly supported the NP. The ideological acceptance of both white sections as constituting a 'white nation' meant that thumping an Afrikaner nationalist drum was no longer a prudent strategy; and in any case, for the rising generations of Afrikaners the old animosities had lost much of their sharpness. Nevertheless, the cultural commissars and other *verkramptes* who retained a mistrust of the perfidious English sought to mount a flanking operation as the 'true' custodians of Afrikaner culture and political traditions. It was a classic case of ethnic outbidding that would receive a major fillip from the breakaway

CP. Floors van Jaarsveld, a leading historian (and a target of *verkrampte* wrath), observed in 1979 that

> ... the old Afrikaner nationalism is now a White nationalism, albeit under Afrikaner leadership. That is why there is so much talk about preserving Afrikaner culture, so much calling up the old myths ... . Afrikaners have been overtaken by the past, and are hesitating to face the future.[34]

The rightwing revolt signalled cracks in the inter-class, urban–rural coalition that had been constructed by an earlier generation of Afrikaner nationalists. The HNP's support-base was largely a mix of working-class Afrikaners and poorer farmers. Its leaders launched regular vitriolic attacks on the Afrikaner *geldmag* (money-power) for its alleged liberal tendencies and for collaborating with its English-speaking counterparts. Rising prosperity had lifted the ratio of Afrikaner per capita incomes to those of English-speakers from 47.8:100 in 1946 to 69.9:100 in 1970; but, despite perceptions to the contrary, income inequality among Afrikaners had widened only marginally.[35]

From 1977 onwards, however, the economy ran into difficulties, and it was widely reckoned that white living standards were declining by 1 per cent per annum. Negative growth of GDP was recorded in 1977 and again in 1982 and 1983. Double-digit inflation and high interest rates became entrenched. The elaborate system of subsidies and other support for commercial agriculture had steadily been stripped away, and farming became an increasingly precarious occupation. An analysis by the University of South Africa's Bureau of Market Research showed that between 1975 and 1980 real personal income per head for whites had declined by 4,4 per cent, whereas that for Africans had risen by 3,3 per cent.[36] Excessive government spending and a decline in the value of the currency aggravated the developing economic crisis.

If the proximate cause of the rightwing revolt was an ideological one, tougher economic times fuelled it. It was easier for rightwingers to invoke the old canard that 'too much was being spent on blacks', and galling for them to learn, according to official figures, that the average wage paid to Africans in the non-agricultural sector had risen from R476 p.a. in 1970 to R2 253 in 1980, an average annual increase of 16,8 per cent, which was far higher than that of whites – although African wages were coming off a very low base and the absolute differentials remained large.[37]

Johann van Rooyen's analysis showed that there was a significant correlation between incomes and support for the CP:

The CP's support declined almost proportionally with the increase
in income per category: among Afrikaners it declined from 39 percent in the lowest income category to 23 percent in the highest.

But, as he suggests, an explanation solely in terms of class did not account for the many Afrikaners from higher income and educational levels
who also supported the CP.[38] The nostrums of Verwoerd retained their
appeal for many, regardless of class.

Apart from class, provincialism was another contributing factor to support for the rightwing. Both the CP and the HNP were strongest in the
rural and mining areas of the Transvaal and Orange Free State, as future
election results would confirm. In the Northern Transvaal especially, white
rural and urban areas were in close proximity to national and homeland
boundaries, and the enormous preponderance of Africans over whites
in a situation of deteriorating security in neighbouring Zimbabwe (as
Rhodesia became in 1980) and in South Africa itself created a frontier-like
atmosphere. In a unique empirical study of white farmers in the north-
western Transvaal, Pierre Hugo found that, apart from chronic financial
problems and intermittent devastating droughts, they

> ... saw themselves surrounded by politically hostile black states,
> whose public pronouncements made no secret of their determination
> to play a role in the demise of white minority rule in South Africa.[39]

Their sense of vulnerability was heightened during late 1985 and 1986
when MK made a concerted attempt to attack white farmers in border
areas by means of landmines, which claimed several lives, including those
of farm labourers.

An opinion poll conducted shortly after its formation in March 1982
showed that the CP already had the support of 18,3 per cent of the electorate; and if the (reduced) support for the HNP were added, over 20 per
cent favoured the rightwing. It seemed ominous. Lawrence Schlemmer,
however, showed that when placed in perspective the apparently burgeoning rightwing could be contained by strong leadership and a determination to confront it:

> [T]he government could be notably more venturesome in embark-
> ing upon reforms that went beyond minor tinkerings with the ap-
> paratus of structural racial inequality. The emergence of a vocifer-
> ous right wing does not contradict this tendency; although still a
> formidable political force – despite its persistently harking back to

obsolete values – demographically the right is shrinking. Previously it had lodged within the protective fold of the governing party; but Mr Botha's initiatives temporarily moved the weight of the party toward the centre, and the right wing, thus exposed, appeared at first glance more significant. The comparatively small size of the group that was prepared fully to support Dr Treurnicht, however, showed that beliefs about the extent of the right wing's influence within the party were somewhat exaggerated.[40]

Schlemmer nevertheless warned that further (ostensibly) liberalising moves would exacerbate the fracturing of Afrikaner unity, and therefore be unacceptable to the NP leadership. *Volkskeuring* (fracturing of the *volk*) was a traumatic experience for Afrikaner nationalists, many of whom recalled the split between Hertzog and Malan in 1934 and the fragmentation of the movement in the early 1940s. The breakaway of the CP in 1982 had contradictory consequences: on the one hand, there was fear that reforms would provide grist to the CP mill; on the other, the departure of Treurnicht and his acolytes removed a millstone from the NP's neck.

Electoral challenges aplenty occurred during 1983. Three by-elections were held in Transvaal constituencies in May, after an imprudent challenge by a Nationalist minister was accepted by the CP as a trial of strength. The minister in question, Fanie Botha, held his Soutpansberg seat by a humiliatingly slashed majority; Treurnicht, who had resigned his Waterberg constituency to take up the challenge, held it despite a substantial share of the vote going to the HNP; but in the elite Pretoria constituency of Waterkloof, the NP won easily, even slightly increasing its majority. The results confirmed the general impression that the Northern Transvaal was a CP stronghold, whereas in middle- to upper-middle-class areas with Afrikaner majorities the NP was relatively safe.

The real trial of strength came in November 1983, in a (white) referendum called by PW Botha in fulfilment of an earlier undertaking to refer any major constitutional change to the electorate. The new Constitution had been enacted into law in September; now voters were called upon to decide whether it should be implemented. In a rancorous campaign the NP, supported by the New Republic Party (the fast-dwindling successor to the United Party), called for a 'yes' vote, while the CP and HNP – joined, ironically, by the liberal Progressive Federal Party – urged their supporters to vote 'no'. Much of the business community (with the notable exception of Harry Oppenheimer, chairman of the giant Anglo American Corporation) lent their weight to the 'yes' campaign, insisting, against all the evidence, that, for all its faults, the new Constitution was 'a step in the right direction' and that a 'no' victory would be hugely damaging to South Africa's economic interests and to the cause of reform generally because it would play into the hands of the CP. It was widely argued that the Constitution represented the limit to which the political constraints on the NP permitted it to go. Moreover, according formally equal status to Coloureds and Indians was, in spite of the pervasive white veto, a historic breach of the colour divide. Much of the press, English- and Afrikaans-language alike, supported these arguments even while pointing out the Constitution's shortcomings. The South African Broadcasting Corporation pulled out all the stops in marketing the new Constitution: it had long been little more than a mouthpiece of the NP; its coverage of the campaign plumbed new depths of partisanship.

For the CP and other rightwing organisations the Constitution was the thin end of the wedge: any dilution of the principle of exclusive white sovereignty spelt the beginning of the end of white rule. Lacking the support of a significant newspaper and being regularly vilified by the SABC made it difficult for the rightwing to get its message across.

The PFP was similarly handicapped, and although Van Zyl Slabbert fought a vigorous and principled campaign, many of its supporters succumbed to blandishments that the Constitution was a 'step in the right direction'. Arguments that the exclusion of Africans would have a dangerously polarising effect, that the new system was actually the constitutionalisation of apartheid, and that excessive powers were being vested in the hands of the State President were all true, but made little impact on supporters who were eager to clutch at any supposedly reformist straw. In a rueful account of the beating the PFP took, Slabbert wondered what alchemy would make the Constitution work:

> I could never quite put my finger on it when reading the enthusiastic supporters of the Yes vote who condemned the constitution. Phrases such as 'it depends on goodwill on all sides for it to work', 'the confusion created by the obvious shortcomings will unleash new forces for change', 'the Nats can never go back after this', seemed to bring comfort to them, but there was never any coherent analysis to back this up or even the slightest empirical evidence to support it. It was thumbsucking and wishful thinking on an impressive scale.[41]

The results of the referendum were an overwhelming victory for PW Botha and the 'yes' campaign: 76 per cent of the electorate voted, nearly 66 per cent voting 'yes' and 33,53 per cent voting 'no'. Estimates suggested that 90 per cent of the 'no' votes came from the right wing. Of the 15 voting districts into which the country was divided for purposes of the referendum, only one, Pietersburg, in the Northern Transvaal, returned a (narrow) majority of 'no' votes. If any comfort were to be derived from the outcome it was that Schlemmer was possibly correct in maintaining that there was a ceiling to the potential growth of the rightwing.

Referenda were not held for the Coloured and Indian categories, a decision that reflected Nationalist fears that either or both would reject participation, and thereby scupper the new system. Prospective Coloured and Indian participants either welcomed or acquiesced in this decision since referenda would be hugely convulsive affairs in communities that were politically fragmented to the extent that it was impossible to determine who, in either case, were the 'real' political leaders. The (Coloured) Labour Party, led by Allan Hendrickse, a Port Elizabeth clergyman, was pivotal in the decision to proceed directly to elections for the (Coloured) House of Representatives.

The Labour Party, founded in 1966, was firmly anti-apartheid, but declined to follow the 'anti-collaborationist' approach of boycotting government-initiated representative institutions that had been a powerful strand in Coloured politics in the Western Cape. It had, accordingly, served in the Coloured Persons' Representative Council, but disenchantment with its effectiveness had soon set in. There was widespread expectation that the party would decline to participate in the Tricameral Parliament, but, although highly critical of the Constitution and continuing to affirm its commitment to an inclusive, non-racial democracy, its national congress decided in January 1983 that it would participate. Hendrickse had concluded that PW Botha was genuine in his reformist moves, and, moreover, that other strategies of resistance were futile: 'We believe one should fight where one can be seen and heard.'[42] It seemed, furthermore, that Chris Heunis, the Minister of Constitutional Development and Planning and the government's marketer-in-chief of the new system, had twisted Hendrickse's arm to accept direct elections to the new Parliament, thereby eliminating the need for a referendum. A further consideration in persuading the Labour Party to participate was that they would lose their salaries should they boycott the new system, but by participating they would earn the same as white MPs.

The elections to the Coloured and Indian Houses were little short of farcical. The Labour party won 76 out of the 80 elected seats for the House of Representatives in a poll in which only 30,9 per cent of registered voters voted. The National People's Party, led by Amichand Rajbansi, led by one seat in the House of Delegates, giving it 18 out of the 40 elected seats, in a poll in which only 20,29 per cent of registered voters voted. In both cases the number of registered voters was substantially lower than the numbers who, by virtue of age, would have been eligible to register as voters – which showed that the campaign to boycott voting had been preceded by large-scale refusal to register.

Little need be said about the actual operation of the new Constitution. Slabbert's Nationalist interlocutor who predicted that 'the bloody thing' would not work was correct. Consensus politics, supposedly the system's operating principle, was more honoured in the breach than in the observance, and the deadlock-breaking mechanism, in the form of the NP-dominated President's Council, had to be invoked on several occasions.

Both Hendrickse and Rajbansi were appointed to the Cabinet, as ministers without portfolio, but neither survived for more than a few years. Hendrickse's exit stemmed from an episode that indicated the extent of Botha's reforms: during January 1987 Hendrickse and a number of senior members of his party defied the law by going for a swim at a Port Elizabeth beach reserved for whites. This infuriated Botha, whose notoriously short temper appeared to be worsening. He demanded that Hendrickse either issue a public apology, or resign from the Cabinet, or face the (unpalatable) prospect that fresh elections be held for the Coloured House in May, coinciding with 'white' elections. Hendrickse declared that for him and his colleagues the swim had been in accordance with the dictates of their consciences and with party policy, which was implacably opposed to discrimination. But, he continued, no affront to Botha had been intended, and he apologised if their action had been interpreted in this way. Botha accepted the apology and Hendrickse remained in the Cabinet. The apology, however circumscribed, seriously damaged Hendrickse's standing as leader of the Labour Party and a spate of resignations followed.   ·

Relations between Botha and Hendrickse continued to deteriorate in 1987. During August Botha lost his temper in the course of a debate in the Coloured House, after being subjected to severe criticism. He launched what De Klerk called a 'personal and humiliating attack' on Hendrickse.[43] Hendrickse lashed back shortly thereafter, declaring that Botha's behaviour resembled that of 'a rat trapped in a corner'.[44] This was too much for Botha, who dropped him from the Cabinet.

Rajbansi's career as a minister ended ignominiously: during 1988 he was suspended from Parliament after a committee of the Indian House found that he had been guilty of misusing public funds. Further evidence of Rajbansi's corrupt behaviour was produced by a commission headed by a retired judge, who recommended that he should never again be appointed to an official or semi-official post. He was thereupon dismissed from the Cabinet.[45]

* * *

Ideally, constitutions should provide an institutional framework for governance and for the effective management of conflict. Even on its own terms
the Tricameral Constitution achieved neither. The interdependent relationship among all groups in South Africa made the distinction between
'own' and 'general' affairs senseless. Had the distinctions been cultural,
and not racial, a case might have been made for giving cultural groups some
autonomous say in regulating their own cultural affairs. The Coloured
people, however, were neither culturally distinctive nor culturally homogeneous, although some 80 per cent were Afrikaans-speaking and many
belonged to the Coloured branch of the NGK – the Sendingkerk. Nor,
given their heterogeneous origins, could they be described as a 'racial'
group. Yet it was central to the Constitution that 'race', as determined by
the Population Registration Act, was the organising principle.

   The system did, however, produce some unanticipated consequences:
politicians from the different Houses were forced to listen to one another and to debate one another, sometimes in the joint debates in the
large new chamber (known by cynics as the 'Great Hall of the People'),
and sometimes when white ministers spoke in the Coloured or Indian
House. For many white politicians it was a sobering experience. FW de
Klerk writes:

> There was genuine political interaction and accountability. White
> cabinet ministers had to report to the coloured and Indian houses
> on their activities. They were exposed to criticism and indignation
> over the injustices of apartheid. They were also taken to task over
> the remaining elements of discrimination. Sometimes government
> ministers were shouted down and often they had to listen to moving
> protestations and views that they had never before experienced or
> heard so directly. This regular contact, debate and interaction broad-
> ened the attitudes of all those involved.[46]

An even more significant unintended consequence was the massive alienation that their exclusion from the system provoked among Africans.
The argument used in the referendum campaign, that Africans had their
own political institutions, namely bantustans and local authorities in
the 'white' areas, was absurd. By the early 1980s over 40 per cent of the
22 million-strong African population lived in the 'white' areas, substantially outnumbering the combined population of Coloureds, Indians and
whites. Even moderate bantustan leaders expressed strong opposition to
the exclusion of Africans. More than any other single factor, the outrage caused by the Tricameral Parliament generated forces that led to the

downfall of apartheid. In a perverse way it was indeed 'a step in the right direction'.

*　　*　　*

From the NP's point of view, the supposed accommodation of Coloureds and Indians forced the question of African political rights to the top of the agenda. Increased unrest, guerrilla attacks by MK, and growing international isolation accompanied by the tightening of sanctions were inexorably pushing Botha and his government to acknowledge that the time for decisive action had come. There was also the looming question of the continued incarceration of Nelson Mandela, by now the most celebrated political prisoner on earth. What if he died in prison? At 64 years of age in 1982 this was not an unrealistic possibility; and the potential consequences could be devastating. Tough character that he was, Mandela refused release unless it were unconditional; but, as Botha recognised, he could not be released into a political vacuum without possible destabilising effects. In short, he could not be released unless it were into a negotiating process, and this implied, in effect, the involvement of the ANC. Botha's thinking was far off this prospect.

Early in 1983 Botha appointed a Special Cabinet Committee (SCC) charged with the task of examining options for the political future of Africans. It was chaired by Chris Heunis, the minister responsible for constitutional issues, and included De Klerk and other senior ministers. The SCC faced a difficult task: it accepted at the outset that the old formulation of separate development had had some success, but that it could not be the complete solution since no more than 40 per cent of the African population (an optimistic projection) could ultimately be accommodated in the bantustans. Moreover, it acknowledged that attempts to link urban Africans with their supposed homelands might work satisfactorily for certain people in certain areas, but that it was not universally applicable.[47]

The SCC made heavy weather of its work. Its point of departure was the primacy of the statutory group as the building block of any future constitutional development: 'group interests, especially those of Whites, were the first condition of anything that the NP was prepared to accept regarding blacks [Africans].' But there were differences of opinion in the NP about the extent to which the group approach could serve as a basis for further reform. An 'own community life' based upon the Group Areas Act was deemed to be a cornerstone of any new constitution, but even this sacred cow was challenged within the NP. The first four years of the SCC's deliberations achieved little, and Heunis was plunged into gloom, declaring that further reform was doomed if it was directed by a cumbersome committee of people with underlying political differences.[48] According to Heunis's son, Jan (who was chief state law adviser in the presidency), Heunis (senior) was denied permission to meet Mandela, evidently because Botha was anxious to keep contact with him in the hands of securocrats – the term used to describe ministers and officials from the security and intelligence departments.[49]

It was against a background of mounting tumult in the country and divided counsels inside the NP that Botha delivered the so-called Rubicon speech to an NP Congress on 15 August 1985. It was an epoch-making speech whose catastrophic impact probably hastened the end of apartheid, as well as provoking more opposition to Botha inside his party. In preparing the speech Botha asked for, and received, inputs from Heunis and others, including the Department of Foreign Affairs. A senior official of the latter, Carl von Hirschberg, drafted a strongly reformist contribution. Minister RF 'Pik' Botha and his officials spent the period immediately prior to 15 August whipping up expectations that PW Botha would announce a major breakthrough in reform, which would have been welcomed by President Reagan, Margaret Thatcher and other Western leaders who were under strong pressure to impose sanctions.

News of the supposed impending breakthrough inevitably leaked to the media, which added to the buzz of anticipation. PW Botha was infuriated by the leaks, and demanded to know who had been responsible. His fury caused him utterly to misread the situation: he was principally a party man, and the tone of the speech he ultimately delivered suggested that it was addressed mostly to the party faithful, with little regard to the millions inside and outside the country who watched it on television. The speech was Botha at his truculent, defiant, finger-wagging worst. It began with a tirade against those who had dared to anticipate, even prescribe, what he should say, followed by an onslaught on the 'irresponsibilities and destructive actions of barbaric Communist agitators and even murderers who perpetrate the most cruel deeds against fellow South Africans'. This was vintage Botha.

There would be no 'abdication and suicide' by whites and other minority groups. While prepared to negotiate, this readiness should not be mistaken for weakness. Negotiation would involve 'letting the people speak through their leaders'; there would be give and take – 'we will not prescribe and we will not demand'. But there were limitations. Botha repeated what he had said previously: he would consider releasing Nelson Mandela provided that he gave a commitment not to plan, instigate or commit acts of violence for political ends. He went on to quote from the judge and the prosecutor in the Rivonia trial, with the clear intent of portraying Mandela as a man of violence and a communist.

Beneath this volcanic eruption nuggets of reformist sentiment lay buried. Botha accepted:

- the economic interdependence of all population groups;
- property ownership rights for Africans outside the bantustans;
- the principle that any future constitutional dispensation providing for participation by all South Africans should be negotiated;
- that it would not be possible to accommodate the political aspirations of the various population groups and communities in a 'known defined political system'; and
- that while the granting and acceptance of independence by bantustans formed part of the solution, independence could not be forced on any community. Those bantustans rejecting independence would remain part of the South African nation and should be accommodated within political institutions inside South Africa.

Several of these points were vague and unspecific – reflecting the inability thus far of the SCC to reach agreement – but collectively they spelled unmistakably the demise of apartheid as anything like a coherent ideology. Equally unmistakably, Botha was determined not to give up white control.

Predictably, Botha rejected one-man-one-vote in a unitary system. A fourth chamber for Africans tacked on to the Tricameral Parliament was also unacceptable since the Tricameral system was carefully calibrated to the numerical proportions of the participating groups, and the addition of an African house would upset effective control by the white chamber.[50]

The Rubicon speech was an unmitigated disaster: De Klerk called it 'probably the greatest communication disaster in South African history', adding that the ensuing collapse in the value of the currency meant that it had perhaps cost more than a million rand per word.[51] By 28 August the Rand had declined to 34 US cents, its lowest-ever value. Twenty years later, in response to a question about why PW Botha had not announced far-reaching reforms, Pik Botha said: 'It remains a mystery to me – if you find out, come and tell me too.'

The damage caused was compounded six months later by the torpedoing of the Commonwealth Eminent Persons Group's mission, which attempted to broker a settlement. The EPG arose out of the Commonwealth meeting in Nassau in October 1985, which adopted an Accord that threatened tougher action against South Africa unless the government dismantled apartheid and initiated a process of dialogue with a view to establishing a non-racial and representative government. The EPG, consisting of seven persons, was co-chaired by Malcolm Fraser, a former Prime Minister of Australia, and Olusegun Obasanjo, a former head of the military government of Nigeria.

Botha initially refused to permit the EPG's visit, deeming it 'uncalled for interference'.[52] Nor, he claimed, was he able to reconcile the condemnation of South Africa at Nassau with the proposed attempt to promote dialogue. The British Prime Minister, Margaret Thatcher, was dismayed by Botha's reaction, pointing out that she had stood virtually alone in warding off sanctions. Botha expressed sympathy for her position, but insisted that allowing the EPG would be a sign of South Africa's buckling under pressure, whereupon 'the hunt would be on'. Thatcher reacted sharply, pointing out that 'it would be infinitely more damaging to South Africa's future interests if you were to refuse to have anything to do with the Group'. Botha eventually acquiesced, informing the co-chairmen on 19 December 1985 that he was prepared to approach the initiative 'in a constructive manner'. He warned them that if they saw themselves as a pressure group seeking to force concessions from the government this could do a lot of damage; but if they confined themselves 'in an unprejudiced way' to fostering peaceful dialogue, it could serve a useful purpose.

For its part, the ANC-in-exile was sceptical and wary, Tambo fearing that the initiative might lead to a reduction of pressure on South Africa. 'White South Africa, Botha didn't like it – Pik or PW – but black South Africa didn't like it either,' according to Shridath Ramphal, the Commonwealth Secretary-General.[53] Despite the unpromising, even grudging attitudes, the EPG were able to gain the confidence of many of those whom they interviewed in their shuttle diplomacy during February, March and April 1986. They spoke to a wide cross-section of politicians, businesspeople, clergy and NGOs, including Mandela, whom they were allowed to visit. Mandela stressed that Tambo was the leader of the ANC and that they should see him (which they did), since the views he, Mandela, expressed were his personal views – 'They don't even represent the views of my colleagues here in prison.' Mandela made it clear that he favoured discussions between the ANC and the government. After the meeting he sent word to both government and Tambo: 'I wanted the government to see that under the right circumstances we would talk, and I wanted Oliver to know that my position and his were the same.'[54] His comment foreshadowed what would be the recurring problem of ensuring that his advocacy of negotiations did not evoke suspicions that he was trying to cut a deal behind his comrades' backs.

Predictably, talks with government ministers were sticky. The EPG were sceptical of the government's intentions, concluding that:

> Their actions up to this point do not justify any claim that apartheid is being dismantled. The argument that the considerable change which we have seen is directed to that end founders, irretrievably, on the rocks of 'group rights' and white control.

In response to the government's demand that the ANC renounce (and not merely temporarily suspend) violence as a means of attaining political goals, the EPG commented:

> To ask the ANC or other parties, all of them far weaker than the Government, to renounce violence for all time here and now would be to put them in a position of having to rely absolutely on the Government's intentions and determination to press through the process of negotiation .... It was neither possible nor reasonable to have people foreswear the only power available to them should the Government walk away from the negotiating table.

The EPG were impressed with 'the overwhelming desire in the country for a non-violent negotiated settlement'. They were satisfied that if there were the necessary political will on all sides a negotiated settlement could be attempted. Accordingly, they composed a 'Possible Negotiating Concept' that was forwarded to the government on 13 March. Shrewdly, the EPG sought to hoist the government on its own petard by matching some elements of the Concept with indications they had received from the government. They suggested that the government might give serious consideration to the following steps by declaring that it:

(i) is not in principle against the release of Nelson Mandela and similar prisoners;

(ii) is not opposed in principle to the unbanning of any organizations;

(iii) is prepared to enter negotiations with the acknowledged leaders of the people of South Africa;

(iv) is committed to removal of discrimination, not only from the statute books but also from South African society as a whole;

(v) is committed to ending white domination;

(vi) will not prescribe who may represent black communities in negotiations on a new constitution for South Africa;

(vii) is prepared to negotiate on an open agenda.[55]

More than a month later, Pik Botha replied in terms that the EPG found disappointing, since he appeared to suggest that his government had already done much of what was required of it – which the EPG did not accept. But they were nevertheless encouraged by the use of the term 'suspension' of violence, as compared with 'renunciation', on which the government had previously insisted. It was a slender straw to clutch at. A subsequent meeting with Pik Botha showed a hardening of the government's attitude. On 15 May 1986 – four days before the raids that torpedoed the EPG's mission – PW Botha confirmed the hardened attitude, warning against 'interference by outside bodies', and limiting co-operation in the quest for solutions to those 'who reject violence as a means of achieving political goals'. 'Suspension' had been dropped.

Probably, the exuberant Pik Botha had oversold or overestimated the government's flexibility, giving the EPG the opportunity to weave together stray 'indications' (its term) from ministers (notably Pik Botha, one suspects) into a 'Concept' that in its totality went well beyond what PW Botha and the securocrats were prepared to accept.

Several senior Cabinet ministers, including Pik Botha, were hopeful that the initiative would bear fruit. Pik Botha was especially optimistic that an agreement could be reached on Monday, 19 May: a meeting would be held to agree to a formula for the release of Mandela and the unbanning of the ANC. Monday came, and with it the news that early on that morning the South African Defence Force (SADF) had carried out raids on neighbouring capitals, Gaborone (Botswana), Harare (Zimbabwe) and Lusaka (Zambia). Clearly, these attacks – what cynical critics called 'pre-emptive hot-pursuit' – had been planned some time before. They were followed shortly after by a hit on an alleged ANC home in Swaziland, and attacks on Soviet and Cuban ships in an Angolan port. Ostensibly, the raids on the capitals were a reprisal for an MK attack on Sasol, the oil-from-coal refinery, but few believed this.

The timing of the raids was hardly a coincidence: as the EPG said in its report, 'It was all too plain that, while talking to the Group about negotiations and peaceful solutions, the Government had been planning these armed attacks.' It concluded that 'concerted action of an effective kind' – implying tough economic sanctions – had to be considered, warning that 'such action may offer the last opportunity to avert what could be the worst bloodbath since the Second World War.'[56]

What caused Botha to blow the EPG out of the water, thereby dismaying his few remaining friends in the international community? Chester Crocker, the United States' Assistant Secretary of State for African Affairs in President Reagan's administration, believed that: 'Something snapped in the man; xenophobic anger overtook his common sense.'[57] It was apparent that there were divisions in Botha's government: several re-formist ministers and senior officials in the Department of Foreign Affairs entertained hopes that the EPG could encourage a more credible reform process that would lead to inclusive negotiations. The hardliners in the Cabinet wanted to defer any possible negotiations until the domestic in-surrection and the armed struggle had been comprehensively defeated. Moreover, the security forces needed little encouragement to mount raids on alleged ANC bases.[58]

PW Botha himself never liked the idea of 'foreign meddling', and may well have played along with the EPG initiative to gain some favour with Margaret Thatcher and President Reagan. Botha, moreover, was dismayed and infuriated by the international community's refusal to acknowledge the extent of his reforms. In the event, the EPG debacle was a seminal episode in Botha's presidency. As Thatcher predicted, international con-demnation and intensified sanctions were the consequence. Increasingly, the Botha government was seen not only as intransigent, but also incor-rigible. It was no coincidence that Botha's reform efforts, some of which had been significant, ran out of steam in 1986.

In evidence to the TRC, Pik Botha claimed that the EPG 'came closer to success than most people realise'. The raids had not been discussed at any meeting where he had been present. Magnus Malan, Minister of Defence at the time, said much the same thing, adding that the SADF had wished to launch attacks on the capitals in late April 1986, which PW Botha had approved.[59] The attacks, however, were postponed until mid-May, in fact until the very day that the EPG and the government were due to make a major breakthrough. In his autobiography Malan claims that the SADF was not aware of the meeting with the EPG and that it 'was not a factor in his considerations'.[60] PW Botha, however, must have been aware of the timing.

It was also a low point in the relationship between the securocrats (including PW Botha) and the Department of Foreign Affairs, many of whose senior members had grave misgivings about official policies, and were, in turn, accused of 'less than loyal support' by PW Botha.

The failure of the EPG's mission, ironically, let the ANC and its inter-nal surrogates off the hook. Mandela had gone further than many of his colleagues, in exile or in prison, were prepared to go as far as potential negotiations were concerned. Frankly, they were not ready for them. In a shrewd assessment, Patti Waldmeir observes that the ANC's judgement was that 'the balance of forces had tipped decisively in their favour as the township revolt gathered pace; they were not ready for compromise'. She cites Tambo's outrage on being told by Obasanjo that they were out of their minds to suppose that they could defeat the government.[61]

Despite their failure, the EPG produced a report that was a balanced, essentially fair, account of South Africa's politics in the mid-1980s. Their labours had effectively pin-pointed the prerequisites for potentially successful negotiations that forced the South African government, or at least its genuinely reformist component, to confront the realities of the unfolding situation; and by the same token, they forced the ANC and the UDF to think more seriously about the appalling costs that 'seizure of power' – chimerical aim though it was – might exact. Conflicts have to 'ripen' before they become amenable to possible negotiated accommodations. The critical part of the ripening process is the mutual recognition by the conflicting parties that neither could win on its own terms. The government and the ANC still had some distance to travel.

*　　*　　*

To what extent Botha's intemperate behaviour was a symptom of the impending strokes that he was to suffer in 1988 and 1989 is not known. The first stroke was hushed up; the second, on 18 January 1989, which was severe, precipitated his eventual resignation. Strokes occur after a period of damage to brain cells, and early warning signs commonly include increasingly obsessive concern with order and the gradual breakdown of emotional control. Botha had long been notable for his irascibility and volcanic temper, which were said to have been capable of reducing even ministers to tears. It was not for nothing that he was known as '*Die Groot Krokodil*' (the Big Crocodile), and Tuynhuys, the presidential office in Cape Town, as *Kruithuis* (Gunpowder House).

Early in his premiership Botha floated the idea of a 'constellation of states of Southern Africa' that would incorporate a confederation of independent states each of which would retain its sovereignty and governmental functions. Any state in the region, including the bantustans, that accepted the need for regional cooperation could become a member. The proposal was stillborn, as far as South Africa's immediate neighbours were concerned: their principal aim was to limit their dependence on South Africa as far as possible. Most, moreover, saw Botha's idea as a transparent attempt to buttress 'white' South Africa with a surrounding ring of weak client states. Whatever the case for regional economic cooperation – and it was a strong one – the political price was too high.

Below the level of national and regional constitutional issues, several initiatives were launched in the early 1980s: in 1982 legislation sought to create African local authorities in the 'white' areas. These were supposed to resemble white local authorities: membership would be elected, but only by citizens of South Africa or of 'independent' bantustans who possessed rights to be in the area – which excluded large numbers of people who did not possess these rights. While the new institutions were accorded real powers, their lack of financial viability undercut any potential they may have possessed for making a difference to the lives of the people they were supposed to represent. In the absence, at that time, of freehold rights for urban Africans, the usual source of local authority income, rateable property, did not exist. A senior official of the Western Transvaal Administration Board, PJ Riekert, expressed the optimistic view, no doubt shared by those in government, that the new institutions would

> ... defuse pent-up frustrations and grievances against administration from Pretoria. Local authorities will affect the daily lives of these [African] people more directly and intimately than the more removed activities of the central government.[62]

No prediction could have been wider of the mark. Elections were held for 29 of the new local governments in November and December 1983. Overall, only a 21 per cent poll was recorded (including a mere 10,7 per cent in Soweto), and even this figure was inflated because many of those eligible to register had not done so. Even moderate organisations declined to participate: Mangosuthu Buthelezi, leader of Inkatha, for example, objected to an official pamphlet which, he claimed, said that the local authorities were a substitute for parliamentary rights, and an adjunct of the reviled tricameral system.[63] This was the essential truth; and few credible African leaders would be drawn into a system that was premised on the denial of effective political rights at the centre. Moreover, as the violence that erupted in September 1984 would show, the absence of an adequate financial base was widely perceived by urban communities as an attempt by the state to make the councils themselves responsible for imposing further economic burdens on residents.

Further tinkering with the local authority system occurred in 1985 with the establishment of Regional Services Councils (RSCs) that were to include representatives of local governments of all population groups in regions designated by the Provincial Administration (a central government appointee). The system was aimed at providing certain municipal services, especially bulk services, more cheaply and efficiently. By 1988, 16 such Councils existed (far fewer than the 50 or more originally anticipated) and for the most part they had assumed responsibility for the bulk supply of electricity, water and sewerage services. An important aim was to ensure that infrastructure, facilities and services would be provided in those areas that needed them most – which, in practice, meant urban African townships.

Apart from the benefits of economies of scale and resource allocation to poorer communities, the government claimed that the councils *might* be building blocks for the development of 'power-sharing' at the national level. According to a government publication in 1988:

> It would not be an overstatement to suggest that each RSC is in fact a 'parliament' in miniature in which, for the first time, representatives of all four major population groups meet to decide by consensus on important issues affecting all, including the apportionment of substantial funds collected from taxpayers. If it can be shown at RSC level that consensus politics can work effectively, that representatives of all four population groups can meet and decide together on important issues for the benefit of their region, without one seeking to dominate the other, it would certainly facilitate power sharing at higher levels of government.[64]

It did not work out that way. By 1988 no RSCs had been established in Natal or the KwaZulu homeland, largely because Inkatha rejected the principle: 'they are just another leg of the own affairs and general affairs of the [tricameral] constitution, which Inkatha rejects'.[65] Most blacks took the same view.

A further effort at the same mode of power-sharing occurred in 1985 when provincial councils (elected by whites) were abolished and replaced by multiracial provincial executive committees appointed by the State President. As had happened with RSCs, the new system cut no ice with increasingly militant blacks.

The real significance of RSCs and provincial executive committees was the extent to which they contributed to the massive acceleration in the centralisation of power that occurred in the era of Botha. Pierre du Toit noted:

> Regional service councils represent an elaborate system of control whereby powerholders at central level will gain crucial influence at local level. The system relies ultimately on co-opting subordinate elites into new multi-racial decision-making structures. These elites will have to comply with the rules of the political game dictated by the ruling group at national level – which is politically represented by the National Party.[66]

By 1986, after the abolition of influx control, Botha's reformist impulse ran out of steam. At the beginning of the year he had proposed a 'national statutory council' that would meet under his chairmanship. It was to consist of representatives of the government and of non-independent bantustans, as well as leaders of other African communities and interest groups. Pending a settlement of constitutional issues, the council was to consider and advise on matters of common concern, including proposed legislation. In subsequent speeches Botha elaborated on his proposal: leaders of urban communities would be chosen by the communities themselves; the envisaged council could be the forerunner of a 'state council' that could contribute to the formulation of policy by means of consensus decision-making.

At the same time Botha stated emphatically that he was not prepared to sit around a negotiating table with a gun pointed at his head, the hand-over of power to the revolutionaries being the only item on the agenda. The ANC could participate in the negotiations provided it foreswore violence and ceased to be cat's-paws of the SACP. He would not hand over the country to the tyranny and the 'rotten conditions' (*verrotte toestande*) which the ANC–SACP alliance wanted to impose.[67]

Predictably, proposals for the National Statutory Council (or 'Great Indaba', as Botha thought it might be called) got nowhere. Buthelezi declared it an 'absolute prerequisite' that no serious negotiations could take place until Mandela was released. Likewise, the United Democratic Front, which had become a powerful mass movement and, effectively, the ANC's internal surrogate, rejected the concept: 'We are sure the vote-less people of South Africa will recognise the National Council for the farce that it is, and return it to the dustheap where all the government's other toy telephones and other grandiose schemes lie.'[68]

De Klerk reveals that Heunis, in a desperate attempt to attract more credible African support for the council, had urged Botha to release Mandela, but he would not budge from the conditions he had laid down; nor would Mandela accept anything but unconditional release. In speech after speech Botha berated the ANC for its close ties to the SACP; official publications, the SABC and other bodies spewed forth the same message. A sophisticated pamphlet published in 1986 by the state, *Talking with the ANC ...*, offered a detailed analysis of the SACP's involvement with the ANC, claiming that of the 30 members of the ANC's National Executive Committee appointed in June 1985 no fewer than 23 were also SACP members. It went on to recount how the ANC accepted the SACP's notion of a 'two-stage revolution': the national democratic revolution, in which bourgeois rights and freedoms would be established, followed by the second stage, in which 'capitalist exploitation' is destroyed and replaced by a socialist system. A quotation from the ANC publication *Sechaba* (published in the German Democratic Republic) in September 1985 read:

> We in the ANC know that a *nationalist struggle* and the *socialist struggle* are not one and the same thing, and they do not belong to the same historical period. The two represent two distinct categories of the revolution … . We must not allow our desire for socialism to intoxicate us.

Botha dismissed as 'naïve' the view that the ANC was basically a nationalist organisation, and rejected the argument that there was a parallel between the ANC's attitude to the SACP and the sympathy that some Afrikaners had shown for the Nazis on the principle that 'my enemy's [Britain's] enemy is my friend'. Nor could he understand that the harsh tactics directed against the Communist Party and individual communists, as well as many non-communists, had been counterproductive, giving the SACP and fellow-travellers an enormous propaganda boost as being the most committed opponents of apartheid.

Apart from the considerable power vested in the State President under the Tricameral Constitution, Botha's position was bolstered by two additional factors: the fear that he inspired in Cabinet and NP caucus members, which meant that few dared challenge him; and the centralisation of state power as Botha refined and rationalised the instruments of coercive power in accordance with the requirements of the 'total strategy', the state's response to what it regarded as the communist-inspired 'total onslaught' directed against South Africa. Especially as internal resistance rose in late 1984 and afterwards, the security establishment, comprising principally defence force, police and intelligence personnel (despite rivalries among them), became a powerful pressure group in the administration. It was, in the title of Kenneth W Grundy's book, the militarisation of South African politics.[69]

The focal point of this process was the State Security Council (SSC), originally established by Vorster in 1972, but seldom convened by him. Under Botha, who had been impatient with Vorster's uncoordinated, ad hoc approach to security matters, the SSC assumed major significance, becoming effectively a government within the government, even though it was supposedly only an advisory body. It was chaired by Botha himself and consisted of all ministers in security-related finance and constitutional development, the defence force chiefs, heads of the intelligence agencies, and the directors-general of the line-function departments involved. FW de Klerk, who was co-opted to serve on the SSC in his capacity as one of the senior NP ministers, became a member in the early 1980s.

Although it was ostensibly only an advisory body, the SSC's brief covered all aspects of security – and, given the all-embracing nature of the total strategy, there were few aspects of society that could not be construed as impinging on security. De Klerk, who was soon identified by the 'securocrats' as a dove who could not be trusted with their 'inner secrets' and consequently kept 'out of the loop', soon grew disenchanted with the SSC's activities, which, he said, involved constant interference in the affairs of departments. He confirms the conclusions of many observers:

> Theoretically, the council itself had no decision-making powers and was dependent on subsequent cabinet approval to give effect to its proposals. In practice, it became, in many respects, more powerful than the cabinet. Those occasions when P.W. Botha chose to have Security Council strategies and action plans ratified by the cabinet, often appeared to me to be little more than window-dressing. I disliked being part of a system which I believed was undermining the sound principle of full collective responsibility within the cabinet.[70]

The reach of the total strategy was demonstrated by the introduction in 1979 of the National Security Management System, and the elaboration and refinement of its scope in the violent mid-1980s. James Selfe describes it as 'a militarised bureaucracy, which operates in tandem with the regular civil service to promote the co-ordination of state security action.'[71] Its elaborate structures were premised on the belief that military methods were more effective and quicker than traditional civilian bureaucratic ones.

At the sub-national level were 11 Joint Management Centres (JMCs), each consisting of approximately 60 officials from government departments in the area, usually chaired by a senior police or defence force officer; below were some 60 sub-JMCs and 400 mini-JMCs.

The underlying aim of this complex structure was two-fold: first, to provide an early-warning system for possible flash-points, and to identify and neutralise activists deemed to be 'trouble-makers'; and second, to cut through bureaucratic tangles and swiftly provide amenities or facilities whose absence was a cause of grievances in local communities. This was part of a WHAM or 'Winning Hearts and Minds' strategy. A senior SSC official was quoted as saying of WHAM: 'First we neutralise the enemy, then we win over the people so they will reject the ANC.'[72]

General Magnus Malan, a protégé of Botha who became chief of the defence force in 1976 and Minister of Defence in 1980, defended the system in the following terms:

> The Joint Management System was one of the best systems we ever had .... It allowed us to address a situation like the toilets in Queenstown [in one particular case intelligence reports said a major cause of unrest in Queenstown was a lack of toilet facilities in the black residential areas] or the situation in Alexandra [near Johannesburg], which was at one stage declared a 'liberated' area by the ANC. We [the SADF] approached the Public Works Department and told them they had to rectify the situation. They told us they had no money. 'We don't give two hoots,' we said. 'Find the money and rectify the situation, it's affecting the security of the country.' That was the problem. Other departments didn't realise they were involved in the security of the country. They thought of toilets, full stop. They didn't think how it affected our security.[73]

Botha and the securocrats around him who dominated the administration were sadly mistaken if they believed that providing schools, hospitals, toilets and other facilities – however necessary – could douse the fires of resistance in black communities. Things had progressed too far for palliative measures to have much impact. Moreover, there was little hope of success for the strategy, accepted by Cabinet on 27 March 1985, of driving a wedge between 'the radical minority and the neutral mass'. The document outlining the strategy maintained that those who were responsible for politicising and mobilising the masses were seeking a system that had as its goal the total destruction of the existing order. Incremental adaptations of the system would not satisfy them. It was necessary, therefore, to prevent the further radicalisation of the masses: viable constitutional, economic and social structures and conditions had to be created to draw in 'moderate black opinion-formers'.[74]

In one respect the analysis was correct: incremental tinkerings with the apartheid order, even if of a liberalising nature, not only did not appease the masses or create the political space for 'moderate black opinion-formers' to fill; in fact, they provided encouragement to the militants who interpreted such moves as evidence that the government was being pressurised into making concessions.

The dialectical relationship between liberalising reforms that were intermittently dribbled out and increased resistance from their supposed beneficiaries was acutely noted by De Tocqueville in his study of pre-revolutionary France. His famous remark that 'the most perilous moment for a bad government is one when it seeks to mend its ways' was widely quoted during the Botha era. Few, however, went on to read the subsequent sentences in which he sought to explain why it was precisely in those parts of France where there had been most improvement that popular discontent ran highest. It seemed a paradox:

> Only consummate statecraft can enable a King to save his throne when after a long spell of oppressive rule he sets to improving the lot of his subjects. Patiently endured so long as it seemed beyond redress, a grievance comes to appear intolerable once the possibility of removing it crosses men's minds. For the mere fact that certain abuses have been remedied draws attention to the others and they now appear more galling; people may suffer less, but their sensibility is exacerbated.

In the securocrats' thinking, reform could not be implemented in a climate of protest and violence. Stability had to be enforced, by tough measures if necessary. As the turbulent 1980s unfolded, Botha's government had to focus increasingly on crisis management. From August 1984 onwards protest escalated, often attracting violent responses from the security forces. In the earlier part of the year grievances about the quality of African education and hostility to the inauguration of the Tricameral Constitution and the elections of the Coloured and Indian houses had fuelled protest; but the trigger for sustained protest was the rent increases imposed by African local governments, elected on very low polls, in the PWV (Pretoria-Witwatersrand-Vereeniging) triangle. On 3 Sept 14 people were killed, and by the end of the year the death toll had risen to 149 – or 175 total for the year.[75] By the end of 1987 an estimated 2 681 people had been killed in political violence since September 1984. According to the SAIRR's analysis of the figures for 1986 about 50 per cent of deaths were the result of conflict within black communities, and over 30 per cent were killed by the security forces.[76] The protesters were now targeting local councillors, accelerating the collapse of the local government system. Black police and alleged 'collaborators' and informers were also high on the militants' hit lists.

In July 1985 a state of emergency covering 36 (subsequently 44) magisterial districts was declared, giving the security authorities even more power to detain individuals, ban gatherings and proscribe organisations and publications. A year later the state of emergency was re-imposed on the entire country. It remained in force until 1990, by which time FW de

Klerk was president. During 1986 and 1987 over 3 500 were detained under security legislation. In February 1988 the United Democratic Front and 16 other organisations, mostly affiliates of the UDF, were banned, and the Congress of South African Trade Unions (Cosatu) was prohibited from engaging in political activity.

De Klerk supported these draconian measures, which succeeded in reducing the amount of unrest, but with a growing realisation that heavy-handed efforts to suppress protest did nothing to remove its underlying causes. He writes:

> In the end, the most important effect of the State of Emergency was to force revolutionaries to adopt more realistic perceptions of the balance of power between them and the government. During the anarchic months before June 1986, many of them believed that the tide of internal unrest was irresistible and that further action would soon lead to the revolutionary destruction of the government. By 1988 these perceptions had changed dramatically. The more realistic leaders of the ANC and the internal uprising realised that there could be no quick or easy victory. They also began to accept that a prolonged struggle between them and the government would be so bitter and destructive that there would be little left for anyone to inherit. *This perception was an indispensable pre-condition for the beginning of genuine negotiations.*[77] (Italics added.)

Nelson Mandela was thinking along parallel lines. De Klerk, at this time, was widely believed to be sympathetic to the *verkrampte* cause, an accusation that he vigorously denies: 'If you were leader of the National Party, with Andries Treurnicht ... breathing down your neck, you might even sound like me.'[78] He was nevertheless always careful to uphold the official party line, and also to avoid identification with either wing of the NP. In private, however, his thoughts were changing.

In a comment made in 2006, De Klerk acknowledged that he had often been criticised before becoming President 'for not racing ahead in the pursuit of reform'. He responded:

> Had I done so I would have alienated key players and important constituencies, I would not have become leader of my Party in 1989 and I would not have been able to do the things that I did when I was President. Timing change is of the utmost importance.[79]

Apart from increasing dismay at the failure of apartheid and the injustice it was causing, he had come to recognise the inevitability of negotiating with the ANC. In April 1987 he told the incoming British Ambassador, Robin Renwick, that if he had his way, South Africa would not make the same mistake that had been made in white-ruled Rhodesia, namely 'leaving it much too late to negotiate with the real black leaders'.[80]

Several Nationalists held similar views, but to voice them brought thunderous disapproval down upon their heads. Wynand Malan, a *verligte* young NP MP, for example, told a closed meeting of an Afrikaner organisation (possibly the Broederbond) that it was time to abolish all apartheid laws and to begin negotiating to give full political rights to black South Africans. This was reported to Botha, whereafter Malan was disciplined by the NP caucus. No other NP MP publicly supported Malan, although in the lobby there were murmurings that 'what Wynand said was absolutely correct, it's only his timing that was wrong'.[81] (Malan subsequently resigned from the NP and fought and won his seat as an independent.)

Equally revealing was the repudiation of a comment by Pik Botha at a press conference in February 1986 that, under specified circumstances, he would be prepared to serve under a black President. His explanation was that his remark was the only logical conclusion that could be drawn if the putative President were appointed in terms of structures that had been jointly negotiated. Even so, this was manna for the CP, which immediately wanted to know if what Botha had said was in line with NP policy. PW Botha was thereupon forced to intervene and repudiate his Foreign Affairs minister, declaring that speculation about a future State President was 'purely hypothetical and confusing and did not represent the party's policy'. He added that no minister of the governing party had any right to compromise his party without prior consultation.[82] It was a humiliation for Pik Botha, who was later to say that he had come close to resigning.

Despite the presence of a younger generation of Nationalist MPs who were impatient for the government to get on with reform, the mainstream of the caucus was preoccupied with the threat posed by the CP, which had won six more seats in the 1987 election, raising its numbers to 23 (compared with the NP's 133), and replacing the liberal Progressive Federal Party as the official opposition. At a *bosberaad* (literally 'bush consultation') of ministers and deputy ministers held in March 1988, Kobus Meiring, recently appointed as Deputy Minister of Foreign Affairs, observed with dismay that far too much time was spent on the threat from the right, which had recently wrested two previously safe seats from the NP in by-elections. There was general agreement that one of the major reasons for the CP's success was the non-enforcement of the Group Areas Act and the consequent growth of so-called 'grey areas'. One deputy minister shocked Meiring by boasting of his successful efforts to have a racially mixed couple removed from a 'white' area in his constituency.

This was too much for Meiring, who took his courage in both hands and deplored the lack of 'love and compassion' in what had been said. He proceeded to cite examples of the serious injustices caused by the Act. No one else stood up to agree with his argument, causing him to fear that his political career was about to come to an abrupt end. To his amazement PW Botha fixed his penetrating eyes on him and said: 'Colleagues, everything that this colleague has just said is true and we will have to work on it.'[83] But here was the problem: what could 'improve' or ameliorate an intrinsically unjust law like the Group Areas Act? It was the dilemma faced by all would-be reformers of apartheid: a rotten system could not be reformed; it could only be abolished. This was precisely what the black opposition kept saying. The days of incremental change were over.

Reference has been made to the growth of the securocrats' influence under Botha. As the effective locus of influence shifted to the SSC, Botha grew more isolated, tending to receive only information that had been filtered through his securocrat gatekeepers. If all components of the security establishment accepted the fundamental tenets of 'total onslaught' thinking, there were significant variations among them, as well as within each. Armies are commonly bastions of rightwing, even ultra-conservative, views, but the South African Defence Force, at least at senior levels, was not composed exclusively of bone-headed reactionaries. A number were well-educated, sophisticated and able. Several were protégés of PW Botha in his time as Minister of Defence. Magnus Malan was a case in point: having risen rapidly through the ranks, he was appointed Chief of the Army in 1973 and Chief of the Defence Force in 1976. In 1980, Botha appointed him Minister of Defence. Malan fully shared Botha's views on reform and total onslaught; indeed he was one of the principal architects of the doctrine.

Malan's translation from a supposedly politically neutral post to a political one may be read as symptomatic of the militarisation of politics; and indeed it was, although care must be taken not to exaggerate its extent. Though Anglo-Boer War generals had been the first three Prime Ministers after 1910 (Louis Botha, JBM Hertzog and JC Smuts), there was a strong tradition that the military must accept civilian control, and not meddle in politics. By and large, the tradition was upheld even during the period of low-intensity war of the 1980s, despite the widespread suspicion that a 'creeping coup' was under way. The military and the political leadership were in close agreement about the total onslaught and the need to maintain white control. It was a partnership symbolised by the close relationship between Botha and Magnus Malan. While the military's influence, along with that of the National Intelligence Service (NIS), was considerable, there is no evidence to suggest that anyone but Botha took the final decisions on major security issues.

Malan confirmed this years later, saying that: 'It was the prerogative of the State President to decide whether something like [the bombing of ANC offices] could be done or not.' He also noted, however, that the military's way of thinking was: 'don't get the minister or the politicians involved, because if we do it's a hell of a risk politically'.[84]

The view that the conflict was 20 per cent military and 80 per cent 'political, psychological and economic' was repeated like a mantra by the generals, who regarded their task as maintaining a shield that would provide the stability required for peaceful change and a political settlement. While the military was confident of being able to maintain security, it continually warned the politicians that they would have to move on the political front. Constand Viljoen, who became Chief of the Army in 1976 and Chief of the SADF in 1980, recalled admonishing the Cabinet on several occasions:

> We were very frank – we didn't exactly chastise them – but it was very good and very sound advice based on our studies. We warned the government that as every year passed their strategic options would become less and less …. From a military standpoint it is imperative, while we are militarily unquestionably strong, to use the time available to us to obtain the most political advantages possible and to exploit all possibilities presented in a pro-active way to find solutions to the vital problems we face.[85]

Viljoen, widely regarded as a 'soldiers' soldier', was popular among the troops under his command. In retirement in the 1990s he moved into rightwing politics and played a critical role in leading the bulk of the right wing into constitutional politics, rather than opting for an extra-parliamentary, counter-revolutionary attempt to derail the settlement.

Although no reliable data exist for the distribution of political attitudes in the SADF, it is highly likely that a substantial percentage of the Permanent Force (professional soldiers), who numbered nearly 30 000 in 1987–8, were supporters of the ultra-rightwing. The AWB was also reputed to have infiltrated the commandos – volunteer groups that operated in the rural areas under the command of the army. Among the 30 000 white members of the South African Police, according to impressionistic estimates, the corresponding figure was about 70 per cent. Historically, the police had been both the cutting edge and the frontline defence of the racial order, with a primary responsibility for enforcing racial laws. The Security Branch, which was something of an elite force within the police, was responsible for the surveillance of political activity and the enforcement of security laws. Its local divisions enforced the security legislation with brutal zeal, routinely using torture on detainees, as well as killing many activists. Police work was badly paid, low in status, and often dangerous – according to official figures, between September 1984 and April 1986, 807 police homes had been attacked, 33 members of the security forces were killed and a further 584 injured.[86] In many cases, the victims were black police, who were widely regarded as 'collaborators' in black communities.

That Eugene Terre'Blanche, leader of the neo-Nazi AWB, and a number of his colleagues and other prominent ultra-rightwingers were ex-policemen is no coincidence. The sympathy that the AWB's views evoked from rank-and-file white police is illustrated by an episode in Pretoria in May 1985 when 4 000 AWB supporters marched to the Pretoria Central police station to deliver a motion of thanks and support to the police for their actions: 'A number of policemen hoisted the leader of the AWB onto their shoulders whereupon, in a short powerful speech, he reaffirmed the AWB's solidarity with our Police Force.'[87]

It is unsurprising that both the military and the police spawned ugly death squads and practitioners of 'dirty tricks' as the conflict intensified during the 1980s. An unleavened diet of total onslaught and '*swart gevaar*' propaganda, together with combat experience in South Africa, on the Namibian border and in Angola, produced battle-hardened men determined to defend the racial order at any cost.

Jacques Pauw, author of two authoritative books on the death squads, writes of the mid-1980s after a state of emergency had been declared:

> The security forces were given extraordinary powers to counter the tide of black resistance. As a result, a new culture took hold in the security forces: one of no accountability and no rules. This soon bred an evil offspring: death squads. These units were never officially formed or sanctioned by the political leaders, but the fruits of the 'total strategy' were soon evident. Anti-apartheid activists disappeared and were mysteriously killed.[88]

Pauw's observations echo the infamous reply elicited from one of the security policemen responsible for the murder of Steve Biko in 1977 when he was asked at the inquest what statute authorised him to keep a man chained for 48 hours: 'We don't work under statutes.'

This was a logical extension of Vorster's comment that you could not fight communism with the Queensbury rules. Despite vast powers to detain alleged activists, by 1985 the authorities had become seriously concerned at their apparent inability to curb resistance. Their response was increasingly to turn to killing them. As the Truth and Reconciliation Commission (TRC) found, when levels of conflict intensified, 'the security forces came to believe that it was no longer possible to rely on the due process of law and that it was preferable to kill people extra-judicially'.[89]

Many of the killers who formed the death squads were psychopaths with criminal records who appeared to derive considerable job satisfaction from their activities. The most notorious of the death squad camps was Vlakplaas, a farm near Pretoria that had been acquired by the police in the late 1970s for the purpose of 'turning' so-called 'askaris' – that is, inducing captured black guerrillas to work for the security forces, invariably by none-too-gentle methods. Two of Vlakplaas's commanders, Dirk Coetzee and Eugene de Kock, became legendary killers. De Kock, according to Pauw, was involved in killing some 70 people between 1983 and 1993.[90] In 1996 he was sentenced to two life sentences and 212 years' imprisonment for his crimes.

No less culpable than Vlakplaas and other death squads was the curiously named Civil Co-operation Bureau (CCB), established in 1986, supposedly under the aegis of the SADF's Special Forces. According to Hamann, the covert operations of the CCB were intended to cause 'maximum disruption to the enemy', and, according to a CCB planning document, disruption comprised five elements: death, infiltration, bribery, compromise or blackmail. The officer in charge of Special Forces, General Joop Joubert, told Hamann that by the mid-1980s it was clear that the ANC was not going to be stopped by 'normal conventional methods' and that 'revolutionary methods' were necessary. These included the elimination of 'ANC leaders and people who substantially contributed to the struggle'; the destruction of ANC facilities and support services; and the elimination of 'activists, sympathisers, fighters and people who supported them'.[91]

With so wide a remit and in the circumstances of the time, it was inevitable that the death squads would seize the opportunity afforded by their lack of accountability and embark upon uninhibited killing sprees. How far up the chain of command authorisation for these 'revolutionary methods' went remains a controversial issue that was to dog FW de Klerk after he became State President. Despite his efforts to rein in the security forces, it was clear that the CCB and other death squads were no longer under the effective control of the government. A judicial commission of enquiry, conducted by Judge Louis Harms, which reported in November 1990, found its investigations blocked at every turn, including by the destruction of documents and blatant lying, by the skilled practitioners of violence and deceit who treated the Commission with the same contempt that they treated everyone from the State President down. Harms, frustrated by the CCB's stonewalling, concluded that its activities 'have contaminated the whole security arm of the state' and that it 'neither knows nor recognizes any higher authority.'

A critical component of the security establishment was the National Intelligence Service, headed by Niel Barnard, a former political science professor who had been hand-picked by PW Botha in 1979. Barnard, a quiet, studious and self-effacing person with impeccable Afrikaner nationalist credentials, quickly proceeded to reform the NIS, turning it into a sophisticated and professional organisation that recruited its personnel largely from university campuses. It was a far cry from NIS's predecessor, the Bureau of State Security (widely known as BOSS) and its fearsome head, General Hendrik van den Bergh, who had been Vorster's trusted henchman. According to one of NIS's agents, Riaan Labuschagne, under Barnard's leadership the NIS

> … moved away from the often ruthless, brutal and ham-fisted image that BOSS had portrayed. Barnard believed in stealth, diplomacy, outwitting and outthinking the enemy. He placed a high premium on intelligence analysts within the service and on the value of validated information.[92]

Barnard became one of Botha's most trusted advisers – a trust that De Klerk maintained after 1989. He was to play a crucial role in brokering talks between the government and the ANC. He told Anthony Sampson that from the early 1980s the NIS had been advising government that 'there was no answer in trying to fight it out'.[93] Barnard's role in setting up meetings between senior NP politicians, including Botha himself, and the ANC was subsequently publicly praised by Nelson Mandela. These and other tentative contacts between the two great antagonists as they groped towards talks are described below.

*   *   *

By the mid-1980s the state of the economy was causing concern. GDP growth rates had averaged 5.5 per cent a year in the 1960s, and 3.25 per cent in the 1970s. For the 1980s the figure had declined to 2.24 per cent, which included negative growth in 1982, 1983 and 1985, and zero growth in 1986. Real gross domestic fixed investment declined annually between 1982 and 1987, reaching record low levels that approached 20 per cent of GDP in the mid-1980s.

The sluggishness of the economy meant rising unemployment, especially for those with few or no skills, which largely meant Africans, especially women and rural dwellers. The exact figure for unemployment was hard to gauge, given the unreliability of official statistics, the exclusion from national estimates of the 'independent' bantustans, and differing definitions of unemployment. Estimates in 1987 varied from a conservative 1.5 million unemployed to as high as 6.1 million. A survey conducted by Market Research Africa found that 25 per cent of Africans in the metropolitan areas were unemployed, the worst affected (and politically most volatile) being those under the age of 34.[94] Rates for country towns and the rural areas were appreciably higher. Figures produced by the Development Bank of Southern Africa for the labour market absorption capacity showed a steady decline beginning in the late 1970s, worsening rapidly in the 1980s to reach 68.7 per cent in 1988.[95] For young African school-leavers finding work became increasingly difficult. It was a factor that contributed powerfully to the volatility of township conditions.

Economic travails prompted a good deal of soul-searching. Apart from government over-spending and a decline in confidence among investors as the political crisis intensified, economic sanctions, including those informally applied by foreign consumers, exacted their toll. 'How much did apartheid cost?' was the question raised by Michael Savage in 1986. In a clinical dissection he isolated seven costs of apartheid:

- direct costs involved in implementing and maintaining apartheid programmes;
- indirect costs;
- enforcement costs involved in applying and policing apartheid;
- lost opportunity costs, including lost investment, and limitations on the development of skills;
- punitive costs resulting from embargoes and sanctions;
- the human costs resulting from the hardships inflicted by apartheid;
- the regional costs imposed upon neighbouring states, forced to defend themselves.[96]

As Savage acknowledged, disaggregating specifically apartheid-related costs from general budgetary allocations was a well-nigh impossible task. Moreover, quantifying the human costs in monetary terms could be done to a limited extent that reflected 'only faintly the appalling toll that apartheid exacts on its victims'.

A previous attempt to cost apartheid, cited by Savage, was undertaken in 1977 by a prominent liberal businessman, LG Abrahamse. Stressing that his estimates were 'very conservative', Abrahamse concluded that had apartheid, with all its wastefulness, not been applied for the previous 30 years, 'it would not be unreasonable to assume that GNP per capita would have been some 50 per cent higher', and that for the year 1976 apartheid had cost R13 billion. Using the same conservative assumptions, Savage calculated that in the year 1985 apartheid had cost R56 billion. He showed also that between 10 per cent and 21 per cent of the annual budget was devoted to financing the machinery of apartheid. Broadly similar estimates were made by Stephen R Lewis, who concluded that had South Africa been able to achieve from 1975 to 1987 the growth rate it had experienced between 1946 and 1975, the 1987 real GDP would have been 45 per cent higher than it actually was. The bulk of this difference, he said, could be attributed to the economic burdens imposed by apartheid and the effort to preserve white domination.[97]

A critical cost of apartheid – and the instability that it was assumed it would cause – was impossible to quantify: how much growth in GDP was foregone because investors, foreign and domestic, were inhibited by considerations of risk?

The quantifiable direct costs of apartheid that were itemised by Savage, such as consolidation of the bantustans, the multiplication of legislatures and departments and segregated facilities, were only one hugely expensive dimension. The efficient working of the economy was seriously skewed in other ways as well by politically driven allocation of resources. As international hostility to apartheid grew, the government moved to mitigate the possible effects of sanctions by seeking to make South Africa more self-sufficient in critical areas of production with Sasol, an oil-from-coal plant; Mossgas, a plant to convert offshore gas into liquid fuel; Armscor, an armaments manufacturing enterprise directed by law 'to meet as effectively and economically as may be feasible the armaments requirements of the Republic'; and stockpiling of various commodities, notably oil, which was stored in disused mineshafts, and widely believed to have been sufficient to tide South Africa over for some three years in the event of a more comprehensive oil embargo.

Defence of the racial order also entailed major increases in defence spending, which rose steadily to consume 14.7 per cent of the budget in 1987–8. As Seán Archer noted in a careful analysis:

> ... on balance, defence expenditure probably constrains sources of economic expansion like the volume of investment and pre-empts the use of labour skills up to the highest educational and occupational categories.[98]

Compounding the economic problems was the intensification of the international drive to impose tougher sanctions. In general trade sanctions, disinvestment and informal consumer boycotts of South African products had some impact in further weakening the economy, but the likelihood that they would force Botha's government to the negotiating table was always remote. Devious ways of evading trade sanctions were found, and, with the assistance of a number of shady middlemen, the oil embargo was largely circumvented. Kevin Davie showed that many oil-producing countries supplied oil to South Africa in spite of having endorsed the embargo. They included Saudi Arabia, the United Arab Emirates, Qatar, Omar, Iran and Egypt. At a time when there was a glut of oil it was hardly surprising that some oil-producing states would not heed the embargo. According to the Shipping Research Bureau of Amsterdam, which monitored the supply lines to South Africa, the embargo was subject to 'massive violations'. Nevertheless, there was a cost, estimated to have been R80 billion since 1979, a figure that includes the cost of off-shore exploration for oil, the creation of the Mossgas facility and Sasol.[99]

Disinvestment by foreign companies, while obviously a negative comment about South Africa's future stability, had little impact on the Botha regime. In a caustic comment Simon Jenkins says the departure of foreign firms caused 'little more than a shudder of disquiet. To Botha, they were the enemy finally folding its tent.'[100] Few companies actually withdrew lock, stock and barrel – Kodak was an exception. Many sold their operations to local companies, often at fire-sale discounts, usually making franchising arrangements with the new owners.

Far more significant than any of the sanctions mentioned above was the debt standstill initiated by Chase Manhattan Bank in July 1985 and followed thereafter by other international banks. The decision meant that South Africa's maturing loans were being called in and borrowing facilities were terminated. Chase Manhattan denied that its motives had been political, saying that the risk of political and economic instability became too high for its investors. This was probably only partly true, since Chase Manhattan, and indeed all American firms that had business links with South Africa, were under intense pressure from some of their shareholders and activists to withdraw.

The denial of borrowing facilities and the requirement of repaying existing debt – R60 billion, of which R34 billion was short-term, owed by banks, private companies, the state and public corporations, and the South African Reserve Bank – was a huge blow to business confidence that was compounded thereafter by Botha's Rubicon speech. Having long been de- pendent on foreign capital for financing domestic investment and current account deficits, South Africa could no longer borrow from abroad; in- stead, it had to export savings to reduce debt. Moreover, growth had to be limited to 2 per cent to reduce imports. Since the population growth rate among Africans was 2.7 per cent (excluding the 'independent' bantustans whose inclusion would have made it even higher) this represented an un- tenable situation that could only mean worsening unemployment.

It was not only the virtual cessation of long-term direct foreign invest- ment that hobbled growth: South African capital, increasingly apprehen- sive of political instability, looked abroad for more lucrative and less risky investment opportunities. Carolyn Jenkins suggests that this flight of do- mestic capital may have exceeded that caused by disinvestment, whose effects were in any case somewhat mitigated by buy-outs by local compa- nies. She indicates that between 1980 and 1985 the total direct investment abroad increased in real terms by 105.2 per cent.[101]

The implications of these developments were not immediately ap- parent to Botha and the securocrats in his inner circle. Robin Renwick, the British Ambassador, recounts the amazement of Gerhard de Kock, Governor of the Reserve Bank, at the response of the security chiefs to be- ing told that the haemorrhaging afflicting South Africa would eventually be fatal, a view that they could not grasp: they responded 'that all that was required was to imprison a few thousand more agitators and South Africa's problems would be solved.'[102]

In public, the government's response to the tightening noose of sanctions was, predictably, one of defiance. More perspicacious members of the rul- ing elite realised that this was dangerous, but they did not say so, at least in public. There were compelling political reasons why the Nationalists could not be seen to be making concessions to an increasingly hostile world. 'Meddling in South Africa's internal affairs' was anathema to the growing xenophobia of a substantial number of whites, especially those of rightwing persuasion. Botha, moreover, was infuriated by the failure of much of the international community to give him credit for the reforms that he had made. He could not understand that reforms, even significant ones, cut little ice abroad while he still clung to the basic neo-apartheid framework – and Mandela remained in prison.

Opinion polls among whites told a similar story of hardening atti- tudes: authoritative surveys carried out by the South African Institute of

International Affairs in 1986 and 1988 reflected the process: in 1986 in response to the statement 'The South African economy is strong enough to prevent economic sanctions hurting our country', no fewer than 71 per cent of respondents disagreed, and 27.3 per cent agreed. The correlation between support for particular parties and their response to the statement was strong: 54.8 per cent of CP supporters disagreed, compared with 90.2 per cent of PFP supporters; NP supporters found themselves between these poles with 66.5 per cent disagreeing.

The same item was included in the 1988 survey: 51.6 per cent disagreed, while 46.5 per cent agreed. André du Pisani, who analysed the findings, concluded:

> Supporters of the NP and the CP have the greatest faith in the South African economy's ability to withstand the harmful effects of sanctions. They are the least likely to be intimidated, and their racial policies are furthest removed from the international norms. At the other end of the spectrum, PFP supporters are overwhelmingly convinced of the damage that sanctions could inflict … . In general, the data suggests a hardening of attitudes among a growing number of whites – a more defiant mood against a 'meddling' international community.[103]

Broadly similar responses were obtained in a survey of white opinion conducted in April and May 1989 for the Investor Responsibility Research Center of Washington DC: 18 per cent of whites believed that South Africa could cope 'easily' with total sanctions; another 62 per cent believed that the country would cope with 'some difficulty'. Only 16 per cent believed it would cope badly. The authors concluded that:

- As the gap widens between the changes whites are prepared to accept and what they believe is being demanded by outsiders, the possibility declined that sanctions could play a role in pushing whites towards change.
- As long as the sanctions campaign is perceived by many whites to be demanding white capitulation, there is a danger that whites could get locked into a counterproductive cycle of behavior in which considerable economic costs would be borne before the changes required to get sanctions lifted would be made.[104]

A plausible interpretation of the data cited above is that sanctions not only hardened white attitudes but also played into the hands of the CP and other ultra-rightwing organisations. The rapid growth of the CP during the mid-1980s was affirmed by its winning 27 per cent of the votes in the 1987 election and 31 per cent in 1989. The movement launched in December 1989 Treurnicht to boost support to one million votes, thereby enabling it to win the next parliamentary election, looked an appallingly realistic possibility. Many whites were also convinced that the sanctions drive would not cease until there had been capitulation to the ANC. Moreover, such incremental reforms as were implemented would not be requited by the lifting of at least some sanctions: on the contrary, such reforms would be construed as proof that sanctions were working, thus providing an impetus for ratcheting up the pressure until apartheid finally collapsed. In fact, however, Botha's reformism ran out of steam by 1986. Clearly Botha did not want to allow the perception to develop in his support-base that he was caving in to international pressure, which was also why the Commonwealth EPG initiative was torpedoed.

Few advocates of sanctions, domestic or international, could offer a coherent projection of what sanctions might achieve. For many, sanctions were an expression of moral outrage that should be enforced come what may; radical proponents hoped that intensified sanctions would lead to economic collapse, thereby precipitating a revolutionary situation; others hoped that sanctions would nudge the NP to the negotiating table by raising the cost of enforcing apartheid. Archbishop Desmond Tutu, the most prominent domestic advocate of sanctions, argued passionately that they were the only possible means of avoiding a bloody outcome of the conflict.

The extent to which blacks favoured sanctions was disputed. While the ANC spearheaded the international campaign, and was supported internally by the UDF, and no significant black leader, with the notable exception of Buthelezi, voiced public opposition to sanctions, survey data suggest that there was considerable ambivalence on the street. The surveys had to be viewed with some caution since it was a serious offence to advocate sanctions. The most important internal proponent, Archbishop Desmond Tutu, could get away with doing so because the state recognised that prosecuting and convicting him would have played into the hands of sanctions lobbies abroad. A further difficulty with survey data was that responses were determined in important respects by how the questions were framed.

In spite of the apparently contradictory findings of six major surveys of black opinion, what emerged was the conclusion that many blacks supported sanctions, including disinvestment, provided that the costs incurred by workers were not too high. The qualification referred to job losses.

Similar conclusions were drawn from the behaviour of the trade unions, whose major federation, Cosatu, backed sanctions and disinvestment from its inception in 1985. By the late 1980s, however, a more cautious, ambivalent note entered the views expressed by many individual, affiliated unions. Some had demanded 'negotiated withdrawal' by foreign companies, meaning that generous terms had to be negotiated with workers well beforehand. After General Motors had announced in October 1986 that it was to sell the South African operation to a local company, efforts were made by some of the unions involved to establish guidelines for future withdrawals. Apart from a demand that departing companies should give timeous notice of their intentions, other minimum conditions were laid down, including:

- A guarantee that no retrenchments took place.
- The new owners must recognise representative unions.
- Severance pay from the departing company of one month's wages for every year of service.
- A guarantee that benefits would not be prejudiced.
- A year's guarantee of full earnings.

In another case, where a union demanded similar terms, the employers accused it of 'wanting to have its disinvestment cake and eat it too'.[105] Despite the widespread fears that sanctions would exacerbate already high unemployment, Cosatu stuck to its guns and maintained its symbolically important alignment with the ANC.

Precisely how much unemployment was attributable specifically to the effect of sanctions is virtually impossible to estimate. Market reactions to perceived risk were closely intertwined with sanctions in their effect on unemployment and it is impossible to distinguish between their respective impacts.

How then are the effects of sanctions to be weighed in accounting for the erosion of apartheid? Was Sampson correct in claiming that international pressure and sanctions brought down apartheid?[106] Or was De Klerk closer to the mark in asserting that 'sanctions did more to delay the process of transformation than they did to advance it'? He acknowledged that sanctions did serious damage to the economy, costing it 1.5 per cent of the annual growth rate during the 1980s and early 1990s, as well as making South Africa more inward looking, less competitive, and creating serious long-term distortions.[107]

Clearly, sanctions *did* make the imposition of apartheid more expensive, especially if the crippling debt standstill is added to the mix. Another possible factor is that the ostensibly defiant attitude of many whites to international pressure may well have embodied resentment of their pariah status while masking a desperate desire to be accepted back into the international community, not least in the arena of sport. At this level, having their noses rubbed in international ostracism may have had some effect on limiting white intransigence. So, at least, it has been argued, but the argument enters the realm of speculation.

*　　*　　*

By the 1980s, business had become seriously concerned about future stability and profitability of the economic environment. To generalise about business as if it were a homogeneous entity with a shared outlook on politics is misleading: different sectors had different stakes in the racial order; (white) English-language firms generally took a different view from their Afrikaner counterparts, who supported the NP; and small and big businesses tended to have differing interests.

Successive government leaders had made it clear that criticism of apartheid by business was unwelcome. Given the range of sanctions that a highly dirigiste government could impose on business leaders who voiced criticism, together with their politically mixed personnel and client bases, few failed to heed the repeated warnings to keep their noses out of politics. The consequence was that business protest tended to be episodic, as in the aftermath of Sharpeville in 1960 or the Soweto Uprising of 1976–7, or concerned with issues that directly affected business, such as the job colour bar, which exacerbated the chronic shortage of skilled workers.

If business lacked the political leverage directly to persuade government to abandon or at least modify apartheid, leading figures in the private sector nevertheless believed that the long-run consequence of sustained economic growth would be to undermine apartheid. Harry Oppenheimer was among the first to express this view: apartheid sought to keep people apart, whereas sustained growth would bring them together. Oppenheimer's views were put into more theoretical form by Michael O'Dowd, an executive director of Anglo American and, in major respects, its resident social philosopher. The 'O'Dowd thesis' argued that the intensity of conflict and injustices of society were not abnormal when compared with the stages of evolution of other industrialising societies; but the comparative evidence suggested that 'when the supply of unskilled labour ceases to appear inexhaustible and the ruling minority starts to find that it actually needs the rest of the population' a new period of reform may gather momentum 'until the antagonism between the rulers and the ruled has been so far diminished by improving living standards and sustained economic progress that the rulers, or some of them, find it actually preferable to compromise with the ruled than to oppress them and constitutional reform in a democratic direction begins'. Major reform, he predicted, would begin about 1980.[108] Whatever its merits, the O'Dowd thesis provided a powerful rationale for business to continue doing what it did best, namely, to create wealth and provide employment. Whether O'Dowd or his Marxist critics, who postulated a contingent if not symbiotic link between capitalism and apartheid, were correct is examined in the conclusion.

The turbulent 1970s and 1980s ended the detachment from politics that many in the private sector maintained. As Zach de Beer, an Anglo American director and a prominent liberal politician, put it, they were forced to confront the reality that they could not 'do good business in a rotten society'.[109]

In the aftermath of the violence of 1976–7, which had prompted another vigorous round of business activism, a new strategy emerged in late 1976 under the auspices of the Urban Foundation, a finely balanced coalition of black and white business leaders, representing as much as 60 per cent of the country's business assets, and headed by Jan Steyn, a humane judge with a strong commitment to social justice. Vorster acquiesced in the formation of the Foundation, admonishing it not to meddle in politics, to which it readily agreed, having eschewed any notion that it was preparing to become a political pressure group. Apart from its activities as a conduit for the funding of housing, education and other community services, the Foundation's principal strength was its high-quality research on urbanisation. At a time of government's hesitant, even dickering, efforts to reformulate urban policy, the Foundation realised that strategically aimed research could help nudge policy in the right direction. Its policy director Ann Bernstein said:

> Key government officials and politicians no longer have the lodestone of apartheid to guide each and every decision. In this context of uncertainty, government is likely to be influenced by detailed new policy recommendations which offer it a way out of its many impasses far more than broad and generalized calls for change.[110]

By avoiding a confrontational approach to government, the Urban Foundation was able to exert significant influence in securing property rights for urban Africans and in prompting the abolition of influx control in 1986.[111]

Business had been encouraged by Botha's unprecedented (for a Nationalist leader) commitment to private enterprise and to political reform. His remarks that the attainment of stability required that the private sector be allowed to work as efficiently as possible, and his commitment to privatisation and deregulation were viewed as hopeful portents of a better working relationship between government and the private sector than in the past.[112] Summits between government and business leaders in 1979 and 1982 strengthened their optimism and, from Botha's point of view, helped to harvest considerable business support for the Tricameral Constitution.

Widespread disillusion with the pace and the evident lack of focus soon set in and accelerated as violent resistance resumed in late 1984. Some believed that they had been duped, allowing themselves to be co-opted into Botha's strategy. Gavin Relly, Oppenheimer's successor as chairman of Anglo American, stated his views bluntly:

> Piecemeal reform in the current [1986] style is now identified clearly in the black mind as tinkering with apartheid and only a visible process of political negotiations that symbolizes real intent to share power will end the stonewalling tactics pursued by many black political leaders.[113]

During September 1985 Relly led a small delegation of businessmen (including three editors) to a meeting with the ANC in Zambia. President Kenneth Kaunda, who had taken the initiative in arranging the meeting, was deeply concerned that an 'imminent explosion' would occur in South Africa. As the host government to the ANC-in-exile, his country was vulnerable economically and militarily to South Africa. Sensible people, he said, should meet to use what was now a 'threadbare opportunity' to avert that explosion. According to Hugh Murray, one of the delegation, PW Botha had originally given his 'implicit blessing' for the meeting, but after the extensive publicity during the run-up, he had withdrawn it. He did not, however, appear to be 'totally closed'.

Despite frank exchanges and widely differing views, the meeting was cordial. On the ANC side, Oliver Tambo was flanked by other ANC heavyweights, including Thabo Mbeki, Chris Hani and Mac Maharaj, indicating the importance that the ANC attached to the meeting, which they possibly saw as a means of further isolating the government by driving a wedge between it and the private sector. The businessmen were impressed with the calibre of the ANC delegates, whom Tony Bloom, chairman of the Premier Group, described as 'highly intelligent, intellectual and very articulate'. He was not convinced by Tambo's account of the ANC's relationship with the SACP, believing it to have stronger influence than Tambo had indicated, particularly as over half of the membership of the National Executive were SACP members. He acknowledged, though, that the ANC delegates had avoided 'traditional Marxist-Leninist jargon and dogma', even if Tambo was emphatic that 'monopoly capital would be nationalised', and Mbeki had said that 'clearly the press would have to come under state control'.[114]

Business activism continued into 1986. In January officials of the Federated Chamber of Industries (FCI) held talks with the ANC prior to releasing its *South African Business Charter of Social, Economic and Political Rights*, which was an unequivocal call for the establishment of a liberal-democratic form of government, based upon non-discrimination, universal suffrage, civil rights and the rule of law. The FCI claimed full support from its approximately 10 000 member firms, but there were murmurings that the scope and tenor of the Charter reflected the invidious position of its chairman, John Wilson of Shell SA, who was under pressure from his British and Dutch principals to distance Shell as far as possible from apartheid. That the Charter's call was excessively strong meat for many in the business community was reflected in its failure to become a rallying point for business's political demands.

A further foray into the political arena by the FCI in June 1986, in which it dissociated itself from 'the strategy of political repression and economic isolationism to which the South African government is apparently committed', evoked a menacing rebuke from Botha:

> Kindly do not trouble me with your points of view if you are not prepared to take the trouble of familiarizing yourself with mine. Your assessment of the government's position is quite ridiculous. Unless you too come to grips with the reality of the security situation in this country and act accordingly, you are bound to pay a heavy price. This is not a threat – it is a considered warning.

It was hardly surprising when Tony Bloom remarked that 'English-speaking business has about as much effect on government policy as a ping-pong ball bouncing off a stone wall.'[115]

Worse was to follow. In January 1987 Chris Ball, managing director of Barclays National Bank, was vigorously attacked by Botha for having caused his bank to lend R150 000 to a client to fund newspaper advertisements commemorating the seventy-fifth anniversary of the ANC and calling for its unbanning. Ball denied that he or the bank had any knowledge of the advertisements prior to their publication. Not satisfied, and clearly irritated by Ball's spirited response challenging him to repeat his accusations outside Parliament, Botha appointed a judicial commission to investigate whether Ball had been involved. It was a serious abuse – by no means unprecedented – of the function of judicial commissions to employ one, headed in this case by a politically reliable judge, to nail political opponents. Predictably, the Commission found that Botha's accusations were true and, in the process, made some highly critical remarks about Ball's credibility.[116] Not long after this episode Ball left the country, joining what was by now a significant exodus of businesspeople, professionals and young white males anxious to avoid the mandatory two-year military call-up.

By 1987 not only had Botha's reform programme run out of steam, but his behaviour had become increasingly erratic and unpredictable. Undoubtedly the sustained crisis of the mid-1980s was taking its toll. As an example of his bizarre behaviour, Raymond Ackerman cites a demand by Botha that business should deduct money directly from black employees who were refusing to pay rents for their state-owned houses as part of a concerted campaign. He described it as 'a preposterous idea', and noted ruefully that apartheid policies 'sat next to us at board meetings, forming a silent quorum dictating decisions, if so permitted, because they impacted on every facet of business one way or another'. [117]

Despite the chilly relationship between government and business, one initiative, undertaken by Anglo American, had a beneficial impact on reformist thinking inside government and on key groups in white society. This was an exercise in scenario-building, based upon the work of local and overseas futurologists. Clem Sunter and other Anglo American officials sought in their work to identify trends and processes in what they termed 'winning nations'. Extrapolating from the global scene to South Africa enabled them to present two scenarios: the 'High Road' and the 'Low Road'. Which route was taken depended critically on political decisions.

The High Road presupposed minimal sanctions; small (though not weak) government; decentralised power; and joint negotiation with all who wished to participate. South Africa could become a high-growth democratic society. The Low Road, on the other hand, projected a downward spiral of increased sanctions, a more controlled economy and further centralisation of government, eventually leading to confrontation and conflict in 'Fortress South Africa', reducing the country to a wasteland.

In 1986 Sunter and his colleagues decided to present their material to a wider audience, and over the next two years they addressed 230 groups, including the Cabinet, comprising up to 30 000 people. It is impossible to estimate what influence the engagingly-presented 'roadshows' exerted. In a retrospective account Sunter recalls that many audiences regarded the negotiation route as 'a pipe dream': after all, 'no group in the world had ever negotiated themselves out of power on their own turf'. Nevertheless, as he remarked, fantasy became reality.[118]

Little in the foregoing account of business–government relations in the 1970s and 1980s supports the notion, advanced by some Marxists, that business benefited from apartheid. The argument may have been true for mining and commercial agriculture in an earlier phase of history when repressive labour policies facilitated capital accumulation. In an empirical analysis of the views of Nationalist ministers and MPs, Schlemmer was interested to learn which interest groups were, in their belief, most influential. He found that business interests were not spontaneously mentioned at all, and no respondent suggested that the corporate sector had any particular influence on government: 'There is no evidence from any of the interviews, or in any action or response by the government, that the National Party is a handmaiden to capital.'[119]

* * *

Space considerations preclude detailed analysis of other opposition institutions and groups: opposition parties to the left of the NP, notably the Progressive Federal Party, the English-language press, universities, churches, and a number of pressure groups such as the Black Sash, the South African Institute of Race Relations and the End Conscription Campaign all played a part in destroying the moral legitimacy of apartheid and exposing its cruelties. The combined effect of their efforts was that a significant minority of whites were not stampeded into a racial laager. At least as far as whites were concerned, South Africa never degenerated into a full-blown totalitarian society in which all forms of dissent were stamped upon. To be sure, there were severe limitations on the expression of opposition. Marxists, radical liberals and even an outspoken editor like Donald Woods, for example, felt the lash of authoritarian government and, in some cases, the attentions of death squads[120] and other forms of dirty tricks or harassment.

Although grievously restricted in what it could report and whom it could quote, the press nevertheless remained a valuable conduit for opposition views and, in spite of the legal minefield it had to traverse, it could still report on developments in the country. Likewise, the four English-language universities made what use they could of the amount of academic freedom that survived – and, especially in the 1980s, took what gaps they could find, whether legal or not, to admit students of all races.

The Black Sash, an organisation of middle-class white women established in 1954, tirelessly monitored the impact of apartheid, notably the pass laws, on black people; and their advice offices sought to assist those enmeshed in the coils of the apartheid bureaucracy.

For the PFP the 1980s were hard times. Its parliamentary representation remained at one MP, the redoubtable Helen Suzman, from 1961 to 1974 when the number rose to seven; it gained further seats in 1977, becoming the official opposition, and reached the apex of its representation in the 1981 election, winning 26 seats (out of 165). Thereafter its fortunes declined. As noted above, it took a bad beating in the referendum on the Tricameral Constitution in 1983, and suffered a body blow in 1986 when its leader F van Zyl Slabbert precipitately resigned his seat, declaring that Parliament had almost no relevance at all. The 1987 election campaign saw the Nationalists vigorously attacking the PFP for being 'soft on security' and sympathetic to the ANC. Support slumped to 19 seats, and the Conservative Party, with 22 seats, replaced it as the official opposition.

Given what appeared to be the inherent dynamic of white politics, a liberal party like the PFP had no hope of winning a general election. Over 90 per cent of its support-base were English-speakers, mostly drawn from the middle to upper-middle classes. While not dismissing the role of Parliament as a forum of protest against exploitation and injustice, Slabbert offered cogent arguments against its relevance: it had no relevance for representative government because it excluded the vast majority of South Africans; it had no relevance for accountable government since it had effectively transferred its sovereignty and accountability to the powerful executive presidency; and it had no relevance for the constitutional change of government since it had made it constitutionally impossible for the majority peacefully to change the government. The fundamental opposition to apartheid was extra-parliamentary, and increasingly Parliament had become less significant in influencing the relationship between the power-holders and their extra-parliamentary challengers.[121]

Apart from the hammering that white liberals had received from the Black Consciousness movement, the PFP was also accused of legitimating an unjust parliamentary system by participating in it. Moreover, its opposition to sanctions and violence rendered it suspect in the eyes of militants. What alternative did the PFP have but to soldier on? It represented a bloc of some 20 per cent of the white electorate, and played some role (it is impossible to be precise) in influencing the Nationalists to recognise that apartheid was both unjust and unworkable, and in pointing the way to a negotiated settlement. A number of the PFP's MPs were exceptionally able people: Helen Suzman, Colin Eglin and Ken Andrew, among others, commanded a wider audience than those who voted for their party. Suzman's role as a critic, spanning a parliamentary career that began in 1953 and ended in 1989, was especially remarkable. Apart from prising information out of ministers by way of parliamentary questions, she took the trouble to visit political prisoners, which, in the case of Robben Island, resulted in a marked improvement of conditions. She was also a great believer in seeing situations for herself and ensuring that her speeches were factually correct – in 36 years she was never once tripped up on a point of fact. It is difficult to resist the conclusion that her formidable logic and debating skills had some influence, if only by a process akin to osmosis, on her opponents (however unlikely they would be to admit this).

It is also likely that Botha's successor, FW de Klerk, recognised that the Democratic Party (formed by the merger of the PFP with independent candidates after the 1987 election) provided him with a cushion of safety against possible future inroads by the CP. In the election of September 1989 the NP's parliamentary majority was significantly reduced: from 123 seats won in 1987 it now held 93, and for the first time in decades it had failed to win more than 50 per cent of the votes cast. The CP, however, won 39 seats, possibly winning a small majority of Afrikaner votes, and over 20 per cent of the overall vote. The DP pushed up the PFP's seats from 19 (plus the single successful independent) to 33. De Klerk would have surmised that he could rely on the DP's support for the quantum leap he would take in February 1990.

Whether these considerations, jointly or severally, trump Slabbert's arguments for the near-irrelevance of Parliament remains a debatable issue. It is worth noting, however, that the fundamental change initiated by De Klerk in February 1990 *did* come through Parliament; and also that De Klerk, while critical of the excessive powers vested in the state presidency, nevertheless used them to do so.

* * *

PW Botha's departure from the political scene in 1989 was ignominious. He had suffered a stroke during 1988, which was hushed up, and another, presumably more serious, on 18 January 1989. While recuperating he sent word on 2 February to the chairman of the NP caucus that the office of the State President and the leadership of the NP should be separated so that the state presidency could then 'to a considerable degree, become a unifying force in our country'. He requested that the caucus elect a new leader. That neither the Cabinet, let alone the caucus, had any prior inkling of

Botha's astonishing decision is an indication of the gulf between him and his party. The extent to which the strokes had impaired his judgement remains an open question; but how could so canny and experienced a party man make what was to prove a massive error of judgement? By cutting himself off from his caucus he destroyed his power-base, and this would prove to be decisive in his downfall.

On receiving Botha's missive a small group of ministers decided that, in the interests of preventing a drawn-out and divisive election, the new leader should be elected immediately. In the third round of voting, Chris Heunis and Pik Botha having been eliminated in the first two, De Klerk beat the young and personable Minister of Finance, Barend du Plessis, by the narrow margin of 69 votes to 61. De Klerk wrote:

> This voting pattern carried with it an interesting message. My interpretation of it was there was an urgent desire among many members of the caucus to move quickly ahead with reform. The unexpectedly strong showing of Du Plessis resulted from his image as a *verligte*, as opposed to my more centrist image. It also indicated a taste for renewal in the party itself. The Young Turks had become tired of what they regarded as the exaggerated deference that was paid to seniority and experience.[122]

Immediately after the election the party closed ranks, each of the losing candidates pledging loyalty to De Klerk, whose acceptance speech had strongly emphasised the need for reform: 'I said that we had reached a point where we would have to take bold initiatives'.

The problem now was how to cope with the awkward situation of diarchy: who called the tune – De Klerk as leader of the party that made policy, or Botha as State President who was responsible for implementing it? Botha's domineering style and his touchy, suspicious nature, exacerbated by the strokes, made him determined not to play second fiddle to anyone. What De Klerk called his subtle undermining continued after his return to office in March. Inevitably it provoked a backlash. De Klerk and his colleagues would not put up with what was becoming an intolerable situation; increasing numbers of NP MPs and NP-supporting newspapers were calling for Botha's resignation. With an election due on 6 September the issue was damaging the NP. As a wag put it, Botha had made zoological history by transforming himself from a crocodile into an albatross in three months! The showdown was approaching rapidly.

The dénouement occurred at a special Cabinet meeting called by Botha on 14 August. The flashpoint was Botha's hearing of De Klerk's and

Pik Botha's intention to visit President Kaunda of Zambia, of which he claimed (incorrectly, according to Pik Botha) he had not been apprised, in violation of the protocols governing ministerial visits to foreign countries. At the Cabinet meeting Botha asked each minister for his views, and with hardly an exception, the collective opinion was that he should resign. His temper flared only when one minister said that 'the PW Botha I knew before your stroke is not the same man I know after your stroke'. Insisting that he was perfectly fit, Botha now insulted several ministers and claimed that visiting Kaunda was walking into a trap that he had set to get the South Africans to negotiate with the ANC.[123] Nevertheless, he acquiesced in his fate and resigned, repeating the substance of his accusations in a television interview that confirmed to many that he was no longer fit to be State President. He subsequently allowed his membership of the NP to lapse.

Botha's hardline approach to security and his obsessive concern with retaining the principle of compulsory group affiliation have obscured the important changes that occurred under his leadership. As this chapter has shown, some of his reforms tore down major pillars of the racial order. Even the ill-fated Tricameral Constitution had the unintended and perverse effect of intensifying the decisive conflict of the 1980s and accelerating the decline of the Nationalists' morale. At the ideological level, he had administered the *coup de grâce* to the traditional notion of apartheid by declaring that the peoples of South Africa constituted 'one nation', even if it was 'a nation of minorities'. By driving out the conservatives in 1982 he had irrevocably split the NP and the wider Afrikaner nationalism, without which occurrences the transition would almost certainly have been far more protracted and even bloodier than eventually was the case. It should not be forgotten, moreover, that despite his visceral mistrust of the ANC and their communist allies, the first tentative, even furtive, contacts between representatives of the government and the ANC occurred on Botha's watch.

The most appropriate epitaph on PW Botha was written by Brian Pottinger: 'Botha ... had shown that he had the wit to identify crises but insufficient wisdom to resolve them.'[124]

CHAPTER 8

The Growth of Black Resistance
in the 1980s

The transition began in earnest when the leaderships of the contending forces, black and white, recognised that the conflict was deadlocked: neither side was capable of winning an outright victory and imposing its will on the losers. It is mistaken to regard the conflict as one between two monolithic antagonists: there were internal conflicts in both. Nevertheless, it was obvious that the ANC and the NP were the major players; and the *relatively* peaceful character of the transition owed much to their ability to mobilise and retain their respective support-bases while leading them into a negotiated settlement.

Black resistance in the 1980s had its roots in what had gone before, but its scope, intensity and durability was far greater than what had occurred in 1960, after Sharpeville, or in 1976–7 in the Soweto Uprising. While there can be no doubt that the black opposition forced the pace and pushed the country into a deadlock, there can equally be no doubt that developments in the white bloc were a critically important component of the process. The trajectory of the transition is best understood as a dialectical interaction between the consolidation of black resistance and the growing recognition among white elites that the old racial order had to change. With some oversimplification, the process can be summarised as the hardening of black resolve and the weakening of white resolve. This observation does not imply that the security apparatus and the ferocity with which it was deployed was weakened: the contrary was true.

﹡   ﹡   ﹡

At the beginning of the decade the Minister of Justice, Kobie Coetsee, warned against 'a false sense of security', saying that there were indications that the activities of 'terrorist organisations' were on the increase.[1] He was right. Several guerrilla attacks took place during 1980, including an attack on the oil-from-coal plant, Sasol, which caused R58 million worth of damage. As disquieting for the state was the evidence of widespread support in townships for the guerrillas and their organisation, MK.[2] Funerals for those killed in violence had become symbolic occasions for the expression of opposition.

MK's numbers had been augmented by the exodus of 1976–7; over the ten-year period after 1977 an average of 1 250 recruits were trained annually so that by 1987 over 12 000 had been trained, of whom some 5 000 were active in the country.[3] Like the imprisoned ANC leaders on Robben Island, the MK leadership was startled by the ferocity of those coming from the violent townships. Ronnie Kasrils, a senior MK commander, compared them with the recruits of the 1960s:

> That generation had received their experience in the non-racial politics of the Congress Movement. This generation was unacquainted with the ANC, which had been outlawed most of their lives. They were young and had grown up in a political void. The only whites they had known were arrogant school inspectors, township supervisors and swaggering thugs in uniforms.[4]

Many bristled with a grim impatience to receive training, then return to South Africa as fighters and overthrow the regime. The extent to which armed struggle could damage the state became an issue of some contention, the romantic revolutionaries believing that a war of liberation could succeed, whereas more sober-minded counsels suggested that what became known as 'armed propaganda' could facilitate mass mobilisation inside the country and push the government to the negotiation table, but not topple the state. Why take on the enemy where he was strongest, namely in his ability to use force and coercion?

MK's tactics changed after a 1978 visit by Slovo, Tambo and others to Vietnam, where they took advice from General Giap, the renowned guerrilla leader. Vietnam was utterly unlike South Africa in major respects, but the achievement of successively defeating the French and the Americans was inspirational. Similarly, guerrilla war in Rhodesia, while not defeating the state's security forces, had nevertheless pushed the illegal Rhodesian Front regime up against the ropes.

Giap's advice led the ANC and MK to develop a three-year plan in which armed struggle was incorporated into a political strategy, based upon building a mass movement inside South Africa and a strengthened

underground network. As Kasrils put it: 'The organisation and mobilisation of the masses was the prerequisite for the development not simply
of military operations but of a fully-fledged people's war.'[5] As of 1980,
MK had no bases in the country: attacks would have to be launched from
outside with a view to raising the masses' morale by attacking spectacular
targets – such as Sasol, and a daring rocket attack on the South African
Army base at Voortrekkerhoogte in Pretoria on 16 June 1981. During
1981 and 1982 over 60 attacks took place, mostly against police stations,
rail tracks and electricity installations. As mobilisation increased, inside
bases, and even training facilities, would become more feasible.

Officially, the security authorities boasted about their ability to thwart
guerrilla attacks. During 1982 Louis le Grange, the Minister of Law and
Order, claimed that the whole internal MK network had been identified and disrupted during 1981; and a senior police officer maintained
that 'every deed of terror committed in the Republic was being solved'.[6]
These were probably exaggerations, intended to reassure an increasingly
nervous white public; but it was undeniably the case that MK fighters
suffered a high capture or mortality rate, attributable to a considerable
extent to the penetration of both the ANC and MK by informers, as well
as tighter border surveillance. Oliver Tambo himself admitted this to an
American journalist who had quoted to him a police boast that the state
had informers 'all the way to Moscow'. Tambo responded:

> He was right! He was right! ... They've been giving us a rough time,
> making us work very hard. At one time there was a group of ten, and
> only one of them was genuine.'[7]

By the early 1980s ANC strategy had crystallised into four interlocking
components: mass mobilisation, underground organisation, armed propaganda, and the international isolation of the apartheid state. Moreover,
the development of the labour movement's muscle was regarded as critically important.

The difficulties of infiltrating trained guerrillas into the country, securing safe houses and storing arms caches were immense. If the ANC
was riddled with informers, so were the townships. With the squeeze put
on surrounding states that offered sanctuary and entry points, infiltration became even more difficult. In 1985, however, MK managed to move
some 150 cadres into South Africa who, according to Barrell, were able
to increase the number of attacks to 135 in 1985, compared with 44 in
1984.[8] Kasrils gives a slightly higher figure of over 150 operations annually after 1985.[9] The cost was high: according to an MK officer quoted by

Barrell the average survival time of an individual guerrilla was about six months.[10]

The intensification of conflict in townships in many parts of the country in 1984 and after provided a more protective environment for guerrillas, increasing numbers of whom had begun to be trained inside South Africa. As Tambo explained it, in answer to a question about where MK had its bases:

> In South Africa. A base for the ANC does not mean a place where you have an army and equipment in an independent country, and you go away and you come back there. We don't have that. Any such bases are inside South Africa, secret places we go to, we go in and out of, secret places from which we do our reconnaissance of targets and to which we return. Our bases are the ordinary people themselves who are at work every day, who are cadres of our army. And a lot of training is going on in the country, not of the best sort naturally, in those conditions, but there are a lot of cadres around.[11]

High levels of penetration by informers, harsh conditions in the Angolan camps where most guerrillas were based, boredom and frustration were a combustible mix. Discontent simmered for several years. MK commissars, mostly SACP men, and Mbokodo, the security organisation, developed a reputation for brutality that led to mutinous behaviour which assumed serious proportions in early 1984. Four commissions (two of them appointed by the ANC) and Amnesty International investigated allegations of human rights abuses in MK camps and found extensive evidence of torture, executions and other inhumane treatment.

A survivor of the Angolan camps, Mwezi Twala, has described the brutality that prevailed, which he attributes, partly at any rate, to the grip that SACP members had taken over MK:

> During my years in exile [since 1975] I had trained and waited for the day when I would return to eliminate South Africa's white minority regime and destroy apartheid once and for all .... [O]ver the years I had seen the takeover of the true ANC and its ideals by a communist element which had, like a creeping cancer, silently eaten its way to total power and destroyed it just like the disease that destroys a healthy body. For this reason the ANC/Communist Alliance had destroyed every vestige of democratic principles and had, as communism had done wherever it took root, replaced happiness and vision with misery and helplessness except for the sycophants, the yes-

men and women. All I had done during my service to the true ANC ideal was to criticise those activities that were communist-inspired and unacceptable to hundreds like me. For this I had been labelled a dissident and suffered torture and near death many times .... [12]

The Truth and Reconciliation Commission reached similar conclusions about the prevalence of torture, finding that gross violations of human rights were committed against suspected enemy agents and mutineers in particular.[13] Other accounts maintain that ferocious punishment was meted out to critics of the ANC or MK leadership or as a means of settling old scores and intimidating dissenters.[14]

Further evidence of rough treatment of ANC exiles was provided by Terry Bell, himself an exile and former principal of the primary school for the children of ANC exiles in Tanzania:

[A] political and economic elite wielded grossly disproportionate privileges. Bribery, force and the threat of force or isolation were the main means of holding the ranks together. ANC members soon discovered that advancement to the privileged elite, to scholarships or even to necessary medical treatment abroad, depended on not falling foul of the leadership.

Bell attributes this to the 'inordinate amount of influence' that the SACP exerted over the ANC.[15]

In 1985 ANC strategy shifted towards 'people's war', meaning that guerrilla activity would now link with mass mobilisation. As Thabo Mbeki explained it:

The general orientation of the armed struggle up to this point has been what we have called 'armed propaganda' .... Now it is necessary to move beyond that point, it is necessary to move to what we call 'people's war'. We're saying this now because in fact there is not only a mass popular opinion in favour of armed struggle – there is a mass popular willingness to carry it out.[16]

The effect was the mutual reinforcing of township resistance and guerrilla activity: new life was breathed into MK, and increased MK action was a source of inspiration to militants. It was also to confirm the ANC's pre-eminence in the struggle.

Its rival, the Pan-Africanist Congress, with its armed wing, the Azanian People's Liberation Army (Apla), had long been rent by factionalism, and, in comparison with the ANC and MK, its resources were meagre. It lacked the ability to absorb the large number of militants who fled the country in 1976–7. Apla's predecessor, Poqo, had fizzled out in the 1960s. It had been a genuinely terrorist organisation, engaging in random acts of violence against whites. No fewer than 23 Poqo members had been convicted and hanged for the murder of five white civilians in Transkei in 1963. Apla's attacks in the 1970s and 1980s were far fewer than MK's. As one of its commanders told the TRC, in the mid- and late 1980s 'we lost more comrades in armed robberies than in actual armed confrontation with the enemy forces'.[17] It was not surprising that it was unable to fire the imagination of township activists to the same extent as MK.

From its inception MK had been determined to avoid being tarred with a terrorist brush, terrorism being defined by the ANC as military attacks on civilians by armed groups or individuals. In 1977 the ANC became a signatory to the Geneva Convention on the humanitarian conduct of war. In its submission to the TRC the ANC said that it had never deviated from its belief that it was not only morally wrong but strategically sense-less to attack civilian targets. Inevitably, civilians would be caught in the crossfire, and on occasion, MK operatives violated ANC policy and did attack civilian targets. This became a trend in late 1987, and MK com-manders were instructed by the ANC's National Executive Committee to reassert ANC policy regarding the avoidance of purely civilian targets.[18] Subsequently, the ANC tendered its apologies to the TRC for the loss of civilian lives that MK operations had caused.

During 1985 a decision was adopted to take the struggle to the white areas. In a broadcast on the ANC's Radio Freedom, Tambo said:

> We cannot and should not allow a situation of relative peace and tranquillity to obtain in the white areas of our country while the black townships are in flames. We must take the struggle into the white areas of South Africa and there attack the apartheid regime and its forces of repression in these areas which it considers its rear.

Part of the new strategy was to persuade whites that their security was illusory, and to persuade some – young army conscripts, for example – to join the struggle against apartheid.

Another category whom the ANC sought to dissuade from continu-ing to serve the apartheid state was black policemen. Although they were regarded as 'collaborators', and hence as legitimate targets for assassi-nation, a few, it was believed, might be 'turned' to act as 'moles' who would provide useful information to MK. How many were recruited is not known. The extent to which they were targeted can be inferred from official figures: from September 1984 to April 1986, 807 police homes were attacked, 33 were killed and 584 injured.[19]

In mid-1987 nearly half of the approximately 56 000 members of the police force were black, including 20 000 Africans. Awareness of the dangers did not appear to be an overwhelming deterrent to enlistment: in 1985–6 nearly 2 000 Africans applied to join the force.[20] The apparent anomaly of blacks' joining the principal instrument of their repression can be explained largely in economic terms: whatever the dangers and drawbacks, police work was at least a job in times of growing unemployment. Similar motives no doubt prompted many of the 2 260 Africans who applied to join the permanent force of the army in 1987.[21]

Between 1976 and 1989 approximately 1 200 guerrilla attacks occurred. The figure was possibly higher, since attacks in the independent bantustans were either excluded or under-reported. Further estimates, which cannot be regarded as entirely reliable, suggest that between June 1976 and August 1986 428 guerrillas had been either captured or killed by the security forces, with a further 78 guerrillas captured or killed and an estimated 771 persons killed or injured in attacks between January and June 1988.[22] Compared with the death and injury toll in other forms of political violence, this was a relatively small proportion; and it was also small in comparison with the number of deaths caused by other liberation movements such as the National Liberation Front (FLN) during the Algerian civil war between 1954 and 1962, in which 300 000 lives were lost.

By the mid-1980s it was evident that there were differing emphases within the ANC. Highly tentative and clandestine feelers to the ANC were being put out by the government; and the efforts of the Commonwealth Eminent Persons Group in 1985–6 to broker a negotiated settlement had put the possibility of negotiation on the radar screen, albeit as a tiny blip. Hardliners in the ANC and, especially, the SACP dismissed the idea, insisting that 'total seizure of power' was the aim of the struggle, and that armed struggle was critical to this strategy. Ellis and Sechaba maintain that the SACP, which dominated MK, had put its faith in armed struggle, which it regarded as the heart of its strategy.[23] Premature attempts to engage the government in negotiations, it was reasoned, might squander the advances made by the armed struggle. It was for this reason that Operation Vula was conceived in 1986. It was a very small group, convened by Tambo, and, given the need for tight security, its formation and membership were kept a closely guarded secret, even from MK and certainly from the exile community in Lusaka. Although it was later claimed that Vula had been established as an 'insurance policy' lest negotiations failed, the actual intention was to put high-ranking MK operatives into South Africa to move guerrilla war towards a 'people's war' in which the forces on the ground were co-ordinated and aligned with the other strands of ANC strategy. According to Vula's leading operative, Mac Maharaj, the primary aim of Vula was 'to build the long-term capability of MK to fight a protracted people's war'. He argued that 'the regime will only talk about negotiations when they see that the mass struggle and the underground struggle are heating up.'[24] The ANC would not countenance 'forswearing violence' as a precondition for entering into negotiations, as Botha demanded. The capacity to wage armed struggle was regarded as a bargaining chip in any negotiating situation.

By 1985 Nelson Mandela was beginning to rethink ANC strategy. He had been amazed when the Minister of Justice, Kobie Coetsee, had visited him in a Cape Town hospital prior to his undergoing a prostate operation in August 1985. Coetsee, probably one of the earliest Cabinet members to recognise the inevitability of negotiating with the ANC, was, according to Mandela, 'altogether gracious and cordial'. He was offering an olive branch. On his return to prison, Mandela resolved to do what he had long pondered: begin discussions with the government.

> I had concluded that the time had come when the struggle could best be pushed forward through negotiations. If we did not start a dialogue soon, both sides would soon be plunged into a dark night of oppression, violence and war .... We had been engaged in the armed struggle for more than two decades. Many people on both sides had already died. The enemy was strong and resolute. Yet even with all their bombers and tanks, they must have sensed that they were on the wrong side of history. We had right on our side, but not yet might. It was clear to me that a military victory was a distant if not impossible dream. It simply did not make sense for both sides to lose thousands if not millions of lives in a conflict that was unnecessary. They must have known this as well. It was time to talk.[25]

As Mandela realised, his thoughts would be controversial, especially among many MK guerrillas who remained strongly driven by the vision of seizing power in a 'people's war'. It would be several years before the conflict had ripened to the point where negotiation would become a possibility.

To what extent the armed struggle contributed to accelerating the transition is a debatable issue. There is no doubt that MK's exploits struck a resonant chord among many black people and helped to funnel considerable popular support towards the ANC. Lodge and Nasson argue plausibly that MK's most significant contribution to the liberation struggle was 'helping the ANC exercise political leadership over constituencies it was unable to organise directly'.[26] Unrest and guerrilla attacks also ensured that South Africa's problems received a higher profile in the international community, thereby further contributing to the isolation of the government and the growing perception that a racial civil war was inevitable and imminent. In purely military terms, however, MK's impact was little more than an irritant. Hopes by some that the security forces would be stretched thin, that there would be significant defections or a widespread decline in the will to fight were not realised. 'Seizure of power', in which MK would play a major role, became an increasingly remote prospect, as Mandela's thoughts suggested.

If anything, the armed struggle tended to heighten white resistance to a transition to democracy. Security checks in many public places, and posters prominently displayed in official buildings depicting mines, bombs and other devices for which the public should be on the lookout, testified to a measure of jumpiness among whites, especially after the rise in civilian deaths in attacks from 1985 onwards. A number of young whites, mostly English-speakers, left the country to avoid the military call-up. Overall, however, evidence suggests that white opinion hardened as the armed struggle and unrest intensified. For example, a survey conducted for the South African Institute of International Affairs in January 1988 showed that 73 per cent of whites believed that the police and the army were strong enough to control unrest; nearly 80 per cent agreed that 'South Africa should militarily attack terrorist/guerrilla bases in its neighbouring states'; 78 per cent disagreed with the contention that the government exaggerated the communist threat; and 61,7 per cent disagreed with the view that 'the government should negotiate directly with the African National Congress (ANC) to try to find a solution to South Africa's racial problems' (the latter figure reflecting an increase from 58 per cent who disagreed in the 1986 survey).[27]

White opinion was affected by official propaganda, notably the highly partisan news selection and views of the South African Broadcasting Corporation's radio and television services. Manipulation was facilitated by the crudeness and often bloodcurdling nature of ANC publications, notably *Sechaba*, and the Marxist-Leninist jargon in which they were written. These publications were banned inside the country, although some circulated clandestinely, but the government allowed itself to publicise selected extracts for the purpose of confirming to whites the correctness of its policies.

*   *   *

The intensity of protest in the mid-1980s derived from the confluence of three issues in particular: the continuation of the crisis in black education; the inauguration of the Tricameral Parliament; and the imposition of substantial rent increases by discredited community councils that were widely considered to be corrupt. The issues were part of the bigger demand for the comprehensive rejection of apartheid and its replacement with the extension of political rights to all in a non-discriminatory system. Popular anger needed channelling, organisation, and a focus, which it received principally from the United Democratic Front (see below). National and local organisation was undergirded by the rise of an astonishing array of civil society bodies, notably local community 'civics', that mobilised what Jakes Gerwel called 'enormous social energy' which was harnessed in the cause of a democratic society.[28]

A further critical factor in the growth of resistance was the poor state of the economy, to which reference has been made. Apart from a brief spurt between 1987 and 1989, thanks to a rise in commodity prices, the economy remained in the doldrums for much of the decade, and dipped again in the early 1990s. Although there was some coincidence between adverse socio-economic conditions and unrest, Kane-Berman suggested that there were other intervening variables: during the 1980s the Pretoria-Witwatersrand-Vereeniging triangle accounted for more than half of the violence in the country despite having per capita incomes that were double the national average.[29]

*   *   *

The rise of black resistance in the 1980s reflected the growth of black leverage on several fronts. It was insufficient to topple the state, but it was able to create a deadlock: the state could not eliminate resistance, even if the security forces remained firmly in control; but the black opposition grew sufficiently strong and resolute to thwart the effective implementation of a coherent policy (if one existed).

'Leverage' is an admittedly imprecise concept. As used here it refers to resources that are, or can be, mobilised for the purpose of extracting reforms and/or frustrating the implementation of policies. Resources can be tangible or quantifiable – like sheer numbers, economic muscle (including degree of economic indispensability and worker power), skills and educational levels, and military capacity. Less tangible resources include morale, capacity for organisation and discipline, quality of leadership, and strategic skill. Racial consciousness or ethnicity is a major political resource, as the rise of both Afrikaner nationalism and Black Consciousness showed.

Some of the most important bases of leverage are listed below;[30] their significance, and the impact of less tangible ones, will be shown in succeeding pages.

- Sheer numbers: between 1960 and 1985 the African population increased from nearly 11 million to nearly 25 million, over 40 per cent of whom lived in the 'white' areas and were permanently urbanised.
- In 1960 12,47 per cent of the African population were at school; by 1984 the figure had risen to 22,51 per cent (excluding the 'independent' bantustans).
- In 1960 there were 835 Africans in Standard 10; by 1985 the number was over 107 000.
- In 1963 there were approximately 1 900 Africans attending universities and a total of 72 received degrees; by 1985 there were 43 500 and 5 082 received degrees.
- In 1972 about 3 per cent of African workers were members of trade unions; by 1988 the figure was at least 30 per cent. In 1987 nearly 6 million man-days were lost as a result of strikes, representing a massive increase over the 10 558 lost in 1978.
- In 1965 middle-level manpower was only 20 per cent black; by 1985 the figure was 40 per cent; for high-level manpower the corresponding figures showed a rise from 25 per cent to 30 per cent.[31] Another estimate, based on census figures, showed that in 1952 75 per cent of all Africans in employment were unskilled labourers; by 1980 that figure had declined to less than 25 per cent, the remainder being employed in occupations that implied some degree of skill.[32]
- By 1985 Africans accounted for 32 per cent of personal disposable income, a figure that was projected to rise to 41 per cent by 2000. The figure implied formidable consumer power which could be, and was, used as a political weapon.

The trends mentioned above are the matrix in which black assertiveness increased, particularly in the 1980s. There were two sides of the coin: the steady haemorrhaging of the traditional concept of apartheid; and the acquisition of significant leverage by blacks. In the title of John Kane-Berman's book, which is a detailed account of the processes summarised above, South Africa's silent revolution was under way – and it was irreversible.

*   *   *

The educational system for Africans and, in particular, the Afrikaans language requirement, had been the spark that ignited the uprising of 1976–7. By the end of the 1970s the government had begun to institute reforms: the Afrikaans requirement was hastily dropped, legislation in 1979 provided for instruction in the mother tongue (the vernacular African language) up to and including Standard Two, whereafter the wishes of parents had to be taken into consideration in determining which of the official languages – English or Afrikaans – was to be used where the mother tongue could not be. Overwhelmingly, urban Africans wanted English to be used as soon as possible, but the Department of Education and Training, which controlled African education in the 'white' areas, dragged its feet, hoping that the mother tongue could be used even after Standard Two. Ultimately the Department had to give way, and regulations were promulgated authorising the use of English from Standard Three onwards.[33]

Verwoerd's views on what 'Bantu Education' should achieve had been repudiated, together with his insistence that funding should be derived from a separate Bantu Education Account, which received annually a fixed amount of R13 million from the General Revenue Account plus a proportion of the poll tax levied on Africans. From 1972, funding for African education came from the Consolidated Revenue Account, with the result that financing for African education was greatly increased: Hyslop calculates that the Department of Education and Training's budget increased from R143 million in 1978–9 to R709 million in 1984–5, reducing the disparity in spending on African children compared with white children from 18:1 in 1970 to 7:1 in 1984.[34] The principle of compulsory education for African children was accepted in 1980, but only painfully slow progress was made in implementing it.

In 1980 the government asked the Human Sciences Research Council to conduct an investigation into the schooling system with the aim of recommending all-round improvements, including making available education of the same quality for all population groups. Professor JP de Lange, rector of the Rand Afrikaans University, was appointed chairman, and a fairly diverse group of 25 (including eight blacks) were appointed as members. Ideologically the Committee was heterogeneous, including both conservatives and liberals, which precluded reaching a consensus on the philosophy and purposes of education. For this reason, the focus was on the provision of education.

The principal recommendation in what was a wide-ranging review of the education system was: 'Equal opportunities for education, including equal standards in education, for every inhabitant, irrespective of race, colour, creed or sex, shall be the purposeful endeavour of the

State.' In a White Paper published in November 1983, the government accepted this recommendation and other broad principles enunciated by the Committee, but balked at the recommendation for a single ministry, insisting that education must remain an 'own' affair that had to take place 'within the context of the particular group's own culture and frame of reference'. Education, in other words, had to remain firmly within the apartheid mould. Nevertheless, accepting the principle of equal opportunity in education showed that 'the centre of gravity of the education debate had shifted: the idea of equality no longer had to be argued'.[35] The argument would henceforth be whether 'separate' could ever be 'equal' – the issue dealt with by the United States Supreme court in the Brown case of 1954.

Thinking among even relatively moderate blacks had gone beyond what government was prepared to concede: moderates and militants alike regarded educational issues as a component of the wider issue, namely, apartheid itself. As they had in 1976–7, educational grievances would quickly shift to embrace the entire discriminatory order. After the high drama of 1976–7, the intensity of the pupils' protest declined (many of the leading activists had fled the country), but grievances continued to rankle. During 1980 there were extensive protests and boycotts in many areas, including among Coloured people in the Western Cape, but over the following two years protest was sporadic, tending to peter out. In 1983, however, it flared up again, and some 10 000 pupils participated in demonstrations and boycotts in all four provinces and several homelands.[36] The spirit of resistance was anything but dead.

A significant new organisation, the Congress of South African Students (Cosas), was founded in 1979. Its principal activists were battle-hardened 'veterans' of 1976–7. Monique Marks quotes a young pupil from the Diepkloof area of Soweto:

> That thing of 1976 made me to hate white people – I am sorry to say that. So at school they explained to me what was going on and I tried to find a way of helping my people, only to find that Cosas was the only organisation available to me at the time. So I joined Cosas so I could do something to end this thing in our country ... I was very proud of my involvement because as I grew up I told myself I wanted to fight for the people. I wanted to avenge the people who had been killed.[37]

Cosas began as a Black Consciousness organisation, but soon shifted into the ANC's sphere of influence by accepting the Freedom Charter

and committing itself to non-racialism and democracy. With the formation of the UDF in 1983, Cosas became, in effect, the school wing of the
movement.

During 1983 and especially 1984 the tempo of resistance increased: new
targets of popular opposition, in addition to the perennial opposition to
what was called 'gutter education', were readily found. The new system
of local government for Africans, legislative attempts by means of the
so-called 'Koornhof Bills' to regulate influx to urban areas, and the enactment of the Tricameral Constitution were grist to the opposition's mill.
A further impetus to protest was given by proposals to increase rent and
service charges in townships in the Vaal Triangle, at a time of deepening
unemployment and rising inflation. African local councillors, who had
been elected on uniformly low polls, were widely perceived as corrupt
lackeys of the apartheid state, and hence were prime targets (often literally) for militants.

A critical background factor in the African pupils' revolt of the 1980s
was the huge increase in numbers at the secondary level (from Standards
6 to 10). This had political implications since, generally, the higher the
standard the more disposed pupils were to militance. According to
Hartshorne's calculations, between 1975 and 1988 overall numbers grew
more than five times; Standard 6 enrolments increased three-and-a-half
times; Standard 8 increased more than six times; and Standard 10 21
times. As he points out, even a benign, democratic government would
have been hard put to cope with the surge.[38]

By the mid-1980s secondary schooling for Africans had virtually dis-
integrated, and Coloured schooling in the Western Cape was disrupted
on many occasions. During 1984 some 40 000 African pupils boycotted
school between July and August; in November about 400 000 African pupils joined a stay-away on 5 and 6 November; and by the end of the school
year in December 220 000 in various parts of the country were boycotting
school. On 25 August, the day of elections for the (Coloured) House of
Representatives, an estimated 800 000 pupils and university students (including 630 000 Coloureds) boycotted classes.

In 1985 and 1986 boycotts continued in many parts of the country. The
involvement of Coloured pupils was a notable feature that reflected not
only the alienation of particularly younger Coloured people, but also the
impact of the UDF and a range of community organisations. Even the
banning of Cosas in August 1985 made little difference to the intensity of
feeling. Local organisations, moreover, filled the vacuum to a considerable
extent. An attempt by the state to restrict boycotts in the worst affected
areas was ignored.

Figures for detentions and arrests between 1984 and 1988 vary considerably: some were detained in terms of 'normal' security legislation, others under the regulations imposed by the partial, and thereafter total, states of emergency. Moreover, figures from the 'independent' bantustans, which were also affected by protest, were not included in those released by the Minister of Law and Order. An unofficial estimate put the number of persons detained under the emergency regulations of between June 1985 and September 1988 at 32 000.[39] Of those eventually charged, 7 710, no fewer than 5 819 were aged 20 or younger. The role of youth as the cutting edge of resistance was self-evident. This was perhaps unsurprising, since over 50 per cent of the African population was below the age of 20 in 1980.

By the time of its banning in 1985 Cosas had developed into a mass movement; with the establishment of the UDF in 1983, and a sub-structure of youth organisations were affiliated with a wider movement that could reasonably claim to be the biggest mass movement in South African history.

'Youth' was an elastic category, including a fairly wide range of ages from under 14 years to nearly 30. It was also a politically charged term, referring as much to an 'attitude of mind' as age.[40] The label was analogous to the designation of all 'non-whites' as 'black', black referring less to skin colour than to common subordinate status. As the recession of the 1980s deepened, unemployment among Africans increased significantly, hitting young people especially hard: a survey conducted in 1979 of unemployment in Johannesburg, the Reef, Pretoria, Durban, Port Elizabeth and East London found that almost 50 per cent of all unemployed Africans were aged between 16 and 24 years.[41] The figure would rise even higher in the 1980s. Hartshorne calculated that in the decade 1980–89 over a million African candidates wrote the matriculation examination, of whom nearly 50 per cent failed. He estimated that over the decade some 400 000 left school with no certificate, and 150 000 dropped out of secondary school every year. Together these categories formed 'a disruptive and explosive sector of society'.[42]

*　*　*

As in 1976–7, grievances about the educational system, including specific or local ones, soon broadened into a generalised protest against apartheid: 'Bantu Education' was the product of the apartheid planners' frame of mind and, consequently, improvement in the quality of education was not possible unless and until the entire edifice of the unequal society was swept away. The school pupils, including many Coloureds, were joined by students from the black universities, also in periodic tumult during the 1980s, as well as some from the 'white' English-medium universities, where Nusas still dominated student politics.

An older generation of Africans, while hating Bantu Education and its patent aims, had nevertheless acquiesced in the new system, reflecting the effective cowing of African protest in the 1960s and early 1970s. A widespread response was that poor-quality education was better than none. Moreover, it was reckoned, bright, conscientious pupils could beat the system with a supreme effort. In an article lamenting the appalling conditions in many African schools, Raks Ramogale, a professor of English at the University of Venda, compared his school experience with the situation in 2000:

> ... many of us in leadership positions today were groomed by the self-same schools. But of course we went to these schools in a different era. I ... can clearly recall that the learning environment then was not, in spite of material scarcity and the harsh rule of apartheid ideologues, as desolate as it is today. Then there was a sharp sense of academic purpose and scholastic excellence was a common value. For us then, excellence had an important political implication: it was a blow for freedom, an act of struggle. We – pupils and teachers – worked hard and sought to excel because to do so was to contribute meaningfully to the failure of apartheid's grand design: the oppression of blacks through the intentional expansion of mediocrity.[43]

The events of 1976–7 had opened a generational rift that went far beyond the normal adolescent chafing against the bonds of authority; the turbulent 1980s, during which school boycotts and its accompanying slogan 'Liberation now, Education later' were frequent, widened the rift, causing anguish to many parents, including older community leaders, who had made major sacrifices to put their children through school. Nomavenda Mathiane, a journalist with an acute sense of what ordinary people in Soweto were feeling, expressed resentment that was typical of the older generation:

> As things stand in Soweto and most townships, schooling has long ceased to be an educational matter. It is political ... . The education of the black child has moved from the parents and educationists into the political arena. The tragedy of this situation is that, in view of the prevailing political climate, the more fortunate black parents

have removed their children from trouble-torn schools and have either taken them to the homelands or to white [private] schools. Those children left behind who wish to go to school cannot, and woe unto those who dare to against 'the will of the people'.[44]

For many parents, education represented the only hope for their children to obtain work, however limited the possibilities of doing so. There was also the practical consideration that school attendance fulfilled a de facto child-minding function when the parents were at work, which often involved travelling long distances and lengthy absences from home. Owing to the dislocation caused by the migrant labour system, influx control and the institutionalisation of insecurity in the urban areas, many households, perhaps over 50 per cent, were headed by women, which added to the strain of caring for children. Women's problems were exacerbated by the macho attitude of many men, which commonly expressed itself in serial sexual liaisons that often involved violence against women.

The townships were violent places. Aside from the conflicts between police and protestors, crime and gangsterism were rife; violence in spousal and interpersonal relationships was also common. It is no exaggeration to say that violence was woven into the very fabric of everyday township life. What is striking about a collection of diaries of Soweto children, aged between 12 and 14, written in 1982, is the matter-of-fact way in which violence, some of it horrific, is described by the young writers. For example, a 13-year-old girl's entry for 21 September 1982 reads:

> I left home at 6.30am and arrived at school at 7.30am. I saw, on my way, a boy and his mother fighting for not going to school. His mother said, Sipho go to school, otherwise I am going to call the teachers to come and fetch you. Sipho said, When you call them I'm going to stab you in your mouth, because you are talking nonsense, leave me alone. I don't need school ... .[45]

Respect for one's elders was a fundamental part of traditional African culture; but during these turbulent times it was subverted, if not destroyed. The columns of African newspapers and other publications in the 1980s were filled with lamentations of parents, teachers and community leaders about the wildness and uncontrollability of many youngsters. Aggrey Klaaste, a respected *Sowetan* journalist, asked plaintively how it was that these 'lovely kids' had been turned into 'monsters', as he described seeing a group of smartly dressed youngsters about to kill a hapless victim.[46]

School principals were in a peculiarly invidious position, being responsible to a harshly bureaucratic state department, but also unable to exercise authority over their pupils. Mathiane quotes a frustrated Soweto headmaster deploring the collapse of the educational mission:

> In the past we felt hopeless with Bantu Education. Educationalists claimed that the longer a child stayed at school the more difficult it was to undo the harm done by Bantu Education. So year in and year out we turned out a frustrated product. But at least they knew their limitations and worked from that premise. Today, we have a zombie who comes to school, squanders his pocket money at break and goes home without having touched a book. The teacher can do nothing.[47]

Variations on this theme occurred in many areas, even in small towns that had previously been relatively unaffected by protest and the violence that invariably followed. Grahamstown, a small city in the Eastern Cape, provides an example. CW Manona, a social anthropologist who observed events between 1984 and 1986, described how efforts by church and civic organisations to mediate between pupils and parents with a view to ending the school boycott achieved nothing: 'The parents left the meetings dejected, as students argued for more action.' He concluded:

> Black societies traditionally have been structured on the dependence of children on their parents and elders – teachers also were not to be questioned or criticised. All this has changed, and the change has been a great shock for the older generation. Civic and political structures were put in place and run by the youth who, despite the disruptions, were better educated than their elders. This has led to a widened generation gap.[48]

Anecdotal evidence suggested another consequence of school boycotts and the violence: continued exposure to dangerous, life-threatening conditions increases the procreative urge among males. This was probably a factor in the heightened sexual activity that resulted in increasing teenage pregnancies. Many of the 'comrades' or 'young lions', as the youthful militants were called, abandoned whatever restraints remained, proclaiming the slogan 'Have a baby for the revolution!' Thokozani Xaba describes the phenomenon of 'struggle masculinity' which was accompanied by chauvinist attitudes and behaviour towards women:

> During [the 1980s] being a 'comrade' endowed a young man with

social respect and status within his community. Being referred to as a 'young lion' and a 'liberator' was an intoxicating and psychologically satiating accolade. This was especially so to young men who were members of a group with low social status and who came from families where accolades of any kind were hard to come by. The accolades would have given any young man an idea of himself that was disproportionate to reality. Such accolades also came along with the kind of power and respect which attracted women to men. As such, 'young lions', especially those in leadership positions, were coveted by women.[49]

The dangers of 'the struggle' produced a sense of excitement and exhilaration at the prospect of liberation, which they believed to be imminent. What Seekings calls 'a culture of militaristic camaraderie' seized the youth, imbuing them with a sense of collective power and freedom from restraints.[50]

Nothing in the preceding paragraphs should be construed as a blanket generalisation about youth or as implying that they were a homogeneous category. Research by Seekings, Gill Straker and Monique Marks suggests significant variation among leaders and, especially, followers. Some were battle-hardened veterans of 1976–7, and folk memories of those times remained vivid. Straker notes that the leaders, far more than others, came from families with histories of resistance.[51] According to Marks, many of the followers, while wanting change, had only limited political understanding and little notion of what activism involved.[52] From several accounts it is clear that heavy peer group pressure was applied to those reluctant or hesitant to join. Pupils who did not wish to boycott school, or wanted to write examinations, were often threatened, and even whipped, by militants. Strong-arm methods were also used against others who declined to observe stay-aways from work or to participate in boycotts of white-owned shops. Describing Soweto in 1986, Mathiane writes:

> [The] situation in Soweto is such that people live in fear. There is a strongly believed myth that the students are a faceless and leaderless mob and nobody dares question their actions. The leader who survives these days is the one who endorses whatever the youth says, be it right or wrong. People have opted for popularity with the students because opposing them is to invite being 'necklaced'.[53]

'Necklacing' was a hideous method of killing people by trussing them in a petrol-soaked tyre and igniting it. Its victims included alleged police informers (so-called *impimpis*), local councillors, political opponents and others who dared cross the paths of militants. According to police statistics, 406 people were 'necklaced' between September 1984 and December 1989.[54] It was a barbaric practice that outraged many senior leaders, including Archbishop Desmond Tutu. Although it was never condoned or encouraged by the UDF or the ANC, their outright condemnations were either slow in coming or ambivalent.[55]

The issue came to a head in a notorious speech made by Winnie Mandela, wife of the imprisoned Nelson Mandela, in April 1986:

> We have no guns – we have only stones, boxes of matches and petrol. Together, hand in hand, with our boxes of matches and our necklaces we shall liberate this country.[56]

The speech caused a storm of protest, nationally and internationally. Apart from being a propaganda gift to the government, it was a huge embarrassment to the ANC and the UDF. Winnie Mandela remained popular among young militants, a popularity that would even survive surrounding herself with a group of young thugs, curiously named the Mandela Football Club, which would terrorise Soweto in the late 1980s, as well as being implicated in several kidnappings and murders.

It was perhaps inevitable that young criminal elements would attach themselves to the militants – many of whom deplored their criminal activities and drug-taking habits. The so-called 'com-tsotsis' (the word is an abbreviated combination of 'comrade' and 'tsotsi', the latter meaning 'young gangster') operated in the slipstream of the militant activists, with the violence of the struggle often masking their own criminal violence. Theft of goods owned by non-Africans could be claimed as 'repossession', implying that the goods in question – or the means whereby they were obtained – had been wrongfully acquired from Africans.

The com-tsotsis were an embarrassment to the leaders of the youth movements, who were often idealistic, dedicated and even austere or moralistic in their outlooks. Criminal activity, moreover, gave the authorities useful material to paint all of the young activists as criminals. Schlemmer writes:

> There is undoubtedly a minority among youth which is anti-social, deeply enmeshed in gang culture and which has a criminal predisposition. There is also a minority of youth which may be characterised by 'organised or semi-organised' socio-political alienation … [who] may be at least available for confrontation and violence in

the township ... these are minorities. One dare not understand all township youth in these terms. The passive majority remains largely invisible.[57]

Many among the 'passive majority' were followers who were swept up by peer group pressure or by a sense of excitement or both. By the end of 1984, when serious and enduring revolt had begun, an estimated one million black youths had participated in mass protest, which included a significant proportion of the six million pupils in black schools.[58] Lodge estimates that some 50 000 or so teenagers and young adults 'carried [the UDF] through its most assertive and powerful phases'.[59] Again, assuming that he is referring principally to the more dedicated activists who contributed the bulk of the leadership category, 50 000 was a sizeable figure, indicative of the scale and intensity of the revolt. Youth organisations, moreover, formed the large majority of the UDF's affiliates. Restraining the young militants and channelling their energies into constructive action would be a recurring problem for the relatively sober-minded and cautious leadership of the UDF.

*   *   *

The initiative for the formation of the UDF came from a speech by Allan Boesak delivered in January 1983. As mentioned, Boesak was a young theologian from the NG Sendingkerk, who had obtained a doctorate in theology from a Dutch theological institute. A fiery orator, he quickly attracted a considerable following in the Coloured community and rose steadily in the church hierarchy, becoming president of the World Alliance of Reformed Churches in 1982.

In his speech Boesak called for the formation of a front to oppose the government's constitutional plans. His call struck a receptive chord and planning began for the establishment of the United Democratic Front, which was formally launched at a mass rally in Cape Town in August 1983. Structurally, the UDF was a federation of affiliated organisations that precluded membership of individuals. By the time of its banning in February 1988 the UDF claimed to have between 700 and 800 affiliates, giving it a total membership of 2.5 million.

The ANC had no known direct hand in the creation of the UDF, although its formation accorded with the ANC's recognition that a mass-based above-ground organisation was a necessary complement to waging a 'people's war'. In August 1979, following the visit of an ANC delegation to Vietnam, the Politico-Military Strategy Commission reported to the ANC's National Executive Committee that the struggle had neglected some areas of crucial importance. It recommended a programme of action 'round which mass activity can be generated at all levels of our society'. This involved creating a 'nation-wide popular liberation front':

> We must bring about the broadest possible unity of all national groups, classes and strata, organisations, groups and prominent personalities around local and national issues. This means we must combine illegal with legal and semi-legal activity to ensure such mass mobilisation and to establish our presence and influence wherever the people are.[60]

Broadly, the UDF fitted this specification. It was, moreover, apparent from its selection of patrons (largely honorific roles) and presidents where its sympathies lay: all were ANC stalwarts, the patrons including Nelson Mandela, Govan Mbeki and Walter Sisulu. With few exceptions, the affiliating organisations were headed by ANC members or sympathisers. Similarly, the National Executive Committee was composed exclusively of ANC-aligned people.[61] It accepted also the ANC's long-standing internal practice of requiring that the majority of leadership positions be occupied by Africans. Moreover, although it was not formally adopted until 1987, it was clear from the UDF's inception that the majority of its affiliates supported the Freedom Charter. It was hardly surprising that many regarded the UDF as the ANC's internal surrogate, despite its denials that this was the case.

It is perhaps surprising, in view of these open indications of support for the banned ANC, that the state did not immediately ban the UDF on grounds that it was 'furthering the aims of a banned organisation'. Given its previous record of proscribing organisations that it deemed to be threats, why did it not try to nip the UDF's growth in the bud, prior to its becoming a movement that played a major role in destroying the old order? It was indeed effectively banned in February 1988, but not before it had made a considerable impact. It was not as if the state had any doubts about the UDF's ANC leanings, nor about its implacable opposition to the Tricameral Constitution and the entire apartheid system.

The conventional explanation for the state's apparent toleration of the UDF was that heavy-handed action against a leading opponent would have diminished the legitimacy of the elections for the Coloured and Indian houses of the Tricameral Parliament, held in August 1984. This was probably so, but if it was tolerance it was certainly 'repressive tolerance' of a Marcusean kind, and it did not extend to office-bearers of the

UDF or to leading figures in a number of its affiliates, who commonly set the pace in orchestrating local protests. Many were banned or detained over the next few years, and UDF-inspired activity was subject to continual police harassment. Perhaps the strategy was to hollow out the UDF by neutralising its key figures. Although the UDF was hard hit, it was to some extent able to counter the strategy by having a second rung of replacement leaders whose low profiles had not yet caught the attention of the security police.

Undoubtedly the vigorous campaign waged by the UDF against the Tricameral Constitution played a part in the derisorily low registration and voter turnout. This was achieved in spite of the failure to meet its target of one million signatures for a petition rejecting the Constitution and the so-called 'Koornhof Bills', and demanding instead a non-racial democratic system. Eventually hardly one-third of the target was met, which the UDF attributed, with some justification, to police intimidation.

The irony of the new system's effect of driving home to some Nationalists the human costs of apartheid has been noted; the flip-side was that the introduction of the Constitution spawned the UDF, which in turn precipitated the long crisis that was instrumental in eventually causing the downfall of apartheid.

FW de Klerk supported the 'firm action' taken by the state, which he believed was necessary to create a peaceful climate for negotiation, but:

> I also began to realise that the initiatives that we were planning at that stage to extend political rights to black [African] South Africans were inadequate to defuse the growing crisis. In my mind, the development of a meaningful framework for black political rights became a matter of the greatest urgency.[62]

Many tributaries flowed into the main stream of protest. Not all were initiated by the UDF; but the UDF's achievement was to provide a national focus: to change the metaphor, local and regional issues, of which there were many, could be woven into a national tapestry of protest, thereby greatly augmenting its force. It was, moreover, a two-way process: local communities with local grievances, often with no history of overt protest, were emboldened by being part of a country-wide movement; while the demonstration effect pulled yet others into the protest. Commonly, local issues arose spontaneously, although, no doubt, they were inflamed by the prevailing country-wide atmosphere.

The crisis that gripped South Africa in the mid-1980s was sparked by what an eye-witness, Johannes Rantete, called the 'Sebokeng Rebellion of 1984'.[63] Sebokeng, about 40 miles south of Johannesburg, had a population of over 500 000. It was one of a cluster of townships in the Vaal Triangle that fell under the Lekoa Town Council, which had been elected on a derisory 14.7 per cent poll in November 1983. In many respects what began in Sebokeng on 3 September 1984 established a pattern that was broadly replicated in many other townships.

Patrick Noonan, a Catholic priest who lived in Sebokeng, describes 'the incubation period', beginning in 1982, when frustrations and resentment were building up, and 'natural networking by highly motivated like-minded people' was occurring. Bad conditions in schools, growing unemployment, inflation and poor municipal services all fanned the flames of resistance. The ANC's Radio Freedom, broadcast from Lusaka, was avidly listened to. During 1982 an 'action committee' was formed that later transformed itself into the Vaal Civic Association, which became an affiliate of the UDF.[64]

By late August 1984 momentum was building up and demands had crystallised. The last straw had been a decision by the Lekoa Town Council to raise rents by R5.90 per month, in spite of the inability of many residents to pay even the existing charges. Apart from demanding that the increase be scrapped, and the rental be reduced to R30, an emotionally charged meeting decided to call a stayaway from work and school for 3 September, and to demand that councillors resign or face the boycotting of their businesses (often, in the opinion of the community, acquired by corrupt means). Approximately 60 per cent of workers and virtually all school pupils heeded the stayaway call.

By the end of the day, after a protest march which was broken up by police, 14 people lay dead, many others were injured, and councillors' homes had been attacked. Clearly it had been a display of community solidarity and anger that the police were not going to ignore. According to figures collated by the Vaal Ministers Solidarity Group – clergy who played a vital role in the events – 72 people were killed in the Vaal Triangle between 2 September and 1 January 1985.[65] Predictably, the police and the Minister of Law and Order insisted that the protest was 'artificially instigated' by outside agitators. While it was true that some were dissuaded from going to work through fear of reprisals, the widespread community anger did not need agitators to stir many into action.

Police and army platoons deployed in the townships exacerbated the tensions by heavy-handed action. Little had been learned about less draconian methods of crowd control since 1976–7. In response to an interviewer's questions, senior police officers maintained that the use of minimum force in unrest situations was difficult to implement for four reasons:

the police were almost invariably outnumbered by expanding crowds; the open terrain of townships heightened their vulnerability to being surrounded and cut off; and high temperatures and breezes commonly rendered tear gas ineffective, as well as making it difficult to wear heavy protective gear. Many police or young soldiers, moreover, were young, poorly trained, and often terrified out of their wits.[66]

The Southern African Catholic Bishops' Conference, hardly a radical body, produced a report in November 1984, whose opening paragraph read:

> The allegations in the affidavits and statements in our possession describe an alarming carelessness or disregard for the people, property, feelings and even lives of the inhabitants of South Africa's black townships. The overwhelming impression created by the affidavits as a whole is that the police behaviour in the townships resembled that of an occupying foreign army controlling enemy territory by force without regard for the civilian population and, it appears, without regard for the law.

The report went on to enumerate and substantiate allegations that included reckless or wanton violence; damage to property; provocative, callous or insensitive conduct; and indiscriminate or reckless use of teargas. It noted, moreover, that while both black and white police had been involved, 'in most cases there seems to have been a preponderance of young white policemen'.[67] For the most part they were drawn from that class of whites who felt most threatened by black resistance, and consequently had a proclivity towards ultra-rightwing views.

The police dismissal of these views was unconvincing. At the same time, however, it should be recalled that police were among the prime targets of protesters. According to official figures, between September 1984 and February 1985 five African council members and four African policemen were murdered; 109 African councillors were attacked; 56 African policemen were injured; 143 African schools, six churches and nine clinics were destroyed; the homes of 66 council members were destroyed; and 147 council members were forced to resign from local councils, which in a number of cases caused the councils and community services to collapse completely. Even the police acknowledged that by mid-1985 violent unrest prevailed in most important African townships in the country, with the exception of Soweto.[68]

The actions of the police in dealing with demonstrations, marches and other gatherings came under judicial scrutiny after 20 Africans (nine of whom were 16 years or younger) were killed by police fire at Uitenhage (in the Eastern Cape) in March 1985. They were part of a procession of between 3 000 and 4 000 that was walking to a cemetery to attend funerals of people killed in previous police action which, unbeknown to them, had been banned. Their proposed route took them through a 'white' part of Uitenhage.

The commission of inquiry was headed by a conservative judge, DDV Kannemeyer, who, despite substantially whitewashing police behaviour, was unable to avoid some critical observations. Allegations that the marchers' intention was to attack whites or that the majority were armed were rejected. He conceded that the police were 'clearly deeply disturbed and frightened by what they saw', but nevertheless found that they were not equipped with non-lethal weapons, such as teargas, rubber bullets or birdshot:

> Had the holding of funerals not unnecessarily been prohibited on doubtful grounds there can be little doubt that the procession would have passed through Uitenhage without incident .... Had proper equipment been available the gathering may well have been dispersed with little or no harm to the persons involved.[69]

Comparable findings emerged from an analysis by Johan Olivier, who examined the details of 657 events ('ethnic collective action' in his designation) in the Pretoria-Witwatersrand-Vaal Triangle between 1970 and 1984. His conclusion was that 'the mere presence of police at events increased the subsequent rate of collective action by 39% over events where police were not present'; and if the police opened fire, the rate increased by 56 per cent.[70] The meaning was clear, and indirectly confirmed Kannemeyer's finding, that police reaction triggered even greater anger. Helen Suzman urged the Minister of Law and Order to keep police away from funerals, especially those of people who had been killed by the police: 'Their very presence is like a red rag to a bull.' She pointed out that at several large funerals, including those of Sobukwe and Biko, the police had been sensible enough to keep a low profile and there were no confrontations.[71]

Being the primary source of control and the frontline defence of apartheid, maintaining law and order meant protecting the racial order. Brogden and Shearing observed:

> Externally, the SAP [South African Police] has been closely identified with the executive branch of government, an instrument of National Party partisanship. Political accountability remains minimal. There

is none at all to the black majority population. But even for white society, accountability is very limited.[72]

Police actions could expect to be defended by the Minister of Law and Order, and pertinacious questioning by the likes of Helen Suzman was commonly fobbed off on the pretext that it was 'not in the national interest' for the required information to be disclosed.

The frontline defence of apartheid meant enforcing racial legislation. No law was more vexatious to Africans than that providing for influx control (until its abolition in 1986), which branded the police as the hated instrument of injustice rather than as protectors of ordinary people from crime. The surge of protest in the 1980s compounded the hatred by creating regular confrontation between the police and protesters.

Many of the white police shared the views of the Conservative Party (which boasted about its support among police), and even the AWB. They shared the anti-communist paranoia propagated by 'total onslaught' thinking. It was very likely that some, when confronted by protesters, abandoned restraint and succumbed to the urge to shoot indiscriminately, or engaged in other forms of provocation. There was, moreover, clear evidence of police collaboration with Inkatha in the Natal conflict (see pp. 331–342).

It is no argument in mitigation of police behaviour to suggest that on occasion protesters themselves deliberately sought to provoke the police, which was often not difficult to do. Ernie Wentzel, a leading liberal advocate who appeared for the defence in many political trials, thought that the frequency with which stones and petrol bombs were thrown at the police suggested that many activists seemed intent on provoking the police to react violently so that government action to restore order could be discredited.[73] If this indeed was the strategy, it succeeded, and deflected any criticism of their own role in confrontation.

According to Khehla Shubane, Soweto's relative quiescence in 1984–6 was attributable to a combination of factors: organisational weakness, the absence of key community leaders who had been drawn into national and regional UDF structures, conflict among rival organisations, and the rise of a home-owning middle class that was able to find new job opportunities in Johannesburg. This was to change after mid-1986 when the Soweto Civic Association organised the community into street committees and called for a rent boycott as a way of protesting against an illegitimate local council that had been elected in 1983 on a 10.7 percentage poll.[74]

Two other factors became prominent in the uprising of the mid-1980s: first, funerals of those killed in conflict became highly significant symbolic occasions where, apart from cathartic outpourings of grief, political activism was given a regular added impetus by graveside speeches, invariably delivered by activists themselves. Noonan, who officiated at a number of funerals, describes one such occasion:

> Like other funerals, it was supercharged with the youth dominating the proceedings but at the same time, respecting the wishes of the presiding ministers and priests. In speech after speech they vented their anger and frustration. Anti-government rhetoric was interspersed with freedom songs and declarations of 'Amandla!' [Power!] accompanied by clenched fists punctuating the air.[75]

Highly politicised funerals, which served as occasions for mobilisation, were nothing new – the funerals of Steve Biko in 1977 and Robert Mangaliso Sobukwe in 1978, and many of those killed in the 1976–7 uprising, were equally politicised – but the scale of deaths in the 1980s was far greater. Attempts by the police to limit attendance met with only scant success. In a number of cases mourners and the police clashed, with the result that funerals begat yet more funerals. On the other hand, where police kept a low profile, sometimes by prior arrangement with the organisers, funerals took place without violence. The Catholic Bishops' report described police conduct at funerals in the Vaal Triangle as 'particularly provocative':

> Although in some cases funerals took place without the necessary permission that was required for any gathering of more than two people, if the police had maintained a lower profile during these sensitive occasions, the bitterness they created would have been avoided.

The report listed several occasions on which apparently gratuitous beatings were meted out to mourners.[76]

A second factor of importance in the turbulent 1980s was the phenomenon of the 'turbulent priest' and the role of churches over the period. While prominent clerics such as Archbishop Desmond Tutu, Allan Boesak, Frank Chikane and Beyers Naude were well-known activists, there were many others in local communities who supported 'the struggle' by identifying with the plight of their congregants. Noonan's account of the Vaal Triangle uprising contains many references to the individual or collective role of clergy, black and white, in protecting their flocks (as best they could), comforting the bereaved, burying the dead, collecting affidavits, allowing clandestine meetings of activists to take place on church

premises, providing sanctuary, and acting as intermediaries between communities and the authorities, and between rival political organisations.
Above all, the churches bestowed a theological legitimacy on the morality
of the struggle, though many, including Tutu, opposed the recourse to
violence that exponents of 'liberation theology' had endorsed.[77]

While churches and bodies like the South African Council of Churches
clearly played an important role in the downfall of apartheid, two questions remain: first, to what extent, if any, did the fact that nearly 80 per
cent of South Africans describe themselves as Christians (including over
30 per cent of the African population who were adherents of the many
independent African churches) impose at least some moral bounds on the
ferocity of the conflicts? Secondly, did the dogmatic moralism of a number
of religious bodies, or individuals within those bodies, promote an inflexibility of attitude that was hardly helpful in creating a negotiating climate
to facilitate the compromises that would be necessary if a settlement were
to be reached? Neither question allows a straightforward answer.

The UDF was a secular organisation whose affiliates included people
of several faiths. As the names of the patrons and presidents show, however, prominent Christian clerics were closely involved. Mark Swilling
notes that the rhetoric of ministers, imams and Gandhians of the Indian
Congress was more conservative than that of many of the more radical
working class leaders.[78] The UDF was a multi-class front, and inevitably it was ideologically heterogeneous, its principles being couched in the
broadest of terms that could be accepted across the board.

At its inception the UDF had targeted the Tricameral Constitution and
the 'Koornhof Bills'. It played little or no role in the Vaal Triangle uprising, although the Vaal Civic Association, a UDF affiliate, was actively
involved. The uprising transformed the struggle, and hugely widened its
parameters, both in terms of geographical spread and the scope of demands, which became more explicitly aimed at eliminating apartheid and
replacing it with majority rule. A powerful weapon, the stayaway protest strike, which had had mixed success in the past, was relaunched on
5 and 6 November 1984. An estimated 500 000 workers in the Pretoria-
Witwatersrand-Vereeniging area stayed away on both days. By mid-June
1988, 70 stayaways, some national and some regional, organised by various bodies, had taken place.[79]

Consumer boycotts, also used in the past with mixed success, also became frequent, especially in the Eastern Cape, with its long tradition of
organised opposition, and the Transvaal. The record shows that in many
cases the boycotts had a severe impact on white-owned businesses, sometimes forcing the owners to negotiate with the organisers or, rarely, even

to make representations to government about the hardships that apartheid inflicted on Africans. In a few cases, sympathetic white businesses were exempted from boycotts.[80] The downside of the strategy was that violators of the boycott were sometimes liable to rough treatment, such as being forced to drink cooking oil or liquid soap 'illicitly' bought from white shops.

From the start the UDF faced problems that derived from its organisational structure. Its affiliates retained their autonomy, which meant that the national leadership had difficulty in laying down policies to which the affiliates and the regions would adhere. It was a less troublesome issue in the earliest phase, when there was a high degree of consensus in opposing the Constitution. Indeed, such was the anger that it was often the case that local affiliates were the tail that wagged the national dog. In spite of this problem, the UDF succeeded in providing a national focus for protest.

Eighteen months after its formation, Trevor Manuel, branch secretary in the Western Cape region, acknowledged that the UDF was far from monolithic:

> Divisions were blurred in the euphoria of the Front's formation, but different opinions and perspectives are emerging. It is necessary to do battle at an ideological level to define a clearer ideological stance.[81]

On the other hand, Patrick 'Terror' Lekota, the national publicity secretary, cautioned that forging a coherent ideological programme would undermine the concept of the Front; but unity in action 'did give birth to common perceptions, programmes and styles of work'.[82]

Ideological heterogeneity and its multi-class character largely explain the UDF's caution in formally adopting the Freedom Charter; it was only in mid-1987 that it did so, although in the intervening years since 1984 a number of affiliates had already adopted it. The Freedom Charter itself was ideologically a 'catch-all' document that was broad enough and vague enough to enable the various ideological strands in the Congress Alliance (with the notable exception of the Africanists) to accept it. As Lodge notes, however, different interpretations could be placed on the Charter. He identifies three distinct tendencies in the UDF's leadership and the intelligentsia: middle-class nationalists, often from an older generation of activists; 'national democrats' who supported the ANC/SACP's programme for a 'two-stage' revolution; and socialists, intent on ensuring that working-class objectives should prevail.[83]

A significant innovation in the mobilisation of communities for protest was the civic organisation, commonly referred to as 'the civic'. Many, like the Port Elizabeth Black Civic Organisation (established in 1979) preceded the formation of the UDF, but the great majority were formed in 1983 and after. Typically the civic was an association of residents, formed to protest against local conditions, notably housing and rents, but feeding into the country-wide protest – and, reciprocally, drawing added impetus from the national focus. Eighty-two civics were represented at the launch of the UDF in 1984.[84] By 1987 perhaps as many as 500 civics existed, including a number in rural areas. It reflected an unprecedented degree of mobilisation. Collectively they constituted one of the UDF's principal driving forces. What was also notable was the mushrooming of civics among the Coloured people of the Western Cape.

There was considerable variation in the make-up of civics and their effectiveness. One of the most effective and efficiently run civics was the Cradock Residents' Association (Cradora), which was established in 1983 on the initiative of Matthew Goniwe, a young science teacher at the local African high school. His transfer to another town early in 1984, for obvious political reasons, sparked a major boycott and intense community resentment. Cradora's strength lay in the street committee system in the African township of 17 000 people. It was highly effective, ensuring that the entire community could be rapidly mobilised. Goniwe's organisational talent was used to set up civics in several other Karoo towns and on the Eastern Cape coast. Goniwe was obviously regarded as a major threat by the security police, who murdered him and three other UDF officials in July 1985.

Draconian security legislation, extended by successive states of emergency, had a disruptive effect on the UDF's activities. Fifty UDF members and supporters had been detained during 1984 around the time of the Coloured and Indian elections, and by August 1985, 45 out of the 80 national and regional executive members of the UDF were either in detention or awaiting trial – or had been assassinated.[85] Eleven UDF activists or officials were recorded as missing or as having been assassinated. The scale of the crackdown can be inferred from figures released by the Minister of Law and Order showing that in 1985 nearly 19 000 persons had been arrested for 'unrest offences' including public violence, arson and murder, of whom 72 per cent were under the age of 20.

In the same year 114 trials of persons charged with political offences took place: 2 368 were charged, but 2 067 were acquitted. Fifty-five persons were charged with high treason in seven trials.[86]

Of the treason trials, in which those convicted could face the death penalty, the so-called Delmas (a town east of Johannesburg) trial was especially significant because, effectively, the UDF was charged with being a surrogate of the ANC and conspiring to overthrow the state by violence. Patrick Lekota and Popo Molefe, both senior national office-bearers in the UDF, and 20 others stood accused. Three were eventually acquitted after a lengthy trial which began in October 1985 and ended in November 1988. Lekota, Molefe and Moss Chikane (a former executive member of the UDF's Transvaal region) were convicted of treason and sentenced to lengthy terms of imprisonment. The trial judge found that they had 'been part of the UDF's conspiracy to render South Africa ungovernable and to overthrow the government with violence'. A year later, however, the Appellate Division of the Supreme Court overturned the verdict of the lower court on a technicality, finding that the trial judge had erred in dismissing one of the assessors, Professor Willem Joubert (a liberal Afrikaner who had signed the UDF's one million signatures campaign), without allowing either Joubert or the defendants to be heard on the matter.

Despite this and other legal victories, the disruptions of the UDF caused by arrests, trials, tough enforcement of emergency regulations and ongoing harassment by vigilantes weakened its ability to orchestrate national or regional campaigns. Local campaigns such as rent and consumer boycotts continued, however, though largely outside of the UDF's initiative. By September 1986 rent boycotts affected approximately 50 townships countrywide and many African local governments had ceased to function because of the loss of their principal source of revenue and the attacks on councillors.[87] For many occupiers, though, non-payment reflected inability to pay as much as opposition to the councils.

Despite the mauling it was receiving, the UDF managed to survive. Indeed, survival became the priority. Its (first) annual conference, held in April 1985, proclaimed the theme 'From Protest to Challenge ... Mobilisation to Organisation'. It passed resolutions demanding the scrapping of all discriminatory legislation and practices, the release of political prisoners and the repeal of all security legislation, as well as the disbanding of the army, police and other 'repressive apparatuses'. In August the UDF sent a memorandum to foreign governments and businesses, and to South African business organisations, urging them to break diplomatic, economic, military and sporting ties, declaring that continued participation in the economy sustained apartheid.[88]

It was technically a serious offence to advocate economic sanctions, but the state declined to prosecute, possibly because consistency would have required it also to prosecute Desmond Tutu, winner of the Nobel Peace Prize in 1984, who was to become the (Anglican) Archbishop of Cape Town in 1986. Tutu, probably the best-known African leader after

Mandela, was the most influential advocate of sanctions, believing them to be the only alternative to the violent overthrow of apartheid. The international shockwaves that Tutu's arrest and prosecution would have caused outweighed any advantages to be derived from silencing the pertinacious cleric. Already heavy-handed efforts to suppress the uprisings had cost Botha's government much of whatever international credibility it retained, and overshadowed the significance of his reforms.

*　*　*

At the ANC's Consultative Conference in Kabwe, in June 1985, Tambo lavished praise on the UDF, describing it as 'that outstanding example of the political maturity of our people'. Proclaiming the 'Decade of Liberation', he said that Conference would be remembered as a 'council-of-war that planned the seizure of power by these masses [referring presumably to people mobilised by the UDF]' and a prelude to taking the country 'through the terrible but cleansing fires of revolutionary war to a condition of peace'. This was heady, though romantic, even Fanonesque, stuff. Tambo was on firmer ground in saying that apartheid was in 'a deep and permanent general crisis from which it cannot extricate itself'. He noted also that the mass offensive was directed at the very machinery of apartheid, 'at making our country ungovernable'. All of this despite his candid acknowledgement that the ANC's organisation inside the country was 'relatively weak'.[89] According to Mac Maharaj, a leading MK cadre, the aim of ungovernability was to neutralise blacks who had been co-opted into apartheid structures:

> We realised that the epicentre of the revolt would be in the urban areas and that the instruments lay in the urban councils and their adjuncts: civil service, the police, and so on. Apartheid had even begun to use black police as its frontline shock troops. This was the context in which ungovernability arose. We would make it impossible for the regime to use any of its usual instruments, even indirect ones, to maintain control.[90]

Making the country 'ungovernable' became the catch-phrase of the time. Although the UDF as such never explicitly endorsed it – which would have had serious legal repercussions – it certainly resonated with the sentiments of militants, who shared Tambo's view that the seizure of power was possible, and, in their belief, even imminent. The collapse of many African local councils, the disruption of schooling and continuing violence obviously were serious manifestations of crisis. The imposition of a countrywide state of emergency on 12 June 1986 and the presence of over 30 000 troops in townships were acknowledgements by the state of the need for crisis management, which became the *leitmotif* of the following years. Tambo acknowledged that not all areas of the country and not all sections of the oppressed had responded with equal vigour and determination, thereby enabling the state to concentrate its forces on certain areas.[91] The insurrection, in other words, although extensive, was not countrywide. However popular the quest for 'ungovernability' became, the extent of the crisis never remotely threatened to topple the state. From time to time 'no-go' areas were created in some townships, but they were invariably of short duration. The claim made by the Commissioner of Police, General PJ Coetzee, in August 1986, that the state remained in full control of the country, was substantially accurate.[92] But effective administration was nevertheless rendered impossible in many towns.

Complementing 'ungovernability' and substituting a new type of authority for discredited state institutions was 'people's power', a concept that referred obliquely to zones liberated by the 'people's war'. It implied that where administration had collapsed, communities themselves should assume responsibility for the provision of day-to-day services such as garbage removal and street cleaning, as well as welfare and judicial functions. The better-established the network of street and war committees in any township, the more effective 'people's power' was likely to be. 'People's power', moreover, was not merely a practical response to the disruption of state-provided services: it was also a means of consolidating the gains that mobilisation had made. As Zwelakhe Sisulu put it in 1986:

> The reason that people's power strengthens us ... is that our organisation becomes one with the masses. It becomes much more difficult for the state to cripple us by removing our leadership, or attacking our organisations. Instead they confront the whole population and occupy our townships. As our people make increasing gains through the exercise of people's power, experience the protection of our mass organisations, and frustrate the attacks of the regime, the masses tend to consolidate their position and advance. In other words, people's power tends to protect us and constantly opens up new possibilities, thereby taking the struggle to a new level. This explains why people's power is both defensive and offensive at the same time.[93]

This was an optimistic view, which Sisulu was careful to qualify by warning that 'transfer of power' was not imminent.

Two important dimensions of people's power concerned the administration of justice and the vexed question of education. Ideally, 'people's courts' would, according to Sisulu, act on a mandate from the community and operate under its democratic control. [94] The range of issues that came before these courts varied 'from the ownership of a puppy, to marital disputes and political offences'.[95] The main aim was, according to a UDF activist from a Pretoria township, rehabilitation:

> ... to re-educate the wrongdoer and make him a better person. You have to see this from our point of view. The community must be the judge and must see that justice is done. It has reaped tremendous rewards. Many people who opposed us have been converted and now work with us – even policemen.[96]

One aim of these courts was to prise loose some of the functions of the white-controlled state by diverting people from 'white man's courts' and, regarding crime prevention and prosecution, the police. To some extent they invoked ideas of restitutive justice and community involvement in the judicial process that had operated in traditional African societies. In addition, the hope was that the people's courts would undercut the extreme forms of 'justice' meted out by undisciplined youth and 'kangaroo courts' – a serious problem in many townships, as well as providing a propaganda boon to the state.

School boycotts were another source of contention in many black communities. Many parents shared the children's hatred of apartheid and their condemnation of 'gutter education'. But boycotts in perpetuity, at least until fundamental change was achieved? Or, as the slogan of the times put it, 'Liberation now, Education later!'? There were also calls for 1986 to be 'The Year of No Education'. These questions raised serious issues. In December 1985 the Soweto Parents' Crisis Committee had urged pupils to return to school in 1986; but the response was mixed. An estimated 250 000 African pupils (or 4 per cent of the total number of African pupils in schools) continued to boycott classes.[97]

The divided views of Sowetans can be gauged from the acid remarks of Mathiane:

> When we first heard the call for 'Liberation now, Education later', we were told the students were going to stand united until liberation was achieved. What has happened is the opposite. The well-off children have left the township schools. The poor have stayed in the townships,

where they have long forgotten education and now have forgotten liberation too .... Every parent who could by any means afford it, has removed their children. They have gone to private schools, home-land boarding schools, or to live with relatives. Among those to leave were students who incited others not to attend.[98]

After the ANC had informed a UDF delegation that pupils should return to schools – their 'trenches' – a new strategy emerged under the aegis of the National Education Crisis Committee, an umbrella organisation with country-wide representation. At a meeting on 29 and 30 March 1986, a number of demands, both political and educational, emerged. Essentially, people's power was to incorporate 'people's education'. Zwelakhe Sisulu described the new strategy as not merely denouncing 'gutter educa-tion' but also as saying 'Forward with People's Education, Education for Liberation!' There were several strands to the concept: an attempt to de-fuse divisive issues by linking parent, teacher and student structures in 'people's committees' that would assume increasing control over the run-ning of schools; an educational system that involved 'education at the ser-vice of the people as a whole, education that liberates, education that puts the people in command of their lives'. An Education Charter was to be drawn up to articulate 'the type of education people want in a democratic South Africa'.[99] In concrete terms, little came of the education project; it was heavily stomped on by the authorities.

Another factor underlay the call to return to schools: the recognition that boycotts dispersed the pupils, making it more difficult to mobilise them for protest. The authorities were well aware of this, and during 1986 several attempts were made to prohibit the use of schools for political purposes and to exclude boycotting pupils from future enrolment. Little came of their efforts, and 1986 was another year of disrupted education.

The countrywide state of emergency, declared on 12 June 1986, had begun to take its toll. According to official figures released in June 1987, in the preceding 12 months unrest incidents had decreased by 85 per cent, deaths by 82 per cent, and attacks on the security forces by 89 per cent. Moreover, according to the police, the downward trend continued for the rest of 1987.[100] Over 27 000 people were detained in 1986, under 'normal' security legislation and in terms of emergency regulations. Nearly 30 per cent of detainees were pupils, students and teachers, and 70 per cent were members of UDF affiliates or UDF office-bearers.[101]

In an interview, conducted in 2001, Johann van der Merwe, who was head of the Security Branch in the mid-1980s (and later, National Commissioner of the police), revealed his scepticism about the effectiveness of detentions: detaining people did not work and, in fact, had a negative influence. 'If one detains a person who was not really involved, he soon became involved on his release – that we learned from very hard experience.' He continued:

> So from the outset I said to my members to make sure that whenever they detain a person, they had sufficient information that he was in fact involved. It was a difficult situation, because we had to rely on informers for our information, some of them reliable, and some of them unreliable …. Most times the informers are so close to the detainee that when we disclose in court our reasons for detention, the detainee would immediately know whom the informer is. This was one of the main problems, and that was also the time they started the necklacing of people, and I think they killed more than 500 of our informers that way.[102]

Van der Merwe's attempts to persuade Botha and his Minister of Law and Order, Adriaan Vlok, that detention did not work and that a political solution was required, were rebuffed. Botha was adamant that detention be retained, insisting that 'there was no other way to deal with these matters'. Judging by the figures for incidents of unrest, detention, as well as other tough measures, did have an impact, but it was only a short-term one that heightened popular anger.

Faced with heavy-handed repression, as well as attempts to cut off its sources of foreign funding, the UDF could do little more than mount a 'holding operation'. Nevertheless it survived 1987, and continued to articulate popular demands. Prior to the parliamentary elections for the (white) House of Assembly on 6 May 1987, the UDF published an uncompromising call, aimed particularly at white voters, denouncing all reformist proposals that fell short of its own demand for universal franchise in a non-racial unitary state. In particular, supporters of the liberal Progressive Federal Party were urged to 'abandon the myth of change through parliament' and join the majority 'in building an anti-Nationalist front that will isolate the Nationalists from all support and ultimately unseat this government'.[103]

The call did little more than handicap the PFP, which had already been damaged by Van Zyl Slabbert's decision to withdraw from Parliament. Many young whites, especially students, declined to vote, contributing to the loss of seven seats by the PFP, which was replaced as the official opposition by the Conservative Party. The CP captured six seats from the NP, giving it a total of 23 – and it could have been 30 were it not for a number of constituencies where the ultra-right vote was split by the HNP's participation.

*　*　*

In February 1988 the UDF was effectively banned, along with 18 other organisations, 16 of which were UDF affiliates. By this time the UDF had between 700 and 800 affiliates, giving it an overall membership of some 2.5 million. Its remarkable achievement was to have survived at all: the 'holding operation' had lasted for over two years, during which time the UDF had managed to continue articulating demands and providing a focus for grievances. Much of the driving force came from the grassroots. The mushrooming of 'civics' and other local organisations released enormous social energy as pent-up frustrations expressed themselves in mass mobilisation. Heribert Adam and Kogila Moodley wrote of the UDF that it had 'many generals but an undisciplined army. It served more as an embodied sentiment than an effective tool for action'.[104] There was truth in this comment, but the 'embodied sentiment' nonetheless had powerful inspirational force.

Mandela praised the UDF for producing 'an extraordinary crop of young leaders'. Cosatu and the UDF, he continued, 'had in some measure been surrogates for the ANC inside South Africa during the 1980s'.[105] This was judiciously expressed. Despite the government's continued insistence that the UDF was a creation of the ANC and was committed to promoting revolution, this could never be proved. Despite close alignment with the ANC's ideology, as expressed in the Freedom Charter, and occasional communication and consultation with the ANC, there was no evidence to show that the UDF followed directives given by the ANC. It did not, and could not, publicly endorse the ANC's commitment to a 'people's war'. Indeed, senior UDF officials considered the ANC's quest for a 'seizure of power' to be hopelessly unrealistic. The state remained in control, but the UDF's 'politics of refusal' had effectively destroyed PW Botha's constitutional programme. It was one of the ironies of the 1980s – and an unintended consequence – that the Tricameral Parliament, intended to entrench racial division and white control, had led to a burgeoning display of solidarity that transcended the racial categorisation prescribed by apartheid. Arguably, these factors were the biggest single force behind the making of the deadlock out of which the transition was to emerge. Walter Sisulu was correct in his assessment that the UDF had 'decisively turned the tide against the advances being made by the PW Botha regime'.[106]

If the UDF was only 'in some measure' a surrogate of the ANC, it

nevertheless played a major role in ensuring that the ANC was re-established as the strongest force in black opposition politics. Its consistent
demands for the release of Mandela and other political prisoners and the
unbanning of the ANC struck resonant chords with the growing international pressure on the government. In alliance with Cosatu, the UDF res-
urrected itself early in 1989 as the Mass Democratic Movement (MDM),
a broad alliance of anti-apartheid organisations with no Constitution or
membership lists.

That the UDF became the biggest organisation among blacks was significant. It far eclipsed the residual Black Consciousness organisation, the
Azanian People's Organisation (Azapo), with which it clashed violently on
a number of occasions. It also challenged Inkatha in Natal, but without
being able to establish a decisive competitive advantage. The potentially
anti-white thrust of BC had been substantially neutralised after 1976–7,
when the great majority of the activists who fled the country were, in one
way or another, accommodated by the ANC – and helped to pull it out
of the doldrums. It was the ANC's leaders, both in jail and in exile, who
were hugely more inspirational and higher in stature than their bickering
counterparts who had succeeded Robert Sobukwe as leaders of the PAC.

Whatever criticisms may be made of the Freedom Charter, its racially
inclusive terms – 'South Africa belongs to all who live in it, black and
white' – provided ideological legitimacy for discountenancing the development of a stridently anti-white movement that might have encompassed
a majority of black activists. There was no inherent reason why the humiliations of racial discrimination should not have generated a black racist backlash. There was undoubtedly plenty of anti-white sentiment at
grassroots level which, to some extent, had been given organisational embodiment, but without being able to gain majority support.

By adopting the Freedom Charter and committing itself to non-racialism the UDF cleaved to the ANC tradition. It tried hard to attract white
support, and succeeded in doing so, if only to a limited extent, especially
among students at the English-medium universities, whose leaderships,
together with that of Nusas, had become increasingly radicalised in the
1970s and 1980s. Moreover, UDF spokesmen urged pessimistic whites
(and there were many of them in the 1980s) not to emigrate, but to stay
and contribute to a non-racial, democratic solution.[107]

Why this racially inclusive approach was maintained has never been
convincingly explained. Could it be attributed simply to the ANC's tradition, which derived from its earliest days when it was little more than
an elite politely requesting release from racial discrimination? Was it the
role of non-African communists in the Congress Alliance, which certainly

helped to break down the anti-white sentiments of Mandela and other ANC Youth Leaguers in the 1940s? Did the communists' analysis of social dynamics in terms of class, more than race, facilitate a capacity to distinguish between the system and the colour of those who enforced it?

An example of the latter ability was provided by Mandela, who had been amazed at a kind remark made by a prison officer named Badenhorst: he had been noted for his 'callous and barbaric' behaviour, but on his departure from Robben Island he wished the prisoners good luck. Mandela noted that there was another side to his nature:

> It was a useful reminder that all men, even the most seemingly cold-blooded, have a core of decency, and that if their hearts are touched, they are capable of changing. Ultimately, Badenhorst was not evil; his inhumanity had been foisted upon him by an inhuman system. He behaved like a brute because he was rewarded for brutish behaviour.[108]

The comment is perhaps more revealing of Mandela's generosity of spirit than of Badenhorst's potential humanity.

It was not only white communists who demonstrated a commitment to ending apartheid: liberals such as Peter Brown (national chairman of the Liberal Party – which disbanded in 1968 rather than submit to legislation that prohibited interracial parties), Alan Paton, Helen Suzman, Colin Eglin and many others devoted entire lifetimes to opposing racism. White society, despite consistently returning NP governments, was never monolithic in its commitment to maintaining apartheid. Despite the sneers directed at white liberals for being 'insufficiently progressive', 'captives of privilege', 'supporters of capitalism', etc. etc., they played an important role in destroying the legitimacy of apartheid. That white and black never confronted one another as cohesive blocs was a significant part of the explanation for the relatively peaceful nature of the transition.

Other factors also inhibited the growth of black counter-racism. There was a widespread recognition, however intuitive or inchoate, of racial interdependence and that whites were here to stay. Threats to 'drive them into the sea' would not only heighten the intransigence of whites, but also if implemented, cause the collapse of the economy. These beliefs were noted in the survey of urban African attitudes by Theodor Hanf and his associates in 1977. Group interviews included the following typical comments:

- It's not that we don't like the whites. We like them but we don't like

at all what they are doing to us. They must share with us what belongs to us all.

- If the whites left? I wouldn't feel happy. I would miss them. We have
  become too used to them being here, to working with them. We
  need them too. And they still owe us a lot.
- If the whites left the country there would be a terrific mess. It would
  be like being in a bus with no driver. Everyone would try to drive the
  bus even if they couldn't drive.

Though substantial majorities expressed racially tolerant views, the sur-
vey nevertheless showed that there were also racial prejudices among
Africans, especially among the less educated and poorer strata, but that
Africans were relatively less racist than whites.[109]

By the 1980s the ANC occupied the high moral ground internationally
and domestically. Nelson Mandela was the world's most famous political
prisoner; and domestic activists like Archbishop Desmond Tutu enjoyed international prestige, signified by his winning the Nobel Peace Prize in 1984.
To a considerable extent the opposition to apartheid was couched in moral
terms: it would, accordingly, have been folly to tarnish its reputation by
yielding to any temptation to respond to racism with counter-racism – not
that any of the prominent leaders appeared to have been so tempted.

Concerns with moral issues were prominent in the UDF, especially with
the involvement of so many clergy in its ranks. Seekings draws attention
to this aspect by quoting Patrick Mosiuoa Lekota on the necessity of
avoiding counter-racism:

> In political struggle, the means must always be the same as the ends.
> How else can one expect a racialistic movement to imbue our society
> with a nonracial character on the dawn of our freedom day? A politi-
> cal movement cannot bequeath to society a characteristic it does not
> itself possess.[110]

The views described above did not go unchallenged. Critics pointed out
that, notwithstanding the inclusive tenor of the Freedom Charter, the
ANC did not admit whites to membership until 1969, and then, so it
was rumoured, only via the SACP. Many white liberals, while staunchly
opposed to apartheid, were deeply suspicious of the close ties between
the ANC and the SACP. They argued that the ossified form of Marxism-
Leninism for which the SACP stood was embodied in states whose au-
thoritarianism was even worse than that of apartheid. Moreover, how
could they fight bravely for democratic freedoms in South Africa (as

many communists did), while simultaneously accepting uncritically the systematic negation of democratic freedoms in communist states, to say nothing of their approval – shared by the ANC – of the suppression of the Hungarian uprising in 1956 and the quashing of Czechoslovakia's Prague Spring in 1968? And was the SACP's self-designation as a 'vanguard' party compatible with any notion of a multiparty system in a pluralist society?

These issues had been hotly debated for decades. Socialism was widely supported in the ANC and Cosatu. The UDF, given its multi-class make-up, was more muted and its economic proposals were diffuse, as could be inferred from the divergent interpretations placed on the economic clauses of the Freedom Charter. Many in the UDF, however, considered themselves to be socialists. In no case, however, was what was understood by socialism spelled out: the socialist vision was far more an angry protest against the extreme degree of inequality and the capitalism *manqué* that operated in South Africa. That the appeal of the socialist vision was little more than anti-capitalism is clear from remarks made by Tutu, who expressed his loathing of capitalism, deeming it 'all competition and selfishness':

> Are people happy under capitalism? No, from everything I have seen capitalism gives unbridled license to human cupidity, to the law of the jungle. Capitalism and the free enterprise system – it is unfreedom, it is morally repulsive.[111]

Another question was whether mass mobilisation in the form of marches, demonstrations and other activities provoked violence – and if so, was it not wrong to encourage protesters in the fairly certain knowledge that there would be a violent response from the police? There can be little doubt that mass mobilisation *did* provoke violence. Had the black population remained passive in the 1980s the death toll would have been far lower. The issue is, however, that in the absence of legitimate channels for the exercise of political rights and freedom of expression, and in the face of the structural violence of the state, the resort to mass mobilisation was well-nigh inevitable. The UDF had consistently foresworn violence, and tried hard to prevent mass mobilisation from degenerating into unruliness, but it was powerless to curb 'an undirected, often suicidal, street militancy'.[112] The *zeitgeist* of the times suggested, to the youth especially, that with a few more pushes the state would be toppled.

It was inherently improbable that mass mobilisation could be a match for the heavily armed and often trigger-happy security forces. Despite a trickle of white dissenters, who either went to prison or emigrated rather than be conscripted, and even the existence of a few 'moles' inside the security apparatus, the state's coercive power remained immune to revolutionary overthrow.

It became the height of political incorrectness to criticise the 'liberatory' or 'defensive' violence of the black opposition in anything resembling the same terms as the violence of the state.[113] Of course the 'primary cancer' (a phrase coined by Bishop Peter Storey) was apartheid; and in the absence of effective political rights it was likely that political competition would assume physical, often violent, forms. Moreover, the solidarity of whites (unsuccessfully) mandated by the 'total onslaught' strategy was partially reflected in the drive for solidarity in black townships. Anyone who weakened the drive or collaborated with 'the system' was fair game for militants, often with brutal consequences.

Between September 1984 and December 1989 nearly 400 people were 'necklaced' and another 395 died by burning. Necklacing appalled Tutu, who, in July 1985, plunged into an angry crowd to rescue a man who was about to meet this fate. On another occasion, when a young woman had been 'necklaced' for allegedly being an informer, Tutu expressed his outrage:

> If you do this kind of thing again, I will find it difficult to speak for the cause of liberation …. If the violence continues, I will pack my bags, collect my family and leave this beautiful country that I love so passionately and deeply.[114]

It was not only Tutu who was dismayed by the often gratuitous violence. Joe Thloloe, a columnist on the *Sowetan*, for instance, deplored the growth of intolerance that crept into black politics, declaring that the logic of what was happening was that 'if I do not agree with your politics I have to annihilate you ….'[115] African journalists received dire threats should they not toe the party line by writing critically of the ANC or the UDF.

Severe tensions between UDF supporters and Azapo also led to violence. Azapo was far smaller, but it had pockets of support in Soweto, Port Elizabeth and elsewhere. Penetration proved to be 'easy meat' for the state's *agents provocateurs*, who appear to have enjoyed some success in fanning the flames of conflict.[116] Not all of the killings, however, could be attributed to such machinations. Exact figures are unavailable, but the number could have been over 200, and several hundred homes were destroyed. Rian Malan, who interviewed a number of Azapo activists in

Soweto, found them bitter about the lack of media publicity accorded to attacks on them by UDF activists, and the failure or likely inability of the UDF leadership to stop the violence:

> Many UDF leaders thought there was no war at all; the black community was simply cleansing itself of collaborators and rightwing vigilantes .... The UDF seemed to be turning into something of a headless monster, its most capable leaders rotting in jail while the rank and file ran amok.[117]

* * *

A particularly horrifying massacre occurred in Sekhukhuneland, part of the Lebowa bantustan, in April 1986, when 32 bodies and, later, a further 11, were discovered. All were allegedly victims of witch-burning during a campaign to eliminate collaborators and witches. According to Malan's account, the 32 were 'hurled alive into pits of flame'; and an eye-witness described how he had seen his wife burned to death 'while youth sang freedom songs'. The unfortunate victims were accused of using witchcraft to retard the struggle. The killers were said to be 'comrades', supporters of the UDF.[118]

Belief in witchcraft was common in traditional African societies; and typically, witch-hunting was aimed at the supposed enemy within the gate. During times of acute social tension accusations of witchcraft increased sharply. The circumstances of Lebowa in the 1980s conformed to this pattern: apart from the sharp conflict between the homeland authorities and ordinary people, the turbulence of the towns and cities washed over into rural areas. An anthropological study of Lebowa by Isak Niehaus showed

> ... how Comrades exploited popular discontent: they attacked witches in an attempt to eliminate evil in order to attain legitimacy as a political movement. Indeed, these attacks became linked to a broader challenge to the state's control of local government, the courts and schools.[119]

The stresses of the times exacerbated many latent tensions among urban African populations. Apart from the hostility to local councillors, police and other state functionaries, and inter-generational issues, severe conflict arose between urban 'insiders' and 'outsiders', that is, between people who regarded themselves as town-rooted and those who saw themselves as rural and regarded their spells in the city as temporary, and little more than a means of earning money. The distinction between 'insiders' and 'outsiders', of course, lent itself to government manipulation that aimed at emphasising and deepening the cleavage between the two categories.

While the salience of the distinction should not be exaggerated (as government officials were wont to do in the interests of proclaiming the strength of outsiders' ties with their homelands), there were real issues involved. Commonly, for example, the townspeople looked down upon the migrant outsiders as uncouth, rude country bumpkins, who not only threatened their jobs, but also preyed upon their womenfolk. For their part, the migrants resented the supercilious attitudes of the urbanites, and the ways in which they mocked them as yokels.

There was more to the conflict than that. The migrants, who typically lived in single-sex hostels or in shack settlements such as Cape Town's Crossroads, bitterly resented efforts by the young comrades to press-gang them into stayaways (which cost them earnings), consumer boycotts and other protests. Moreover, being ordered around by mere youngsters violated their traditionalist view of the respect that the young should accord their elders.

Variations on these themes played themselves out in several parts of the country. In Cape Town, for example, *witdoeke* (vigilantes, so named because they wore white headscarves) were involved in clashes with comrades in May 1986 that resulted in 44 deaths and the destruction of 60 000 shacks.[120] Despite their denials, there was little doubt about police involvement, either by active encouragement of the *witdoeke* or by turning a blind-eye to their raids. Far higher death tolls were recorded in the violence between Inkatha and the UDF/ANC in Natal and the Transvaal in the 1980s and early 1990s. According to estimates, between September 1984 and 1994 over 21 500 people were killed in political violence.[121] Of these roughly 3 000 were killed by the security forces, suggesting that the remaining 18 500 died in internecine violence, mostly in Natal. This fact should not be interpreted as an argument in mitigation of apartheid, even if both rightwing and leftwing authoritarian governments elsewhere, including in Africa, had killed many more people: it was an evil system and, moreover, apartheid was the primary cancer underlying the violence. Nevertheless, brutality was not the monopoly of the state's security forces. Jill Wentzel's book, *The Liberal Slideaway*, published in 1995, was a powerful reminder that it was an over-simplification to see the conflict as 'Hitler versus the Cosby Family', as a cynical journalist had dubbed accounts that ignored or played down violence emanating from the black side. The wider truth was that South Africa was involved in a 'low-intensity' civil war, and war invariably brutalises all antagonists.

* * *

The rise of the independent trade union movement in the 1970s and 1980s was a major tributary that swelled the river of opposition to apartheid. Prior to 1979 African trade unions had had a long history, but they were never officially recognised and, while nominally legal, trade union organisers were hounded by the state and by many employers. Economic domination was one of the pillars of white rule, and nothing that could potentially threaten it was tolerated.

Strikes by African workers had long been illegal, and when they occurred, they were often met with mass dismissals and police action. Legislation in 1973 theoretically made provision for legal strikes, but in practice the law was so circumscribed that the status quo was effectively maintained.

The watershed for the re-emergence of African unions occurred early in 1973 in the Durban area when over 61 000 African workers in nearly 150 companies either went on strike or engaged in work stoppages.[122] As far as one could tell, the strikes were spontaneous, and a demonstration effect caused them to spread from enterprise to enterprise. The principal issue was abysmally low wages, which shocked many whites, including the media, when details were made known. The authorities' reaction was restrained: police kept a low profile, and none of the strikers was prosecuted.

A survey conducted by the Institute for Industrial Education concluded that, although the strikers had achieved only limited gains, the strikes had contributed to a growing sense of solidarity:

> The workers struck because of low wages and the feeling that the employer would not do anything to remedy the wage levels unless drastic action was taken. They feel that the strikes were productive, but they remain very dissatisfied. Having discovered that the strike is an effective weapon, the majority are fully prepared to use it again. It may well be, therefore, that the most significant change wrought by the strikes is not in the workers' living standards, but in their sense of their own potential power.[123]

The concluding sentence was prophetic: new unions emerged, and existing ones grew rapidly; and strikes, even though technically still illegal, continued throughout the 1970s, although not on so large a scale as in 1973. Equally important, issues regarding the status and rights of African workers became firmly established on the national agenda. More enlightened employers recognised that there was no effective alternative to granting union rights. In 1974 Harry Oppenheimer called upon employers to note that African unions were not illegal and that where they were representative of the workforce and responsible they should be regarded as legitimate bargaining partners. The Association of South African Chambers of Commerce (Assocom) also expressed support for the principle of granting registered trade union rights to African workers.[124]

In Parliament, however, Helen Suzman (the Progressive Party included some of the more liberal employers among its supporters) was the lone voice advocating the extension of full trade union rights for Africans, a call that, in 1973, was still excessively strong meat for the ruling NP and the official opposition. She also made a critical point about the underlying change in the economy: as it grew, increasing numbers of African workers would be absorbed into the economy, which would strengthen their bargaining power:

> The more he [the African worker] is drawn into our industrial structure as a semi-skilled and as a skilled worker, the more irreplaceable he is and the greater power he will get to demand more rights.[125]

In the past it had been common for employers, often with the assistance of the police, to fire striking workers and recruit replacements from the large (and growing) pool of unemployed people. This was possible when Africans were confined to the ranks of unskilled workers and were considered to be, in the notorious phrase used by Nationalists, 'interchangeable units of labour'. Increasingly complex techniques of production, however, required more skilled operatives. Where were they to be found?

By the 1970s the chronic shortage of semi-skilled and skilled workers had caused the wholesale granting of exemptions from job reservation restrictions. Increasing numbers of Africans were better educated and they were beginning to climb up the occupational ladder. Although it still occurred, the old strong-arm method of 'firing-and-hiring' became increasingly less practicable. Moreover, as workers and communities became more militant, firing strikers was liable to cause even greater militancy, including sympathy strikes and consumer boycotts that targeted offending firms.

The following table, derived from a study by the Human Sciences

Research Council in 1984, showed that Africans had made steady gains in middle-level occupations:[126]

JOB DESCRIPTION	WHITES		AFRICANS	
	1965	1981	1965	1981
Clerical	83.1%	65.5%	9.1%	17.8%
Sales	72.7%	59.6%	15.2%	25.0%
Artisan	85.5%	73.1%	0.4%	5.9%
Foremen and supervisors	76.7%	56.9%	13.5%	26.5%

Another factor conducive to unionism was the changing scale of industrial and other enterprises: they were becoming larger, employing more workers, thus facilitating their mobilisation in trade unions.

By the late 1970s multinational corporations were beginning to feel the pressure of international criticism that would, by the early 1980s, become pressure to disinvest. It made sense to try to neutralise these pressures by accepting the unionisation of their workforces, as well as abolishing internal discriminatory practices. The Wiehahn Commission, noting these pressures and declaring stoutly that it would not be influenced by them, nevertheless concluded that it would be naïve to ignore them:

> The presence of multinational subsidiaries of multinational enterprises within a country's borders creates a conduit through which strong influences and pressure can be exerted .... The Commission is aware that, while the State can readily withstand and curb foreign pressures and influences, this is much more difficult for subsidiaries of multinational enterprises.[127]

Clearly it had been the state's intention to use registration of unions as a means of exerting control over their activities, in particular preventing them from using their muscle for political purposes.

Among the first issues to confront the emerging union movement was whether to register and participate in the industrial council system. The unions that opposed registration argued that it would lead to greater control by the state and, moreover, inveigle them into a bureaucratic system that would diminish worker control of their leaders. Other unions, however, disputed this: 'They saw the new laws as a site of struggle. These laws could provide some spaces where unions could win workers' rights.'[128] The debate was a divisive one; underlying it was the old question of whether to participate in or to boycott state-initiated structures.

Whether to participate in industrial councils raised the same issue.

These councils were viewed with suspicion by the emergent unions as bureaucratic, racist institutions in which management, white unions and the state colluded at the expense of black workers. Moreover, the councils operated on an industry-wide basis, whereas the unions were plant-based, having decided that their priority was to build solid organisations within individual factories. The burgeoning growth of the unions in the early 1980s, fuelled by a wave of strikes, called for a new approach that could link workers in the same industry and create a more cohesive force. Led by the Metal and Allied Workers Union (Mawu), the new strategy involved participating in the council structure as a means of mobilising on a national basis while retaining a power-base at factory level.[129] Ironically, the growing influence in the industrial council of the National Union of Metalworkers of South Africa, formed by a merger of Mawu and other unions, prompted some employers to seek to revert to plant-level bargaining. The decision to 'opt in' to an officially sponsored structure played a significant role in promoting union growth and cohesiveness. It also resolved the debate about registration.

By the early 1980s, another even larger issue had arisen: the relationship between unions and political organisations, which became more pressing as political tumult engulfed black communities. It was virtually inevitable that, in the absence of political rights for Africans, trade unions with largely African memberships would press for political as well as economic rights. The earlier experience of the South African Congress of Trade Unions (Sactu), a part of the Congress Alliance, served as a cautionary reminder of the perils of premature involvement in the political struggle.

Sactu was formed in 1955, explicitly as a part of the Congress Alliance and conscious of the close connection between workers' demands and the struggle for political rights. From its inception Sactu was targeted by the state and many of its officials were banned, 23 being charged (and subsequently acquitted) with treason in 1956. Despite the hostile environment Sactu struggled on: by 1961 it claimed 46 affiliated unions with over 53 000 members of all races, mostly Africans. The banning of the ANC in 1960 was followed by a severe crackdown on Sactu officials, some of whom were involved in MK activities, making it impossible to continue with any measure of effectiveness. Although it was never banned, it survived in name only. The unions of the 1970s and 1980s were anxious to avoid a similar fate.

Differing union traditions crystallised in the early 1980s as a debate between the 'workerist' and the 'populist' unions. The workerist unions, while by no means unmindful of political issues, believed that their primary focus should be on the shop floor, where they would concentrate on building a strong union that would be less vulnerable to persecution. According to Doug Hindson:

> While recognising the connection between economic exploitation and political oppression, the unions held back from full engagement in political struggles outside the work-place, arguing that to take up issues which they had little chance of winning at that stage, and thereby risk destruction of the unions, was politically senseless.[130]

A major exposition of this perspective was given in an address by Joe Foster, the general secretary of the Federation of South African Trade Unions (Fosatu), in 1982. He declared emphatically that while Fosatu was not going to stand on the political sidelines, 'we would only be dreaming of change if we do not strengthen and build our unions into large and effective organisations.' He noted that at its inception in 1979 Fosatu had stressed its independence of any political organisation; but, as the numbers and importance of workers grew, political movements would try to recruit them.

The notion of a working-class movement with its own identity, which was central to Fosatu's thinking – and which, according to Foster, did not yet exist – would be diluted by premature involvement in broad, multi-class fronts:

> It is, therefore, essential that workers must strive to build their own powerful and effective organisation even whilst they are part of the wider popular struggle. This organisation is necessary to protect and further worker interests and to ensure that the popular movement is not hijacked by elements who will in the end have no option but to turn against their worker supporters.[131]

The 'elements' to which he referred were the nationalist elite who dominated the political movements and who, when in power, would be very likely to be co-opted by the forces of capitalism, as had occurred in several independent African states.

There was another consideration, pointed out by others: the black working class was not homogeneous in its political views, which ranged from militantly radical to relatively conservative. The issue came to a head with the question of whether to affiliate to the UDF, which the UDF repeatedly asked the unions to do. Although a few of the newer (and populist) general unions did so, Fosatu and other independent unions declined. Affiliation might jeopardise the quest for trade union unity, which appeared to be making some progress by 1983. The issue, however, would spark splits in several unions.[132]

The opposing point of view derived from the proposition that black workers were members of communities before they were workers; and they could not abstract themselves from community political issues that vitally affected them and their families. This position was forcefully stated by Sisa Njikelana, who argued that the distinction between trade union struggles and the mass struggles engaged in by political and community organisations was exaggerated:

> Are workers' struggles for higher wages that unrelated to rent boycotts or bus boycotts? Even those community and other struggles which are not so clearly economically based, such as those waged in the schools for a free and better education system, are issues which directly affect the working class. These issues link to community-based and often more political struggles directly to the economic struggles being waged by the unions. Then the broad democratic front which takes up these wider struggles, undoubtedly represents the interests of the working class to the extent that the working class must combine economic struggles with political struggle. It must be recognised that the economic struggle cannot be successful or even conducted on a large scale if workers have not won elementary political rights such as the freedom to organise without the threat of bannings, detentions and the violent breaking of strikes.[133]

This was a persuasive argument – but then so was Foster's. Both perspectives contained valid points. Eventually, however, the dispute was overtaken by events in the townships, and the unions who shared Foster's views had to compromise and forge alliances with the political movements – or face marginalisation.[134] Nevertheless, the compromise did not jeopardise the workerist unions' key principles: strength on the shop-floor and the democratic accountability of union leaders and shop stewards to their members.

It required several years of tough negotiation in the early 1980s to achieve a greater measure of unity among the different trade union groupings. In November 1985 the Congress of South African Trade Unions emerged from this process, incorporating eight affiliates of Fosatu, which disbanded, and 25 others, most of them previously unaffiliated. Cosatu claimed a paid-up membership of nearly 450 000. The largest affiliate was the National Union of Mineworkers (NUM), which had a membership of 100 000 and had broken away from a rival federation, having sensed that the tide was moving towards the Charterists. Its general secretary was a young man named Cyril Ramaphosa, born in 1952, who had trained as a lawyer and cut his political teeth in the BC movement in the 1970s, during which time he had spent two long spells in detention. His considerable negotiating skills, honed in bargaining with the mining industry, were to be highly significant in the future constitutional negotiations.

The old fault-line in African politics reasserted itself in the negotiations for unity. The Council of Unions of South Africa (with 12 affiliates and 150 000 paid-up members) and the Azanian Confederation of Trade Unions (with eight affiliates and 75 000 members) both jibbed at the principle of non-racialism, which the embryonic Cosatu insisted upon. Consequently, neither would affiliate; in October 1986 they amalgamated to form the National Council of Trade Unions (Nactu), claiming by 1989 28 affiliates and about 250 000 signed-up members. Nactu asserted its full commitment to the national liberation struggle, but declared that it would not affiliate to any political organisation. Its PAC/BC roots, though, could be inferred from its requirement that its leadership should be drawn from the African working class.

At Cosatu's founding conference Ramaphosa adroitly straddled the workerist/populist issue – which, by 1985, was in any case being overtaken by political events:

> [T]he struggle of workers on the shop floor cannot be separated from the wider struggle for liberation .... Our most urgent task is to develop unity among the workers. We would wish COSATU to give firm political direction to workers. If workers are to lead the struggle for liberation, we have to win the confidence of other sectors of society. But if we are to get into alliances with other progressive organisations, it must be on terms that are favourable to us workers. Where we do plunge into political activity, we must make sure that the unions under COSATU have a strong shop-floor base not only to take on employers, but the state as well. Our role in the political struggle will depend on an organisational strength.[135]

Cosatu committed itself to building a non-racial working class movement and to restructuring the economy 'in the interests of the working class', among other resolutions. It favoured socialism, but it was unspecific about what model it had in mind, although its president, Elijah Barayi, subsequently said that Cosatu would nationalise the mines and take over some of the big businesses. More commonly, socialism was invoked as a kind of mantra that expressed hostility to the existing form of capitalism.

Although Cosatu was committed to non-racialism, there were in fact few whites in Cosatu unions, though substantially more Coloured and Indian workers were members. The membership of its unions was over-whelmingly African. Whites, however, especially young idealistic gradu-ates, were prominent among union officials. Indeed, the union move-ment's first martyr of the 1980s was a young white doctor, Neil Aggett, general secretary of an unaffiliated union, who committed suicide in 1982 after being savagely tortured by the security police while in detention. White students belonging to Nusas formed Wages Commissions in the aftermath of the 1973 strikes which were critical to the lift-off of union-ism in the mid-1970s.[136] Whites also founded journals such as the *South African Labour Bulletin*, which was devoted to practical and theoretical discussion of union matters.

Despite its commitment to participating in the political struggle, Cosatu declined to become an affiliate of the UDF. Nevertheless, the choice of the word 'Congress' in its title suggested its political bent. In December 1985 Jay Naidoo, the general secretary, met ANC leaders in Harare, which caused some grumbling among affiliates, who claimed, correctly, that they had not been consulted beforehand. Nevertheless, the move towards a closer relationship could not be stayed, Cosatu's leader-ship being well aware that the ANC was by far the most popular politi-cal organisation among Africans in general, as well as among rank and file members of its affiliated unions. Cosatu was determined not to allow itself to be subordinated to the ANC's policies and strategy, however. It denied accusations that it was a mere front for the ANC, a denial that was echoed by the ANC although it expressed strong support for Cosatu and urged unaffiliated unions to join it. Further talks between Cosatu and senior ANC leaders were held in March 1986. In a statement Cosatu said that the fundamental problem facing South Africa was the question of political power and that it could not be resolved without the full par-ticipation of the ANC 'which is regarded by the majority of the people of South Africa as the overall leader and general representative'.[137]

At its second annual congress in July 1987 Cosatu took a further step towards political engagement by adopting the Freedom Charter, which it described as encompassing 'the minimum demands of the democratic majority'. A strong minority, said to be about one-third of the delegates, opposed this move, some declaring that the Charter did not go far enough and needed to be complemented by a workers' charter, others arguing that adoption would be politically divisive.[138]

Cosatu also embarked on further political campaigns, including de-mands to release Mandela and other political prisoners, unban proscribed organisations and permit the return of exiles. It also campaigned to have 1 May and 16 June declared public holidays, and supported its demands with stayaway strikes. Among its more narrowly economic projects was its campaign for a living wage – which appeared to have some success, unionised black workers being the only section of the working population to achieve wage increases above the inflation level in 1987.[139]

Cosatu's emboldened political campaigns came at some cost: predictably, the state regarded it as a prime target. During 1987 Cosatu's Johannesburg headquarters were badly damaged by a bomb (an attack subsequently acknowledged by the Minister of Law and Order to have been authorised by him); other Cosatu offices and those of affiliates around the country were attacked and damaged; a number of unionists were refused passports; and, according to an unofficial count, 167 union officials and members were detained under security legislation during 1987 (representing 24 per cent of the total number of detainees), and a further 406 were detained under the emergency regulations. Other estimates put the figure even higher. A high percentage were members of Cosatu affiliates.[140]

During the 1980s membership of the independent union movement grew dramatically: by the end of 1985 a total of 1.5 million workers were members of registered and unregistered unions, meaning that approximately 15 per cent of the total workforce was unionised – low by the standards of developed economies, but growing, in contrast to the tendency in advanced capitalist states for trade union membership to decline.[141] While the traditional white unions were in a process of steady decline, Cosatu grew rapidly: from a membership of over 450 000 at its inception in 1985 it grew to over 721 000 in 1987, and by the end of 1991, to 1.26 million. Between 1979 and 1991 total trade union membership rose nearly fourfold, from 700 000 to 2.7 million, representing 53 per cent of the workforce in the non-agricultural sector.[142]

The strength of the independent unions, especially those affiliated to Cosatu, lay in their tight shop-floor organisation. By the end of 1985 the unions were organised in 43 500 workplaces, had signed 450 plant agreements and employed over 12 500 shop stewards.[143] The new labour dispensation initiated in 1979 had, moreover, created opportunities for unions to challenge employers through the Industrial Court, which was empowered to adjudicate on unfair labour practices, including dismissals, failure to negotiate with a registered trade union that was representative of the employees, and failure to follow equitable procedures prior to retrenchments. Despite initial suspicions about the Court, most unions used it to consolidate worker rights. In 1987 over 2 300 cases were referred to the Court, which was an indication of confidence in the even-handedness of its rulings. Many employers, however, did not share this view, and brought few cases to the Court.

The developments described above show the unmistakable growth of trade union muscle, muscle that could be flexed, ultimately, by labour's most powerful weapon: the strike. Between 1980 and 1988 the number of strikes involving black workers – including work stoppages, but excluding stayaways for political reasons – increased dramatically, from 207 in 1980 to 1 148 in 1987, declining slightly to 1 025 in 1988. Over 400 000 African workers struck in 1986, and 572 000 in 1987.[144]

Most of the strikes occurred because of work-related issues, including retrenchment, recognition agreements, wages and dismissals. What was remarkable was that the strikes took place at a time of rising unemployment and economic hardship. In 1986, when over 1.3 million man-days were lost through strike action, workers, overwhelmingly African, lost over R23 million in wages. This suggests that the political climate and trade union conscientisation had hardened worker attitudes to the extent that they were prepared to lose wages and even run the risk of retrenchment. Between 1984 and June 1988, 70 stayaway strikes took place, 11 being organised by trade unions, 41 by regional civics, and 17 by alliances that probably included unions.

The most significant strikes of the 1980s were the stayaways in the Transvaal in late 1984 and the mineworkers' strike in August 1987. The latter has aptly been described as 'the most important trial of strength between a black union and employers in South African history'.[145] It occurred, moreover, in an industry that was historically resistant to African trade unionism. It also reflected the growing leverage of the NUM under the skilful leadership of Ramaphosa.

The mineworkers' strike was bigger and longer in duration than the previous large-scale strike that was forcibly broken in 1946. The 1987 strike lasted for three weeks and involved between 220 000 and 330 000 African miners on 33 of the 99 gold and coal mines belonging to mining houses that were members of the Chamber of Mines. Although neither the NUM nor the Chamber claimed victory, the strike cost the NUM dear: 50 000 employees were dismissed, and violence between strikers and non-strikers, and between mine security and strikers, led to some 30 deaths (estimates vary).[146]

In February 1988, at the same time as the effective banning of the UDF and other extra-parliamentary organisations, restrictions were imposed on Cosatu, requiring it to confine its role to trade union work. It was the culmination of several years of attacks on Cosatu's political activities by government ministers. The restrictions, nevertheless, left Cosatu organisationally intact, but restricted its capacity to mount political campaigns. Police vigilance and harassment remained intense.

Cosatu, together with Nactu, called for a three-day stayaway in June 1988 in protest against proposed labour legislation which, in their view, was 'part of a broader strategy to suppress democratic opposition and worker organisation'. The stayaway was fairly successful in the Transvaal, Natal and Eastern Cape, but was a failure in the Western Cape.[147] It was nevertheless claimed to have been the largest stayaway strike in South African history.

The legislation that sparked the industrial action was enacted into law in 1988, but not promulgated: it significantly tightened up what had hitherto been an open-ended definition of an unfair labour practice, outlawed sympathy strikes, and extended the criminal liability for strike action. The stayaway strike, however, succeeded in inducing the government not to implement the legislation and, furthermore, paved the way for future corporatist arrangements involving the state, the private sector and labour. It had been yet another demonstration of labour's muscle.

Cosatu may have been hobbled, but the tight shop-floor organisation of its unions enabled it to retain significant muscle. It was also able to remain fairly cohesive in spite of internal differences. The workerist/populist dispute, which appeared to have subsided in the heady mid-1980s, was still a factor; there were fears that the growth of a class of skilled African workers would form a 'labour aristocracy' whose interests would differ from those less skilled; and the increasing divestment of foreign companies was of concern to their employees, in spite of Cosatu's support for the international sanctions campaign.

The de facto banning of the UDF meant that it was down, but by no means out: many of its affiliates and young activists were, apart from routine police harassment, unaffected by the ban. The situation nevertheless pointed to Cosatu's becoming the major component of the internal resistance movement. It was in these circumstances that the Mass Democratic Movement emerged in the course of 1988 and early 1989. There was no formal founding event or Constitution; indeed, its title was acquired through repeated use of a term that reflected the approach. It was nevertheless reasonably clear that Cosatu and the UDF were the main backers, inspired no doubt by the ANC's call for 1989 to be a 'Year of Mass Action for People's Power'. There was another powerful source of inspiration: the strengthening sense of *fin de siècle* generated by the widespread belief that for all its bluster and heavy-handed security measures the Nationalist government was up against the ropes. The ructions inside the NP during much of 1989 appeared to confirm this view.

The closest to a definition of what the MDM was and what it stood for was given in August 1989 by one of its leaders, Titus Mafolo, a former member of the UDF's executive. He said that the expression MDM had been used prior to the banning of the UDF because it reflected the views of mass democratic organisations involved in the struggle. Mofolo said that the MDM was made up of various political, religious and cultural organisations, including the UDF, Cosatu and the National Education Crisis Committee. It was, he added, part of the wider liberation movement. It stood for:

- the mass approach to struggle;
- alliances and campaigns on the basis of unity in action and united mass action behind a common programme;
- constituent organisations should be accountable to their constituencies and memberships;
- working-class leadership in the struggle for liberation and the acceptance of the African majority as the main force in the struggle; and
- collective rather than individual leadership that is both democratic and accountable.[148]

During 1989 the MDM sustained, even increased, the momentum of protest. A sense of expectation emboldened activists. The release of political prisoners that began in May extended to the unconditional release in October of seven ANC heavyweights, including Raymond Mhlaba, Andrew Mlangeni and Walter Sisulu. Could the release of Mandela be far off? And was it not very likely that he would be released into a negotiating situation, and not a political vacuum?

Detainees embarked on hunger strikes; a defiance campaign launched in July 1989 emulated the 1952–3 campaign by deliberately breaking apartheid laws; and organisations and individuals declared themselves 'unbanned'.

A high point was reached in September 1989 when elections were held for all three Houses of the Tricameral Parliament. The MDM launched a vigorous campaign against 'racist' elections and called for a two-day stay-away in protest, which was widely observed. Once again low percentage polls were recorded for both the Coloured and Indian Houses. Violence occurred in various parts of the country, at least 19 deaths being recorded in the Cape Peninsula, where opposition to the Tricameral Parliament was most vehement.

*   *   *

Little has been said thus far about political developments in the bantustans, largely because the major political developments occurred in the urban areas. There was nevertheless restiveness in most of the bantustans, which accommodated roughly 50 per cent of the entire African population. The migrant labour system ensured that there was a constant oscillation of people between the rural areas and the towns – and direct contact where bantustans abutted major centres such as Pretoria, Durban, Pietermaritzburg and East London, and workers commuted to work in white-controlled areas. Significant numbers of youths, sent by their parents to rural schools to escape the violence of the urban areas, threw their weight into 'struggle' concerns, ensuring that these backwaters were not isolated from the urban tumult.

Many migrants retained a rural focus, encapsulated in closed groups of fellow-migrants, and despised urban ways, especially the systematic violation of traditional values, including the lack of respect shown to older people by urban youngsters. They were, however, not immune to the resentments caused by living in a discriminatory society and to the loss, actual or potential, of South African citizenship. Nor were they unaware that most of the bantustans were controlled by unrepresentative, corrupt and authoritarian leaders, surrounded by small cliques who depended on the leaders' patronage, and all of whom benefited mightily from grants and loans provided by the South African government. Not one of the bantustans was able to generate even 50 per cent of its revenues from domestic sources. In virtually all of the bantustans opposition politics was either prohibited or subject to severe restraint and harassment.

As noted above, the historical function of the bantustans was twofold: as labour-reservoirs for the white-controlled economy, and as standing pretexts for the denial of civic rights to Africans in a common, multiracial society. After 1959, as Verwoerd's vision of the separate development of independent African states based on the bantustans unfolded, the second function obviously came into prominence. An additional function was the use of bantustans as repositories for 'relocating' ('dumping' is the more appropriate word) people deemed 'surplus' to the requirements of white South Africa. As a device for deflecting peoples' aspirations away from political rights in a unified South Africa, the bantustans were a palpable failure – even more, they undoubtedly strengthened popular commitment to resistance. Hopes by apartheid planners that the 'citizens' of these territories would develop ethnic identities appropriate to their respective bantustans were unfulfilled. People were certainly aware of their ethnic identities as Tswana, Venda, Zulu, and so on, but it did not preclude an equal awareness among most that they were also Africans in the supra-ethnic sense, with a claim to common South African citizenship.

In a survey for the 1979 Ciskei Commission, chaired by GP Quail, Schlemmer found evidence of ethnocentric attitudes, but large majorities, over 90 per cent among most categories of Ciskeian Xhosa, agreed with the statement: 'There is no real difference between African people – we can easily forget tribal differences and stand together.'[149] Among Zulu-speakers in KwaZulu/Natal and in urban Transvaal areas, only minorities – between one-fifth and one-quarter in KwaZulu/Natal itself – defined themselves as 'primarily Zulu'. The survey, conducted by Schlemmer for the Buthelezi Commission in 1980–1, found that 'there is *substantial minority* pride in ethnic identity, rather less aggressive tribalism, but near-majority concern that ethnic characteristics should not be obliterated in a [new] political dispensation.'[150] The existence of a strong Zulu identity was not surprising: apart from being the largest African ethnic cluster, the Zulu had a long history of resistance to colonial rule, a monarchy that was widely revered, and, in Inkatha yeNkululeko yeSizwe (later becoming the Inkatha Freedom Party), led by Mangosuthu Buthelezi, the bantustan party with by far the most popular support, and a strong proponent of Zulu ethnic interests.

Despite the obvious failure of bantustans to provide a 'solution' to the racial question, the government continued to tinker with them in the hope that they would offer at least a partial accommodation. It was obviously for the purpose of reducing the number of Africans in the country that the government decided in 1982 to excise KaNgwane, the 'homeland' of some 160 000 South African-born Swazi, and Ingwavuma, a bloc of KwaZulu territory, and cede them to the independent state of Swaziland, a former British High Commission Territory, which had long demanded this. (The pre-colonial Kingdom of Swaziland had lost two-thirds of its territory to white concessionaires in the nineteenth century.) The bantu-stan authorities in both KaNgwane and KwaZulu were outraged by this high-handed action, and launched actions in the Supreme Court. In both cases the government's actions were found to be invalid, and the excisions had to be aborted.

During 1985 the security authorities concocted a bizarre plan, called Operation Katzen, in a desperate attempt to quell resistance in the Eastern Cape. It envisaged bringing together the Transkei and Ciskei bantustans as a 'united nation of Xhosa-speakers' who would support the South African government and assist in stamping out unrest.

A 'united Xhosa nation' had long been an ambition of Transkei's President Kaiser Matanzima, who had for this reason opposed the 'independence' granted to Ciskei in 1981. The plan, which was to involve the assassination of Lennox Sebe, President of Ciskei, failed dismally.

Unfortunately for those who had devised Operation Katzen, details of the plan of action and other dirty tricks were subsequently leaked by one of their operatives to General Bantu Holomisa, who had assumed control of Transkei in a military coup in December 1987. Holomisa's revelations were to be a source of acute embarrassment to the South African government as they dribbled out in the early 1990s. The leaked secret operational files also revealed plans to eliminate leading ANC activists in the Eastern Cape, including Matthew Goniwe, who together with three others, was murdered by the security police in 1985. At Mandela's behest Holomisa periodically leaked files to the *New Nation*, an ANC-supporting newspaper, enabling Mandela to use the information to pressurise De Klerk into making more concessions during the negotiations.[151]

Coups d'état and attempted coups occurred in other bantustans aside from Transkei: an attempted coup in Bophuthatswana early in 1988 failed, thanks to the intervention of the South African army; but unpopular and corrupt leaders in Ciskei and Venda were removed in 1990.

Among the bantustans, two stood out as being significantly different from the others: KaNgwane and KwaZulu. The difference lay not in their economic circumstances – both were poverty-stricken and utterly dependent on subventions from the South African government – but in the character of their respective leaders. Enos Mabuza, Chief Minister of KaNgwane, a commoner and former educationist, was implacably opposed to apartheid and made no secret of his support of the ANC. In March 1983 he led a delegation of his party, the Inyandza National Movement, to consult with an ANC delegation led by Oliver Tambo in Lusaka. The two delegations exchanged views on their respective strategies, and jointly concluded that no negotiated settlement was possible while leaders were imprisoned and the Pretoria government refused to accept that South Africa should be governed by all its people. The ANC accepted Inyandza's bona fides as 'part of the forces fighting for a democratic South Africa', and its commitment to non-violence. According to Mabuza's curriculum vitae, he occupied a unique position:

> He has successfully maintained a balancing act on the tightrope of South African politics between his position in an apartheid-created structure and his acceptance by the extra-parliamentary groups and liberation movements. The [Inyandza National Movement] was accorded the status of an 'integral' part of the democratic movement by the ANC in 1986 and its President has come to be recognised as

'a comrade within the system'. Despite his strong anti-apartheid stance he has earned the respect and ear of senior RSA government members.[152]

The respect and acceptance accorded by the ANC to Mabuza contrasts sharply with its revilement of Buthelezi and Inkatha. Why this should have been so needs explanation. As described above, Buthelezi, with the connivance of the ANC, had revived the long-dormant Inkatha in 1975, renaming it the Inkatha Freedom Party in 1990. As the administrative structures in the fragmented homeland grew, Inkatha's claimed strength grew to one million members by 1985, and to 1.5 million by the end of the 1980s. In 1972 Buthelezi had become Chief Minister in the KwaZulu Legislative Assembly, a position that afforded him the opportunity to consolidate his regional power-base and also to enhance his role as a significant actor in national politics. Control of the Legislative Assembly, in what was effectively a one-party system, also offered possibilities of patronage from which non-Inkatha members were routinely excluded. High office as a bantustan leader, moreover, gave Buthelezi a substantial degree of immunity from state repression.

Buthelezi had been consistent in his advocacy of federalism. In 1974 he proposed federal arrangements that sought to reconcile white fears with black aspirations: since conventional federal systems could not obviate contests for power at the centre, he envisaged a system with three types of state: (1) states in which the interests of an African ethnic group were paramount; (2) states in which white interests were paramount; and (3) special or federal areas which were multi-ethnic in character in which no particular group interests were designated. There would nevertheless be a common federal citizenship in addition to a state citizenship. The federal parliament would consist of representatives of the constituent states.[153]

Broadly similar views were expressed by the Buthelezi Commission in 1982, although its recommendations encompassed only KwaZulu and Natal. More concrete proposals emanated from the KwaZulu Natal Indaba of 1986. Some 39 organisations deliberated with the intention of formulating proposals for a single legislative body for the joint areas of Natal and KwaZulu. It was stressed that no consideration was given to the possibility of independence for the proposed regional entity. The core of the proposals was a consociational system in which the first legislative chamber would be elected by universal franchise (that is, all races), and a second chamber of 50 members would be composed of 10 members each from designated 'background groups': Africans, Afrikaans-speakers, Asians, English-speakers and a 'South African' group, consisting of those who declined to be assigned to a racial/ethnic group or did not belong to any of those designated. All legislation had to be passed by both chambers.

The Indaba proposals enjoyed substantial support across the envisaged joint region, being favoured by the IFP, the Progressive Federal Party, and a few other political groupings, as well as much of the white business community. The NP, however, rejected the proposals, even though it had sent observers to the deliberations: power-sharing that included Africans was not on PW Botha's agenda. Notwithstanding the government's rejection, the National Intelligence Service and some local Broederbond branches requested briefings. The UDF and Cosatu decried the entire Indaba exercise, regarding it as a forerunner to the potential balkanisation of the country, as well as an attempt by Buthelezi to consolidate his control over an enlarged region. The proposals evoked strong opposition. The possibility that implementation of the Indaba proposals could threaten potential ANC hegemony was clearly a major cause of the hostility.

In response Buthelezi observed:

> Our involvement in the Indaba incurred the wrath of the ANC and its allies. We were accused of treachery and of attempting to fragment the struggle for liberation! All this and more when we honestly set out to show that a non-racial democracy was possible within South Africa and hopefully that our example, if permitted to operate, would take hold elsewhere and spread throughout the rest of the country. If this proliferation of democracy became a reality, quite obviously an entirely new constitutional dispensation ... would be negotiated and put into practice.[154]

During 1986 politics appeared hopelessly deadlocked and violence raged, especially in Natal. The Indaba proposals, whatever their inherent problems, were at least an attempt to create an opening in an intractable situation. Even if the spectrum of organisations represented in the Indaba was limited by the refusal of the right and the left to participate, it nevertheless showed that negotiation could produce substantial consensus across racial divides. It is possible, even likely, that had the government agreed to the implementation of the Indaba proposals, majority support among all races in KwaZulu and Natal could have been gained. The militants would have done their best to sabotage the new system, adding fuel to the ongoing violence. Whether the potential demonstration effect, posited by Buthelezi, would have resulted in similar regional accommodations elsewhere remains an imponderable.

Even Buthelezi's detractors had to concede that his outspoken criticism of apartheid and his widely reported verbal skirmishes with Nationalist ministers helped to end the apparent quiescence in African politics in the late 1960s. But at the same time that he became a national figure, the phenomenon of Black Consciousness was rising, and, in time, its organisations and their leaders would become Buthelezi's bitterest foes. Nevertheless, by the mid-1970s, Buthelezi was perhaps the best-known African leader. Surveys conducted by Theodor Hanf and his associates between 1974 and 1977 found that he was the most admired African leader by 44 per cent of respondents, surpassing ANC leaders nominated by 22 per cent, including Mandela, who was named by 19 per cent.

Buthelezi, moreover, was found to have support 'far beyond' the Zulu. The authors acknowledge, however, that their findings were skewed because it had not been possible to include in the survey the urban African population of the Eastern Cape, the historic heartland of the ANC. They also acknowledged the 'uninterrupted popularity' of Mandela and Sobukwe, despite their having been out of the political spotlight for more than a decade.[155]

The multi-layered conflict that developed in Natal and spread to the Transvaal in the 1980s and early 1990s defies easy explanation; nor is it possible to assign more blame to either one of the conflicted parties, Inkatha and the UDF/ANC, or to the malevolent activities of the practitioners of 'dirty tricks' operating from within the state's security apparatus. Much of the literature on the conflict, either explicitly or implicitly, is hostile to Inkatha, blaming it as the primary cause of violence, but the view taken here is that a more nuanced account is required which maintains that all three were heavily implicated in the conflict, and that none did enough to end it. What follows is neither a detailed account of the conflict, nor an attempt to ascertain who threw the first stone. The tragedy is that it claimed over 10 700 lives in KwaZulu and Natal between 1976 and 1994, nearly 90 per cent occurring between 1989 and 1994. Several hundred more fatalities occurred in the Transvaal in conflicts between Zulu hostel-dwellers and other urban people.

Despite rumblings of disapproval from some in the ANC and overt hostility from BC sources inside South Africa, Tambo, who had known Buthelezi since the 1950s, continued to encourage the build-up of Inkatha after 1975. According to his biographer, Tambo 'hoped to mentor Buthelezi, highly intelligent and keenly sensitive, to utilise legal space so as to open up opportunities for the ANC's separate underground activity'.[156]

Things fell apart after a meeting in London in October 1979, attended by Inkatha and ANC delegations led respectively by Buthelezi and Tambo.

Buthelezi presented his proposals in a prepared document, whose introduction read:

> I am aware that some of my followers would like to see Inkatha challenge the ANC's position and you are aware that some of your followers would like to challenge Inkatha's position. We are both however aware that the peasants and the workers in South Africa would rebuke us bitterly if any sense of rivalry was ever evidenced between us.

Buthelezi's case for Inkatha rested on the proposition that when the people were offered 'constructive political involvement by engaging the forces of oppression in the mechanisms of oppression, the masses respond'. He proceeded to list the various manifestations of hostility to Inkatha emanating from the ANC in exile, international anti-apartheid movements, the BC movement, and others. It would be tragic if the liberation movement were to be divided: 'The idiom of Africa is towards single party systems.' Opposition required that 'a central and dominating force begins to regulate black opposition to apartheid. The vehicles for this dominant force are Inkatha and the African National Congress.'

The critical question Buthelezi put to the ANC was this: 'Will the ANC in exile publicly acknowledge the fact that Inkatha is a vital force in the struggle?' It was followed by subsidiary questions, most of them asking the ANC to call off criticisms of Inkatha by other organisations, domestic and foreign.[157]

The meeting was supposed to be secret, but to the ANC's anger a report of it was published in the (Johannesburg) *Sunday Times*. Each side blamed the other for the leak, although Suzanne Vos (later, in 1994, an Inkatha MP), who reported the story, insisted that one of the ANC exiles had been responsible.[158] Others, however, believed that Buthelezi himself may have been the source.

Although the two-and-a-half day meeting had been cordial, it was clear that scepticism about Inkatha had been growing in the ANC, no doubt heightened by the recent influx of uncompromising BC youth who vigorously opposed having any truck with bantustan leaders, especially with Buthelezi. Buthelezi reciprocated the hostility: his opposition to radicalised youth may well have been sparked, or increased in intensity, by an incident at Sobukwe's funeral in Graaff-Reinet in 1978 when Buthelezi was insulted and jostled by angry youths who put his life in danger and forced him to flee. Benjamin Pogrund, an eye-witness to the episode, said to his wife: 'That man with his enormous pride has been totally humiliated. God knows what price South Africa will be made to pay for it.'[159]

The belief had grown that Buthelezi was trying to promote himself and Inkatha as equal in status to the ANC, which claimed exclusive rights to being considered as the premier liberation movement. There were also major policy differences between the ANC and Inkatha: the ANC supported 'armed struggle', whereas Inkatha opposed it; the ANC actively encouraged economic sanctions, which Inkatha opposed; and Inkatha favoured a federal system for a future democratic political system, while the ANC wanted a unitary system, fearing that federalism would not only hamstring the power of the central government but might also provide a backdoor method of accommodating the bantustans. There were, moreover, lurking suspicions that Buthelezi was fundamentally a Zulu ethnic nationalist.

In a retrospective analysis of the rupture, Tambo, in an address in 1985, took some of the blame himself. He acknowledged his hopes that Buthelezi would use the legal space afforded by the bantustan system to create a mass movement focused on the struggle for a united, democratic and non-racial society:

> Unfortunately, we failed to mobilize our own people to take on the task of resurrecting Inkatha as the kind of organization that we wanted, owing to the understandable antipathy of many of our comrades towards what they considered as working within the Bantustan system. The task of reconstituting Inkatha therefore fell on Gatsha Buthelezi himself who then built Inkatha as a personal power base far removed from the kind we had visualized, as an instrument for the mobilization of our people in the countryside into an active and conscious force for revolutionary change …. Later, when he thought he had sufficient of a base, he also used coercive methods against the people to force them to support Inkatha.[160]

By the mid-1980s the UDF, and thereafter Cosatu, had become exactly 'the kind of organization that we wanted'. Inkatha was dispensable.

Buthelezi's retrospective view lamented the deaths of many thousands and the consequences:

> Had we joined forces in 1979, the terrible destitution of the people would not have been aggravated by the violently destroyed and disrupted communities. There would not be the legacy of bitterness and hatred that there now is. There would not be a whole generation of young people who have known only a decade of the hideous black-on-black violence and killing for political purposes.[161]

The parting of the ways opened the floodgates for ever-increasing acrimony. The ANC's propaganda organs launched blood-curdling attacks on Buthelezi, the most notorious of which was a call by John Nkadimeng, a trade unionist and member of the ANC's national executive committee, in November 1986:

> It is clear that the puppet Gatsha is being groomed by the West and the racist regime to become a Savimbi [the Angolan guerrilla leader] in a future free South Africa. The onus is on the people of South Africa to neutralise the Gatsha snake, which is poisoning the people of South Africa. It needs to be hit on the head.[162]

Nkadimeng's comments reflected a widespread sentiment in the ANC. Patti Waldmeir writes that ANC officials in Lusaka during the mid-1980s 'made no secret of the fact that they would like to kill him'.[163] Thoughts of assassinating Buthelezi, however, were abandoned. Nevertheless, the stream of unrelentingly hostile propaganda targeting him continued, contributing to a climate of opinion in which Inkatha members were regarded as legitimate targets. Many of the more vituperative examples were included in Inkatha's submission to the TRC. Typically, he was condemned as a 'tribalist', 'a frontrunner in the service of Botha', 'an enemy of the workers' strikes', a 'blood-soaked gangster', 'a tyrant'. Moreover, the historical validity of Buthelezi's claim to be the traditional 'prime minister' to the Zulu monarch was disputed, an allegation that deeply offended him.[164]

The fierce rhetoric from the ANC, and comparable responses from Inkatha, raised the political temperature on the ground, predisposing rivals to regard the conflict in 'zero sum' terms, implying that only one winner could emerge. It made violence virtually inevitable.

An evangelist, Michael Cassidy, who played an important role in bringing Buthelezi and Inkatha into the 1994 election, sums up the basis of ANC hostility:

> [T]here was a failure ... to understand accurately the feelings and the dangerously intensifying emotions of the Inkatha Zulus. The problem seemed to lie in the fallacious view among many that KwaZulu was simply another artificial apartheid creation, an anachronistic Bantustan and tribal relic run by a Pretoria surrogate with no popular support. All therefore that was required was to tighten the political thumbscrews and if that failed to entertain the notion of the so-called military solution. This would silence what one opposition camp

leader called 'the howling dogs of Ulundi [the capital of KwaZulu]'. KwaZulu and Inkatha and the so-called Zulu problem were basically an over-inflated political bubble, pumped up by Pretoria and Zulu traditionalism, which, once popped, would evaporate into the ideologically thin air whence it came.[165]

For its part the ANC was anxious to prevent a 'tribalistic' fragmentation of the liberation movement, and to abort the development of counter-revolutionary organisations such as Unita in Angola or Renamo in Mozambique. It could accommodate the Inyandza National Movement because Mabuza was evidently prepared completely to subordinate its goals to the ANC's, even if it maintained a non-violent strategy.

Buthelezi and Inkatha, however, posed different issues: not only was KwaZulu far larger than KaNgwane in population terms, but Buthelezi was not prepared to be an obedient surrogate of the ANC. He understood African liberation politics – indeed, practised a robust version himself – and believed, with some justification, that the ANC's aim was hegemonic control of the struggle, as well as of a future democratic South Africa. Equally worrying to the ANC was the possibility that Inkatha might forge alliances, not only with other bantustan leaders and Tricameral Parliament politicians, but also with sympathetic whites who approved of Buthelezi's opposition to sanctions, his support for private enterprise, and his hostility to the radical unions of Cosatu.

Even Buthelezi's sympathetic biographer regards his failure to appreciate the political significance of Cosatu as a serious misjudgement.[166] Hardly less serious was the close link between Inkatha and the United Workers of South Africa (Uwusa), established in 1986 as a counterweight to Cosatu. Uwusa was little more than a 'sweetheart' union in relation to Inkatha: it imported the rivalry between the UDF and Inkatha onto the shop-floor. Uwusa's first foray into industrial action was to provide strike-breaking workers to replace Fosatu/Cosatu workers at a factory near Pietermaritzburg, causing several deaths in resulting clashes. Revelations of covert funding by the state subsequently destroyed its (limited) credibility, and it faded from the scene.

While Buthelezi retained a strong support-base among the peasantry of rural KwaZulu, it was evident in the early 1980s that support among non-Zulu and urban populations was declining. Heavy-handed action against children boycotting schools and anti-Inkatha university students damaged his standing among the youth who were a critical stratum of the resistance in the 1980s. Buthelezi's problem was exacerbated by demographic factors: 50 per cent of the African population of KwaZulu and Natal were under the age of 16; and urbanisation was proceeding at nearly 5 per cent per annum, with the consequence that increasing numbers no longer lived in relatively tight-knit rural communities. Huge informal settlements developed around the major cities and towns. Technically these settlements were located in KwaZulu, this being a homeland whose territory abutted urban areas. Attempts to incorporate several established Durban townships into KwaZulu created another flashpoint for conflict as many residents objected to the change.

Buthelezi's ability to straddle the difference between being a traditional leader and a modern politician, heading a mass organisation, had been an advantage in earlier days when something of a vacuum existed in African opposition politics. By the late 1970s and 1980s this had become more difficult: it was one thing to manipulate the symbols of Zulu history and to invoke the authority of the Zulu monarchy; but it was another simultaneously to appeal to a broader, inter-ethnic constituency. Inkatha's membership and its support base had always been overwhelmingly Zulu. As Buthelezi's national appeal eroded and that of the UDF/ ANC increased, he was increasingly forced to concentrate on shoring up his ethnic base. He had always insisted that he was no narrow Zulu chauvinist and that there was no inconsistency between his Zulu and South African identities – indeed, that they were mutually reinforcing. Many rank-and-file Inkatha members, however, did not share this sophisticated view and, moreover, were susceptible to the belief that they were fighting the 'Xhosa-dominated' ANC. Conflicts with Xhosa-speaking Mpondo, migrating from Transkei to Natal in search of work, sharpened anti-Xhosa sentiment as competition for scarce resources increased.

A difficult question, not amenable to an easy answer, if, indeed, to *any* answer, is the extent to which a historic fault-line among Zulu-speakers was a factor in the conflict. Originally the Zulu were a small chiefdom, but in the 1820s its scale and militarist character were built up into a formidable state by Shaka, whose military genius and ruthlessness conquered and absorbed surrounding chiefdoms that were unable to flee. The *Mfecane*, as this massive population displacement was known, dramatically reduced the size of the African population of Natal, as distinct from the Zulu heartland north of the Tugela River.

In 1843 the British annexed Natal, whereupon displaced people steadily began returning to their ancestral homes. By 1847 the African population was at least 100 000, and by 1871 the figure was 300 000. The pioneer of indirect rule, Theophilus Shepstone, re-established chiefly rule on the small (and generally barren) reserves that were allocated to Africans. Hereditary chiefs were recognised, and when none could be located 'chiefdoms' were artificially created from fragmented clans, and commoners were elevated to chieftainships. In many cases appointed chiefs were the beneficiaries of Shepstone's patronage.

Bishop John W Colenso, noting in 1854 the divisions among the Natal Africans, most of whom were refugees or returning refugees, observed that 'the name of Zulu has come to be applied to all, indiscriminately, who came beneath [Shaka's] power, and subsequently that of his brothers, Dingaan and Panda'. Of the 100 000–120 000 Africans in the colony, he observed, they looked up to the Queen of England 'with affection and reverence as their protector and friend'. But, he warned presciently, this would dissipate as neglect, hut taxes and other burdens of colonial rule bore down on them.[167]

As a consequence of missionary work and the (limited) provision of education, a distinctive *kholwa* (literally 'believers') class emerged, by whom the first demands for greater equality with whites were voiced. The earliest modern political movements, forerunners of the ANC, were composed exclusively of *kholwa*. The distaste of many *kholwa* for traditional culture was a common theme in the African press of the late nineteenth and early twentieth centuries. In rejecting demands to abolish the Zulu military system in 1878, Cetshwayo, the Zulu king, voiced his distaste for those Zulu-speakers, including *kholwa*, who were under colonial rule in Natal:

> The king and nation will consider it a humiliation, and a descent from their proud position as independent Zulus to the lower and degrading position of Natal Kafirs, to agree to this demand.[168]

Despite their frustration at the restrictions that were imposed upon them, a number of *kholwa* fought on the side of the British army in the Zulu War of 1879. A mounted contingent from Edendale, a mission centre near Pietermaritzburg, 'were all devout Christians, who rose every morning before the rest of the camp to hold their services and sing hymns'.[169] A mixed picture emerges from the Bambatha Rebellion of 1906. This was essentially a peasant uprising precipitated by the imposition of a harsh poll tax at a time of economic hardship. It was put down with great brutality by the Natal authorities. *Kholwa* fought on both sides, but the majority who supported the rebellion were apparently members of independent churches that had broken away from the white-controlled denominations. John Dube, the most prominent *kholwa* in the Colony, who subsequently became President of the Native National Congress in 1912, urged the readers of his newspaper *Ilanga lase Natal* to refrain from joining the revolt and to stay loyal.[170]

Whether, by the 1970s and after, the descendants of *kholwa* venerated the past glories of the Zulu kingdom to the same extent as traditionalists from the Zulu heartland is doubtful. The possibility (and it is no more than that) is that, even if blurred by the passage of a century, intermarriage and urbanisation, differing degrees of identification with 'Zulu-dom' remained – and could be reactivated if political provocation sparked it. It is doubtful whether any UDF or ANC supporters shared Buthelezi's view of Zulu history and his invocation of past sovereignty, expressed in a speech to the KwaZulu Legislative Assembly in 1994:

> We were defeated militarily but never crushed. We most certainly never relinquished our Zuluness and we never renounced our Zulu sovereignty. When we were dragged into the Act of Union [1909] without even so much as a by-your-leave, we took with us our sense of who we were, where we came from and where we intended to be going. We also took with us our Zulu sovereignty.[171]

Buthelezi had consistently expressed these sentiments. By 1994, however, there was an added sense of urgency since the ANC appeared intent on comprehensively dismantling the bantustans. For Buthelezi it was vital to retain control of the KwaZulu bantustan apparatus: it was symbiotically linked to Inkatha, and a major source of its patronage. Chiefs who were the scaffolding of Inkatha's popular support were tightly controlled, being obliged not to become members or promote the objects of any organisation 'of which the aims are the unconstitutional overthrow of the Government'.[172] The monarchy, moreover, was widely venerated by Zulu, and buttressed claims that Zulu sovereignty continued to exist. The establishment of the KwaZulu Police in 1980, alleged by critics to be little more than 'Inkatha's private army', soon became another instrument of control.

Antagonists in ethnic conflict are commonly distinguished from one another by 'markers' such as cultural (including language) or phenotypical characteristics. It is commonly observed that the conflict in Natal could not be characterised as ethnic since the combatants were all Zulu-speakers (except in the case of the Mpondo). Broadly this is correct, but it is subject to two qualifications. First, Inkatha supporters could generally be identified because they spoke 'deep Zulu', whereas the *amaqabane*, 'comrades' who played a prominent role on the UDF side, spoke *tsotsi taal*, a heterogeneous mixture of English, Afrikaans, Zulu and 'some slang words from God knows where', and greeted one another with the word '*Heytha!*', which had become loaded with political implications.

Secondly, the comrades used provocative and insulting terms to taunt Inkatha supporters: thus, *theleweni*, meaning 'the one who pours us over a cliff', was said to infuriate them; hardly less insulting was the description of Inkatha supporters as *klova*:

> [I]f you say someone's a *klova* you also mean he's a fool, or rather a bumpkin, an unsophisticated, someone who swallows his toothpaste because he doesn't know better. When the *amaqabane* call Inkatha people *klova*, they mean they're like children, they haven't grown up to the twentieth century yet.[173]

For youthful comrades to use such language against the generally older Inkatha men was regarded as an intolerable violation of the traditionalist code that demanded respect for elders.

There are echoes in the insults of common stereotypes of rural people by urbanites. They had been a feature of clashes between migrants and townspeople elsewhere in the country; but the situation in Natal was different since the traditionalist targets of these and other insults had the backing of a powerful movement that was close by and bitterly resented the enemy's muscling in on 'its' turf.

What happened in Natal resembled a civil war. The following overview is necessarily brief. Of the extensive literature describing it, the best is the encyclopaedic book by Anthea Jeffery, *The Natal Story*, which is massively detailed, and possesses the additional merit of presenting both sides' respective understandings of the conflict.[174]

Fundamentally the conflict revolved around political competition. It could not be reduced to a struggle for control of scarce resources, such as land, access to water, or jobs, although there can be little doubt that the dire poverty of many of the region's inhabitants sharpened the antagonisms. Other areas of the country that were occupied by Africans were hardly less impoverished, yet the competition for scarce resources did not spill over into violence. The unique element in KwaZulu-Natal was the presence of a powerful movement (Inkatha) that would not allow itself to be rolled over and eliminated by the UDF and the ANC, or even permit them to invade what it regarded as its turf.

The competitive aspect of the conflict reached a climax when Inkatha began a recruitment drive in the Pietermaritzburg area, including the Edendale Valley, late in 1987. From September onwards through to February 1988 fatalities in the Natal Midlands region rose rapidly, reaching over 600 by mid-October 1988. The UDF accused Inkatha of using coercive methods to force people to join it or face being driven out of the area – or worse. Predictably, Inkatha denied this, insisting that they were acting in self-defence. The truth was that the respective leaderships of the two organisations, both ostensibly committed to non-violence, had little power to control the combatants. Archie Gumede, a national president of the UDF and its leading figure in Natal, expressed a sense of helplessness:

> The affiliates [of the UDF] are totally autonomous. The UDF itself does not have the machinery to supervise the activities of its affiliates ... I am not able to control 10-year-olds. The only people we believe can make a meaningful agreement are the ones in jail – Mandela and Sisulu.[175]

Similarly, Buthelezi disclaimed responsibility for the violence perpetrated by Inkatha-supporting chiefs in the Midlands: there was

> ... no nexus whatsoever between those chiefs and myself as president of Inkatha or between them and Inkatha as an organisation. If they are members of Inkatha then that is incidental ... I am unable to control the manner in which they act in their capacity as chiefs.

Both statements contained elements of truth: by 1988 the conflict had developed a momentum of its own that made it resistant to peace-making efforts by the local (white) business community, the churches, and the respective leaderships of the UDF and Inkatha. In the absence of effective control, warlords filled the vacuum, often extracting money from those under their control, and, of course, keeping the conflict alive.[176] Ancient inter-clan feuds were incorporated into the conflict, rivals positioning themselves on opposing sides.

In October 1988 the ANC was informed that Buthelezi wanted to end the conflict: Margaret Thatcher, the British Prime Minister, offered her services as an intermediary, but the ANC rebuffed the initiative, saying that 'the time has not arrived to speak with Gatsha [Buthelezi] or even Thatcher.'[177]

In an analysis of the conflict, Alexander Johnston makes the critical point about the 'localisation' of the conflict, which was an important cause of the inability of political leaders and would-be peace-brokers to end the violence:

> ... political competition between the IFP and the ANC in KZN is inextricably mixed with other dimensions of conflict: crime, tribal and

factional disputes and intergenerational tensions are fertile sources
of violence. Participants in these struggles often show keen opportunism in approaching one or other of the main parties for help, and
are met with matching eagerness to exploit tensions. Central to this
kind of relationship is the phenomenon of 'warlordism', in which
powerful local figures act as brokers for the interests of squatters,
hostel dwellers or other marginalised groups, attaching themselves
to one or the other political party in the process, but not always placing themselves under their control. Individuals or cliques of this sort
tend to have their own conceptions of what it means to 'belong to'
or be associated with the ANC or the IFP. The general impression of
localised conflict is reinforced by the fact that peace pacts between
ANC- and IFP-supporting groups seem to hold in some areas and
not in others.[178]

Localisation often meant that violence occurred in areas that were difficult to police. Rugged terrain, deep valleys, and roads that were often
little more than tracks made rapid responses difficult, if not impossible.

The role of the South African Police and the KwaZulu Police was a
highly contentious one. There were undoubtedly 'good cops' among the
SAP, who properly saw their duty as preventing or restraining violence
and arresting those responsible for attacks; but, given the rightwing proclivities of many white policemen, it was inevitable that the predominant
view was that the UDF and associated 'comrades' were the enemy. The
role of the KwaZulu Police, effectively controlled by Inkatha, was even
more openly partisan.

In a cautiously worded analysis, Anthony Minnaar writes:

> [One] has to question the role of the South African and KwaZulu
> Police. At the very least certain elements have been guilty of turning
> a blind eye to the activities of Inkatha vigilantes, allowing them free
> rein to attack ANC areas and to drive out ANC activists. At worst
> they have colluded and assisted in a number of attacks, protected
> Inkatha cadres from counterattack, assisted in transporting arms to
> certain areas, and refrained from arresting Inkatha members openly
> guilty of leading attacks.[179]

The TRC reached similar conclusions in its investigations of the violence.
It had access to a State Security Council document of 1989 which claimed
that in 1985 the Inkatha Central Committee had decided 'that the whole
of KwaZulu and Natal must be turned into a so-called 'no-go' area for

the UDF, regardless of the consequences'. The TRC, whose membership included no one with a background affinity to Inkatha, largely ignored the impact on Buthelezi and Inkatha of the UDF's 'ungovernability' campaign, as well as the alleged threat posed by MK, which led, in turn, to Inkatha's request to the SADF in 1986 to train 200 Inkatha supporters for paramilitary purposes, including defence and a 'strike capacity'.

Of the security forces' complicity in the violence the TRC reported:

> Both [vigilante groups and security force members] perceived the same enemy, and were perceived as the same enemy. Security Force members who testified before the Commission spoke of the various ways in which the security forces had collaborated with Inkatha in attacks on the UDF. This included warning Inkatha supporters of impending attacks, disarming ANC supporters, arming Inkatha supporters, transporting Inkatha attackers and standing by while Inkatha supporters attacked people.[180]

Buthelezi's role in the downfall of apartheid has been underestimated, at least by the ANC, which came to regard him as a mere extension of the apartheid government. This was an injustice to him: by refusing to accept independence for KwaZulu he prevented the loss of South African citizenship by over six million Zulu – the biggest ethno-linguistic cluster in the population. As FW de Klerk acknowledged, Buthelezi 'made a major contribution to the demise of grand apartheid by refusing adamantly to accept independence for KwaZulu and by insisting on the release of Nelson Mandela and the unbanning of the ANC before he would enter into constitutional negotiations with the government.'[181] Nelson Mandela, who had known Buthelezi since the 1950s and regarded him as one of the ANC's 'upcoming young leaders', similarly acknowledged Buthelezi's role, while pointing out also that he was 'a thorn in the side of the democratic movement'.[182]

Tragically, the violence that wracked Natal and KwaZulu in the 1980s – and had extended to conflict between Zulu hostel-dwellers and townspeople in the Transvaal – was to continue, even intensify, in the 1990s. It threatened to derail the transition.

*　*　*

By the end of the 1980s, a sense of impending change was in the air. De Klerk had given no hint of the momentous scale of the changes he was to announce on 2 February 1990. The black internal opposition, though mauled by the security apparatus, had survived, and had not backed down from any of its core demands. The state was too strong to be overthrown; 'ungovernability' had not been achieved on any widespread, durable scale, although the effectiveness of government had been severely impaired. 'Seizure of power' remained an unrealistic goal. In short, the contending forces were deadlocked: unless a settlement could be negotiated, bloodshed, misery and the creation of a wasteland stared South Africans in the face.

CHAPTER 9

Groping Towards Negotiation

On his way into Parliament on 2 February 1990 FW de Klerk turned to his wife Marike and said, referring to his forthcoming speech: 'After today South Africa will never again be the same.' He had said much the same thing at a social function the previous evening, leaving the guests abuzz with excited anticipation. Apart from the Cabinet and some trusted officials, no one else knew what was to come. Mindful of the consequences of the hype prior to Botha's Rubicon speech and the subsequent let-down, De Klerk had been careful to impose strict secrecy on his ministers; not even the NP caucus was told about the scope of the initiatives he would announce.

Subsequent to his historic speech, De Klerk repeatedly denied that he had undergone a Damascene conversion during 1989. He insists that he took his 'quantum leap' in 1985–6 when the NP abandoned apartheid by pulling down some of its major institutional and ideological props and accepted that South Africa was 'one nation'. He insisted that he was carrying forward policies initiated by Botha. His speeches, beginning in 1986, show a consistently reformist slant, even when facing fierce CP opposition. He remarked to the American and British Ambassadors in 1986 and 1987, respectively, that South Africa should learn a lesson from white-ruled Rhodesia and not leave it too late to talk to the real leaders of the African population.

De Klerk was widely regarded as a conservative, and he had been expected to do little more than tinker with apartheid. In a retrospective explanation of his conservative image, De Klerk said:

> It is stupid to be vociferously right at the wrong time or to move so
> far ahead in the right direction that your followers can no longer hear

344

or see you … . I was often criticized before I became President for not racing ahead in the pursuit of reform. Had I done so I would have alienated key players and important constituencies, I would not have become leader of my Party in 1989 and I would not have been able to do the things that I did when I was President. Timing change is of the utmost importance … .[1]

In the campaign prior to the election on 6 September 1989, the NP, under severe assault from the Conservative Party, appeared to be offering the mixture as before: there was an emphasis on the urgent need for reform, but also the usual quota of ANC-bashing, including a denial by De Klerk that the existing NP position on talking to the ANC had changed:

> I want immediately to say that that is not so … . The NP says that it is prepared to negotiate with all who do not engage in violence, and who are committed to peaceful solutions. As long as the ANC disqualifies itself in this respect, we are not in favour of negotiating with the ANC.[2]

He appeared also to maintain the NP's policy on group rights, saying that only when people feel secure in a group context (*groepsverband*) would they be prepared to run the risk of sharing power.[3] Provision had to be made for 'own' power bases, within which each group would control its interests. He attacked the Democratic Party's federal proposals, which would leave whites a practically powerless minority in every region; moreover, the DP's refusal to endorse a group's right to retain 'own' schools, residential areas and amenities amounted to 'forced integration'.[4] NP policy was firmly against majority rule or 'simple majoritarianism', as it was termed: whatever Constitution was negotiated should not permit the domination of one group by another: as De Klerk put it: 'Domination by a majority is as unacceptable as domination by a minority. After all, the worse case in history [Nazi Germany] of domination and oppression was committed by a majority.'[5]

In a parliamentary speech delivered shortly after his election as leader of the NP, and almost exactly a year before his historic speech in 1990, De Klerk spelled out his views on the need for a 'totally changed South Africa' and the constitutional mechanisms that he advocated. On the critical issue of 'groups' he said:

> … the NP is not as ideologically obsessed with the group concept as has been suggested by many critics in this debate … . Our strong

emphasis on group rights, alongside individual rights, is based on the reality of South Africa and not on an ideological obsession or racial prejudice. All the lip service being paid to a so-called non-racial society is pure nonsense. There is no such thing as a non-racial society in a multiracial country. However closely we may co-operate, however near to each other we may move, South Africa will retain its diversity, and that diversity will remain a powerful and often beneficial force which must be reckoned with.

He added that the NP was not bound to any particular measures and that it would seek to find a mutually acceptable basis for the maintenance of 'group security', which he acknowledged was a sensitive issue.[6]

Despite De Klerk's protestations of his commitment to a country free of racial discrimination, critics dismissed the concept of 'group rights' as a form of neo-apartheid, designed to ensure that whites would retain ultimate control or at least possess a veto. In March 1989 heavyweight criticism of the concept came from an unexpected quarter, the South African Law Commission, a body consisting of judges and lawyers. In a working paper, it denied the juridical validity of 'group rights' since a 'group' is not a legal person. This did not mean, however, that minorities should not be protected, since failure to do so 'would be to invite endless conflict'. In its interim report the Commission concluded that individual rights could be invoked to protect cultural, religious and minority rights without the necessity of determining 'groups' by referring to race or colour: 'It is an error of logic to suppose that the protection of [minority] rights can only take place through a group; in fact, juridically it can only take place through an individual.'[7]

It has been necessary to belabour the point about 'groups' since it had been, and would continue to be, a sticking point in the quest for a negotiated settlement. De Klerk's arguments, however, could not be dismissed out of hand: he was surely right to warn against the 'tyranny of the majority', however unjust the preceding minority domination had been; and his claim that there is 'no such thing' as a non-racial society in a multiracial country is also substantially correct if by this he meant that senses of identity and group interests would not disappear even under a formally non-racial, democratic Constitution. On the contrary, they would be powerful forces shaping politics, especially in a state like South Africa with its legacy of division and conflict.

De Klerk was prepared to be flexible in the interest of reaching a settlement, as he indicated in his first meeting with Nelson Mandela on 13 December 1989. Mandela declared flatly that the NP's concept of group rights was unacceptable to the ANC, adding that 'if it was his true intention to preserve apartheid through the Trojan horse of group rights, then he did not truly believe in ending apartheid'. De Klerk listened attentively, and then said that his aim was no different from Mandela's; Mandela had acknowledged the reality of white fears of black domination, and 'group rights' was a mechanism whereby the NP proposed to deal with them. Mandela was impressed with this response, but said that the idea of 'group rights did more to increase black fears than allay white ones'. De Klerk said, according to Mandela, 'We will have to change it, then.'[8]

South Africa's transition underlines the importance of leadership of the contending parties: it was vital to keep their respective constituencies in line, to prepare them for the inevitable compromises, and to have some flexibility. It was also important that mutual trust be built up. The relationship between Mandela and De Klerk went through some rocky rapids, but ultimately held firm. The first meeting established a reasonably cordial rapport: De Klerk was impressed with Mandela's aristocratic bearing and his warmth and charm; Mandela found that De Klerk, unlike NP politicians of the past, listened to him, which was a novel experience. Both reached the conclusion that they could do business with each other.[9]

De Klerk had assumed the presidency at an inauspicious time: domestic insurrection, isolation by much of the international community, and an economy that was never far from crisis ensured that the going would be tough. Moreover, there were doubts about the solidity of the NP's support base. As noted, the NP's share of the votes cast in the 1989 election had dropped below 50 per cent, and it lost 27 seats, while the CP's representation increased from 22 to 39. The NP, with 93 seats, still enjoyed a handy majority, but 29 constituencies were considered vulnerable to the CP, having NP majorities of less than 1 500. The liberal Democratic Party (DP) had also won some seats from the NP, raising its representation to 33, with 21 per cent of the votes. De Klerk knew that he could rely on the DP's support in any genuinely reformist move, which meant that nearly 70 per cent of the white electorate supported reform. But what kind and scale of reform?

Surveys of white opinion in the late 1980s suggested strong opposition to negotiating with the ANC: in 1988 nearly 62 per cent of whites (including 78.5 per cent of Afrikaans-speakers) opposed the idea, which was 4 per cent higher than the figure for 1986.[10] A survey of white student opinion conducted in mid-1989, with a large sample (over 4 000) found that over 90 per cent of Afrikaans-speakers were unsympathetic to the possibility of an ANC-controlled government. This figure included 31.7 per cent who said they would rather emigrate, and 44.1 per cent who claimed that they would physically resist.[11] A poll published in February 1990 found that only 54 per cent of NP supporters and 44 per cent of all white voters supported the unbanning of the ANC, PAC and SACP. Moreover, support for the CP had increased by 12 per cent between November 1989 and February 1990, suggesting that it would win at least 38 per cent of the white vote in a hypothetical election.[12]

De Klerk was not unduly fazed by these data. He knew that opinion surveys commissioned by the government in the late 1980s had consistently shown that the ANC enjoyed the support of some 60 per cent of the total population. Excluding the ANC would ensure that negotiations failed, and this would make the ANC and its huge internal constituency even more militant. If there were to be any hope of peace, engagement with the ANC was imperative.

Two factors were helpful to De Klerk in pushing for inclusive negotiations. First, South Africa had succeeded in extricating itself from the Namibian imbroglio – with considerable assistance from the United States, the Soviet Union and the United Nations. The protracted negotiating process culminated in general elections in 1989 and independence in March 1990. Although difficult, Namibia's transition had eventually proved smoother than anyone might have dared to hope. It was perhaps a dress rehearsal for what could possibly be achieved in South Africa, as well as being a sign that under Gorbachev foreign adventures by the Soviets would be stopped, and that negotiated settlements should be sought in Namibia, South Africa and elsewhere by political rather than violent means. Indeed, Shubin claims that Gorbachev had become less and less interested in anything to do with liberation struggles or developing countries.[13]

The second factor was the steady unravelling of the Soviet Union and the roll-back of its domination over much of Eastern Europe, which was symbolised by the destruction of the Berlin Wall on 9 November 1989. The collapse of communism destroyed whatever credibility the total onslaught doctrine retained, as well as reducing fears that the SACP would remain as a kind of ideological Trojan Horse within the ANC. For some time the Nationalists' strategy had been to try to drive a wedge between the ANC and the SACP, in the belief that there was a potential cleavage between African nationalists and communists. It had not succeeded: the symbiotic relationship was far too strong. Despite this failure, the collapse of communism 'created an opportunity for a much more adventurous approach than had previously been conceivable':[14] a gap had opened, and De Klerk took it.

Apart from insisting that the ANC foreswear violence as a prerequisite for participating in negotiations, Botha had demanded that it also sever its links with the SACP. This the ANC flatly refused to do. In his memorandum to Botha, sent prior to their meeting in August 1989, Mandela reiterated the ANC's view, denying that it was under the SACP's control: 'Which man of honour will desert a life-long friend at the insistence of a common opponent and still retain a measure of credibility with his people?'[15] To the ANC it was intolerable that its foe should try to determine who could, and who could not, be included in a negotiating team. In short, no SACP, no ANC.

De Klerk was realistic enough to recognise that the SACP was no longer the threat that it was believed to pose and, moreover, that refusing to unban it would keep it underground where it could possibly have more nuisance value than might be the case if it were to operate as a lawful organisation in the glare of public scrutiny. In any case, the dual membership arrangement between the ANC and the SACP would enable SACP members easily to participate in ANC negotiating teams by wearing their ANC hats. There was resistance in Cabinet to De Klerk's view that the SACP should be included in the number of organisations to be unbanned, but his pragmatism overcame it.

Not having been a member of the inner circle surrounding Botha, nor having held a ministerial portfolio with direct security concerns, De Klerk was out of the loop as far as security issues were concerned. In his capacity as Transvaal leader of the NP he served on the State Security Council, but he maintains that his involvement was peripheral: he and other ministers not involved in security matters 'were not informed of the innermost operational secrets of the security forces – and we were not encouraged to ask too many questions about them'.[16] The extent to which De Klerk knew about, condoned, or acquiesced in the 'dirty tricks' activities of elements in the security forces would be an issue that dogged him in the following years.

De Klerk was unaware that stealthy emissaries of the state and, in some cases, private citizens acting with Botha's knowledge were actually meeting ANC representatives, usually in Europe or Lusaka. Equally in the dark was Chris Heunis, the Minister of Constitutional Development and Planning, whose duties included attempting to persuade 'moderates' to participate in negotiations to be convened by the government. Apart from visits to Mandela by the Minister of Justice, Kobie Coetsee, and subsequently by Heunis's successor, Gerrit Viljoen, his constant interlocutor was Niël Barnard, the young Director of the National Intelligence Service. Mandela, who overcame his initial reluctance to have dealings with Barnard, found him to be 'exceedingly bright, a man of controlled intelligence and self-discipline'.[17] As noted, although Barnard's Afrikaner nationalist credentials were impeccable, he had become convinced by the early 1980s that it would be futile to try to fight it out with the ANC, and in regular briefings to the Cabinet and State Security Council he argued this proposition.

Despite his visceral mistrust of the ANC and his opposition to majority rule, Botha nevertheless gave permission to Coetsee and Barnard to pursue contacts with Mandela. Such contacts had to be conducted in the strictest secrecy because a leak would have been manna from heaven for the CP – and a huge embarrassment for Botha, who would have had difficulty explaining how these contacts could be reconciled with his fierce opposition to the ANC. For Botha the problem remained: he could foresee the awful consequences of Mandela's dying in prison, but could he be released into a political vacuum, and could Botha avoid accusations of political weakness? By the end of his presidency Botha had made no fewer than six offers to release Mandela, but with conditions that Mandela found unacceptable.

In a newspaper interview in 1992,[18] Barnard describes receiving official approval to engage in dialogue with Mandela to ascertain whether he could play a role in bringing about a political settlement. Together with his deputy, Mike Louw, and two other officials, from May 1988 onwards, Barnard had held many discussions with Mandela, initially in Pollsmoor Prison (near Cape Town) and subsequently at Victor Verster Prison (about 50 kilometres from Cape Town), where Mandela had been accommodated in a comfortable house in which he could hold discussions in private. (At the time of his transfer to Victor Verster in December 1988, Coetsee brought a case of wine as a housewarming gift!)

Barnard's team sought to ascertain whether Mandela really wanted a peaceful solution. At various times Mandela acknowledged that the ANC did not possess the military capacity to overthrow the state or even to drive it into a corner: South Africa was different from what occurred in Zimbabwe or Angola and Mozambique. The question posed to Mandela was whether the ANC would remove the major obstacle to negotiation by renouncing violence, which, according to Barnard, was nothing more than criminal behaviour. In reply, Mandela insisted that it was the state that was responsible for the violence that left the oppressed with no alternative but to resort to violent methods of self-defence. Mandela appreciated his interlocutors' argument that the NP, having repeatedly insisted that the ANC foreswear violence as a precondition of participating in negotiations, could not now suddenly announce talks with the ANC without losing credibility. For talks to begin, the ANC had to make some compromise so that the government would not lose face with its constituency. Mandela conceded that this was a fair point, but that it was a dilemma that the government itself had to resolve. Tell your people, Mandela advised, that peace and a settlement would be impossible without involving the ANC: 'People will understand.'[19]

It was not bloody-minded obstinacy that caused the ANC to refuse to renounce violence as a precondition: its capacity – however ineffective – to wage guerrilla war was a bargaining chip, part of the ANC's arsenal of resources. Another factor, of which Mandela must have been aware, was the probability that if the ANC leadership were to suspend the armed struggle there would be an angry backlash from MK operatives and many township militants who remained committed to the chimerical hope of seizing power. It was the obverse of the risk that Botha faced. Moreover, there were enough precedents elsewhere for negotiations, or at least talks about negotiations, to take place even while antagonists remained locked in combat.

The talks with Mandela raised another issue: the perennial question of whether he was a communist. No, he replied, but there were aspects of communist ideology that attracted him; and he certainly would not budge on the question of the ANC's severing its ties with the SACP. And what about minority groups' fears of black domination? Mandela referred them to the ANC's long history of seeking to unite all South Africans, as stated in the preamble of the Freedom Charter:

> I told them that whites were Africans as well, and that in any future
> dispensation the majority would need the minority. 'We do not want
> to drive you into the sea,' I said.[20]

Early in 1989 Mandela put several requests to Coetsee and Barnard: he wished to speak to the State President, wanting to make sure that Botha heard the points he had made directly from him: 'He would see that we were not wild-eyed terrorists, but reasonable men.' With a view to such a meeting he prepared a memorandum that set out the ANC's position on the key issues that divided the government and the ANC. He envisaged two stages: a discussion to create the proper conditions for negotiations, to be followed by the negotiations themselves. He urged Botha to seize the opportunity to break the deadlock.[21]

Barnard pressed Botha to agree to a meeting: Botha had nothing to lose, and even if the meeting was not a success he could always claim that he had tried to establish an understanding. But if it were a success 'he would be honoured in history as the person who took the initiative in the process'. Botha pondered the issue for some time and eventually assented. On the morning of 5 July Mandela, resplendent in a new suit, was taken secretly to Tuynhuys, the presidential office. Botha, according to Mandela, was 'unfailingly courteous, deferential and friendly', and even, to his astonishment, poured the tea.[22] Mandela, as well as Coetsee and Barnard, had been apprehensive that Botha might display his volcanic temper, but nothing of the kind happened.

Botha had made it clear to Barnard beforehand that the meeting would only be an informal conversation, and not negotiation. Pleasantries were exchanged, with both elderly men enquiring about each other's health. They talked about Afrikaner history, about which Mandela had read in prison, various African leaders and states, and the questions confronting Africa. Mandela touched on some of the issues that were central to the ANC, but declined to press Botha, not wishing to misuse the occasion to carry on so serious a conversation. Botha insisted that since 1978 he had gone out of his way to combat violence: instead of violence people should rather solve their problems around the negotiating table. Mandela, he continued, was in a position to contribute to a peaceful solution; however, 'he should not forget the contribution the Afrikaner could make in that respect'. The Afrikaner was ready to talk and to make a positive contribution. Mandela, in turn, assured him that the ANC leadership did not differ from the government about this. Indeed, he said, there was no party inside or outside Parliament that had a better record of commitment to peace than the ANC. Mandela also raised the issue of Walter Sisulu's release, saying that if Sisulu abused his new-found freedom, Botha would have every right to doubt Mandela's word, but that the converse was also true. Botha informed him that the decision to release Sisulu had already been taken, and that if he were thereupon to embark on a 'new propaganda campaign', Mandela's honour would be on the line. (Sisulu, together with several other long-serving prisoners, was eventually released in October 1989.)

The meeting ended with mutual good wishes and Botha's inviting Mandela to keep in touch.[23] A bland press release from Coetsee was issued three days later to a surprised country. Even if substantive issues had hardly been raised, the symbolism of the occasion was huge: if the State President of one of the most reviled regimes on earth and the world's most famous political prisoner could enjoy a cordial conversation, could Mandela's release be far off? And did the meeting not presage the inevitability, indeed even the imminence, of negotiations? It was not necessarily a breakthrough, but at least it signified that a firmly closed door was now slightly ajar. It was a sign that the conflict, which heretofore had not 'ripened' sufficiently to be amenable to a negotiated settlement, was now approaching the requisite state of ripeness.

It was not difficult to reconcile Botha's hostile public attitude to the ANC, and his insistence on imposing conditions for negotiations that the ANC would not meet, with what was happening behind the scenes. Although his stated view was that the ANC were little more than 'terrorists and communists', he knew that any leaked report of the clandestine dealings with ANC representatives would be a propaganda bonanza for the CP. Niël Barnard and Kobie Coetsee were his point men for talking to Mandela, but Botha also inspanned the services of several private citizens to take soundings from the ANC, always on the basis of 'deniability'. For its part, the ANC was keen to reciprocate, being intensely interested in knowing what was happening inside the ruling bloc.

The best-known of these private citizens were two Stellenbosch University professors, Willie Esterhuyse, a philosopher, and Sampie Terreblanche, an economist, both of whom were Broederbonders with impeccable Nationalist credentials who acted as informal advisors to the government. Both, although *verligtes*, had robustly attacked Stellenbosch colleagues whom they considered to be *oorbelig* ('overly enlightened', implying 'too liberal'). Willem de Klerk, brother of FW de Klerk, was also a member of the group of some 20 prominent Afrikaners who met senior ANC figures on a dozen occasions between 1987 and 1990.[24] Amazingly, news of these meetings did not leak out. Although Botha and the NIS were kept informed, even the Cabinet was left in the dark. The meetings were not negotiations – as Waldmeir pithily describes them, they were 'talks … about whether to talk … about talks'.

Another clandestine emissary to the ANC was Richard Rosenthal, a respected liberal lawyer who, in 1987, when on the verge of emigrating, wrote to Botha offering his services to facilitate the delicate initial stages of the preparatory work that might lead to formal negotiations. Rosenthal was contacted by Stoffel van der Merwe, the Deputy Minister of Constitutional Planning, and a protégé of Botha's, and over the ensuing 18 months he engaged in shuttle diplomacy as a go-between involving Thabo Mbeki of the ANC and Van der Merwe. His account is a unique analysis of mutual perceptions in the run-up to the eventual inception of the negotiating process.[25]

Non-official contacts with the ANC increased after 1985, despite strong criticism from Botha. The contacts became a steady stream. Apart from the business delegation, led by Gavin Relly, whose meeting with the ANC in 1985 was described above, other delegations included opposition politicians, sports administrators (including the venerable Danie Craven, head of the South African Rugby Football Union), students and various NGOs. The most significant of these visits was that organised by F van Zyl Slabbert under the aegis of the Institute for a Democratic Alternative for South Africa, an organisation established by him after his withdrawal from Parliament in 1986 for the express purpose of engaging with extra-parliamentary organisations. The 60-strong delegation, mostly Afrikaners who had already rejected apartheid, met an ANC group in Dakar, Senegal in June 1987 for intensive discussions. Slabbert's initiative predictably evoked a furious reaction from the white establishment.

None of these encounters, of course, involved negotiations. What they achieved was to strengthen support for the principle of negotiating with the ANC, now increasingly accepted as inevitable among sections of the Afrikaner elite. Grassroots white opinion, however, remained generally hostile. For De Klerk, coming into the presidential office after the election of 6 September 1989, the political context for major reform was hardly propitious: Botha's protracted and messy departure from office had damaged the NP; the threat of popular insurrection remained high and the violence in KwaZulu and Natal seemed unstoppable. The economy, despite a small upswing in 1988–9, remained in crisis. Although the NP had won the election, it had lost 17 seats to the CP, whose parliamentary representation increased from 22 to 39 seats, and 12 seats to the Democratic Party. The CP won over 680 000 votes (or 31.2 per cent of the total number cast), compared with 1.03 million for the NP. Estimates suggested that some 40 per cent of Afrikaners had supported the CP. While the NP continued to enjoy a viable majority in Parliament, the growth of the CP and support for it in the army, police and bureaucracy was menacing. There was a possibility that further support might accrue if radical reforms were initiated and/or if there were a breakdown of security.

De Klerk, who came from a highly political background (his father had been a Cabinet minister in the 1950s and 1960s), was a lawyer by profession. After becoming an MP in 1972, his rise in the hierarchy was meteoric. He was appointed a Cabinet minister in 1978 and served in various portfolios. He was elected leader of the NP in the Transvaal in 1982, giving him an influential position as a provincial baron. He was appointed chairman of the Ministers' Council in the (white) House of Assembly in 1986, a position that required him to become an advocate of the 'own affairs' concept that was central to the Tricameral Constitution. He ruefully observes that his role as a spokesman for white 'own affairs' resulted in his being labelled as a *verkrampte* – 'an image with which I had to live until I became leader of the National Party in 1989'.[26] De Klerk's reputation as a conservative was aggravated also by his habit of criticising ostensibly reformist measures that in his view were half-baked since, being piece-meal, they did not form part of a coherent vision of reform. Willem de Klerk writes of his brother:

> He had deliberately built up a conservative image and a flexible pro-file. In Afrikaner politics, power is based on conservative thinking; in the long run it gains you confidence, and once you have that, you can do magical things with the Afrikaner. That was FW's strategy, not rigid conservatism.[27]

While De Klerk strenuously denied any sympathy for the *verkramptes* – and robustly attacked the CP on many occasions – he equally strenuously avoided identification with any of the groupings inside the NP. He saw himself as a 'team-player' who loyally supported official policy, at least in public. By the early 1980s it was obvious to De Klerk that apartheid was failing catastrophically and, moreover, that its human costs were im-mense – and mounting, since it could be enforced only by coercion, which invariably entailed confrontation. No lasting solution, he believed, could be built on injustice.

Despite his cool – and, during 1989, stormy – relationship with Botha, De Klerk never failed to give him credit for smashing the major ideologi-cal pillar of separate development, namely that the population consisted of 'separate nations'. The shift had occurred in 1985–6. De Klerk told his brother:

> When those of us in the inner circles – courageously led by PW Botha – had reached the conclusion that our policy had to shift from separate development to power-sharing, I gave it my full support … . I took a leap in my own mind, more decisively than many other National Party politicians, that power-sharing with blacks was the right course for a new political dispensation … . I made it emphatically clear that the logical consequence of our policy was the inclusion of blacks in any new political system.[28]

De Klerk would learn, during the negotiating process of the early 1990s, that his proposals for power-sharing would be rejected by the ANC, which demanded undiluted majority rule, save for some sops to minority cultures (as provided for in the Freedom Charter) and, even-tually, as a purely temporary expedient, a multiparty government of national unity. Any institutional device for protecting minority rights was dismissed out of hand as a 'white veto' or 'neo-apartheid'.

During 1989 De Klerk, speaking with greater authority as party leader and thereafter also State President, clarified his views, while not offering specific institutional details. According to Stoffel van der Merwe, as told to Rosenthal, De Klerk had told a group of *verligte* Afrikaners early in 1988 that there were four options:

1. To capitulate to the dominant black majority.
2. To 'dig in'; resist demands for power-sharing, and do whatever might be necessary to maintain white domination.
3. To make adaptations and adjustments to the Constitution, whilst maintaining white control through 'indirect means'.
4. To confront the necessity for fundamental constitutional change, recognising democratic principles, but negotiating to prevent the domination or subordination of any group.[29]

De Klerk had plumped for option 4. His speeches during 1989 reiterated themes that elaborate it. First, power-sharing was to preclude 'simple majoritarianism' in a 'winner-take-all' political system. He attacked the DP for allegedly acquiescing in majority rule, saying that this would lead to minorities becoming practically powerless. Secondly, it was necessary for each group to have its own power-base and its own community life in which it could maintain its own language, traditions, habits and view of life (*wêreldbeskouing*). Only when people felt secure in a group context (*groepsverband*) would they be prepared to run the risk of sharing power. At the same time, he said that the NP was not ideologically obsessed by the concept of groups. Indeed, it wished to move away from the current definition of groups (in the Population Registration Act) to one that was acceptable and based upon the principle of free association. The NP had a fairly open approach to the formation of new groups, and it was possible that a 'so-called' non-racial group could arise through a process of freedom of association. At the same time, he declined to be specific or to offer a blueprint of what the final institutional provision for this form of minority/group protection would be. It was, moreover, untrue that the government had ever considered adding a fourth chamber for Africans to the Tricameral Parliament. De Klerk was at pains to stress that his proposals were not intended as a covert form of white domination. The protection of minorities, he insisted, was not apartheid, provided it was done with acceptability and justice.

De Klerk was reaching for a consociational model, different from the sham-consociationalism embodied in the tricameral system. Although sneered at by his opponents, including the ANC, his concerns were legitimate. Non-racialism (apart from the elimination of all discriminatory laws) was chimerical, an aspiration that had not been achieved in any multi-ethnic or multiracial society. 'Group' voting preferences would continue to be salient. He acknowledged that Belgian or Swiss methods of managing cultural diversity in politics could not simply be transferred into a South African context, but nevertheless constitutional and political mechanisms were necessary to ensure that minorities were not subjected to the tyranny of the majority. As De Klerk put it:

> There is no way in which all the people of this country will suddenly forget who they are; where they come from; where their roots are; what their goals and motivations and their basic cultural outlooks on life are. There is no way in which everybody is suddenly going to say we are now in a new entity in which all differences have disappeared. Numbers will not really make any difference if South Africa is governed on a basis of consensus by the chosen majorities of its population groups.[30]

The problem for De Klerk and his party was two-fold: first, what was a 'group', and who decided on its parameters for purposes of inclusion in the Constitution, assuming that 'race classification' as prescribed by the Population Registration Act fell away? Secondly, while minorities are legitimately entitled to rights in order to protect themselves against the tyranny of the majority, the Afrikaner/white minority was no ordinary minority: it carried the historical baggage of oppressive domination of the majority. Was it not chutzpah to demand minority rights, especially if the perception among opponents was that this was a ploy to preserve at least neo-apartheid?

De Klerk had no option but to stress proposed safeguards for minorities if his programme of reform were to be saleable to a white electorate, more of whom might otherwise be tempted by the siren calls of the CP. Accordingly, majority rule was unacceptable, and no substantial changes would be made without consulting the electorate. De Klerk subsequently sought to allay suspicions that this was the case, saying:

> What has made the concept of minority rights suspect is that in the past we definitely used it to signify white rights. We are working on a clean sheet now, and our accent on minority rights is by no means a form of hidden apartheid … . Minorities must be formed by voluntary association, they must not be racist groupings; and no discriminatory basis must be built into minority rights.[31]

The NP's campaign preceding the election of September 1989 contained the usual quota of anti-ANC rhetoric. In reply to the question whether the NP's position on talking to the ANC had changed, De Klerk denied that it had, saying it was prepared to negotiate with any organisation that did not engage in violence and was committed to peaceful solutions. As long as the ANC disqualified itself in this respect, the NP was not in favour of negotiating with it.[32] This was partly electoral rhetoric; a few days later, he singled out Mandela, who by his commitment to peace had 'included himself among those who are prepared to cease violence and with whom [we] can negotiate'.[33] De Klerk's statements pointed to a way around the dilemma created by the NP's insistence that it would negotiate only with organisations that foreswore violence, a pre-condition that the ANC, including Mandela, rejected. If, however, a commitment to seeking peaceful solutions became the criterion, a cessation of violence would surely follow. Accordingly, foreswearing violence could be downplayed, if not dropped, as a requirement.

A sense of urgency pervaded De Klerk's speeches and interviews throughout 1989. South Africa, he said, stood on the threshold of a completely new system, and he asked voters to give him a mandate to enter the following phase: 'The NP is ready with everything it has to break out of the current deadlock'.[34] Many in the opposition remained sceptical of his intentions, believing that he would tinker with existing institutions rather than attempt radical reform. Typically, an editorial in *Business Day* commented, less than a month before the election:

> On the constitutional front ... we can look forward to another 5-year spell of fruitless Heunis-like maneuvers to draw fringe leaders of the black communities into negotiations. Meanwhile, of course, expensive and corrupting efforts will be made to sustain the tricameral Parliament, rather in the manner in which the Bantustans have been sustained, in the hope that legitimacy will come with the passage of time. The De Klerk presidency, on this front at least, is more likely to differ in style than in substance from the awful Botha years.[35]

According to her private secretary, Margaret Thatcher was equally disparaging of De Klerk's likely intentions, saying he was 'just another bloody Boer'.[36]

Despite the CP's gains, De Klerk insisted that the September election had given him a mandate for fundamental reform. He could also derive some comfort from the growth of support for the DP, which, together with the votes cast for the NP, accounted for 70 per cent of the white electorate's votes. Little in the NP's campaign, however, had prepared its supporters for the scale of changes that were to come.

On coming into office De Klerk moved swiftly to dismantle the 'securocratic' state that Botha had created: the National Security Management System was abolished, the State Security Council was downgraded to the status of a Cabinet committee, and an investigation of all secret operations of the security forces was ordered. Having been concerned at the eclipsing of the Cabinet by securocrats in Botha's presidency, De Klerk now insisted on the full restoration of cabinet government: 'In my team there was no place for inner circles and no by-passing the cabinet. All important decisions were taken by the cabinet, which was given full access to all the facts that could influence its decisions.' In similar speeches to senior police and military officers, he told them that their duty was to be absolutely impartial and that they 'would no longer be required to promote or oppose any political cause'.[37] The text of the speeches was leaked to the press.

De Klerk had reason to be concerned about the political loyalty of the police and the army, both of which were deeply steeped in apartheid thinking. There were good grounds for believing that support for the CP and other ultra-right organisations was strong, especially among the police. De Klerk had not been part of the securocrat complex, which he mistrusted – and which, in turn, mistrusted him, especially when he made it known that their previous influence would be drastically curtailed. Domestically, the police, and regionally, the army, were the ultimate guardians of the apartheid state. To demand of them a 180-degree turnaround while simultaneously requiring their loyalty was bound to be difficult, but De Klerk was determined to do so. Only later in the transition process would he learn that elements in the security forces were intent on sabotaging his reform initiative.

In (undated) interviews with Hilton Hamann, General Georg Meiring, who became chief of the army in 1990, says that De Klerk's decision to unban the ANC was a complete surprise 'which made life terrible for us'. A meeting of the intelligence community, presumably late in 1989, advised against releasing Mandela – 'it's going to cause havoc in the country'. De Klerk rejected the advice, saying that he was going to release him 'because in jail nobody can make mistakes'. Despite these negative views, Hamann found that most of the generals, with the possible exception of Constand Viljoen (who had retired in 1985), supported De Klerk, as did General Magnus Malan, Botha's hawkish protégé whom De Klerk had retained as Minister of Defence.[38]

In opting for a blitzkrieg, De Klerk consciously sought to seize the initiative and to convince supporters and opponents alike that the NP had now indeed crossed the Rubicon. Total secrecy had been necessary to ensure that the speech would have maximum impact: neither the NP caucus nor ministers' wives knew beforehand just how far-reaching it would be. Even the local media, adept at sniffing the political wind, were caught by surprise. De Klerk had decided

> ... to take a quantum leap .... I knew what I announced would cause great concern to many followers, but decided to announce everything at once, rather than to do so in a piece-meal fashion. That gave us the tremendous advantage of gaining the initiative, as opposed to appearing to be giving in to pressure.[39]

As De Klerk knew, he was taking a risk – but what alternative was there? His autobiography mentions a Cabinet gathering early in December 1989, where all of the issues were discussed, including 'fall-back positions should things go wrong'.[40] But what realistic fall-back position would there be once Pandora's Box had been opened? Certainly it would not be possible to stuff the contents back inside: an unbanned ANC, together with other unbanned organisations, was bound to show militance, even unruliness, as it jockeyed to strengthen its hand in the negotiating situation. In a retrospective observation, De Klerk said that the process

> ... was rather like paddling a canoe into a long stretch of dangerous rapids. You may start the process and determine the initial direction. However, after that the canoe is seized by enormous and often uncontrollable forces. All that the canoeist can do is to maintain his balance, avoid the rocks and steer as best he can – and right the canoe if it capsizes. It is a time for cool heads and firm, decisive action.[41]

*   *   *

Before the mid-1980s the ANC had given little serious thought to the possibility of a negotiated settlement, which seemed an utterly remote prospect. From its inception in 1912 to the late 1940s, the ANC's stance had typically been one of humble supplication – or so its internal critics alleged – until the revolt spurred by the Youth League had stiffened its resolve. After its banning in 1960 and the decision thereafter to form MK, all thought of supplication, petitions and the like disappeared, to be increasingly replaced by notions of revolutionary overthrow of the state and the 'seizure of power'. The SACP, often a source of ideological and strategic thinking, called in 1962 for a 'national democratic revolution which will overthrow the colonialist state of White supremacy', though it did not completely dismiss all prospects of a non-violent transition to the democratic revolution.[42]

The ANC's consultative conference in Morogoro in 1969 reaffirmed the centrality of the armed struggle in ANC strategy, though insisting that MK was subordinate to the political leadership. Moreover, it was made clear that military force could succeed only if it attracted the active support of the mass of the people. 'Conquest of power', nevertheless, was the goal. The ANC's Radio Freedom, in a broadcast in 1969, proclaimed that the apartheid government must be removed by force: 'This land of ours was taken away by bloodshed, we will regain it by bloodshed.'[43] The context of Morogoro was the considerable disaffection among MK soldiers, many of whom were highly critical of the ANC leadership. By 1969 MK had yet to engage in action on South African soil, but many of its soldiers were eager to go back and fight, which caused the ANC leadership to over-estimate their readiness for battle and their likely capacity to pose a threat to the apartheid state.

The ANC was offended by President Kenneth Kaunda's initiative in orchestrating the Lusaka Manifesto on Southern Africa in 1969. The document, signed by 14 independent states of East and Central Africa, pleaded for liberation to be achieved without physical violence: 'We would prefer to negotiate rather than destroy, to talk rather than kill.' Without explicitly saying so, the Manifesto appeared to endorse the view taken by conservative states like Ivory Coast and Malawi that there should be dialogue with the repressive regimes of Southern Africa. The Manifesto, which was subsequently endorsed by the Organisation of African Unity and the United Nations, was drawn up without consulting the ANC or the PAC. Tambo, while appreciating the problems that these regimes created for the signatories, responded by pointing out that Vorster's strategy of seeking dialogue with African states was essentially a trap, designed to fragment Africa's united hostility to apartheid. It was necessary that the armed struggle continue; Tambo stipulated: 'It is only when our tactics can, at a given historical phase, produce no further changes that we should change the tactics.'[44]

Tambo must have known that any thought of genuine negotiation was not even remotely in Vorster's mind: his government might ostensibly 'consult' with supposed leaders in an attempt to lure them into apartheid structures on a take-it-or-leave-it basis, with the proviso that those who declined would be on the receiving end of the security police's attentions.

Moreover, for the ANC to concur with the Lusaka Manifesto's anodyne tone would have been interpreted by the government as a sign of weakness, confirmation that the strong-arm actions of the 1960s had succeeded.

It was not until the mid-1980s that the possibility of a negotiated settlement was entertained by some – by no means all – in ANC leadership circles. The key figure was Mandela, whose conclusion in August 1985 that the time for negotiation had come was quoted above. Shortly before, the ANC had held a national consultative conference at Kabwe, Zambia. The political report of the National Executive Committee (NEC), presented by Tambo, proclaimed the gathering to be 'a council of war that planned the seizure of power by [the] masses'. The ANC, of course, was buoyed by the 'deep and permanent general crisis' into which the apartheid state had fallen, and the widespread mobilisation of protest in many parts of the country. If 'seizure of power' remained the *leitmotiv* of the proceedings, the possibility of negotiations now at least appeared on the radar screen.

The report acknowledged that there had been speculation about negotiations between the ANC and the government, but it remained convinced that Pretoria was 'not interested in a just solution', and that its main concern was

> ... to use the question of negotiations to divide our movement, de-mobilize the masses of our people by holding out the false promise that we can win our liberation other than through its overthrow. It also seeks to improve its image internationally. In any case, it is clear that no negotiations can take place or even be considered until all political prisoners are released.

While these comments appear to dismiss the possibility of negotiations, the NEC immediately qualified them, saying that

> ... we cannot be seen to be rejecting a negotiated settlement in principle. In any case, no revolutionary movement can be against negotiations in principle.[45]

At this stage, however, the ANC's belief was that the crisis besetting the state would ultimately force it to sue for a settlement. On this reading, there could be no negotiations unless they were tied to the transfer of power – in effect, capitulation, which was not on Botha's agenda, nor that of any member of his government. The ripening process still had some way to go. Commonly, antagonists do not agree to negotiate a settlement until *both* recognise that the conflict cannot be won on either's terms;

in other words, that a stalemate has been reached and that continuing pursuit of a unilateral victory would result in appalling loss of life and destruction of property.

Mandela had recognised the 'no-win' situation and the need for the antagonists to talk; but this did not mean that he would allow himself either to be separated from his ANC colleagues in Lusaka or to be used as a cat's-paw by the state. He showed his mettle, as well as his understanding of what negotiation meant, early in 1985 when he received an offer (the sixth) from Botha to be released from prison provided that he 'unconditionally rejected violence as a political instrument'. He sent a message to the government rejecting the offer, but also saying that he believed that 'negotiation, not war, was the path to a solution'. To allay possible suspicions that he was contemplating a separate deal with Botha, he sent a message out of prison that was read by his daughter to cheering crowds in a Soweto stadium: 'What freedom am I being offered while the organization of the people remains banned? ... Only free men can negotiate. Prisoners cannot enter into contracts.'[46]

By the 1980s Mandela's iconic status, both domestically and internationally, was enormous. Not only did this cause intensifying worldwide interest – and pressure on the government – but the symbolism of courage and commitment to principle represented by Mandela was perhaps the ANC's most important asset. Moreover, domestically, demands for his release became a rallying cry for large-scale mobilisation and protest.

In April 1982, Mandela, Walter Sisulu, Raymond Mhlaba, Andrew Mlangeni, and (later) Ahmed Kathrada were suddenly transferred from Robben Island to Pollsmoor Prison, near Cape Town on the Peninsula. It was a move designed to diminish the symbolic aura surrounding Robben Island as well as to stop their influencing the other political prisoners.[47] Ironically, the move, in due course, facilitated Mandela's secret dialogue with the government.

As Mandela shrewdly realised, one of the obstacles to initiating the process of talks about negotiations was the reluctance of either side to be seen as the initiator, lest it be interpreted as a sign of weakness. Apart from the long record of mutual demonisation, there were political dangers for both sides that inhibited any opening move. The further danger was that continuing mutual demonisation could turn into something resembling a self-fulfilling prophecy. Botha's intense concern for the secrecy with which his stealthy emissaries met ANC representatives reflected the danger of potential political fallout if knowledge of the meetings were leaked; similarly, ANC leaders, whether Tambo or Mandela, had to tread with care lest talks with government emissaries be interpreted by more insurrectionist-minded followers as 'betrayal' or 'selling out'.

Mandela was determined to scythe through the obstacles. While he always described himself as a disciplined member of the ANC and also recognised that the decision to talk to the government could be taken only by the leadership in Lusaka, he nevertheless went ahead: 'There are times when a leader must move out ahead of the flock, go off in a new direction, confident that he is leading his people the right way.'[48]

Late in 1985 Mandela underwent prostate surgery. He was informed on his return to Pollsmoor that he was being separated from his colleagues and moving to 'a kind of splendid isolation' in better accommodation. He seized the opportunity:

> I chose to tell no one what I was about to do. Not my [Pollsmoor] colleagues upstairs nor those in Lusaka. The ANC is a collective, but the government had made collectivity in this case impossible. I did not have the security or the time to discuss these issues with my organization. I knew that my colleagues upstairs would condemn my proposal, and that would kill my initiative even before it was born.[49]

Mandela's hope that his initiative could be kept confidential was in vain: after a meeting with Kobie Coetsee, a warder told Kathrada about it, and kept them informed of subsequent developments. They easily grasped what was happening: Mandela had decided 'to engage the enemy in talks, aimed at initiating dialogue with the ANC'.[50] Mhlaba and Mlangeni readily approved what Mandela was doing; Sisulu, according to Mandela, was 'uncomfortable, at best, lukewarm'. He was not opposed in principle to negotiations, but he 'would have wished that the government initiated talks with us rather than our initiating talks with them'. Kathrada was resolutely opposed, declaring that it would appear like capitulation. In his own account, Kathrada acknowledges that, as the secret talks progressed, he realised that his initial judgement had been flawed, 'but I was never really reconciled to this course of action.'[51]

The apparent failure of the Commonwealth EPG's mission in 1986 has been described. In the short term it was indeed a failure, yet, even if through an intermediary, the ANC and the government had been forced to confront what would be required if a negotiating situation were to arise. The EPG's Report crystallised for both sides the central issues in a way that became a template for initiating a future negotiating process.

The ANC was initially disappointed with the Commonwealth Heads of Government's Nassau Accord on Southern Africa's compromise decision to establish the EPG, instead of intensifying sanctions. It believed that the proposal had been designed to assist in relieving pressure on the South African government. Nevertheless, it agreed to meet the mission, as did Mandela and other ANC-aligned movements like the UDF.

Despite their misgivings, Tambo and the ANC's National Executive Committee accorded the EPG a warm welcome. Although its views on the prospects for negotiations were pessimistic, the ANC was curious to learn about the government's response to the EPG's mandate. Thus far, according to the ANC, 'it appeared that the Botha regime was interested not in negotiations but only in pursuing a war against the people'. Such reforms as Botha had introduced were merely a response to the increased pressure being exerted on the government. But:

> If the Government was prepared to shift its ground and indicate its readiness for fundamental change this would impact on the ANC view. Their assessment was, however, that nothing had changed and nothing would change. If that proved to be the case, then the conditions for negotiation did not exist.

As described in the EPG's Report, the ANC laid down some fundamental prerequisites before negotiation could even be considered: first, that Mandela be released and that the government talk to authentic leaders, not those whom it designated as 'leaders'; second, that it declined to renounce violence prior to its being satisfied that the government was ready to negotiate transition to a non-racial system: 'For the ANC to renounce violence now would be to reduce itself to a state of helplessness.' Moreover, the ANC pointed out, there were ample precedents, including in Zimbabwe, for negotiations to take place to end hostilities, even while violence continued.

The forcible termination of the EPG's mission, ironically, let the ANC and its internal surrogates off the hook. Mandela had aroused suspicion among his colleagues in prison or in exile by going further, as far as potential negotiations were concerned, than most of them. The mood in Lusaka was deeply mistrustful of the government's intentions.

In spite of the confirmation of the ANC's belief in the untrustworthiness of the government that the torpedoing of the EPG had caused, the idea of a negotiated settlement could no longer be ignored either by the government or by its opponents, domestic and exiled. As it happened, most of the items in the EPG's Concept were subsequently incorporated in the ANC's declaration on its negotiating position.

Although dismayed at the turn of events, Mandela refused to give up his quest for dialogue between the ANC and the government: 'often, the most discouraging moments are precisely the time to launch an initiative'. He was able to set up an appointment with Kobie Coetsee in June 1986 at which they spoke for three hours, Mandela being 'struck by his sophistication and willingness to listen'. Coetsee's questions went to the heart of the matter: under what circumstances would the ANC suspend the armed struggle? Mandela replied, as he had to the EPG, that the ANC could not be expected unilaterally to suspend violence, but if the government and the ANC were to synchronise their expressed intentions to negotiate and to declare a ceasefire, there should be no problem with its implementation. He agreed that he and his colleagues would have to take active steps to persuade their followers to desist from violence and to respect the negotiating process, which meant that it was up to the government to ensure that the process's credibility was maintained.

Mandela was encouraged by the conversation, sensing that the government was trying to find a way to break out of the stalemate: 'In ghostly outline, it was the beginnings of a compromise.' Further meetings with Coetsee took place in 1987.[52] At this stage, however, neither side knew how negotiations could be initiated, even if the political will had been there. Frene Ginwala, a former aide to Tambo, said in 1991 that:

> ... all of us were convinced in the many years of liberation struggle that victory was certain. That was one of our favourite slogans. But, there was never a clear cut and unequivocal scenario of how that victory was going to come about and what would actually happen. A move to a people's war and the possibility of insurrection were avidly debated .... And many a fantasy was woven of an embattled regime regrouping around the Voortrekker Movement [Monument?] behind a laager formed of ox-wagons and Caspirs, tanks, sneeze machines, rocket launchers and so on, while in the cities and countryside ordinary people took over public buildings, factories and the institutions of power. We had visions of MK Commanders striding at the head of their troops into Pretoria, Johannesburg and all the cities of South Africa, while people formed spontaneously into a national convention to write the new constitution.[53]

Although these comments contain some hyperbole, they capture the spirit of romantic revolutionism that was widespread. It paralleled the attitudes of some diehard whites who claimed that they would resist until the last drop of blood, etc. Stoffel van der Merwe acknowledged to Richard Rosenthal that although the government was committed to a policy of constitutional dialogue, 'it did not know how to begin'.[54]

By 1987, and with the failure of the EPG still fresh in their minds, the insurrectionist spirit still prevailed in the ANC. In May Tambo told a meeting in London that a 'terrible collision between ourselves and our opponents is inevitable'. Many battles would be fought and many lives would be lost throughout the region, yet, whatever the cost, 'there is no doubt that we will win'. He reiterated that, given the conditions laid down by the government for participating in negotiations, the onus could not be placed on the ANC to take the initiative. But: 'If the key to negotiations were in our hands, we would long [ago] have used it to open the door.'[55]

*   *   *

Both government and the ANC had come to accept the principle of negotiation, though with vastly differing meanings attached to the concept. For the mainstream ANC, negotiation would effectively be about the government's terms of surrender and the mechanics of transferring power. For Botha, the obverse was the aim: to crush the ANC and to impose an NP-designed 'solution' on the country. These apparently inflexible public postures, however, were belied by the informal talks that were being conducted behind the scenes. Significant players on either side recognised that neither the ANC's nor the government's official views would prevail: a negotiated compromise was inevitable, and the terms of that compromise would be determined by the strength that either party brought to the bargaining table.

Apart from growing international pressure on both sides to reach out for a mutual accommodation, certain domestic factors were also creating a climate that would eventually be conducive to negotiation. First, the battering that the UDF had experienced caused some of its more thoughtful members to reconsider the strategic options available to the liberation movement. The UDF had viewed the EPG with the same suspicion as the ANC, but it had nevertheless co-operated, spelling out prerequisites for negotiation that were virtually identical to the ANC's. Moreover, the UDF had borne the brunt of the security forces' repression in the harsh years after 1984: it was entitled to express its views. In an interview with Waldmeir, Valli Moosa, general secretary of the UDF in the Transvaal and an important figure nationally, expressed his impatience with the ANC's romantic approach to revolution: 'Whenever I met with ANC leaders, the question I asked over and over was, How exactly are we going to take over?' It was not possible to overrun Pretoria: there was a stalemate. He recalled that the ANC leadership had attacked him and other UDF representatives for even suggesting that there could be a stalemate:

'We were given a lecture on insurrection and sent back to prepare for it.' As Waldmeir observes, Moosa was not yet advocating negotiation, but he – and no doubt a number of his colleagues – had reached the critical point of recognising that the contending forces were deadlocked.[56] It was but a short step to accepting the inevitability of negotiations.

A second set of factors were of a different order: even in the heat of the struggle in the 1980s, negotiations between mostly ANC-aligned 'civics' and white local governments or between African trade unions and business had been shown to facilitate the management of conflict. In many local communities 'civics' articulated popular grievances, as well as long-term demands. The more immediate issues were discontent over rent increases, corrupt councillors, consumer boycotts, forced evictions and the right of 'civics' to organise. Most of these issues were amenable to settlement; longer-term demands, such as for single, non-racial and democratic municipalities, could not be met at the local level, and would have to await a national settlement. Cas Coovadia, former general secretary of the Civic Associations of Johannesburg, wrote:

> The parties involved in the negotiations agreed to negotiate because of an underlying stalemate. On the one hand the state was unable to forcibly end the rent boycott that was crippling the local fiscal system, while on the other hand the civic associations were unable to force the collapse of the state. Gradually it became clear to both sides that they were interdependent: the communities needed to survive and the state had a responsibility to create a functioning, fiscally viable urban system.[57]

Likewise, on the industrial relations front, the independent unions quickly acquired the art of negotiation, often to the discomfiture of (white) managements. Both the unions and management learned many lessons about negotiation as a process 'which could also be extended into the political arena'.[58]

However localised and patchy, these manifestations of negotiated settlements steadily seeped into the political cultures of both blacks and whites. Johannes Rantete observes that while the idea of national political negotiations was not yet on the ANC's agenda, it was not indifferent to local negotiations that addressed the rent crisis, despite initial suspicions: 'This lukewarm acceptance of local-level negotiations was later transformed into a force within the movement as more pro-negotiations arguments were advanced.'[59] Negotiation, in time, would come to be viewed as another 'site of struggle', thus enabling the concept to be more easily assimilated into ANC strategic thinking.

A third source of encouragement for the idea of negotiation came from the steady procession of (some 70, mostly white) groups visiting the ANC, either in Lusaka, Europe or, as in the case of the group led by Slabbert, Dakar. The ANC were not only pleased to see fellow-South Africans, and hear first-hand knowledge about home, but were also encouraged by what they interpreted as an increasing desire among whites to abandon apartheid. In conversation with Rosenthal, Thabo Mbeki, the ANC's Director of Information and Publicity and Secretary for Presidential Affairs, pondered the stream of visitors:

> With all these people wanting to come and talk to us, who is it that still wants old-style apartheid? Van Zyl Slabbert and Wynand Malan [a former NP MP] don't want it. The Afrikaans Churches assure us they don't want it. The Rugby Unions don't want it. So who does? Is it just PW [Botha] and Magnus Malan? The NIS also says it doesn't want it, as do the Generals. It suggests that there may have been an important shift in South Africa.[60]

Mbeki – son of Govan, who had been sentenced to life imprisonment together with Mandela – was the diplomatic face of the ANC, and one of its rising stars. His pipe-smoking affability, charm and sweet reasonableness allayed the suspicions of many white visitors that the ANC were little more than a bunch of murderous terrorists. As he put it: 'They expect monsters and find themselves talking to human beings!'[61] Afrikaners were assured that their culture would not be endangered in a non-racial democracy.

Beneath the cordiality of the visits, invariably lubricated by copious quantities of whisky, lay a deadly serious intent on Mbeki's part: to detach visitors ideologically from the grip of the apartheid mindset and convert them into proponents of negotiations with the ANC. Since it was virtually an act of rebellion for the visitors – apart from the stealthy emissaries – to have any dealings with the ANC, it was a comparatively easy task: most had already broken with apartheid. Moreover, many were high-profile people; their role in white-anting the establishment could be significant, and could even lead to an informal coalition. Reciprocally, Mbeki and his colleagues learned a great deal about Afrikaner politics and minority fears.

Undoubtedly the meetings contributed to a growing sense among some whites that negotiations which included the ANC were inevitable (as even Pik Botha had acknowledged) and that the outcome need not necessarily be catastrophic for whites. Indeed, there was every chance that life under an ANC government could be appreciably better than it was in the current violence-wracked garrison state, with a contracting economy and an ever-tightening noose of isolation.

Together with Mandela, Thabo Mbeki had become the leading protagonist of a negotiated settlement, an issue that was controversial in the ANC. Mbeki, born into a highly political family, had left South Africa in 1962. Crucially, he enjoyed Tambo's support. As a protégé of Tambo, he had risen quickly in the ranks of the ANC and the SACP, becoming a member of the ANC's National Executive Committee in 1975 and the SACP's Central Committee in 1970.[62] His years abroad included a year's military training in Moscow. In these earlier years he was said to display a fierce loyalty to the USSR. By the late 1980s, however, it was apparent that his enthusiasm for Marxist-Leninist systems had declined and that he was moving in a social-democratic direction. (He allowed his membership of the SACP to lapse after returning to South Africa in 1990.) His involvement with visiting whites and his insistence that they, too, could be part of the liberation struggle incurred the suspicion of both radical insurrectionists and Africanists in the ANC. Worst of all, he gained the reputation of a 'moderate'; in the paranoid circumstances of exile, rumours even circulated that he was a spy for the apartheid government. Moreover, it was alleged, he was meeting visitors 'without a mandate' – despite Tambo's approval.[63]

As the end of apartheid drew nearer, it was imperative that the 'broad church' be held together so that a united front could be presented. A split or paralysing disunity would have played right into the hands of the enemy. It required all of Tambo's considerable diplomatic skills to maintain unity. In an adroit straddling act, he continued to insist that the armed struggle and negotiations were complementary. For him

> ... it was imperative that the ANC be prepared, if and when the time came, to enter into negotiations ... his nightmare had been that even if the ANC were able to 'hear' and translate the message [about possible negotiations] from the regime, the movement would not be *politically* prepared for such a meeting. The result would be that the ANC would lose its initiative and so the balance of power would once again become skewed. As president, Tambo could not afford to spell out openly the complexities and contradictions of the situation and so risk division within the ANC at this sensitive time.[64]

Tambo's inability openly to risk providing details about the unfolding situation was paralleled by the extreme secrecy shrouding the activities of Botha's stealthy emissaries. When Rosenthal mentioned to Mbeki the NP's claim that it had sustained political costs as a consequence of its reforms, Mbeki responded that the ANC, too, had suffered high political costs for insisting upon a non-racial struggle. Just as the NP had shed support to the CP, so the ANC had to cope with the rivalry of the PAC and Azapo. Young people were becoming impatient with ANC policy: 'We also have a need to confront our own "political monsters".'[65] This exchange underlined a critical question in a potential negotiating situation: could the main antagonists keep their more radical (or racist) followers in line? Or would racial outbidding destroy any initiative?

The build-up of pressure on the ANC to negotiate continued: apart from major Western governments and the frontline states, the ANC's major backer, the Soviet Union, was indicating that negotiation was its favoured course. Nevertheless, as Shubin shows, Soviet support for the ANC, if more uncertain, continued.[66] The Soviets, moreover, supported the American-brokered agreement reached in December 1988 between Angola, Cuba and South Africa that led to the independence of Namibia in 1990. While the ANC expressed support for the agreement, it meant also that its Angolan bases had to be moved. In turn, this meant that MK would no longer have bases in a state that adjoined South Africa, or, as in this case, South African-controlled territory. It was a setback for MK, even if many of its guerrillas were by now being recruited and trained inside South Africa. The prospect of Namibian independence, however, was a gain that outweighed any drawback: the final section of the *cordon sanitaire* was to be removed. But the agreement also spurred the ANC into readying itself for a possible negotiating situation. There was another unspoken consideration: having won the diplomatic battle against the government, it would have appeared churlish for the ANC to shut the door on the negotiations that much international opinion was advocating.

Tambo's fears about the ANC's being politically unprepared for negotiations were well-founded. The stealthy emissaries were surely harbingers of at least talks-about-talks; and since 1987 the ANC had begun to receive messages from 'influential people' in the South African military establishment that 'either an agreement would have to be reached by 1990 or the country would be destroyed'.[67] No independent confirmation of this report exists, none of the message-senders having acknowledged what they had done. Quite probably, though, it had some effect on the ANC leadership since it was not in their interest to inherit a wasteland, which would have been the possible consequence of a protracted civil war.

During 1988 Tambo set up a small team to prepare a document setting out the ANC's terms for negotiations. The draft, heavily criticised at first, eventually became the Harare Declaration. Steve Tshwete, a former Robben Island prisoner and thereafter MK's national commissar, subsequently recounted how difficult it had been to sell the idea of negotiations to the ANC rank-and-file, especially MK operatives: 'I don't think we succeeded in pushing it across, partly became we were half-hearted ourselves.' Tambo had recognised sooner than most of his colleagues that changing circumstances might require fresh strategies, and he warned about being caught off-guard, as Zimbabwe's Patriotic Front, led by Robert Mugabe, had been in the late 1970s. As Tshwete described Tambo's argument about the pressure exerted by Mozambique, which had suffered mightily from the Rhodesian war,

> Those guys [the Patriotic Front] had to be taken to [Lancaster House in London, where the final pre-independence negotiations were conducted in 1979] kicking and crying. It was said to them, if you don't want to go to negotiate, then you are pulling out of Mozambique ... *A Luta Continua* – from home. End of story. So we must avoid this situation. When the moment for negotiations comes, it must find us ready; and we should not start to fumble.[68]

Despite Tambo's persuasiveness and his diligent quest for consensus in the ANC's exile community, resistance to the idea of negotiating with the enemy remained strong. Which side would take the initiative? The question was converted into 'who would blink first?' The insurrectionists continued to portray parleying with government spokesmen as a sign of weakness, a first step down the slippery slope of capitulation.

The SACP, a major source of strategic influence in the ANC, remained insurrectionist in its orientation, although it is apparent that there were divisions, no doubt exacerbated by the unfolding of *perestroika* in the Soviet Union, and the growing ambivalence of its attitude to revolutionary wars in the developing or colonial world. Waldmeir says of the SACP's leading theoretician, Joe Slovo, that he 'continued to argue for the outright seizure of power'.[69] Other reports, however, suggest a more nuanced view. Shubin quotes his saying in 1988:

> The SACP is for political settlement. The experience of the national liberation movements in other countries proves its feasibility .... The question is not 'to talk or not to talk?' but 'with whom to talk and about what?'[70]

Allister Sparks makes a similar comment, with Slovo adding that: 'If there were any prospects of settling this thing peacefully tomorrow, we would be the first to say let's do it.'[71]

On the other hand, at the SACP's congress held in Havana in April 1989, the new party programme's last chapter, said to have been written mostly by Slovo himself, retained the insurrectionary perspective, while acknowledging that this did not conflict with the possibility of a negotiated transfer of power. Slovo nevertheless remained ambivalent: as late as June 1989; he still distinguished negotiation from 'the real thing', by which he meant a people's war.[72]

Chris Hani, another SACP heavyweight as well as being a member of the ANC's NEC and Chief of Staff of MK, reported in 1989 to a meeting of the ANC's National Working Committee that the uncertainty caused by the international community's pressure for a negotiated settlement and rumours of the Soviet Union's supposed withdrawal of support had had an effect on the membership, 'some of whom believe we are preparing for negotiations'. Shubin says that Hani's comments did not signify opposition to negotiations, only that he and most ANC leaders did not believe that the time had yet come for them: the ANC needed to be stronger, and its underground network strengthened. The meeting was concerned to reassure ANC members that it was not about to 'sell out'.[73]

Hani's caveat raised a critical point: negotiations do not conjure settlements out of thin air. Their trajectory and the respective strengths of the negotiating parties are determined by the amount of bargaining resources each brings to the table. The decisions about if and when to negotiate depended on either party's assessment of its rival's strength and staying power. By the late 1980s South Africa's contending forces were clearly deadlocked: decisions to negotiate depended critically on the mutual recognition of this fact. At best, such recognition was patchy – on both sides.

Despite the ascendancy of the insurrectionist perspective, which proclaimed either the seizure of power or negotiation merely about the terms of surrender, the ANC began to draft its negotiating framework during 1989. A readiness to negotiate would be underpinned and complemented by an intensification of the revolutionary struggle that would force the government to the negotiating table. Hani even suggested the targeting of white civilians as part of the intensification process, but this was opposed by senior ANC leaders, who were anxious to avoid the ANC's being tagged as a 'terrorist' organisation. To be sure, whites might inadvertently be caught in the crossfire, or MK operatives in the field, beyond the immediate control of their officers, might violate standing orders (as happened on several occasions) and kill civilians, but these instances were different from the deliberate targeting of civilians as a matter of policy. The ANC, uniquely among liberation movements, had subscribed to the Geneva Convention, which prohibited deliberate attacks on civilians in time of war. Nevertheless, it declined to dissociate itself from those responsible for such attacks.

Historically, the ANC had had a tradition of seeking conciliation. It had been eclipsed, but not extinguished, after the ANC's banning in 1960. The tradition was embodied in many of the older ANC leaders, notably Tambo and Mandela. The conciliatory and insurrectionist strands were not easy to reconcile in the same movement, except by dint of insisting that negotiation proceed hand-in-hand with intensified struggle. But even this yoking together of contrasting paradigms did not fully resolve the issue. As Rantete notes, although a broad consensus about negotiations was achieved within the ANC, SACP and the (internal) Mass Democratic Movement, 'the question of negotiating to achieve limited victories or to strengthen a revolutionary seizure of power' provoked intense debate that continued well after the unbanning of the ANC in February 1990.[74]

In January 1989 Mandela, now housed at Victor Verster Prison, began to prepare a memorandum to present to PW Botha. Apart from more comfortable accommodation, he could receive more visitors and was also permitted to communicate with colleagues on Robben Island, in Pollsmoor and even Lusaka. He was aware that his continuing meetings with ministers and officials were arousing suspicions; and he knew also that his thinking about the future was way ahead of most of his colleagues. The memorandum was eventually completed in March, but its preparation had coincided with Botha's illness and convalescence so that it was not until 5 July that he was taken to the presidential office in Cape Town.

Mandela's memorandum is one of the seminal documents of modern South African history, combining as it does an unyielding commitment to principle with a conciliatory sensitivity to the fears of minorities.[75] He prefaced his remarks by emphasising that although he was a 'loyal and disciplined' member, he had drafted the memorandum without consultation with the ANC, who he nevertheless hoped would endorse his action. He also insisted that the step should not be interpreted as the beginning of actual negotiations, but only as the more limited one of bringing the ANC and the government to the negotiating table.

He firmly rejected calls from the NP for the ANC to renounce its links with the SACP, which would be 'a violation of the long-standing and fruitful solidarity' that the two organisations had maintained. In majestic prose he explained why he had chosen to act:

... my intervention is influenced by purely domestic issues, by the civil strife and ruin into which the country is now sliding. I am disturbed, as many other South Africans no doubt are, by the spectre of a South Africa split into two hostile camps – blacks on one side (the term 'blacks' is used in a broad sense to indicate all those who are not whites) and whites on the other, slaughtering one another; by acute tensions which are building up dangerously in practically every sphere of our lives, a situation which, in turn, foreshadows more violent clashes in the days ahead. This is the crisis that has forced me to act.

The body of the memorandum focused on the three main issues that the NP had long invoked to rationalise its rejection of unbanning or negotiating with the ANC. First, the question of violence. Mandela explained how it was that the ANC was forced to adopt violent methods of resistance after decades of having 'diligently sought peaceful solutions'. The government, however, had ignored the ANC's demands, and even met them with force. In a sentence aimed at Afrikaner sensibilities, he observed that South Africa's history confirmed the vital lesson that 'Africans as well as Afrikaners were, at one time or other, compelled to take up arms in defence of their freedom against British imperialism'. (Whether Botha could appreciate the parallel is not known, but he certainly grew up with vivid family memories of the 'methods of barbarism' employed by the British Army in the Anglo-Boer War.)

Mandela concluded that the ANC's refusal to renounce violence was not the real problem facing the government; rather, it was not yet ready for negotiation and for the sharing of political power with blacks:

> It is still committed to white domination and, for that reason, it will only tolerate those blacks who are willing to serve on its apartheid structures. Its policy is to remove from the political scene blacks who refuse to conform, who reject white supremacy and its apartheid structures, and who will insist on equal rights with whites. This is the reason for the government's refusal to talk to us, and for its demand that we disarm ourselves, while it continues to use violence against our people.

Secondly, he addressed the topic of the SACP and the wider issue of the ANC's attitude to communism. He denied that the ANC was dominated by the SACP or that it was communist in its ideology. He omitted mention of his (erstwhile?) sympathy for the Soviet system and his possible membership of the Communist Party. Mandela insisted that the SACP accepted the leading role of the ANC and that SACP members who also joined the ANC became fully bound by its policy as set out in the Freedom Charter.

Mandela's exposition was unlikely to satisfy the NP, or, indeed, many opponents of apartheid who were leery of the ANC's close ties with the SACP. The truth was that the ANC and the SACP, although organisationally separate, were symbiotically linked to the extent that without Soviet assistance to the SACP and the ANC, the ANC would possibly not have survived the brutal decades after 1960. In her review of Shubin's book Irina Filatova writes:

> ... without Soviet assistance the ANC as we know it would not have existed and South African history would have been very different. Without it there would either have been no armed struggle – or it would have been a greatly reduced armed struggle – and it would have been much more difficult for the ANC to become the main symbol of struggle against the apartheid regime.[76]

Many ANC members who were not also SACP members shared a similar outlook. A heady mix of nationalist and communist views was not uncommon elsewhere in Africa, including in Angola and Mozambique.[77] It was understandable: apart from the Soviets' consistent opposition to imperialism (other than its own brand) and its material support of liberation movements, Marxism-Leninism offered an ideological understanding of colonialism and a strategic guide to ending it. Its appeal to many grievously oppressed people was obvious. Moreover, however spuriously, it appeared to offer a quick-fix solution to the problems of underdevelopment and inequality. By targeting communism with such unrelenting hostility the government persuaded many blacks of the truth in the old adage that 'my enemy's enemy is my friend'.

In addition to his defence of the ANC's ties to the SACP and his rejection of any demand that they should be severed, Mandela raised a challenging question: the government's refusal to have any dealings with the SACP was inconsistent with its own policy, for had it not concluded treaties with Angola and Mozambique? It would be difficult, if not impossible, to reconcile its preparedness to work with these Marxist regimes for the peaceful resolution of mutual problems, while uncompromisingly refusing to talk to the SACP. (Interestingly – and perhaps not coincidentally – Kobie Coetsee had been struck by the same point a few years before in relation to the Nkomati Accord, signed in 1984 by South Africa and

Mozambique, then led by an avowedly Marxist-Leninist government.)

The third issue raised in Mandela's memorandum was the most difficult of all: how to reconcile majority rule in a unitary state with white fears of black majority domination and their insistence on structural guarantees to avoid this. He offered no advice on how such reconciliation could be achieved, except to say that both parties would have to compromise in a negotiating situation for which a proper climate must be prepared. In an earlier meeting at Pollsmoor with a government group that included Coetsee and Barnard the same question had arisen: how would the ANC protect the rights of the white minority? Mandela replied:

> I said there was no organization in the history of South Africa to compare with the ANC in terms of trying to unite all the people and races of South Africa. I referred them to the preamble of the Freedom Charter: 'South Africa belongs to all who live in it, black and white'. I told them that whites were Africans as well, and that in any future dispensation the majority would need the minority. 'We do not want to drive you into the sea.'[78]

While Botha was evidently impressed by Mandela as a person – as were all of the NP government people who met him – his reaction to the cogently argued memorandum is not known. Given his almost obsessive concern with 'group rights', his visceral anti-communism, and his repeated insistence that the ANC lay down its arms before becoming eligible to negotiate, it would have been virtually impossible to accept any of Mandela's major points. A few days before his resignation on 14 August 1989, Botha expressed his regret to some officials that he had not moved faster with reform; but, having painted himself into an ideological and strategic corner, it is difficult to see how he could extricate himself without a humiliating recantation of virtually everything he had previously proclaimed. Moreover, Botha and the NP had little faith in Mandela's assurances, undoubtedly sincere though they were, that the white minority would be fairly treated under majority rule.

Reaction to Mandela's meeting with Botha and his ongoing meetings with ministers and officials provoked suspicion, even outright hostility, among many ANC and MDM members.[79] Although Tambo's fears had been allayed by personal messages conveyed by George Bizos, a leading Johannesburg advocate and ANC sympathiser, others suspected that he was cutting a deal behind their backs. It was believed, wrongly, that Mandela had offered whites 'structural guarantees' to protect their position. Govan Mbeki, who had been released from prison in 1987 and restricted to Port Elizabeth, had long differed politically from Mandela and at times was barely on speaking terms with him. On reading a summary of Mandela's memorandum all of his old suspicions about Mandela's reliability were revived, and the word went out in UDF circles that he should not be visited. Allan Boesak, a key figure in the UDF, accused him of acting without a mandate – an egregious offence in the UDF. It was not until the full text of Mandela's memorandum was received in Lusaka that belief in his integrity was restored. The episode had nevertheless underlined the tensions in the ANC and its internal allies.

Nothing in what Mandela had written contradicted the Harare Declaration, the ANC's statement of its negotiating position. It was drafted under the careful supervision of Tambo, and the final version was approved by the ANC's National Working Committee. Tambo had been eager to obtain the support of the Frontline States, which had been severely affected by apartheid, and also to pre-empt any attempt by foreign powers to shape the conditions for negotiation. The document was released on 21 August 1989 by the OAU.[80] It proved to be a propaganda triumph for the ANC, consolidating its occupation of the moral high ground, and confirming support for its position in Africa and much of the international community. It also succeeded in its aim of ensuring that the ANC would not be caught unprepared should a negotiating situation arise.

The Declaration's premise was:

> We believe that a conjuncture of circumstances exists which, if there is a demonstrable readiness on the part of the Pretoria regime to engage in negotiations genuinely and seriously, could create the possibility to end apartheid through negotiations. Such an eventuality would be an expression of the long standing preference of the majority of the people of South Africa to arrive at a political settlement.
>
> We would therefore encourage the people of South Africa as part of their overall struggle to get together to negotiate an end to the apartheid system and agree on all the measures that are necessary to transform their country into a non-racial democracy. We support the position held by the majority of the people of South Africa that these objectives and not the amendment or reform of the apartheid system should be the aims of the negotiations.

It then proceeded to list elements of its goal, a united, democratic and non-racial state, which drew on the previously published Constitutional Guidelines and outlined its conditions for an acceptable climate for negotiations: 'at the very least' the government should release all political prisoners and detainees unconditionally; lift all bans and restrictions on all proscribed and restricted persons and organisations; remove all troops from the townships; end the state of emergency and repeal all legislation that circumscribed political activity; and cease all political trials and executions. These, the Declaration continued, were the necessary conditions for free political discussion.

Furthermore: a mutually binding cease-fire that suspended hostilities should be achieved by discussion, whereafter the parties could negotiate the necessary mechanism for drawing up a new Constitution. An interim government should be formed to supervise the drafting and adoption of the Constitution, as well as governing the country and effecting the transition to the new democratic order. Once the Constitution had been adopted 'all armed hostilities will be deemed to have formally terminated', and the international community could lift sanctions. In the meantime, however, the campaign for mandatory and comprehensive sanctions was to be intensified.

It was a reasonable, even conciliatory, statement, although De Klerk would jib at some of the points, notably the idea of an interim government. The Declaration also finessed the insurrectionist strand of the ANC, which had wanted a tougher, more revolutionary statement. By August 1989, however, there were reasonable grounds for hoping that South Africa was on the cusp of genuine negotiations, and Tambo and Thabo Mbeki were anxious not to alarm Western governments, future foreign investors and the local business community, whose support would be necessary to facilitate the transition process, and, when the time came, to reconstruct the conflict-ravaged country. As they well knew, unbridled militancy would play into the hands of the ominously burgeoning right wing.

Finessed though they may have been, the insurrectionists were far from acquiescing. Militant action continued even as negotiations got under way. Some referred to these activities as the 'Leipzig Option', meaning mass action of the kind that had toppled communist governments in Eastern Europe. Then there was Operation Vula, a plan that was discovered by the police in July 1990 and provided an early jolt to the build-up of mutual trust in the earliest phase of pre-negotiations.

Prior to his first meeting with De Klerk on 13 December, Mandela drafted a memorandum in which he praised him for unconditionally releasing eight ANC heavyweights, including Sisulu, Kathrada and Raymond Mhlaba, and also for his recent inaugural speech, in which he had pleaded for reconciliation and a new spirit and approach. He understood De Klerk's plea to embrace all, and not only homeland leaders and other functionaries in apartheid structures whose 'principal role has been, and still is, to make the struggle for majority rule in a unitary state far more difficult to achieve'. Mandela reiterated his readiness to facilitate negotiations, but decried the government's approach: 'No serious political organisation will ever talk peace when an aggressive war is being waged against it.' Moreover, he insisted, the ANC had repeatedly expressed its willingness to negotiate, provided that a proper climate existed: 'readiness to negotiate is in itself an honest commitment to peace'. He also pointed out that it was only dialogue with the ANC and other mass-based organisations that could bring an end to the violence.

Mandela raised the vexed issue of group rights, which were totally unacceptable to him and the ANC because they smacked of a backdoor way of retaining a form of apartheid.[81]

The meeting enabled both men to size each other up and to conclude that they could do business with each other. De Klerk was impressed by Mandela's dignity, courtesy and self-confidence: 'He was every inch a Tembu patriarch and bore the mantle of authority with the ease of those who are not troubled by self-doubt'.[82] He told his brother subsequently that he had 'no doubt that we will get along well on a give-and-take basis.'[83] For his part, Mandela was struck by the 'novel experience' of meeting a Nationalist leader who listened carefully to what he had to say, without reacting quickly. He quotes De Klerk as saying 'my aim is no different than yours'. He 'seemed to represent a true departure from National Party politicians of the past'.[84] Mandela's colleagues in Lusaka were soon informed of this apparently promising first encounter between the two leaders who were destined to preside over the transition.

In a detailed account of the meeting with De Klerk, addressed to Tambo, Mandela described him as 'a strong, cautious but flexible man who is prepared to adapt to new ideas and to meet new challenges'. He warned that these were his personal impressions and that the ANC should not be guided by them, but by 'harsh reality'. According to Mandela, De Klerk said that his efforts to normalise the situation were being impeded by the ANC's calls to intensify pressure; this was making his position more difficult and causing consternation among his supporters and giving 'lethal ammunition' to the right wing: 'If events continue on this course, we would soon be knocking at Tuynhuys [the presidential office in Cape Town] to see Dr Treurnicht, except that he would not speak to us.' De Klerk, said Mandela, was careful to say that he was not making these comments in a spirit of confrontation 'but in order to reach understanding with us'.[85]

Mandela and De Klerk were indeed an 'odd couple'. Both were nationalists, but with backgrounds and aims that were as historically divergent as it was possible to imagine. The NP had finally recognised that apartheid was dying and that a new, inclusive system had to be negotiated, but the ideological gulf was wide. Equally wide apart were the proposals on the mechanisms for negotiation itself. Despite the goodwill and cordiality of the meeting, the NP and the ANC remained profoundly suspicious of each other. At least some degree of mutual trust would have to be built up if negotiations were to have any hope of success.

In the four turbulent years after 2 February 1990 the relationship between De Klerk and Mandela would go through rocky passages, sometimes appearing to push the country to the brink of civil war. Somehow it held. Both men recognised that the other was a vital partner. Mandela realised that De Klerk was the only white leader who could take the white population out of the corner into which apartheid had painted them; and De Klerk realised that Mandela's towering authority would be vital to keeping the volatility of the masses within bounds as the process got under way and popular expectations burgeoned.

CHAPTER 10

Getting to the Table

As he had intended, De Klerk's speech on 2 February 1990 caused a sensation. Finally the Rubicon had been crossed; De Klerk had seized the initiative and at least some small part of the moral high ground. Few had anticipated that this reputed conservative, schooled in the tough arena of Afrikaner politics in the Transvaal, would go as far as he did. The man had been misread, even though hints of what was to come had been dropped: apart from the release of Sisulu and other long-term prisoners, De Klerk had allowed protest marches, previously forbidden in terms of the state of emergency, 'since they were essential for the democratization process that we envisaged'. Despite the advice of his security advisors, De Klerk was prudent enough to realise that if marches and demonstrations were banned, their organisers would go ahead anyway and defy the law, inevitably prompting clashes with the police.[1]

It was undoubtedly the most important speech ever delivered in the South African Parliament.[2] Urging political leaders inside and outside Parliament to cease laying down new conditions for participation in negotiations that would delay their inception, De Klerk proceeded to drop his bombshell:

- The prohibition of the ANC, PAC, SACP and a number of subsidiary organisations was being rescinded.
- People serving prison sentences for membership of these organisations would be released.
- Emergency restrictions on the media and on 33 organisations, including the UDF, Cosatu and the extreme right-wing Blanke Bevrydingsbeweging (the White Liberation Movement), were to be lifted.
- Detention under the emergency regulations would be limited to six

months, and detainees would have the right to legal representation and a medical practitioner of their own choice.

De Klerk stressed that law and order would be maintained. The unbanning of organisations did not in the least signify approval or condonation of terrorism or crimes of violence committed by their members in the past or which might be perpetrated in the future. He announced his intention to lift the countrywide state of emergency as soon as circumstances permitted. South Africa had been embroiled in conflict, tension and violent struggle for decades: 'It is time for us to break out of the cycle of violence and break through to peace and reconciliation.'

In a parliamentary speech a few days later, De Klerk's Minister for Constitutional Development, Gerrit Viljoen, spelled out the nature of the deadlock:

> ... the South African Government realizes that the continued successes achieved by its security forces cannot free it of its ultimate obligation to seek a political solution. Instead of remaining entangled in a long-drawn-out violent conflict, without the prospect of ultimate victory, it is in the interests of all parties to find a negotiated solution.[3]

The programme De Klerk announced included a new, democratic Constitution; universal franchise; no domination; equality before an independent judiciary; the protection of minorities as well as of individual rights; freedom of religion; a sound economy based on proven economic principles and private enterprise; and dynamic programmes directed at better education, health services, housing and social conditions for all.

The impending release of Nelson Mandela was announced in the concluding section of the speech: he was to be released unconditionally on a date to be determined. Mandela, De Klerk said, could play an important part in achieving the goal of a new democratic order: 'he has declared himself to be willing to make a constructive contribution to the peaceful political process in South Africa'. There was no longer any reasonable excuse for the continuation of violence, he continued. Past allegations that the government refused to talk to activists or that the banning of their organisations had prevented normal activity were no longer valid.

De Klerk had opted for what he called his 'quantum leap' partly because it gave him the initiative and partly because he realised that the previous practice, under PW Botha, of allowing incremental reforms to dribble out without any overall vision of where they were going was not

only ineffective, but also dangerous: it gave the reforms' intended beneficiaries the impression that government was responding to their pressures,
which, in turn, sharpened their demands, exactly as De Tocqueville had
observed. As De Klerk said in 1997: 'If one has to cut off the tail of a dog,
it is much better to do so with one clean and decisive stroke.'[4]

* * *

The far-reaching implications of De Klerk's speech wrong-footed opponents of the NP at both ends of the spectrum. Despite its extensive
preparation of demands for particular procedures and goals for the negotiations, the ANC was unprepared for what had happened. Sparks, reporting on the mood in Lusaka immediately before the speech, found that
'almost every member of the [ANC's] national executive committee had a
different response to what was happening', doves like Thabo Mbeki being
encouraged, and hawks like Chris Hani remaining deeply suspicious and
demanding that the armed struggle be intensified.[5]

The venerable Walter Sisulu, recently released from prison and on a
visit to Lusaka, was shocked by the volume of protest voiced by the rank
and file at an ANC meeting. Hawks were horrified by a statement made
by Secretary-General Alfred Nzo that the ANC lacked the capacity to
intensify the armed struggle to any significant extent. Sisulu, who enjoyed
the respect of all shades of opinion in the ANC, was able to mollify feelings by declaring that the ANC would intensify the armed struggle, while
simultaneously working towards a negotiating situation. He noted how
badly the ANC was missing the skilled diplomacy of Tambo, who was recuperating in Sweden after a severe stroke suffered in August.[6] In another
comment Sisulu observed that it was not easy for the ANC to sit down
and negotiate because many of the youngsters were not really interested
in negotiating: 'That's why I say that this chap De Klerk is moving too fast
and can create problems for us.' The ANC, he continued, had to educate
its people, and for that, time was needed.[7]

The hawks had a point: a premature commitment to negotiate, and the
possibility that the viscerally mistrusted government was leading them
into a trap, held disastrous potential implications for the ANC. For the
government, too, a failed attempt at negotiating a settlement would have
undercut the doves in the NP and the ANC, and given an enormous boost
to the hardliners on both sides. De Klerk's speech had nevertheless presented both sides with a *fait accompli*. The challenge in the pre-negotiat-
ing period would be to build sufficient mutual trust to enable the process
to go forward.

If the ANC and the NP government were the two major players in the conflict, Inkatha's Mangosuthu Buthelezi could also legitimately claim to be one of the premier players, as Mandela described him. Mandela praised Buthelezi for his consistent stand against being drawn into negotiations before all political prisoners had been released. Buthelezi had memorably described PW Botha's proposed National Council as a 'castration chamber' and refused to have anything to do with it. Apart from the release of Mandela and other political prisoners, Inkatha had insisted that before negotiations could begin, amnesty be accorded to exiles and refugees, organisations be unbanned, the state of emergency lifted and press freedom restored. In addition, key apartheid statutes governing group areas, separate amenities and population registration should be repealed. There should also be a statement of intent that the Tricameral Parliament would be replaced by a system acceptable to the majority.

Buthelezi was pleased with De Klerk's speech, saying that his sincerity could no longer be doubted and that he had created a situation from which there could be no going back.[8] Despite an amicable telephone conversation between Mandela and Buthelezi shortly after his release, the hostility between Inkatha and the ANC/UDF would intensify during 1990 and beyond. Determined not to be marginalised by the 'big two', Buthelezi dug his heels in and would prove to be an awkward negotiating partner, regularly engaging in perilous brinkmanship.

On the white side of the political divide, reactions were predictable: the CP, the official opposition in the House of Assembly, was reduced to spluttering rage, bewilderment and, most significantly, utter confusion about its options now that the political arena was about to change so fundamentally. Its electoral progress since 1982 had convinced it that victory was ultimately attainable through the ballot box. By-elections in a string of constituencies between June 1990 and February 1992 showed a substantial swing to the CP, enabling Treurnicht to claim that if the results were extrapolated to the national level it would mean that the CP enjoyed majority support among whites. True or not, it was an alarming possibility that would force De Klerk to test it in March 1992. Nevertheless, in committing itself to parliamentary methods of opposition, the CP distinguished itself from some wilder elements of the far right who spoke bellicosely of 'fighting to the last drop of blood' to defend Afrikanerdom.

For the DP, which had won 33 seats with over 20 per cent of the vote in the election of September 1989, De Klerk's speech was a vindication of policies that it and its predecessors had long propounded. Some 12 per cent of former NP voters had supported it. There were concerns in the NP about the inroads that the DP was making, but also interest in what Willem de Klerk termed its policy's 'considerable marketing value'. The NP had now stolen its clothes, but it had nevertheless helped to prepare a way for De Klerk's 'quantum leap'.[9] Parliamentary politics had been widely dismissed as 'irrelevant' and as 'legitimating the system' by many of the UDF/MDM camp; but, even if the DP's policies fell short of what the ANC was demanding, its sustained critique of apartheid over three decades had had an impact on a growing number of NP supporters. Despite the restrictions on the flow of information and pervasive censorship, South Africa remained a sufficiently open society for opposition parties and newspapers to express sharp criticism, and, as Willem de Klerk acknowledged, this had been effective.

De Klerk was pleased by the reaction to his speech, and the support he had received from his caucus, the DP and the Coloured and Indian Houses of the Tricameral Parliament. International reaction was also favourable, encouraging him to hope that sanctions would be lifted, notwithstanding the demands of the ANC and its internal allies that they be retained. 'We had achieved our objective of convincing our friends and foes alike that the National Party had made a paradigm shift.'[10] De Klerk deliberately pushed back the date of Mandela's release so that his thunder would not be stolen. Eventually, he and Mandela agreed on 11 February, after Mandela had initially demurred, wanting an additional week to enable the ANC to ready itself for what would clearly be a tumultuous occasion.

Tumultuous it was. Mandela wrote: 'As I finally walked through those [prison] gates ... I felt – even at the age of seventy-one – that my life was beginning anew.'[11] Forty-five minutes later his motorcade reached Cape Town, where an enormous, restive crowd awaited his (late) arrival on the Grand Parade, in front of the city hall from whose balcony he would speak, watched by millions of television viewers in South Africa and around the world.

It was a tough, uncompromising speech, written, it is said, by tough, uncompromising ANC/UDF supporters, who imposed the collective stamp of the ANC on it.[12] Having thanked his colleagues in the struggle, Mandela went on to insist that the circumstances which had necessitated the armed struggle still existed: 'We have no option but to continue.' Covering himself against rumours that he had been negotiating behind the ANC's back, Mandela denied this, saying that he had done no more than to insist that the government and the ANC meet. Moreover, he continued, there were demands in the Harare Declaration that had to be met before negotiations could begin. The core of the speech was a demand that the struggle be intensified:

Our struggle has reached a decisive moment. We call on our people to seize this moment so that the process towards democracy is rapid and uninterrupted. We have waited too long for our freedom. Now is the time to intensify the struggle on all fronts. To relax our efforts now would be a mistake which generations to come will not be able to forgive. The sight of freedom looming on the horizon should encourage us to redouble our efforts. It is only through disciplined mass action that our victory can be assured.

The toughness of Mandela's speech, softened by a reference to De Klerk as a man of integrity, was geared to his immediate audience, many of whom were ANC/UDF sympathisers, and the wider ANC domestic constituency and exiles, many of whom continued to doubt the wisdom of parleying with the NP government. His views on future economic restructuring were also calculated to resonate with the views of radical socialists. In a letter written shortly before his release and publicised in the press, Mandela had said that nationalisation of the mines, banks and monopoly industry was the policy of the ANC (as implied in the Freedom Charter) and 'a change or modification of our views in this regard is inconceivable'.[13] He expressed substantially the same views in the speech and in a subsequent press conference.

It was at the press conference, held at Bishopscourt, Archbishop Desmond Tutu's episcopal home, that Mandela displayed a more conciliatory tone, thanking the (predominantly white) press for having ensured that his name remained in the public eye, and reassuring whites that they had a critical role to play in any new dispensation. 'We did not want to destroy the country before we freed it, and to drive whites away would devastate the nation … . there was a middle ground between white fears and black hopes, and we in the ANC would find it.'[14]

De Klerk was disappointed by Mandela's speech, as were many whites, especially businesspeople, who shuddered at his endorsement of nationalisation. If he had not known it already, De Klerk now fully realised that the road ahead would be rough. If he and Mandela had generated mutual respect at their meetings, this fell short of warmth or even the promise of the 'personal chemistry' that facilitates difficult negotiations. Both were politicians, leaders of the major rival organisations – and politicians, by definition, seek to obtain the best possible deal for their constituencies with the bargaining resources available to them. Statesmen go beyond satisfying their constituencies, and seek to act in a broader interest that encompasses the entire polity. De Klerk and Mandela met this criterion: they were bound together in 'antagonistic co-operation'[15] which obliged them to recognise that neither could ride roughshod over the other. De Klerk possessed the full panoply of the power of incumbency plus significant support in the white community; Mandela enjoyed massive legitimacy among the black population.

The time for 'talks about talks about talks' had now passed, and the pre-negotiation phase proper was about to be entered. The obstacles to negotiation had to be cleared away, which would involve formal meetings between government and ANC representatives.

The first such meeting took place at Groote Schuur, the historic Cape Town residence of the head of state, between 2 and 4 May 1990, but not before the first of many spats between De Klerk and Mandela. This arose out of the killing by the police of eight demonstrators in the troubled township of Sebokeng on 26 March. The police claimed that the 50 000-strong demonstration had been illegal and that they had been forced to defend themselves when fired upon; Mandela, on the other hand, contended that the demonstrators were unarmed and that most had been shot in the back while fleeing: 'This sort of action angered me like no other, and I told the press that every white policeman ... regarded every black person as a military target.' He announced the suspension of the talks, scheduled for 11 April, and warned De Klerk that he could not 'talk about negotiations on the one hand and murder our people on the other'.[16] It was widely believed, however, that Mandela's decision, which had been backed by the ANC's NEC, had actually arisen from fears in the ANC of losing radical support by appearing too conciliatory to the government, thereby creating a sense that the ANC had been stampeded into negotiations. For his part, De Klerk expressed amazement that the ANC should suspend the proposed meeting, which was intended precisely to replace violence with peaceful negotiation.[17]

Subsequent spats revolved around the same issue, and threatened on some occasions to derail the negotiations. Both men faced severe problems – Mandela with the insurrectionist strand in the ANC's support-base; De Klerk with a police force that was ill-prepared to cope with large-scale demonstrations, and a legion of practitioners of 'dirty tricks' who would do their best to sabotage the negotiating process. Variations on a similar theme of controlling violence – coming from both sides – have characterised other apparently intractable conflicts such as those in Northern Ireland and Israel/Palestine.

The initiatives of early 1990 gave an added fillip to violence, especially in Natal. The realisation that an inclusive, democratic election lay somewhere down the road sharpened the edge of political conflict. During 1990, 3 699 deaths in political violence were recorded, an increase of 163 per cent over the toll in 1989. Of these deaths, 1 811 occurred in Natal alone. Other fatalities caused by rivalry between the ANC and Inkatha occurred on the Witwatersrand. The violence seemed unstoppable.

Notwithstanding this inauspicious background, the meeting at Groote Schuur took place in a cordial atmosphere, despite the government's initial jibbing at the inclusion of the much-demonised Joe Slovo in the ANC delegation. The objection got nowhere after Mandela put his foot down, and Slovo duly took up his seat around the table. The skill, logic and pragmatism of many of the ANC delegates took their government counterparts by surprise. Thabo Mbeki observed that 'within a matter of minutes, everyone understood there was no one in the room who had horns'.[18]

The Groote Schuur meeting was not intended to produce agreements on constitutional issues or on constitution-making procedures. The intention was to clear away obstacles to a peaceful process of negotiations. The Minute agreed to by both parties committed them to seeking a resolution of the existing climate of violence and intimidation from whatever quarter. There was agreement to define political offences, to advise on norms and mechanisms for dealing with the release of political prisoners and the granting of immunity for political offences committed inside and outside South Africa. The government undertook to review security legislation in the light of the need to ensure normal and free political activities, and committed itself to lifting the state of emergency. Finally, channels of communication between the ANC and the government would be established in order to curb violence and intimidation.[19] The wording of the Minute concealed difficult issues that would take time to resolve: how did one define a 'political offence', and under what circumstances should such offenders be granted amnesty?

Both De Klerk and Mandela were pleased with the successful outcome of the deliberations. The ANC had not formally agreed to suspend the armed struggle, but its commitment to a peaceful process of negotiation was hardly consistent with continued guerrilla activity. In any case, MK actions had dwindled to insignificance in 1989–90. According to Shubin, there were only between 600 and 700 MK soldiers inside the country, and another 2 000 outside, although 200 to 300 young people left every week to join up.[20] De Klerk's sense was that the ANC could, at that stage, make no further concessions because it did not want its more radical supporters to suppose that it was conceding too much, too soon.[21] This was probably correct.

The goodwill generated by the Groote Schuur meeting did not last long. Early in July 1990, police investigations in the Durban area uncovered Operation Vula and jumped to the conclusion that it was a plot hatched by the SACP to overthrow the government even while negotiations were under way.[22] Prima facie this was a plausible interpretation of the documentation seized. De Klerk was dismayed: 'For a moment the whole negotiation process was in jeopardy. The securocrats felt that their worst suspicions regarding the real intentions of the ANC/SACP alliance had been proved.' When Mandela was confronted by De Klerk, he seemed 'genuinely surprised'.[23] Mandela himself writes: 'I was taken aback because I knew nothing about it.'[24] In Waldmeir's account, Mandela was furious, not at De Klerk, but at his own people.[25] Joe Slovo assured Mandela that Vula was a 'moribund operation', and claimed that De Klerk was trying to drive a wedge between the SACP and the ANC.

The belief that Vula was an exclusively SACP operation turned out to be untrue, although several, perhaps most, of its key personnel were SACP members. The plan had been conceived under Tambo's close supervision in 1987. It was intended to circumvent the difficulty of maintaining links between domestically based insurgents and the operational command outside the country.

Ronnie Kasrils, a key figure in the project and a leading figure in MK, welcomed the plan, saying that for years they had been trying to establish strong underground structures to confront a formidable enemy:

> We had often debated that what we lacked was a senior leadership inside the country, capable of taking decisions on the spot and linking up with the emergent mass movement. Although the possibility of negotiating with the Pretoria government was arising, expectations of progress were generally uncertain and the ANC remained banned. With popular protest soaring, most in our ranks argued that underground leadership was more necessary than ever.[26]

The project was kept secret: not even the ANC's security department was aware of it. Tambo selected the key operatives who were infiltrated into South Africa.[27] The operatives, led by Mac Maharaj and Siphiwe Nyanda, built up underground structures and a highly sophisticated communications system that was used by Mandela to communicate with Lusaka during his final spell in prison. According to police sources, substantial quantities of arms and ammunition, together with computer orders for further advanced weaponry, were discovered at two 'safe houses'.

The same sources linked Operation Vula to discussion at an SACP consultative conference held at Tongaat, Natal, on 7 May 1990, the minutes of which appeared to suggest that the inception of negotiations created legal space for the possibility of an uprising:

> We need to bear in mind that there is a tremendous uncertainty
> about a smooth and simple negotiated solution .... we must build
> our revolutionary forces side by side with the negotiation process.
> These revolutionary forces cannot simply be legal ones. Neither can
> they simply be forces that apply pressure on the government so as to
> force it to make the necessary concessions demanded of (by?) our
> negotiating team. But a great deal of work is going to have to be
> planned and organized in a clandestine way. This brings us to our
> strategic perspective. Where is the limit to the pressure of the masses
> which must be exerted against the existing power block? The only
> logical answer is a nationwide uprising.[28]

While neither the veracity nor the context of this document can be independently established, it seems a plausible account of the emerging ANC
strategy that negotiations were a 'site of struggle'; what could not be
achieved at the negotiating table could be won by mass action. Moreover,
the underground structures put in place would serve as a fall-back position if negotiations failed. As Kasrils put it, 'We cannot be too sure of the
real intentions of FW [de Klerk]. We've got to put in place an insurance
policy.'[29] The original idea behind Operation Vula had been changed in
the new circumstances.

Of the operatives arrested, Maharaj, Nyanda and six others were
charged with attempting to overthrow the state by force. Two of those arrested were killed in detention. In March 1991 all charges were dropped,
and the operatives who had been in hiding were indemnified against prosecution. Mandela later welcomed all associated with Operation Vula
back to the 'overt legal structures of the ANC', declaring that they had
been acting on the instructions of the ANC, and denying that it had been
an SACP plot to seize power by violent means. Moreover, he did not deem
the project to have been inconsistent with the ANC's participation in the
negotiating process.

De Klerk, although disturbed by what he regarded as a breach of the
fragile (if it existed at all) trust that was being established, had little option but to acquiesce in these developments. Operation Vula, after all,
had been conceived well before 1990, and even if unanswered questions
remained about the insurrectionist tone of the SACP document quoted
above, it made more sense not to allow the process to falter.

However much the ANC tried to explain it away, the uncovering of
Operation Vula sent shockwaves through an already apprehensive white
community, and provided the CP with an unexpected propaganda bonanza. It would have been difficult, if not impossible, for De Klerk to

proceed with negotiations unless the ANC agreed to a suspension of the armed struggle. Slovo, who had been wrongly identified as one of those implicated in Operation Vula, seemed to have grasped this point.

The public at large appeared favourable to the idea of a negotiated settlement. Even before De Klerk's speech, a survey conducted for the South African Institute of International Affairs in January 1990 found that 52.3 per cent of whites favoured negotiations with the ANC, compared with the 36.2 per cent affirmative responses to the same question in 1988. But, worryingly for De Klerk, 61.5 per cent of Afrikaners opposed the idea in 1990, though this was down from 78.5 per cent recorded in 1988. He was walking a political tightrope. More encouraging was the response to a poll conducted in July 1990 for the Institute for Black Research: in response to the question 'Do you support the current talks between the ANC and the National Party?', 74.5 per cent of the 3 725-strong sample responded affirmatively, including 75.9 per cent of Africans, 78.4 per cent of whites, 75.2 per cent of Coloureds and 72.2 per cent of Indians.[30]

Despite the support from the public at large, Mandela, too, was going out on a limb, as far as many ANC activists were concerned. He recalls that Slovo approached him privately before an ANC NEC meeting in July 1990, suggesting that the ANC voluntarily suspend the armed struggle to assist in creating a more favourable climate for negotiations and also to give De Klerk something to show his supporters that his initiative was bringing benefits. At first Mandela rejected the idea, believing that the time was not yet ripe. On further reflection, however, he changed his mind, concluding that if the process were to go forward the ANC had to take the initiative. Slovo, moreover, had impeccable credentials as a militant and was therefore the ideal person to make the proposal to the NEC since he could hardly be accused of capitulating.

Slovo's proposal, firmly supported by Mandela, eventually prevailed at the NEC, but only after several hours of tough debate, during which opponents of the idea claimed that 'we were giving De Klerk's supporters a reward, but not our own people'. Mandela countered this argument by insisting that the purpose of the armed struggle was always to bring the government to the negotiating table and that its suspension could always be revoked.[31] Not all of the insurrectionists would necessarily have accepted Mandela's view of the purpose of armed struggle.

Immediately before the next meeting with the government in Pretoria on 6 August, the ANC announced its unilateral suspension of the armed struggle. It was a clever strategic move, acknowledged as such by De Klerk, because it gave the ANC the moral high ground and made it appear that the decision had been reached of their own volition and not at the government's insistence. Slovo acknowledged afterwards that 98 per cent of ANC supporters 'thought the decision was a sellout'.[32] But, Slovo insisted, the purpose was to break the logjam, adding that at the start of the meeting, Mandela had emphasised that 'time was not on our side, that the longer the process was stretched out, the more time would be given to those who would like to sabotage the process'. The militants were not convinced. To reassure its supporters, the ANC was forced to take out newspaper advertisements declaring that the armed struggle had not been abandoned, and MK had not been dissolved: 'we have not forfeited our right to self-defence ... continued suspension is conditional on the behaviour of the South African police and defence force'.[33]

There was another dimension to the militants' unhappiness: the circumstances of exile combined with the strong 'democratic centralist' influence of SACP members had created a 'top-down' style of leadership, notwithstanding Tambo's diplomatic skills. Moreover, (well-founded) paranoia about government spies in the organisation had further weakened the tolerance of differing internal views or criticism of the leadership that might create openings for attempts to provoke disunity. These factors made for a clash with the style developed by the UDF and Cosatu, for both of which 'top-down' leadership was anathema. In May 1990 Cosatu joined the ANC and SACP to form the 'Triple Alliance'. At the same time, the UDF was being severely haemorrhaged by the co-optation of many of its leading figures by the ANC, which badly needed their organisational skills and knowledge of local communities; it was dissolved in 1991.

It was not long before Cosatu was expressing criticism of its new-found partners: the alliance was ineffective; inadequate consultation had preceded the suspension of the armed struggle; and there were complaints about Mandela's 'imperial' leadership style. 'The style of many exiles is top-down, commandist – very different from the Mass Democratic Movement.'[34] There was also resentment of Cosatu's being treated as a junior partner. These and related issues would rumble on for the next decade and beyond. The ANC had traditionally been a 'broad church', as Mandela described it. The incorporation of many UDF supporters and the alliance with Cosatu would make it even broader.

The Pretoria Minute, signed by the ANC and the government on 6 August 1990, was a major step in the negotiation process.[35] Apart from the ANC's undertaking to suspend all 'armed actions and related activities' with immediate effect, and a commitment by both sides 'to do everything in their power to bring about a peaceful solution as quickly as possible', agreement was reached on the phased release of political prisoners and the granting of indemnity from prosecution to returning exiles. Concern was expressed about the general level of political violence and intimidation, especially in Natal. Both parties agreed to undertake steps 'to promote and expedite the normalization of the situation in line with the spirit of mutual trust obtaining among the leaders involved'. De Klerk had previously lifted the country-wide state of emergency, except in Natal, but he now undertook to consider lifting it in Natal as well 'in the light of the positive consequences that should result from this accord'. He also committed his government to an ongoing review of security legislation 'to ensure free political activity'. Finally, the Minute acknowledged that the ANC and the government were not the only parties involved in the process of shaping the new South Africa, and urged others to commit themselves to peaceful negotiations. The way was now open to proceed towards negotiations on a new Constitution, concluded the Minute hopefully.

The optimistic spirit of the Minute was, unfortunately, submerged by the opened floodgates of violence: 'mutual trust' was to be strained to breaking point; and the 'positive consequences' that should have flowed from the accord were hard to discern. As noted, 1990 was the most violent year in modern South African history, approximately 50 per cent of fatalities occurring in Natal, and 40 per cent in the Transvaal. Mutual recriminations, especially between the ANC and Inkatha, made it difficult, if not impossible, to determine which organisation was mainly responsible. In the light of hindsight it was an error not to have included the Inkatha Freedom Party (IFP), as it now called itself, in the Groote Schuur and Pretoria meetings. Buthelezi, after all, was one of the 'premier players', as Mandela had described him, and the IFP, like the ANC, was deeply implicated in the violence. Mandela's personal relationship with Buthelezi was close and respectful, sentiments that Buthelezi reciprocated. Moreover, although Buthelezi had not taken umbrage at not being invited to the Groote Schuur and Pretoria meetings, his *amour propre*, always fragile, might have been fortified by his being fully recognised as a premier player from the inception of the negotiating process.

Hindsight, however, also suggests that, despite Mandela's inclination, most of the ANC leadership would have rejected any thought of Buthelezi's inclusion in the meetings. This surmise is based upon the thwarting by the ANC in Natal of Mandela's early efforts to meet Buthelezi, whom he had thanked for his long-standing support shortly after his release. Mandela's wish to meet Buthelezi to try to resolve their differences was vetoed by the ANC in Lusaka. Equally unsuccessful was his effort to arrange for Sisulu to accept an invitation to visit the Zulu king. The carnage in Natal horrified Mandela: he told a rally in Durban, attended by 100 000 people, two weeks after his release, to

Take your guns, your knives and your pangas [machetes], and throw
them into the sea! Close down the death factories. End this war
now![36]

Mandela acknowledged that while there were 'fundamental differences'
between Inkatha and the ANC, Inkatha was to be commended for its
demands over the years for the unbanning of the ANC and the release of
political prisoners, as well as their refusal to participate in negotiations
before the creation of the necessary climate: 'We recognize that in order
to bring the war to an end, the two sides must talk.' He hoped that one
day it might be possible to share a platform with Buthelezi. It would be
nearly a year before the two leaders actually met.

Mandela's heartfelt call for the violence to cease was disregarded. The
carnage continued unabated: in the three months up to the end of March
1990 nearly 700 deaths had occurred in Natal. It is not possible to answer
the counterfactual question whether the violence would have abated had
Mandela and Buthelezi embarked upon a joint peace mission urging
violence-wracked communities to end the war; but it was at least worth
trying. Any thought of such a joint initiative would have been rejected by
the Natal regions of the ANC, which contained its own quota of warlords,
determined not to allow Buthelezi the chance of enhancing his credibility
by joint appearances with Mandela.

A third preparatory meeting between the government and the ANC
took place in Cape Town on 12 February 1991 and resulted in the DF
Malan Accord. Coming soon after a tense meeting between De Klerk
and Mandela, the Accord was hailed as a breakthrough: following on the
ANC's earlier suspension of all armed actions, the Accord confirmed that
the ANC, 'with specific reference also to Umkhonto we Sizwe and its or-
ganized military group and armed cadres' would refrain from the following actions:

(i)   Attacks by means of armaments, firearms, explosive or incendi-
      ary devices.
(ii) Infiltration of men and material.
(iii) Creation of underground structures.
(iv) Statements inciting violence.
(v)   Threats of armed action.
(vi) Training inside South Africa.

The Accord 'accepted the principle that in a democratic society no political party or movement should have a private army'. Nevertheless, it was
noted that although MK was no longer an unlawful organisation, it was

vital that control over cadres and arms within the country should be exercised to ensure that no armed actions or related activities occurred.[37]

De Klerk and Mandela announced acceptance of the Accord in a joint statement, but expectations that this would lead to a cessation or a reduction of violence were to be dashed. It was a chimerical hope that the practitioners of violence, many of whom were out of control, would heed what the leaderships of the ANC and the government were ordering. Alleged violations of the Accord would lead to a blazing public row between Mandela and De Klerk.

Violence would continue for the duration of the negotiating process, causing it to lurch from crisis to crisis, though not derailing it. A new and sinister factor entered the picture: the involvement of elements in the security forces in encouraging and assisting attacks on the ANC, or turning a blind eye to such attacks by IFP supporters. More than anything else, this so-called 'third force' activity threatened the process and inflicted serious political damage on De Klerk. One simple fact saved the transition: De Klerk and Mandela both knew that they needed each other.

The unbanning of the ANC and other organisations had immediately created an exuberant sense that liberation really was now at hand, but it also sharpened the cutting edge of political conflict among rivals, not only between the ANC and the IFP, but also between the ANC and the much smaller Azapo. Having suspended the armed struggle and failed to persuade the international community to intensify sanctions and to continue to isolate the government, the ANC's major remaining weapon was mass action, which included protest marches and gatherings. According to police figures, during 1990 and the first seven months of 1991, 10 889 gatherings were held, of which 1 360 were authorised, 851 took place without authorisation, although the gatherings were planned in advance, 8 608 were classified as 'spontaneous', and in 70 cases permission was sought but denied. Remarkably, only in three of the 9 529 cases of technically illegal gatherings or demonstrations did controversy arise because of riot police action.[38] During late 1989 De Klerk had authorised demonstrations and marches as part of a process of 'normalising' political activity, but, as the number of technically illegal and spontaneous gatherings showed, it was beyond the capacity of the state to regulate or control them – which in many cases, no doubt, was precisely what the organisers sought to demonstrate. Promoting 'ungovernability' could not be turned off like a tap.

Much of the mass action occurred spontaneously or was organised by 'civics' independently of the ANC, and in many cases it targeted local issues such as rents, consumer boycotts, school issues and locally enforced discrimination. In response to an interviewer, Raymond Suttner, head of the ANC's department of political education and an SACP member, explained the rationale for mass action:

> The general goal of mass action is to emphasise the mass national character of the movement for democracy. It seeks to emphasise and draws strength from the isolation and narrowness of support of the De Klerk government. It is a broad strategy with symbolic significance. It demonstrates the disparities in actual support. It is also a means of bringing pressure on the government; and forcing them to concede things which reason and logic alone cannot dictate … . This is the most basic form of action employed throughout the country. We need it to strengthen our hand at the negotiating table, to increase our battalions.[39]

Another reason was that participation in mass action was cathartic. In a number of violence-wracked townships the militant youth were demanding guns. Impatience, frustration and an urge to lash out at the state or political opponents combined to form a highly combustible mix which a single incident could ignite.

It was not only blacks who engaged in mass action: the ultra-right, albeit with smaller battalions, also sought to torpedo the transition with its own forms of aggressive action. In 1990, 52 acts of rightwing violence were committed for which 91 persons were arrested. Of these attacks the most serious occurred near Durban in October when three members of the AWB opened fire on a bus, killing seven blacks and wounding 18. It was a retaliatory action for an earlier attack on whites by militant young blacks. The three rightwingers were convicted and sentenced to death (but, in view of the suspension of the death penalty, none was executed). In another case, court proceedings in November revealed that members of a small group called *Die Orde van die Dood* (The Death Order) admitted to plans for the assassination of seven Cabinet ministers. Between the beginning of 1991 and the end of 1993 some 40 shooting episodes (which may be an underestimate) occurred, several of which involved fatalities. Apart from the AWB and the CP, most of the ultra-rightwing groups were tiny, as well as evanescent – but, for all that, dangerous.[40] The country trembled on the brink of even worse violence after two extremists assassinated Chris Hani on 10 April 1993.

Notwithstanding the severe criticism to which the police were subjected and the support for the ultra-right in their ranks, the police were efficient in infiltrating rightwing groups, tracking down offenders and having them successfully prosecuted. Police sources claimed an 85 per cent success rate in arresting rightwing terrorists.[41] The most notable case was the episode on 9 August 1991 at Ventersdorp, a village in the Western Transvaal that was a stronghold of the ultra-right. Some 2 000 AWB members tried to prevent De Klerk from speaking at a public meeting, but were thwarted by the deployment of 2 000 police. In the fracas that ensued three AWB members were killed and 48 (including six policemen) were injured. Numerous Africans were assaulted and several were rescued by the police. For the ultra-right the battle of Ventersdorp was traumatic: it was, said one of its leading lights, the beginning of the Boers' Third War of Liberation. De Klerk was not going to submit to the humiliation of having a meeting cancelled or disrupted: having to back down in the face of the AWB's threats 'would have been tantamount to admitting that free and fair elections would be impossible'.[42]

The episode had also been a test of the police's institutional loyalty. It was the first occasion since 1922, the year of the great Witwatersrand strike, that white protesters had been killed by the security forces. Many AWB members no doubt hoped, even expected, that segments of the force deployed at Ventersdorp would break ranks and come over to their side, but nothing of the kind happened. It was true, however, that elements of both the police and army had other ways of seeking to derail the negotiations – or, at least, of weakening the ANC. De Klerk was repeatedly blamed by the ANC for these activities, with Mandela on occasion accusing him of deliberately fomenting them, or at least of not doing enough to curb them. The truth was more complex than this conspiracy theory, even if conspiracies lay at the heart of the 'dirty tricks' that occurred. De Klerk angrily rejected Mandela's accusations of his complicity, asserting that the ANC itself was deeply involved in the violence in Natal and elsewhere in the country. Responding to Mandela's repeated accusations of police connivance at or indifference to violence, De Klerk would ask him to provide evidence and names of witnesses so that investigations could be made:

> We, from our side, regarded many of Mandela's representations as the height of hypocrisy – given the ANC's own deep involvement in violence in Natal and throughout the country – as well as its apparent unwillingness to rein in members and supporters who were clearly involved in violence. If Mandela was so concerned about violence why would he not agree to meet with Chief Minister Buthelezi to try to resolve the issue?[43]

De Klerk had a point, but then so did Mandela, as subsequent revelations would show. The wider issue was that De Klerk could not control renegades in the security forces, and neither Mandela nor Buthelezi could fully control their followers.

In an analysis of the violence, prepared as a confidential document for the National Consultative Conference in December 1990, the ANC attributed primary responsibility to perpetrators who belonged to an organisation that was not independent of the state:

> ... they are an arm of the establishment, with the backing or at least tacit support of forces from the highest government echelons, and they are commanded by circles well-established within the state machinery. The controllers and, in many cases, the immediate commanders are white. This applies also to those units which come from the KwaZulu bantustan structures. The open, direct role of the SAP and SADF has been documented … . The actions of these units is not an aberration, but reflects the confidence of forces acting within the ambit of state policy with the support of command structures going all the way up.

The strategy, according to the document, reflected a more aggressive stance by the NP government against the liberation movement, with the intention of inducing fear, despondency and destabilisation in black communities; heightening frustration among people and causing them to wonder whether the pre-February situation was not better; discrediting the ANC; creating a pretext for repressive measures; and switching violence on and off at given moments, thereby creating the impression that the state was indispensable for achieving peace. Some of the forces sought to derail the entire negotiating process. The broader quest was to weaken the ANC and prepare the way 'for the kind of transition which serves the interests of capital and the privileges of the white minority'. Moreover, the strategy was to ensure that the transition was controlled and managed by the regime.

In response, the document recommended, the ANC must strive even harder to consolidate its mass base 'while at the same time striving for national hegemony, i.e. to be seen more and more as a representative of the interests of "the nation"/society as a whole'. In addition to its traditional mission of building the unity of the African people and anti-apartheid forces in general, the ANC should engage bantustan leaders, chiefs and the independent churches. Regarding Inkatha, it would be a 'costly error' for the liberation movement to seek to isolate or exclude it: 'maximum space' should be given to those in Inkatha who genuinely wanted peace. The ANC should engage Inkatha at various levels, encourage local peace initiatives, and arrange for a meeting between ANC and Inkatha delegations, led by Mandela and Buthelezi.[44]

A key sentence in this document concerned the ANC's striving for 'national hegemony' in an attempt increasingly to represent society as a whole. It was a typical attitude among African nationalist movements elsewhere. According to Marina Ottaway, the 'fiction' of dominant liberation movements was that 'they embodied the aspirations of the entire population'.[45] Although the ANC rejected the idea of a one-party state – the exiles had seen enough of its baneful consequences in Zambia, Tanzania and elsewhere – its commitment from the very beginning in 1912 had been to unify the African people. Moreover, it was mindful of the potentially disruptive consequences of ethnic conflict, as well as the devastation caused by civil wars in Angola and Mozambique. The danger was that the putative 'general will' could be ruptured by competing 'partial' wills, to use Rousseau's terms.

Buthelezi, despite his being no mean practitioner of a de facto one-party system in KwaZulu, doubted the ANC's commitment to multiparty democracy, and feared its intention of imposing its own hegemonic rule, as well as destroying his power-base in KwaZulu, as part of a wider project to dismantle the bantustans. He had long insisted that KwaZulu was no mere creation of the apartheid state: on the contrary, it was the historic heartland of the Zulu nation, even if colonial conquest had greatly reduced its size. Buthelezi, stung by the ANC's refusal to acknowledge his role in ending apartheid, was increasingly being forced to fall back on his KwaZulu and Natal redoubt, as well as to thump a Zulu ethnic drum. Apart from Mandela, Jacob Zuma, the only Zulu in the ANC's national leadership, was critical of the strategy of isolating Buthelezi, saying: 'It was important for Buthelezi to feel welcomed, embraced, and part of the process.' Had this happened and Buthelezi had succumbed to the Mandela charm (which would have been a distinct possibility), 'you could have had absolutely the end of the problem'.[46] But being treated as a pariah only hardened Buthelezi's resolve:

> I ... will not be the one who lays himself down before the ANC's war machine to be mangled and trampled upon in the ANC's march forward to supremacy over all.[47]

Mandela and Buthelezi and their respective delegations eventually did meet in Durban on 29 January 1991 with the aim of ending the violence, which according to the joint statement had claimed over 8 000 lives and caused millions of rands of damage. Both parties committed themselves to taking steps to prevent violence and destruction and to uphold political tolerance and freedom of political activity. Forced recruitment, mutual vilification and intimidation were to be ended, and joint tours of all affected areas by Mandela and Buthelezi were to commence. The accord called also for the security forces to act without political bias.[48] Sadly, the agreement had little effect.

The ink on the accord was barely dry when further serious violence occurred, and continued for the next few years, making the well-intentioned commitment to peace look hollow. The figures for deaths in political violence in KwaZulu/Natal were:

1991	1 684
1992	1 427
1993	1 489
1994	1 464.

To these must be added the death toll in political violence involving IFP supporters and (mostly) ANC supporters countrywide. The total figures, including those in KwaZulu/Natal and other homelands, for the whole country were:[49]

1991	2 706
1992	3 347
1993	3 794
1994	2 434.

The hopes expressed in the accord that the commitments made by the ANC and IFP leaderships would percolate down to the grassroots proved to be idle ones. The conflict had become localised to a considerable extent and, moreover, it had acquired a self-perpetuating momentum that made it resistant to the blandishments of leaders. Warlords (on both sides), who often extracted protection money from the communities under their control, gun-runners, *sangomas* (so-called witchdoctors who sold protective medicines) and criminals who preyed on defenceless people, had all developed a stake in perpetuating the conflict.

Apart from its apparent inability to dent the IFP's support in Natal, and the hammering both it and the IFP were inflicting on each other, the ANC's Southern Natal region was experiencing other problems. At a regional conference in late 1990, a group of former Robben Island prisoners presented a document containing their analysis of the weaknesses of the region: an absence of African leadership, especially local,

402   THE RISE AND FALL OF APARTHEID

which gave 'enemies', specifically Buthelezi, the opportunity to attack the ANC leadership, depicting it as non-African, non-Zulu, Indian-controlled, and Xhosa-led.[50] The comment about the absence of *local* African leadership was almost certainly a reference to the regional leader, Patrick Mosiuoa Lekota, a Sotho who had emerged from the BC movement through the UDF to a fairly senior position in the ANC. It was not long after his deployment to Natal in 1990 that the position of regional leader came up for formal election and Lekota was voted out in favour of Jacob Zuma. It was – and still is – taboo to talk about so-called 'tribalism' in the ANC, but it is probable that Lekota's ousting was an expression of ethnic preference as well as a move to deflect IFP criticism of having a non-Zulu leader.[51]

In a speech to the ANC's Consultative Conference, held in December 1990, Mandela listed 'at least four clearly identified groups of comrades who bring different strands of experience' to efforts to re-establish the ANC as a legal political organisation. These were: the soldiers of MK; former political prisoners; the exiles; and those who participated in the internal struggle who were 'probably the most attuned to the popular mood'. These four strands, Mandela continued, had the potential of enriching the ANC 'provided we recognize the value of each and work towards weaving them into a robust cord so that they are mutually reinforcing'.[52]

There was tough talking at the Conference. Tambo, who had recently returned after 30 years in exile and was very frail, created a storm by mildly suggesting that the ANC should re-evaluate the advisability of urging the international community to retain sanctions. Much of the West wanted to reward De Klerk for his initiative and to encourage him to do more, so that sanctions were being scaled down in any case. The danger, Tambo warned, was that South Africa faced 'international marginalisation', and the possibility that the ANC would inherit a seriously ravaged economy. Although the speech had been approved by the ANC's NEC, Tambo's comments on sanctions were rejected by the militants, whose views carried the day.[53]

Mandela's own speech was an uncompromising attack on the government in general and De Klerk in particular for dragging their feet in clearing away obstacles to negotiation, notably concerning the return of exiles, the release of political prisoners and the removal of the final vestiges of discriminatory legislation. His most serious accusation, however, was that 'elements' in the government were orchestrating a campaign of counter-revolutionary violence aimed at weakening the ANC and discrediting the concept of 'disciplined mass action'. The government, he alleged, was interpreting the ANC's suspension of the armed struggle 'so as to cast us in the role of a surrendering belligerent'. Ceasefires, he warned, were by their nature temporary and conditional.[54]

Even this strong language did not shield Mandela and his colleagues in the leadership from outspoken criticism by the militants. An analysis in the *Weekly Mail* detected unease among many delegates about the fruitfulness of negotiating with De Klerk. There were organisational problems in getting the ANC off the ground, tardy recruitment, tensions between the exiles and 'inziles', a lack of strategic direction, and a seeming inability to deal with allegations concerning violence: 'Overall, there is a strong feeling that these problems have allowed the government to seize the initiative and dictate the course of negotiations.' Above all, there was resentment of the 'top-down' style of leadership.[55]

In his closing speech a chastened Mandela acknowledged that mistakes had been made and he welcomed the frank criticism: 'The leadership has grasped the principle that they are the servants of the people and that they must seek guidance from the masses in taking important decisions and in the formulation of policy.' He declined, however, to heed the demand that there should not be confidential discussions between the leadership and members of the government. 'We are not prepared to neglect our duties as the leadership because of views which … are totally unreasonable.'[56]

At this stage, the issue of political prisoners was as important as any other, and predictably it created yet another source of tension between the government and the ANC. In his speech of 2 February 1990, De Klerk promised amnesty to prisoners who had been convicted merely by virtue of their being members of a banned organisations or because they had committed an offence that was classified as such because of a prohibition on one or other of the banned organisations; but those convicted of offences such as murder, terrorism or arson, ostensibly for political reasons, would not be eligible. Not long thereafter, the Indemnity Act was passed, which granted indemnity to persons who in the process of conflict and in the pursuance of a cause may have committed some or other offence. The legislation applied to prisoners, those awaiting trial, and exiles who wished to return.

What constituted a 'political offence' was to be the criterion for deciding who was eligible for amnesty or indemnity. De Klerk was prepared to accept the guidelines suggested by Carl Norgaard, a Danish legal scholar, that had been used in Namibia.[57] While granting that there was no universally agreed-upon definition, Norgaard accepted that there was a considerable degree of international consensus on what types of offence could be classified as 'political', and what factors should be taken into account. Since the question of amnesty was at issue, and reconciliation was a fundamental aim, Norgaard argued that it was inappropriate to adopt a strict or narrow approach. He listed six factors that should be taken into consideration: motivation; circumstances in which the offence was committed; the nature of the political objective; the legal and factual nature of the offence, including its gravity; the target of the offence, for example government personnel or property or private citizens; and the relationship between the offence and the political objective, including the proportionality between the offence and the objective.

De Klerk read the Norgaard principles as excluding from the definition of 'political' offences that had involved the gratuitous murder of civilians or a high degree of premeditated violence: 'I believed that violent crimes, such as cold-blooded murder and assassination, should under no circumstances be allowed to go unpunished, irrespective of who had committed them.'[58] He had in mind persons convicted of 'necklace' murders or attacks that killed innocent civilians, such as Robert McBride, an MK member, whose bomb attack on a Durban bar in 1986 had killed three people and injured 69. There were white rightwingers, too, who had committed equally appalling crimes.

The ANC would have none of this, and demanded the unconditional release of all political prisoners, regardless of the severity of their crimes. This had been one of the core principles of the Harare Declaration, and Mandela recognised that there was growing impatience among his constituency at the slow pace of the process. Mandela had made it clear, after the signing of the Groote Schuur Minute in May, that there would be no negotiations unless political prisoners, including 80 who had been sentenced to death and were awaiting execution, were released immediately, political trials were suspended, and the approximately 20 000 exiles were allowed unconditionally to return. (The death penalty's having been suspended by De Klerk meant that the lives of those awaiting execution were spared.) Ironically he also had to deal with the remarkable refusal of 25 MK prisoners on Robben Island to accept amnesty because 'they would leave only after a victory on the battlefield, not the negotiating table'. Why, one asked: after spending a lifetime fighting the government, 'now I have to ask for a pardon from them?' Eventually they were persuaded to accept amnesty.[59]

There was a wide discrepancy between the number of prisoners deemed eligible for release by the government and the number demanded by the ANC. In terms of the Pretoria Minute, indemnity would be granted as from 1 October 1990: it was hoped that the process would be completed within six months, but no later than 30 April 1991. The phased release began in September 1990 and by the end of February, 270 had been released and a further 760 applications were at an advanced stage of being processed. By the supposed 'envisaged latest date' at the end of April, 933 prisoners had been released. The ANC claimed that there were still some 5 000, but De Klerk insisted that there were fewer than 200. The process dragged on: by mid-July the ANC said that there were over 800 political prisoners, including some 166 in 'independent' Bophuthatswana. Penuell Maduna, a senior member of the ANC's legal affairs department, acknowledged at the end of July that almost all of the clearly identifiable cases of those eligible for release had been identified, but that there were outstanding 'unrest prisoners' it was still examining.[60] The issue had by no means been fully resolved: during 1992 it would flare up again, causing a serious spat between De Klerk and Mandela.

During July 1991 a 'bombshell' (De Klerk's word) hit both the government and Inkatha. Press reports revealed that substantial amounts had been paid from state resources to Inkatha and its (nominally independent) trade union offshoot Uwusa: R250 000 had been given to Inkatha for staging rallies and R1.5 million to Uwusa, over a number of years. Buthelezi claimed to know nothing about the payments, one of his senior lieutenants saying that he had not informed him because he knew that Buthelezi would disapprove. When the bombshell exploded Buthelezi repaid the R250 000 to the state.

More embarrassing revelations occurred when it became known that the SADF had provided training in 1986 for some 200 members of the KwaZulu Police to enable them to protect senior members of the KwaZulu government from ANC attacks. It seemed at the time, according to De Klerk, legitimate to have done so, given the levels of violence in the region and the targeting of Inkatha officials. The KwaZulu Police, however, were justifiably viewed by the UDF and the ANC as little more than Inkatha's private army, and many participated in attacks on perceived opponents, often with the connivance of the security forces.

Buthelezi, on the other hand, was adamant that something had to be done to stop the killing of Inkatha officials, of whom 170 had died by September 1991, together with over 1 000 ordinary members. Temkin writes that arms were being supplied, with the connivance of elements in the security forces, especially to Inkatha supporters who 'unlike the ANC (through Umkhonto we Sizwe), would otherwise have not had access to these'.[61] Whatever mitigating circumstances may have been argued, Inkathagate, as the funding scandal was termed, and the SADF's training of KwaZulu police members, damaged Inkatha by contradicting its claimed independence of action and underlining its dependence on the South African government.

All of this confirmed Mandela's suspicions that De Klerk had a double agenda, talking peace while fomenting violence. The state, he said, bore responsibility for the carnage in Natal and elsewhere when ANC and Inkatha supporters clashed. That there was direct involvement by elements of the security forces, including senior officers, in the violence could hardly be doubted – a fact that was confirmed in evidence given to the Truth and Reconciliation Commission, whose Report says:

> Security Force members who testified before the Commission spoke of the various ways in which the security forces had collaborated with Inkatha in attacks on the UDF. This included warning Inkatha members of impending attacks, disarming ANC supporters, arming Inkatha supporters, transporting Inkatha attackers and standing by while Inkatha supporters attacked people.[62]

De Klerk's response to the Inkathagate revelations was to declare that what had happened was 'totally unacceptable' in the circumstances prevailing after 2 February 1990. He immediately announced a package of measures aimed at preventing any recurrence. They included:
- the prohibition of all secret funding of political parties and organisations;
- a requirement that secret projects had to be conducted within the law;
- the immediate cessation of all special projects run by the security forces outside their legitimate line of operations;
- an advisory committee, headed by Professor Ellison Kahn, a distinguished legal scholar, was appointed to review the necessity of existing secret projects and the adequacy of control mechanisms – subsequently 41 secret projects were terminated.

De Klerk's concerns about the involvement of elements of the security forces in illegal operations had been growing:

> I was angry and frustrated by the tardy and ineffective implementation of my repeated instructions to eliminate all questionable activities. I also began to suspect that some elements in the security forces might be dragging their feet or willfully undermining my initiatives.

He gave a firm undertaking that 'relentless action' would be taken against any security force members found to be assisting or inciting Inkatha members or any other organisation to commit violent actions.[63]

De Klerk's first effort to uncover the truth about hit squads ended in failure. This was the appointment of a judicial commission headed by Judge Louis Harms in January 1990 which was to report on 'alleged incidents of murders and other unlawful acts of violence committed in South Africa and the homelands in order to achieve, effect or promote constitutional or political aims in South Africa'. The commission, whose report was published in November 1990, achieved nothing, its efforts to obtain evidence being frustrated by the stonewalling tactics of the principal focus of its enquiry, the curiously named Civil Co-operation Bureau (CCB).

The CCB had been created in 1986 as part of the SADF's Special Forces. Its primary task had been to cause 'maximum disruption' to the enemy by means of killing, infiltration, bribery, compromise of people and blackmail. To bring revolutionary organisations, notably the ANC, to a halt would require going beyond 'normal conventional methods'. The personnel of the CCB included an odd hodge-podge of men from the SADF, police (mostly 'riff-raff', according to a senior general) and outsiders, some with alleged criminal connections.[64] Who exactly in the top echelons of government and the security forces knew about the CCB and its murderous proclivities is a controversial issue: Magnus Malan, a former chief of the SADF who was appointed as Minister of Defence in Botha's Cabinet in 1980, insisted that he knew nothing of the CCB's activities – and, indeed, he alerted De Klerk to the problem in January 1990. Despite having been given a supposedly full briefing on the SADF's range of operations, De Klerk, too, knew nothing about the CCB: 'I realized that despite all the assurances I had been given about the bona fides of the SADF's covert operations, something was seriously amiss.'[65] This was the trigger for the appointment of the Harms Commission.

Deep suspicions about the actual nature of the CCB's role were raised when David Webster, an academic activist, was gunned down on 1 May 1989. It was widely believed that he was murdered because he had uncovered evidence about the SADF's continuing support for the Mozambican rebel group, Renamo, as well as collecting information about death squads operating in South Africa.[66] Although two CCB operatives were suspected, the evidence against them was deemed inconclusive by the prosecution. At the inquest the presiding judge said that 'the truth was not told on who killed Webster because many of the suspect witnesses were professional liars who made their living in deception and who were unblushingly resourceful in building up tissues of conflicting falsehoods.'[67] It would be nine years before Ferdi Barnard, a CCB operative, was convicted of Webster's murder.

The Harms Commission encountered the same problem with CCB

witnesses, some of whom wore bizarre disguises while testifying. Harms got nowhere: the proceedings were often farcical, causing him to lament that there had been a 'basic lack of evidential material that might put some flesh on the bones'. Moreover, 'willing, trustworthy witnesses did not come to the fore'. To add to the judge's difficulty, the CCB had destroyed or hidden all of its files and ignored the instructions of the Minister of Defence and the chief of the SADF to co-operate fully with the Commission. In short, the CCB treated the Commission with the same contempt with which it treated other officials from the State President down. In reality, it was out of control.

Even though the wool had been pulled over his eyes, Harms concluded that the CCB's activities 'have contaminated the whole security arm of the state' and that it 'neither knows nor recognizes any higher authority'. Controversially – and, as it transpired, incorrectly, since the horrors of Vlakplaas had yet to be uncovered – Harms found that there was no evidence of hit squads in the police; and that Magnus Malan, the Minister of Defence, was only 'politically responsible' and therefore could not be held responsible for the activities of the CCB.[68] Malan, on learning of the CCB's activities, and even before alerting De Klerk to the situation, had ordered its disbandment. There is every likelihood, however, that erstwhile members continued their murderous ways.

The violence continued, damaging De Klerk's credibility and giving grist to the ANC's mill: in 1991 there were 2 510 fatalities in political violence; in 1992, 3 347; and in 1993, 3 706. Up to 90 per cent of cases occurred in Natal. Mandela's anger and the sharpness of his attacks on De Klerk increased exponentially. In April 1991 he discussed his doubts about De Klerk with the ANC's NEC, which believed that the violence was government-inspired and that it was upsetting the climate for negotiation. De Klerk responded to the surge of violence by calling a multi-party conference to be held in May, but Mandela replied that it would be pointless 'since the government knew precisely what it had to do'. Talks with the government were thereupon suspended.[69]

De Klerk was acutely aware of the damage being caused to the negotiating process and to himself. He also found it galling to be accused of conniving in the violence when he knew that the ANC itself was also heavily involved. According to De Klerk: 'News, reports and evaluated intelligence continued to stream in, implicating the ANC in violence, crime and intimidation.'[70] Mandela's iconic status and the albatross of apartheid's legacy that weighed De Klerk down, notwithstanding his efforts to jettison it, ensured that greater credence was given by much of the local and international media to Mandela's accusations than to De Klerk's denials of his own complicity. A more balanced analysis of what lay behind the violence, and a more realistic apportionment of culpability, was unlikely to emerge in the volatile conditions of the transition. Ultimate responsibility for safeguarding the lives of citizens lies with the head of state: De Klerk fully acknowledged that the buck stopped on his desk, but he was learning that the state is no monolith, unquestioningly obeying the commands of its head, however much power is formally vested in him.

In the aftermath of the Inkathagate revelations and the failure of the Harms Commission, De Klerk availed himself of the opportunity created by the retirement of three Cabinet ministers to shift Magnus Malan and Adriaan Vlok from their portfolios – Defence and Law and Order, respectively – to minor ones. Both men were hawks and had been the target of sustained criticism from the ANC and demands for their removal. Although De Klerk denied that the shifts were a caving in to these demands, it was apparent that the controversy in which they were mired made it impossible for them to continue in their posts.

Probably, De Klerk was beginning to develop doubts about the extent to which some of his ministers and a number of securocrats were being entirely honest with him. Vlok, for example, 'did not keep the subtle degree of distance from his department that ministers are wise to maintain'.[71] Very likely, the police generals controlled him, rather than the other way round. In an acerbic comment, Ken Owen described Vlok as: 'Amiable, bumbling, he tries to sound fierce, but sounds comical .... he is putty in the hands of the police.'[72] It was not until near the end of De Klerk's presidency in 1994 that Vlok informed him that he was going to apply for amnesty for having authorised several illegal acts, including the destruction of Cosatu House in central Johannesburg in May 1987; the placing of dummy explosives in several cinemas around South Africa in June 1988 to provide a pretext for the banning of *Cry Freedom*, the film about the murder of Steve Biko; and in August 1988 rendering Khotso House (headquarters of the South African Council of Churches) in Johannesburg 'unusable'. Vlok claimed that PW Botha had ordered the attack on Khotso House – which Botha denied. He had also accused an ANC activist, Shirley Gunn, of complicity in the episode, while congratulating the Vlakplaas operatives who had actually been responsible.[73]

It proved more difficult to pin culpability on Magnus Malan for involvement in illegal actions. Unlike Vlok, he did not apply to the Truth and Reconciliation Commission for amnesty, the granting of which was largely dependent on a full confession of involvement in human rights abuses. In May 1995 Malan was one of 20 accused of killing 13 people in KwaMakutha (KwaZulu-Natal) in 1987. The state alleged that the killers were members of a hit squad trained by the SADF to eliminate UDF/ANC members during the 1980s. Malan and his co-accused were eventually all acquitted in a controversial verdict. Malan opposed attempts to have the trial quashed, in spite of a belief that the ANC had brought pressure to bear on the prosecution to prefer charges. He was eager to be vindicated. In his evidence to the TRC, Malan apologised for having given orders that led to the death of innocent civilians caught in the cross-fire – 'this is part of the ugly reality of war'. But he insisted that he had never ordered, or been approached for authorisation by any member of the SADF, to kill political opponents of the government.[74]

De Klerk was perhaps too trusting of some of his Cabinet colleagues' bona fides. He prided himself on being a 'team-player', and expected members of the team to be upfront and honest with him. Waldmeir asserts that ministers regularly lied to him. She quotes an unnamed minister:

> Every time we would discuss it, they [unnamed] would try to convince us that there was no third force. I was present several times when De Klerk challenged first [Adriaan] Vlok [his first police minister] and Hernus Kriel [Vlok's successor]. He said to them, 'But how do you explain this?' He really got into them. But they always had convincing answers. I think it was a question of trusting the people who advised him.[75]

Vlok's not informing De Klerk of his past involvement in criminal dirty tricks, or at least resigning when De Klerk's rejection of illegal police activities became clear, was reprehensible; and thereafter lying to the Cabinet compounded his offence. Pik Botha, Minister of Foreign Affairs, was contrite in testifying to the TRC that he could have done more in the State Security Council, Parliament and the Cabinet 'to ensure that political opponents were not killed or tortured by government institutions'. No one in the previous government could say that 'there were no suspicions on our part that members of the South African Police were engaged in irregular activities'. Leon Wessels, the former Deputy Minister of Law and Order, was even more frank: 'I ... do not believe that the defence of "I did not know" is available to me, because in many respects I believe I did not want to know.'[76] The question of whether more could have been done by government to halt the violence is considered below. Whether the ANC is as blameless as Mandela's allegations implied must also be considered.

By early 1991 De Klerk was becoming dangerously exposed on both his right and left flanks. The CP continued to make menacing gains in a series of by-elections, even in constituencies hitherto considered safe NP seats:

- June 1990: Umlazi – NP majority slashed to 547, a swing of over 20 per cent to the CP;
- January 1991: Randburg – NP wins, but CP vote increased by 120 per cent;
- March 1991: Maitland – NP wins but CP obtains 34.4 per cent of the vote, compared with the combined CP and HNP share of the vote of 7.9 per cent in 1987;
- November 1991: Virginia – narrowly won by the NP in 1989, but won by the CP with a majority of over 2 000;
- February 1992: Potchefstroom – a safe NP seat for decades, won by the CP with a majority of 2 140, reversing the NP's majority of nearly 2 000 in 1989.

De Klerk was deeply concerned that his mandate was eroding. Extrapolations from these results suggested that the CP would win a general election. The trend eventually caused De Klerk to call a referendum on 17 March 1992 among white voters to decide whether the negotiation process should continue.

Notwithstanding the evident surge in support for the CP De Klerk proceeded with legislation that removed the last remaining statutory pillars of discrimination, except for those that denied the vote to Africans in a central Parliament, and provided for separate votes for the Coloured and Indian Houses of the Tricameral Parliament, which would have to await a constitutional settlement. Furthermore, by the end of 1990 the NP opened its membership to all races in the hope that it would win support even from the erstwhile victims of apartheid. The legislation repealed in 1990–1 included the land laws of 1913 and 1936 (which together allocated 13.7 per cent of the country to Africans), the Group Areas Act, the Reservation of Separate Amenities Act and the linchpin of apartheid, the Population Registration Act (which divided the entire population by 'race'). An undertaking was given in 1991 that future education policy, while remaining an 'own affair' pending the abolition of the Tricameral Parliament, would be non-discriminatory, although still subject to the NP policy that education would be governed by the principle that 'groups' would be entitled to 'an own culture, language or religion'. Although increasing numbers of state and private schools had opened their doors to all races, the actual extent of effective desegregation was limited, mostly owing to the comprehensive system of *de facto* residential segregation that would long outlive the formal repeal of the legislation (principally the Group Areas Act) that enforced it.

All of these reforms gave ammunition to the ultra-right, which objected vociferously to the removal of the barricades that decades of discrimination had erected around white exclusivity and privilege. Conservative agricultural groups objected to the repeal of the land legislation; CP-controlled local authorities opposed the desegregation of municipal facilities, as well as the impending prospect of non-racial local government. Blacks fought back with their most effective weapon, consumer boycotts, which had a devastating effect on numerous businesses, whose owners in many cases were forced to recognise that maintaining segregation was unaffordable.[77] The most difficult issue was inevitably going to be the desegregation of white schools. A survey showed that between 1989 and 1991 the number of whites favouring school desegregation rose slightly from 20 per cent to 27 per cent, while those favouring the retention of racially segregated schools rose from 49 per cent to 59 per cent.[78]

The potential thrust of the ultra-right was considerably neutralised by the inability of the major organisations to agree upon a strategy, let alone a goal. Much the biggest of the organisations was the CP, which since its inception had pinned its hopes on wresting power from the NP by electoral means. As the 'respectable' face of the ultra-right, it eschewed violence, although one of its MPs, Koos Botha, was convicted in 1991 of attempting to blow up a multiracial school for the children of returning ANC exiles in Pretoria, and an ex-MP, Clive Derby-Lewis, was found guilty of involvement in the assassination of Chris Hani in April 1993.

De Klerk's announcement in February 1990 threw the CP into confusion over how to react to the changed circumstances. Andries Treurnicht now had to engage in a tricky balancing act as factions with differing strategies emerged. The more realistic faction, led by Koos van der Merwe, argued that the CP should enter the negotiations and be prepared to settle for a smaller *volkstaat*, while the hardliners, led by Ferdi Hartzenberg (a minister in PW Botha's Cabinet until he resigned in 1982), wanted the restoration of apartheid in its full Verwoerdian rigour. The hardliners prevailed, and after Treurnicht's death in April 1993, Hartzenberg assumed the leadership. Five MPs resigned in August 1992, constituting themselves as the Afrikaanse Volksunie; Koos van der Merwe had previously been expelled for advocating participation in the negotiations, and he eventually joined Inkatha.[79]

As has been noted, the inability of the various ultra-rightwing organisations to agree upon the boundaries of a putative *volkstaat* thwarted their potential thrust as a unified counter-revolutionary force. Whatever boundaries were proposed, the project was nevertheless still-born because in no single magisterial district of the country or constituency held by the CP did whites constitute a majority. Moreover, as the NP pointed out, exactly the same demographic imbalance was true of every white-owned farm: black farm workers invariably outnumbered their white employers. Few whites, however strong their rhetorical commitment to a *volkstaat*, would have been prepared to uproot themselves from their farms or jobs (many were employed in the public service, police or defence force) and relocate to a *volkstaat* that was bound to be an isolated pariah state, un-recognised by the international community and, of course, by a prospec-tive new government with a strong commitment to an undivided South Africa.

These considerations persuaded some ultra-rightwingers that a *volk-staat* could not be achieved by means of a forcible 'unilateral declaration of independence'; rather, the best chance of success lay in seeking to ne-gotiate it. The major figure in subsequent efforts to do so was Constand Viljoen, a man of great integrity who had been chief of the South African Defence Force until his retirement in 1985.

Notwithstanding the lack of unity on the ultra-right, either collectively or as individual segments, it was a dangerous threat to the transition. Opposition to the prospect of an ANC-dominated government was wide-spread among white members of the police, the army and the public ser-vice, as well as among working class Afrikaners and white farmers. There was ominous talk in some quarters of a coup, or at least of a 'creeping' coup, whereby co-operation with the De Klerk government was either withheld or sabotaged. It can also be assumed that the practitioners of dirty tricks, assassinations, and other attacks on the ANC were strongly committed to thwarting the transition by sabotaging De Klerk's initiative. Violence emanating from these sources continued throughout the period of negotiations, despite De Klerk's efforts to nail those responsible.

*   *   *

In the face of the often deadly violence directed against it, the ANC main-tained an air of injured innocence, blaming De Klerk for both commis-sions and omissions. Yet, as De Klerk caustically observed, the ANC itself was deeply implicated in the continuing violence, a fact that it was reluc-tant to acknowledge.

To his credit Mandela did eventually acknowledge this unpalatable fact, in a speech at a funeral near Pretoria in April 1993:

> There are members of the ANC who are killing our people. We must face the truth. Our people are just as involved as other organizations that are committing this violence. And people who are doing that

are no longer human beings, they are animals. It is no use when I speak the truth for you to say: 'No, no, no no.' You want me to blame Inkatha only. I am not going to do that. It is true that the government is involved in the violence. It is members of the army, members of the police force, members of their intelligence service who are also behind this violence, because they want to cripple and weaken the ANC. But I am not going to criticize only the government and Inkatha.

These comments were a 'striking reversal' of Mandela's previous views on the origins of the violence, as Rich Mkhondo notes.[80] The unhappy truth, though, was that neither De Klerk, nor Mandela, nor Buthelezi was able fully to exercise control of their followers. During the early 1990s and beyond, as organisations sought to reach a political accommodation, violence, like a contrapuntal theme, threatened, disrupted and, on occasion derailed the process, bringing the country to what seemed like the brink of civil war.

While acknowledging that apartheid was the 'primary cancer', it is also true that strategies adopted by opponents of apartheid in the struggles of 1976–7 and the mid-1980s created a matrix in which violence, intimidation and other strongarm tactics came to be regarded as 'normal'. Apart from the deliberate assassination of black official functionaries, alleged informers and political rivals (notably in the conflict between the UDF/ANC and Inkatha), intolerance extended to dissidents who refused to toe the party line in communities where a single organisation was dominant.

Pressures were exerted even on black journalists for allegedly not reporting to the satisfaction of militants. Thami Mazwai, a senior journalist on the *Sowetan*, who could hardly be accused of being a 'stooge' or a 'sellout', told a seminar in August 1990 about a new type of censorship:

> We have a situation in which journalists are far less exposed to arrest, detention and incarceration by the government than they used to be, but are being threatened and manhandled by political activists in the townships … and are being told to toe the line 'or else'.

What had been created was 'a monster that has now become uncontrollable'. Another journalist, Connie Malusi, attributed the climate of political intolerance to the 'culture of resistance politics' which 'assumed ideological homogeneity among black people'.[81]

The campaign for 'ungovernability' encouraged by the ANC in the mid-1980s was an inevitable response to the temper of the times. An unrelenting

hatred of 'the system' caused many youngsters to seize any opportunity
to attack official buildings or vehicles – but also to loot shops and liquor
stores. Lawlessness and the abandonment of restraint led many into crim-
inality. Solomon Marikele, a veteran of the turbulent Vaal Triangle unrest
of the mid-1980s, whose education had been comprehensively disrupted,
candidly described his slide into crime:

> Mostly those who are there, they were students. So they saw they
> can't go further with education and now they have to repossess [a eu-
> phemism for 'steal'], there is nothing we can do, we need to survive.
> This is our country, so we have to take anything from them [whites],
> bring [it] to us. They've got money, we've got nothing. They will buy
> and we will steal … .[82]

The strategy of making the country ungovernable was legitimate, from
the UDF's and the ANC's point of view, but the lawlessness, violence and
propensity to violence that it entailed could not be summarily stopped by
command of the leadership when new political circumstances emerged in
1990. Buthelezi had predicted in 1986 that reducing the country to ungovernability would cause it to remain ungovernable after liberation.

An aggravating factor was the return of MK soldiers, some of whom
had been brutalised by years of difficult and dangerous conditions, and
many of whom retained an insurgent disposition that was sceptical of the
call for peace, if not downright opposed to it, especially as the violence
raged on.

Inexplicably, the government had authorised the carrying of 'traditional weapons' in public by Zulu in August 1990. This was in response
to demands from Inkatha that Zulu custom required the carrying of such
weapons as part of a man's accoutrement on cultural occasions. The
weapons actually carried often included spears, knobkerries, wooden
sticks, and even sharpened axes. Despite an attempt to outlaw the more
lethal weapons and a court ruling that the authorisation of such weapons
was invalid, Inkatha supporters continued to carry them. For the ANC it
became a major issue.

In response to the violence directed against defenceless communities,
the ANC decided in 1991 to establish self-defence units. If the state could
not, or would not, provide protection, then communities were entitled
to undertake their own defence, as many were demanding. In spite of
government disapproval, the ANC went ahead. MK soldiers were to train
community members and also to play a leading role in the units themselves. While it is true that these units did offer some protection, their

activities led to increased polarisation and even more violence, as the government had warned. Mkhondo, who was sympathetic to the plight of communities and condemned the state's failure to protect them as racist, nevertheless writes:

> The ANC's call to arm the people was not the way to democracy; it was more likely the path to chaos. The ANC's assurance that the defence units were not designed as elements of a private ANC political army was less than reassuring ... the township fighting showed starkly that all political organizations, including the government, have been unable to instill discipline among unruly members, let alone control them. It was not surprising that, a few months after the formation of the units, there were reports that [their] members were running amok in the townships, conducting kangaroo courts, killing opponents and even fighting among themselves. Some were arrested for crimes such as armed robberies.[83]

The violence in Natal and Transvaal, and the sheer viciousness of the conflict between Inkatha and ANC supporters, approached the scale of civil war – one, moreover, with strong ethnic overtones. It evoked images of the horrifying civil wars in Angola and Mozambique, as well as the anti-Ndebele pogroms in Zimbabwe in the early 1980s. There was something resembling a cruel Catch-22 situation: on the one hand, there was an imperative need to reach a political settlement and establish a democratic polity through which conflicts stood a chance of being peacefully managed; on the other, the approach to negotiations and the possibility of inclusive elections in the near future heightened political competition, thereby increasing the possibility of violence.

If elements in the state's security apparatus were intent on sabotaging negotiations, they had their counterparts in both the ANC and Inkatha, who either believed that negotiations were futile or that political ground had to be defended and expanded by violence – or both. A prime example in the ANC's ranks was Harry Gwala, a self-confessed Stalinist who had spent years in jail for political offences and, in 1990, became leader of the ANC's Midlands region in Natal. Despite the embarrassment that his bellicose utterances caused the ANC's national leadership, Gwala enjoyed huge support in the region. When the editor of the *Natal Witness* referred to Gwala's 'armies of the night', Gwala retorted that the newspaper had underestimated his strength by not mentioning his 'armies of the day'.[84] He scorned peace initiatives, asking:

How many people have been killed since the Mandela-Buthelezi celebrated bearhugs – thousands! If people think the struggle will be
won through negotiations and peace accords alone, they are naïve.[85]

Maverick though he was, Gwala's popularity showed that he articulated
the views of many ANC militants, and not only those in the Natal caul-
dron. While few other senior figures in the ANC matched Gwala's extrem-
ism, remarks by some were hardly calculated to serve the cause of peace.
In what he described as 'a very confrontational meeting' with Mandela,
De Klerk accused him of repeated violations of the DF Malan Accord,
and claimed that the ANC had been involved in numerous armed attacks.
He also quoted several of Chris Hani's statements about the spread of
MK's preparedness for action that were bound to incite violence: 'the
ANC was going to get what we want, all the weapons are here'; and 'if
told, MK would to back to the bush, irrespective of what the NEC ... is
saying. We will get the mandate from the people and not from the executive of the ANC.'

According to De Klerk's account, Mandela demanded to see the evidence, and challenged him to prosecute those who had committed crimes.
De Klerk assured him that they did indeed have detailed evidence, but that
'the problem would not be solved simply by proceeding with prosecutions'.[86] He considered Mandela's attacks 'outrageous' and declined to
answer them publicly and in kind.

De Klerk was receiving a bad press. Mandela's stature, on the other
hand, ensured that his allegations were widely publicised and believed.
Certainly there was truth in what he said, especially concerning the involvement of elements in the security forces in promoting violence. In
his autobiography Mandela writes that he never sought to undermine De
Klerk 'for the practical reason that the weaker he was, the weaker the
negotiations process'.[87] However, while he was undoubtedly under pressure from his grassroots to lash out at De Klerk, his *ad hominem* attacks
sometimes went too far and in fact did damage De Klerk.

Vindication of the ANC was aided not only by Mandela's occupation
of the moral high ground but also by the sympathy for the ANC shown by
most of the organisations, domestic and foreign, that monitored violence.
Violence committed by the ANC could be justified either by deeming it
'defensive' violence, or, prior to 1990, by the broader concept of armed
struggle, deemed by some theologians to be a 'just war'. In either case,
blaming apartheid invariably trumped any criticism of ANC complicity or excesses committed in the name of the struggle. There was much
for which apartheid could be held directly or indirectly responsible, but

stifling critical analysis of the militants' behaviour hardly assisted the quest for peace – and, moreover, did little to encourage peaceable sentiments among Inkatha members.

Determined efforts by the South African Institute of Race Relations to present a more balanced perspective were greeted with scepticism, if not hostility. In particular, Anthea Jeffery's meticulous analyses of the violence in Natal and of the Truth and Reconciliation Commission's findings avoided a partisan approach, but provided both sides of the story, while exposing the omissions, errors and 'disinformation' contained in other accounts of the violence produced by domestic and foreign monitors.[88]

Further efforts to curb violence were started in September 1991 with the signing of the National Peace Accord (NPA) and the establishment of the complementary Commission of Inquiry into the Prevention of Public Violence and Intimidation, headed by Judge Richard Goldstone. The NPA was the resurrection of a conference on violence convened by De Klerk in May, in which the ANC declined to participate, Mandela saying that the conference was 'pointless' since the government knew precisely what it had to do – which might have been news to De Klerk.[89]

Subsequent efforts by church and business leaders bore fruit, however, and leading figures from the ANC, Inkatha and NP were drawn into the preparation of a draft peace accord. Eventually 29 political parties and other organisations signed the Accord, including the ANC, NP, Inkatha, Cosatu and a range of homeland governments and parties. Notably absent from the list of signatories were the CP and the AWB; the PAC and Azapo also declined to be associated with 'an undemocratic regime' but expressed agreement with the NPA's principles. It was a lengthy document whose preamble committed the signatories to ending the scourge of political violence that 'jeopardizes the very process of peaceful political transformation and threatens to leave a legacy of insurmountable division and deep bitterness in our country'. The Accord provided for a code of conduct to be adhered to by all signatories; a code of conduct to be observed by every police official; guidelines for reconstruction and development aimed at addressing the worst effects of violence in local communities; and dispute resolution committees at regional and local levels operating under the overall aegis of a National Peace Secretariat.[90]

Despite the high hopes created by the NPA, levels of violence increased after the signing. This suggested that the practitioners of violence on all sides were largely out of control. On the other hand, as the chairman of the National Peace Committee, John Hall (a leading businessman), said, 80 per cent of the country was peaceful, and the death toll in political violence was lower than the annual number of road deaths. This was not of much comfort to ravaged communities, many of whose members were not necessarily politically partisan but had been caught in the withering crossfire. Judge Goldstone, whose involvement in investigating political violence had been intense, told an interviewer in April 1993 that it was 'almost illogically naïve and pessimistic' to dismiss the NPA. Had it not been for the many local dispute resolution committees, 'I don't think any sensible person could doubt but that the level of violence would be much worse'.[91]

Goldstone's investigations were to play a major role in bringing to book some of the major practitioners of dirty tricks. His appointment as chairman of the eponymous Commission was an interesting reflection of De Klerk's determination to root out violence – although, to be sure, he was careful to appoint a judge, after consultation with other parties, with a reputation for fairness and opposition to apartheid that would make him generally acceptable, and to the ANC in particular. De Klerk says of Goldstone that he developed 'a healthy respect for his fairness and his thoroughness … . As a result of his work, we were slowly able to escape from the miasma of unfounded allegations, accusations, disinformation and propaganda which had previously shrouded the question of violence.'[92]

As a law student in the 1950s, Goldstone became active in student politics, becoming an executive committee member of Nusas. He was appointed to the bench of the Transvaal Supreme Court in 1980, and in 1982 he delivered a judgement that effectively ended prosecutions under the Group Areas Act. Subsequently he was able to use his judicial position to visit detainees incarcerated under the emergency regulations. He tried hard to persuade the police officers to adopt a more humane attitude and to ameliorate the grim conditions under which detainees were held.[93] By and large, Goldstone's relationship with De Klerk was a co-operative one, as it was with Mandela. His pertinacity and single-mindedness invariably ensured that his requests were granted – and that the Commission's independence was fully recognised.

The developments recounted in this and the preceding chapter constitute what I William Zartman has termed the 'prenegotiation' phase, described by him as beginning

> … when one or more parties considers negotiation as a policy option and communicates this intention to other parties … . [P]renegotiation is the span of time and activity in which the parties move from conflicting unilateral solutions for a mutual problem to a joint search for cooperative multilateral or joint solutions.[94]

Following Zartman's terms, a 'hurting stalemate' prompted leaders on both the ANC and NP sides to reach out for a negotiated settlement, a decision in both cases that was informed by calculation of the costs and benefits of a potential agreement, as well as the costs of failure to reach one. Both De Klerk and Mandela were obliged to estimate and consolidate the support in their respective support bases for an accommodative policy 'to prepare the home front for a shift from a winning to a conciliatory mentality'.[95] As the evidence has shown, this was no easy task for either leader: De Klerk had to face down a counter-revolutionary force on the radical right, mostly of erstwhile NP supporters; and Mandela first had to persuade his colleagues in the leadership that the alternatives to a negotiated settlement implied an appallingly high cost, and then, in the pre-negotiation phase itself, continually had to douse the fires of militancy, ignited by angry, violence-wracked communities.

CHAPTER 11

Opening Pandora's Box

The pre-negotiation period had shown profound, seemingly intractable difficulties, many of which would continue even after formal constitutional negotiations got under way. The negotiations appeared to pose an insuperable task: how could two such opposed organisations as the ANC and the NP ever hope to reach a constitutional settlement, given their respective histories, their radically different constitutional proposals, and a serious difference of opinion over the mode of drawing up a new Constitution? And then there were the problems posed by Inkatha and the militant ultra-right. Only a supreme optimist could have hoped that 'sufficient consensus' (the term that came to be used) could emerge from this maelstrom of contending forces.

The ANC produced its *Constitutional Guidelines for a Democratic South Africa* in 1988, declaring them to be a conversion of the Freedom Charter 'from a vision for the future into a constitutional reality'.[1] They were premised on the view that a Constitution could not merely be a dry legal instrument; it had also to incorporate provisions for corrective action that guaranteed 'a rapid and irreversible redistribution of wealth', as well as the promotion of 'the habits of non-racial and non-sexist thinking, the practice of anti-racist behaviour and the acquisition of genuinely shared patriotic consciousness'.

The *Guidelines* were briefly stated general principles, amounting to the demand for majority rule in a unitary, democratic and non-racial state. State policy would promote the growth of a single national identity, while recognising the linguistic and cultural diversity of the people; the state and all social institutions were to be under a constitutional duty to eradicate racial discrimination and to take active steps to eradicate the inequality that it caused; the advocacy or practice of racism, fascism, Nazism or the incitement of ethnic or regional exclusiveness or hatred were to be outlawed. Subject to the prohibition of the advocacy and practice of racism, basic rights and freedoms were to be guaranteed, including the right of parties to take part in political life (which meant that a one-party state was not being contemplated).

Proposing a unitary state suggested rejection of a federal system, advocated in varying forms by the NP, Inkatha and the Democratic Party. Sovereignty of the people, said the *Guidelines*, was to be exercised through one central legislature, executive and administration, but provision was to be made for the delegation of the central government's powers to 'subordinate administrative units for purposes of more efficient administration and democratic participation'.

The *Guidelines* included economic clauses that suggested the ANC's continuing adherence to socialist – or at least social democratic – views, as the Freedom Charter had implied. The state was to have the power 'to determine the general context in which economic life takes place and define and limit the rights and obligations attaching to the ownership and use of productive capacity'. The economy was to be mixed, but the private sector was obliged to co-operate with the state in realising the objectives of the Freedom Charter. Only property for 'personal use and consumption' was to be constitutionally protected, although another clause mentions ownership of land, but not its constitutional protection.

Affirmative action was mentioned as an instrument of economic redress, but how it would be enforced was not spelt out, other than briefly in relation to land reform: apart from the abolition of all racial restrictions relating to land, affirmative action would be enforced in implementing land reforms, 'taking into account the status of victims of forced removals'. Affirmative action was endorsed also in the elimination of discrimination against women, while provision was made for a charter protecting workers' trade union rights to be incorporated into the Constitution.

Overall, the *Guidelines* proposed what Mandela often referred to as his wish for an 'ordinary democracy'. Given the variation in forms of the democratic state, what was to be regarded as 'ordinary' to some extent begged the question. Could an ordinary democracy cope with the problems posed by a deeply divided society? How, for example, could the 'tyranny of the majority' be avoided, especially in view of the probability that voting would cleave largely to racial divisions? This was a question that troubled the NP in particular.

That the ANC should propose a straightforward system of 'majoritarian' democracy was understandable and inevitable, given its long history of opposition to an undemocratic, discriminatory system. Moreover, as the virtually certain winner of a majority of votes in a future inclusive election, it was disinclined to heed any objections to equating democracy with majority rule; or to allow itself to be constrained by a system so loaded with mechanisms for minority protection that the majority 'must be constitutionally disempowered and deprived of the capacity to effect changes which will rescue them from subordination'.[2]

* * *

It was not until September 1991, on the eve of the commencement of constitutional talks, that the NP published a formal statement of its proposals.[3] In the intervening months since February 1990, however, De Klerk and his ministers, notably Gerrit Viljoen, the Minister for Constitutional Development, had enunciated a number of principles that were incorporated into the statement. In addition, the South African Law Commission produced a massive *Report on Constitutional Models* which contained a wealth of data on constitutional structures drawn from many states.[4]

A review of De Klerk's and Viljoen's speeches during 1990–1 illustrates the thinking that lay behind the NP's proposals. The following principles emerged (with date and speaker noted):

- 'The politics of confrontation so typical of the Westminster system and our history, have to make way for the politics of consensus' (De Klerk, 17 April 1990).
- There were three basic alternatives: partition, 'simplistic majority rule', and power-sharing. Partition, as propounded by the CP, was 'an unattainable dream in the face of the realities of South Africa'. 'We believe that majority rule is not suitable for a country like South Africa because it will lead to domination and even the suppression of minorities. This applies both to a unitary system and to the typical geographic federation' (De Klerk, 17 April 1990).
- '... power-sharing endeavours to find a balance between fair and complete participation in government at every level by every citizen on the one hand, and the effective protection of minorities against domination and the dismantling of their values, on the other' (De Klerk, 17 April 1990).
- 'We have all along explicitly committed ourselves to a balance between universal franchise and the majority's power on the one hand and protection of minority rights and interests on the other hand, provided this is done in a non-racial and democratic fashion .... the effective way in which interest groups, including minorities, in the political field articulate and promote their interests is through

organizing themselves in political parties. Therefore, we believe political parties, rather than groups defined in cultural or ethnic terms, are the instruments through which the rights of political minorities should be protected. Political parties ... must be given a democratic chance. Parties should not, after unsuccessfully attempting to attain a majority, be relegated to a semi-relevant opposing critic. 51% of the votes should not entitle a party to 100% of the political power. Minority parties must specifically be enabled also to take [an] active and effective part in the governing process' (Viljoen, 8 October 1991).

- 'In achieving an acceptable system of checks and balances the concerns of the minorities will of course have to be accommodated in such a way that the claims of the majority are not disregarded and in fact overridden by minority domination. The will of the majority must remain an essential prerequisite for decision-making' (Viljoen, 9 May 1990).

- There should be 'maximum devolution of power to lower authority structures – government closer to the people who are directly affected by decisions':
  - 'Those who wish to live in particular communities ... must be able to do so in the New South Africa; but without laws that require people or limit them to do so';
  - 'own schools (be it in the context of language, religion or culture) can be established, with equal state support, but, again, without anyone being obliged by law to do so';
  - 'A Supreme Court with testing power over government legislation and the executive in terms of the constitution – i.e. no longer absolute sovereignty of Parliament of the British tradition' (Viljoen, 8 October 1990, translation).

In addition to these general principles, De Klerk reiterated an undertaking given previously that once the negotiations had been completed and a draft Constitution drawn up, it would be submitted to the electorate of the (white) House of Assembly by way of an election or a referendum. Should the electorate approve the draft it would be enacted into law by the Tricameral Parliament.

De Klerk's response to the barrage of criticism from the CP, claiming that he had not obtained a mandate from the (white) electorate, was to insist that he had done so in the election in September 1989. The NP's manifesto had proclaimed the goal of an undivided South Africa, with a common citizenship and the right of every citizen to participate in government at all levels, with the proviso that there should be no domination.

Since a new Constitution had yet to be negotiated, the NP could not foretell what its final terms would be, but it was adamant that it would have to provide for minority protection and the safeguarding of property in a free-enterprise system. The NP's principles invited cynicism from those who had experienced over 40 years of apartheid: a constitutional state in place of the sovereignty of Parliament, a consensus-driven political process and the avoidance of 'winner-take-all' outcomes were not features of parliamentary rule under the Nationalists. Yet, if De Klerk were to carry a majority of whites into a new dispensation he was obliged to reassure his constituency that the NP would not merely cave in to the ANC's demands for straightforward majority rule.

De Klerk and his colleagues, moreover, were aware that when an inclusive, democratic election was eventually held, the NP would be a distinctly minority party. Surveys commissioned by the government itself in the late 1980s showed a consistent pattern (that was, in fact, closely mirrored in the actual results of the election held in April 1994): the ANC would win roughly 60 per cent of the votes. As the prospective winner, the ANC was likely to oppose minority protection or power-sharing as a covert effort to retain white privilege. Similarly, proposals for a federal system were construed as a device that would enable the wealthier regions – where most whites lived – to retain their wealth.

If the ANC was proposing a 'progressive' Constitution that paved the way for a massive programme of social upliftment and racial equalisation, unfettered by major restraints on its power, the NP's proposals, while representing a break with the apartheid past, were essentially defensive, aiming particularly to calm white apprehensiveness at the momentous changes that were imminent. Persuading the ANC to accept even watered-down versions of the NP's principles would be a hard sell.

The core of the model proposed by the NP, and incorporating the principles quoted above, was an elaborate system of protection for minority parties. The First House of a bicameral Parliament would be elected by universal franchise with an electoral system based on proportional representation; the Second House would be smaller than the First and would represent the regions, each of the nine suggested in the model being given an equal number of seats to be filled in regional elections. Each party winning a specified minimum amount of support in a regional election would be given an equal number of the region's seats in the Second House. (It was not surprising that Joe Slovo of the SACP bitingly described this as a proposal for a 'House of Losers'.)

The Second House was pre-eminently for minority protection, the assumption being that ethnic minorities or categories would look to parties to represent their interests. Legislation that affected minority or regional interests would require a higher majority to be passed, as would constitutional amendments.

The proposed executive provided further participation for minority parties: it would be a collective entity, to be known as the Presidency, consisting of the leaders of the three biggest parties; chairmanship of the Presidency would rotate on an annual basis, and decisions, including Cabinet appointments, would be taken by consensus.

The framers of the proposal clearly had in mind the 'magic formula' whereby multiparty Swiss governments were formed. The extensive devolution of power in the Swiss system also influenced the model. The Swiss system, however, was *sui generis,* and whatever its merits it was difficult to imagine the successful transplant of a variant to the radically different circumstances of South Africa, where a tradition of compromise and a political culture embodying 'amicable agreement' had yet to emerge – if it were ever going to emerge.

The document made it clear that the model was not necessarily 'an unchangeable final proposal': it could be changed through further consideration by the NP and as a consequence of negotiations and in the light of the South African Law Commission's Report, when it was published. Indeed, the proposals bore the hallmark of an opening bid in the forthcoming constitutional talks. Predictably, they were greeted with scorn by the ANC as well as many opinion leaders in white opposition circles, and dismissed as a form of 'neo-apartheid'.

It was true that the model was far too cumbersome to have worked successfully in practice; but in dismissing it so scornfully the critics ignored important issues that the model indirectly raised. For example, could 'an ordinary democracy' (whatever that meant) succeed in South Africa's circumstances? That racial/ethnic identities would remain salient – and perhaps even sharpened – in the circumstances of competitive democracy was a probability that was either ignored or dismissed as conservative scaremongering. Ethnicity was a taboo issue among opponents of apartheid: it was assumed to be the consequence of apartheid planners' attempted manipulation and/or a variant form of class consciousness. Donald Horowitz's challenge to this kind of thinking was largely ignored:

> So strong is the aversion to official group categories that the very existence of politically significant ethnic groups is denied. And denial is not too strong a term for describing the studied neglect of ethnicity that characterizes current discourse .... the confluence of

South African opposition with this more general stream of scholar-
ship has produced something close to silence on ethnicity in South
African scholarly and political discourse.[5]

The backlash against any form of minority protection was a consequence
of the enforced 'group' membership that was fundamental to apartheid.
It started with 'race classification' under the Population Registration Act,
and proceeded via the designation of bantustans for specific African ethnic groups and the creation of the Tricameral Parliament that gave constitutional force to compulsory group membership.

No doubt, a (prospectively) minority party such as the NP might have
received more support in its quest for minority safeguards had it not been
saddled with the historical guilt of apartheid. Its proposals could be dismissed by the ANC as attempts to limit the powers of a new government
and to entrench white privilege, land ownership and the distribution of
income, which were 'cunningly designed cloaks under which to perpetuate the system of white minority domination'.[6]

Whatever truth there was in this allegation, it was equally true that
South Africa was a deeply divided society, with a long history of conflict, and such societies are notoriously infertile ground for sustaining
democratic polities. Moreover, even if the ANC were likely to win the
first election with some 60 per cent of the votes, as most polls and other
projections suggested, 40 per cent of the other votes would be distributed
among other parties – notably the NP, which hoped to win 30 per cent
overall, and the IFP. Most of these smaller parties would have their support bases in minority groups, however configured. Proportional representation could go some of the way in making every vote count, thereby
ensuring that, electorally at any rate, a winner-take-all outcome could be
avoided. But what about power in government? De Klerk's argument that
51 per cent of the vote should not confer 100 per cent of the power on
the winners had *prima facie* validity, not only in the light of a democratic
theory appropriate to divided societies, but also for the pragmatic reason
that minorities excluded from power where it mattered most, namely in
the national executive, could potentially become a dangerously alienated
and destabilising force. Some means of lowering the stakes in the founding election had to be found.

Buthelezi's Inkatha Freedom Party was also a significant actor in the
unfolding drama, and its constitutional demands could not be brushed
aside. Until the very eve of the election in 1994 Buthelezi would engage
in brinkmanship, causing his opponents to consider him a spoiler. Even
though he was fighting an ever-diminishing corner, he was not going to

allow his claims to be ignored in the name of 'sufficient consensus' between the ANC and the NP. Whether the IFP had the capacity to scupper the negotiating process and the eventual election became a critical
question.

Buthelezi's exploration of federalism had begun as early as 1974 and
continued with the Buthelezi Commission and the KwaZulu Natal Indaba
in the 1980s (see chapter 8). Writing in 1990, Buthelezi warned blacks that
the prospect of government in a unitary state based on universal franchise
frightened whites. While he and the vast majority of blacks favoured such
a system, they had to put South Africa first and 'be prepared to look at
a federal system, a canton system, or any other kind of system in which
the fundamental principles of democracy ... are preserved.' The Inkatha
Declaration of 1990 listed the human rights that should underpin 'whatever democratic system is finally adopted', but added that provision should
be made for the protection of minority rights provided that they did not
violate the principles of democratic government. Moreover: 'There shall
be no domination of one group by any other group.'[7] In due course, as
the exigencies of the negotiating process increased and the IFP's position
weakened, the bland statement of 1990 was replaced with a far more extreme demand for federalism.

The Democratic Party, lineal descendant of the Progressive Party, could
claim a consistent record of staunch support for civil rights and the rule
of law, as well as of federalism. Of all the significant parties that were
involved in the process it alone had a longstanding commitment to liberal
democracy. Its ranks included seasoned politicians like Helen Suzman,
Colin Eglin, Zach de Beer and Ken Andrew, which enabled the DP to
punch above its weight in the negotiations, even if its electoral support
was small, as was to be shown in the 1994 election.

*   *   *

The wide differences among the parties in regard to their constitutional
proposals were matched by equally wide differences about how a new
Constitution was to be drawn up. The ANC held fast to the Harare
Declaration's terms: discussions between the liberation movement (primarily the ANC) and the government, first to suspend hostilities, and
thereafter to agree upon the necessary mechanism for drafting a new
Constitution. In addition:

> The parties shall agree on the formation of an interim govern-
> ment to supervise the process of drawing up and adoption of a new

Constitution; govern and administer the country, as well as effect the transition to a democratic order including the holding of elections.[8]

The ANC insisted that only an elected body, a constituent assembly, could draft the Constitution. It should be elected by universal franchise on a common voters' roll by proportional representation. The ANC and its alliance partners, the SACP and Cosatu, launched a campaign in March 1991 to achieve this object. Mandela told the ANC National Conference in July that attaining the objective of a constituent assembly could not be achieved solely via negotiations:

> It will require the generation of mass support .... We reject the regime's contention that mass mobilization stands in the way of the negotiating process. In the absence of voting rights, the only power we can exercise is the power and the strength of our organized people.[9]

There was a *prima facie* logic to the ANC's demands: if, as the NP had repeatedly said, a new Constitution should be drawn up by all parties 'with a proven basis of support', the ANC retorted that there was no better way of proving a basis of support than an election. But, the NP responded, the ANC's proposal was putting the political cart before the constitutional horse. Viljoen argued on 7 June 1991 that the election of a constituent assembly as advocated by the ANC 'would leapfrog the whole negotiating process, would predetermine its outcome. The elected majority will decide and that is where negotiation will end.' This would amount to a simple 'transfer of power to the masses', thereby eliminating a broad multiparty involvement in the making of the new Constitution. All parties in the process, he continued, must be treated as having an equally legitimate stake in participation and in the outcome, and dominance of one or a few parties over others was to be avoided. An election held under current circumstances would be problematic: 'At a moment in our history when we need reconciliation and compromise, an election would have a highly confrontational effect.'

The NP was also opposed to the idea of an interim government: De Klerk rejected the proposal because it would create a constitutional vacuum and rule by an unelected government. South Africa was a sovereign state with a lawfully elected government that would continue to govern in terms of the existing Constitution until it was replaced. But there were possibilities of a more flexible arrangement: on 15 May 1991 Viljoen mooted the idea that, were the negotiation process to proceed expeditiously, 'a natural development could be that an informal, influential leadership corps would emerge that will inevitably have very persuasive influence' on governmental decisions even before a new Constitution came into force. De Klerk expressed his readiness to consider expanding the Cabinet to include a 'relatively broad spectrum' of competent individuals; but this would require the consensus of the multiparty negotiating forum. These were tentative thoughts, but they were the germ of the Transitional Executive Council which eventually came into existence in September 1993. The ANC's concern was that the NP government would use the power of incumbency and its role as both 'player and referee' to the disadvantage of other parties. De Klerk indignantly disavowed any such intention.

Buthelezi's rejection of an elected constituent assembly was as unequivocal as the NP's. Firmly convinced of the ANC's drive for hegemony, he quoted ANC sources declaring their intention to 'smash' Inkatha and deprive it of its political base. The Harare Declaration 'makes assumptions about the supremacy of the ANC and was drawn up to reflect the assumption that the only negotiations of any importance ... will be negotiations between the ANC and the SA Government.'[10] He warned also that the civil wars in Angola and Mozambique would be child's play compared with the conflict that would erupt if large groups were left out of the negotiating process. Exacerbating Buthelezi's fears of the ANC's intentions was a deepening suspicion that the NP and the ANC were preparing to cut a deal that would effectively exclude the IFP or relegate it to a peripheral role. It was a suspicion that would grow.

Buthelezi's opposition to sanctions, and the compatibility of the IFP's and the NP's proposals, might have suggested that there was sufficient common ground for an alliance, but the NP ministers who dealt with Buthelezi found him prickly and obstructive. Moreover, they realised that any overt move towards alliance-building at an early stage of what were bound to be delicate negotiations would have inflamed already tense relations with the ANC, despite their frequent dismissals of Buthelezi as a government puppet; and for De Klerk the big prize was, indeed, a deal with his major adversary, the ANC. For his part, Buthelezi would have liked nothing more than to be welcomed into the 'liberation struggle' club and to have his undoubted role in undermining apartheid acknowledged. Perhaps Mandela might have accepted Inkatha, if only in the interests of black solidarity, but whatever his private inclinations were, there is little doubt that any such move would have provoked uproar in the ANC.

Both proponents and opponents of the view that an elected constituent assembly should be the constitution-making body could mount persuasive cases for their respective points of view. That they were poles apart seemed ominous, since the issue was so important that it was difficult to see how negotiations could begin unless it was resolved. Eventually, how-ever, it was resolved by an ingenious squaring of the circle.

*   *   *

1991 was another tumultuous year, and it would not be the last. It began promisingly enough with general agreement among the bigger parties to the convening of a multiparty conference to discuss the future of the ne-gotiating process and, hopefully, to reach agreement on the shape of a for-mal constitution-making body. Not long thereafter, on 12 February 1991, the DF Malan Accord was signed whereby the ANC agreed to suspend armed action, though MK would not be disbanded.

The violence continued unabated, however, strengthening ANC suspi-cions of the state's complicity. In April the ANC directed its demands to De Klerk by way of an open letter and when he failed to respond to its satisfaction it suspended talks with the government. Further embarrass-ment for both the government and the IFP occurred when news of the Inkathagate scandal emerged. The effect of these developments on the negotiating process was two-fold: first, the ANC demanded an interim government with increased stridency, especially with a view to ensuring that the security forces came under multiparty control; and secondly, it re-peated its insistence that the government could not be both player and ref-eree. In a tough speech to the ANC National Conference in July, Mandela said that it was 'incorrect and unacceptable' that one of the parties to the negotiation should continue to govern the country on its own. An interim government, broadly acceptable to the various parties, would take on the character of a transitional government of national unity.[11]

If the government was embarrassed by scandal and its inability to stop the violence, the ANC was experiencing its own problems. Organisationally, it was sluggish and inefficient, symptoms of a long-banned movement's efforts to transform itself into a legal body ready to do battle with its opponents in a negotiating situation. In a leaked, confidential report the outgoing Secretary-General, Alfred Nzo, told the Conference that the ANC lacked 'enterprise, creativity and initiative. We appear very happy to remain pigeonholed within the confines of populist rhetoric.'[12]

The election of Cyril Ramaphosa as Secretary-General not only brought his organisational skills to the ANC, which badly needed them; his im-peccable credentials as a radical unionist and MDM activist also helped to bridge the gap between the old guard, personified by Mandela, and a rising generation of younger militants, less inclined to compromise than their elders. Ramaphosa, a seasoned and wily negotiator (as employers in the mining industry could confirm), was able to tilt the ANC away from its past tendency to break off talks every time there was violence: the practitioners of violence could not be allowed to exercise a veto over the negotiating process; instead, the ANC should use the violent outbreaks as opportunities for extracting more concessions from the government.[13] Ramaphosa had learned an important lesson about the dynamics of conflict and negotiation: postponing negotiation until the violence had been ended provided those intent on thwarting negotiations with an incentive to continue their activities.

Not long after Ramaphosa's appointment, he and Roelf Meyer, then Deputy Minister of Constitutional Development, met at the trout farm of a mutual friend who thought it would be a good idea for the two men to meet. Neither knew that the other would be a fellow-guest. How the experienced fly-fisherman Ramaphosa removed a hook from the hand of the inexperienced Meyer was a story that gained legendary status. The trust that was built up between them was the foundation of the 'Cyril–Roelf' back-channel that played a critical role in keeping the subsequent negotiations on track. Despite widely differing backgrounds, Meyer was in some respects Ramaphosa's counterpart in the NP. Both were relatively young and both were pragmatic as well as affable; and both were rising stars in their respective organisations.

Meyer was appointed Deputy Minister of Law and Order in 1986 and Deputy Minister of Constitutional Development in 1988. His spell at Law and Order, where he was responsible for the National Security Management System (see chapter 7), was an eye-opener: it gave him 'a far clearer – and more disturbing – understanding of our security and sociopolitical situation …. I had been put on a new learning curve.'[14] In August 1991 Meyer replaced Magnus Malan as Minister of Defence, a portfolio he occupied for nine months. Thereafter, in May 1992, he succeeded Viljoen as Minister of Constitutional Planning and became also the government's chief constitutional negotiator. Although he enjoyed De Klerk's full confidence and support, his appointments were not well received in all quarters. The securocrats mistrusted him, and his lack of military experience led many army officers in particular to view him with ill-concealed contempt. Similarly, more conservative members of the NP Cabinet and caucus grew uneasy at his relationship with Ramaphosa, especially when it became evident that he was directing the steady jettisoning of many of the NP's (unworkable) constitutional proposals, though with De Klerk's agreement.

As 1991 dragged on and the violence continued, damaging uncertainty afflicted the country, exacting a toll on an already troubled economy. Even by the spring, nearly 18 months after De Klerk's speech, the government and the ANC had still not begun to talk about constitutional issues. They were preoccupied with removing obstacles, such as the release of political prisoners, the question of amnesty, the return of exiles, and, above all, ending violence. Mandela's call in January for multiparty talks had been agreed to by the government and other parties, but nothing had yet been done to convene them. The meetings that led to the signing of the National Peace Accord in September had provided valuable experience of multiparty co-operation, but the focus had been on violence, not a Constitution. Nevertheless, reaching agreement was a prelude to the multiparty talks that began in December.

*   *   *

A chance encounter between Meyer and Joe Slovo led to the initiation of arrangements for the Convention for a Democratic South Africa (Codesa). The two men had discussed what was delaying the start of formal constitutional talks; both agreed that the time was ripe. Shortly thereafter, in mid-October, Mandela called for the convening of the talks, whereupon Ramaphosa telephoned Meyer to say that his instructions were that talks could begin: 'When can we start?' Meyer, in turn, was authorised to start the preliminary arrangements for which he and Ramaphosa would be largely responsible.[15]

Delegations from 19 parties and administrations duly assembled at the World Trade Centre near Johannesburg Airport on 20 December 1991, amid high expectations among the public that the uncertainty of the past two years could be ended. As a preliminary, a Declaration of Intent was signed by 16 of the parties. It was a bland document, long on ideals, but short on critical details. Nevertheless, by committing the signatories to a 'united, democratic, non-racial and non-sexist state in which sovereign authority is exercised over the whole of its territory', it showed that South Africans of all persuasions had come a long way towards a final break with apartheid.

Buthelezi's IFP and the governments of 'independent' Ciskei and Bophuthatswana initially declined to sign the Declaration. Buthelezi, joined by the Ciskei government, suspected that the phrase 'an undivided South Africa' precluded the federal option. Bophuthatswana insisted that it could not be party to a document that potentially affected its status without the formal agreement of its government. Subsequently, both the IFP and Ciskei did sign, having been reassured by way of an amendment that 'undivided' did not rule out federalism. Bophuthatswana, led by

President Lucas Mangope, held out, no doubt hoping that this strategy would help to secure a better deal. It was a vain hope: the writing was on the wall for all of the bantustans, their reintegration into an undivided South Africa being merely a matter of time – and sustained pressure.

Apart from its commitment to a non-racial democratic state, the Declaration proclaimed other visionary ideals. Summarised, they included:

- to work to heal the divisions of the past;
- to strive to improve the quality of life of our people;
- to create a climate conducive to peaceful constitutional change;
- to set in motion the process of drawing up and establishing a Constitution;
- that the Constitution will be the supreme law, guarded over by an independent, non-racial and independent judiciary;
- that there will be a multiparty democracy with regular elections on a common voters' roll, with an electoral system to be based on proportional representation;
- a separation of powers with appropriate checks and balances;
- an acknowledgement of cultural diversity; and
- an entrenched and justiciable bill of rights and a legal system that guarantees equality before the law.[16]

The 19 parties and organisations represented at Codesa belonged to two categories: first, what can be described as 'system' parties, including the South African government: the NP, DP, IFP, parties from the Coloured and Indian houses of the Tricameral Parliament and other homeland governments and parties, 15 in all; and secondly, four 'anti-system' organisations, the ANC, the SACP, and the Natal and Transvaal Indian Congresses (which were represented as a single organisation).

Notable absentees were the PAC and the CP. Despite having been involved in some of the preparatory work for Codesa, the PAC declined to participate, alleging that the ANC and the government were 'in cahoots', and that they were initiating all decisions at the preparatory meeting and all other parties were 'rubber stamping' them. Codesa, moreover, was not elected democratically and was incapable of delivering a constituent assembly.[17] The PAC's tactics and its principal policy demand, restoration to the indigenous people of all the land alienated by white settlers, were no doubt part of a strategy of racial outbidding.

Notwithstanding the belief of some of its MPs that boycotting Codesa was unwise, the mainstream CP, buoyed by the hope that its string of by-election victories would enable it to thwart negotiations, refused to

participate. In an advertisement, the CP, HNP and other ultra-right organisations said that Codesa was doomed to failure 'because it does not
have the approval or the support of the majority of the white nation'.
Furthermore, Codesa was 'a recipe for conflict, bloodshed and domination
through numbers' and it was a 'travesty of democracy because different
peoples and different races can never form a single nation'. Non-racialism
was a myth and there could never be freedom without self-government in
one's own territory.[18]

The ANC showed little overt concern about the PAC's attempted racial outbidding, but it was worried by the apparent erosion of De Klerk's
support base indicated by the CP's gains in by-elections. While it would
not budge from its own fundamental principles or soften its criticism of
De Klerk, its recognition of the disaster that would befall South Africa
were the CP to eclipse the NP was brought into sharper focus. Possibly,
the ANC was nudged into greater readiness to make concessions to the
NP; but, more likely, potential catastrophe made the ANC determined
to get its hands on the levers of power sooner rather than later. It also
forced the ANC to acquiesce in the whites-only referendum called by De
Klerk in March 1992 to test support for continuation of the negotiations.
However bitter the recriminations between them, the underlying reality
was that Mandela and De Klerk, and their respective organisations, had
sunk all of their political and moral capital into making a success of the
negotiations: failure would mean disaster – and rivers of blood. In his
autobiography Mandela wrote:

> I never sought to undermine Mr de Klerk, for the practical reason
> that the weaker he was, the weaker the negotiation process. To make
> peace with an enemy, one must work with that enemy, and that en-
> emy becomes your partner.[19]

Even as Codesa got under way, the gulf between the ANC and the NP, as
well as the IFP, remained wide. The ANC's intentions regarding Codesa
were different from those of the NP. Shortly before the opening Joe Slovo
said: 'We don't want to negotiate the Constitution at Codesa, that's the
task of an [elected] representative body.' The NP, he added, would try
to transform Codesa into a constitution-making body, but 'We are going to resist that.'[20] The NP, indeed, hoped that Codesa might produce a
Constitution, but its hopes were tempered by recognition of the ANC's
implacable insistence on an elected constitution-making body. Somehow
a compromise had to be found between two seemingly irreconcilable
positions.

Apart from set speeches delivered by the leaders of each of the delegations, the first session of Codesa was notable for a blazing row between De Klerk and Mandela, conducted in the full glare of the assembled dignitaries and of local and international television. The background, according to De Klerk, was his admonition of Mandela, prior to the signing of the National Peace Accord in September, that the ANC had breached 'every single provision' of the DF Malan Accord, which required the suspension of armed action and related activities by the ANC and MK. Even though MK was no longer an unlawful organisation, the Accord also declared that 'in a democratic society no political party or movement should have a private army'. Mandela may well have retorted that the government's complicity in violence was also in violation of the Accord, and, regarding MK, since South Africa was not yet a democratic society, it was not obliged to disband. Nevertheless, De Klerk's account says that he subsequently received assurances from the ANC that it would honour its commitments under the Accord – which it failed to do. Almost certainly, the truth was more complex: whatever the terms of the Accord, or De Klerk's denials of complicity, significant elements of MK and the state's security forces were out of control, but neither leader could easily acknowledge this.

Mandela had accepted De Klerk's request to make the final speech on day one of Codesa. On the advice of some of his colleagues, De Klerk opted to make a sharp attack on the ANC's alleged violations of the DF Malan Accord. The decision to do so had been preceded on the eve of Codesa by the intensive discussion about whether Codesa should go ahead or whether the NP should postpone it until a satisfactory undertaking to implement the Accord had been received from the ANC. According to Kobie Coetsee, who had contacted the ANC, they had promised to make rapid progress in implementing outstanding issues. The NP's Policy Group eventually reached consensus that it would be 'catastrophic' to cancel Codesa, but that the issue was so serious that it could not be swept under the carpet. Coetsee was instructed to inform Mandela that Codesa would go ahead, but that he should know that De Klerk would make sharply critical remarks about the ANC's breaches of the Accord. Coetsee duly reported that the message had been conveyed to Thabo Mbeki, who promised to inform Mandela. Coetsee also reported that the ANC had expressed understanding for his concern at the delays and the fact that De Klerk would have to take a strong line.[21]

But something went seriously amiss. For reasons that are unclear, the message never reached Mandela, who was taken aback and infuriated by De Klerk's attack. De Klerk described the ANC as the only party at

Codesa with its own armed wing and secret arms caches, which had not been brought under control as required by the DF Malan Accord: 'An organisation which remains committed to an armed struggle cannot be trusted completely when it also commits itself to peacefully negotiated solutions ... we will have a party with a pen in one hand while claiming the right to have arms in the other.'

Believing that he had been tricked into allowing De Klerk the final speech of the day, Mandela strode to the microphone to deliver the most blistering attack ever on a South African head of government. Describing De Klerk as 'the head of an illegitimate minority regime', he denied having any foreknowledge of his attack, despite having had a bilateral discussion with him the previous evening. The gravamen of Mandela's attack was familiar: joint control of MK and its weapons would occur only when the ANC had an effective say in government, which would be 'our government' and the army would be 'our army'. Turning De Klerk's own phrase against him, he accused the government of 'talking peace while at the same time conducting a war against us'. If De Klerk could not control renegade elements in the security forces or stop the illicit disbursement of funds (to Inkatha) 'then he is not fit to be head of government'.[22]

Fortunately, both men's tempers cooled, and in a public show of reconciliation they shook hands. Mandela had made it clear in his onslaught that no useful purpose would be served by the ANC's trying to undermine the NP – or vice versa – 'because we want the National Party to carry the whites in this initiative'. But, as Waldmeir observed, Mandela appeared to regard De Klerk 'as a kind of handmaiden to help him deliver the new South Africa' to the ANC.[23] This was not on De Klerk's agenda, and had it been, his ability to 'carry the whites' would have been destroyed.

The row caused a breach between De Klerk and Mandela that was never fully healed. As noted, Mandela's *ad hominem* attacks wounded De Klerk, who declined, however, to respond in kind. At least the episode dispelled the myth, believed by parties to the left of the ANC and to the right of the NP, that the two parties were in cahoots. It had been made abundantly clear that they were rivals, still separated by wide divisions. Whether it was prudent of De Klerk to have raised the issues in this particular forum is debatable: perhaps it would have been wiser to keep plugging away in bilateral discussions; perhaps he and his colleagues wanted the problem exposed in the most public possible way. In a retrospective interview, some years after he had resigned from the NP, Meyer thought that it had been mistaken because the (failed) attempt to put pressure on the ANC was 'at the wrong time and place, and to our discredit'.[24]

The high drama temporarily overshadowed an important initiative

suggested earlier in De Klerk's speech to overcome seemingly unbridgeable differences about how a Constitution should be drawn up. He proposed a two-phase process: an Interim Constitution would be drafted by
Codesa, in terms of which a fully inclusive Parliament would be elected,
and would thereafter sit as a constitution-making body, producing the
final Constitution, incorporating pre-agreed 'immutable constitutional
principles'. Before coming into operation, the Constitution would have
to be certified by the proposed Constitutional Court as complying with
those principles. Between the election of the interim Parliament and the
ratification of the final Constitution, the country would be governed by
an elected transitional multiparty government. If accepted, De Klerk said,
'the core demands of both sides would be essentially satisfied'.[25] It was
potentially an ingenious way of squaring the circle. But, as the difficulties
experienced at Codesa showed, a settlement was still a long way off.

*   *   *

The business of Codesa was conducted by five Working Groups, with
each party represented on each Working Group by two delegates and two
advisors. The areas of discussion allocated to each group were:
1. To consider the creation of a climate for free political participation
    by levelling the political playing field, curbing intimidation, ending
    political violence, and making recommendations for the release of
    political prisoners and the return of exiles. It had also to consider
    the role of the international community.
2. To consider constitutional principles and how a constitution-mak-
    ing body should function.
3. To consider transitional arrangements, including an interim
    government.
4. To debate the future of the bantustans.
5. To consider time-frames.

The Working Groups were constituted on 20 January 1992 and began to
operate shortly thereafter for two days at the beginning of every week,
enabling parliamentarians, ministers and other functionaries of government to devote the remaining three days to their normal duties. Codesa
had an excessively cumbersome structure, despite the heroic efforts of
the support staff to function efficiently, and the work schedule imposed
enormous strain on, for example, Cabinet ministers who were required
to manage demanding portfolios as well as to engage in even more demanding negotiations. Gerrit Viljoen, the leading intellectual in the NP

and a man listened to with respect across the political spectrum, was an early victim, being forced to retire through illness from Working Group 2, whose deliberations were central to Codesa.

As the most inclusive forum ever assembled in South Africa, it was inevitable that Codesa would eclipse Parliament as the principal focus of politics. This changed, if only temporarily, when De Klerk announced on 24 February 1992 that a referendum among white voters to test their support for continuation of the reform process would be held on 17 March. As noted, the victory of the CP in the Potchefstroom by-election on 19 February had sent an alarm signal to the NP. Potchefstroom had been a safe NP seat since 1915, apart from an interregnum between 1938 and 1948 when it was held by the United Party.

Both the NP and the CP had thrown everything they had into the preceding by-election campaign. De Klerk insists that he did not shy away from the logical consequences of NP policy and there was no attempt to adopt a *verkrampte* stance to woo doubtful Nationalist supporters. The Potchefstroom result was, he said, 'devastating'. It was now uncertain whether the NP could win a general election; and it was equally uncertain whether it could win the referendum that De Klerk had decided to call. At a meeting of the NP's Federal Council on 20 February, when De Klerk announced his decision, there was shock and some resistance; but De Klerk was adamant: he and the NP could not continue with negotiations without obtaining a mandate. De Klerk acknowledged, with some understatement, that NP policies 'had undergone a fair amount of adaptation' since the mandate received in 1989. There was more shock at the ensuing NP caucus meeting when De Klerk informed MPs of his decision. Indeed, he was sure that had the issue gone to a vote a majority would have opposed him. As party leader, however, he was empowered to take the decision: 'I decided to bite the bullet and to resign as leader … if the referendum did not produce a positive result.'[26]

Referendum day was to be 17 March 1992, and the question put to voters was:

> Do you support the continuation of the reform process that the state president started on 2 February 1990 and which is aimed at a new constitution through negotiations?

The referendum would be a decisive encounter. It was no exaggeration to say that the future of the country depended on the outcome. The ANC grumbled about the principle of the referendum's racial exclusivity but acquiesced. Mandela even called for whites to vote 'yes' and warned that a victorious 'no' vote would be a declaration of war against the majority.

The DP threw its weight behind a 'yes' vote, but ran its own vigorous campaign. The referendum would be one of the rare occasions on which English-speaking whites, most of whom were anti-NP voters, could possibly make a decisive difference. Much of the business community, heartened by the steady erosion of sanctions but deeply apprehensive at the possibility of a 'no' victory, publicly supported the 'yes' campaign and opened their wallets to fund it. Another factor that surely influenced voters was the readmission of South Africa to international sport – indeed, the national cricket team was at that very time playing in the World Cup series in Australia, and doing rather well. The entire team publicly called for a 'yes' vote in the knowledge that a 'no' victory would inevitably mean that the barriers to international participation would go up again.

The NP campaigned robustly on the basis of its power-sharing proposals, asking voters to 'vote "yes", if you're scared of majority rule'. A new Constitution 'must contain or address' a range of principles, including:

- Domination by a majority, or the possibility of a one-party state will be precluded;
- Your property will remain your own – no government will be able to confiscate it through expropriation or nationalization;
- A free market economy;
- Job and pension security for civil servants;
- Strong regional government;
- The maintenance of language and cultural rights, including the choice of community-oriented education.[27]

Another leaflet reiterated that Codesa had not usurped the authority of Parliament: consensus-decisions adopted by Codesa would have to pass through the normal parliamentary channels before becoming law. The tenor of much of the NP's campaign rhetoric must have made the ANC blanch, but sensibly they did not intervene. Cosatu, moreover, had been dissuaded from embarking on a mass action campaign directed against the 'whites-only' aspect of the referendum, lest this should boost the 'no' vote.

The NP was merciless in its attacks on the CP and its allies, which accused the NP of having allied itself with the ANC, SACP and Cosatu to bring a communist-dominated black government into power. An NP pamphlet rejected this, declaring communism to be a 'devastating ideology', which had been nourished by the inequalities and frustrations caused by apartheid that the ultra-rightwing was seeking to perpetuate. Propaganda also exploited the AWB's close alliance with the CP, depicting the AWB as armed neo-Nazi thugs. A newspaper advertisement proclaimed: 'free with every CP vote, the AWB and all they stand for.'[28] However zealous the CP was, it could match neither the NP's and DP's access to resources nor their favourable press coverage. Treurnicht, moreover, was denied equal television and radio coverage, which was slanted in favour of a 'yes' vote. All of these factors contributed to the huge 'yes' vote victory – 68.7 per cent of the number of votes cast in an 85 per cent poll. Most voters, it seemed, on being asked, as many were, 'Do you want to talk or shoot?', chose the former.

For the referendum, the country was divided into 15 regions. In only one, Pietersburg in the northern Transvaal, strong CP country, did the 'no' vote win – but not by an overwhelming majority. Even in other regions where the CP held a majority of the parliamentary constituencies, the 'yes' vote won, if only by slender margins. An estimated 79 per cent of English-speaking voters supported the 'yes' vote: over 85 per cent voted 'yes' in Durban and Cape Town and 78 per cent in Johannesburg, these being cities with large concentrations of English-speakers; 38 per cent of Afrikaans-speakers voted 'no'.

For De Klerk, who had fought a tireless campaign, the outcome was a triumph. At the time when he called the referendum, informed estimates and poll data predicted a 55:45 win for the 'yes' vote. De Klerk's personal estimate was even lower, that he would win 53 per cent – a Pyrrhic victory which would give hope to the ultra-right that all was not yet lost. Receiving what he called an 'unambiguous mandate' carried another benefit: it would no longer be necessary to refer the inevitable major constitutional change back to the white electorate.

The referendum strengthened De Klerk's hand and sowed confusion in the ranks of the ultra-right, which fragmented even further. Although the 'no' vote had been comprehensively beaten, dangerous elements remained, now made desperate by the tide of events. There were strong pockets of support for the ultra-right in the security forces, in the bureaucracy and among employees of critical sectors such as mining. There was, moreover, a pool of well-trained and, in many cases, battle-hardened troops who had completed their military service and returned to civilian life. The pool, which could have numbered 250 000, contained men of all political persuasions in the white population. A significant number were probably supporters of the ultra-right who might have responded to a call to arms issued by, say, disaffected generals in the event of a collapse of negotiations and the outbreak of widespread disorder and violence.

The ANC regarded the outcome of the referendum with mixed feelings: obviously there was relief that the menace of the ultra-right had been tamed, and therefore it was no longer necessary for the ANC to restrain its attacks on the NP lest this should play into the hands of the CP and its allies. On the other hand, the ANC believed that the NP's renewed confidence had emboldened it to the point where it had become arrogant, even cocky. It was, as an ANC member put it, content to keep on 'kicking for touch', trying to spin out the negotiating process for as long as possible, meanwhile clinging to power. Mandela was convinced that the government was hoping that 'the longer we [the ANC] waited, the more support we would lose'.[29] Moreover, the ANC believed that the NP's hope for a protracted process would ensure that a Codesa-made Interim Constitution would be difficult, if not impossible, to amend, making it de facto the final Constitution. Strongly entrenched regions with significant powers would not be amenable to reintegration into the more unitary form of state desired by the ANC.

Predictably, the government denied these allegations, but hardliners in the Cabinet wanted as protracted a process as possible, and were reluctant to make concessions to ANC demands. The hardliners were counterbalanced by younger, more pragmatic and *verligte* ministers, like Roelf Meyer, Sam de Beer, Leon Wessels and Dawie de Villiers, who were eager to reach a settlement. They recognised that the longer the negotiations were drawn out the more support the NP might lose. Wessels and De Villiers had both made public apologies for the hurt caused by apartheid, which evoked some resentment among more conservative colleagues.

On becoming Minister of Constitutional Development in May 1992, after Gerrit Viljoen's withdrawal because of ill-health, Meyer also became chairman of the Beleidsgroep vir Hervorming (the Policy Group for Reform), a Cabinet committee consisting of ministers, senior officials and others co-opted as necessary. This committee was responsible for managing the negotiating process and framing policy proposals for consideration by the Cabinet and the State President. Meyer said of some of the senior Cabinet heavyweights that they were less than enthusiastic about the negotiating process and the direction it was taking:

> Against considerable opposition, I sometimes had to insist to cabinet and the president that certain crucial inevitabilities had to be accepted. Certain quarters still regarded the whole process as a tactical exercise to see how little could be 'given away' while retaining as much as possible of the old order. I was not prepared to accept this approach. It was not only fundamentally dishonest but would not contribute to the kind of solutions the country needed … . Not all of us in the [Policy Group for Reform] had made the personal paradigm

shifts which were necessary if we were to achieve the constitutional reform required to be able to face the future with confidence. We had different views on what real democracy meant and on how it could or should be achieved.[30]

Comparable problems were affecting the ANC as the negotiations got under way. There were signs of a greater readiness to reconsider aspects of strategy. Rantete noted a 'sweeping mood of sobriety creeping into the ANC leadership', though this did not imply modification of its goals.[31] Nor was 'tactical flexibility' intended as a concession to what the ANC regarded as the NP's obduracy. De Klerk had insisted that no constitutional vacuum would be allowed to develop: the existing government and the Tricameral Parliament would remain in power until a new Constitution was enacted into law. The ANC was now having second thoughts about the advisability of its demand for an (unelected) interim government of which it would be part. The consequence might be that the ANC would be saddled with responsibility for decisions over which it did not have complete control. As an internal discussion document said:

> The ANC would become part of a structure vested with complete responsibility for running the country. At the same time such an interim government would be a power structure which would be unable to address in any meaningful way the on-going socio-economic crisis, to effectively transform the apartheid power institutions and the racial imbalances which it will inherit at every level. In such circumstances we run the grave risk of discrediting ourselves in the eyes of our constituency.[32]

The risk alluded to was real. Codesa's proceedings took place behind closed doors, heightening suspicions among ANC militants that deals were being cut that compromised what they regarded as principles of near-canonical status. The negotiations at Codesa proceeded at a leisurely pace, partly because of its two-days-per-week schedule and partly because of the intractability of the issues involved, notably in Working Group 2. Workings Groups 1, 3 and 4 made good progress with their respective briefs (Working Group 5, dealing with time-frames, had little to do since it was dependent on the agreements reached in other groups).

By May 1992, agreement in Working Group 2 had not been reached, and worse, seemed incapable of being reached. It came as no surprise when on 15 May the ANC's chief negotiator in the Working Group, Cyril Ramaphosa, announced that the deadlock could not be broken and that the ANC delegation was withdrawing. The proximate cause of the breakdown was the inability of the NP and the ANC to agree on the voting percentages required for the constitution-making body to adopt a new Constitution; but the underlying causes were deeper, going to the heart of the political divide.

Codesa had begun with an encouraging flourish: all but one of the parties agreed on the broad principles contained in the Declaration of Intent. Now it was necessary to move from principles to the mechanics of how power was to be distributed. And how far could Codesa go in deciding upon those mechanics? The ANC wanted the Constitution to be drawn up by an elected constituent assembly, perhaps, as the Harare Declaration allowed, based upon prior agreement on principles between the liberation movement and the regime. The NP government, having conceded the principle of an elected constitution-making body, nevertheless wanted Codesa to draft as much of the Constitution as possible, leaving little for the elected body to do. The ANC wanted exactly the opposite, with as much as possible left over for the elected body.[33]

Of the several substantive constitutional issues that were incapable of resolution two stand out as crucial: the extent to which regions should be allocated significant original powers, and the 'meaningful participation of political minorities'. The first raised the question of federalism, to which the NP, IFP, DP and some of the homeland parties were committed, but which the ANC and its allies viewed with suspicion. The ANC appeared to accept the principle that powers delegated from the centre to lower tiers should be entrenched in the Constitution, but the agreement was more apparent than real. Delegation of powers, in the ANC's view, did not exclude concurrent powers shared by the centre and the regions or the power of the centre to override the regions.

The issue of minority participation yielded little more: agreement was reached in March with the principle that 'a new Constitution should provide for effective democratic participation of minority political parties consistent with democracy', the last three words having been added at the insistence of the ANC. The vagueness of the wording rendered the principle virtually meaningless: it could accommodate the NP's elaborate proposals for minority safeguards and, simultaneously, the ANC's view that proportional representation, the rights of opposition parties and a vigilant civil society gave sufficient possibilities of effective participation to minority parties.

This was the heart of the matter: the NP wanted to see its proposals constitutionally entrenched, while the ANC did not want to see its potentially hegemonic power constitutionally fettered in perpetuity. The ANC and its allies argued that the ANC was a 'catch-all' party that would seek votes from across the racial spectrum. Moreover, the ANC anticipated that parties in a future democratic system would become parties based upon common interests and values, rather than race or ethnicity. Besides, Mandela was frequently on record as distinguishing 'majority rule', which he favoured, from 'black majority rule', which he opposed.

The difficulty with the NP's proposals was that the record of constitutionally-enforced multiparty governments was not encouraging, as earlier examples in Cyprus and Northern Ireland showed. There was, however, a strong case for the argument that broad-based coalitions, which allow the possibility of minority party participation in government, are a *sine qua non* if there is to be any hope of sustaining democracy in deeply divided societies.

The difficulty with the ANC's proposals was that nowhere has 'simple majoritarianism', even if qualified by proportional representation, some degree of federalism and a justiciable bill of rights, succeeded in securing democracy in a divided society. Moreover, examples of party systems that have shifted from being racially or ethnically based to being based around interests and values are rare, if they exist at all. Voting in ethnically/racially divided societies tends strongly to be not only an expression of interests but an affirmation of identity as well. Political competition in such societies, moreover, is liable to strengthen this kind of bloc voting since ethnic or racial solidarity is a political resource that often proves irresistible to politicians.

The lesson to be learned from comparative experience was that constitutions per se can only go some of the way in bridging divisions of the past and creating an institutional framework for peaceful co-existence. The critical variable in securing these goals lies less in complex constitutional architecture than in the development of a political culture in which majority aspirations are tempered by recognition of the need not to ride roughshod over minority interests, and the avoidance of 'winner-take-all' outcomes. Codesa's Working Group 2 revealed profound disagreements about the very nature of democracy that boded ill for reaching a settlement.

The breakdown of Working Group 2, and consequently the entire Codesa enterprise, occurred because of what seemed like a technical, perhaps even trivial, issue. The NP government had accepted the principle of an elected constitution-making body operating within the framework of an Interim Constitution. But who was to draw up the Interim Constitution? Only Codesa was on hand to be able to do so. The ANC accepted this, in spite of the NP's demand that its proposed senate, with

its inflated representation of minority parties, be involved in the constitution-making process. The ANC also insisted that what it termed the
constituent assembly should be subject to a time-frame which required it
to draw up a Constitution within four months: should it not be able to do
so, it would be dissolved and new elections held.

In a debate prior to 15 May, the government insisted on a 70 per cent
majority for decisions in the (elected) constitution-making body, and a 75
per cent majority for decisions concerning the Bill of Rights, regions and
the structure of government. The ANC countered with a demand that the
figure be a two-thirds majority on all issues. After consulting with allies
the ANC appeared to compromise, accepting the 70 per cent figure and 75
per cent for the Bill of Rights, provided that the NP agreed that the senate
be democratically elected and shorn of minority parties' inflated strength.
It demanded also a deadlock-breaking mechanism to ensure that its opponents could not spin out the process, while remaining in power: if the
constitution-making body could not agree on a Constitution within six
months, a draft Constitution acceptable to a simple majority of delegates
would be submitted to a referendum, and if two-thirds of the electorate
supported it, the Constitution would be adopted.

The figures proposed by the NP were carefully calibrated to comply
with what the NP and its allies expected to win in an election: 30 per
cent for the NP and perhaps another 10 per cent for other parties who
shared the NP's view that the ANC should not be able to write its own
Constitution, even though the ANC itself doubted whether it could win a
two-thirds majority – indeed, some opinion polls indicated that the ANC
might win 45 per cent of the vote.[34]

The ANC concluded that the high figures demanded by the NP were a
trap aimed at ensuring that an Interim Constitution drawn up by Codesa
could be kept in force indefinitely because the NP and its allies would
have a veto power over decisions made in the body drafting the final
Constitution.

At the crucial meeting of Working Group 2 on 15 May Cyril Ramaphosa,
the ANC's chief negotiator, went head-to-head with Tertius Delport,
Deputy Minister of Constitutional Development, who had succeeded
Gerrit Viljoen as the NP's leader in the Working Group. Ramaphosa decided to spring his own trap, by agreeing that the ANC would accept voting figures of 70 per cent for the Constitution and 75 per cent for the Bill
of Rights, but demanding that if the constitution-making body failed to
pass the final draft by the required majority within six months, it would
then be submitted to a national referendum, and if more than 50 per
cent of the voters approved it, it would be adopted. De Klerk instructed

Delport to hold firm, pointing out that if Ramaphosa's proposal were adopted, the ANC could simply spin out the process for six months, thereafter submitting its preferred draft to a referendum, which it would very likely win.[35]

Ramaphosa had deliberately engineered the deadlock and the ensuing breakdown of Codesa, saying that he wanted to demonstrate that 'we are dealing with an enemy that will not give in easily'.[36] One may ask how else he expected the 'enemy' to behave, particularly after the bruising referendum a mere two months before in which it had explicitly assured voters of its opposition to majority rule? His comment suggested yet again that the ANC expected the NP to be little more than the midwife who delivered the country into ANC control.

But there was another reason for causing the breakdown: the negotiators at Codesa had become locked into a cosy environment that separated them from their grassroots constituencies. Outside the walls of the World Trade Centre the violence raged on, continuing to ravage communities. The ANC's grassroots were growing increasingly restive. Mkhondo writes:

> CODESA did not falter over a dispute about voting percentages; it faltered because too many people saw it as dragging on interminably and doing little to address black expectations. The ANC was seen by its constituency as lacking aggression and meekly giving in to the government. Disenchantment with the snail-like pace of CODESA threatened to wipe out grassroots support for ANC negotiators, sharply reminding them to pay greater attention to their supporters' demands. The extent to which black frustration and anger limits the ANC's room for negotiation cannot be ignored. Leaders of the ANC and their allies had to show their followers they were tough negotiators.[37]

The breakdown of Codesa signalled the beginning of a long, bleak winter of discontent. Gloom descended on the land, and the economy registered the widely felt decline of confidence. South Africa seemed more polarised than ever.

De Klerk and Mandela met shortly after the breakdown, and both tried unsuccessfully to talk up the achievements of Codesa. True, some of the Working Groups had achieved significant agreements, but the central issues remained unresolved. Mandela acknowledged that the issues upon which Codesa had foundered were 'difficult', but not 'insoluble'.[38] Both he and De Klerk agreed that the negotiating process had to be kept alive.

In reality, neither had any alternative option. Another glimmer of hope was the resurrection of the 'Cyril–Roelf' channel. Meyer records that 10 minutes after Mandela and Ramaphosa had appeared on television to announce that no further negotiations would take place, Ramaphosa telephoned him to ask when they could talk. Throughout the critical months from June to September they remained in regular contact.

Meyer's disquiet over the 'give-as-little-as-you-can' attitude of some of his hardline Cabinet colleagues has been noted. Writing several years after his resignation in 1997 from the NP, he blamed the intransigent stance of the hardliners for the collapse of Working Group 2: he had argued vigorously for accepting the 70 per cent proposal, and making concessions to the ANC as a quid pro quo: 'Afterwards I often asked myself what would have happened if my standpoint had won. We would have got more than we got later on [in 1996] – which was two-thirds and not 70%.'[39]

The cessation of negotiations breathed new zeal into the minds of militants in the ANC alliance, many of whom remained sceptical about negotiations. Some now called for the 'Leipzig Option' – mass demonstrations that would paralyse the country and force the government out of power, as had happened in Leipzig, effectively crippling the communist government of the German Democratic Republic. A forcible seizure of power was a chimerical hope, but 'rolling mass action' could certainly inflict considerable damage on an already reeling economy, as well as on white morale.

The initiative for the mass action campaign was taken by Cosatu, which had been miffed at the rejection of its demand to be represented at Codesa by a separate delegation. In March 1992 it announced a plan for mass action in support of its demands, which included an interim assembly to be appointed by the end of June, elections for a constituent assembly by the end of the year, and a democratic Constitution to be in place by the end of 1993. It threatened a general strike if its constitutional and economic demands were not met.

Cosatu's plans included marches, demonstrations, factory occupations and boycotts, in addition to stayaways and a general strike of not less than three days. According to the general secretary, Jay Naidoo, mass action would be used as an alternative to Codesa, a view that accorded with the ANC's belief that rolling mass action 'would display to the government the extent of our support around the country and show that the people … were not prepared to wait forever for their freedom.'[40]

The programme was for a four-phase campaign, beginning on 16 June (the anniversary of the beginning of the Soweto Uprising in 1976) and proceeding through a general strike and, finally, to 'exitgate', at which point the government was supposed to yield power.

The campaign was to be a trial of strength: could the ANC and its allies hold the country to ransom and thereby secure political gains? There was little point in huffing and puffing about 'blackmail'. The DP's chief negotiator, Colin Eglin, wisely observed that the ANC had made a political assessment that it was time to mobilise to secure its constituency: 'Without recourse to the vote, one of the few remaining options is mass action.' But, as he acknowledged, it placed the negotiation process at risk because mass action could develop its own momentum and possibly could be hijacked by people who did not want a negotiated transition.[41]

*   *   *

Exactly one day after the start of the mass action campaign, an appalling episode occurred in the Southern Transvaal township of Boipatong, south of Johannesburg. Late on the night of 17 June, residents of the adjoining KwaMadala hostel, nearly all of them Zulu supporters of the IFP, attacked Boipatong and the surrounding informal settlement of Slovo Park. Forty-five people were killed and 22 severely injured. The episode proved to be a turning point in the transition process, and therefore deserves special attention.

The ANC was outraged, and Mandela led the charge with some wild accusations against De Klerk, whose visit to Boipatong shortly after the tragedy to express his sympathy with residents had to be aborted because of the residents' hostility. De Klerk hints that the demonstration had been organised by the ANC, who allegedly had also instructed the community to withhold co-operation from the police in their inquiries.

In an emotional speech in Boipatong on 21 June, Mandela accused De Klerk of shedding crocodile tears for the victims and of having the capacity to stop the violence but not using it:

> ... just as the Nazis in Germany killed people not because they were a threat to the state, but because they were Jews, the National Party regime is killing our people simply because they are black. They are killing our people in an effort to stop the ANC getting into power .... I can no longer explain to our people why we keep on talking peace to men who are conducting a war against us, men of corruption who kill innocent people.[42]

An exchange of acrimonious letters followed, with Mandela repeating his accusation of the regime's complicity in the violence, and De Klerk vehemently denying this as 'a lie'. In an annexure to his letter to Mandela of 2

July, De Klerk demanded that the ANC account for its direct and indirect involvement in over 30 000 incidents of violence and the murder of over 6 000 persons since February 1990.

The negotiation process, dormant since mid-May, now seemed all but dead, although Mandela stopped short of saying so, declaring it to be 'in crisis', and ratcheting up the ANC's demands as a condition of resumption. De Klerk had no intention of giving in, declaring some of them to be 'outrageous'. He requested a face-to-face meeting with Mandela, which was rebuffed, Mandela saying that such a meeting 'would suggest that we had something to talk about, and at the time we did not'.[43]

Subsequent investigations of what had happened revealed a different account from Mandela's. Two journalists, Rian Malan and Denis Beckett, unearthed information which showed that the murderous attack, admittedly a peculiarly appalling one, was the latest in an ongoing series of clashes. According to an IFP informant, the KwaMadala hostel was 'a refugee camp for Zulu-speaking Inkatha members driven from their homes by ANC-inspired arson and violence'. The ANC, on the other hand, produced a 30-page document listing acts of violence committed by hostel dwellers. 'The area is a virtual war zone inhabited by people who hate and fear each other.'

Who threw the first stone (metaphorically and sometimes literally) was not possible to ascertain, any more than it was in Natal. According to Malan and Beckett, the build-up to the massacre of 17 June began on 13 June, when ANC-supporting comrades started to hunt down Zulu, some of whom were not even IFP supporters. A woman was necklaced because of her romantic involvement with a Zulu hostel dweller, and two other IFP members were also killed thereafter. The police appeared powerless; indeed, they were unaware of what had happened. The local police commandant told the journalists that there was so much violence he could no longer keep track of it: 'He showed us a tome containing brief records of just four or five days' worth of mayhem .... It was the size and thickness of a London telephone directory.'[44]

But what of the main charge made by Mandela and ANC-aligned organisations of police complicity in the attack, which in turn proved De Klerk's culpability? The TRC's finding in 1998 did little more than recycle earlier claims made by the ANC, that:

> KwaMadala hostel residents, together with the police, planned and carried out an attack ... that the police colluded with the attackers and dropped them off at Slovo Park .... white men with blackened faces participated in the attack.[45]

In a devastating critique of the TRC's findings, Anthea Jeffery showed how the TRC had ignored earlier conclusions, which, even if the TRC had disagreed with them, ought to have been challenged, and if necessary rebutted. De Klerk's undertaking to ensure that those responsible for the massacre were brought to justice was fulfilled in June 1994 after some 30 hostel dwellers had been prosecuted: six were each sentenced to 18 years' imprisonment and 19 others received sentences of between 10 and 15 years. The trial judge examined the alleged role of police involvement with care, since it was a pivotal issue, but found that there was no truth in the allegation. Indeed, some 120 witnesses from the communities that had been attacked offered no evidence that police vehicles had ferried the assailants into the area. In 1999 the Supreme Court of Appeal upheld the trial court's finding.[46]

The Goldstone Commission also investigated the massacre. Goldstone had been asked by De Klerk to appoint a leading international jurist to sit with him in the inquiry. Goldstone's choice was former Chief Justice of India, Proful Bhagwati, who readily accepted. He also requested and obtained the assistance of a leading British criminologist, Professor Peter Waddington, and two senior officers from the London Metropolitan Police. Neither the Commission nor its co-opted experts could find evidence of police involvement, although Waddington made some scathing criticisms of the inefficiency of the police's investigation.[47]

The Boipatong massacre entered the mythology of the struggle, and provided encouragement for the proponents of the Leipzig Option. There was a sequel to the massacre in 2000 when the TRC's own amnesty committee granted amnesty to the IFP supporters from KwaMadala Hostel, finding that they had perpetrated the killings on their own, without police help, and in revenge for repeated attacks by ANC supporters. The committee also found that alleged 'eyewitness' evidence of police involvement was 'untruthful' or mistaken.[48]

Unhappily for De Klerk and his party, by the time that refutation of police involvement in the massacre emerged, the damage had been done. The ANC consolidated its occupation of the moral high ground, with much international opinion accepting its version of the episode, although the Security Council of the United Nations declined to apportion blame for the violence at its meeting in mid-July. The violence and the breakdown of negotiations led President George H Bush to offer United States mediation in the conflict, but both De Klerk and Mandela declined, saying in effect that South Africans would sort out their problems by themselves.[49] Nevertheless this was a signal by the international community of intensified diplomatic efforts to get the process back on track.

Without implying that the ANC welcomed the Boipatong massacre – Mandela's distress and grief were heartfelt – it breathed life into the mass action campaign. The winter of discontent would continue. At an emergency meeting of the NEC on 23 June 1992, the ANC broke off negotiations, including bilateral negotiations. It would keep the situation under continuous review, and its response would be determined by the 'De Klerk regime's' reaction to the ANC's demands for an interim government of national unity and the election of a sovereign constituent assembly. Furthermore, it demanded the termination of all covert operations by members of the security forces, the phasing out of migrant labourer hostels and a ban on the carrying of all dangerous weapons in public, including so-called cultural weapons. It called upon the United Nations Security Council to convene and discuss measures to stop the violence.

Mandela declared that 'the negotiation process is completely in tatters ... the gulf between the oppressed and the oppressor has become unbreachable'.[50] In his address to the Security Council on 15 July, he reiterated many of the allegations levelled against De Klerk, insisting that the violence was

> ... a cold-blooded strategy of state terrorism intended to create the conditions under which the forces responsible for the introduction and entrenchment of the system of apartheid would have the possibility of imposing their will on a weakened democratic movement at the negotiations table.

Mandela's speech also contained several sideswipes at Inkatha, which, he alleged, was financed by the government and had 'permitted itself to become an extension of the Pretoria regime, its instrument and surrogate'.[51] Buthelezi, who also addressed the Security Council, was infuriated by these accusations, which further alienated him from the negotiating process. Subsequent developments would increase his fury, with dangerous consequences.

Mandela's anger was genuine. He recognised that the apparent failure of the negotiations to deliver tangible results played into the hands of the ANC's militants, who now demanded direct action with increasing stridency:

> Calls for a seizure rather than a transfer of power dominated the language of grassroots activists. The Boipatong slaughter sparked anger, not only against the suspected perpetrators, but also against

leaders of the ANC who were perceived as having been too soft in their negotiating stance at CODESA.[52]

Mass action, with the support of the PAC, dominated the political stage for the next three months. Apart from marches, demonstrations and other forms of protest that occurred in many parts of the country, a national stayaway was called for on 3–4 August, to be followed on 5 August by the occupation of city centres and other strategic points. The success of the stayaway was disputed: Cosatu, which had taken the lead in orchestrating the mass action campaign, claimed that 90 per cent of formal sector employees, or four million people, had stayed away on day 1, but spokesmen for business countered that the number was far less: since agriculture, mining and the public service had not been affected, hardly more than 2.5 million workers could have stayed away.[53] The stayaway was nevertheless costly, in terms of both lost production and business confidence, already badly shaken by the bleak political outlook. Moreover, it was a portent of possibly worse disruption to come.

Mandela was unconcerned at the alarm expressed by the business community: 'Our economy has been so mismanaged it can hardly be hurt by mass action.'[54] But soon after saying this he would receive a severe jolt on being shown evidence of the dramatic downward spiral of the economy. Regarding itself as 'a government in waiting', the ANC did not want to inherit an economic wasteland.

Yet another appalling slaughter occurred on 7 September 1992 at Bisho, capital of the 'independent' Ciskei. It occurred during a march of an estimated 70 000 people organised by the ANC to protest against the authoritarian rule of Ciskei's military dictator, Oupa Gqozo. The Ciskei was part of the Eastern Cape, historically the ANC's heartland, but under Gqozo free political activity was prohibited, and violations were savagely dealt with. The ANC's NEC had authorised the march, believing no doubt that the ramshackle bantustan and its unpopular leader was a more vulnerable target than those in white-controlled areas. The aim was to march from the South African side of the 'border' into Bisho itself and hold a 'people's assembly' for 24 hours to demand freedom of speech and association.[55]

Despite pleas from De Klerk to Mandela to call off the march, it went ahead and ended in tragedy. The Ciskeian authorities' attitude, hardened by threats from ANC leaders that the marchers would occupy Bisho until Gqozo gave up control, refused to allow the demonstrators into Ciskei. Eventually, however, a decision by the Chief Magistrate of Ciskei, made in the early hours of the day of the march, allowed the demonstration to take place in the Bisho stadium, a stone's throw from the border. Senior officials of the National Peace Secretariat urged the organisers to adhere to the ruling and hold the demonstration *inside* the stadium. 'I told them I could not assure them of that,' responded Ronnie Kasrils, one of the principal organisers.[56] It was apparent that there was no intention of heeding the ruling.

Counsel for the ANC and its allies subsequently told the Goldstone Commission, which investigated the episode, that by the time the Magistrate's decision was received, 'the [ANC] alliance had firmly committed itself to a march into Bisho', which it regarded as a fundamental right and the Ciskei regime's attempts to curtail it as invalid. That a human rights culture was poorly developed in Ciskei would be a costly lesson for a breakaway group of marchers, led by Kasrils, who had run out of the stadium through a gap in the razor wire barricades which provided a route into Bisho.

Trigger-happy Ciskei soldiers opened fire 'for a prolonged period and quite indiscriminately,' the Commission found. Twenty-nine demonstrators were killed and hundreds were injured. In a meticulous report, the Goldstone Commission condemned the behaviour of the Ciskeian soldiers in the strongest terms; it also condemned the ANC for having approved its followers' running through the gap as irresponsible, unfortunate and unjustified. The Commission noted with approval how mass organisations and the police had quickly learned to co-operate in ensuring that demonstrations went off peacefully 'which would have been unthinkable only a short while ago'. But if organisations violated the ground-rules and engaged in unpredictable actions, tragedies like the Bisho episode could occur.[57]

The Bisho episode spelt an end to the Leipzig Option and tilted the balance back towards negotiation. Mandela, apparently angry with both De Klerk and his own militants, nevertheless defended Kasrils. He realised that however much frustration led to the tragedy, the ANC's image had been damaged, and that a return to the negotiating table was the only feasible option.[58] A proposed march on Ulundi, the capital of KwaZulu, where even more volatile conditions could be expected, was quietly dropped.

In an interview, Mandela acknowledged that 'loyal friends' of the ANC, both local and domestic, had expressed 'reservations' about what had happened, but he insisted that the primary responsibility was Gqozo's. Nevertheless, he committed the ANC to adhering to the guidelines for mass action laid down by the NPA and the Goldstone Commission. He denied that there was conflict between radicals and moderates in the ANC, but conceded that 'if we don't do something visible to show that we are fighting against oppression, those who are demanding the resumption of the armed struggle are going to prevail.'[59]

Intense diplomatic pressure and recognition of the danger that mass action could spin out of control combined with another looming factor, impending economic crisis, to push the ANC and the NP government back to the negotiating table. The economic crisis had its roots in the mismanagement of the economy over several decades. The economy had performed poorly since the mid-1970s; low growth had continued through the 1980s, and negative growth had been recorded in 1990 and 1991. Inflation hovered around 15 per cent, business confidence had declined, foreign and domestic investment was sharply reduced, and there had been a substantial outflow of capital that had accelerated in the 1980s. The imposition of sanctions and the refusal of foreign banks in 1985 to roll over loans aggravated the situation. Apart from the worldwide recession, South Africa was in the grip of a devastating drought, which not only severely affected the agricultural sector, but also had knock-on effects on consumers.

Another source of uncertainty was the ANC's commitment to nationalisation of the commanding heights of the economy, including land, as proclaimed by the Freedom Charter. Mandela had reiterated this commitment shortly after his release. It became an article of faith in the ANC, especially among its radicals. Nevertheless, as the fears of the (white) business community and many in the international business world became apparent, a less dogmatic attitude was adopted. In May 1992 the ANC assumed a more pragmatic stance: companies would be nationalised according to the balance of evidence rather than on ideological criteria. Nationalisation remained the ANC's policy, but it was not intended to be a 'holy cow'. Decisions would be taken in the light of the international climate and the need to generate confidence and, hence, growth.[60]

It was into this economic morass that Derek Keys, a successful businessman, stepped in May 1992 as Minister of Finance. He proved to be an inspired choice. He set about constructing a 'picture of reality' in the form of a number of slides (prepared by a senior banking executive) that could be shown to illustrate the problems faced by the economy. The picture showed that since 1980 funds that should have gone into investment had, instead, gone into government consumption and expenditure, supporting failed bantustans and fighting insurgencies at home and in the region. The consequence was that real growth, above the rate of population increase (2.2 per cent in 1992), became less and less possible. Macroeconomic trends pointed to an unsustainable situation.

Keys seized every opportunity to present what became known as 'the dirty pictures' to those concerned. He warned that government was verging on the brink of a debt trap caused by the excessive government expenditure and consumption that was leading to dangerous deficits. At a presentation to the ANC's economic team in August 1992, Keys's obvious integrity and honesty of purpose impressed the ANC, notably Trevor Manuel, who readily agreed to the creation of a National Economic Forum, comprising representatives of business, labour, government and the ANC. As Waldmeir observes, Keys confronted ANC policy-makers with the unpleasant reality that they would not inherit a rich country with lots of surplus cash to devote to black economic upliftment: 'They would have tragically limited room for economic manoeuvre.'[61]

Manuel briefed the ANC leadership, armed with the 'dirty pictures'.[62] It had a galvanising effect, and played no small part in expediting the ANC's return to negotiations. Another consequence was to induce the ANC to dilute or even abandon some of its more radical economic ideas.

*   *   *

Throughout the winter of 1992 Cyril Ramaphosa and Roelf Meyer had remained in communication via the 'channel'. During the negotiations Meyer had become increasingly uncomfortable with the NP's constitutional proposals, becoming convinced that 'a true participatory democracy' was the only option:

> I was determined not to have anything to do with the variety of unrealistic schlenters ['fast ones'] and tricks which were still thought by some on our side to be viable options. Loaded majorities, rotating presidents, weird protective mechanisms for minorities (meaning whites, in this context) and the like would simply not bring the stability a new constitution had to ensure – apart from having had no chance of being accepted by other parties. A truly democratic constitution, based on individual rights and with all the necessary inbuilt checks and balances to ensure the separation of the powers of the state, was the only option .... And we had to accept the full consequences of such a dispensation. It was not always easy to sell this concept to my colleagues.[63]

In spite of rifts in the Cabinet, agreement was reached on constitutional proposals drafted by Francois Venter, a legal academic from Potchefstroom who was one of the government's advisors. The proposals were appended to De Klerk's reply of 2 July to Mandela during their exchange of salvoes. They dealt with principles that should govern a transitional dispensation, including:

- A transitional Constitution must be a complete Constitution.
- It should replace the current Westminster system with a constitutional state.
- It should accommodate South Africa's diversity of community interests.
- It should be bicameral, with an executive council directly elected by all voters, which, in turn, would appoint the Cabinet.
- An independent judiciary, with judges appointed by a non-political body.
- A charter of justiciable rights.
- Autonomous regional and local government.
- Special provisions to safeguard the army, police, the auditor-general and other state functionaries against political manipulation.
- Amendment of the transitional Constitution would require a 70 per cent majority and 75 per cent for the charter of rights.
- If the transitional Constitution were not replaced within three years, a general election would be held in terms of the Constitution.
- The transitional Constitution could be amended or replaced only within the framework of general constitutional principles agreed to at Codesa and certified as complying with them by a constitutional chamber of the Appellate Division of the Supreme Court.

Venter's proposals satisfied Meyer's criteria, and after their approval by Cabinet they became the basis of the NP government's negotiating position. They represented a significant change from the NP's earlier proposals: gone were the 'unrealistic schlenters and tricks' to which Meyer objected. Apparently the NP had acquiesced in majority rule – though subject to checks on the majority's power. The sovereignty of Parliament, which enabled it to make or unmake any law, had been a principal feature of South Africa's traditional Westminster-style system: the proposed constitutional state fettered parliamentary powers in significant ways.

De Klerk's approval was obviously pivotal. Theoretically he could have dug in his heels after the breakdown of negotiations and resisted ANC demands, but he was savvy enough to recognise that, especially after Boipatong, the tide had turned in the ANC's favour, and he also realised that it was critical to the country's interests that negotiations be resumed and pushed through to a conclusion as soon as possible, even if this meant making significant concessions to the ANC. Meyer writes:

> At the time, the negotiating team and I enjoyed the president's full confidence. He supported us in cabinet on most of the important issues and encouraged us – and me personally – to carry on in the direction that had been taken .... Everyone of a realistic view – especially the president himself – knew by then that the tide of real change and reform had gained its own momentum and would have to be carried through to its full consequences.[64]

In the run-up to the signing by De Klerk and Mandela of the Record of Understanding on 26 September 1992, three difficult issues presented as demands by the ANC had to be resolved: the banning of dangerous weapons, including those carried by Zulu on ceremonial occasions, the fencing of hostels, which housed mainly Zulu migrant workers, and the release of all remaining political prisoners. As the first two were of importance to Inkatha, both Meyer and De Klerk had held prior discussions with Buthelezi, seeking to allay his suspicions that a deal with the ANC was about to be cut behind his back. Both emphasised that the objective of bilaterals with the ANC was to persuade them to return to the negotiating table.

On September 17 De Klerk and Buthelezi met for two hours in which they discussed the ANC's demands, the Goldstone Commission's recommendations on hostels and the issue of releasing political prisoners. According to De Klerk, Buthelezi was noncommittal, though it was clear that he had not liked what he heard.[65] Buthelezi's account of the meeting is somewhat different: he repeated what he had said before, namely that the ANC's approach was that all that was necessary was agreement between the government and the ANC. He expressed further demands, including the disbandment of MK; the seating of the Zulu king and the KwaZulu government (in addition to Inkatha) at the negotiating table; and that the government had to cease creating the perception that negotiations were seen as bilaterals between De Klerk and Mandela. Furthermore, he told De Klerk that Inkatha was reviving federal proposals that had been drawn up by the KwaZulu Natal Indaba in 1986.[66] As De Klerk anticipated, serious problems with Buthelezi lay ahead.

All three of the ANC's demands posed difficulty, but none caused De Klerk more anguish than the question of releasing the remaining political prisoners. He had accepted the guidelines drawn up by Norgaard, and many political prisoners had been released; but the ANC's demand, presented emphatically by Mandela, was for the release of all of its imprisoned members, regardless of the severity of their crimes. They included MK operative Robert McBride, who had placed a car bomb outside a Durban bar, resulting in the deaths of three young women, and others convicted of 'necklace' and other murders (one of whom said on release that 'I felt happy watching him burn'.[67])

De Klerk was outraged by Mandela's insistence on their release, and his 'bullying tactics' in threatening to call off their forthcoming meeting. In a telephone conversation Mandela warned De Klerk to accede to his demands: 'Because you know in the end you are going to give in. Because if you don't we are going to humiliate you. And I will see to it that that happens.'[68] De Klerk's initial inclination was 'to turn Mandela down flat' and risk a further delay in resuming negotiations. A number of his Cabinet colleagues, however, argued that he should acquiesce in the interests of the bigger issue. He notes that it was possible that some of the securocrats favoured the virtually unrestricted definition of a political crime in their own interests: when a new government was in power a number of them feared that they could be prosecuted for human rights violations, including murder. Were this to happen, the previous release of convicted ANC murderers might serve as a precedent for their being granted amnesty.[69]

De Klerk faced a painful dilemma: he could not release convicted ANC members without also releasing whites convicted of politically motivated crimes. The most controversial in the latter category was the sickening case of Barend Strydom, a former policeman, who claimed to be leader of a lunatic fringe group calling themselves the *Wit Wolwe* (White Wolves). In November 1988 Strydom had cold-bloodedly killed seven Africans in the centre of Pretoria before he was overpowered and disarmed by a courageous African passerby. It was ascertained that he had murdered another African shortly before. Strydom was sentenced to death, but escaped the gallows because the death penalty had been suspended. On his release from prison in 1992, he showed no remorse, maintaining that his victims were 'enemies of the Afrikaner people and were justifiably killed'.[70] The mentality of Strydom and others of his ilk was illustrated by another comment made by him:

> Each black person threatens the continued existence of whites, even an 88-year old woman. They are known to breed very fast: Scientists have shown that the oxygen is decreasing. This is the fault of blacks. They are threatening the life of the entire planet.[71]

De Klerk's distaste for the indemnity legislation he had to push through Parliament was compounded by the no-win political situation in which he had been landed: many whites were angered by the release of convicted ANC members, who were by far the greatest beneficiaries of the legislation; and many blacks were angered by the release of Strydom. On both counts De Klerk was politically damaged. The disagreement between the government and the ANC was reflected in the Record of Understanding, and the issue of the identification of those to be released was deferred for further attention. Nevertheless the parties agreed that 'all prisoners whose imprisonment is related to political conflict of the past and whose release can make a contribution to reconciliation should be released'. What 'contribution' the release of the likes of Strydom and the necklace murderer quoted above could make was not clear. But, as Mkhondo observes, 'the more extreme the case, the more it brought home the price that has to be paid for reconciliation'.[72]

The government had already shifted ground, beginning with De Klerk's acceptance of a two-phase process of constitution-making, which he announced at the opening of Codesa in December 1991. Moreover, the 'schlenters and tricks' had been dropped from NP proposals.

In his introductory remarks before the meeting with Mandela on 26 September, he said:

> I believe that it is of fundamental importance that we must move as quickly as possible to the situation of a government of national unity, a government of national reconciliation – representative of all role-players. I believe that – under the leadership of such a government of national unity – we must move as quickly as possible to a completely new constitutional dispensation.[73]

These comments reflected the shift in De Klerk's position. Crucially, they were mirrored by a strategic shift in Joe Slovo's thinking. Even as early as the time of the collapse of Codesa in May, Slovo had come round to the idea of a government of national unity, differing from De Klerk's proposal in that it would only be a temporary device.

Slovo committed his thoughts to a paper that was circulated privately and published subsequently in the SACP's journal, *African Communist*.[74] Slovo's ideas opened the way for a historic compromise with the government – but not before fierce debate in the ANC. Slovo's major premise was that the ANC was not dealing with a defeated enemy, which made the revolutionary seizure of power an unrealistic goal: there was 'no prospect of forcing the regime's unconditional surrender across the table'. The outcome of negotiations would inevitably be less than perfect when measured against the liberation movement's long-term objectives: if such an outcome were unacceptable 'then we should cease raising false expectations by persisting with negotiations'.

Slovo warned against underestimating the danger of counter-revolution following a major transformation. The extreme right would target whites in the bureaucracy and security forces who feared for their economic security: because racism had given them a monopoly of skills and experience, their potential for destabilising a new democracy was enormous. Consideration should be given to measures that would undercut their insecurity by honouring existing contracts and pension rights. (As the ANC would learn, to its cost, solicitude for the security of civil servants, police and soldiers could not be limited to whites: it had also to benefit their counterparts in the bloated bureaucracies and armies of the homelands.)

The key test for the acceptability of a compromise, Slovo continued, was that it did not permanently block the move to non-racial democratic rule. It was necessary, therefore, to lay down certain 'bottom lines':

- The future Constitution had to be drafted by a democratically elected, sovereign constitution-making body.
- This body would be limited only by the Declaration of Intent adopted by Codesa and such other *general* constitutional principles which the key actors agreed should be binding.
- The powers and functions of regions must be determined by the constitution-making body.
- Effective structures had to be put in place to ensure a free and fair election.
- Time-frames and deadlock-breaking mechanisms had to be provided for the constitution-making body.
- The Tricameral Parliament and the executive had to be dissolved upon the election of the constitution-making body, which would also serve as a legislative body in the interim.
- No minority veto in any shape or form would be tolerated.
- The entrenchment of compulsory power-sharing as a permanent feature of a future Constitution was unacceptable.
- The constitution-making body could not be bound in such a way that a future democratic state would be constitutionally prevented from effectively intervening to redress racially accumulated imbalances in all spheres of life.

Despite these boundaries that compromises could not be allowed to cross, there were 'certain retreats from previously held positions which would create the possibility of a major positive breakthrough in the negotiating process without permanently hampering real democratic advance'. The principal retreat was a 'sunset' clause in the new Constitution that would provide for compulsory power-sharing for a fixed number of years in the period immediately following adoption of the Constitution. The executive would be composed on a basis of representation that was proportional to the election results. The power-sharing executive would take decisions according to procedures 'which would not paralyse its functioning'.

Secondly, the boundaries of regions (later termed provinces) and their powers and functions would be determined exclusively by the constitution-making body – but, Slovo argued, the ANC should make its position clear in all essential detail. Was it unprincipled, he asked, rhetorically, for both main parties (the ANC and the NP) to attempt to reach a bilateral understanding on those issues to which they would be committed in the constitution-making process? This raised the tricky question whether the new Constitution was to be unitary, as the ANC demanded, or federal, as the NP, Inkatha, Democratic Party and other minor parties demanded.

None of these 'retreats' or concessions would permanently block the way to 'real democracy', but they would facilitate the negotiation process and 'would situate us indisputably in the moral high ground and weaken the capacity of the more extreme hard liners within the regime's camp to block an early agreement.'[75]

Both Thabo Mbeki and Mandela had hinted at a similar deal earlier, but neither had spelt out proposals with the same detail as Slovo had done. In May 1991 Mandela told a predominantly Afrikaner group in Stellenbosch that simple majority rule 'may not be enough to work purely on one-person one-vote, because every national group [meaning the broad colour categories] would like to see that the people of their flesh and blood are in government'. Subsequently, he said:

> The ordinary man ... must look to our structures and see that as a coloured man I am represented ... and an Indian man must also be able to say, 'I am represented.' And the whites must say, 'There is Gerrit Viljoen. I have got representation' ... especially in the first few years of democratic government ... [we may have to do] something to show that the system has got an inbuilt mechanism which makes it impossible for one group to suppress the other.[76]

Mandela's generosity of spirit, and, even more, Slovo's concrete proposals attracted strong criticism from more radical ANC and SACP supporters. Pallo Jordan, a bright Marxist intellectual (though not an SACP member), weighed in with an attack on Slovo for assuming that the ANC and the NP could co-operate in government when their relationship was one of conflict. Moreover, his proposals would entrench in power a bureaucracy with no sympathy for the ANC's constituency and an interest in undermining democracy. If implemented, the proposals 'would amount to capitulation to some of the core objectives of the regime'.[77] Similar objections came from other radicals. More would follow when the deal was done, and the ANC and the NP had agreed to the idea of a government of national unity (or GNU, as it came to be termed).

The issue was not discussed at the signing of the Record of Understanding. It was still a hot potato in the ranks of the ANC, and it was not until the meeting of the ANC's NEC in November that Slovo's proposals were accepted – and then only after a two-day debate in which 62 of the 80 members spoke.[78] Acceptance proved to be a critical ingredient of the eventual settlement.

Apart from the difficult issues mentioned above, the Record of Understanding created the framework within which subsequent negotiations would take place. The agreement included proposals for:

- A democratically elected constitution-making body that would be bound only by agreed constitutional principles, functioning within a fixed time-frame and having adequate deadlock-breaking mechanisms.
- The constitution-making body would act as an interim Parliament, and there would be an interim GNU.
- Provision would be made for national and regional government during the transition, as well as justiciable rights and freedoms.

Furthermore, agreement was reached on the right to peaceful mass action within the parameters established by the National Peace Accord and the Goldstone Commission. The ANC and the NP committed themselves 'to do everything in their power to calm down tension and to finding ways and means of promoting reconciliation'. The ANC agreed urgently to consult its constituency about its current programme of mass action.[79]

Buthelezi's reaction was predictable – and immediate. For him, the Record of Understanding was a 'betrayal': he would not be bound by its terms, nor would he return to the negotiations until MK had been disbanded and a multiparty negotiating forum had agreed to restructure the process in such a way that it would no longer be vulnerable to ANC disruption. He maintained that an elected constitution-making body could not be representative in the existing climate of intimidation. He was dismayed by the proposed ban on 'cultural weapons', pointing out that ANC supporters were regularly armed with sophisticated guns. As far as the fencing off of the hostels was concerned, it resembled 'ethnic cleansing in Yugoslavia'.[80]

464 THE RISE AND FALL OF APARTHEID

Buthelezi's anger marked the end of the road in his relationship with De Klerk; his earlier respect and trust had evaporated, despite De Klerk's efforts to persuade him that the bilateral talks with the ANC were no more than an effort to restart the negotiations. There had never been a formal alliance between the NP and Inkatha, despite the ANC's insistence that Inkatha was essentially a puppet of the government. Nevertheless, there were significant commonalities: both parties favoured a federal system, a market-driven economy, and the formation of a bloc to oppose the ANC's hegemonic aspirations. If Buthelezi now found the NP untrustworthy, and believed that it had lost control of the negotiating process (which, in fact, it had never really had), the NP considered Buthelezi to be an awkward and prickly character, and therefore an unreliable ally.

For Buthelezi, it had now become a trial of strength: could his support base, largely confined to KwaZulu and Natal, flex its muscles sufficiently to thwart a deal between the ANC and the NP; a deal that, he believed, would inevitably see an ANC-dominated process attempting to dismantle not only the homeland institutions, but also the institution of traditional leaders, including conceivably the Zulu monarchy? Buthelezi's fears were not unfounded: younger militants in the ANC were contemptuous of an institution that smacked of backward 'tribalism', especially if it provided the scaffolding for Inkatha's power. The monarch, in the person of Goodwill Zwelithini, who was Buthelezi's nephew, however, was widely revered among Zulu (of all political stripes) – and for that reason was an important political resource, which was effectively controlled by Buthelezi.

Buthelezi gave warnings of serious conflict if the ANC and NP tried to ride roughshod over Inkatha's vital interests:

> If anyone looking to the future of South Africa expects Inkatha to vanish, they [had] better go and reread their Zulu history ... . I serve [notice] that Inkatha is a national political force and the KwaZulu government is an historical reality which can only be ignored at the peril of the negotiation process.[81]

These comments indicated that Buthelezi, deeply offended at not being regarded as one of the big three leaders, was determined to show that a settlement could not be achieved without his agreement. Even so, his position continued to weaken: his support base outside rural KwaZulu was shrinking, and as foreign perceptions of his apparent obstructiveness increased, international support declined.[82]

Buthelezi's tactics, encouraged by hardline white advisers, had knock-on effects on both the ANC and the NP. Angry ANC militants in Natal stepped up their anti-Inkatha invective; but Buthelezi's demand for federalism contributed to the ANC's having a closer look at the federal option. Conservatives in the NP, unhappy at the concessions that De Klerk had made, took a more favourable view of Inkatha's strategy and proposals, and retained the hope that an alliance with Inkatha could be formed.

In the immediate aftermath of the Record of Understanding, Buthelezi made a desperate move to establish an anti-ANC bloc: on October 6 the so-called Concerned South Africans Group (Cosag) was formed in Johannesburg: it was an improbable grouping of white rightwing organisations, including the CP, the Afrikaner Volksunie and the Afrikaner Vryheidstigting, and homeland leaders, Buthelezi, Gqozo (Ciskei) and Lucas Mangope (Bophuthatswana). Cosag was (loosely) united in opposition to the trend of the negotiations: it demanded the abolition of Codesa and its replacement by a more representative body; a halt to the implementation of the Record of Understanding, and the disbandment of MK, before negotiations could be resumed. The formation of the group, however, could not conceal major divisions of strategy and goals. Even among the Afrikaner organisations there were differences about where a *volkstaat* should be established, and whether to participate in negotiations. Gqozo, Mangope and Buthelezi shared an interest in holding on to their homeland fiefdoms, but only Buthelezi could claim a large support base. Moreover, the racism of the white rightwingers was soon apparent and soured relations with their African counterparts.[83]

Consorting with white rightwingers was an error of judgement on Buthelezi's part, no doubt occasioned by his desperation. It damaged him politically. His next move, to refurbish the KwaZulu-Natal Indaba proposals, was equally imprudent, especially since the constitutional proposals put forward on 1 December 1992 in the name of the KwaZulu Legislative Assembly, at the behest of Buthelezi, went significantly further than what the Indaba had advocated, by verging on a demand for secession. The draft proposed that KwaZulu *and* Natal become a member state of a federal South Africa in which decentralisation would be taken to an extreme limit. For example, no federal law would be able to override any state law and no federal taxes could be imposed on the state without its express permission. Moreover, a state militia would be established, but no federal armed forces would be allowed to be stationed in KwaZulu-Natal.

Buthelezi proposed that the draft Constitution be submitted to a referendum of the electorates of KwaZulu and Natal, and if ratified 'it would become the supreme law of the land ... in spite of whatever course negotiations at central level happen to take.'[84] He denied vehemently that the

draft was 'secessionist'; but it could be described as confederal in character. With the predictable exception of the CP, no other significant party
supported the proposal. If the constitutional proposals had little chance
of being politically feasible, they had no chance of being economically
viable: like all the bantustans, whether independent or not, KwaZulu was
an economic hostage of the central government, which provided some
two-thirds of its revenue. Moreover, while many in the (white) business
community of Natal were sympathetic to Buthelezi and apprehensive of a
future ANC-controlled central government, they were opposed to a rash
political manoeuvre.

Probably, Buthelezi was flying a kite, demanding an exaggerated form
of federalism, thereby making a symbolic statement. De Klerk had
warned Buthelezi of the consequences of confrontation, but he discerned
beneath his suspicions a desire to return to some form of multiparty negotiations, which De Klerk attributed to growing fear of marginalisation.[85]
Brinkmanship was all very well: but if it failed the costs could be high, as
Buthelezi must have realised. Accordingly, he left the door slightly open,
but yet more brinkmanship was to come.

✳   ✳   ✳

The ANC had regarded the Record of Understanding as a triumph: 'They
caved in on everything,' proclaimed Slovo.[86] In an indignant response,
published in 1997,[87] to Slovo's claim (quoted in Waldmeir's book), Meyer
disputed the contention that all of the concessions had been made by
the NP. The Record of Understanding, he said, was merely the smoke-
screen behind which the ANC could return to the negotiations without
loss of face. Moreover, it contained no new constitutional agreements and
merely ratified earlier ones. It also represented a significant climb-down
by the ANC if one compared the demands for a virtual transfer of power,
contained in the Harare Declaration, with the phased process insisted
upon by the NP and now accepted by the ANC. Constitutional continuity, the basis of a system that would be more federal than unitary, and the
entrenchment of rights – including property rights, language and cultural
rights, and the right to mother-tongue education – all represented agreement to NP demands.

The NP's revised constitutional stance owed much to the recognition by
Cabinet members who were close to De Klerk, notably Meyer, that its earlier proposals were unworkable – and, moreover, that persisting with them
would make an eventual settlement impossible. De Klerk came around to
this view, realising that it was imperative to keep the negotiations on track

even if this meant abandoning earlier constitutional proposals. A delicate question, however, arose: would 68.7 per cent of the white electorate have voted 'yes' in the March referendum had they known what the implications of the Record of Understanding would be? Several years later De Klerk would be subjected to criticism for 'surrendering'. The criticism is unfair: the strong currents of the river favoured the ANC in massive surges, and any attempt to resist them would have been fruitless – and caused hugely intensified conflict. It is difficult to see what alternatives De Klerk had.

At the meeting of the NEC on 25 November 1992, the ANC ratified what had been achieved, noting that while there had been a shift in the balance of forces, and that the regime was divided and had suffered a renewed crisis of legitimacy, it still commanded 'vast state and other military resources' and the support of powerful economic forces. The ANC continued to insist that the regime was trying to weaken the liberation movement by low-intensity conflict: 'objectively, the counter-revolutionary violence and the growing potential of long-term counter-revolutionary instability acts as a resource for the regime'. The NEC acknowledged that, while the ANC commanded majority support, it suffered 'many organisational weaknesses' and was 'unable to militarily defeat the counter-revolutionary movement or adequately defend the people'.

Negotiation was therefore the preferred option: the Democratic Revolution for the attainment of majority rule would proceed in phases. The document warned that ANC strategy would need to consider the army, police and civil service: 'If the transition to democracy affects all the individuals in these institutions wholly and purely negatively, then they would serve as fertile ground from which the destabilisers would recruit.' This was precisely the warning that Slovo had sounded – and it was a realistic one. The NEC also took into consideration the possibility of incorporating Slovo's other recommendation: a GNU – 'provided that it does not delay or obstruct the process of orderly transition to majority rule and that the parties that have lost the election will not be able to paralyse the functioning of government'. This was 'fundamentally different' from power-sharing, which entrenched vetoes for minority parties.[88]

As the document showed, it was the ANC's view that the counter-revolutionary forces bent on destabilisation were part of a deliberate strategy of the state. The smouldering issue exploded on 16 November 1992 when the Goldstone Commission made public revelations of serious criminal behaviour on the part of senior army officers aimed at aborting the transition. Normally, Goldstone presented the Commission's reports to the State President, who thereafter promptly released them. On this occasion,

468 THE RISE AND FALL OF APARTHEID

to De Klerk's annoyance, Goldstone took the unprecedented step of revealing evidence that his investigators had found to a press conference.

The evidence was startling: for the first time hard evidence about the
existence of a 'third force' had been obtained. The saga began when a
Mozambican named João Cuna went to the *Vrye Weekblad*, an Afrikaans
newspaper that had been prominent in claiming the existence of a third
force, saying that he was controlled by whites who had forced him to participate in attacks on ANC activists in the Pietermaritzburg area. On reading the *Vrye Weekblad* report, Goldstone decided that the Commission
should investigate Cuna's allegations. In the company of an investigator,
Cuna identified the hotel in Pietermaritzburg, which was able to produce
the credit card slip for payment of his and his controllers' stay. The slip
was in the name of the Africa Risk Analysis Consultancy, which turned
out to be a front organisation for an office of Military Intelligence named
the Directorate of Covert Collection, with headquarters in Pretoria. This
Directorate was a shadowy organisation, whose personnel included a
number of operatives formerly belonging to the equally shadowy Civil
Cooperation Bureau that had been disbanded on De Klerk's instructions.
His instruction that none of the operatives should ever again be employed
in the Defence Force had been ignored.[89]

Armed with a search warrant, and supported by police, the Goldstone
Commission's investigators raided the Africa Risk Analysis Consultancy's
offices and seized files relating to Ferdi Barnard, essentially a hitman, now
apparently engaged in efforts to blackmail ANC and MK operatives.
Unfortunately the Commission's legal punctiliousness caused it to refrain
from a general search of the offices on grounds that a warrant authorising
it to do so would certainly have led to an application for a court interdict
forbidding a so-called 'fishing expedition'.

Notwithstanding its limited scope, the raid produced explosive material which Goldstone revealed at his press conference. It was the breakthrough, the smoking gun. De Klerk observed of the SADF that it possessed a 'steel-belted culture' that made it disdainful of civilian control,
and even more resentful of outside intrusion into its operational domain.
In a vivid simile he described his relationship with the security forces as
resembling:

> ... a man who had been given two fully grown watchdogs – say, a
> Rottweiler and a bull terrier. Their previous owner [a not-so-thinly
> disguised reference to PW Botha] had doted on them. He had given
> them the tastiest morsels from his table and had allowed them to run
> free and chase cats all over the neighbourhood. I had to put a stop to

all that. As a result, they did not particularly like me – although they had an ingrained sense of obedience. When I took them for walks in the neighbourhood, I put them on leashes and stopped them from chasing cats. I could determine the general direction in which they would move, but they would walk at their own pace, sometimes wanting to go back, sometimes straining to chase a passing cat, sometimes walking happily in my direction. I could guide them, but I knew that if I pulled too hard, I might choke them – or they might slip their collars and cause pandemonium in the neighbourhood.[90]

That the SADF had an ingrained tradition of obedience to civilian political control was generally true in 'normal' times, during which both government and the security forces were jointly committed to preservation of the apartheid order. De Klerk's initiative, however, had shaken the previously unquestioned alignment. Even if it were true that most of the top brass in the army supported the new direction – several generals had previously insisted that South Africa's conflict could be resolved only by means that were 80 per cent political and 20 per cent military – there were doubters, whose numbers increased in the lower ranks of the officer echelon. Some had doubts that were so great that they resolved to thwart the transition.

De Klerk's announcement on 2 February 1990 had taken the SADF by surprise. De Klerk had had no illusions about the institutional power of the security forces and their capacity to resist or undermine his efforts. Goldstone's revelations now set the stage for a showdown. A Military Intelligence operative told the TRC that De Klerk's initiative 'took the foundation of the securocrats from beneath their feet'. They were caught unawares, having been steeped in the belief that the communist-controlled ANC was the enemy:

> [T]hey sat with the question, where to go now. Then individual commanders developed individual strategies ... The last resort lay with the far right. By train violence, taxi wars, Boipatong, etc., can't we create anarchy?

While allowance must be made for exaggeration (and, in the case of Boipatong, factual inaccuracy), his comments reflected the thoughts of some securocrats and ex-securocrats who sought to link up with right-wingers in an attempt to prevent the transition, or at least to strengthen the bargaining position of those trying to negotiate a *volkstaat*.[91]

On several previous occasions, De Klerk had interrogated the security establishment about the existence of a 'third force', but each time they would convincingly deny its existence. Goldstone's precipitate revelation of (untested) evidence 'shocked and dismayed' him, making him recognise that the allegations had to be thoroughly investigated. While the Goldstone Commission would continue its probe, De Klerk decided to appoint Lieutenant-General Pierre Steyn, chief of the SADF staff, who was an air force general, to conduct an in-depth investigation to get to the root of the illegal activities. It was the start of one of the most decisive episodes in De Klerk's presidency.

De Klerk was fully aware of the risks involved: since the SADF was the ultimate guarantor of the state's security and stability at a time of considerable turbulence, he could not afford to alienate it or weaken its morale. De Klerk made no mention of the possibility of a coup, being convinced that the great majority of serving officers would abide by the rule of obedience to the civilian authority.[92] Nevertheless, rumours abounded – mostly, no doubt, spread by the ultra-rightwingers. Heribert Adam and Kogila Moodley alluded to the possibility of a 'soft' coup, whereby the security establishment would withhold its cooperation:

> If certain policies were pursued, [De Klerk] was advised, security could not be guaranteed (personal interviews, various dates 1990-92). One of his planned overseas visits was almost canceled because of this looming rebellion. A reputed judge [unnamed], commissioned to evaluate the attitude of leading military figures, reported after extensive interviews that most expressed intense resentment of the government's course and displayed varying degrees of cynicism.[93]

American diplomats doubted that there was much stomach among the Afrikaner community at large for organised violence, but questioned the loyalty of elements among the Citizen Force and the Commando Force. Opinions on this varied, but Ambassador Princeton Lyman raised the critical question: who would organise and lead such an uprising?

> Scattered resistance was worrisome, but it could not threaten the transition. The real threat would be if there was leadership on the right sufficient in stature to mobilize these groupings and overcome the historically fractured right-wing politics among them, and to do so with the skill to make such an uprising politically significant.[94]

Such a figure of the requisite stature, capable of leading a politically significant uprising, was entering rightwing politics at roughly this time: Constand Viljoen, who had been appointed chief of the army in 1976, and chief of the SADF in 1980, a position he held until his retirement in 1985. Viljoen, a man of great integrity and personal magnetism, stood head and shoulders in calibre above other rightwing leaders. Moreover, as the archetypical 'soldiers' soldier', he was immensely popular among the troops he had commanded. His formal entry into rightwing politics occurred in May 1993 when he became leader of the Afrikaner Volksfront, an alliance of over 20 rightwing groups committed to forging unity on the right and promoting an Afrikaner *volkstaat*.[95] Viljoen was destined to play a critical role in the turbulent months leading up to the election in April 1994.

General Steyn's appointment, and his wide-ranging brief, caused dismay and consternation among many of the SADF's top brass. But De Klerk was determined to press ahead: alleged third force activity had already inflicted considerable political damage on him and he could not afford to sustain much more. Steyn was put in immediate overall command of the SADF's intelligence operations, with instructions to review them and to put in place a proper division of responsibility between the SADF, the police, and National Intelligence. Action would be taken against those violating the law or undermining official policy.[96] De Klerk wanted to be able to state categorically that military intelligence had ceased illegal activities.

On 18 December 1992 Steyn presented De Klerk with his preliminary findings, which were disturbing. Rogue elements were operating outside the control of the political and military command. Some 'had been involved in, and in certain instances were still involved in, illegal and unauthorized activities which could be prejudicial to the security, interests and well-being of the state'. According to Dave Steward, then Director-General in the Office of the President, the government was confronted with a situation where the top structure of the SADF

> ... was either no longer in control of several key units or was itself condoning or involved in actions that were illegal or in direct contravention of the policy and express intentions of the government. It was either a question of gross incompetence, gross insubordination or active subversion of the state.[97]

De Klerk and some of his ministerial colleagues listened in astonishment as Steyn presented his findings:

> He [Steyn] alleged that some units had been illegally stockpiling weapons in South Africa and abroad; that they had been providing

arms and assistance to elements within the IFP; that they were in-volved in the instigation and perpetration of violence; and that they were involved in activities to discredit the ANC and to sabotage the negotiation process .... Time and again, he indicated that these ac-tivities had been unauthorized or self-initiated.[98]

Steyn stressed that much of his information was based on unconfirmed re-ports that were insufficient to secure criminal convictions. Further inves-tigation would be needed. But De Klerk had to respond quickly: because the negotiation process was accelerating, those eager to thwart it were likely to step up their activities, thereby plunging the country into more violence. On the other hand, De Klerk noted, 'it would have been the height of folly to dismantle the command structure of the South African Defence Force and cripple the force's morale, without clear and indisput-able evidence.'[99]

De Klerk faced a dilemma: as Steyn made clear, the evidence was *prima facie* alarming, and sufficient to suggest that the transition could be de-railed by a combination of mass action, heightened insurgency, attempted secession by KwaZulu and a rightwing uprising. It was potentially a highly combustible mix.

De Klerk took the tough decision to instruct Steyn and General Kat Liebenberg, chief of the SADF, to identify those possibly guilty of of-fences and those whose services would no longer be required in view of the impending restructuring of intelligence activities. A total of 23 of-ficers, including two generals and four brigadiers, were either forced into compulsory retirement or placed on compulsory leave, pending further investigations. Essentially, they had been fired.

Liebenberg, never an enthusiastic supporter of the transition, was deeply unhappy about these developments, but had to acquiesce – or face dismissal, which De Klerk had seriously considered. In mid-1993, how-ever, he was retired, and replaced by General Georg Meiring, whose brief was to cut the ties between the SADF and the right wing.[100]

Given the haste and the inconclusive evidence on which De Klerk was forced to act, it was inevitable that some innocent officers were caught in the dragnet. One was General Chris Thirion, deputy head of Military Intelligence. Thirion was a dedicated soldier who saw his duty as combat-ing insurgency to create a climate of security in which politicians of all stripes could negotiate a democratic dispensation – in other words, the '20 per cent military, 80 per cent political' formula. Thirion was deeply embittered by his dismissal, and demanded in vain that he be tried or court-martialled. He declined to apply for amnesty to the TRC – which, in any event, could find no evidence of his involvement in human rights abuses. Subsequently, Thirion sued De Klerk, and the matter was settled out of court. De Klerk has acknowledged that innocent people, including Thirion, whom he described as a 'loyal officer', were among the 23, and apologised, while insisting that he had been obliged to take drastic steps, and pointing out that he had been dependent on the army itself for the list of names.[101]

The 'Night of the Generals', as the episode was termed, predictably caused an uproar. Magnus Malan, former chief of the SADF and Minister of Defence from 1980 until he was shifted to the Ministry of Water Affairs and Forestry in July 1991, considered De Klerk's action to have been an error of judgement, though without suggesting what else he might have done in the circumstances.

Since many of the alleged criminal activities had occurred when Malan was the responsible minister, De Klerk offered him the choice of resigning with the 23 or riding out the storm. Malan was indignant, insisting that nothing irregular had occurred on his watch because he had his finger on the pulse of the army. Moreover, he knew most of the 23, and asserted that they were honourable people who would not commit these improprieties, especially against the state.[102]

Malan's injured innocence was misplaced: the nefarious activities of both the CCB and the Directorate of Covert Collection had occurred, apparently without his knowledge, while he was Minister of Defence. Moreover, even though further investigation produced no evidence that would stand up in a court and none of the 23 was prosecuted (and some were exonerated), the circumstantial evidence of what De Klerk called 'a veritable rat's nest of unauthorized and illegal activity within military intelligence' was overwhelming. Hard evidence that substantiated many of Steyn's findings emerged only several years later when officers and other members of the security forces, apprehensive of prosecution for human rights abuses, confessed their crimes to the TRC in exchange for amnesty.

Allegations of De Klerk's complicity in state-sponsored violence damaged him politically and dogged him well after 1994. A consideration of the question is a necessary digression. The TRC grilled him as if he were a criminal in the dock – in marked contrast to the kid-glove treatment accorded to ANC witnesses, notably Winnie Mandela. De Klerk refused to be browbeaten, sticking to his insistence that he had not known about, or even less authorised 'anti-terrorist' strategies that involved illegal actions. In his written submission, he said:

In dealing with the unconventional strategies from the side of the Government I want to make it clear from the outset that, within my knowledge and experience, they never included the authorization of assassination, murder, torture, rape, assault or the like. I have never been part of any decision taken by Cabinet, the State Security Council or any Committee authorizing or instructing the commission of such gross violations of human rights. Nor did I individually directly or indirectly ever suggest, order or authorize any such action.[103]

At the public hearing of the TRC on 14 May 1997, De Klerk (now under oath) could not be budged. He readily accepted overall moral and political responsibility for his government's part in the conflicts of the past, and acknowledged that 'our security legislation and the state of emergency created circumstances which were conducive to many of the abuses and transgressions of human rights'. He found the revelation of atrocities that poured forth at the TRC 'as shocking as anybody else'. He emphasised that during his presidency he had avoided cover-ups and, had he been able to ascertain the facts now being revealed, he would have charged all of those involved with murder.

De Klerk had been astounded by Steyn's findings. He was equally astounded when Goldstone informed him on 20 February 1994 that the Commission had uncovered information about the activities of the supposedly disbanded Vlakplaas Unit in fomenting violence aimed at derailing the transition and destabilising the country. Goldstone's informant claimed that the operations had been carried out under the command of the deputy-commissioner of the police, Lieutenant-General Basie Smit, and the head of the police department of counter-intelligence, Major-General Krappies Engelbrecht. Goldstone's observations about De Klerk's reaction to these revelations are relevant: 'The spontaneity of his reaction convinced me that he had no knowledge of the allegations of complicity in the violence of the most senior police officials.'[104]

De Klerk's written and oral testimony before the TRC satisfied neither the Commission nor the ANC. The chairman of the TRC, Archbishop Desmond Tutu, and his deputy, Alex Boraine, dismissed his explanations as inadequate at a press conference on the day following De Klerk's appearance on 14 May 1997. It was not only strange behaviour for a commission's leadership to pass judgement on evidence it had only just heard, but very likely a violation of the legislation of 1995 that established the TRC and enjoined impartiality upon it. The NP, on behalf of De Klerk, took the Commission to court, and the matter was settled only when Tutu and Boraine offered an unqualified apology.

Another round in the conflict between De Klerk and the TRC was fought late in 1998 when the TRC had completed its first five volumes, in which De Klerk was accused of a 'lack of candour', failing to make full disclosure of gross violations of human rights, and of being 'morally accountable' for concealing evidence of violations that were known to him. De Klerk, who had done his best to cooperate with the TRC, in spite of his deep misgivings about its impartiality, was infuriated and immediately applied for a court order to forbid publication of the findings against him. The order was granted, and the TRC was forced to excise the relevant page prior to distribution of the report.[105]

Boraine's account of the TRC is spattered with attacks on De Klerk: 'aghast' when De Klerk repeatedly insisted that he had not known what had been happening, he quoted Eugene de Kock (of Vlakplaas notoriety), saying:

> [De Klerk] simply did not have the courage to declare: yes, we at the top level condoned what was done on our behalf by the security forces. What's more, we instructed it should be implemented. Or – if we actually did not give instruction, we turned a blind eye. We didn't move heaven and earth to stop the ghastliness. Therefore, let the foot soldiers be excused.[106]

Jacko Maree, an NP MP at the time, recalls that when the question of Vlakplaas and De Kock came before the caucus, De Klerk told them that 'he would not lift a finger to help De Kock, that no-one was above the law, and that killing for political reasons was unacceptable'. As Maree suggests, if De Klerk had been party to the Vlakplaas set-up, he would have had sympathy with De Kock.[107]

De Klerk's misgivings about the TRC were well-founded: of the 15 commissioners who signed the report in 1998, none had a background of support for, or affinity with, either the NP or IFP, the two political organisations found to have been responsible for most human rights violations. (Wynand Malan had been an NP MP, but had resigned in 1987, citing disagreement with fundamental parts of official policy.) Although the legislation of 1995 establishing the TRC precluded the appointment as commissioners of persons with a high political profile, critics immediately claimed that a majority of those appointed had at least ideological affinities or sympathies with the liberation movement. Tutu himself, although a man of great personal decency and integrity who had tried to keep himself politically non-aligned, had nevertheless been a patron of the UDF and an ardent advocate of sanctions. Apart from the commissioners, the staff of some 500, including the critically important investigators, were preponderantly sympathetic to the liberation struggle. Buthelezi described the TRC as a 'politically characterized body which derives from, and is appointed by, political institutions'.[108] De Klerk's view of its composition was similar: he had tried to persuade Mandela (now President), who had the final say over appointments, to choose an ideologically more balanced commission, but Mandela declined.

Many of the human rights abuses that the TRC investigated had occurred when PW Botha was State President, during which time De Klerk was not in the securocrats' loop. He had sought Botha's cooperation in preparing the NP's submission to the TRC, but had been given a brush-off. Nevertheless, he could emphatically aver that neither the Cabinet nor the State Security Council had ever taken a decision in his presence to authorise illegal actions. The truth about how such actions were authorised, and by whom, remains shrouded in mystery.

During 2007, when the National Prosecuting Authority decided to prosecute Vlok and General Johan van der Merwe, former Commissioner of Police, further allegations of De Klerk's complicity were expressed. In a press interview, Van der Merwe emphatically denied that neither Cabinet or the SSC had ever given instructions for the illegal use of violence: 'Only PW Botha did so, in his personal capacity.'[109]

Further clues were provided by Adriaan Vlok, Minister of Law and Order in De Klerk's Cabinet (until his demotion to the Ministry of Correctional Services in 1991), who had strongly identified with the police under his ostensible ministerial control. In an interview in September 2006, he said that PW Botha had been 'very strong' on the need-to-know principle: often, after a Cabinet or State Security Council meeting,

> He would say to one or two ministers present and even heads of department: 'Can you please stay behind?' This was the case in the Khotso House [headquarters of the South African Council of Churches] bombing .... With operations he would congratulate us and say 'that was good work and I am happy with you' .... He was particularly happy that there was no loss of life.

The probability is that after blandly worded resolutions had been adopted by Cabinet or the Council, orders went to the line-function departments and thereafter to operatives on the ground. The action taken in consequence was often far more vigorous, indeed, lethal, than the original resolution had indicated. Vlok admitted using words like 'neutralise' for dealing with UDF activists and 'troublemakers', and he told police in trouble-spots to *maak 'n plan* (make a plan):

We had to know what the influence of leader figures [was] and their role in creating a revolutionary climate. We talked about how we could limit these people. But never that we should kill them.[110]

Vlok did not explain how operatives would not assume that words like 'neutralise', 'eliminate', 'take out' or 'destroy' could have any meaning other than 'kill'. A number of the security operatives who were prosecuted or sought amnesty took refuge in the 'we-were-only-obeying-orders' defence that was discredited in the Nuremberg Trials; but it was true that they were subjected to considerable pressure from their commanders, and, during the time of PW Botha, from politicians. Pik Botha observed that in many, though not all, cases

> ... members of the security branch believed that they were doing what was expected of them. And the less the rest of us knew about their methods the better, especially for our consciences. How the terrorists were to be fought was the security forces' business and task. The total onslaught demanded total resistance.[111] (Translation.)

De Klerk made a somewhat different acknowledgement to Tutu's biographer who asked him about the murder by security police of four activists in 1984:

> I never knew about this and I was never part of any policies authorizing it. But where maybe I failed was not asking more questions, not going on a crusade about things ... following up on a slight uncomfortableness you feel here and there ... . In my case, I'm not saying I didn't want to know. But I do think, with the advantage of hindsight, that I was at times maybe not strong enough on following up on my instincts. But that doesn't take away from the fact that at no time was any decision taken of which I was part, where I felt, 'This is actually authorizing assassination or cold-blooded murder.'

He went on to recount an episode where he had exploded angrily in front of three (unnamed) 'top security people' during the 1980s after killings had occurred. De Klerk had respect for them: 'And they took me aside and on their words of honour they assured me that my suspicions on that particular occasion were unfounded.'[112] As was the case with some of his ministers, De Klerk learned to his cost that he could not trust certain key officials either.

Notwithstanding his genuine abhorrence of violence and a punctilious concern for upholding the law, De Klerk was unable to persuade the TRC that his efforts to eradicate illegal actions were sincere. The question that the TRC and other critics failed to answer – or even to ask – was: why would De Klerk encourage, sponsor or condone violence that was aimed at sabotaging the transition into which he had sunk all of his moral and political capital? And why would he support the activities of his sworn political enemies on the right wing? The accusation made no sense. Nor was the (marginally) milder accusation that the violence sought to weaken the ANC in the negotiations persuasive.

If anything, the anger evoked by the violence strengthened the ANC, and made its negotiating stance more intransigent. It also inflicted political damage on De Klerk, weakening his possible support base among Africans: according to polls conducted early in 1992, 80 per cent of urban Africans expressed satisfaction with his leadership, some even ranking him higher than Mandela.[113] Although 14 per cent of the NP's vote in the election of April 1994 came from Africans, this was only three to four per cent of the total African vote, and came mainly from older, more conservative and often rural voters.[114] It is impossible, though, to say whether the NP's share of the African vote might have been bigger had it not been for the sophisticated and effective barrage of anti-NP propaganda launched by the ANC, principally in response to the violence.

Despite its concerted and zealous efforts to pin complicity on De Klerk, the TRC was unable to do so. John Allen, who had been Tutu's press secretary before becoming the TRC's communications director, describes the TRC's finding as displaying an 'embarrassing weakness'. He also notes: 'No evidence was ever forthcoming implicating De Klerk in violence.'[115] This did not prevent a stream of allegations against him. Typical was the snide observation by Anthony Sampson – citing the TRC's finding circumstantial evidence that the signing of the Record of Understanding had led to a decline of third force violence – who claimed that this 'clearly suggested that De Klerk was able to curb violence when he wished to'.[116] There was indeed a decline that lasted until April 1993, but there was not a shred of evidence, circumstantial or otherwise, to link this with manipulation on De Klerk's part. The decline may have been attributable to a decision by the ANC to call a halt to the violence because it had largely achieved its goals in the Record of Understanding – but there was not a shred of evidence to suggest this either.

The TRC held the ANC accountable for various human rights abuses, both before and after 1990, and blamed it for contributing to the spiral of violence by arming and training self-defence units in a volatile situation in which they had little control over their actions. It also found that the

success of so-called 'third force' activities was 'at least in part a consequence of extremely high levels of political intolerance, for which all parties to the conflict are held to be morally and politically accountable'.[117]

This attempt at even-handedness between the NP and the ANC caused
the ANC, unsuccessfully, to seek amendments to the final draft of the
TRC's Report. Seven commissioners supported the ANC's demand, and
seven opposed it. Only Tutu's vote decided the matter. An application to
court was also unsuccessful. The IFP and Buthelezi also challenged the
TRC's findings in court, causing the Report to be amended in some respects, and allowing the inclusion in the final report of a statement by the
IFP contesting other findings.[118]

Buthelezi, also accused of complicity in violence, lashed back angrily
at his accusers, challenging them to prove what the TRC had failed to
do, namely that he had ever personally ordered, authorised or approved
the death of a single human being during that conflict; but that he had
authorised Inkatha supporters to 'defend themselves from attack'.[119] It
is probably true that Buthelezi never personally sanctioned violence or
instructed Inkatha warlords to attack their opponents. Nevertheless, it is
difficult to resist the conclusion that Inkatha supporters often considered
attack to be the best form of defence. Much the same was true of the
UDF/ANC.

The TRC, despite having been presented with voluminous documentation regarding ANC threats to Inkatha after the breakdown of relations
in 1979, declined to assign primary blame for starting what became virtually civil war. The closest the Report came was a single sentence:

> The ANC, having failed to make Inkatha the vehicle for its inroads
> into the important rural constituencies, now embarked on a propa-
> ganda onslaught against Chief Buthelezi and Inkatha.

Both the UDF/ANC and Inkatha were deeply implicated in violence and it
is difficult, if not impossible, to determine who threw the first stone, and
which organisation was responsible for most human rights violations.
The TRC's statistics, derived from violations reported to it, showed that
at least three times as many victims of 'severe ill treatment' belonged to
the ANC/UDF as to the IFP and other groups. ANC supporters were also
the overwhelming majority of victims of 'associated violations'. *Prima
facie* this suggests that Inkatha, together with the police, were the major
perpetrators of violence. This may be true, but the findings have to be
viewed with caution because first, many victims probably had no known
political affiliations or even preferences, and secondly, as the Commission

acknowledged, the antagonism of the IFP to the TRC inhibited many of its supporters from coming forward to tell their stories, even after the deadline for submissions was extended.[120]

De Klerk was angered by the TRC's Report, which, he believed, had vindicated his early misgivings about the bias that its composition was likely to cause: 'its agenda was to discredit and humiliate me'. While acknowledging that the TRC had uncovered brutal deeds, and afforded victims the cathartic opportunity of testifying, he argued that

> ... the TRC pursued its investigations of gross violations of human rights perpetrated by the security forces with a vigour and zeal that was quite lacking in its investigations of necklace murders, black on black violence, and the assassination of members of the IFP.[121]

Political violence continued right up to the election of 1994 – and beyond. The country trembled on the brink of a major conflagration when, on 10 April 1993, Chris Hani, a leading figure in the ANC Alliance and a strong contender to succeed Mandela, both as leader of the ANC and President of South Africa, was assassinated by two rightwingers.

CHAPTER 12

Negotiating the Interim Constitution

The years 1993 and 1994 were no less turbulent than the preceding ones. A series of pacts between the NP and the ANC enabled 'sufficient consensus' to be achieved on the terms of an Interim Constitution and the mode of drafting both it and the final Constitution. The concept of 'sufficient consensus' (meaning that if the ANC and the NP agreed the process could go forward) angered the IFP and Buthelezi to the extent that they boycotted much of the negotiations. Moreover, however fragmented it was, the ultra-rightwing remained a menace, manifesting itself in the near-catastrophic assassination of Chris Hani and other violent attacks. The question was: would 'sufficient consensus', as understood, be sufficient to withstand onslaughts on it from the IFP and its new-found allies on the ultra-right? Did they collectively possess enough muscle to abort the transition?

The imminence of fundamental change and an inclusive, democratic election spurred the contending parties into ever-more zealous and robust action. The consequence was that violence continued unabated, with fatalities recorded in 1993 exceeding those in preceding years.

Debates about constitutional models took place up and down the country, involving politicians, academics, journalists and others. Academics, in particular, sought to locate South Africa within a paradigm based upon comparative transitions, notably those occurring in southern Europe and Latin America. The South African case, however, was unique in significant respects: in some (limited) ways it resembled the decolonisation process – but South Africa was not a colony; in other respects, it resembled conflicts in Northern Ireland, Palestine/Israel and other troubled societies, but, again, the differences were profound. In truth, the South African case was *sui generis*. Whether South Africa could sustain a democratic polity, given its long history of conflict and the massive socio-economic inequalities between white and black, was a much-debated question.

* * *

In a series of bilateral meetings beginning in November 1992 and continuing into 1993, the ANC and the NP thrashed out a number of issues, and agreed to propose a multiparty planning conference to be held early in March 2003 to plan for the resumption of formal negotiations. The ANC was anxious for the multiparty negotiations to resume, and for contentious issues between it and the NP to be resolved beforehand so that, in Ramaphosa's words, 'when we get to the multiparty table the negotiation will be smoother and there will be less chance of deadlocks developing'.[1]

At the planning conference, there was agreement that the Multiparty Negotiating Process (MPNP) should meet on 1 April 1993. Twenty-six organisations attended the April meeting, including the IFP, the CP, the Afrikaner Volksunie, the PAC and three delegations of traditional leaders. It was hailed as the most representative gathering ever in South Africa's history. The unwieldy and fragmented structure of Codesa was replaced by a more streamlined one. The critical forum was the Negotiating Council, consisting of four delegates plus two advisors per party. Negotiations were facilitated by Technical Committees, consisting of five or six non-party experts who considered written submissions from the parties and acted as compromise-seekers. A sub-committee of the Planning Committee, consisting principally of Mac Maharaj and Fanie van der Merwe, was a highly effective deadlock-breaking mechanism.[2] The critical factor in facilitating the negotiating process was the meaning now attached to 'sufficient consensus': it was famously defined by Ramaphosa as 'if we and the National Party agree, everyone else can get stuffed'.[3] This approach suited the ANC and NP, but inevitably it led to the alienation of the IFP, while Buthelezi engaged in more brinkmanship.

The MPNP's start had seemed auspicious, but the country's hopes were dashed very shortly thereafter when Hani was assassinated on 10 April. Hani lived in the predominantly Afrikaner town of Boksburg, east of Johannesburg. He was gunned down in the driveway of his home and died instantly. An alert neighbour, a young Afrikaner woman, noted the getaway car's registration number, and the two assassins, Janusz Waluz, a vehemently anti-communist Polish immigrant and member of the AWB, and Clive Derby-Lewis, a former CP MP still active in ultra-rightwing circles, were quickly arrested and charged.

Hani was general secretary of the SACP and chief of staff of MK, and, at 51, he was a rising star in the ANC alliance whose huge popularity may have made him Mandela's successor. He was a militant, initially hesitant about the wisdom of negotiating with the NP government but committing himself wholeheartedly to the process once it got under way. Mandela said of him:

> He was a great hero among the youth of South Africa, a man who spoke their language and to whom they listened. If anyone could mobilize the unruly youth behind a negotiated solution, it was Chris.[4]

In an autobiographical pamphlet Hani wrote that in the current situation 'the decision by our organization to suspend the armed struggle is correct and is an important contribution in maintaining the momentum of negotiations'.[5]

Hani had been a man of action, rather than an ideologue or theoretician. His embrace of communism probably owed much to his being appalled by the poverty of rural Transkei where he had grown up. Shortly before his assassination, according to a German businessman he had sat next to when flying back to South Africa after visiting countries in Eastern Europe, he had said that communism was 'dead'.[6] (Whether he had discussed this with his party comrades and what implications it might have had is not known. While there is no reason to doubt the businessman's account, it is surprising that Hani would offer so fundamental a recantation to a stranger.)

The assassination could have sparked a countrywide conflagration: as it was, rioting and looting caused some 70 deaths and substantial damage to property. A stayaway of approximately 90 per cent of the black workforce, plummeting business confidence and increased emigration of whites took their economic toll.

Prudently, De Klerk realised that he could do nothing to calm the angry masses: 'this was Mandela's moment, not mine'.[7] In a televised address, repeated three times, Mandela spoke with statesman-like gravitas, appealing for peace and 'disciplined expression of our emotions'. He stressed that it had been a young Afrikaner woman who had risked her life to ensure that the assassins were arrested. The killing, he continued, was 'a national tragedy that has touched millions of people, across the political and colour divide'. He acknowledged that young people had lost a hero, but appealed to them, as the leaders of tomorrow, to show restraint: 'Your country, your people, your organizations need you to act with wisdom.'[8]

Over two million attended 85 rallies held across the country, and 120 000 attended Hani's funeral service in Soweto on 19 April. On this occasion Mandela's speech was less irenic in tone, much to De Klerk's anger. Mandela claimed that the assassination was 'no aberration', being consistent with a pattern of 'unsolved' killings:

> There has been a deliberate and massive propaganda offensive against Umkhonto we Sizwe, its cadres and leadership. No effort has been spared to criminalize both MK and Chris Hani. This has deliberately created a climate of acceptance when an MK cadre is assassinated, as dozens have been over the past months … . Those who have deliberately created this climate that legitimates political assassinations are as much responsible for the death of Chris Hani as the man who pulled the trigger, and the conspiracy that plotted his murder.[9]

De Klerk, despite some of Mandela's palpably unfair comments, recognised that Mandela's tough words were aimed at assuaging the anger of the 'unruly youth'. His televised address and the funeral oration certainly contributed to dousing the potential conflagration, but this did not prevent booing and jeering from some in the crowd when Mandela mentioned that he had received messages of sympathy from De Klerk and when he reiterated his intention to work with De Klerk for a democratic settlement.[10] Indeed, one of the main thrusts of his speech was a demand that the process be accelerated, which bore fruit when on 1 June the MPNP's negotiating council agreed that the first election should be held on 27 April 1994.

Waluz and Derby-Lewis were convicted of murder and sentenced to death, which was commuted to life imprisonment since capital punishment had been suspended. Their subsequent appeal for amnesty was denied. It emerged in the course of police investigations that the weapon used in the assassination was one of a number stolen from an SADF armoury by a fanatical rightwinger some years before. A search of Waluz's home turned up a hit list containing the names, among others, of Mandela, Pik Botha, Slovo, Maharaj and Goldstone.[11] It is worth remarking that, amidst the violence of the transition, no other major political figure was assassinated. Whether this was attributable to tight security measures (absent on the day in Hani's case), good fortune or, most probably, a mixture of both is impossible to say. Small and fragmented as they were, the ultra-rightwingers had nevertheless demonstrated that the fanaticism of some was dangerous.

Hani's assassination had given the country a glimpse into the abyss. Contrary to what many rightwingers had hoped, the killing, far from causing a breakdown or even a significant delay in negotiations, had actually been a spur to speeding up the process. Once again considerable strain had been put on the relationship between De Klerk and Mandela, but both realised that it was imperative to reach a settlement as soon as possible. This put pressure on the MPNP. The agreed date of the election was only a year away, and, given its emotional significance, it would be difficult, if not impossible, to postpone it. Many in the NP, including Meyer and De Klerk, realised that they could no longer govern effectively on their own: Mandela's role in the aftermath of Hani's assassination had underlined that. Even less could they create the conditions required for vitally-needed faster economic growth. The practical effect was to force the NP into making more concessions.

The tenseness of the times was aggravated by violence directed against whites from another quarter which had appeared to be largely inactive until 1990: the PAC's armed wing, Apla. The PAC/Apla strategy was an attempt to outbid the ANC in racial terms: 'settlers', as whites were termed, were fair game, as the slogans 'One settler, one bullet' and 'One hand grenade, ten settlers' suggested. There were a number of attacks on farmers and public places frequented mostly by whites. Civilians were deliberately targeted: Apla's chief commander, Sabelo Phama, told a television interviewer in April 1993 that 'he would aim his guns at children – to hurt whites where it hurts most'.[12] Brutal attacks occurred in the Eastern Cape and in Cape Town during 1992 and 1993. Measured by the number of fatalities, the worst occurred during a service at St James Church in a suburb of Cape Town on 25 July 1993 when an Apla group burst in during a service attended by 1 000 people, opened fire with machine guns and threw two hand grenades into the congregation. Of the 11 dead, four were Russian sailors. Equally appalling attacks, though with fewer fatalities, occurred at a golf club in King William's Town, at hotels in East London and Fort Beaufort, and at a pub near Cape Town. These were callous actions, made even worse by the total lack of remorse shown by the perpetrators. Apla's Director of Operations, Letlapa Mphahlele, told a media conference in 1997 that he was offering neither regret nor apology for the lives lost, and said that his 'proudest moment was seeing whites dying in the killing fields'.[13]

The PAC had declined to suspend the armed struggle, and in any case it had little or no control over Apla's estimated 120 operatives in South Africa. Mounting evidence from intelligence sources during 1992 and 1993 suggested that Apla was using Transkei as a base, with the connivance of General Bantu Holomisa, the military ruler. De Klerk had tried, unsuccessfully, to persuade Holomisa to cease assisting Apla; now, given what he had been assured was hard evidence, verified independently by two groups, that a house in Umtata, capital of Transkei, was being used by Apla, he authorised the SADF to raid the house, specifying that minimum force should be used. Pik Botha had opposed the raid, but the then chief of the Defence Force, General Georg Meiring, had remonstrated with him, asking: 'Minister, if these people [Apla members] come into South Africa again and execute another attack against civilians, are you going to explain it to the people?' Botha had no answer.[14]

Unfortunately for De Klerk, the raid on 8 October 1993 was botched, and five teenagers were killed, allegedly because the SADF soldiers believed that they were reaching for weapons.[15] Whether the house was, or had been, an Apla 'safe house' is not known. Despite his expression of deep regret, the episode inflicted more damage on De Klerk.

Apla's violence had no direct effect on the course of the negotiations, although it ruptured the tenuous relationship between the PAC and the NP. The wanton killings horrified many, including the ANC leadership. They heightened the insecurity among whites, and undoubtedly reinforced racist stereotypes. Police sources reported that Apla's activities had caused a rightwing backlash that included shooting at African occupants of vehicles on country roads.[16] Few whites, however, considered how fortunate they – and South Africa – were that the NP's principal negotiating partner was the ANC, and not the PAC, with its ill-disguised anti-white racism.

White insecurity, and a perception that it was being forced to make ever-more concessions to the ANC, rubbed off on the NP: from the high point of the referendum in March 1992, when 68.7 per cent of whites voted in favour of continuing the negotiating process, support declined from late 1992 into 1993. White support for the NP, according to polls, dropped from 56 per cent in July 1992 to 28 per cent in July 1993, but rose thereafter. No fewer than 31 per cent recorded responses of 'uncertain/don't know/will not vote' at the end of 1993. While Coloured and Indian support was significant, African support declined from 8 per cent in mid-1992 to less than 1 per cent a year later: the barrage of criticism directed at the NP by the ANC had taken its toll.[17] The impact of these trends caused consternation in the NP, and enabled Meyer and his more liberal colleagues to press home the viewpoint that it was in the NP's interest to reach a settlement swiftly, before its support and bargaining power declined further, even if this meant making concessions to the ANC.[18]

*   *   *

The MPNP resumed its labours late in April, now under considerable pressure to produce an Interim Constitution in time for Parliament to enact it into law before the end of the year. To facilitate comprehension of a complex trajectory, milestones on the road to settlement are listed below,[19] prior to an examination of the issues involved.

- April and May 1993: Technical Committees established.
- 1 June: Negotiating Council agrees that sufficient progress has been made to agree to 27 April 1994 as the date of the first election. Instructions given to Technical Committee on Constitutional Matters to draft an Interim Constitution.
- 15 June: IFP calls on Council not to consider recommendations of Technical Committee and to consider proposals for a federal Constitution. This is rejected in a vote.
- 22 June: Council calls for establishment of the Independent Electoral Commission and the Independent Media Commission.
- 2 July: MPNP agrees that:
    1. it should adopt constitutional principles providing for strong regional and national government;
    2. these constitutional principles to be binding on the constituent assembly and justiciable by a Constitutional Court;
    3. a commission will make recommendations on regional boundaries;
    4. MPNP shall agree on legislation for levelling the playing field and promoting conditions conducive to the holding of free and fair elections; and
    5. MPNP shall agree on a transitional Constitution.
- 31 July: Agreement is reached on a proposal for nine regions.
- 25–28 October: ANC and NP reach agreement on the Interim Constitution, including a government of national unity, a provision agreeing to deputy presidents, the required percentage of the national vote to elect a deputy president and the right to membership of the Cabinet. The NP abandons its claim to a veto over decisions of Cabinet.
- 16 November: Mandela and De Klerk reach agreement on final issues.
- 18 November: MPNP ratifies Interim Constitution.

The fundamental trend of the negotiations was that the NP's bargaining power had declined to the extent that it had had to abandon some of its earlier proposals, receiving a few concessions in return, and that the IFP, by excluding itself from the process, had lost out comprehensively. The outcome of negotiations broadly reflects the respective bargaining powers of the negotiating parties. When the process started in 1990 the NP and the ANC (including its allies) had a rough parity of bargaining resources, the NP having the advantage of incumbency, the power of state resources, and extensive support in the white population, and the ANC having numbers and a mass-based following.

As the narrative has shown, mutual recognition of a deadlock, or 'hurting stalemate', prompted the quest for a negotiated settlement. From mid-1992 onwards, however, the scales tipped in favour of the ANC: the NP government, while in no danger of being forcibly ejected from office, found that it could no longer deploy its resources with any degree of effectiveness, its legitimacy having declined. The ANC, on the other hand, was not subject to comparable restraints and *could* deploy its resources with maximum effect: numbers, increasing mobilisation and support, the capacity for mass action, including strikes, and command of the moral high ground in much of the international community, inexorably shifted the balance of influence in its favour. As Slovo put it in a triumphant assessment of the MPNP's outcome:

> ... negotiations are a terrain of struggle which, at the end of the day, depend on the balance of forces outside the process. It was the link between the negotiations and our mass struggle that played an absolutely key role.[20]

Of the issues that the MPNP had to resolve, two stand out: the question of regional government – whether South Africa should be a federal or unitary state, and power-sharing. The NP favoured a federal system and power-sharing, both of which the ANC opposed. The regional issue, of course, was complicated by the IFP's demand for an extreme form of federalism that would give virtual autonomy to KwaZulu and Natal; and by the demands of the ultra-rightwing for a *volkstaat*. From the inception, the ANC had demanded a unitary state, with regional administrations that were little more than conveyor belts of policies determined by the central government.

The ANC mistrusted the federal concept for three interlinked reasons: first, it was regarded as a way of according 'respectability' to the bantustans by converting them into regions of a federal state. The ANC was implacably opposed to the entire bantustan idea, and the ethnic basis on which they had been demarcated. Secondly, the ANC believed that federal regionalisation would prevent the establishment of an all-powerful, indeed, hegemonic, central government by creating countervailing centres of power. Thirdly, it was believed that a federal system would entrench the existing pattern of regional inequalities by enabling wealthier regions to protect themselves against measures aimed at reducing economic disparities.

In a robust criticism of federal proposals, Kader Asmal, an academic lawyer and one of the ANC's constitutional advisors, insisted that federation could not succeed if it was imposed on a previously unitary state or where nearly half the country's wealth was locked into one geographical area, namely the Pretoria-Witwatersrand-Vereeniging Triangle. He argued that the proponents of federalism were animated principally by the idea that 'less government is good government', thereby depriving the central government of the power to allocate resources and to establish central standards for economic reconstruction.[21] It was a clear indication of the ANC's dirigiste intentions.

The ANC's rejection of federalism was similar to that of the majority of African nationalist movements elsewhere. In the heady days of Africa's liberation from colonial rule, 'nation-building' was the universal quest, and federalism was regarded as a system that would thwart mobilisation for its attainment. Anti-federalism also reflected hegemonic aspirations in circumstances where fissiparous tendencies were common, actually or potentially. Benyamin Neuberger wrote:

> The African opponents of federalism are not so much concerned with the division of power as with the creation of power. For them, order and stability loom much more important than pluralism and compromise with their odium of sectorialism and particularism.[22]

It was ironic that the NP, having been the architect of a highly centralised system of government that culminated in the abolition of provincial councils in 1986, had now become a supporter of federalism. It was equally ironic that the NP, in spite of the centralising thrust of government, was a federally structured party, and had been so since its inception.

The NP's embrace of federalism reflected the new reality of imminent control of government by the ANC. If the power-sharing proposals for a multiparty executive at the centre were unlikely to get very far, then federalism could reasonably be regarded as another form of power-sharing. Political considerations supported this view: the Western Cape was certain to be demarcated as a region, and, since Africans were a demographic minority there, and Coloured support for the NP was substantial, the NP believed that it could win control in an election. Depending on how many regions would be established, and what their boundaries would be, yet others might also be won. Federalism might also help to stanch the haemorrhaging of support by erstwhile NP supporters to the IFP (a poll taken in January 1993 showed that 19 per cent of white voters supported the IFP).[23]

That calculations of political gains or losses should have shaped the debate on regional government was hardly surprising; indeed, they were inevitable. A more abstract, though no less pertinent, argument advanced by the DP was that a federal system was desirable because it erected barricades against an overbearing and potentially tyrannical central government. The DP and its antecedent parties could claim a long record of support for the federal idea for this reason. An earlier generation of federalists had made the identical argument in the debates that preceded the unification of South Africa in 1909. Olive Schreiner, a novelist as well as a pioneer feminist and liberal, for example, wrote:

> The special danger of centralized democratic States is always the tendency to fall a prey to the tyranny of sections, of large interests, or of strong individuals. The walls of each self-governing State [in a federation] are so many barricades, each one of which must be broken down before any oppressive over-domination can absolutely succeed; and, behind any one of which a successful resistance may take place when others have fallen. In short, it makes for freedom.[24]

Another irony was the extent to which the debates of the 1990s mirrored those at the (all-white) National Convention in 1908, where the great protagonists of a unitary South Africa were Smuts and John X Merriman, Prime Minister of the Cape Colony, whose misleading argument maintained that the underlying unity of the white 'races' (meaning Boer and Briton) rendered federation unnecessary. The differences between the 'races' was 'superficial and would disappear' said Merriman; Smuts held the hopeful view that the units coming together in South Africa were not 'independent powers but brothers'.[25] To extend the irony even further, the strongest proponents of federalism were the delegates from Natal! They eventually acquiesced, expressing satisfaction with the few (pseudo-) federal sops thrown in their direction.

Albie Sachs, one of the ANC's leading constitutional experts, observed the parallels between the two constitution-making processes, noting that Smuts's key aspiration was to bring Boer and Briton together – just as the ANC now wanted 'all the people of our country to feel they are part of one evolving nation'. The provinces of the old South Africa, he said, had similar powers to the ones that the ANC was now proposing.[26] The evolution of that system showed that it was little more than a unitary system with some federal fig-leaves.

*   *   *

By common consent most parties in the MPNP stopped using the word 'federalism' – the so-called 'F' word – in debates, and spoke instead of regional powers and functions. Subsequently the acronym 'SPR' came into use. This was a shorthand and neutral way of combining 'States, Provinces and Regions', each one of which was perceived as connoting a particular form of constitutional structure. 'SPR' covered all possibilities, and could be used without committing the user to any one. Given the ANC's hostility to federalism, abandonment of the term facilitated more constructive debate about what role SPRs might actually play in the future system.

According to Meyer's account, the ANC 'underwent a fundamental change of mind' at a bilateral meeting with the NP in January 1993. It now accepted, he claimed, that authority should be rolled downwards, rather than delegated, meaning that the central government could no longer remove powers and functions that it had rolled down. This shift, together with an agreement on power-sharing for a five-year period, had, over the course of the bilateral negotiations between December 1992 and February 1993, opened the way to a new political dispensation: 'We entered a new phase in the negotiation politics because pragmatism and co-operation in [the] national interest had set in.'[27]

In his eagerness to reach agreement with the ANC on basic issues, Meyer exaggerated the extent which the ANC's change of mind was 'fundamental'; although there had been some sign of greater flexibility, which opened up the possibility of a settlement. There had been mutual recognition between the two parties that it was misleading to view federal and unitary forms of government in dichotomous terms: formally unitary systems could permit a substantial degree of decentralisation, and federal systems could be highly centralised. Unitary and federal systems are located on a continuum, containing a penumbral zone in which there may be a substantial overlap. Moreover, in all modern systems, whether formally federal or unitary, central and regional governments interact, co-operate and interpenetrate in myriad ways. In a famous comment about American federalism, Morton Grodzins observed that it resembled a marble cake rather than a layer cake.

The shift in the ANC's thinking was its recognition that strong regional governments did not preclude a strong central government. This point had been brought home by visits to federal systems, sponsored by several federal states. As early as September 1992 the United States had suggested that a federal structure was most appropriate for South Africa's circumstances, arguing that federalism did not mean a weak central government that was incapable of rooting out apartheid and its vestiges. Moreover, by responding reasonably on this issue the ANC could perhaps parry or neutralise the IFP's extreme confederal demands. The American Ambassador, Princeton Lyman, an acute observer of local politics, made repeated efforts to persuade the ANC to address Buthelezi's demands for federalism: 'Until it was addressed the ANC could not expose other, deeper sources of his [Buthelezi's] resistance to the negotiations under way, nor convince other parties that the ANC had made a serious effort to reach agreement.'[28]

It was German federalism that had the most influence. An ANC delegation found that the relationship between the *länder* (states) and the centre was similar to what the ANC was proposing, namely, that with two relatively small exceptions, the *länder* and the central government had concurrent powers, with the centre having the decisive say in the event of conflict. The delegation also approved of the German system's principle of equalisation whereby a higher proportion of state funding went to poorer than to wealthier states.[29]

At a national conference held in March 1993 the ANC finalised its regional policy. It proposed a minimum of four and a maximum of ten regions within a system that allowed for regional variety without taking away the principle of a single, united country. Thozamile Botha, head of the ANC Commission on Local Government, said that of the various political systems the ANC had examined, none was purely federal or purely unitary: all were mixtures, and the system the ANC proposed was a combination:

> Powers are being given to the regions and we are saying those powers should be protected to the extent that they are original. But we are not proposing that regions should be given exclusive powers to undermine the centre. The centre remains with the right to override the regions on issues of national interest.

Furthermore, regional boundaries, powers and functions should be entrenched in the Constitution; and while the central government should not have the power to dismiss a regional government, a regional government that encountered serious problems could request the centre to act, whereupon it would stand down. Until elections could be held the central government would take charge.

Regional representatives or senators would represent regional interests in the national Parliament, fighting to ensure that the interests of their regions were protected at national level. There would be a consultation mechanism linking regional governments and representatives of the respective regions at the centre.

As far as the allocation of powers was concerned, the central government would have exclusive jurisdiction over defence, national security and foreign affairs; but functions such as, for example, health, education, development and planning would be exercised concurrently by the regions and the centre, with the centre having the power to set national standards.[30]

An earlier discussion paper had set out a framework to which the ANC would adhere:

> Regions would not be able to contradict national policy as expressed in national laws, but they will help to shape such policy and have considerable scope in relation to how best to implement it. If one takes health as an example. It is difficult to imagine the huge health problems of the country being solved in a piecemeal way. We will need national policies in relation to training, the creation of health delivery services, immunization, health education, notification of diseases and so on. At the same time, it will be impossible for the centre to decide on every question of where hospitals or clinics should be built. There has to be regional decision-making and implementation within the context of regional development policies and in touch with regional needs and sensibilities.[31]

Thozamile Botha did not believe that the differences among the parties were irreconcilable, but he ruled out an Afrikaner *volkstaat*:

> Although we have to take into account linguistic and cultural differences, we cannot use ethnicity or racial considerations as determinants of boundaries.[32]

The ANC's proposals were a far cry from federalist ideas that the NP had considered in September 1992 (and subsequently dropped). The NP's suggestion, presented in a technical report, was that a function ought to be carried out at the lowest tier of government, where it could be most effectively implemented. In line with this, it was argued, the central government's functions should be limited to defence, national security, foreign affairs and constitutional planning; major functions, including education, finance, taxation, trade, health, mining, police, roads, water affairs and welfare could be allocated to the SPRs. At the conference where the report, written by a government advisor, was discussed, De Klerk made it clear that no final decisions on federalism were being taken: the purpose was to discuss the issue, and to prove 'once and for all the ridiculousness of the assertion that federalism is an instrument of clinging to power'.[33]

It was quite clear that the ANC would never accept a highly decentralised system, notwithstanding the NP's disavowal of any ulterior motives. Why, then, did Meyer accept the ANC's supposed 'fundamental change of mind' with such alacrity? Was it a case of clutching at straws in a negotiating situation in which he recognised just how far the NP's bargaining power had weakened? Was it the advice of bureaucrats who pointed out that national standards and guidelines were vital for many line-function ministries, and required a strong central government? Moreover, as Richard Humphries and his co-authors point out, the NP's sobering experience with the wretched quality of governance and the pervasiveness of corruption in the bantustans had raised serious doubts about the likely administrative capacity of SPRs that incorporated them.[34] Guarantees that mass retrenchment of officials in these swollen bureaucracies would not occur meant that the same officials would have to be employed in the new SPRs.

All of these possible explanations are plausible, but perhaps the decisive one was the recognition of how urgent it was to reach agreement with the ANC. There were two reasons for this: first, the date for the first election, 27 April 1994, was by now virtually set in stone, and could not be postponed without risk of serious disturbances and the possibility of rupturing the fragile 'sufficient consensus' slowly being built up between the ANC and the NP. Secondly, the (white) House of Assembly had been elected on 6 September 1989 (and De Klerk elected as State President on 14 September) for a constitutionally-stipulated five-year term. A general election would have to be held within 180 days of the term's expiry. De Klerk could have changed the constitutional provisions, but he would have been reluctant to do so: it would have offended his sense of constitutional propriety and it would have given the CP and assorted ultra-rightwing allies a last-gasp opportunity to achieve the unlikely, but not impossible, result of defeating the NP. The concessions that the NP had had to make and the continuing violence, especially that targeting whites, might well have resulted in a humiliating denting of the NP's prestige, as well as aggravating racial polarisation.

Humphries *et al* write:

NP strategists insist that it did not want stronger regional powers. But the transition had to be complete by the end of its term of office in mid-1994. Since they expected it to take much longer than that to wear down ANC opposition to stronger powers, they concluded that there was not enough time to secure what they wanted. Their goal, therefore, was an interim constitution which would allow regional pressures for greater powers, if they emerged, to erode the scope of the centre. Winning one province was crucial to the strategy because it would provide a base to push for more powers, although they also hoped for regional pressures within the ANC and the [still to be established] constitutional court. Instead of seeking a constitution which guaranteed regional powers, they banked on one which would offer room to press for them.[35]

The reference in the last sentence to the potential political dynamic that strong regional government could generate was significant. Federal systems create political sub-systems at the regional level, and these, in turn, tend to federalise national parties. If the NP welcomed this possibility as a brake on the potentially hegemonic power of an ANC-dominated national government, this was precisely why the ANC opposed it. As a 'broad church', the ANC had to be mindful of internal divisions that could threaten its overall unity, especially in future times when the binding power of shared commitment to the struggle began to lose its force. Slovo noted how at ANC or SACP national meetings 'regions jealously (and correctly) guard their jurisdiction over those areas on which they are most informed and with which they are most connected'.[36] The more power vested in the regions, the more assertive regional ANC parties were likely to become. Regions, accordingly, had to be kept on a tight leash.

Secondly, there was the 'Inkatha problem': apart from the bad name that Buthelezi's demands had given federalism, there was apprehension in the ANC that he might try to emulate Unita (União Nacional para a Indepêndencia Total de Angola), the Angolan nationalist movement that was fighting a bloody civil war in Angola against its rival, the governing MPLA (Movimento Popular de Libertação de Angola).[37] Although Buthelezi had never threatened the Unita option, his bellicose warnings left little doubt that a comparable conflict was a possibility if the ANC and NP tried to impose an unacceptable (because insufficiently federal) Constitution on his political heartland: 'The South African government and the ANC are making deals behind our backs …. If this happens, Zulus will not listen. I see at the very least massive civil disobedience in Natal, and at the most civil war. I shudder when I say this because it is something you do not say lightly.'[38]

This could not be dismissed as mere bluster: although it might have been exactly that, the possibility of an insurgency or rebellion with the assistance of the IFP's Cosag allies had to be taken seriously.

Buthelezi's opposition to the modus operandi of the MPNP, especially the concept of 'sufficient consensus', was total. Underlying his brink-manship was a huge resentment at not being regarded as one of the 'big three' political leaders, a sentiment that manifested itself in an apparent determination to demonstrate that no settlement was possible without the IFP's being one of its architects. Since the signing of the Record of Understanding between the government and the ANC in September 1992, Buthelezi's alienation from the negotiating process and his mistrust of De Klerk and the ANC had festered. He opposed the idea that an elected body should draft the final Constitution (knowing that the IFP would be a distinctly minority party in such a body). Instead, he argued that the Constitution should be drafted by a committee of experts and thereafter submitted to a national referendum, having been approved by the multi-party conference. No revolutionary movement such as the ANC, he con-tinued, had ever drawn up a Constitution that enabled opposition parties to unseat it in an election:

> A constituent assembly, vested with the power of the electoral suf-frage, will not feel bound to follow any principle. As any other body, it will claim the greatest amount of power possible, and will draft a constitution which will bring under its scope and will organize the greatest amount of powers possible.[39]

Buthelezi was unique among bantustan leaders in the way he was able to fuse modern and traditional political styles. His role as the Zulu mon-arch's Prime Minister allowed him, after he had effectively ensured that the King remained out of politics, to control him, but also to use him as a political resource when required. The monarchy was the capstone of traditional leadership in KwaZulu, which, in turn, was the custodian of the IFP's support-base. The King, Goodwill Zwelithini, was not an im-pressive figure in the mould of some of his predecessors like Cetshwayo or Dinuzulu. Despite his ambitions to be a monarch who exercised real power, like his Swazi counterpart to whom he was related by marriage, he remained merely a figurehead. He was no match for Buthelezi, who kept him on a tight rein and ensured that no rival centre of influence devel-oped around him. Buthelezi had been especially vigilant in ensuring that 'alien' forces were kept out of what Inkatha regarded as its turf. These forces included the usual suspects, the UDF/ANC and Cosatu, but also, after its establishment as a national organisation in 1989, the Congress of Traditional Leaders of South Africa (Contralesa), which was aligned to the ANC and was committed to fighting 'tribalism and ethnicity' and 'schooling chiefs about the aims of the South African Liberation Struggle'.[40]

Notwithstanding his lack of real power, the King was a powerful symbol of Zulu unity and respected as such by many Zulu ANC supporters, including Jacob Zuma, the most prominent Zulu in the ANC hierarchy, who was to be the ANC's candidate for the premiership of KwaZulu-Natal in the election of 1994. The King's symbolic value suited the IFP's purposes, as its lack of countrywide support forced it to defend the Zulu heartland and to beat a Zulu ethnic drum (while accusing the ANC of being 'Xhosa-dominated'). It was not only the fragmented KwaZulu bantustan that was at issue: both the King and the IFP demanded the restoration of the whole of the historic, pre-colonial territory that had been brought under Zulu control by King Shaka by 1834.

After the ignominious collapse of Bophuthatswana and Ciskei during 1994, Slovo had exulted 'two down, one to go'. The 'one' referred to KwaZulu (Transkei and Venda already being governed by military dictators who were firmly in the ANC camp). Slovo's comment infuriated Buthelezi, who lashed back, declaring that if the ANC tried to destabilise KwaZulu as it had done in Bophuthatswana and attempted in Ciskei, 'a conflict of awesome proportions will be unleashed to the tragic detriment of South Africa and the democratic process'.

A notion of 'Zulu-ness' had survived, though with varying degrees of intensity determined by locality, class, education and other factors. It was strong among the Zulu peasantry, and even sharpened by their experiences as migrant labourers on the Witwatersrand in the 1970s and 1980s, when political conflict developed. For many traditionalists, folk memories of a golden age of Zulu military prowess were also woven into their sense of identity.

Negative intra-African stereotypes had been shaded, though not eliminated, by the weight of common opposition to racial discrimination. The Zulu were widely regarded as 'fierce', 'cruel', or 'prone to violence' – stereotypes that had existed for decades. The Xhosa, on the other hand, were regarded by many Zulu (and other ethnic groups) as 'clever', 'cunning', or 'crafty'. Horowitz, who reviewed survey data, noted that while the white/black conflict was pre-eminent, there were limits to intra-African ethnicity; but that there was 'a substructure of allegiances and divisions available for activation when a new context brings African politics into the foreground'.[41] This is precisely what occurred between IFP-supporting Zulu and the allegedly Xhosa-controlled ANC once political space had opened up and competition intensified. There was a grain of truth in the allegation that the ANC was Xhosa-dominated: most of the heavyweight figures of recent decades were Xhosa-speakers, including Mandela (and his wife, Winnie), Tambo, Sisulu, Hani, Govan Mbeki and Thabo Mbeki. None, however, could be described as a 'Xhosa nationalist'; indeed, all fully subscribed to the ANC's taboo on 'tribalism'. That Xhosa-speakers were prominent in the ANC owed far more to the earlier and more intensive penetration of the ANC's heartland, the Eastern Cape, by missionaries and teachers than to any ethnic favouritism.

Two other facts are germane: first, several ANC presidents-general had been Zulu: Pixley Seme, John L Dube and Albert Luthuli; secondly, in the 1994 elections, the ANC ran strongly in those provinces even where Xhosa-speakers were small minorities. Even in KwaZulu-Natal an estimated 40 per cent of Zulu voters supported the ANC, compared with 55 per cent who supported the IFP.[42]

Buthelezi's championing of the King's claim to be seated at the MPNP failed, just as it had at the earlier negotiations. The ostensible reason for the ANC's refusal to allow this, despite the government's approval, was that if the Zulu King attended there could be no reasonable grounds for refusing the claims of other ethnic kings (so-called 'paramount chiefs'). Undoubtedly the ANC regarded Buthelezi's demands as a ploy to win support for the IFP, which, in fact, had achieved some success. Many militants in the ANC, moreover, regarded chieftainship as symbolic of 'backward tribalism' that should be dispensed with in a new democratic order. The impact of white rule had perverted the institution in major ways – for example, by undermining the sanctions that constrained chiefly power. Nevertheless, as the ANC would learn, traditional leaders retained considerable influence especially among rural people, and it would prove impossible to dispense with them. It was a lesson that had been learned in other parts of sub-Saharan Africa. Mandela, being himself of royal Thembu stock, needed no persuasion. The Interim Constitution of 1993 gave far-reaching recognition to traditional leaders, including provision for provincial Houses of Traditional Leaders and a national Council of Traditional Leaders.

Throughout 1993 the American government, through Ambassador Lyman, tried hard to persuade Buthelezi to return to the MPNP, and the ANC to moderate its rejection of federalism (in which he had had some success):

> We were pressing the parties to recognize and respond to the issues
> of federalism …. But by being absent from the negotiations, Inkatha

gave credence to the charge that its real goal was to delay, even pre-vent, an election.[43]

Inkatha's fears were real. It had no faith in the ANC's readiness to abide by principles agreed to by the MPNP that would have to be incorporated into the final Constitution. This referred to the ingenious way in which the constitution-making circle was to be squared. The final Constitution would be drawn up by Parliament sitting as a constitution-making body, but it would be bound by constitutional principles, of which there were eventually 34, appended as a schedule to the Interim Constitution. The still-to-be established Constitutional Court would have to certify that these principles had been incorporated in the final Constitution.

The compromise had been a point of some contention in the ANC, whose radicals wanted an elected constituent assembly to have unfettered power to draft the Constitution. Lyman urged Slovo to avoid insisting that the Interim Constitution would be subject to 'total revision' by the constituent assembly – and was gratified when Slovo took the point and proposed to the MPNP that the phrase be dropped.[44]

The violence raged on. Buthelezi's threats of civil war were mostly warn-ings of what might occur if an unacceptable Constitution were imposed on KwaZulu. Others in the IFP camp were less inhibited: unbeknown to Buthelezi, some members of Inkatha set up a 'security committee' to or-ganise military resistance to the impending Constitution. The committee did little more than discuss the issue, agreeing optimistically that it would be logistically impossible for the South African army to invade and oc-cupy KwaZulu. An IFP demand that MK be disbanded was rejected by the MPNP, whereupon it began to train 'self-protection' units; by March 1994 some 3 000 trainees had completed their training.[45]

Buthelezi's brinkmanship would continue into 1994, the *denouement* coming only days before the election. He was encouraged in his hard-line approach by his Italian-American constitutional advisor, Mario Ambrosini, and his confidant, Walter Felgate. Moderates in the IFP, such as Frank Mdlalose and Ben Ngubane, although strongly committed to federalism, were decidedly unhappy about the role played in the negotia-tions by Ambrosini and Felgate, but could do little to curb their influence. De Klerk was also critical of them:

> Time and again, when we appeared to be making progress, they [Ambrosini and Felgate] would get into a huddle with Buthelezi and the whole process would once again freeze up. We found Buthelezi's senior black advisors far more approachable and reasonable.[46]

The motley assortment of ultra-rightwing organisations and bantustan leaders linked together as Cosag was superseded in October 1993 by the Freedom Alliance (FA), comprising the same members but incorporating the Afrikaner Volksfront (AVF), which consisted of 21 parties and organisations. It was led by a Directorate consisting of four retired generals, including Constand Viljoen as chairman. The Directorate reported to the Afrikaner Volksfrontraad, which was dominated by the CP. The Directorate produced a plan of action, which included among its goals the promotion of unity among Afrikaners and a demand that 'we as a people wish to maintain our identity and therefore would strive for an area inside South Africa where we as a people would govern ourselves through the concept of self-determination'. It rejected the direction taken at the MPNP as 'completely unacceptable' since it was based on 'individual liberalism'.[47]

Despite the aim of achieving greater unity, the AVF was soon dogged by the same problems that had confronted the ultra-right previously, namely differences over strategy and an inability to agree on where a putative Afrikaner enclave, or *volkstaat*, should be located. The ultra-right had not confronted the basic issue that there was no region, not even a white-owned farm, where whites outnumbered blacks. A partial exception to this was the arid Northern Cape, which Carel Boshoff (Verwoerd's son-in-law), chairman of the Afrikaner Vryheid Stigting (Afrikaner Freedom Foundation), advocated. No one else wanted it, he explained. The bleakness of the area, however, meant that very few Afrikaners, however rightwing, would be prepared to sell their farms or suburban homes and trek to a wasteland. (A small community of some 600 souls, called Orania, was subsequently established.)

A more immediate issue than the location of a *volkstaat*, however, was the strategy for acquiring it: was it to be by negotiation, by a combination of seizure and force (a kind of unilateral declaration of independence), or some permutation of these methods? It was evident that there were serious divisions regarding strategy. In his submission to the TRC, Viljoen said that a 'negotiation process' was part of the strategic thinking of the Directorate. In consultation with Ferdi Hartzenberg, a hardliner who was chairman of the AVF's *Raad* (Council) and Treurnicht's successor as CP leader, the Directorate started a secret process of bilateral negotiation with Mandela in August 1993, which continued with Thabo Mbeki until the eve of the election in April 1994. The CP, however, had withdrawn from the MPNP in July 1993, expressing outrage at the decision to approve the election date with sufficient consensus. It demanded 'unequivocal recognition' of the Afrikaners' right to self-determination. Shortly thereafter, Hartzenberg further demanded a 'whites-only' referendum on the impending Interim Constitution. He was no doubt encouraged by an opinion poll published in October which indicated that the AVF enjoyed much the same support among whites as the NP.[48]

Viljoen was troubled by the CP's withdrawal, which had been taken unilaterally and without reference to the AVF or its Directorate. He was even more troubled by the behaviour of the swaggering thugs of the AWB and its leader, Eugène Terre'Blanche, who were also members of Cosag and thereafter the Freedom Alliance. On 25 June 1993 the AVF had received permission to hold a protest meeting outside the World Trade Centre in Kempton Park where the MPNP's deliberations were being held. The careful arrangements set up by the protest's organisers and the authorities were comprehensively violated when several hundred AWB supporters, many of them drunk, led by Terre'Blanche, invaded and vandalised the building, shouting racist abuse and tearing up documents. In the midst of the chaos, there was a moment of pure bathos: one of Terre'Blanche's aides approached an official, saying '*Die leier wil pis*' ('The leader wishes to piss').

It was potentially a dangerous situation: Jan Heunis, a government legal adviser who witnessed the invasion, was convinced that violence, which could have led to civil war, was averted by two young policemen who threatened the mob with automatic weapons and forced a retreat.[49]

The rampage caused over R700 000 in damage and resulted in the arrest of 60 people, many of whom were subsequently charged and convicted. Several police officers were injured in the scuffles, despite a decision by the police not to use force inside the building. The Goldstone Commission, while critical of the role of the police, nevertheless agreed that had force been used 'a bloodbath could well have ensued'.[50] Criticism was expressed that what the Commission called 'a dereliction of duty' and the ineffectiveness of the police showed their underlying partiality. Given the injuries sustained and the arrests made, it is hard to sustain the criticism. That errors of judgement were made is true – and deserving of the Commission's strictures – but the allegation of a partisan response was unproven.

The ugliness of the episode and the uncontrollable behaviour of the AWB dismayed Viljoen. He told the TRC that this unplanned action 'was the first of virtually every action which we undertook which in some way ended with an opposite result as was planned'.[51] Clearly, the courteous and decent Viljoen was embarrassed by his loutish allies.

Viljoen emerges from the transition with honour, as the leader of a significant bloc of white opinion who opted, after considerable hesitation, to join the process rather than attempt to sabotage it. As a military man he was inclined to distrust politicians, but he was thrust into becoming one himself after requests from a gathering of farmers to become active in the process 'in order to give strategic guidance to the Afrikaner peoples'.[52] Viljoen was no ordinary conservative. He was not personally a racist, and, indeed, was offended by the unbridled racism of many of his newfound allies. In his submissions to the TRC he acknowledged that 40 years of apartheid had destroyed 'the original Afrikaner ideals of freedom from bondage, when they themselves assumed the characteristics of imperialist rule in South Africa'. Moreover, he said,

> ... we have to admit that the historic struggle of the Afrikaner for freedom and self-realization did not bring about the sensitivity that was needed in order to understand the same motivations and concern when they came from the black people.[53]

In 1996, when it was apparent that the quest for a *volkstaat* was failing, Viljoen told the TRC that the Freedom Front (the party he founded in 1994 to contest the election) accepted that 'the offensive political policies of the past had to be replaced with non-racial governance'; but he warned that 'non-racial structures do not finally guarantee that racialism has been overcome'. Non-racialism, moreover, did not exclude a 'healthy sense of solidarity within distinct communities'.[54]

The fighting talk of the farmers who had summoned Viljoen to leadership did not sway him. He told Allister Sparks:

> I'm not for fighting .... I'm not available for that role – for the moment .... I have accepted the fact that we have switched from a military strategy to that of negotiation.[55]

The critical phrase was 'for the moment', which suggested that circumstances might arise which, he deemed, required a violent response. Ambassador Lyman, who was doing his best to persuade both Buthelezi and Viljoen to participate in the elections, quoted Viljoen as saying that only the retired generals of the Directorate had the strategic vision lacking in the hardline politicians who were unwilling to compromise: ironically, Viljoen said, 'the generals were preventing war'. Viljoen nevertheless kept the option of a war of resistance open as a last resort – but many of his followers kept pushing him. He told Lyman that it might be possible to seize and then defend a *volkstaat* without civil war:

> My idea was not to start a new Anglo-Boer War [1899-1902] with

people joining in. My idea was to demarcate, like the UDI [Unilateral Declaration of Independence in Rhodesia/Zimbabwe], a certain area, say the Eastern Transvaal, and say to the negotiating persons, 'Look here, you either demarcate this into a *Volkstaat* for the Afrikaner, or if you attack us we will resist. We're not going to attack you.'[56]

Viljoen had considered the possibility of a coup. He believed that he could raise some 60 000 men, many of them highly trained. In a conversation with Georg Meiring, chief of the Defence Force, Viljoen had said, 'You and I and our men can take this country in an afternoon,' to which Meiring replied, 'Yes, that is so, but what do we do the morning after the coup?'[57] Meiring, whose remit on appointment had been to sever the links between the Defence Force and the ultra-right, also told Viljoen that: 'If you are really going to do what you say you are going to do, we'll have to stop you.' Asked by an interviewer whether he really would have been prepared to tackle Viljoen head-on if he had taken up arms, he replied: 'Yes, sure, because there was no wisdom in doing it.'[58]

In an interview published in 1999, Viljoen denied that it was ever his idea to 'recapture the old South Africa', stage a coup, or take command. They wanted a *volkstaat*, but the problem was: where? 'I had troops ready, everything, but didn't know which area to defend.' He added:

I never worked on dividing the defence force. It was not my idea to cause violent insurrection. But had I decided on the violent option, there would have been a number of soldiers who would have followed me. It was reassuring, but it also placed a heavy burden on me. It would have destabilized the SADF and would have been a mechanism for instability.[59]

In his submissions to the TRC, Viljoen acknowledged that preparations for armed resistance had been mandated, including stockpiling of weapons and explosives, and logistical arrangements. Having failed to persuade the Demarcation Committee of the MPNP to consider a *volkstaat*, it seemed to him that 'some large-scale action would be necessary'. It was necessary for the AVF:

1. to have a stick available. The stick of the ANC was mass action violence. We needed one too.
2. certain actions had to be started during this process – to show the stick. This led to a number of actions of sabotage. This was done in a way to avoid loss of life and gross violations of human life.

3. As it became clear that mainly through the action of Mr De Klerk the 'volkstaat before 27 April' mandate would not be achieved, planning was directed at declaring a certain area inside South Africa as a volkstaat and to use the Volksfront force to defend it should it be attacked.[60]

Unlike anyone else of significance on the ultra-right, Viljoen had supported the release of Mandela and the initiation of negotiations with the ANC, in spite of his intense dislike of the communists in its ranks. In his view, however, things had gone awry since then. He told the TRC:

We felt betrayed and confused by Mr De Klerk's overnight change from total war to being a dove of peace. Let me say it: we did not believe him and most important, we did not trust his negotiating capacity ... [Conservative Afrikaners'] ideas of self-determination were scorned at in the negotiating forums. They witnessed the NP negotiators fold one after the other. They saw with disbelief how the NP tried vainly to match the concept of majority rule with their invention of power-sharing.[61]

Viljoen's contempt for De Klerk was ill-concealed. To some extent De Klerk reciprocated, describing Viljoen as 'inexperienced' in politics and, 'at times, quite naïve'.[62] Having fought vigorous political battles with the ultra-rightwing for more than a decade, it was impossible for De Klerk to make any concessions to the *volkstaat* idea – upon which he and the NP had long heaped scorn – without giving a fillip to the CP's electoral hopes.

Being unable to make headway with De Klerk and his negotiators, Viljoen turned to Mandela, whom he first met in August 1993, thanks to the efforts of his identical twin brother, Braam, an academic theologian with strong liberal views who had good contacts with the ANC. In spite of their political differences, the brothers were close, and, apart from helping Constand to meet Mandela, Braam assisted with the effort to explore the concept of 'self-determination' that was central to the AVF's aims.

The meeting with Mandela and some of his colleagues went well. Mandela viewed the possibility of an ultra-rightwing insurrection with considerable apprehension, especially in the light of the alliance with the IFP. Many in the ANC, including Slovo, believed that the IFP could be crushed, and some, no doubt, were itching to do exactly that: if 'marching to Pretoria' had been denied them, then 'marching to Ulundi' would at least be a consolation prize. The emergence of a popular figure like

Viljoen, with an ability to raise a substantial militia, changed the equation. In grave terms Mandela said to Viljoen and his fellow generals:

> If you go to war I must be honest and admit that we cannot stand up to you on the battlefield. We don't have the resources. It will be a long and bitter struggle, many people will die and the country may be reduced to ashes. But you must remember two things. You cannot win because of our numbers: you cannot kill us all. And you cannot win because of the international community. They will rally to our support and they will stand with us.[63]

The essential truth of Mandela's words must have struck a resonant chord in Viljoen's mind. Although he had not yet fully eschewed the violent option, his instincts were pointing towards negotiation. As Meiring had tartly pointed out, the UDI option created the same dilemma as that of the dog chasing a bus: what did it do when it caught it? Whatever territory was eventually chosen as a *volkstaat* (and it seemed unlikely that agreement on this could ever be achieved among the *volkstaters* themselves) would have a large black demographic majority: would they be subject to discrimination and/or forced removals, and would their continued subjugation not provoke a sustained uprising that would require massive coercion to contain? Moreover, any putative *volkstaat* would be an economic hostage to the rest of South Africa, whose new rulers would not hesitate to turn the screws on it. In short, the *volkstaat* concept was pure chimera.

In spite of this unpromising prognosis, the ANC, in its efforts to neutralise the possibility of ultra-rightwing insurgency, entered into a lengthy series of meetings – over 20 in all – with Viljoen. De Klerk was not put out at Viljoen's choice of the ANC as the AVF's bilateral negotiating partner. If Mandela could use his legendary charm to woo the AVF into the elections, 'I would not get in their way'. The NP's negotiators would continue to try developing a framework that could accommodate Viljoen, as well as Buthelezi and Mangope of Bophuthatswana.[64]

Mandela and Viljoen were impressed with each other: Mandela appreciated Viljoen's directness and his obvious honesty of purpose; Viljoen found Mandela and his colleagues reasonable and flexible, prepared to hear him out – even if the ANC had not the slightest intention of conceding a *volkstaat*. Viljoen told Ambassador Lyman, 'I think I can trust Mandela. But can I trust all those Communists around him?'[65]

In follow-up meetings, Mbeki and his colleagues, notably the amiable and conciliatory Jacob Zuma, probed the *volkstaters'* proposals, hoping that Viljoen would be forced to recognise their utter impracticability: Mbeki 'just kept asking him questions which he could not answer'.[66] It was a shrewd strategy, far more likely to be productive than a blunt rejection. Mbeki, who had had long experience of seeking to allay Afrikaner fears of majority rule, sought to reassure Viljoen that Afrikaners would be culturally secure under an ANC government, and that their identity would not be threatened. Mbeki appeared to have some empathy for Afrikaners, regarding them as indigenous Africans, worthy of inclusion in his understanding of 'Africanism'.[67]

Progress towards agreement, however, remained slow. Both Mbeki and Viljoen came under fire from their respective camps when knowledge of their negotiations became public. Ramaphosa, the ANC's chief negotiator, took a far harder line, as did his NP counterpart, Meyer: both wanted a speedy resolution. Eventually the Interim Constitution was adopted by the MPNP on 18 November 1993 and was ratified by Parliament on 22 December.

An important innovation, produced as a draft bill by the MPNP and enacted into law by Parliament, was the Transitional Executive Council (TEC), whose principal function was to facilitate the transition in the run-up to the election by promoting a climate for free political participation, and also to monitor governments and administrations to ensure that they could not derive electoral advantage from incumbency of office. It was, according to De Klerk, 'a limited form of power-sharing', but not a parallel government. The ANC, not wishing to be saddled with the responsibility of shared government, agreed.

The TEC was a multiparty body whose participants were required to renounce violence as a condition of membership. Its work was divided among sub-councils dealing with regional and local government, law and order, stability and security, defence, finance, intelligence and foreign affairs. The ANC was especially eager to ensure that strict control was exercised over the security forces: in effect, joint control was to be maintained.

In tandem with the TEC, two other important bodies were created: the Independent Electoral Commission and the Independent Media Commission. The latter's function was principally to ensure that public broadcasting services and state-financed publications avoided bias, and afforded parties the opportunity to participate in discussions, as well as to advertise, provided that all parties were afforded similar access.

Predictably, the CP, the IFP and the Bophuthatswana government opposed the TEC, the CP declaring it to be 'a constitutional revolution that will transfer power to the ANC/South African Communist Party alliance', and the IFP and Bophuthatswana vehemently objecting to the prospect of their internal affairs being subject to what Buthelezi called 'foreigners' ruling the 'Zulu nation'. Buthelezi also threatened military resistance to any potential TEC incursion onto Inkatha's turf.[68]

In spite of the long series of bilateral talks, neither the IFP nor the AVF appeared anywhere close to participating in the forthcoming election. No member of the Freedom Alliance attended the plenary meeting of the MPNP that approved the Constitution. Viljoen announced that acceptance of the Constitution was the beginning of a violent takeover by the communist-inspired ANC. He was reported as calling on AVF supporters to undergo military training and prepare to defend themselves. Buthelezi said that the IFP would meet the new Constitution with 'determined resistance'; and Hartzenberg reiterated his demand for a *volkstaat* in a confederation (whose constituent units would be sovereign).[69]

*   *   *

At this point it is necessary to describe what the Interim Constitution contained, and how it fell short of the demands expressed by Viljoen, Buthelezi and others. The Interim Constitution was to be the template for the final Constitution that would be drafted by the Parliament to be elected in April 1994. The final Constitution, however, was required to incorporate Constitutional Principles, of which there were eventually 34. To repeat: this was the ingenious way in which the constitution-making conundrum was to be resolved.

The Constitution was premised on the assumption that all of the bantustans, independent or otherwise, would be incorporated in the new dispensation, and that there would be a common citizenship. Nine provinces were demarcated on the strength of the MPNP's Commission on the Demarcation/Delimitation of SPRs. No single bantustan was retained intact as a province. For example, Transkei and Ciskei were grouped together with a white-controlled area to constitute Eastern Cape Province; KwaZulu was joined with Natal as Natal Province; and Venda, Gazankulu and Lebowa were included in Northern Transvaal Province. Demarcation largely followed the nine 'development regions' identified earlier by the Development Bank of Southern Africa.[70]

The provisions concerning provinces (the term that replaced SPRs) reflected the series of compromises reached in the MPNP and with Viljoen and Buthelezi. Amendments aimed at bringing the latter and their organisations into the election were enacted early in 1994, even after the Interim Constitution had been passed by Parliament. When the MPNP ratified the final draft of the Constitution on 18 November, Slovo had crowed that it would not be *'remotely* a federation …. We've managed to give them devolution, without losing control.'[71] Meyer, on the other hand, had claimed, optimistically, that 'we have a regional dispensation which has all the hallmarks of federalism'.[72] Meyer probably believed that it was at least a proto-federal Constitution, and that once provinces were established they could use the political space accorded to them, however limited, to press for more powers. But the reverse could occur.

Underpinning the 'sufficient consensus' was the illusion of agreement between the ANC and the NP concerning provincial powers whose actual extent was shrouded in vagueness. With the date for the founding election, 27 April 1994, set in stone, the NP's ability to resist the ANC's demands on provincial and other issues, such as the GNU, had declined. De Klerk and Meyer had recognised, prudently, that moving the election date backwards was impossible. Agreement on the Interim Constitution had to be rushed for this reason. Parliament began its final sitting of the year on 22 November, and if the Constitution were to be enacted into law this was the last opportunity to do so. It was a powerful lever in the hands of the ANC, already dominant in the negotiations. In November, immediately prior to the agreement on the Constitution, an unnamed government negotiator was quoted as saying that the NP 'was bargaining from such a weakened position that it could achieve no more'. Another said that the task of the government negotiators was 'to sell off the family silver as gracefully as possible'.[73]

Schedule 6 of the Interim Constitution listed the legislative competences of the provinces, which included a number of important ones: agriculture, education at all levels, excluding university and technikon education, health services, housing, local government (subject to important limitations on a local authority's power to make by-laws), police (again, subject to significant limitations), regional planning and development, roads, tourism, trade and industrial promotion and welfare services. These powers, however, were not exclusive, but concurrent ones, capable of being exercised jointly with the national government. The principle of concurrency reflected the ANC's view that governmental powers and functions should not, and in fact, could not, be divided between the centre and the provinces. According to Nicholas Haysom, an advisor to the ANC, concurrency was the 'pre-eminent prism' through which both the Interim and final Constitutions' allocation of competences should be viewed: 'both levels of government, national and provincial, would have an interest in a lengthy list of functional areas of social life'.[74]

The national government was to possess major powers of control over provincial governments: an act of Parliament would prevail over a provincial law, provided that it applied uniformly in all parts of the country. The national government was given extensive 'overriding' powers to prevail over provincial laws when:

- the act of Parliament deals with a matter that cannot be effectively regulated by provincial legislation;
- the act of Parliament deals with a matter that, to be performed effectively, requires to be regulated or co-ordinated by uniform norms or standards that apply generally throughout the Republic;
- the act of Parliament is necessary to set minimum standards across the nation for the rendering of public services;
- the act of Parliament is necessary for the maintenance of economic unity, the protection of the environment, the promotion of interprovincial commerce, and protection of the common market in respect of the mobility of goods, services, labour, or the maintenance of national security; or
- the provincial law materially prejudices the economic, health or security interests of another province or the country as a whole, or impedes the implementation of national economic policies.

Interpretation of these provisions promised lucrative pickings for constitutional lawyers. As a legal scholar observed, 'the language is so loose, that whether we actually get a federation is being left to the judges [of the yet-to-be-established Constitutional Court].'[75]

The centralising thrust of the Constitution was reinforced by the provisions governing the financial resources available to provincial governments. Provinces were to be entitled to 'an equitable share of revenue collected nationally to enable it to provide services and perform its power and functions'. The share allocated to each was to be recommended, in accordance with guidelines, by a Financial and Fiscal Commission. Provinces were debarred from imposing income tax or value-added or other sales taxes, but they might, with the authorisation of national legislation, on the recommendation of the Commission, impose surcharges on taxes. Early in 1994, as an inducement to the IFP and others reluctant to contest the election, an amendment to the Constitution gave provinces exclusive competence to impose taxes, levies and duties on casinos, gambling, wagering, lotteries and betting. It was an inducement of limited value: as the ANC made clear, the central government would retain overall control of finances available to provinces.

Other sops were thrown to Buthelezi and Viljoen in the flurry of last-minute amendments early in 1994: instead of a single ballot for elections to both national and provincial legislatures, separate ballots would be required. The ANC had insisted on a single ballot, arguing that double ballots would be confusing to first-time voters, many of whom were illiterate. The double ballot, however, would give greater scope to voter choice, enabling voters to support one party nationally and another provincially.

A second sop was the special recognition that could be given to traditional monarchs when provinces adopted their own Constitutions. KwaZulu/Natal (the name was amended from being merely Natal), however, was specifically required to make such provision for the Zulu monarch, a provision that was buttressed by an amendment to Constitutional Principle XIII, which required that the recognition of a traditional monarch by a provincial Constitution was also to be recognised and protected in the final (national) Constitution.

For Viljoen and the AVF the inducement was the insertion into the Constitution of a Volkstaat Council as a 'mechanism to enable proponents of the idea of a Volkstaat to constitutionally pursue the establishment of such a Volkstaat'. It was to consist of 20 members, elected by members of Parliament who support the establishment of a *volkstaat*. The implication was that only *volkstaters* who participated in the election and were elected to Parliament would have the right to establish the Council. The Council's brief was wide: it was to study possible boundaries, the constitutional relationship with government, and the feasibility of the idea. Furthermore, another Constitutional Principle (number XXXIV) was added, giving the right of self-determination to 'any community sharing a common cultural and language heritage, whether in a territorial entity within the Republic or in any other recognized way'. The final Constitution could give expression to any particular form of self-determination provided there was substantial proven support for it within the community concerned.

Despite the sops thrown his way, Buthelezi remained obdurate: the concessions were insufficient, and they did not meet his fundamental demand that the (final) Constitution be written by experts and only thereafter submitted to a referendum. It was a demand that reflected his intense resentment of being relegated to a subordinate role in the hierarchy of negotiators; but it also reflected his fear that the constitution-making process would eventuate in a blueprint for ANC hegemony, which was by no means an unrealistic view. Moreover, the violence of the preceding decade – which continued unabated – had created real fear in the minds of many IFP people. Ambassador Lyman recounts an incident when he asked one of Buthelezi's more moderate officials why it was that the constitutional guarantees being provided did not meet the IFP's concerns: 'He turned to me, with a look I will never forget, and said, "When the election is over, they will kill every one of us."[76] The fears were groundless, but real nevertheless.

There were differences of opinion in both the ANC and the Cabinet about how to handle Buthelezi. In both a hard line predominated, expressing frustration with Buthelezi's brinkmanship, but Mandela and Mbeki remained eager to draw him in. Before a meeting with Buthelezi in Durban on 1 March, Mandela told a rally that 'I will go down on my knees to beg those who want to drag our country into bloodshed'.[77] At the meeting Mandela turned his inimitable charm on Buthelezi, 'stroking' him, according to Waldmeir, and readily conceding Buthelezi's demand to submit their political differences to international mediation in exchange for the IFP's agreeing to register provisionally for the election.[78]

By March Buthelezi's isolation had increased considerably. Apart from domestic pressure, the Western powers, notably the USA, were pushing him to participate. Moreover, opinion polls indicated that the ANC was running at least neck-and-neck with the IFP, if not eclipsing it, even in its KwaZulu-Natal stronghold. For example, a poll conducted for the SABC in the province asked respondents to rank their favoured leaders on a scale of 1-10: The results were:

King Goodwill Zwelithini	6.64
Mandela	5.8
Buthelezi	5.37
De Klerk	5.04

Jacob Zuma, who was to be the ANC's candidate for the provincial premiership, received a negative rating from nearly half of the sample. The high ranking of the King, and the accompanying wish that he be the titular head of the province, showed that reverence for the monarchy crossed political boundaries, but even his supporters believed that it was wrong for him to be so politically involved with the IFP. A large majority of respondents, 84 per cent, rejected separation, wanting the province to be part of South Africa.[79]

Buthelezi sustained serious political damage in March when the Goldstone Commission revealed evidence implicating senior police officers, including the Deputy Commissioner (the second most senior police officer in the country) in supplying guns, hand grenades and mortars to three senior members of the IFP, including Themba Khoza, chairman of the IFP's Transvaal Region. It was also revealed that training in the use of weapons was being given to IFP members. The Commission also provided evidence of hit squads that were operating in the KwaZulu Police, which was 'dragging its feet' in investigating this criminal activity.[80] Whether

Buthelezi knew of these machinations and approved them is unknown: either way his possible response would have been to aver that the IFP was entitled to take whatever steps it deemed necessary to defend itself, given the continuing legal existence of MK and the involvement of some of its cadres in violence.[81]

Events in the nominally independent bantustan of Bophuthatswana conspired to cause the implosion of the Freedom Alliance. Bophuthatswana had received 'independence' in 1977 and had been ruled since then by the Bophuthatswana Democratic Party, led by Lucas Mangope, who was President of the country. The most that one could say about Bophuthatswana was that it was the least unsuccessful of the independent bantustans. Despite Mangope's authoritarian proclivities and heavy restrictions on opposition parties, the façade of a democratic state had been retained, and it generated approximately 32 per cent of its revenue from internal sources – roughly double that of any of the other three independent bantustans.[82] Since the inception of Codesa in 1991, Bophuthatswana had resisted reincorporation. Mangope regarded its independence as the restoration to the Tswana people of the sovereignty that had been lost when Bechuanaland had been annexed to the Cape in 1885. Predominantly Tswana Botswana, which was contiguous with Bophuthatswana, however, shunned dealings with a state that it did not recognise.

By March 1994 protest was approaching boiling point. It had been simmering for several years: in February 1988 disaffected elements in the army and police had deposed Mangope and detained the heads of the army and police as well as various Cabinet ministers. On the same day as the coup President Botha intervened, sending in an army detachment which reinstated Mangope. The levels of protest increased after the unbanning of the ANC in 1990. Although the ANC had never been formally banned in Bophuthatswana, Mangope was adamant that it would not be allowed to mobilise in the territory. Mangope's small support-base in the population of approximately two million encouraged the ANC to believe that it was being denied access to several hundred thousand potential supporters, just as Gqozo was attempting to do in Ciskei. Mangope's well-founded belief was that the ANC was eager to destabilise Bophuthatswana and force its reincorporation into South Africa.

Mandela urged Mangope on several occasions to allow his people to decide their political future, but he would not listen. In mid-1993 it was announced that Bophuthatswana was planning to draft a Constitution for a proposed region in South Africa which kept its legislative, economic and legal powers intact.[83] 'Our bottom line', said Mangope, was that Bophuthatswana would not consider giving up control of its security forces.[84] Given the forces ranged against Bophuthatswana this was to enter the realm of fantasy. It led immediately to turbulence, with civil servants, anxious about their jobs and pensions, demanding that Mangope hold a referendum on the question of reincorporation – which he declined. The situation deteriorated rapidly, with students and ordinary citizens joining the anti-Mangope protests. Extensive looting of shops in the capital, Mmabatho, occurred.

On 8 March 1994 a Cabinet committee of the South African government decided to put the security forces on alert and also to address an urgent appeal to Mangope to participate in the election. Mangope, however, turned to Constand Viljoen with a request that he dispatch a paramilitary force to bolster Mangope's own army and to act as a deterrent to the ANC, which, in Mangope's view, planned to overthrow his government. According to Viljoen's account, the plan was to strengthen Bophuthatswana's security 'for a few days' to gain enough time for its Parliament to meet to make a decision on participation in the election. (Whether this was, in fact, on Mangope's agenda is not known.) Mangope had turned to Viljoen as the key figure in his FA ally, the AVF, but with the specific instruction that no AWB members would participate in the operation.

What followed on 11 March was a critical moment in the transition.[85] Viljoen mobilised over 4 000 generally well-trained men, 1 500 of whom were to be given arms by the Bophuthatswana Defence Force. It was an astonishingly swift call-up, an indication of the military muscle available to the AVF. Unfortunately, and to Viljoen's chagrin, the AWB had heard of the impending showdown and could not resist unleashing their *Ystergarde* (Iron Guard) militia on Mmabatho – with disastrous consequences: an ill-disciplined rabble, some 600-strong, went rampaging through the streets, firing wildly and shouting racist abuse. The 'Battle of Bop' was on.

Predictably, the Bophuthatswana Defence Force was infuriated – and mutinied, turning their guns on the AWB rabble. Viljoen's men were forced to withdraw, though not before three AWB men were killed, two of them cold-bloodedly executed. Some 60 people were killed in the fracas. The South African army, awaiting developments nearby, moved in and took control, ousting Mangope, thereby disproving the view that the army's loyalty was suspect. Waldmeir, who was an eye-witness to the battle, observed:

> The army had chosen sides. It would not support Viljoen – and without the South African Defence Force, he could do nothing. The threat of organized right-wing resistance was no more.[86]

This was true, but it did not stop the AWB's belligerence, which took the form of a series of bomb attacks on buildings and rail tracks and, in the week prior to the election, car bomb attacks that killed 21 people.[87] Whatever capacity it may have had to disrupt the transition had disappeared.

The real significance of the Battle of Bop was that it proved to be Viljoen's Rubicon. He blamed De Klerk for orchestrating the AWB's action through 'third force activity', aimed at deliberately derailing the AVF's cause. (No evidence for this allegation existed, and, *prima facie*, it is inherently implausible.) On his flight back from Mmabatho, however, Viljoen's ambivalence about the use of force ended. He had always insisted that it was a last resort:

> I myself reserved the right to make the final decision as to how much of this force was to be used at what time. This was necessary because the controlling body of the Afrikaner Volksfront was constituted mostly of politicians and academics [who] did not always understand the implications of a full-scale war in a revolutionary situation such as existed ... during the run-up to the election and the transition process. My stated position was that I can only resort to forceful means if all my other strategies fail.[88]

Viljoen's earlier testing of the waters for negotiating a *volkstaat* had resulted in the humiliation of being booed by a 20 000-strong crowd in January. Now, however, it was clear, after the Bophuthatswana fiasco, that the thugs of the AWB would wreck any military operations. Accordingly, he resigned from the AVF, taking with him most of the generals and nine CP MPs into his new party, the Freedom Front, whose list of candidates was immediately registered with the Independent Electoral Commission. It was not only the military fiasco that led to Viljoen's change of strategy: it is evident that Mandela's and Mbeki's wooing of him had had some success. Viljoen recalled how Mbeki had referred to the Freedom Charter's clause declaring that all national groups shall have equal rights. Mbeki said to him, 'for national groups, read ethnic groups'. 'At that moment,' said Viljoen, 'he acknowledged ethnicity and we reached an agreement on including group rights in the Constitution.'[89]

Viljoen's withdrawal, the downfall of Mangope's regime, and the subsequent collapse of Gqozo's rule in Ciskei achieved what both the ANC and the NP had long wanted, namely the break-up of the FA. 'Two down, one to go,' exulted Slovo. The remaining 'one' was Buthelezi's IFP, which many in the ANC now wanted to crush and thereafter to disband KwaZulu's structures. Buthelezi, more isolated than ever, remained defiant, saying:

I warn that should the ANC attempt to destabilize the KwaZulu government, as it destabilized Bophuthatswana and as it threatened de-
stabilization in the Ciskei, a conflict of awesome proportions will be
unleashed to the tragic detriment of South Africa and the democratic
process.[90]

It was no idle threat: the IFP's support in KwaZulu was far greater than
Mangope's had been in Bophuthatswana. Although Buthelezi had 'provisionally' registered the IFP for the election after meeting Mandela on
1 March, this was subject to international mediation on the outstanding
constitutional issues. His brinkmanship was not over, and it would still
cause high drama.

Precisely what international mediation was meant to achieve was never
clear. Buthelezi's critics believed that his underlying motive was to delay
the election in order to re-open basic constitutional questions and thereby
postpone the IFP's day of reckoning at the polls. Predictably, the parties
involved, the ANC, IFP and the NP government, could not agree on the
terms of reference for the mediators. The mediators, in the form of Lord
Carrington, a British politician, and Henry Kissinger, a former American
Secretary of State, duly arrived on 11 April – and went home after a few
days of watching the frantic, but fruitless, manoeuvring among the parties. Kissinger quickly recognised that the date of the election was a decision that South Africans should make: it was 'a poison tree that the
mediators should not touch'.[91] Since this was the key issue in the dispute,
successful mediation was impossible. On departing Kissinger said: 'I have
never been on such a catastrophic mission and its failure now has cataclysmic consequences for South Africa.'[92]

In the meantime the security situation was deteriorating. On 28 March,
local IFP leaders, apparently without consulting the national leadership,
organised a provocative march on the ANC's headquarters, Shell House,
in central Johannesburg. What happened, and who caused what, remains
in dispute, but 53 demonstrators were killed. The ANC claimed that the
mob had tried to enter the ANC building, but were repulsed by armed
guards. A judicial inquest, however, rejected the ANC's contention, maintaining that there was no *prima facie* evidence to show that the building
was about to be attacked, and finding also that the 'barrage of fire was ...
grossly excessive'.[93] Given the sensitivity of the issue, De Klerk was loth
to have the police, already suspected of complicity in the attack, search
the building. Mandela promised full co-operation, but the ANC declined
to hand over weapons or to assist in establishing the circumstances of the
affray. Needless to say, further bitterness between the ANC and the IFP

was the consequence.[94] It made the prospects for the IFP's participation in the election even more remote, especially when De Klerk felt obliged to impose a state of emergency on Natal on 31 March.

By mid-April it appeared as though only a *deus ex machina* could bring the IFP on board – and, lo and behold, such a *deus* appeared, in the form of Washington Okumu, a portly Kenyan theologian and long-time friend of Buthelezi. He had been persuaded to come to South Africa to assist the would-be mediators by the evangelist Michael Cassidy. What followed was a remarkable sequence of events that resulted in Okumu's persuading Buthelezi to participate in the election.[95] It was touch-and-go, attributable to good luck and, so Buthelezi and Okumu claimed, divine intervention. Okumu's achievement was convincing Buthelezi that staying out of the election would consign him to the dustbin of history and involve his followers in a bloody conflict that they would ultimately lose. There was also evidence that large numbers of IFP supporters wanted to vote; moreover, like their counterparts in Bophuthatswana and Ciskei, public servants in KwaZulu would get anxious about their salaries and pensions should the IFP opt to boycott the election. Like all of the bantustans, KwaZulu was overwhelmingly dependent on the central government for its revenues – and an ANC-controlled government was unlikely to hesitate to turn the screw on it.

Buthelezi saw the wisdom in what Okumu had said, and recognised that the election date was unalterably fixed. A document drafted by Okumu was approved by Buthelezi and the IFP Central Committee, and thereafter by the NP government and the ANC. All three parties accepted a 'Memorandum of Agreement for Reconciliation and Peace' on 19 April. It was agreed to 'recognise and protect the institution, status and role of the constitutional position of the King of the Zulus and the Kingdom of Zululand'; provisions for this were to be made in the provincial and national Constitutions. Any outstanding issues in respect of the monarchy and the 1993 Constitution were to be addressed by way of international mediation, which was to commence as soon as possible after the elections.

Mandela and his colleagues, particularly Ramaphosa, must have swallowed hard before accepting the Agreement, but, as Mandela had said, he was prepared to go down on bended knee to beg those who wanted to plunge the country into bloodshed. In fact, agreement had cost the ANC little, and now gave it the opportunity to campaign in KwaZulu, which, previously, had been largely a no-go area. Indeed, Buthelezi's obduracy may well have cost the IFP more votes than the concessions had gained it.

De Klerk concealed his irritation at Buthelezi's tactics, and his suspicion that the IFP had all along been planning a last-minute entry into the election: 'I could not exclude the possibility that for the past few months they had been playing games with us and the ANC.'[96] It was clear from the speed with which the IFP's electoral machine swung into action that it had been readied to do so for some time. De Klerk's surmise was probably correct.

For the Independent Electoral Commission, chaired by Judge Johann Kriegler, the IFP's entry a week before the election presented a logistical nightmare: stickers bearing the IFP logo had to be pasted on to ballot papers that had been ready for some time; voting stations had to be identified and additional staff trained. Somehow they coped.

The challenge facing the IFP was to win control of KwaZulu-Natal, which would be a close contest. Its chances of winning much elsewhere were slender. For Viljoen's Freedom Front, having been refused a referendum among Afrikaners, it was necessary to demonstrate extensive support for a *volkstaat*, which Viljoen said, remained his 'all-consuming obsession':

> If we were to establish a volkstaat on a legal basis, there is a legal requirement: we have to prove our support among the Afrikaners. The government refuses a referendum before April 27. A referendum after April 27 is unthinkable. The only alternative open to us … is to take part in the elections and then to use the votes for the AVF as indication of this support. This is a difficult idea to accept, but our critics gave us no choice.[97]

Since neither the CP nor any of the other ultra-rightwing organisations was participating in the election, Viljoen hoped to win a large share of their votes, plus some from disaffected NP supporters who believed that De Klerk had sold them down the river. Opinion polls offered mixed messages: in November 1993 a Markinor/Gallup poll showed that 28 per cent of whites were in favour of a *volkstaat*; but only 22 per cent believed it to be a viable option, and a mere 14 per cent claimed that they were prepared to trek to a *volkstaat*.[98]

* * *

The tortuous process of reaching agreement (and it was tenuous) on provincial powers had been a dominant issue in the MPNP, but it was not the only one. The issue of how a government of national unity (GNU) should be structured, and what powers minority parties in it should exercise, remained unresolved until late in October 1993. There had been a tacit agreement between the NP and the ANC that the question of power-sharing, as the NP termed it, or a GNU, which the ANC had accepted, should be deferred until all of the other difficult issues had been resolved.[99]

On the one hand, Slovo's proposal for sunset clauses had been accepted by the ANC (reluctantly by some); on the other, the NP's proposal for a rotating presidency remained on the table. In an interview with the *Financial Times* in June 1993, De Klerk set out his view that the principle of power-sharing should be part of the final Constitution. The NP was still negotiating to have it included among the Constitutional Principles by which the drafters of the final Constitution would be bound. The 'winner-take-all' system, he continued, was 'the worst possible model which there can be for South Africa'. Proportional representation and strong regional government were insufficient:

> There must be limitation of the power of any government, also when it comes to the executive, not to such an extent that it must be a lame duck government but to ensure, as the founders of the American constitution did, there won't be misuse of power.

De Klerk advanced the possibility of an executive committee or inner Cabinet consisting of representatives of the major parties who would decide policy principles. There would be a rotating chairperson of the Cabinet whose decisions would be taken by consensus, not by a head-count. Consensus government, he insisted, was not the same as a minority veto.[100] In another statement De Klerk proposed that all of the President's major powers should be exercised on the advice of the GNU. He proposed also an SADF advisory council made up of a single member from each party in the (future) National Assembly: no presidential decision concerning the promotion or appointment of the chief of the SADF or any of its three services, or promotions to the rank of brigadier or higher, could be made except in accordance with the council's advice.[101]

Slovo's response was swift and acerbic: it was not for De Klerk to decide how the country would be run for the five-year duration of the GNU: he wanted, Slovo continued, 'a majority president to be without teeth, or, at best, false teeth'. To expect a new government, certain to be dominated by the ANC, to be hamstrung by the requirement of consensus was asking too much. It was necessary to negotiate a GNU in which there would be tension between majority rule and allowing minorities to have a meaningful role, but the majority party would have to be at the helm of the state.[102]

Quite early in the MPNP Meyer had become convinced that a GNU which functioned according to a mechanically applied formula could not work. He accepted the necessity for a GNU as an interim device, but, unlike De Klerk, he opposed its being incorporated into the final Constitution:

> It would be impossible to give permanence to an agreement which was essentially undemocratic and therefore not lasting. The GNU concept was not a form of coalition government, it was a forced agreement of co-operation between opponents and not between two parties who have found common ground.

Meyer records that he had difficulty convincing some of his colleagues, who wanted a GNU to be a permanent feature. The lack of agreement lasted for nine months. De Klerk, according to Meyer, was persuaded early on that the GNU could only be a temporary device, but refrained from publicly committing the NP government to this position, presumably because of deep divisions in the Cabinet.[103] As noted above, in mid-1993 he was still proposing the notion of a cooperative executive. Only two other (younger) Cabinet members, Leon Wessels and Dawie de Villiers, consistently supported Meyer's view. Meyer told Waldmeir that when the three of them appeared at Cabinet meetings 'they were treated like so many Trojan horses sent by the ANC'.[104]

De Klerk's critics accused him of stubbornly clinging on to power, or of wanting the constitutional outcome to leave him with significant influence in the new government. He had, after all, campaigned on a policy of power-sharing in 1992. That the system which the NP had proposed was likely to be unworkable is true, but this did not negate the arguments that De Klerk advanced. In his autobiography, he quotes the respected British political scientist Vernon Bogdanor saying:

> Some kind of power-sharing has been a feature of governments in all societies that have successfully overcome their internal divisions; I am not aware of any divided society that has been able to achieve stability without power-sharing.[105]

For the ANC, power-sharing, other than as a temporary device, was unacceptable: it amounted to thwarting the will of the majority by giving minority parties a veto. Nor was the federal form of power-sharing acceptable. Despite Meyer's protestations to the contrary, the Interim Constitution's provision offered only a weak version of federalism, subject to overrides by the central government; and even weak federalism could be largely negated if the polity were to be dominated by a single party, namely the ANC.

There was another dimension to the power-sharing issue: even if it were to be temporary, how would decisions be taken in Cabinet? The terms of agreement embodied in the Interim Constitution were:

- The President was to be elected by a joint sitting of the National Assembly and the Senate;
- Every party holding at least 80 seats out of the 400 National Assembly seats would be entitled to designate an Executive Deputy President from among the members of the National Assembly;
- The Cabinet was to consist of not more than 27 members appointed by the President in consultation with the Executive Deputy Presidents and the leaders of parties participating in the GNU;
- 'The Cabinet shall function in a manner which gives consideration to the consensus-seeking spirit underlying the concept of a government of national unity as well as the need for effective government.'
- Five per cent of the total vote entitled a party to representation in the GNU.

There had been no agreement on the mode of decision-making in the GNU even as late as 17 November 1993. The hardliners in the Cabinet wanted decisions to be taken by a two-thirds majority, which would have given minority parties a possible veto. De Klerk, however, had come round to accepting that requiring a head-count for decisions would not work:

> By that time I had already presided over a cabinet for four years. In all that time, we had never voted on any decisions. We had openly discussed matters and ministers had frankly expressed their views. In the end I had articulated what I thought was a general consensus. Sometimes I personally did not agree with the consensus – but that then became the decision of the cabinet. I felt that an impossible situation would be created if the cabinet were to have to vote on every matter that came before it. If the minority parties consistently thwarted the will of the majority it might in the end cause intolerable strains on the whole constitutional edifice. On the other hand, if we were to adopt a non-confrontational, non-voting approach, all participants would probably be able to exercise real influence on decision-making.[106]

In effect, what this meant was that the NP government had acquiesced in majority rule, notwithstanding obeisance to the 'consensus-seeking spirit'. As Mandela said: 'Majority rule will apply – we just hope we will never have to use it.'[107] His comment followed a bruising encounter with De Klerk late on the night of November 17.

A few days before, Mandela had petulantly remarked that the ANC did not want De Klerk to serve in any government 'as he was indifferent to township killings'; but while this was the feeling of the ANC, it could not keep him out of the GNU if the NP polled more than 5 per cent of the vote. It was a comment that was unworthy of Mandela, and it provoked an immediate response from the NP's four provincial leaders (including Roelf Meyer, who was acting leader of the Transvaal, and the Cape leader, Dawie de Villiers, two of the three 'Trojan horses'). They deplored the 'untold damage' that Mandela's remarks could do to the delicate constitutional process and the cause of national reconciliation. It was, they alleged, a calculated attempt to diminish De Klerk's stature. 'He [Mandela] repeatedly sets blacks against whites and accentuates black/white divisions – despite the lip service which he pays elsewhere to non-racialism.'[108]

It was a legitimate response to what had been an ill-considered remark. Moreover, it was difficult to reconcile this side of Mandela with the more generous one that could say:

> I never sought to undermine Mr de Klerk, for the practical reason that the weaker he was, the weaker the negotiations process. To make peace with an enemy, one must work with that enemy, and that enemy becomes your partner.[109]

Mandela knew that De Klerk's co-operation was vital to ensure that the transition was successfully concluded. He said to the assembled guests at a dinner party: 'My worst nightmare is that I wake up one night and De Klerk isn't there. I need him. Whether I like him or not is irrelevant, I need him.'[110]

De Klerk had his own problems, which Mandela's gratuitous insult did not help. Hardliners in the Cabinet were dismayed by the concession of what was effectively majority rule. Tertius Delport, the Minister for Local Government, was not convinced by Meyer's argument that the NP's most hopeful option was to allow a convention of power-sharing in the executive to develop naturally. He is said to have shrieked at De Klerk, 'What have you done? You've given South Africa away!'[111] The deal, however, was done, and there was nothing that Delport and his recalcitrant colleagues could do, short of resigning, which would have been a one-way ticket into the political wilderness. De Klerk emphatically denies what sounds like the inverse of the Delport story, namely that on being informed of Meyer's conceding majority rule in the negotiations, he exclaimed to Meyer, 'My God, Roelf, you have given away the country.' Meyer also denies that any such exchange with De Klerk occurred. It was, in any case, inherently improbable that Meyer could have taken so momentous a decision without prior consultation with De Klerk. Meyer confirms that De Klerk never said anything of the kind.

A similar remark was attributed to De Klerk by Georg Meiring, chief of the SADF, who quotes his saying, 'We really needn't have given in so easily.' Meiring responded that he, De Klerk, had never used 'your strong base to negotiate from, you never used the military as a base for strength, which you had available to you, you never wanted to use it.'[112] That De Klerk made such a comment was denied by his (former) Director-General, Dave Steward.[113]

What Meiring had in mind in using the military as a base for strength, presumably in the negotiating process, is unclear. Undoubtedly, the greater use of force – which is the prime function of militaries – could have prolonged the survival of the old order, but the costs would have been enormous. Hammering those engaged in mass action? Forcing strikers back to work at gun-point? Detaining thousands of activists? It would not only have been the physical toll, but also the economic costs of a further tightening of the sanctions noose and the virtual cessation of investment. The greatest cost of all would have been further polarisation, that might have made an eventual settlement difficult, if not impossible. During a retrospective analysis, delivered in 2003, De Klerk acknowledged that, had he wanted to, he could have used the army to crush dissenters and thereby cling on to power for some time, but that 'would have been over the bodies of hundreds of thousands of young men and women, and I couldn't live with that'. He added that people would be imprisoned without trial and 'I could not live with that either, because it is morally unjustifiable.'[114]

*   *   *

If power-sharing and provincial powers had been the major issues in the MPNP, other difficult ones had also to be resolved. These included language/cultural rights, property rights, and the composition and function of the judiciary.

Given the centrality of language in the rise of Afrikaner nationalism, it was not surprising that the NP should put up a fight for retaining the status of Afrikaans as an official language. Throughout its history the NP had struggled, successfully in the end, to ensure that Afrikaans-speaking children could receive an education in their mother-tongue from the lowest school grades up to university in exclusively Afrikaans-medium institutions. Over 40 years of NP rule had ensured that this goal had been substantially achieved. By 1991 Afrikaans was the second most widely spoken language (after Zulu), being the home language of 83 per cent of Coloured people and 58 per cent of whites, numbering altogether 5.7 million people.[115]

The ANC's attitude to linguistic diversity was expansive and seemingly generous. The Freedom Charter had proclaimed that 'All people shall have equal right to use their own languages, and to develop their own folk culture and customs,' and much the same approach was contained in the Constitutional Guidelines. How, though, was such expansiveness to be given constitutional form? A Working Document issued by the ANC's Constitutional Committee in 1990 set out provisions that were largely incorporated in the Interim Constitution: It identified 11 languages, including nine Bantu languages, one or more of which could be designated as the language 'to be used for defined purposes at the national level or in any region or area where it is widely used' where it was reasonable to do so. Language or languages would be prevented from being used for purposes of domination or division. The reference to division partly reflected fears that language might be used as a focus for ethnic mobilisation among African ethno-linguistic groups: the inclusive approach was intended to pre-empt any such possibility.

The sensitive issue of the medium of instruction in schools was dealt with in terms that appeared to be comprehensive but also contained 'escape clauses':

> Subject to the availability of public and private resources, and limitations of reasonableness, primary and secondary education should wherever possible be offered in the language or languages of preference of the students or their parents.[116]

Who determined whether resources were available, and who decided what was reasonable? In time this would prove to be a bone of contention.

Language-conscious Afrikaners were wary of the ANC's intolerant attitude to Afrikaans, 'the language of the oppressor', as many Africans called it. The ANC did not fully grasp how emotive an issue it was. Many held the (unstated) view that English would become the dominant language of public life.[117] The NP had little option but to accept the ANC's position on languages, although, as a kind of consolation prize, they secured a clause providing that 'Rights relating to language and the status of languages existing at the commencement of this [Interim] Constitution shall not be diminished'. (The provision was omitted from the final Constitution of 1996.)

Schlemmer asserts that the decision to have eleven official languages at the national level was taken in 'bad faith':

> It makes it impossible to match opportunities to rights in practice and this makes it ever more plausible for the government to backtrack on its constitutional commitments, pleading costs and practicality.[118]

By November 1993, when the MPNP agreed to the language provisions, many in the ANC remained apprehensive of an Afrikaner backlash that centred on language rights and straddled intra-Afrikaner political divisions. Whether the recognition of 11 official languages was part of a deliberate plan to dilute the influence of Afrikaans and to facilitate the spread of English as a lingua franca – as many Afrikaners came to believe – cannot be categorically confirmed. The ANC denied any such Machiavellian intention.

Resolving the property clause involved what De Klerk called a 'titanic struggle'. 'Property' was a metaphor for the big question: what kind of economic system would a democratic South Africa have? During its long years of exile, the ANC had been influenced by Marxism-Leninism, even while remaining primarily a nationalist movement. Whatever the predisposition of most activists, the ANC never formally declared itself a socialist movement. Obviously, its priority in these times was fighting apartheid, a preoccupation that left little time for reflection on an economic future without apartheid. Neither the Freedom Charter nor subsequent policy statements up to, and including, the Constitutional Guidelines of 1988 had devoted much attention to economic issues. Likewise, internal movements such as the UDF and Cosatu had engaged in little more than anti-capitalist rhetoric: 'socialism' was a battle-cry, unaccompanied by any programmatic proposals. Nevertheless, in the second half of the 1980s, when it seemed that a negotiated settlement was becoming a possibility, the ANC's economic thinkers began to engage economic issues more intensively.[119]

Mandela's call for nationalisation of the commanding heights of the economy shortly after his release was merely echoing the relevant clauses of the Freedom Charter. It caused a stir in the local business community and a sharp decline on the Johannesburg Stock Exchange. The reaction was nevertheless a factor in prompting the ANC to intensify its examination of economic options. The collapse of the Soviet Union and the repudiation of state socialism by its Eastern European allies further diminished the enthusiasm of many, though not necessarily SACP members, for the kind of command economy that had so conspicuously failed. Leading figures, led by Thabo Mbeki (who allowed his SACP membership to lapse in the early 1990s), looked with increasing interest to Scandinavian-style social democracy as a model to be emulated.

The ANC Constitutional Committee's Working Document of 1990 offered slightly more detail than the earlier Constitutional Guidelines. Economic legislation was to be guided by the principle of encouraging collaboration between the state and the private, co-operative and family sectors; all natural resources 'which are not owned by any person at the time of coming into force of this Constitution, shall belong to the State', which would have the right to regulate their exploitation, grant franchises, and determine royalties. The Document went further than the Guidelines, which had limited constitutional protection to 'property for personal use and consumption':

> No persons or legal entities shall be deprived of their possessions except on grounds of public interest or public utility, including the achievement of the objectives of the Constitution.
>
> Any such deprivation may be effected only by or pursuant to a law which shall provide for the nature and extent of the compensation to be paid.
>
> Compensation shall be just, taking into account the need to establish an equitable balance between the public interest and the interest of those affected.

It was further provided that disputes could be referred to a special independent tribunal, with the right of appeal to a court. Essentially the same proposals were advocated by the ANC in the MPNP.

In major respects future economic policy was a fundamental issue in the transition. Whites were apprehensive that a socialist and/or populist ANC government would embark on a massive programme of redistribution that might include wholesale dispossession of white-owned property. The ANC was conscious that its black constituency was overwhelmingly poor, many also having been the victims of dispossession, poor education and the deliberate withholding of access to skills. Redress was a crucial demand; but the ANC leadership was aware that it had not defeated the oligarchy and that the productive capacity and skills of the overwhelmingly white-owned formal economy were vitally necessary to tackling the manifold problems that lay ahead. How, then, was the legacy of inequality to be tackled?

Albie Sachs described the options in stark terms:

> Two options were being urged on us. The one was to adopt a Constitution and Bill of Rights that would scrap apartheid laws, but establish the constitution as a Chinese wall against any attempt to alter the social and economic status quo. The other and opposite option was simply to require the new government to confiscate the spoils of apartheid and share them out amongst those who had been dispossessed. While this approach had the immediate attraction of correcting historic injustice, it could not be realistically advanced in the context of an anticipated negotiated transition to democracy. Furthermore, its adoption would have led to capital flight, the destruction of the economy and international isolation just at the time when the people would most be wishing to enjoy the benefits of their ages-old struggle.[120]

The issue pointed to the need for a trade-off as part of a negotiated settlement. Crudely put, the ANC would enjoy relatively unfettered majority rule, subject to certain constitutional constraints; and whites would be allowed to continue their domination of the private sector, subject to very important qualifications aimed at redressing inequality, including affirmative action, black economic empowerment, land redistribution and restitution, and a progressive levelling of inequalities in the provision of services by means of an expanding floor of enforceable minimum rights. Like an inarticulate major premise, the terms of the trade-off were never stated publicly by either the ANC or the NP. Indeed, both would have denied its existence. It was real, nevertheless, even though it did not preclude skirmishes over the property clause.

The fundamental issue was the ANC's fear that iron-clad protection of property rights would frustrate efforts to implement redistributive policies, especially those relating to land. On the other hand, the NP and DP, representing white constituencies, insisted that the protection of property was a universally recognised fundamental right in modern liberal-democratic systems. It was a critical component of a free-market economy, whose absence from the Bill of Rights would deter investors.[121] Despite vehement opposition from its more radical members and allies, such as Cosatu, as well as the PAC, the ANC eventually acquiesced. It recognised that without acquiescence, the negotiations would possibly grind to an inconclusive halt.

During the negotiations, leading members of the ANC, including

Mandela, Sisulu, Ramaphosa and others, had been left in no doubt about the likely consequences of implementing radical redistributive policies by leading captains of industry. A radical critic describes the outcome in scathing terms, declaring that the language and tone of ANC documents on economic policy were similar to those emanating from the business community:

> The capitulation did not occur unchallenged, however. From 1992 onwards, the ANC's policy resolutions had increasingly hedged progressive state regulation with caveats clearly aimed at mollifying business. This triggered angry reactions within the ANC's grassroots constituency and COSATU. During the negotiations process, consultation by the ANC with its membership and political allies was patchy and perfunctory, and the relationship between the negotiations and economic policy formulation virtually non-existent.[122]

'Capitulation' was perhaps an exaggeration: the property clause in the Interim Constitution's Bill of Rights bore the hallmark of a compromise, which incorporated at least some of the ANC's demands. The relevant parts of the clause read:

> 28(1) Every person shall have the right to acquire and hold rights in property and, to the extent that the nature of the rights permits, to dispose of such rights.
> (2) No deprivation of any rights in property shall be permitted otherwise than in accordance with a law.

A further sub-section of the clause provided that property rights could be expropriated for public purposes only, subject to the payment of agreed compensation or, failing agreement,

> ... to the payment of such compensation and within such period as may be determined by a court of law as just and equitable, taking into account all relevant factors, including, in the case of compensation, the use to which the property is being put, the history of its acquisition, its market value, the value of the investments in it by those affected and the interests of those affected.

There was little in these provisions that would have been out of place in a democratic system. The NP was satisfied, especially with the requirement that market value be taken into account.

Another clause (8(3)(b)) provided that communities or individuals dis-possessed of rights in land by past unfair discrimination were entitled to claim restitution. A Commission on Restitution of Land Rights was to be established to investigate the merits of claims and to mediate in the event of disputes. These provisions were aimed particularly at remedying the injustices perpetrated by the Group Areas Act, 'black spot' removals and other forced evictions carried out in the process of homeland con-solidation. They did not, however, address the injustices of the large-scale alienation of African land that had occurred in the past, creating the stark figure of 13.7 per cent as the total share of the country's land to which Africans could lay claim. The issue would have to await redress by future legislation.

The property clause was a far cry from what Albie Sachs had described (and rejected) as confiscation of the spoils of apartheid. If it was not as iron-clad as some ardent free-marketeers wished, it was nevertheless as reasonable a provision as the NP was likely to get in the prevailing circum-stances of massive structural inequality. For the ANC there were at least possibilities of expropriation and restitution of dispossessed land, if only after complex, prescribed procedures.

The clause (8) in the Bill of Rights, providing for equality before the law and prohibiting unfair discrimination, was more directly circumscribed by a sub-clause permitting measures 'designed to achieve the adequate protection and advancement of persons or groups or categories of per-sons disadvantaged by unfair discrimination' – in other words, affirma-tive action. The issue was extensively debated, but within the context of a general agreement among the ANC, NP and DP that affirmative action was a necessary instrument for redressing inequality. Whether affirmative action represented a derogation from the principle of equality before the law would depend on how it was enforced: rigorous and inflexible en-forcement could lead to a situation in which all were equal before the law but some were more equal than others.

The debate about the judiciary, and in particular, about the appoint-ment of judges, was difficult. There was agreement among the par-ties that South Africa was to be a 'constitutional state', in which the Constitution would be the supreme law to which legislation, admin-istrative decisions and the exercise of executive power would have to conform. This represented a clean break from the past Westminster-type system that enshrined the sovereignty of Parliament, meaning that with few exceptions its power was untrammelled. The new Constitution would include a justiciable Bill of Rights and a Constitutional Court that was to have jurisdiction as the court of final instance over all matters relating to the interpretation, protection and enforcement of the Constitution. It was also to be vested with the power of judicial review of legislation.

Two issues were extensively debated in the negotiations: first, whether the Constitutional Court should be a chamber of the Appellate Division of the Supreme Court (hitherto the apex of the judicial system) or a separate branch of the judiciary. Secondly, how judges were to be appointed became a hot issue. In the past judges had effectively been appointed by the Minister of Justice, after consultation with the judge-president of the division concerned.

Kobie Coetsee, the Minister of Justice, inexplicably could see no reason why the practice of executive appointment of judges should not continue under the new dispensation – and the ANC went along with his view. Political considerations had shaped many appointments under apartheid, which Coetsee was slow to recognise – until the dangers were pointed out by Tony Leon of the DP. If the Constitutional Court was to be the final arbiter of what the Constitution actually meant, and in many cases its decisions would inevitably impinge upon policy issues, then it was imperative that the political factor in appointments should be, if not eliminated, then at least substantially diluted. After a tough fight, the ANC, desperate to reach a settlement, relented: Constitutional Court judges, like others, would have to be drawn from names submitted to the President by the Judicial Service Commission.[123]

There was another issue: given the Supreme Court's poor record of 'executive-mindedness' (with the honourable exception of a few judges) and, more generally, the role of the legal system as an instrument for the enforcement of apartheid, the ANC was strongly opposed to allowing the old order judiciary to continue as before. This was especially so given the role that the courts would be required to play in the new system. Moreover, the existing judiciary was nearly exclusively white and male. If the judiciary was to acquire legitimacy then its composition had to reflect greater representativeness.

While dismissal of conservative judges, especially those with poor track records in handling political trials, was not contemplated, future judicial appointments would be filtered through a new institution, the Judicial Service Commission, a broad-based body whose major de facto function would be to dilute political considerations in the making of judicial appointments. It was charged with the duty of making recommendations to the President, who could make appointments only by acting on its advice. It could also investigate allegations of misbehaviour, incapacity or incompetence on the part of judges, whose removal from office required an address from both the National Assembly and the Senate praying for such removal.

The JSC was to consist of:

- The Chief Justice;
- President of the Constitutional Court;
- One judge-president of a provincial division of the Supreme Court designated by the other judges-president;
- Minister of Justice or his nominee;
- Two practising advocates and two practising attorneys designated by their respective professions;
- One professor of law designated by the deans of all the law faculties of South Africa's universities;
- Four Senators designated *en bloc* by a two-thirds majority of all members of the Senate;
- Four persons, two of whom were to be practising advocates or attorneys, designated by the President in consultation with the Cabinet;
- Where matters concerning a particular provincial division were at issue, the judge-president of the division and the premier of the relevant province.

As noted above, the Constitutional Court would play a pivotal role as 'the court of final instance over all matters relating to the interpretation, protection and enforcement' of the Constitution's provisions. Of more immediate significance was the requirement that the Constitutional Court should certify that the final Constitution had incorporated the 34 constitutional principles (adopted as schedule 4 of the Interim Constitution). An unspoken demand by the ANC was that the Constitutional Court should provide a counterweight to the Supreme Court, which was dominated by 'old order' judges. Membership of the Court was announced in June 1994. Without conclusive evidence that the Court was deliberately packed, it was certainly the case that a majority of its 11 members were at least sympathetic to the ANC: the President of the Court, Arthur Chaskalson and one of the members, Albie Sachs, had been constitutional advisors to the ANC during the negotiations. The political convictions of the other judges were less clear, but none could be described as being imbued with the 'executive-mindedness' that was so marked a feature of many judges in the apartheid judiciary. Whatever the political colouration of the judges, many were jurists of high quality. The omission of John Dugard, the country's leading student of human rights and a prominent liberal, however, was inexplicable.

The type of electoral system to be used evoked less controversy. In April

1991 the ANC's Constitutional Committee recommended list system proportional representation (PR) because it encouraged participation by groups that had significant followings, though fringe parties would be excluded by imposing a threshold of a 5 per cent share of the vote; PR led to a more exact political reflection of the distribution of votes, and avoided the time, expense, and accusations of bias in the process of de-limiting constituencies. But it also noted some of the problems, including the limited direct accountability to constituencies. It recommended the combination of national and regional lists, each being allocated half of the seats in the National Assembly.

While the quest for inclusivity was a well-intentioned break with a single-member first-past-the-post system based on the plurality principle, opting for PR offered other less benign possibilities: it enabled the party leadership to determine which candidates should be placed on the party lists and, especially, the order in which their names would appear. It also meant that SACP members could be included without having their SACP membership identified. The critical issue, however, was the power accorded to party bosses to manipulate the lists to suit their own preferences.

The power of the party leadership was further augmented by the in-clusion as a transitional measure in the Interim Constitution of an 'anti-defection' clause, which required an MP to vacate his or her seat on ceas-ing to be a member of the party on whose list he or she was elected. Ostensibly, the reason for this provision was two-fold: first, MPs were elected by party (and not as individuals as in constituency-based sys-tems), and secondly, it was assumed that party coherence and stability was necessary in the circumstances of a fledgling democracy. Imposing a severe penalty on floor-crossing would act as a strong deterrent; but the clause also gave the party leadership a formidable weapon to ensure the loyalty – and perhaps subservience – of its MPs, who could be expelled were they not faithfully to toe the party line. In all probability the effect would be to increase the centralisation of power and undercut whatever federal potential the Constitution contained.

Given the benefits it had historically derived from the distorting effects, which benefited majority parties, of the old plurality/constituency sys-tem, the NP needed little persuasion on the merits of PR. The DP and its predecessors had long advocated PR, though of a type that incorporated a constituency element.

Since time permitted neither the preparation of voter rolls nor the de-marcation of constituencies, the adoption of the simplest form of PR, namely the party list system, was virtually inevitable. Moreover, given the high proportion of first-time voters, many of whom were illiterate, simplicity in the voting procedure was essential. Accordingly, the ANC demanded that there be a single ballot paper for elections to the National Assembly and to the provincial legislatures. While the single ballot would undoubtedly simplify voting, it was also an abridgement of voter choice: some, perhaps many, might want to vote for one party nationally, and another provincially. The single ballot would also tend in practice to favour the bigger parties and disadvantage smaller parties who might hope to run strongly in particular provinces but poorly at the national level. Under sustained pressure from the DP, the Freedom Front and, especially, the IFP (which was pinning its hopes on winning KwaZulu-Natal), the double ballot was eventually accepted. Efforts to have the President directly and separately elected, notably by Colin Eglin of the DP, did not succeed. Eglin's argument was that the separation of powers, a principle of the Constitution, would be enhanced by direct election, as well as widening voter choice. The ANC's insistence that the President be elected by the National Assembly prevailed. The President, however, would be limited to two five-year terms.

*   *   *

Constitutions, Napoleon said, should be 'short and vague'. The Interim Constitution was the exact opposite: long and extremely detailed, a reflection of the many difficult compromises that keeping the negotiations on track had required. It is no doubt true that the less negotiating parties trust one another, the more detailed a Constitution must be.

The Interim Constitution broke new ground for a state that was emerging from decades of authoritarian rule: it provided for a constitutional state based on the rule of law, with an elaborate Bill of Rights to be enforced by an independent judiciary. All of the basic institutions of the modern liberal-democratic state were to be established, which was a notable achievement since neither the ANC nor the NP could claim strong liberal-democratic credentials as part of their respective traditions. The concept of a (temporary) GNU and the provision for a limited degree of federalism may also have served to lower the stakes of the founding election.

On 18 November 1993 the Interim Constitution was enacted into law by Parliament. De Klerk described it as 'a constitution which, once and for all, will rid this country of the albatross which we have had around our neck for 300 years'. He continued, declaring that the NP had not only realised its goals, but had also succeeded in committing most of the other parties 'juridically and emotionally to a fair and reasonable constitution .... No party has won.'[124] In his autobiography, written two years after he had withdrawn the NP from the GNU, he was more circumspect about the Constitution:

> It was not exactly what we would have wanted when we set out at the beginning of the negotiation road: we would have liked to have seen something closer to the power sharing in the Swiss or Belgian models; we would have liked more clearly defined rights for the regions and minorities. But we were satisfied that we had substantially succeeded in achieving the total package that I had spelled out as our bottom line during the referendum [of 1992] ... .[125]

The ANC achieved substantially what it had wanted: perhaps even hegemonic power was within its reach, as Buthelezi had long feared. It had made some concessions, but none that would seriously impede its grip on political power. It is worth noting that in their long years of exile in parts of Africa, many ANC members had seen close up the ravages that poor governance and, in particular, excessively long tenure of office by leaders, had caused. They were also determined to disprove the widespread cynicism, especially in the West, about African states' supposed inability to sustain effective, democratic government.

Moreover, since the ANC had been the principal victim of state violations of human rights, it was determined that never again should this occur in South Africa. In significant respects the elaborate Bill of Rights was a reaction to the past. One example suffices to illustrate this contention: major human rights abuses had occurred under periodic states of emergency, during which executive power was even less restrained than in 'normal' times. Section 34 of the Interim Constitution limited the declaration of states of emergency to times when the security of the state was threatened by war, invasion, general insurrection or national disaster. A declaration could be in force for 21 days and could not be extended without approval by a majority of at least two-thirds of the National Assembly. Any superior court would be competent to enquire into the validity of a declaration of a state of emergency. Persons detained under a state of emergency would be entitled after no longer than 10 days to apply for a writ of *habeas corpus*, and a court could order their release if it were satisfied that their detention was no longer necessary to restore peace and order. These provisions represented a world of difference from the apartheid order, where, even in 'normal' times, detainees were stripped of their rights and placed at the mercy of the state.

*   *   *

Given its legacy of deep division and severe conflict, South Africa was hardly a promising candidate for durable democracy. The depth and resilience of the 'sufficient consensus' underpinning the Interim Constitution remained open to doubt. The founding election in April 1994 would provide the first, but by no means the last, test.

CHAPTER 13

The Founding Election

As the April 1994 election approached, excitement mingled with apprehension gripped the land. It seemed, until the very last minute, that neither the IFP nor the FF would participate; and that both, individually or jointly, might cause disruption or bloodshed. Nearly 3 800 deaths had occurred in political violence during 1993, and 1994 seemed as though it could be worse: during March, when the election campaign was in full swing, 537 deaths were recorded, an average of 17.3 per day. April began looking as though the death toll could be worse, but it turned out to be slightly lower, although still serious: 436.[1] Bomb explosions in several towns in the Transvaal, including Johannesburg, during April claimed the lives of 31 people. According to the police this had been the work of the AWB, which hoped to disrupt the election and intimidate prospective voters. Some 40 AWB members were arrested, a number of whom were convicted and received lengthy prison sentences.

The AWB's efforts were futile: bomb attacks made little impact on the millions who were eagerly anticipating the opportunity to exercise their newly acquired rights as citizens. The critical test to be faced by the election would be: was the new democratic system 'the only game in town', implying that no significant political force would attempt to operate outside its ambit, and that the results would be accepted (or at least acquiesced in) by all participants?[2]

* * *

Control of the election was vested in the Independent Electoral Commission (IEC), established by statute in mid-December 1993.[3] Its chairman was Judge Johann Kriegler, one of the sharpest legal minds in the country and possessed of a rugged sense of independence. The membership was as broad-based in terms of race, gender and political affinity as was likely to be achieved: it included Dikgang Moseneke, a senior advocate and a former member of the PAC, Helen Suzman, the doyenne of white liberals, and Zak Jacoob, a Durban advocate. Subsequently, five foreign members, including a Zimbabwean and an Eritrean, were also appointed as commissioners. While criticism would be directed at the IEC, the impartiality of the 16 Commissioners was not questioned, despite prior survey evidence indicating a lack of confidence, particularly among Afrikaners and other ethnic minorities. There were, however, many allegations of irregularities at the lower levels, notably at polling stations.

From the outset the IEC faced the likelihood that adhering to the 'immutable' date of 27 April was 'technically and administratively a virtually impossible task' and that the prospects for 'free and fair elections were gloomy from the outset and many doubted whether elections were feasible at all'. Moreover, within four months a massive administrative and supervisory structure had to be built up from scratch. Officials from the existing Home Affairs Department who had had experience in running previous elections – admittedly on a far smaller scale – were 'suspect' and were not used.

According to (dubious) census data, an estimated 22.7 million persons were eligible to vote, of whom 72 per cent had never voted before and a majority of whom were illiterate. There was no question of preparing voter rolls, a process that would have taken several years to complete. Prospective voters would be required to produce identity documents, but a substantial number of otherwise eligible voters did not possess them, and had no hope of obtaining them prior to the election. To avoid having to turn them away, which could have led to anger and violence, the IEC was empowered to issue temporary voters' cards. By 29 April, the last day of the election, over 3.5 million such temporary voters' cards had been issued, of which nearly 1.5 million were issued during the four days of voting. The arrangement lent itself to abuse. De Klerk observed, plausibly, that towards the end of the election people were being issued with temporary voters' cards 'virtually on request'. As he suggests, the sheer volume of such cards issued during the election was a strong indication that a scrutiny of the applicants, especially their ages, could only have been perfunctory.[4]

The scale of the operation the IEC was required to mount was huge: it had to find, recruit and train some 300 000 staff members. Many, one must surmise, were young, unemployed blacks since those already holding down jobs were unlikely to be able to take off four months. Recruitment, the IEC acknowledged, caused 'the first signs of breakdown' that were to continue over the entire period. Kriegler observed that the problem lay in the essentially transitory nature of the organisation:

> You didn't have a company with a long-term objective which could develop a sense of purpose; you had an instant company which was going to disappear in four months' time. This led to problems of morale, communication and logistics. With the best will in the world you couldn't move this amorphous lump sufficiently fast to arrive everywhere you had to arrive in time.[5]

By mid-March fears were being expressed that the IEC would not be ready for the election: moving its headquarters to central Johannesburg, internal disputes, and the problems caused by the change to the double ballot meant that the IEC was well behind schedule. It was said that the Commission's work was like building a ship while already at sea – to which a wag responded, 'Let's hope it's an ark, and not the *Titanic*.'[6]

The logistical problems faced by the IEC were compounded by the last-minute decision of the IFP to participate in the election. Since between 15 per cent and 20 per cent of the total electorate lived in KwaZulu this was an important shift towards the election's inclusivity. Without the IFP's participation the significant number of non-IFP supporters within KwaZulu's borders would have found it difficult, if not impossible, to vote. On 23 March a group of commissioners, led by Kriegler, met Buthelezi, King Zwelithini and Zulu chiefs in Ulundi, where Kriegler, in his words, was subjected to a 'choreographed humiliation', being jeered in the Legislative Assembly when he appealed for their co-operation. Neither Buthelezi nor Zwelithini would budge, forcing the IEC to advise the government that elections could not be held in KwaZulu unless a political settlement was reached.

As noted, Buthelezi announced six days before the election that the IFP would participate. Since the ballot papers had already been printed, stickers bearing the name of the party, its crest and a photograph of the leader had to be printed and appended to the bottom of the ballot papers (causing the NP to lose its bottom slot). Not only these tasks were involved: finding suitable voting stations (549) in KwaZulu and recruiting an additional 13 500 staff was no less demanding. Comparable problems could have been experienced in Bophuthatswana, whose recalcitrant President Mangope had refused all IEC requests for voting facilities and permission to conduct voter education programmes. The ousting of his government solved the problem, however, though leaving the IEC with another rushed job to perform.

While the constitutional negotiators may have produced an exemplary democratic Constitution, it could obviously not ensure that participating parties would necessarily abide by the rules and adhere to the code of conduct to which all had subscribed. South Africa largely lacked a civic culture that was supportive of democratic competition. Intolerance remained at disturbingly high levels. A survey conducted for the Institute for Multiparty Democracy in February 1994 suggested that only 54 per cent of Africans were confident that their voting preferences would not be known by the community. In communities where one party was dominant community pressures, violence and intimidation could mean that voters' choices would be highly constrained.[7]

Pre-election research identified no fewer than 165 no-go zones spread across most of the country where it was difficult or impossible for rival parties to campaign against the dominant party in a particular zone:

> The IEC appreciated from the outset that it would be unrealistic to expect wholly free and fair electioneering by all parties throughout a country characterized by profound ideological, ethnic and socio-political rifts. The country had no tradition of open, vigorous yet fair public debate.

The extent to which no-go zones affected the outcome of the election is considered below.

* * *

The campaign hotted up in February, but in fact it had been under way for more than two years, with all parties earnestly examining opinion polls. From early on it was evident that the election was shaping up to resemble a presidential contest between Mandela and De Klerk. The nature of the electoral system – party lists, with no constituencies – helped in this respect: voters would be voting for parties with leaders who, in the case of De Klerk and Mandela, according to the polls, were significantly more popular than their respective parties. Moreover, ordinary candidates were not listed or made known in any other way in the actual voting process. Another critical factor was that this would be a 'liberation' or '*uhuru*' election that would ensure that the party identified with liberation would reap a substantial electoral harvest.

That the ANC would win the national election was a foregone conclusion, given its massive support among the (African) majority. Mandela warned against complacency: 'for us to proceed as if we are going to have a landslide victory is more dangerous than the opposition from the NP'.[8]

For the NP, it was more than a question of survival: it needed to win a sufficient share of the vote nationally to retain some restraining power on a potentially hegemonic ANC, as well as winning control of at least one province. Pik Botha, with his customary ebullience, expressed the optimistic claim that the NP could even win the election in an alliance with the IFP and other homeland parties.[9] De Klerk was more circumspect, though expressing confidence during the campaign that the NP was attracting growing African support. He wrote:

> According to my calculations, we could be reasonably certain of achieving between 15 percent and 20 percent of the vote, based on our support in the white, coloured and Indian communities. The key to further success would be our ability to break into the black [African] vote. We felt that we had considerable growth potential among black South Africans – particularly with the older and more conservative segments of the population, with the emerging black middle class and with many black South Africans who had developed close personal relations with whites, either as domestic workers or as employees of small businesses. Reliable opinion polls indicated that 10 percent of black voters might fall into this category. If we managed to win their support, we had a good chance of getting somewhere between 25 percent and 30 percent. If our support among black voters proved to be even stronger – in the range between 15 percent and 20 percent – we might even achieve the magical 33 percent.[10]

To what extent funding shaped the election's outcome is a matter for speculation. Election campaigns are expensive, but it is not invariably true that the best-funded party will win. Apart from limited funding provided by the state, the major source had to be obtained from the private sector and party supporters. Which party got what and from whom was never fully revealed, but from what little is known it is clear that the ANC was the principal beneficiary of private largesse, receiving perhaps at least double the combined total of what was received by all the other parties. Having set itself a target of R168 million, the ANC raised R150 million – a tidy sum. It raised 'massive' financial support from foreign governments, including Libya, Indonesia, Malaysia and Taiwan (it withdrew recognition of Taiwan not long after the election).[11] Local companies also supported the ANC generously, no doubt out of a combination of institutional self-protection and a wish to ingratiate themselves with the future government. Waldmeir records, citing a *New York Times* report, that Mandela approached 20 leading businessmen, asking each for a donation of at least R1 million: all but one succumbed to Mandela's arm-twisting.[12] The exception was a 'big company with a pro-apartheid record', whose proffered cheque of R250 000 Mandela refused to accept, telling them it was an insult: 'he expected seven figures.'[13] Further large amounts were collected from American, British and European sources.

De Klerk was surprised at the ease with which the ANC collected funds, but he was able to raise sufficient to enable the NP to mount 'a reasonably imaginative – but not lavish – campaign'. The business community, he said, realised how important it was to limit the power of the ANC, so that some regular donors gave more than usual and others who had not previously been donors provided large amounts.[14] It is quite likely that the quasi-presidential nature of the campaign, with Mandela and De Klerk going head-to-head, meant that smaller parties like the DP and the IFP lost out in relative terms.

*   *   *

Nineteen parties contested the election nationally, and seven won representation, albeit very small in four cases. The ANC, NP and the IFP combined won over 93 per cent of the votes and 377 out of the 400 seats in the National Assembly.

The ANC's biggest electoral asset was obviously Mandela, who campaigned tirelessly and pressed the flesh in time-honoured fashion. His avoidance of demagoguery was conspicuous. His major strength lay in his ability to interact with ordinary people, rather than in formal meetings with set speeches. The ANC, aware of, and sensitive to, allegations that it lacked the experience and know-how to govern a complex society, had prepared itself thoroughly – as, indeed, it had done throughout the negotiations. 'Ready to Govern' and 'A Better Life for All' were its major campaign slogans. Its proposals were outlined by the Reconstruction and Development Programme (RDP), a detailed document that had been through several drafts and included substantial inputs from Cosatu and the SACP. It promised 'a productive social democratic haven', based on an anticipated linkage between redistribution and growth.[15] There were to be extensive reforms of education, healthcare, the rights of women, land and environmental issues and workers' rights.

The most eye-catching promise – and calculated to win support from the ANC's largely impoverished constituency – was to build one million houses, provide running water to one million people and electrify 2.5

million urban and rural homes within the first five years of the new dispensation. Moreover, a massive public works programme would create 2.5 million job and training opportunities over 10 years.

Although the RDP was criticised as being a 'wishlist' and 'fiscally irresponsible', the ANC sought to reassure (particularly white) voters that the funding of the RDP would come principally from a reallocation of existing resources available to the state. During the campaign Mandela went out of his way to reassure the business community that the ANC was not a bunch of wild populists and/or Marxists: the RDP, he said, contained 'not a single reference to nationalization ... not a single slogan that will connect us with any Marxist ideology'.[16]

Mandela hoped to cast the net of support as widely as possible, by making special pitches to white, Indian and Coloured voters. He was concerned that poll data were showing significant support for the NP among Coloured and Indian people. Transformation, he said, inevitably caused concern among minorities, but it was the duty of leadership to address those fears and ensure that minorities feel that they are needed. Regarding whites, he said:

> We attach a great deal of importance to whites. In spite of all the criticism we have made about apartheid, the reality is that whites have had opportunities we have not had .... We want that knowledge and expertise now that we are building our country. That is why I have appealed to them repeatedly not to leave the country at this particular moment, and even to ask those who have left to come back. Because we are going to need them, we are going to rely on them.[17]

Mandela and De Klerk, who would be required to co-operate with each other in the future GNU, remained mostly courteous in their relationship. De Klerk complained bitterly about the behaviour of ANC supporters, which reached a climax when he was hit by a stone at an NP meeting in Kimberley. He was not seriously injured. The incident, he said, made the ANC realise that it would have to take stronger measures to discipline its followers.[18] Mandela took immediate steps to warn ANC members that they would not tolerate intimidation, threats or violence against opponents, although the ANC cautioned other parties to take adequate security precautions when campaigning in areas where many voters were hostile to them.[19]

It is doubtful whether the well-intentioned words of the ANC leadership percolated down to the grassroots level. Hostility continued: in several townships where De Klerk sought to speak, residents considered it an intrusion into 'our areas':

> Almost without fail, when De Klerk enters a township, there is a spontaneous eruption of support for the ANC. At times the intrusion is vocal but cheerfully good spirited; at other times it degenerates into the horrible. On one occasion, ANC supporters showered NP supporters emerging from a hall with spit, jeered at them and burnt their posters with merry abandon.[20]

De Klerk showed courage and pertinacity in seeking votes in African townships; but it was a hard row to hoe, made even harder by the NP's inability to campaign in many, if not most, African townships in the bantustans. His essential message, that he had taken down apartheid and that the ANC had wrecked schools and blocked housing developments, was not what most African audiences wanted to hear. Nor were they disturbed by talk of the influence exerted by communists in the ANC. Whatever De Klerk's achievement – and it was considerable – it could not erase the memory of the policy for which his party had been responsible. Moreover, the election was not only a 'liberation' election, it was also, in a profound sense, an expression of identity that no white politician could counteract or co-opt, especially in the emotional atmosphere of the time.

Mandela's usually benign and conciliatory attitude was blemished by several personal attacks on De Klerk, whom he variously described as a 'coward', a 'weakling', an 'unstable person', and the 'evil mastermind' behind the violence.[21] These comments were not only unfair, they were unworthy of Mandela, whose heroic status, domestically and internationally, placed him beyond criticism, and gave his words an oracular quality. On the eve of the election Mandela spoke of De Klerk in patronizing terms that barely went beyond damning him with faint praise:

> In spite of all the quarrels we've had with Mr de Klerk, he remains quite an interesting chap. He is big. Some of our most unpleasant quarrels have been on a one-on-one basis – we've said very cruel things to each other. One of the things that angered me was the fact that he did not use his capacity to stop the violence, when he could do so. This was the major cause of conflict between us, but he has the capacity of quarrelling with you, and the next moment shaking hands and sitting down to coffee. I don't think we've going to have trouble from Mr de Klerk. I think we're going to work with him very smoothly.[22]

Mandela's repeated attacks on De Klerk ignored the ANC's own complicity in violence – which Mandela himself had acknowledged. Why, if Mandela's accusations were true, would De Klerk wilfully inflict political damage on himself, or refrain from taking action to stop the desperadoes who sought to scupper his project? Undoubtedly, the violence and Mandela's attacks reduced whatever limited support the NP could win from African voters. Survey data between July 1992 and February 1993 had suggested that the NP might win between 6 per cent and 8 per cent of African votes. Any expectation that the NP might pick up votes from smaller African ethnic groups, apprehensive of an allegedly 'Xhosa-dominated' ANC, was also shown to be chimerical. Efforts to persuade IFP supporters to vote for the NP were undercut by the IFP's last-minute decision to participate in the election.

Given its apartheid past, the NP did its best to orientate its campaign to the future. On a number of occasions De Klerk apologized for the injustices committed in the name of apartheid. The NP claimed to be just as eager as the ANC to create jobs, build houses and revamp the education system. It was, however, highly critical of the RDP, which De Klerk maintained was 'wild and irresponsible' in creating expectations that available resources could not meet. This was a fair point, since the elements of the RDP had only been roughly costed. Nevertheless, affordable or not, the RDP spoke to the needs of the broad mass of the ANC's constituency, which could hardly be expected to appreciate budgetary constraints in the highly charged atmosphere of impending liberation. Nor would the poor easily comprehend warnings that exuberant over-spending – even on worthy aims – could result in galloping inflation. Caution was not a quality attuned to the temper of an expectant electorate.

Mandela and his colleagues in the leadership were aware of the dangers. In a press interview Mandela said:

> The people have high expectations and though we have warned them repeatedly that to address their basic needs is going to take years; nevertheless there are those expectations. It is something we must warn against.[23]

Both the NP and the ANC fought hard for majority support of the Indian and Coloured communities. These were intermediate categories in the racial hierarchy, subject to humiliating discrimination, including the devastation of communities by the Group Areas legislation, but it was not so pervasive as the discrimination inflicted on Africans. Both, moreover, had benefited socio-economically from participation in the Tricameral

Parliament, even though low percentage polls had suggested widespread rejection of the system.

Rejection of apartheid and large-scale support for the UDF by Coloured people in the 1980s, however, did not necessarily translate into support for the ANC. The Natal and Transvaal Indian Congresses had had a long record of resistance to discrimination and had been pillars of the Congress Alliance from the 1950s, and several Indians held high positions in the ANC. The Indian community was over one million in size, 80 per cent of them living in KwaZulu-Natal and accounting for 9.3 per cent of the provincial population. The Coloured people accounted for 58.4 per cent of the Western Cape's population in 1993; whites represented 23.7 per cent and Africans 17.1 per cent. Together with Northern Cape, where Coloured people accounted for 52.4 per cent of the population, the Western Cape had a different demographic profile from the remaining provinces.

Since it was very likely that the great majority of Africans would vote for a historically African party, mainly the ANC, the political preferences of Coloured voters would be important. In KwaZulu-Natal it would be a close-run election if the IFP decided to participate: with the ANC and the IFP running neck-and-neck, the distribution of the Indian vote (13 per cent of the provincial electorate, although Indians constituted less than 10 per cent of the provincial population) was potentially of critical importance. It could be safely assumed that hardly any of the white population, 7 per cent of the total, would vote ANC, although some would support the IFP.

It was difficult to imagine that majorities of categories that had experienced apartheid's lash could support the NP; but beneath the obvious hatred of past discrimination lay complicating factors. In the case of Indians, memories of the Durban riots in January 1949 remained vivid, especially among the older generations: rampaging Zulu attacked Indians in the heart of the Indian business area, allegedly in reprisal for an Indian shopkeeper's slapping a young African. In the devastation that followed, 142 people, including 87 Africans and 50 Indians, were killed, and many Indian-owned properties were destroyed or damaged. What exactly caused the violence; whether, as some claimed, it was instigated by whites, or whether it was a manifestation of displaced aggression are important questions, but irrelevant ones: fear of the African majority became ingrained in the perception of many Indians. The pact between the Indian Congress and the ANC and participation of Indians in the Defiance Campaign of 1952 were expressions of a commitment to the struggle for liberation, but to what extent the Indian Congresses' views percolated down to the grassroots was an open question.

Idi Amin's expulsion of Asians from Uganda in 1972 and the endorsement of his action by BC activists contributed to further fears of majority rule among Indians, who were aware of a widespread anti-Indian sentiment among Africans despite the involvement of the Indian Congresses in the Congress Alliance. Many Indians recognised that they were in the classic 'middleman' bind: discriminated against by whites (since well before 1948) who resented their economic competition and their alleged 'penetration' of white residential areas; and resented by many Africans because of alleged sharp practices by many petty Indian traders, whose customers were largely African. A further source of friction derived from the appointment of Indians as supervisors of African workers in industry, and therefore having to demonstrate to their white employers their ability to enforce discipline.[24]

Survey data collected for the Buthelezi Commission in 1982 suggested that while Indian respondents were realistic enough to recognise that fundamental changes were needed, many were nevertheless apprehensive of an African majority in an enlarged KwaZulu (that is, including Natal):

- 34 per cent believed that Africans would accept non-African minorities;
- 22 per cent believed that government would respect guarantees to minorities;
- 49 per cent believed that Indians and Coloureds would be victimised.[25]

Contradictory attitudes emerged among Indians in the 1980s, showing how fragmented a category they were. First was the question of participation in the Tricameral Parliament: the small turnout of Indian voters in 1984 indicated large-scale rejection. Buthelezi's warnings of the 'grave consequences' for the Indians should they participate may have served as a deterrent for some, and reminded many of their vulnerable position in the racial hierarchy.

Many young Indian students and professionals supported the UDF enthusiastically, but survey data in 1985 showed only limited support – 8.7 per cent – among Indians at large. Even more surprising was a survey conducted in Durban in 1985 in which respondents were asked to name their preferred leader of South Africa: 53.4 per cent of Indians named PW Botha, and 3.7 per cent Mandela. Many professed to have no political allegiances, suggesting a belief that in their vulnerable position the wisest course was to keep one's head below the parapet and purport to be apolitical.[26]

The violence that intensified in the mid-1980s and after caused further alienation of many Indians from Africans. Although not directly involved in the Natal conflict, Indians were caught up in a serious episode that started on 6 August 1985 when Indian shops and homes were attacked by African students who marched through the huge informal settlement of Inanda, outside Durban. Several days of sporadic violence and looting ensued, including the destruction of the Gandhi settlement at Phoenix, and 70 people died in the fighting. Order was restored largely by Inkatha and Indian vigilantes. This was a far less serious matter than the 1949 riots, but it evoked bitter memories. A small businessman told an interviewer: 'We never forget that underneath they [Africans] hate us. We have it and they want it'. Another businessman, responding to the question about whom the Indians would align themselves when the transition came, said: 'With the whites, of course, not with the blacks.'[27]

Despite the fragmentation and cultural divisions of the Indian community, many shared these views, while at the same time being sufficiently realistic to acknowledge that an accommodation had to be reached with the African majority.

Survey data gathered regularly between July 1992 and February 1994 showed strong Indian support for the NP: 58 per cent in July 1992, dipping below 50 per cent in 1993, though still registering the NP as enjoying plurality support – 46 per cent in February 1994. Indeed, the NP in KwaZulu-Natal was becoming a predominantly Indian party. The ambiguity felt by many Indians, however, was reflected in the same polls which showed a consistent trend for at least one-third of respondents to be classified as 'No choice/Will not vote'.[28] Other polls suggested an even higher percentage of undecided Indian voters.

Mandela addressed large crowds of Indians, and sought to impress upon them that the ANC would protect their property rights and religious freedom; but he also warned them that to vote for the NP would be a 'betrayal'. Mandela impressed his audiences, but doubts remained: 'He's a wonderful man and I came along to hear what he has to say ... but I think I'm going to vote for the National Party.'[29] How typical this ambivalence was among Indian voters is hard to gauge. It illustrated, however, what the polls were indicating, that Mandela and De Klerk were far more popular than their respective parties.

There were parallels between the voting behaviours of Indians and Coloured people, despite the major difference that Coloureds were a majority in Western and Northern Cape. Like the Indians, the Coloured people were diverse, although 87 per cent were classified as Christian and some 90 per cent spoke Afrikaans. Many felt a cultural affinity with

Afrikaners in spite of the treatment to which they had been subjected under apartheid. Oppression had persuaded some to make common cause with Africans in the quest for liberation, and a small number reached positions of prominence in the ANC or joined MK. During the 1970s BC had attracted many young Coloured university students and high school pupils; and during the 1980s, it was a fiery young Coloured clergyman, Allan Boesak, who had been a key founder of the UDF, to which a large number of Coloured 'civics' and other bodies were affiliated. Organisational links between Coloured and African affiliates, however, were weak.

Despite the intense activism of the UDF and the detention and, in some cases, even killing, of many Coloured protesters, strong elements of conservatism and racism remained deeply embedded in the Coloured community. Aspects of apartheid, such as the Western Cape's being a 'Coloured labour preference area' gave Coloured people a competitive advantage over African workseekers who had, moreover, to cope with the rigorous enforcement of influx control and the destruction of shanty settlements. During the 1980s, however, both the preference system and influx control were abandoned, resulting in an accelerated flow of Africans to the Western Cape. Many Coloured people saw the influx of Africans as a threat: increased competition for jobs and housing, as well as a challenge to their sense of being, together with whites, the prior inhabitants of the province. African migrants were interlopers, 'settlers'.[30]

Further sources of conflict between Africans and Coloureds derived from the common workplace practice of employing Coloured supervisors of African labourers. Although categorically rejected by the activist political elite, who stressed the identity of goals between Coloured and African, a good deal of racism existed, reinforced by the legacy of the past and separate residential areas and schooling. When asked if Coloured people feared Africans, Richard van der Ross, a prominent educationalist and leading figure in the Coloured community, replied:

> It is rather a feeling that there is not enough which is common between [African] and [Coloured] people. Although they share certain things there exists a great gap when it comes to culture, religion, language and attitudes toward family life.[31]

The ANC got off to a bad start in the Western Cape shortly after its unbanning: returning exiles and released prisoners, most of them African, assumed most of the leadership positions in the new structures that were being created. Around the country UDF activists and employees were drawn into the ANC, weakening the UDF, and causing it to lose its *raison d'être*. Boesak remarked bitterly in 1992 that there was a feeling among many Coloured ex-UDF activists that they 'were just being pushed aside, left by the wayside or ignored'.[32] In the light of hindsight this seemed a blunder by the ANC that damaged its electoral chances in the Western Cape by alienating a significant number of activists who might have mobilised many Coloured voters to support the ANC. The UDF had monopolised the limelight in the 1980s, forcing the 'collaborationist' Labour Party into a defensive posture, despite its claim to be using the Tricameral Parliament as a means of frustrating apartheid. But how deep were the UDF's roots in the Coloured community? Seekings, the sympathetic historian of the UDF, acknowledges that 'it is far from clear that the UDF did enjoy such widespread support among coloured people in the 1980s.'[33]

Opinion polls conducted between July 1992 and February 1994 showed fluctuations in Coloured support for the NP and the ANC: from a high of 64 per cent supporting the NP in July 1992, support dipped steadily to a low of 27 per cent in October–November 1993, before rising to 44 per cent in February 1994. Support for the ANC was estimated at 10 per cent in July 1992, rose to 21 per cent in October–November 1993, declining to 10 per cent in February 1994.[34]

It is hard to say whether the fluctuations were attributable to the volatility (indeed, fickleness) of the Coloured electorate, or to the impact of the respective parties in the course of the actual campaign. The data showed, however, that, whatever the reason, the NP remained ahead of the ANC throughout in terms of plurality support.

Both De Klerk and Mandela campaigned vigorously in the Western Cape, exploiting the fact that they enjoyed greater popularity than their respective parties. The ANC was eager to win control of the province. Symbolically, Cape Town was important as the Mother City and the legislative capital. Moreover, the quest for black (including Coloured and Indian people) solidarity was an important component of ANC aims. It was Mandela's fervent hope that the ANC could demonstrate its appeal across racial divisions and disprove the view, common among Coloured people, that the ANC was an organisation whose principal goal was the promotion of African interests. Mandela, in fact, had had to concede that this was so.[35]

The ANC's cause was not helped by infighting in its Western Cape structures that involved domination by an 'Africanist' grouping centred on Tony Yengeni, an SACP member who had also been the head of MK in the Western Cape.[36] He had served as general secretary of the provincial ANC in 1992–3, a position that he lost in 1993. Yengeni's membership of the SACP and his involvement with MK stamped him as a militant, an image that was liable to disadvantage the ANC in the eyes of the many Coloured voters who were deeply religious and opposed to violence.

The appointment of Boesak as party leader in the Western Cape created its own problems: for all his qualities as an orator, Boesak was not popular with some of the old UDF stalwarts. Moreover, his chequered love-life and taste for high living offended many Coloured people who were conservative in such matters. It was apparent early in the 1990s that Coloured support for the ANC in the Western Cape hardly extended much beyond the category of young radicals, mostly students, and well-educated professionals – a profile similar to that of Indian ANC supporters in KwaZulu-Natal.

The NP did not hesitate to exploit Coloured fears of the ANC's potential radicalism and the implications for them of affirmative action. The NP candidate for the provincial premiership was a hardliner, Hernus Kriel, who was Minister of Law and Order (which included control of the police) in De Klerk's Cabinet. Although to some extent he was kept in the background while De Klerk dominated the campaign, Kriel's candidacy was meant to underline the NP's strong commitment to maintaining law and order. Throughout, the NP told voters that it had repudiated apartheid, indeed had broken it down, and was now a reformed party, committed to implementing the RDP. Although heavily outspent by the ANC, the NP was able to ensure that its well-oiled electoral machinery ran an efficient campaign.

Particular episodes played into the NP's hands: for example, the illegal invasion by Africans of a Coloured housing settlement near Cape Town in October 1993 enabled it to hammer away on the theme that housing ownership or occupation would not be safe under an ANC government. The ANC caused itself further damage with a poster put up shortly before election day proclaiming that voting for the NP would be 'sinful': 'Your vote is secret, but not before God. Don't vote NP'. Nor was Mandela's remark that Coloured and Indian NP supporters were 'traitors to the revolution' well received. Moreover, with De Klerk riding well above Mandela in provincial polls, 62 per cent to 17 per cent, Mandela's *ad hominem* attacks on De Klerk as 'a man who does not care about black lives' made little impact, apart from provoking an angry reaction.

For its part the NP did not hesitate to exploit Coloured and Indian fears of African dominance of the polity. Some of its tactics exceeded the bounds of propriety, even by the standards of robust electioneering. After complaints from the ANC, the IEC forced the NP to withdraw a 'comic book' that sought to depict life for Coloured people under ANC rule: its crudest section suggested that the notorious slogan used by some fringe

ANC militants, 'Kill a Boer, kill a farmer' could become 'Kill a farmer, kill a coloured'.[37]

Over 60 per cent of Coloured and Indian voters eventually supported the NP. Unlike the great majority of Africans, Coloured and Indian people appeared to accept that the NP had indeed reformed itself. It was a case of supporting the devil you knew, rather than the devil you didn't know.

Underlying their voting behaviour, however, was a deeper sense that there were more commonalities with whites than with Africans. Moreover, under apartheid all blacks had been unequal, though some were more unequal than others; and while the Tricameral Parliament was an ill-conceived constitutional experiment, aimed at co-opting Coloured and Indians, it had nevertheless secured greater material benefits for them. In this limited sense co-optation had been partially successful, notwithstanding the large-scale boycott of elections by its intended beneficiaries. Fear of the loss of this relative advantage played a significant role. (It was not long after 1994 that there arose among Coloured people the lament that they were 'not white enough under apartheid, but not black enough under the ANC'.)

Given the virtual inaccessibility of many African areas to NP (and DP) campaigners, and the evident lack of support for 'historically white parties', the NP had to focus principally on non-African minorities. It had hoped, however, that if the IFP decided not to participate, many of its supporters would defy the leadership and vote NP. The NP also had to reckon with the possibility of a leakage of support to the Freedom Front, whose leader, Constand Viljoen, was an attractive and popular personality. While the NP claimed to have secured many of its constitutional goals (though how securely could not be foretold), it had failed to obtain the critical one, permanent power-sharing and the avoidance of simple majoritarianism. It had done the best it could, but there was a danger that some, even many, of its supporters would consider that its best was not good enough to protect their interests against a rampant majority.

The NP was not helped by the triumphalist crowing by some leading ANC people: Valli Moosa, for example, described the Interim Constitution as 'the terms of surrender of an undemocratic regime', while Tokyo Sexwale said that De Klerk would enjoy no power when, as anticipated, he became a Deputy President in the new government.[38] Whether these comments displeased Mandela, who had avoided triumphalism and gone out of his way to assure whites and other minorities of their security, is not known. Probably, Mandela's reassurances, however, did help a majority of whites to acquiesce in the inevitable ascendancy of a predominantly ANC government.

* * *

The presidential nature of the election pushed smaller parties to the periphery, even though list system PR with no minimum threshold enabled some to gain at least a toehold in Parliament or in provincial legislatures. For the PAC and the DP especially, the outcomes were bitterly disappointing: they won 1.25 per cent (five seats) and 1.73 per cent (seven seats) of votes for the National Assembly, respectively. At the provincial level, the DP did better, winning a total of 12 seats across the nine provinces, suggesting that a fair number of its traditional supporters had split their votes.

The PAC entered the election campaign as something of a dark horse. It was known to have pockets of support in several parts of the country, and it was assumed that its core demand, the return of the land to its original occupants, would strike a receptive chord among the many land-hungry people. Land, moreover, was no mere 'factor of production': it was laden with highly emotive and symbolic overtones. However important the land issue was, though, the more immediate ones for most Africans were jobs and housing. The militance of the PAC's armed wing, Apla, had resulted in the killing of a number of whites. Together with slogans such as 'one settler, one bullet' and 'whites must leave', the PAC gained an image of being anti-white. Although such an attitude was not true of all in PAC leadership circles, the perception could have impressed many young, angry and militant blacks. Many more blacks, however, appear to have been alienated from the PAC by the wildness and cruelty of Apla's killing sprees – which the PAC declined to repudiate.

Why did the PAC not do better, perhaps even winning 10 per cent of the national vote as some polls had indicated? Its founding leader, Robert Mangaliso Sobukwe, had been one of the most impressive leaders ever to emerge in modern black politics; but his incarceration in 1960 and thereafter banishment to Kimberley snuffed out his political career.

Throughout the 30 years in which it was banned the PAC was wracked by severe internal feuding, with the consequence that it was never able to make much of an impact in the states where it had a presence. Its lack of an effective infrastructure and adequate resources meant that it was unable to accommodate or recruit the large number of young black militants who fled South Africa in the aftermath of the Soweto Uprising of 1976–7. One surmises that the PAC's strong Africanist emphasis might well have appealed more to the BC orientation of the young exiles, but this was not to be.

None of the PAC's subsequent leaders came remotely close to Sobukwe's stature. Clarence Makwetu, who became leader in 1991 after a characteristically bruising contest, was dour, unimaginative and entirely charisma-free, and incapable of igniting potentially militant youth under the PAC banner. The PAC's campaign was disastrous. Saths Cooper described it succinctly:

> The PAC message was not heard at all. It had no cogent election plank. When media opportunity presented itself, it was not effectively exploited. The abiding memory many potential voters had of the PAC was of its president making a public complaint about lack of funds, especially from 'imperialists' and 'capitalists'. The abiding memory many existing voters had of the PAC was its apparent anti-whitism.[39]

The DP and its predecessors had an honourable record of opposition to apartheid and its discriminatory laws and draconian security legislations. The PFP was the first party to predict that the contending forces were headed for a deadlock and that the only way to avert cataclysmic violence was to seek a negotiated, inclusive settlement. White liberals have often been ignored in analyses of the forces that led to the transition. Their pertinacious and sustained critique of apartheid, and the moral weight of their arguments, however, played a significant role in undermining the confidence of many apartheid supporters. All of this, moreover, helped, if only in a small way, to mitigate racial polarisation.

The problem for the DP in the election was that the NP's volte-face had stolen many of its clothes. Moreover, a significant number of (white) voters who had supported it in the 1987 election now shifted support to the NP in the belief that it was important to maximise opposition to the ANC's potential hegemony. According to Reynolds's estimate, white votes for the DP declined from over 430 000 in 1989 to 300 000 in 1994.[40] It was also unable to make inroads into the black vote, including Coloured and Indians who supported the NP for comparable reasons.

The quasi-presidential campaign between Mandela and De Klerk largely eclipsed the leaders of small parties. The DP's leader, Zach de Beer, was widely respected across political divisions, and he remained a good speaker, but at 65 and under heavy and debilitating medication for cardio-vascular disease he had lost much of his fire. He resigned as leader soon after the DP's dismal results were announced. Disappointment, mixed with anger and frustration, was widespread in the DP. Colin Eglin, who had played an important role as a bridge-builder and deadlock-breaker in the negotiations, captured the mood in his autobiography:

> I had anticipated being a member of the new non-racial parliament and enjoying the fruits of more than thirty years of hard work to

make such a parliament a reality. Uncomfortable doubts settled in as the results began coming through from the black townships and far-flung rural areas, and the percentage of DP votes started dropping towards the figure below which I would not be re-elected. At one stage I said to myself: 'How unfair it would be if I ... was voted out of parliament and those bloody Nats, the architects of apartheid who brought South Africa close to the brink of disaster, would enjoy the pleasure and the honour of being members of South Africa's new democratic parliament – which they had fought against for over forty years!'[41]

For the Freedom Front, led by Constand Viljoen, the challenge was to demonstrate that it enjoyed the support of a sufficient number of Afrikaners to warrant consideration being given to the creation of a *volkstaat*. As a referendum among Afrikaners prior to 27 April was out of the question; 'substantial proven support' could be gauged only by how many votes the FF could win. 'Substantial', however, was undefined. Ferdi Hartzenberg, leader of the CP, had declined to take his party into the election unless a definite commitment was provided in the Constitution that a *volkstaat* would be established if there were sufficient support. He said that 850 000 votes should be considered sufficient. The Constitution's provisions, however, were anything but definite, and 'substantial proven support' was a contingent notion. When the ANC and NP rejected Hartzenberg's conditions, the CP opted to boycott the election. Viljoen agreed with the conditions, but nevertheless opted for participation.[42]

Some indication of the extent of support for a *volkstaat* has been noted. That only 14 per cent of those polled would be prepared to trek there did not deter its proponents: FF strategists claimed that the 875 619 (or 31 per cent) 'no' votes in the referendum of 1992 understated the true extent of white opposition to constitutional developments. Had it not been for the NP's short, slick campaign and the overwhelming support of the media for a 'yes' vote, the result would have been some 1.2 million 'no' votes (or 45 per cent).[43] This was a debatable claim, although it is possible that had whites been called upon in a referendum to pronounce upon the acceptability of the Interim Constitution the number of 'yes' votes would have been lower, though still a majority.

The FF hoped to win support from supporters of the fast-eroding CP and AWB who would defy their leadership's call to boycott the election. Disillusioned Nationalists who believed that their negotiators had sold the pass could be another source of votes. Until the IFP's last-minute entry into the election, the FF also hoped that it could persuade many of its supporters who wanted to vote to support it. Survey data suggested that as many as 20 per cent of IFP supporters would vote for the FF in the event of the IFP's non-participation. All things considered, it looked as though the FF might just spring a surprise that would be largely at the expense of the NP.

Despite Viljoen's readiness to participate, he remained wary, having quietly built up an armed militia in order to keep his options open should the negotiations surrounding the FF's entry go awry: it was a case of keeping his powder dry. Successive postponements of the signing of the Accord on Afrikaner Self-Determination by the government and the ANC infuriated Viljoen to the extent of sending out a country-wide mobilisation order to his armed force. Believing that the postponements were a deliberate attempt to avoid signing the Accord prior to 27 April, Viljoen is said to have told his officials that if the government and the ANC did not sign before noon on Saturday, 23 April, he would pull the FF out of the election – and go to war.[44] The threat worked: the Accord was duly signed.

In response to taunts from the CP and AWB that he had reneged on earlier commitments, Viljoen and other FF candidates repeatedly said that the constitutional provisions for a *volkstaat* and Afrikaner self-determination were 'flawed and unacceptable':

> It would serve the FF no purpose to participate unconditionally in the election. Our votes would only be overwhelmed by the ANC vote. The only option is to vote in the election, but to vote for a *volkstaat*. According to the constitution all votes for the FF will be regarded as votes for the *volkstaat*.[45]

Despite a spirited campaign that sought to capitalise on Viljoen's popularity among Afrikaners, the FF's results were a disappointment: nationally, the FF polled 424 555 votes (2.17 per cent, giving it nine seats), which was less than half of the 'no' votes in the 1992 referendum. At the provincial level, it won 639 643 votes (3 per cent of the total number of provincial votes, giving it 14 seats, distributed across seven provinces). In no province did its share of the vote reach double figures, although overall it won approximately 20 per cent of the white provincial vote.

The results were well short of the optimistic pre-election predictions (mostly advanced by the FF itself). According to Van Rooyen's estimates, the FF won 27 per cent of the Afrikaner vote nationally, and 41 per cent provincially. It was the provincial votes upon which the FF had focused, since these would give an indication of 'true and proven' support for the *volkstaat* concept. But their widespread dispersal underlined once more the fundamental problem: how and where would a *volkstaat* be located, and was it possible to find anywhere but a minuscule territory (such as Orania) where blacks were either absent or outnumbered by whites? Moreover, would even the 14 per cent of Afrikaners who were, according to a poll, prepared to trek to a *volkstaat*, ever be able to reach agreement on its location? A further question is whether the ANC – or, for that matter, the NP – actually had the slightest intention of permitting the establishment of a *volkstaat*, irrespective of how many votes the FF won.

Constand Viljoen was rightly praised for bringing the bulk of the rightwing into the election, thereby contributing to its substantial neutralisation, as well as ensuring that the CP and the AWB went into terminal decline. Mandela, who appreciated Viljoen's role in defusing the rightwing threat, paid him the compliment of suggesting that his presence in the Cabinet would strengthen the GNU: although 'not so astute politically ... I have a lot of confidence in him.'[46]

The FF's disappointing results suggested that by 1994 most Afrikaners had acquiesced in the inevitable, namely an ANC-dominated government. In the circumstances, it made sense for them to throw their weight behind the NP as the most promising bulwark against ANC hegemony.

In no province was the electoral battle harder fought than in KwaZulu-Natal, where the IFP went head-to-head with the ANC. Despite Buthelezi's brinkmanship and the IFP's last-minute decision to participate, the IFP electoral machinery had been readied for some time. Given the violence and the control of particular localities by either of the parties, a genuinely free and fair election was not possible. The logistical problems faced by the IEC even before the IFP's decision to participate were massively aggravated when Buthelezi finally opted to participate. The scramble to set up polling stations, employ additional staff and post IFP stickers onto the bottom of the ballot papers has been described. Voter education could make little impact: It looked inevitable that a shambles was in the making.

Despite disavowals from its leadership, the IFP had effectively branded itself as principally a Zulu ethnic party. Throughout the negotiations it emphasised Zulu issues, such as the entrenchment of the monarchy and a demand for a far greater degree of autonomy for KwaZulu-Natal than the Interim Constitution allowed. Optimistic IFP officials claimed that their party could win up to 30 per cent of the national vote, but the polls told a different story: even in KwaZulu-Natal they indicated that the ANC was well ahead.

The actual result in KwaZulu, however, showed that the polls had not fully reckoned with the bedrock of support for the IFP in the rural parts of the province, where traditional leaders held sway. Nationally, the IFP won 10.54 per cent of the vote, giving it 43 seats in the National Assembly; but in KwaZulu-Natal it won 50.3 per cent of the vote, giving it 41 seats in the 81-member provincial legislature. This was an apparently decisive victory over the ANC, which won only 32.2 per cent of the votes, giving it 26 seats. Despite the tension between the IFP and the NP, which won 11.2 per cent of the votes and nine seats, their common opposition to the ANC made it likely that they would co-operate, and, in turn, give the IFP a cushion of support that ensured a comfortable majority. According to Reynolds's estimates, the IFP won approximately 55 per cent of the Zulu vote, compared with 40 per cent for the ANC; 85 per cent of the IFP vote came from Africans, overwhelmingly Zulu.[47]

The outcome of the KwaZulu-Natal election was contested by the ANC, which claimed that there had been so many irregularities (a euphemism for cheating) that the validity of the election was highly doubtful.[48] It is quite possible that a legal challenge might have required the IEC to nullify the result. Many ANC officials wanted to mount such a challenge, and were enraged when Mandela agreed not to do so. Mandela, who had purposely voted in Durban, was aware that a challenge and possible overturning of the result could spark unprecedented violence. He acknowledged that violence and intimidation had dissuaded many ANC supporters from voting, and that the election had been marred by gross irregularities, but: 'We had underestimated Inkatha's strength in KwaZulu, and they had demonstrated it on election day.'[49] De Klerk would similarly waive a challenge to the results.

The climax to the battle between the ANC and the NP came when Mandela and De Klerk debated each other on television on 14 April. Both men had been coached beforehand about what issues would be raised, and the appropriate responses. Mandela attacked De Klerk vigorously, declaring the NP to be the most divisive force in the country. De Klerk, recognising that he and Mandela would have to work together after the election, did not respond in kind to the personal attacks on him, hoping to build up an advantage on points. Near the end of the debate, Mandela, conscious of having been too harsh, produced a trump card by leaning across, taking De Klerk's hand and saying:

> The exchanges between Mr de Klerk and me should not obscure one important fact. I think we are a shining example to the entire world of people drawn from different racial groups who have a common loyalty, a common love, to their common country .... In spite of criticism of Mr de Klerk ... sir, you are one of those I rely upon.

> We are going to face the problems of this country together …. I am
> proud to hold your hand for us to go forward.[50]

De Klerk acknowledged the masterstroke, saying that what had been 'a
certain points victory' for him had been converted into a draw.[51]

*   *   *

Tension mounted as 27 April approached. There were stories of house-
wives laying in supplies of food, bottled water and other requirements
should disturbances lead to a siege situation. Foreign TV crews and journalists rolled in to record what was one of the major historical events
of the late twentieth century. Those who had anticipated violence on a
major scale were surprised (and some, perhaps, even disappointed) that
for the most part, even in volatile KwaZulu-Natal, the election went off
peacefully. In effect, the election was stretched over four days: 26 April
was intended to be a special voting day for the disabled, aged, infirm or
pregnant people, but many eager voters who did not fall into any of the
special categories turned up and insisted on voting. Logistical problems
had seriously affected voting in six former bantustan territories (including Transkei), where transport and communications were primitive. The
IEC's request for 29 April to be declared a voting day in these areas was
granted, probably in response to ANC objections that large numbers of
its supporters had been unable to vote.

   The difficulties experienced by the IEC in readying itself to conduct the
election have been alluded to: that serious problems cropped up during
the election and thereafter when votes were being counted was virtually
inevitable. Judge Kriegler and his fellow commissioners were widely criticised, but the fault lay primarily with the politicians who had set them
an impossible task, whose difficulty was compounded by the last-minute
inclusion of the IFP. In the broadest sense, the election was democratic: in
reality it was more a rite of passage consecrating the transfer of political
power from the NP to the ANC. At a press conference in January, Kriegler
expressed his foreboding about what lay ahead:

> This is not going to be a 12-cylinder, turbo-charged Rolls-Royce
> election …. This is going to be a people's election; an African
> election.[52]

Thus it came to pass. The absence of voter rolls, shaky demographic data
(especially those that determined the supposed fit between population

distribution and the location of voting stations) and a huge staff complement, wholly inexperienced in running elections, combined to make it
inevitable that there would be many problems and irregularities, most
of which could only be solved on the hoof. As Kriegler acidly observed
in one of his bons mots, 'When you live in a brothel, it is hard to remain
chaste.' The following extract from the IEC's account of the election describes the problems surrounding the final count prior to releasing the
overall results:

> On the face of it, the procedures were neat and infallible, if a little
> tortuous. It was all very precisely marked out. Each counting stream
> would handle an average of 60 000 papers. On the morning of 29
> April, all packages of streams would be delivered to their allocated
> counting centres, and would be accompanied in transit by at least two
> IEC officials. The reality bore little relationship to the tidy plans. At
> some counting stations [of which there were 700 countrywide], bal-
> lot boxes streamed in without reconciliation papers, without voting
> station identification, without seals ... and even without escorts.
>   After two days of attempting to reconcile ballots in the boxes with
> the number of ballots issued to presiding officers, it became clear
> that at some counting stations it was quite impossible to do so ....
> One by one, carefully worked out strategies were abandoned. It be-
> came clear that all votes could not be reconciled. Kriegler asserted
> that it was reconciliation of people, not of ballot papers, which was
> what the elections were all about.[53]

Somehow, with the assistance of staff from several leading accounting
firms, order was produced from the chaos. The final tally was announced
on 6 May, although results had begun to dribble out several days earlier.
De Klerk, having long realized that there had never been a possibility of
the NP's winning the election, decided to concede defeat on 2 May, even
though senior NP colleagues were pressing him to challenge the results in
an attempt to have the election declared invalid. It was a difficult decision
for De Klerk to make, but he was aware that a legal challenge, especially
if successful, would cause an uproar and possible violence. He said to his
colleagues:

> Gentlemen, there is one way out of this. I must concede. Once I con-
> cede, nothing else really matters ... the result can take six months for
> all I care, but once I concede, this thing is over .... I didn't start this
> to stop it now.[54]

In a gracious speech De Klerk congratulated Mandela, and held out the hand of friendship and cooperation: 'Our greatest task would be to ensure that our young and vulnerable democracy took root and flourished.' He was told later that his speech had been a major event for some ANC supporters, who had doubted that the NP would yield power to a victorious ANC: 'They thought that we would try to pull some trick; that we would reject the election result or that we would engineer a right-wing coup'.[55]

The results were disappointing for the NP. De Klerk had hoped to win over 30 per cent of the national vote, but the final figure was only 20.6 per cent, barely enough to ensure that he would become a Deputy President and that six NP MPs would be allocated Cabinet posts, including Finance, which would continue to be occupied by Derek Keys, a highly respected figure across party lines.

De Klerk, notwithstanding his early concession, remained convinced that fraudulent voting had clipped approximately 8 per cent off the NP's tally. He wrote:

> To this day I believe that the National Party actually did much better than the formal result of 20 per cent indicated. The fact is that there were enormous irregularities. I am convinced that as many as a million illegal votes might have been cast and allocated to other parties. The parties which benefited from these irregularities were, in particular, the ANC throughout the country and, to a lesser extent the IFP in KwaZulu-Natal. An enormous number of double ballots were cast, despite the measures that the IEC had taken to try to prevent this. We also had reason to believe that towards the end of the election people were being issued with temporary voters' cards virtually on request. The fact that one and a half million such cards were issued during the election is in itself an indication that there could have been very little scrutiny of applicants. Many young people under the age of 18 voted. In many of the voting locations in the heartland of the ANC's then most important power bases, such as the Transkei, there was no real control.[56]

In spite of the disappointing outcome, the NP could console itself, if only to a limited extent, that the racial spread of its support base was wider than that of any other party. Over 50 per cent of its votes came from people of colour, including between 500 000 and 600 000 Africans, according to NP estimates.

Although the ANC leadership had expected to win comfortably, it had warned its followers against complacency. Securing 62.65 per cent of the national vote (252 seats in the National Assembly) was a huge victory, but it fell short of a two-thirds majority. Some in the ANC were disappointed at not crossing this threshold, but Mandela expressed relief:

> … had we won two-thirds of the vote and been able to write a constitution unfettered by input from others, people would argue that we had created an ANC constitution, not a South African constitution. I wanted a true government of national unity.[57]

In other comments Mandela said that winning a two-thirds majority 'would have created tremendous problems; De Klerk would have applied to the court to declare the result null and void'; and in a statement to a newspaper, he acknowledged that 'We have to be very careful not to create the fear … that the majority is going to be used for the purpose of coercing the minorities.'[58]

More vintage Mandela appeared in his autobiography:

> From the moment the results were in and it was apparent that the ANC was to form the government, I saw my mission as one of preaching reconciliation, of binding the wounds of the country, of engendering trust and confidence. I knew that many people, particularly the minorities, whites, Coloureds and Indians, would be feeling anxious about the future, and I wanted them to feel secure. I reminded people again and again that the liberation struggle was not a battle against any one group or colour, but a fight against a system of repression. At every opportunity, I said all South Africans must now unite and join hands and say we are one country, one nation, one people, marching together into the future.[59]

Mandela was undoubtedly concerned about the ANC's poor showing among non-Africans: of the ANC's votes, only 4 per cent came from Coloured voters, 1.5 per cent from Indians, and 0.5 per cent from whites, 94 per cent of its votes having come from Africans.[60] It was perhaps some consolation that the spread of African votes for the ANC across the provinces had seriously dented the claim voiced by some of its opponents that the ANC was a largely Xhosa-dominated organisation: it had run strongly not only in the Xhosa-speaking heartland, where the ANC's major roots lay, but also among the large concentrations of non-Xhosa speakers elsewhere in the country. Only in KwaZulu-Natal did it not sweep the boards among African voters. The breadth of its support clearly showed that the vast majority of Africans saw the ANC as the principal instrument of their liberation.

In constructing the Cabinet of the GNU Mandela had to comply with the constitutional requirements and appoint representatives of the two parties, the NP and the IFP, who had secured sufficient votes to be eligible for inclusion; but he sought to go further, expressing the hope that he might accommodate members of the liberation movement who had not reached the threshold. He warned participants in the GNU that they should not try to interfere in the ANC's RDP which, he claimed, was why the majority had voted for the ANC:

> Nobody will be entitled to participate in the government of national unity to oppose the programme. If there are any attempts to undermine the programme, there will be tensions ... .[61]

In the same speech, however, Mandela promised all members of the GNU that they would not be 'showpieces': 'We do not want to reduce them to rubber stamps.' What this evidently meant was that while robust debate might take place in Cabinet, once a decision had been taken, all members would be expected to support it. As Colin Eglin observed after Tony Leon, leader of the DP, had declined an invitation to join the Cabinet, the prohibition on subsequent public disagreement would have emasculated the opposition.[62]

* * *

In considering the founding election certain issues need to be examined. First, to what extent, if at all, did the election resemble a 'racial census'? In discussing the extent to which parties suffered denial of access to 'no-go' zones, the IEC observed:

> ... the final results indicate that, in general and subject to fairly significant exceptions, the electorate voted along ethnic lines: the ANC drew the bulk of its support from Africans, the NP from whites, coloureds and Indians, the IFP from Zulus, and the Freedom Front from conservative whites. It is highly questionable whether a greater degree of openness in electioneering would have had a significant effect on that broad pattern. Indeed, the two major competitors, the ANC and the NP, tended to concentrate their major efforts in areas where they enjoyed major support.[63]

The IEC did not elaborate on what the 'fairly significant exceptions' were. Majorities of Coloured and Indian people voted for the NP, while sizeable minorities of Coloureds voted for the ANC in the Western and Northern Cape. How does one explain the apparently aberrant behaviour of these majorities who supported a party that had subjected them to discrimination? Fears of majority rule and a sense of being closer to whites ('the devil they knew') largely explain what happened. Neither the Coloureds nor the Indians constituted ethnic or racial groups with over-arching common institutions or leaderships. 'Category' is the more appropriate designation.

The notion of an 'ethnic' or, more appropriately in this case, a 'racial' census does not imply an automatic or knee-jerk reaction to voting opportunity. Like voters everywhere, voting behaviour centres on perceived interests – 'party X will best safeguard and promote my interests'. But in South Africa's case 'interests' have been so totally shaped by, and enveloped in, race that it is virtually impossible to perceive interests other than through a racial prism.

A further consideration, relevant to divided societies, is that voting is also an expression of identity. This is not to assert that ethnic nationalism is 'primordial' in character – nationalist movements can mobilise their potential followers in part by imbuing them with a sense of identity, just as Afrikaner nationalism and Black Consciousness did, in their respective ways. At its core, the ANC is a nationalist movement, capable of inspiring the deepest of loyalties among its members and supporters. Two examples from an anthology of reactions to the 1994 election and the installation of the new government illustrate the point: Mazisi Kunene writes that, suddenly 'like a flash of lightning, I realized that my act of voting was not simply physical; to be honest, it must represent many of those people I knew, who would have liked to have voted, but who died in the struggle'. Elsewhere, he says: 'There was never any doubt that I was ANC; I was born into it. It was part of me, like a limb.' In the same anthology, Njabulo S Ndebele, a distinguished academic and writer, says: 'As I watched the new flag go up, I felt, for the first time in my life, that this country was really mine.'[64] It was a comment similar to DF Malan's after the NP's victory in 1948.

A second issue to be addressed is the all-important one: was it, as the IEC pronounced it to be, 'substantially free and fair'? Throughout this chapter, reference has been made to the manifold problems that occurred, as well as to Judge Kriegler's defensive observations, including the remark that 'administratively the elections were flawed. Politically, however, they were a substantial success.'[65]

The critical point is that the election *had* to succeed. Tim Cohen, a leading political journalist, wrote, after the election:

> The political demands were such that the election would have to be declared free and fair even if it wasn't, because the country, world and history desperately required it to be a success. The election was to be the new South Africa's crowning moment, the culmination of the liberation struggle and the birth of a new era. The enormous weight of a historic moment was in sight and the IEC's job was simply to deliver that moment. To fail would have been to deny the people of South Africa their birthright. Miscarriage was inconceivable.[66]

Cohen's words captured exactly the mood of the times – and the constraints under which the IEC and the contending parties operated.

Despite the acquiescence of all parties in the IEC's pronouncement of the election as 'substantially free and fair', many lingering doubts remained, including rumours that the final results had been 'massaged' to ensure the most benign outcome in the circumstances – 'a designer outcome' in Waldmeir's words.[67] The IEC indignantly denied that any such thing had happened. According to the vice-chairperson, Dikgang Moseneke, whose words were echoed by fellow-commissioner, Helen Suzman:

> It wasn't possible to have manipulated the results, even assuming we had wanted to … . We had parties sitting at provincial voting stations to sign the returns; we had auditors sitting and verifying the results.[68]

While there is no reason to doubt this comment, the alleged irregularities mostly occurred much earlier in the electoral sequence. De Klerk's claim that as many as one million illegal votes might have been cast has a *prima facie* plausibility. Given the IEC's acknowledgement that nearly 1.5 million temporary voters' cards had been issued during the four days of the election, it is inherently implausible that the eligibility of applicants could have been properly scrutinised. 'Double-voting' on a large scale was also alleged, which may have been facilitated by partisan officials and/or the absence or non-functioning of equipment to mark voters' hands. There were also allegations that in some cases balloting papers had been crossed with a vote for the 'right' party before the election day. Unsealed ballot boxes, ballot boxes containing ballots neatly arranged in piles, and not in the jumbles that are found when voters push them through the slots …. And so on. All of these forms of fraud undoubtedly occurred, but the problem is one of proof: once an illegal ballot is inserted into the box it becomes impossible to distinguish it from legitimate ballots.

An equally serious issue was the existence of 'no-go' zones, 165 of them, according to the IEC's data. Could an election be pronounced 'free and fair' if campaigning parties were denied access to areas controlled by their rivals, many of whose supporters believed themselves to be fully justified in preventing other parties campaigning in 'their' areas? Venturing into 'enemy' territory could often prove physically dangerous. Neither the NP nor the DP could gain unfettered access to African areas, urban or rural; and no rival party could campaign freely in areas that were solidly pro-IFP. The African townships of Cape Town illustrate the problem: they were no-go areas for the NP and the DP, which meant that two out of three main parties in Western Cape were denied access to nearly 25 per cent of the provincial electorate.[69]

By the end of the election period, according to the IEC, 3 558 complaints had been received, of which 2 408 related to denial of access for campaigning, canvassing or voter education, and less than one-third to violence or intimidation in relation to public meetings. The IEC accepted that parties had to accept the reality of no-go zones, but denied that this had any significant effect on the outcome of the elections:

> On the contrary, there is reason to believe that the political parties acted wisely in not wasting their efforts on lost causes. Political parties generally concentrate on persuading 'undecideds' and getting their faithful to the polls. Very few of either category are to be found for opposition parties in no-go zones .... It is highly questionable whether a greater degree of openness in electioneering would have had a significant effect on that broad pattern. Indeed, the two major competitors, the ANC and the NP, tended to concentrate their major efforts in areas where they enjoyed significant support.[70]

While broadly true, the IEC's views were a sorry commentary on the quality of the emerging democracy: the essence of democracy is choice, even in constrained circumstances. This was denied.

So far as is known, none of the observers from the 30 local and 97 international organisations disputed the finding that the election was 'substantially' free and fair, although the European Union's Election Unit conspicuously refrained from deeming them 'fair'.[71] It is doubtful whether many of the foreign observers from established democracies would have condoned irregularities of this election had they occurred in elections in their own states, but, then, South Africa was not an established democracy, and it was quite apparent from the campaign and the election itself that it had a long way to go before it acquired a political culture that matched the democratic pretensions of its Constitution.

Still, the election was a start, and even the sharpest of critics of the election's many and varied imperfections acknowledged that the results broadly reflected the wishes of the electorate, over 19.5 million of whom had voted, often enduring long queues to do so. For Africans in particular, the days of the election were a time of exuberance in which even the deadly violence was temporarily suspended. The parties that had participated accounted for perhaps as much as 98 per cent of the citizenry's political preferences, and the three biggest parties alone accounted for over 90 per cent of all the votes cast. It was too soon to claim that democratic institutions were 'the only game in town', to repeat Przeworski's phrase. In a famous maxim, von Klausewitz described war as 'the continuation of politics by other means'. In South Africa's case there were reasons to hope that politics might be 'the continuation of war by other means'.

Conclusion

Why did the transition occur relatively peacefully? How does one explain why the sombre predictions of full-scale revolution, 'fighting to the last drop of blood', and so on, did not come true? This conclusion attempts to draw the different strands of the book together and provide answers to these questions.

A miracle? A negotiated revolution? A 'refolution'? All of the above can be, and have been, used to describe South Africa's transition from being the world's last surviving racial oligarchy to a democratic order. The theme of this book has been that the transition occurred because the principal antagonists, the ANC and the NP, mutually recognised that neither could win the struggle on its own terms: the conflict was deadlocked, and perpetuating it would cause horrifying loss of life and serious damage to a potentially prosperous economy.

Colin Eglin observed that in most comparable situations:

> ... low-intensity civil wars escalate until there is a clear winner and
> loser. South Africa, however, took a unique route, largely because of
> a rare display of leadership: a relatively conservative Afrikaner leader
> decided to negotiate before he had lost, and an imprisoned leader of
> a liberation movement decided to negotiate before he had won.[1]

No single-factor cause satisfactorily explains the transition: it derived from a combination of factors. Shifts in the tectonic plates of society, of course, were crucial: the growing strength of the black bloc and the weakening of the white power bloc, together with its international isolation, explain much of the stalemate that developed; but leadership was the indispensable complement. Both Mandela and De Klerk had to

566

keep potentially unruly support-bases in line. As Peter Clarke writes of (British) political leaders, leadership was important 'not because it is all that matters, but because we literally cannot do without it'.[2]

Another theme is encapsulated in the word 'refolution', invented by Timothy Garton Ash to explain changes in Eastern Europe:

> There was a strong and essential element of 'change from above', led
> by an enlightened minority in the still ruling communist parties. But
> there was also a vital element of popular pressure 'from below'.[3]

While the situations in Eastern Europe and South Africa are not comparable, 'refolution' nonetheless captures the essence of the dialectical interplay between the Afrikaner power bloc and its black challengers.

Without the widespread recognition among whites in general, and Afrikaners in particular, that apartheid had not only failed, but that its lingering residue posed a danger to white survival, the transition could not have succeeded other than at a far bloodier cost than was the case. Piet Cillié, the famed newspaperman (and cynic), observed that 'we had a choice between certain downfall and probable downfall, and De Klerk chose the latter'. But, he added, in South Africa 'the worst never happens'.[4] Many whites shared Cillié's forebodings, in spite of Mandela's reassurances. But what was the alternative? De Klerk has often said that the old apartheid order could have been maintained for another decade or more, but it would have assuredly entailed chaos, bloodletting on a massive scale and economic collapse.

Considering the long-standing and entrenched character of white oligarchical rule, the death toll in the conflict between the 1970s and early 1990s – indeed, over the whole span of apartheid from 1948 onwards – was remarkably low in comparison with other transitions or internal wars. The figures presented here must be viewed with caution since the number of fatalities incurred in particular incidents or in periods of acute conflict is often a politically contentious issue. For example, the official figure for the number of deaths occurring in the Soweto Uprising of 1976 and its (countrywide) aftermath is 575; many, notably Sowetans, believe the actual figure to be much higher.

An estimated 23 000 fatalities in domestic political conflict occurred between 1948 and 1994. This figure includes 131 executions for political offences and 72 deaths that occurred during detention in terms of security legislation. An estimated 21 561 of the fatalities occurred between 1984 and 1994; of these, approximately half – 10 744 – occurred in KwaZulu-Natal.[5] Approximately 3 000 of the fatalities resulted from security force action.

It must be stressed that these figures relate to domestic conflict, and do not include deaths resulting from the apartheid government's regional incursions, such as the border war in Namibia/Angola, so-called 'hot pursuit' into neighbouring territories, destabilisation tactics, and support for insurgent movements in Angola and Mozambique. It is impossible to estimate the death toll, although the EPG appeared to accept as credible a figure of 100 000.[6]

It is not an argument in mitigation of apartheid to point out that death tolls in civil conflicts in Africa and other parts of the world have been far higher.[7] The Algerian colonial uprising (1955–1962), for example, claimed 300 000 lives. This book has produced evidence to show why apartheid was rightly considered to be an evil system. Yet it was not uniquely so if degrees of evil are measured by the number of deaths caused. Why then did the apartheid government become the object of an international obloquy that was unique? The response, that South Africa was unique in enshrining discrimination in its Constitution, is true enough, but hardly a conclusive answer to the question – or, for that matter, much consolation to the victims of injustice in states whose Constitutions, to the extent that they are operative, lack discriminatory provisions. Geoffrey Robertson suggests that South Africa was 'an easy (as well as a proper) target because it had few powerful supporters besides Israel'.[8]

It was an easy target for further two reasons: first, apartheid was an affront to all people of colour – many of whom were, or had been, subject to colonial rule. International bodies now offered platforms from which ex-colonial states could express their hatred of institutionalised racial discrimination. Secondly, and more controversially, many states in the developed world were themselves former colonial powers or had been guilty of their own institutionalised forms of racial discrimination (the USA) or exclusionary practices (Australia). The revulsion that many of their citizens felt for apartheid was genuine, but it may have been mingled with projected guilt, as well as a sense that white people (namely, South Africans) should not do this, whereas blacks could be subjected to less moral condemnation for what was often equally or more abhorrent behaviour. White South African bleats that the international community applied 'double standards' were mostly self-serving cant. Their critics, however, were sometimes guilty of an unconscious and perverse racism that expected whites to display higher standards of conduct than could be expected of blacks.

Charges of genocide were frequently flung at the apartheid government. If the concept is interpreted narrowly, in its original meaning, as an attempt to eliminate a racial or ethnic group, the charge fails. As has been noted, the size of the African population nearly trebled over the years of apartheid, confounding policy planners to the extent that unanticipated population growth was one of the main causes of apartheid's downfall. Moreover, life expectancy among Africans, probably between 30 and 40 years in pre-colonial times, had risen to 63 by 1990.

(It should be an embarrassing fact for the ANC government that, according to researchers at the Harvard School of Public Health, between 2000 and 2005 President Thabo Mbeki's 'denialist' views caused the death of over 330 000 HIV-positive people, as a consequence of deliberate delays in the provision of life-prolonging drugs – which Mbeki deemed 'toxic'.)[9]

* * *

To what extent the De Klerk government's decision to unban the ANC and other organisations and to embark upon the road to democracy is unique in modern history is an intriguing issue: no comparable example comes to mind. De Gaulle's decision to grant independence to Algeria in 1962 required considerable courage and caused turmoil in domestic politics; but Algeria, despite its status as part of metropolitan France, was basically a colony, and shedding a colony was not the same as dismantling a racial oligarchy and (eventually) ceding to power to an African majority.

A stock response to the claim of South African 'exceptionalism' is to argue that De Klerk had no alternative: his decision was de facto acknowledgement that the game was up. It was, however, much more complex than that. Ultimately, De Klerk's decision was less about seizing the initiative and negotiating from a position of strength (although that was certainly part of his reckoning) than it was about the morality of trying to perpetuate a system that had failed. As a staunch *Dopper* (member of the small Gereformeerde Kerk), De Klerk abided by the church's postulate that what was morally wrong could not be politically right. He also had an abhorrence of violence, and he knew that shoring up the oligarchy would exact a toll for which he had no stomach. Unfortunately for him, none of his critics, including Mandela, gave the slightest credence to De Klerk's actual beliefs, or to the extreme difficulty of rooting out renegade elements in the security forces who were intent on thwarting the transition. The result was that his reputation as a man of peace was tarnished. Discrediting De Klerk was part of a deliberate ANC strategy of seeking to monopolise the moral high ground, claiming that the downfall of apartheid was exclusively the result of its efforts. It was not in the nature of liberation movements to acknowledge that others, especially hated opponents, might actually have played a part in dismantling oppression.

So far as is known, De Klerk is the only ex-leader of an authoritarian state to have made a comprehensive apology for the misdeeds of the state whose head he had become. Given his background, it was inevitable that a strong sense of Afrikaner identity, including a firm commitment to apartheid, was woven into his persona. In his earlier apologies, De Klerk insisted that apartheid was a policy espoused by him in good faith, which had gone horribly wrong. The refusal of his critics to accept these apologies, which they considered belated, grudging and insincere, offended De Klerk, who was not the kind of person to grovel – or to repudiate a background that included his entire family. Testifying before the Truth and Reconciliation Commission, he said:

> Let me place once and for all a renewed apology on record. Apartheid was wrong. I apologise in my capacity as leader of the National Party to the millions of South Africans who suffered the wrenching disruption of forced removals in respect of their homes, businesses and land. Who over the years suffered the shame of being arrested for pass law offences. Who over the decades and indeed centuries suffered the indignities and humiliation of racial discrimination. Who for a long time were prevented from exercising their full democratic rights in the land of their birth. Who were unable to achieve their full potential because of job reservation. And who in any other way suffered as a result of discriminatory legislation and politics. This renewed apology is offered in a spirit of true repentance, in full knowledge of the tremendous harm that apartheid has done to millions of South Africans.[10]

A further point that is germane to the relative ease with which the transition occurred derives from the character of the oligarchical society even under apartheid. In spite of major limitations on civil liberties, South Africa never became a full-blown totalitarian state comparable to Nazi Germany or the Soviet Union (at least until the arrival of *glasnost*). That it was authoritarian is undoubted; and it is also true that during states of emergency, when (already limited) freedoms were even further circumscribed, the state appeared, especially to blacks, to warrant classification as near-totalitarian.

Attempts to compare the apartheid state to Nazi Germany are misconceived. Apartheid was bad enough without having to exaggerate its evils. Criticism of the racial order remained possible to an extent that was unthinkable in the Third Reich, the Soviet Union and a wide range of authoritarian states of both leftwing and rightwing orientation. The press was hobbled and prevented from reporting fully on security and defence issues; but a number of courageous journalists and editors, sometimes in the face of their proprietors' disapproval, nevertheless managed to keep the flame of press freedom alight. Likewise, a number of scholars in the English-medium universities and a few of their counterparts in the Afrikaans-medium institutions made good use of their academic freedom (less curtailed than university autonomy) to offer critical analyses of apartheid. A few notable academics and a number of student leaders, however, were banned, detained, prosecuted and, in at least two cases, assassinated, mostly because of their activism rather than for narrowly academic pursuits.

Civil society also proved resilient, and a powerful force for change, especially with the rise of the independent union movement and the mushrooming of 'civics' in the 1980s. The churches were a key element of civil society: apart from using the relatively protected status of the pulpit to convey what were essentially critical messages, condemnation of apartheid as sinful by the major denominations was a further source of delegitimation. The steady withdrawal of theological justifications of apartheid by two of the three Dutch Reformed churches should also be noted.

The private sector, also a key component of civil society, received a roasting from the TRC for its alleged complicity in apartheid:

> Business was central to the economy that sustained the South African state during the apartheid years. Certain businesses, especially the mining industry, were involved in helping to design and implement apartheid policies. Other businesses benefited from co-operating with the security structures of the former state. Most businesses benefited from operating in a racially structured context.[11]

This is a sweeping judgement, but the issue nevertheless raises the question of the relationship between capitalism and apartheid. In very brief terms, three broad perspectives can be identified:

1. 'Economic rationality urges the polity forward beyond its ideology.' Horwitz's comment reflects the hypothesis that capitalism gradually erodes racial barriers by virtue of the economic rationality of market forces.
2. That the origins of segregation and apartheid lie in capitalist development, and that capitalism and apartheid are symbiotically linked.
3. '[I]ndustrial imperatives accommodate themselves to the racial

mould and continue to operate effectively within it. We must look to outside factors rather than to a maturation of these imperatives for an explanation of the disintegration of the racial mould.' (Herbert Blumer)[12]

Consideration of these perspectives generated scholarly warfare in South African universities and elsewhere during the 1970s and 1980s, pitting liberals and Marxists/neo-Marxists against one another. Space precludes a review of the arguments. The following are brief conclusions.

First, South Africa's racial hierarchy had been established well before the development of large-scale mining, which had to adapt itself to the hierarchy. Moreover, group alignments or ethnicities that developed in the twentieth century could not be reduced to class, although class and class-like issues were also evident. Secondly, the genesis of segregation and, after 1948, apartheid cannot be attributed to capitalism: both forms of discrimination were lineal descendants of the racial mould established much earlier. It is, however, true that the mining industry and the (white) agricultural sector colluded to augment labour-repressive legislation and the refusal to recognise African trade unions or to permit strikes by African workers.

As Merle Lipton's seminal work has shown, different sectors had different stakes in apartheid. She posited four broad possible relationships between capitalists and apartheid:

- Capitalists do not want apartheid and have the power to get rid of it;
- Capitalists do not want apartheid, but do not have the power to get rid of it;
- Capitalists want apartheid, and have the power to retain it;
- Capitalists want apartheid, but do not have the power to retain it.

As Lipton acknowledges, these are logical extremes, within each of which there would be variation.[13]

The private sector was anything but homogeneous: apart from the language divide between English- and Afrikaans-speakers, the scale of enterprises – small, medium or large – and even provincial rivalries, especially notable among Afrikaners, limited any possible unified thrust of the private sector. Chapter 7 has noted the cautious approach of capitalists to political issues. It was only after the Soweto Uprising of 1976 and the inception of the turbulent 1980s, accompanied by the threat of sanctions and the loss of foreign borrowing facilities, that a more forthright business activism began. Even then, the upper hand remained with government, as Chris Ball of Barclays Bank learned to his cost. It was evident that Lipton's second possible relationship between capitalists and apartheid was closest to reality.

Direct business activism could achieve little, apart from some powerful symbolic acts such as the visit in 1985 to the ANC by a delegation of businessmen, but the indirect effects of business activity possessed far more erosive power. The demand for labour undermined the economic basis of indigenous African societies, massively assisted by the alienation of land, the imposition of taxes and high rates of population growth. Urban industry created a powerful pull factor, while deepening rural poverty created an equally powerful push factor. Urbanisation is inevitable in developing societies; apartheid sought, with much greater ruthlessness than previous policies, to abort it. Just as earlier calls for a 'return to the land' had failed to persuade urbanising Afrikaners to go back to the *platteland* (rural areas), so efforts to force urban Africans to accept that they were 'temporary sojourners' whose 'real' homes were in the bantustans failed comprehensively.

High economic growth rates until the early 1970s meant that job opportunities, despite increasing unemployment, were vastly greater than in the rural areas. The consequence was the creation of the largest proletariat in Africa, and huge urban concentrations that were the matrix of steadily burgeoning protest.

How many in the business community foresaw the political implications of these processes is hard to say. De Klerk, seemingly, did. He writes:

> My exposure to the management of the economy as cabinet minister during the eighties ... convinced me more and more that it would be impossible to maintain economic growth, on the one hand, and succeed with our homeland policy on the other. I firmly believe that economic growth was a far more powerful agent for change than any of the other factors – including sanctions and international pressure .... The growing economy also led to an accelerated flow of black South Africans from the rural areas to the urban areas. It further undermined Dr Verwoerd's grand vision that, by 1978, the tide to the white cities would have turned.[14]

Another consequence of urbanisation and the exploitative conditions that Africans encountered in the cities was the spawning of a powerful trade union movement, which proved to be one of the major levers causing apartheid's final crumbling. Liberal members of the business community had accepted the need for recognising African unions well before this was eventually achieved. Harry Oppenheimer, the dominant figure in the mining industry, which had long resisted African unionism, had expressed this in the early 1970s. Michael O'Dowd, a director of the Anglo American Corporation, noted that even before legal recognition had been accorded to African unions, employers had begun to negotiate with black workers, unionised or not. Recognition came in 1979:

> This was done with almost universal employer support. This was not because the employers had undergone some mysterious conversion but because the black workers had reached levels of skill where the employers had no option but to negotiate with them. When this point is reached, it is cheaper and more efficient to negotiate with organised workers than with unorganised.[15]

Blumer was technically correct to conclude that 'outside factors' rather than 'industrial imperatives' explain the breakup of the racial mould; but, writing in 1965, he perhaps could not foresee what a powerful force those imperatives had unleashed. While the mould was finally broken by politicians, growth had created the circumstances in which they were confronted by an irresistible tide.

* * *

The narrative has shown how repression under apartheid had become too costly, and, moreover, its often brutal character offended the moral sensitivities of some key members of the regime. PW Botha's reforms – while by no means inconsequential, since some struck down pillars of the apartheid system – were not considered credible by the mass-based organisations in the country and the ANC in exile. Moreover, it was of critical significance that, far from dousing the flames of resistance, they actually inspired mass-based organisation to demand nothing less than the complete abolition of the system.

During the 1980s especially, civil society had grown stronger among blacks, notably in the form of 'civics', unions and churches. Despite the battering many militants sustained, civil society did not entirely lose its resilience, which made repression more difficult. Daron Acemoglu and James Robinson observe:

> When citizens are not well organized, the system will not be challenged and transition to democracy will be delayed indefinitely. Similarly, when civil society is relatively developed and the majority is

organised, repression may be more difficult. Therefore, some degree of development in civil society is also necessary for democratization.[16]

Just as the state was finding the costs of repression too high, so the liberation movement was beginning to wonder whether a revolutionary overthrow of the regime was possible, and whether the costs of the struggle were not also going to be too high. The decisive role of leadership in bringing about mutual recognition of the deadlock has been stressed: both Mandela and De Klerk went far out on a limb, well ahead of their followers, to persuade them that negotiation was the only realistic option.

The traditional political sub-culture of Afrikaner nationalism placed *volksleiers* (leaders of the people) in positions that were supported by respect and deference – virtual deification in the case of Verwoerd. Despite the partial fragmentation and loss of cohesion of the wider movement, the NP remained a disciplined organisation. But it operated within a *herrenvolk* democracy in which elections remained fierce contests. The menace of the ultra-rightwing and its supporters in the police, armed services and bureaucracy was real.

In some respects the ANC's position was comparable: it had always been a 'broad church', but after 1990 it was required to become even broader as various streams had to be incorporated, or at least brought into an alliance: the exile community, MK soldiers, ex-prisoners, and the internal opposition in the form of the MDM and Cosatu all had to be brought into alignment to present a unified front. It was a difficult task because the experiences of the different streams, each of which had its own modus operandi, had differed. Traditionally the ANC prided itself on being a 'collective', but the circumstances of exile and the influence of 'democratic centralism' had imparted to its leadership style a degree of 'top-down' decision-making. This does not imply that Tambo was an autocratic leader: on the contrary, his diplomatic skills had been crucial in enabling the ANC to hold together in the long, dispiriting years of exile. His support of Mandela's unmandated talks with ministers, and eventually with Botha, ensured that the vital opening to a negotiated accommodation was made. But Mandela had to endure damaging rumours that he had 'sold out'.

For negotiations to succeed, the principal antagonists must keep their constituencies in line. Both the NP and the ANC managed to achieve this, despite having to make concessions, which was especially so for the NP. It is extraordinary that neither side suffered any significant defections. It is hardly less significant that, with the conspicuous exception of Chris Hani, no major political figure was assassinated in the course of the transition.

Deeming Mandela to have iconic status has become a cliché, although it is true, as clichés invariably are. His heroic qualities are legendary: courage in the face of a possible death sentence, unflinching commitment to principle when offered conditional release from prison, generosity of spirit and lack of bitterness are testimony to a remarkable human being. These qualities played a significant role in inducing a majority of whites to accept, or at least to acquiesce in, majority rule.

Notwithstanding Mandela's stature, he is not above criticism, some of which has implicitly been made. For example, his claim that he 'never sought to undermine' De Klerk is at best a half-truth. The issue throughout was violence, and Mandela's increasingly acrimonious allegations that De Klerk was not doing enough to curb it, or that he was contemptuous of African lives. Mandela, of course, was speaking to his angry support-base as much as to De Klerk. The allegations that De Klerk was somehow involved in the violence as a means of weakening the ANC – and shoring up Inkatha – were unfair and unfounded, but damaging to De Klerk. It was relatively late in the negotiation period that Mandela acknowledged, sorrowfully, the involvement of renegade ANC elements in violence. Moreover, the ANC's complicity in the most serious violence of all, namely that in Natal, was hardly less blameworthy than Inkatha's. Mandela's failure to heed Jacob Zuma's urging that he meet with Buthelezi sooner rather than later, and instead, to allow the firebrand Harry Gwala to dictate that such a meeting should not take place, was a serious failure of leadership: had Zuma's advice been followed, there was a chance, albeit a small one, that the violence might have been limited.

Mandela's patrician background imbued him with a sense of his status. Critics might have termed it hauteur. Even a close comrade, Albertina Sisulu (wife of Walter), recalled that 'he was a Xhosa aristocrat and his training from childhood had made him the way he was, aloof and sometimes a bit arrogant'.[17] Tom Lodge, a sympathetic but not uncritical biographer, ponders whether there was something more than the issue of violence that complicated his relationship with De Klerk. De Klerk, while at all times courteous, never sought to humiliate Mandela or to make *ad hominem* attacks on him in the way that Mandela appeared to relish doing to him. Neither did De Klerk accord him deference, either in their personal interaction or in his autobiography. Lodge writes:

> Mandela may have sensed his [lack of deference]. He certainly resented any external recognition that De Klerk could claim a share of the credit for South Africa's political transition: his discomfort was

very obvious on the occasions at which they received joint awards ....
Certainly, he felt that he had good reasons for believing that De
Klerk was unworthy of such recognition but, even if he had had no
reason to doubt his adversary's good faith, would he have behaved
differently? Mandela was a patriarchal personality conscious of his
messianic stature: such leaders do not share moral authority easily.[18]

An alternative, perhaps complementary, explanation lies in the DNA of
liberation movements: an inability to share the moral high ground with
rival organisations, what Marina Ottaway has called the illusion that the
entire country could have a single purpose and accept a single representative to speak as the 'mouthpiece of an oppressed nation'.[19] South Africa
had conflicting racial nationalisms, but no 'nation': in 1994 its situation
resembled post-unification Italy, of which Massimo d'Azeglio famously
observed: 'We have made Italy, now we must make Italians.' Could a victorious racial nationalism achieve this in South Africa's case?

Brittle though it was, the relationship between this 'odd couple',
Mandela and De Klerk, survived the transition and continued into the
democratic era. It was not until several years after both had retired that
a measure of mutual cordiality was restored. Mandela spoke gracious
words of praise at a function marking De Klerk's seventieth birthday in
2006:

> There is an almost unspoken realisation and appreciation that we
> quite possibly could have fallen into the destructive racial war which
> everyone foresaw, had it not been for the daring farsightedness of
> FW de Klerk.[20]

Another issue worth remarking is how the NP and ANC, neither of which
had traditions of respect for or appreciation of liberal democracy, came to
agree upon a Constitution that was classically liberal-democratic in form.
For many, though not all, in the ANC, and especially the SACP, attaining
liberal democracy (or 'bourgeois democracy') was merely the first stage
of the National Democratic Revolution whose unfolding would lead to
the second stage, socialism. Fortunately, by 1990 the ANC had rejected all
thought of the one-party state that had had such disastrous consequences
in much of post-colonial Africa. Moreover, there was considerable eagerness among many to demonstrate to sceptics that an African state could
create and sustain a democratic political system.

For the NP, on the other hand, the protection offered by a constitutional
state, governed under the rule of law with secure human rights (notably

including property rights) was the best deal obtainable after the failure to achieve its original quasi-consociational goals.

The ANC knew that South Africa would be a difficult society to govern. The effects of generations of entrenched racial inequality and the burgeoning hopes of the now-liberated oppressed would be difficult to handle within the fragile framework of a democratic polity – one, moreover, in which the rival parties regarded one another as enemies rather than mere opponents. No less than apartheid's master-builder, HF Verwoerd, was overheard (by an Afrikaner clergyman) to say that he would entrench apartheid so deeply in the society that whatever government came to power afterwards would find it impossible to undo what had been done.[21] Impossible? No. Difficult? Yes, indeed.

Sustaining democracy in deeply divided societies is notoriously difficult. The ANC equated democracy with majority rule: while universal adult suffrage is a fundamental component of a democratic polity, the equation is problematic. First, it is often the case in established democracies that no party wins a majority of votes, although, thanks to the distortions caused by some electoral systems, one party may win a majority of seats even with a minority of the votes – as happened in South Africa's 1948 election in the pre-democratic era. Secondly, simple majority rule does not have a good record of consolidating democracy in divided societies in which ethnic or racial identities are salient: it can easily – and commonly does – degenerate into a 'tyranny of the majority' when elections assume the form of a racial census. Undeniably, majorities have rights, but so do minorities (however configured). If ascriptively determined majorities crystallise and use their power to steamroller minorities, denying them influence even in decisions that affect their vital interests, the quality of democracy will deteriorate. Moreover, the comparative evidence from divided societies does not offer much support for the view that the salience of ethnic or racial identities will eventually give way to voting alignments that are shaped more by, say, class, interests or ideology.

These considerations did not bode well for the consolidation and sustainability of democracy in South Africa. Developments after 1994 form no part of this book, although it is recognised that transitions extend well beyond the founding election. More than a decade after 1994, democratic constitutional forms have been maintained, but a single-party dominant system has become entrenched. Democracy has survived, and even if it is democracy of a poor quality, South Africa is nevertheless a vastly better society than it was under apartheid.

Notes

CHAPTER 1

1 Malan, *Afrikaner Volkseenheid en My Ervarings op die Pad Daarheen*.
2 Smuts, *A Century of Wrong*, p 95. (Although written by Smuts, the book was issued by FW Reitz, State Secretary of the Transvaal.)
3 Scholtz, *Waarom die Boere die Oorlog Verloor het*, p 180; Jooste and Oosthuizen, *So Het Hulle Gesterf*, p 30.
4 De Villiers, *PW*, pp 8–9.
5 Quoted in Welsh, 'The Politics of White Supremacy', p 53.
6 Hancock, *Smuts*, vol 1, p 357.
7 Quoted in Steyn, *Trouwe Afrikaners*, p 70.
8 Heard, *General Elections in South Africa 1943–1970*, pp 8–9.
9 Stultz, *The Nationalists in Opposition 1934–1948*, p 8.
10 *Report of the Carnegie Commission*, 1932, para 9.
11 Van den Heever, *Generaal JBM Hertzog*, p 593.
12 Thom, *Dr DF Malan en Koalisie*, p 39.
13 Cillié, *Baanbrekers vir Vryheid*, p 25 (translation).
14 Pienaar, *Glo in u Volk: DF Malan as Redenaar*, p 125 (translation).
15 Albertyn, Du Toit and Theron, *Kerk en Stad*, p 24 (translation).
16 Pienaar, *Glo in u Volk*, p 115 (translation).
17 Scholtz, *Het die Afrikaanse Volk 'n Toekoms?*, pp 113, 116.
18 Slabbert, 'Afrikaner Nationalism, White Politics, and Political Change in South Africa', p 6.
19 Pelzer, *Die Afrikaner-Broederbond*, pp 94, 41 (translation).
20 Slabbert, 'Afrikaner Nationalism', p 9.
21 Pelser, *Die Afrikaner-Broederbond*, p 41 (translation).
22 De Klerk, *The Puritans of Africa*, p 219.
23 Paton, *Towards the Mountain*, p 209.

24 Pienaar, *Getuie van Groot Tye*, p 9.

25 Schoeman, *My Lewe in die Politiek*, p 113.

26 Stultz, *The Nationalists in Opposition*, p 93.

27 Hancock, *Smuts*, vol 2, p 384.

28 Smuts, *The Basis of Trusteeship*, p 10.

29 Quoted in Hoernlé, *South African Native Policy and the Liberal Spirit*, p 1.

30 De Villiers, *Paul Sauer*, p 85.

31 Cillié, *Baanbrekers vir Vryheid*, p 67.

32 Posel, *The Making of Apartheid*, p 1.

33 Scholtz, *Dr Hendrick Frensch Verwoerd*, vol 1, p 43 (translation).

34 House of Assembly Debates, vol 62, 1948, cols 361–3.

35 Pienaar, *Getuie van Groot Tye*, p 16 (translation).

36 Van Wyk, *The Birth of a New Afrikaner*, p 61.

37 Cillié, *Tydgenote*, p 44 (translation).

38 Stultz, *The Nationalists in Opposition*, pp 129–30.

39 Pienaar, *Glo in U Volk*, pp 38, 43.

40 Hancock, *Smuts*, vol 2, p 498.

41 Heard, *General Elections in South Africa*, pp 42, 44.

42 Schoeman, *My Lewe in die Politiek*, pp 136–7.

43 Thompson, *The Cape Coloured Franchise*, pp 57–8.

44 Friedman, *Smuts: A Reappraisal*, pp 185–6.

45 Malherbe, *Never a Dull Moment*, pp 366–72.

CHAPTER 2

1 Quoted in Welsh, *The Roots of Segregation*, p 35.

2 De Kiewiet, *A History of South Africa*, p 75.

3 Macmillan, *Complex South Africa*, p 120.

4 Natives Land Commission: Minute addressed to the Hon. the Minister of Native Affairs by the Hon Sir WH Beaumont, para 69.

5 Report of the South African Native Affairs Commission, 1903–5, para 192.

6 Plaatje, *Native Life in South Africa*, p 17.

7 Rogers, *Native Administration in the Union of South Africa*, p 148.

8 Houghton, *The South African Economy*, p 162.

9 Report of the Transvaal Local Government Commission, 1921 (Stallard Commission), para 268.

10 Smuts, 'Problems in South Africa', p 280.

11 Report of the Native Economic Commission 1930–1932, para 69.

12 Report of the Native Laws Commission 1946-48, para 7.

13 Report of the Interdepartmental Committee on Social, Health and Economic Conditions of Urban Natives, paras 54, 86, 87.

14 Thompson, *Cape Coloured Franchise*, p 55.

15 Report of the Transvaal Labour Commission, evidence, p 730.

16 Quoted in Welsh, *Roots of Segregation*, p 204.

17 Odendaal, *Vukani Bantu*, p 287.
18 Karis and Carter, *From Protest to Challenge*, vol 1, p 53.
19 *Ibid*, p 72.
20 Willan, *Sol Plaatje*, p 153.
21 Report of the South African Native Affairs Commission, 1903–5, para 69.
22 Karis and Carter, *From Protest to Challenge*, vol 1, pp 77–8.
23 Tatz, *Shadow and Substance in South Africa*, p 74.
24 Wickens, *The Industrial and Commercial Workers' Union of South Africa*, p 209.
25 Luthuli, *Let My People Go*, p 102.
26 Mandela, *No Easy Walk to Freedom*, p 92.
27 Karis and Carter, *From Protest to Challenge*, vol 2, pp 209–23.
28 Houghton, 'Economic Development, 1865–1965', p 36.
29 Mandela, *Long Walk to Freedom*, p 92.
30 Karis and Carter (eds), *From Protest to Challenge*, vol. 2, pp 305, 304.
31 Lembede, *Freedom in Our Lifetime*, p 118.
32 *Ibid*, p 85, 22.
33 Karis and Carter, *From Protest to Challenge*, vol 2, p 321.
34 Meer, *A Fortunate Man*, p 120.
35 Mandela, *Long Walk to Freedom*, p 106.
36 Lembede, *Freedom in Our Lifetime*, pp 27–8.
37 Walshe, *The Rise of African Nationalism in South Africa*, p 357.
38 Meer, *A Fortunate Man*, p 67.
39 *South African Communists Speak*, p 184.
40 *Ibid*, p 200.
41 Simons, *Class and Colour in South Africa*, p 575.
42 Mandela, *Long Walk*, p 101.
43 *Ibid*, p 113.
44 Karis and Carter, *From Protest to Challenge*, vol 2, p 306.
45 Vilakazi, *Zulu Transformations*, p 136.
46 Hodgson, 'A Battle for Sacred Power: Christian Beginnings Among the Xhosa', p 87.
47 Lembede, *Freedom in Our Lifetime*, p 117.
48 Van den Heever, *Generaal Hertzog*, p 306 (translation).
49 Memmi, *The Colonizer and the Colonized*, pp 87–8.
50 Mphahlele, *Es'kia*, p 73.
51 Mandela, *Long Walk*, p 13.
52 Mphahlele, *Es'kia*, p 65.
53 Quoted in Wickens, *The Industrial and Commercial Workers' Union*, p 206.

CHAPTER 3

1 *Die Burger*, 15 July 1971 (translation).
2 Brookes, *A Documentary Study of Modern South Africa*, p 22.

3 Bekker, *Eben Dönges*, pp 48–58.

4 Slabbert, *The Last White Parliament*, p 51.

5 Brookes, *A Documentary Study of Modern South Africa*, p 152.

6 Paton, *Journey Continued*, p 181.

7 South African Institute of Race Relations, *Survey of Race Relations 1985*, p 348. (Note: subsequent references are: SAIRR *Survey*, with the relevant year.)

8 Welsh, 'The Growth of Towns', in Thompson and Wilson, *The Oxford History of South Africa*, vol 2, p 241.

9 House of Assembly Debates, vol 64, 1948, col 1654.

10 Van Reenen, *Op die Randakker*, pp 16–7 (translation).

11 Schoeman, *My Lewe in die Politiek*, pp 198–9 (translation).

12 *Ibid*, p 224.

13 JL Sadie, 'Was Professor Tomlinson Verwoerd se Slagoffer?', in *Rapport*, 3 March 1996.

14 AN Pelzer, *Verwoerd Speaks*, p 121.

15 *Ibid*, p 120.

16 Pienaar, *Getuie van Groot Tye*, p 63.

17 Michael Savage, 'The Imposition of Pass Laws on the African Population in South Africa 1916-1984', pp 181–205.

18 Quoted in *ibid*, p 195.

19 *Ibid*, p 186.

20 Helen Suzman, *In No Uncertain Terms*, p 102.

21 Welsh, 'Growth of Towns', pp 194–6.

22 Pelzer, *Verwoerd Speaks*, p 40.

23 Quoted in Scholtz, *Hendrik Frensch Verwoerd*, vol 1, p 295.

24 Quotations from Verwoerd's speech are drawn from Pelzer, *Verwoerd Speaks*, pp 83–4.

25 Horrell, *Laws Affecting Race Relations in South Africa*, p 312.

26 Ken Hartshorne, *Crisis and Challenge: Black Education*, p 197.

27 *Ibid*.

28 House of Assembly Debates, vol 10, 1965, col 627.

29 Pelzer, *Verwoerd Speaks*, pp 275–8, 286.

30 House of Assembly Debates, 7 February 1978, col 579.

31 See Sheena Duncan, 'A birthright stolen', p 11.

32 Platzky and Walker, *The Surplus People*, p 44.

33 SAIRR *Survey*, 1980, p 451.

34 Buro vir Ekonomiese Navorsing Insake Bantoe-Ontwikkeling, *Swart Ontwikkeling in Suid-Afrika* (Pretoria, 1976), p 23.

35 MC Botha, *Die Swart Vryheidspaaie* (Perskor, Johannesburg, 1982), p 101.

36 SAIRR *Survey*, 1981, p 289.

37 De Villiers, *Paul Sauer*, pp 135–6.

38 Scholtz, *Hendrik Frensch Verwoerd*, vol 2, p 151 (translation).

39 Pelzer, *Verwoerd Speaks*, p 375.

40 Dippenaar, *The History of South African Police*, pp 301–2.

41 Slovo, *Slovo: The Unfinished Autobiography*, p 86.
42 D'Oliviera, *Vorster – The Man*, p 125.
43 Dippenaar, *The History of South African Police,* p 300.
44 Dugard, 'The Judicial Process, Positivism and Civil Liberty', p 191.
45 Bizos, *Odyssey to Freedom*, p 250.
46 *Ibid*, p 189.
47 Corder, 'Crowbars or Cobwebs? p 11.
48 Dippenaar, *The History of South African Police*, p 367.
49 Report of the Truth and Reconciliation Commission, vol 3, p 7.
50 Suzman, *In No Uncertain Terms*, p 234.
51 Mathews, *Freedom, State Security and the Rule of Law*, pp 94–5.
52 Report of the Truth and Reconciliation Commission, vol 4, p 101.
53 SAIRR, News Release, 8 August 2003.
54 SAIRR *Survey*, 1988/9, p 532.
55 Amnesty International Report, *Political Imprisonment in South Africa*, p 93.
56 SAIRR *Survey*, 1986, p 858; 1988–9, p 533; and 1989–90, p 152.
57 Dippenaar, *The History of South African Police*, p 341.
58 Pelzer, *Verwoerd Speaks*, pp 125, 127.
59 Carr, *Soweto: Its Creation, Life and Decline*, p 59.
60 Dommisse, *Anton Rupert*, p 169.
61 Mouton, *Voorloper: die Lewe van Schalk Pienaar*, pp 66–7.
62 Interview with Nico Smith in Olivier, *Praat met die ANC*, p 26.
63 Schoeman, *My Lewe in die Politiek*, pp 334–5.
64 D'Oliviera, *Vorster*, p 167.
65 House of Assembly Debates, vol 65, 1969, col 1369.
66 Smith, *Bitter Harvest*, p 164.
67 Richard, *Moedswillig die Uwe*, pp 134–5 (translation).
68 Du Pisani, *John Vorster en die Verlig/Verkrampstryd*, pp 45, 50.
69 Treurnicht, *Credo van 'n Afrikaner*, p 22.
70 D'Oliviera, *Vorster*, p 229.
71 Van der Merwe *et al*, *White South African Elites*, p 62.
72 Adam, 'The South African Power-Elite: A Survey of Ideological Commitment', pp 80, 82, 91.
73 Mouton, *Voorloper*, p 122 (translation).
74 Pienaar, *Getuie van Groot Tye*, p 74.
75 De Villiers, Evidence given to the (Cillié) Kommissie, paras. 1531, 1532, 1549, 1554, 1571.
76 Quoted in Welsh, 'The Policies of Control: Blacks in the Common Area', p 101.
77 House of Assembly Debates, vol 65, 1969, col 356.
78 *Ibid*, col 362.
79 Buro vir Ekonomiese Navorsing insake Bantoe-Ontwikkeling (BENBO), *Swart Ontwikkeling*, p 28.
80 Geyser, *BJ Vorster: Select Speeches*, p 335.

81 *Ibid*, p 343.
82 Quoted in Steyn, *Penvegter: Piet Cillié van Die Burger*, p 255.
83 Scholtz, *Vegter en Hervormer: Grepe uit die toesprake van PW Botha*, p 56 (translation).
84 BENBO, *Swart Ontwikkeling*, p 40.
85 House of Assembly Debates, 1967, col 741.
86 Ackerman, *Hearing Grasshoppers Jump*, p 211.
87 House of Assembly Debates, vol 81, 1979, cols 8027–8.
88 *Die Burger*, 17 August 1979.
89 House of Assembly Debates, vol 81, 1979, cols 8132, 8141.
90 The (Wiehahn) Commission into Labour Legislation, *The Complete Wiehahn Report* Part 6, pp 707, 712.
91 NP van Wyk Louw, 'Foreword' to Botha, *Die Opkoms van Ons Derde Stand*, p v.
92 Quoted in Menzies, *Afternoon Light*, p 206.
93 Geyser, *Vorster: Select Speeches*, p 155.
94 Verslag van die Kommissie van Ondersoek na Aangeleenthede rakende die Kleurlingbevolkingsgroep, pp 361, 462, 513.
95 Geyser, *Vorster: Select Speeches*, p 335.
96 SAIRR *Survey*, 1973, p 283.
97 SAIRR *Survey*, 1976, p 316.
98 House of Assembly Debates, vol 81, 1979, col 8038.
99 Godsell, 'The Regulation of Labour', p 212.
100 Nattrass and Duncan, *A Study of Employers' Attitudes Towards African Worker Representation*, p 16.
101 Godsell, 'The Regulation of Labour', p 213.
102 *Complete Wiehahn Report*, p 30.
103 Wilkins and Strydom, *The Super Afrikaners*, p 233.
104 D'Oliviera, *Vorster – The Man*, p 254.
105 Adam and Giliomee, *The Rise and Crisis of Afrikaner Power*, p 215.
106 Quoted in D'Oliviera, *Vorster – The Man,* p 233.
107 De Klerk, *The Last Trek*, p 63.
108 *Cape Times*, 22 June 1976.
109 *Cape Times*, 28 August 1976.
110 *Die Burger*, 18 June 1976 (translation).
111 *Die Burger*, 21 June 1976 (translation).
112 *Rapport*, 20 June 1976 (translation).
113 *Die Burger*, 18 June 1976 (translation).
114 Mouton, *Voorloper*, p 157 (translation).
115 Cillié, *Baanbrekers vir Vryheid*, p 3 (translation).
116 Van Wyk Louw, *Liberale Nasionalisme*, p 63 (translation).
117 JL Sadie, *The Fall and Rise of the Afrikaner in the South African Economy*, pp 53–4.
118 Hanf *et al*, *South Africa: The Prospects of Peaceful Change*, pp 203, 208, 210.

119 Quoted in Hopkins and Grange, *The Rocky Rioter Teargas Show*, facsimile reprint between pp 116 and 117.

120 Wilkins and Strydom, *Super Afrikaners*, p 214.

121 De Villiers, *Secret Information*, pp 108, 73, 75.

122 Rees and Day, *Muldergate*, pp 10–11.

123 *Sunday Times*, 26 October 2003.

124 De Villiers, *PW*, pp 102–113.

125 De Klerk, *Politieke Gesprek*, pp 82, 86.

126 Pogrund, *War of Words*, p 268.

127 Hyslop, *The Classroom Struggle*, p 144.

128 SAIRR *Survey* 1977, pp 266–7.

129 Van Wyk Louw, *Gedagtes Vir Ons Tyd*, p 105.

CHAPTER 4

1 Luthuli, *Let My People Go*, p 127; see also Kuper, *Passive Resistance in South Africa*.

2 Mandela, *Long Walk*, p 129.

3 Meer, *A Fortunate Man*, pp 116-120.

4 *Ibid*, p 123.

5 *South African Communists Speak*, p 211.

6 Matthews, *Freedom for My People*, p 176.

7 Bernstein, *Memory Against Forgetting*, p 154.

8 Quoted in Fine, *Beyond Apartheid*, p 140.

9 Turok, *Nothing but the Truth*, p 59.

10 Quoted in Fine, *Beyond Apartheid*, p 142.

11 *Ibid*, p 143.

12 Vigne, *Liberals against Apartheid*, pp 49–50.

13 Bunting, *Moses Kotane: South African Revolutionary*, pp 215–16.

14 Mandela, *Long Walk to Freedom*, p 248.

15 Elinor Sisulu, *Walter and Albertina Sisulu: In Our Lifetime* (David Philip, Cape Town, 2002) p 129.

16 Bernstein, *Memory Against Forgetting*, pp 180–1.

17 Luthuli, *Let My People Go*, p 185.

18 Quoted in Gerhart, *Black Power in South Africa*, p 146.

19 Pogrund, *Sobukwe and Apartheid*, pp 93, 102.

20 Sisulu, *Walter and Albertina Sisulu*, pp 136–7.

21 Nkosi, *Home and Exile*, p 3.

22 Karis and Carter, *From Protest to Challenge* vol 3, p 543.

23 SAIRR *Survey*, 1959–60, p 52.

24 Mandela, *Long Walk*, p 224.

25 Pogrund, *Sobukwe and Apartheid*, p 127.

26 Dippenaar, *The History of South African Police*, p 277.

27 Frankel, *An Ordinary Atrocity: Sharpeville and its Massacre*, p 113.

28 Dippenaar, *The History of South African Police*, p 278.
29 Kgosana, *Lest We Forget.*
30 Vigne, *Liberals against Apartheid*, p 118
31 *Ibid*, p 123.
32 SAIRR *Survey*, 1961, p 52.
33 Kgosana, *Lest We Forget*, pp 32–3.
34 Dippenaar, *The History of South African Police*, p 285.
35 *Cape Times*, 30 March 2006.
36 Kgosana, *Lest We Forget*, p 35.
37 SAIRR *Survey*, 1963, p 52.
38 SAIRR *Survey*, 1966, p 75.
39 Mandela, *Long Walk*, p 260.
40 Luthuli, *Let My People Go*, p 235.
41 *Ibid*, p 209.
42 Mandela, *Long Walk*, p 260.
43 Slovo, *Unfinished Autobiography*, pp 147–8.
44 Ronnie Kasrils, *Armed and Dangerous,* p 74.
45 Slovo, *Unfinished Autobiography*, p 146.
46 Karis and Carter, *From Protest to Challenge* vol 3, p 717.
47 Barrell, *MK: The ANC's Armed Struggle*, p 7.
48 *Ibid*, p 13.
49 Bernstein, *Memory Against Forgetting*, p 251.
50 *Ibid*, p 238.
51 Joffe, *The Rivonia Story*, p 53.
52 Mandela, *No Easy Walk to Freedom* (Heinemann, London, 1956), p 189.
53 Bernstein, *Memory Against Forgetting*, pp 240–1.
54 Barrell, *MK*, p 16.
55 Mathews, *State Security and the Rule of Law*, pp 90–5.
56 Joffe, *The Rivonia Story*, p 274.
57 Bunting, *Moses Kotane*, p 274.
58 Ludi, *Operation Q-018*, pp 189–92.
59 SAIRR *Survey* 1966, p 24.
60 Suttner, *The ANC Underground in South Africa to 1976*, pp 59–83.
61 Barrell, *MK*, p 19.
62 Ciskei Commission, *The Quail Report*, p 115.
63 Mandela, 'Whither the Black Consciousness Movement? An assessment', in Maharaj, *Reflections in Prison*, p 54.
64 Mandela, *Long Walk*, p 565.
65 Barrell, *MK*, p 17.
66 Mandela, *Long Walk*, p 325.
67 Sampson, *Mandela: The Authorised Biography,* p 241.
68 Mandela, 'Clear the Obstacles and Confront the Enemy', in Maharaj, *Reflections in Prison*, pp 14–16.
69 Sisulu, 'We Shall Overcome!', in Maharaj, *Reflections in Prison*, p 89.
70 Tambo, *Preparing for Power: Oliver Tambo Speaks*, p 146.

71 Temkin, *Buthelezi: A Biography* (Frank Cass, London, 2003) p 123.

72 Shubin, *ANC: A View From Moscow*, p 74.

73 Slovo, *Unfinished Autobiography*, p 152.

74 Irina Filatova, *Times Literary Supplement*, 23 January 2000.

75 Luthuli, *Let My People Go*, p 154.

76 Tambo, *Preparing for Power*, pp 203–4.

77 Sparg, Schreiner and Ansell, *Comrade Jack: The political lectures and diary of Jack Simons, Novo Catengue*.

78 Mandela, 'Whither the Black Consciousness Movement?', p 43.

79 Evans, *Dancing Shoes is Dead: A Tale of Fighting Men in South Africa*, p 243.

80 Slovo, *Every Secret Thing: My Family, My Country*, pp 35–6, 37–8, 120.

81 *South African Communists Speak*, p 365.

82 Slovo, *Every Secret Thing*, p 109.

83 Ellis and Sechaba, *Comrades against Apartheid*, p 148; Davis, *Apartheid's Rebels: Inside South Africa's Hidden War*, p 51.

84 Shubin, *ANC*, p 119.

85 Breytenbach, *The True Confessions of an Albino Terrorist*, p 75.

86 Karis and Gerhart, *From Protest to Challenge*, vol 5, p 389.

87 Shubin, *ANC*, p 124.

88 Sisulu, *Walter and Albertina Sisulu*, p 220.

89 Shubin, *ANC*, pp 84-7.

90 O'Malley, *Shades of Difference: Mac Maharaj and the Struggle for South Africa*, p 204.

CHAPTER 5

1 Hopkins and Grange, *The Rocky Rioter Teargas Show*.

2 Dippenaar, *The History of South African Police*, p 374.

3 SAIRR *Survey*, 1968, p 16.

4 Schlemmer, 'Factors Underlying Apartheid', p 29.

5 SAIRR *Survey*, 1971, p 41.

6 Biko, 'White Racism and Black Consciousness', pp 192–3.

7 Arnold, *Steve Biko: No Fears Expressed*, p 77.

8 *Ibid*, pp 99–100.

9 Stubbs, *Steve Biko: I Write What I Like*, pp 48–9.

10 *Ibid*, pp 28–9.

11 Arnold, *The Testimony of Steve Biko: Black Consciousness in South Africa*, p 108–9.

12 Mandela, 'Whither the Black Consciousness Movement?', p 41.

13 South African Communists Speak, p 424.

14 Quoted in Karis and Gerhart, *From Protest to Challenge*, vol 5, p 105.

15 Stubbs, *Steve Biko*, p 51.

16 Khoapa, 'The New Black', *Black Viewpoint*, p 64.

17 Ramphele, 'Government-Created Platforms', p 39.

18 SAIRR *Survey*, 1972, p 30.

19 SAIRR *Survey*, 1970, p 243.

20 BA Khoapa (ed) *Black Review 1972* (Black Community Programmes, Durban, 1973), pp 174–5.

21 Ramphele, 'Empowerment and Symbols of Hope: Black Consciousness and Community Development', pp 163–4.

22 Mandela, *Steve Biko: 25 Years On*.

23 Ramphele, 'Empowerment and Symbols of Hope', p 173.

24 Ibid, pp 176–7.

25 *The Star*, 22 April 1976.

26 SAIRR *Survey*, 1975, p 84.

27 Pauline Morris, *Soweto*, p 40.

28 Ibid, pp 44–5.

29 *Rand Daily Mail*, 11 November 1976.

30 Ibid, 2 February 1978.

31 Cited in Morris, *Soweto*, p 47.

32 SAIRR *Survey*, 1976, p 191.

33 *The Star*, 13 May 1976.

34 Quoted in Bonner and Segal, *Soweto*, p 77.

35 *The Star*, 10 October 1974.

36 Hartshorne, *Crisis and Challenge*, p 202.

37 SAIRR *Survey*, 1975, pp 222–3.

38 Edelstein, 'What Do Young Africans Think?', p 114.

39 Quoted in *Verslag van die Kommissie van Ondersoek oor die Oproer in Soweto en Elders van 16 Junie 1976 tot 28 Februarie 1977* (Cillié Commission), vol 1, para 1.14.2.

40 Kane-Berman, *Soweto: Black Revolt, White Reaction*, p 14.

41 Cillié Commission, paras 2.3.3, 2.3.4.

42 *Argus*, 21 April 1976; *Rand Daily Mail*, 3 March 1976.

43 Bonner and Segal, *Soweto*, p 79.

44 Cillié Commission, para 2.3.7.

45 SAIRR *Survey*, 1976, p 321.

46 *Ibid*, 1975, p 95.

47 Hartshorne, *Crisis and Challenge,* p 76.

48 SAIRR, 'South Africa in Travail', pp 4, 6, 7.

49 Cillié Commission, paras 3.10.3, 3.9.1.

50 Schuster, *A Burning Hunger,* p 56.

51 *Ibid*, p 62; Hopkins and Grange, *The Rocky Rioter Teargas Show*, pp 86–7.

52 Brink and Malungane, *Soweto,* pp 51–2.

53 Cillié Commission, paras 3.5.2 to 3.5.9.

54 Herbstein, *White Man, We Want To Talk To You*, p 218.

55 Cillié Commission, paras 3.6.6, 3.6.7, 3.6.9.

56 Van der Merwe, *Peacemaking in South Africa*, pp 93, 94–5.

57 Cillié Commission, paras 3.10.17, 3.9.4.

58 Brink and Malungane, Soweto, pp 60–1.
59 Mashabela, *A People on the Boil*, pp 19-20.
60 Quoted in Bonner and Segal, *Soweto*, p 86.
61 *Survey*, 1978, p 74.
62 Sisulu, *Walter and Albertina Sisulu*, p 249.
63 Kane-Berman, *Soweto*, p 17.
64 SAIRR *Survey*, 1977, pp 144, 146.
65 Quoted in Ndlovu, *The Soweto Uprisings*, p 44.
66 *The Star*, 3 September 1976.
67 Schuster, *A Burning Hunger*, p 91.
68 *Cape Times*, 7 September 1976.
69 Cillié Commission, paras 23.2, 23.2.5.
70 Quoted in Bonner and Segal, *Soweto*, p 91.
71 Cillié Commission, paras 3.2.1, 2.2.2.
72 Tambo, *Preparing for Power*, p 116.
73 Mandela, *Long Walk*, pp 472–3.
74 BA Khoapa (ed), *Black Review*, 1972, p 40.
75 Tambo, *Preparing for Power*, p 127.
76 Barrell, *MK*, p 32.
77 Tambo, *Preparing for Power*, p 129.
78 Biko, *No Fears Expressed*, pp 97–8.
79 Mandela, *Long Walk*, p 473.
80 Lekota, *Prison Letters To A Daughter*, p 175.
81 Brooks and Brickhill, *Whirlwind Before the Storm* chapter 7; Kane-Berman, *Soweto*, chapter 9.
82 Cillié Commission, para 31.4.10.
83 Van der Merwe, *Peacemaking in South Africa*, p 94.
84 Matthews, *Remembrances*, p 14.
85 Mayer, 'Class, Status, and Ethnicity as Perceived by Johannesburg Africans', p 144.
86 Hanf *et al*, *South Africa: The Prospects of Peaceful Change*, pp 325–6.
87 Kasrils, *Armed and Dangerous*, p 122.
88 Shubin, *ANC*, p 201.
89 Ndebele, *Rediscovery of the Ordinary*, pp 64–5.

CHAPTER 6

1 Quoted in Dommisse, 'The changing role of the Afrikaans press', p 97.
2 *Ibid*, p 103.
3 De Klerk, *Die Tweede (R)evolusie*, p 77 (translation).
4 Van Deventer, *Kroniek van 'n Koerantman*, p 181 (translation).
5 Pelzer, *Verwoerd Speaks*, p 723.
6 Steyn, *Van Wyk Louw*, vol 2, p 1064 (translation).
7 Van der Merwe, *Breaking Barriers*, p 85.

8   Brink, 'Samisjdat, tamisjdat, lamisjdat', pp 59–60.

9   *Rapport*, 9 October 2005.

10   *Rapport*, 18 September 1983.

11   Human, *'n Lewe met Boeke*, p 58.

12   *Argus*, 25 May 1982.

13   *Rand Daily Mail*, 17 March 1978.

14   *Argus*, 30 December 1978.

15   Uys, *Elections and Erections*, p 33.

16   Hugo, 'The Politics of "Untruth": Afrikaner Academics for Apartheid', pp 31–55.

17   *Ibid*, pp 35, 41.

18   Holleman, 'The Great Purge', pp 34–48.

19   Hugo, 'The Politics of "Untruth": Afrikaner Academics for Apartheid', pp 35, 41.

20   *Ibid*, p 36.

21   *Rapport*, 17 February 1974.

22   *Sunday Times*, 4 August 1982

23   SAIRR *Survey*, 1958-1959, pp 23–5.

24   Hugo, 'The Politics of "Untruth": Afrikaner Academics for Apartheid', p 48.

25   Hexham, *The Irony of Apartheid*, p 191.

26   *Rapport*, 17 and 24 October 1976.

27   *Sunday Times*, 3 September 1978.

28   Hugo, 'The Politics of "Untruth": Afrikaner Academics for Apartheid', pp 51–2.

29   *Die Burger*, 19 October 1976.

30   *Hoofstad*, 30 January 1978.

31   Lückhoff, *Cottesloe*.

32   *Ibid*, p.116 (translation).

33   Pelzer, *Verwoerd Speaks*, p 263.

34   Geldenhuys, *In die stroomversnellings: Vyftig jaar van die NG Kerk*, p 58 (translation).

35   *Ibid*, pp 60–1 (translation).

36   *Daily Telegraph*, 8 September 2004.

37   Kinghorn, 'Vormende Faktore', p 48 (translation).

38   NGK, *Die verhaal van die Nederduitse Gereformeerde Kerk se Reis met Apartheid*, pp 24–5 (translation).

39   Ibid, p 33 (translation).

40   Geyser *et al*, *Delayed Action*.

41   Smith et al, *Storm-Kompas*, pp 139–140 (translation).

42   Ope Brief, *Die Kerkbode*, 9 June 1982.

43   Esterhuyse, *Broers Buite Hoorafstand*, p 18.

44   *Die verhaal van die Ned Geref Kerk se reis met apartheid*, pp 44-5.

45   NGK, *Kerk en Samelewing 1986* (General Synod of the NGK, 1986).

46   Loubser, *The Apartheid Bible*, p 120.

47 Alant, 'Die Rol van die Kerk in die Moderne Afrikanersamelewing', pp 102–113.

48 Quoted in Bezuidenhout, *Dr Tinie Louw*, pp 28–9 (translation).

49 Sadie, 'The Fall and Rise of the Afrikaner in the South African Economy', pp 23–4.

50 *Ibid*, p 28.

51 Hartmann, *Enterprise and Politics in South Africa*, p 17.

52 *Sunday Times*, 25 April 1971.

53 Dommisse, *Anton Rupert*, p 54.

54 Esterhuyse, *Anton Rupert*, p 115.

55 Dommisse, *Anton Rupert*, p 141.

56 *Ibid*, p 283.

57 Wassenaar, *Assault on Private Enterprise*, p 128.

58 Louis Luyt, *Walking Proud*, pp 135, 161, 169.

59 De Klerk, *Die Tweede (R)evolusie*, p 58 (translation).

60 Sadie, *The Fall and Rise of the Afrikaner in the South African Economy*, p 54.

61 AHI, Submission to TRC, 9 October 1977, pp 8–9 (translation).

62 Viljoen, *Ideaal en Werklikheid*, p 54.

63 Ibid, p 31 (translation).

64 De Klerk, 'Gerrit Viljoen se leierskap van die Afrikaner Broederbond', pp 190–1 (translation).

65 De Klerk, *Die Tweede (R)evolusie*, p 65 (translation).

66 Hugo, *The Politics of Untruth*, p 33.

67 *Rand Daily Mail*, 19 November 1979.

68 Afrikanerbond, *Bearer of an Ideal*, para 7.3.

69 *Ibid*, para 7.

70 Sadie, *The Fall and Rise of the Afrikaner in the South African Economy*, p 56.

71 Pienaar, *Getuie van groot tye*, p 70 (translation).

72 Landman et al, *Wat Kom Na Apartheid?* pp 1, 4 (translation).

73 See the review of Border War writing by JP Smuts, *Die Burger*, 14 July 2007.

74 Du Preez, *Pale Native: Memories of a Renegade Reporter*, p 185.

75 Kombuis, *Seks en Drugs en Boeremusiek*, p 218.

76 Grundlingh, 'Rocking the boat?' The 'Voëlvry' music movement in South Africa, p 505.

77 Du Preez, *Pale Native*, p 206.

CHAPTER 7

1 Scholtz, *Vegter en Hervormer*, p 16 (translation).

2 *Ibid*, p 39 (translation).

3 Abeldas and Fischer, *A Question of Survival: Conversations with Key South Africans*, pp 513, 517.

4 Wiehahn Commission, Part 1, para 3.33.
5 *House of Assembly Debates*, vol 81, 1979, cols 8037–9.
6 *Ibid*, cols 8030–1.
7 *Rapport*, 9 April 2006 (translation).
8. Pottinger, *The Imperial Presidency*, p 93.
9 Wiehahn, 'Industrial relations in South Africa – a changing scene', p 190.
10 SAIRR *Survey*, 1982, p 172; 1983, p 197; 1984, p 318.
11 *Report of the Committee for Constitutional Affairs of the President's Council on An Urbanisation Strategy for the Republic of South Africa* (PC 3/1985), p 161.
12 Cited in *Black Sash*, May 1980, p 3.
13 *Report of the President's Council on Urbanisation*, p 159.
14 *Rapport*, 3 March 1981 (translation).
15 *Report of the President's Council on Urbanisation*, pp 148–9.
16 SAIRR *Survey*, 1984, pp 64–5.
17 *Report of the President's Council on Urbanisation*, pp 173–4.
18 *White Paper on Urbanisation* (nd), paras 5.1.2, 5.1.3.
19 *House of Assembly Debates*, vol 10, 1986, cols 7662, 8780.
20 *Ibid*, col 7675.
21 SAIRR *Survey*, 1984, p 187.
22 *Ibid*; Daan Prinsloo, *Stem uit die Wildernis*, pp 256–7.
23 Suzman, *In No Uncertain Terms*, p 123.
24 SAIRR *Survey*, 1988/9, pp 247–8.
25 *Ibid*, 1983, p 461.
26 Scholtz, *Vegter en Hervormer*, pp 58–9.
27 FW de Klerk, *Last Trek*, p 95.
28 Slabbert, *The Last White Parliament*, p 120.
29 Ries and Dommisse, *Broedertwis*, pp 110–112 (translation).
30 Slabbert, *The Last White Parliament*, p 114.
31 FW de Klerk, *Last Trek*, p 84.
32 *Ibid*, p 87.
33 Ries and Dommisse, *Broedertwis*, p 199.
34 *Sunday Express*, 23 September 1979.
35 Sadie, *The Fall and Rise of the Afrikaner in the South African Economy*, pp 56–7.
36 SAIRR *Survey*, 1984, p 242.
37 *Ibid*.
38 Van Rooyen, *Hard Right*, pp 34–5.
39 Hugo, 'Frontier Farmers in South Africa', p 550.
40 Schlemmer and Welsh, 'South Africa's Constitutional and Political Prospects', p 216.
41 Slabbert, *The Last White Parliament*, pp.116-7.
42 Quoted in Van der Ross, *The Rise and Decline of Apartheid*, p 314.
43 De Klerk, *Last Trek*, p 127.
44 Quoted in Prinsloo, p 196.

45 *Survey*, 1988/9, pp 696-7.

46 De Klerk, *Last Trek*, p 96.

47 Stoffel van der Merwe, MP, … *And what about the Black People?* (Federal Information Service of the National Party, 1985).

48 Prinsloo, *Stem Uit die Wildernis*, p 209.

49 Heunis, *The Inner Circle*, p 61.

50 Quotations are from a verbatim transcript of the speech.

51 De Klerk, *Last Trek*, pp 103, 105.

52 Prinsloo, *Stem Uit die Wildernis,* pp 310–311.

53 Quoted in Callinicos, *Oliver Tambo*, p 586.

54 Mandela, *Long Walk*, pp 517–8.

55 Commonwealth Group of Eminent Persons, *Mission to South Africa: The Commonwealth Report,* pp 43–4, 119, 103–4.

56 *Ibid*, pp 120, 140–1.

57 Crocker, *High Noon in Southern Africa*, p 316.

58 *Ibid*, p 315.

59 Report of the TRC, vol 2, pp 151–2.

60 Malan, *My lewe saam met die SA Weermag*, p 333.

61 Waldmeir, *The Anatomy of a Miracle*, p 97.

62 Riekert, 'Black local government in the Republic of South Africa', p 156.

63 SAIRR *Survey*, 1983, pp 258-9.

64 Bureau of Information, *The Regional Services Councils* (Pretoria, 1988) p 17.

65 *Survey*, 1988/9, p 510.

66 Du Toit, 'Regional services councils: control at local government level', p 75.

67 JJJ Scholtz, *Vegter en Hervormer*, pp 48–9.

68 SAIRR *Survey*, 1987/8, p 780.

69 The book was published by Indiana University Press, Bloomington in 1986.

70. De Klerk, *Last Trek*, pp 115–6.

71 Selfe, 'South Africa's National Management System', p 150.

72 Quoted in Swilling and Phillips, 'State power in the 1980s: from "total strategy" to "counter-revolutionary warfare"', p 145.

73 Quoted in Hamann, *Days of the Generals*, p 58.

74 Prinsloo, *Stem uit die Wildernis*, pp 270–1.

75 SAIRR *Survey*, 1984, p 65.

76 *Ibid*, 1986, p 517.

77 De Klerk, *Last Trek*, pp 120–1.

78 Quoted in Waldmeir, *Anatomy of a Miracle*, p 111.

79 *Concensus*, vol 3, no 4, 2006, p 6.

80 Renwick, *Unconventional Diplomacy in Southern Africa*, p 117.

81 Quoted by Tim du Plessis, *Rapport*, 20 June 2004.

82 Ries and Dommisse, *Broedertwis*, p 135.

83 Meiring, *In Interesting Company,* pp 53–5.

84 Quoted in Hamann, *Days of the Generals*, pp 150–1.

85 *Ibid*, pp 55–7.

86 Dippenaar, *The History of South African Police*, p 779.

87 Beyers and Kotzé, *Die Opmars van die AWB*, p 118 (translation).

88 Pauw, *Into the Heart of Darkness*, p 22.

89 TRC, vol 2, p 220.

90 Pauw, *Into the Heart of Darkness*, p 33.

91 Hamann, *Days of the Generals*, p 143.

92 Labuschagne, *On South Africa's Secret Service*, p 23.

93 Sampson, *Mandela*, p 352.

94 SAIRR *Survey*, 1987/88, pp 294–5.

95 *Ibid*, 2000/1, p 385.

96 Savage, 'The Cost of Apartheid'.

97 Lewis, *The Economics of Apartheid*, p 127.

98 Archer, 'Defence expenditure and arms procurement in South Africa', p 253.

99 Davie, 'How South Africa Gets Its Oil', pp 25–30.

100 Simon Jenkins, 'Good morals, good business?'.

101 Jenkins, 'Economic Implications of Capital Flight', p 180.

102 Renwick, *Unconventional Diplomacy in Southern Africa*, p 118.

103 Geldenhuys, What do we think? A survey of white opinion on foreign policy issues, no 3, May 1986; André Pisani (analysis), *ibid*, no 4.

104 Investor Responsibility Research Center, *The Impact of Sanctions on South Africa*.

105 De Villiers, 'Blowing Hot, Catching Cold', p 72.

106 Sampson, *Mandela*, p 581.

107 De Klerk, *Last Trek*, p 70.

108 O'Dowd, 'South Africa in the Light of the Stages of Economic Growth', pp 25–43.

109 Quoted in Welsh, 'Politics and Business', p 164.

110 Quoted in *ibid*, p 165.

111 Steyn, *Managing Change in South Africa*, p 20.

112 Scholtz, *Vegter en Hervormer*, p 66.

113 Relly, 'A Businessman's View', p 69.

114 From unpublished notes taken by AH Bloom at a meeting at Mfuwe Game Lodge, 13 September 1985.

115 *New York Times*, 18 August 1986.

116 SAIRR *Survey*, 1987–8. pp 88–9.

117 Ackerman, *Hearing Grasshoppers Jump*, p 208.

118 Sunter, *The World and South Africa in the 1990s*, p 10; and *The High Road: Where Are We Now?* p 100.

119 Schlemmer, 'South Africa's National Party government', pp 21, 23.

120 Laurence, *Death Squads: apartheid's secret weapon*.

121 Slabbert, *The System and the Struggle*, pp 92, 96.

122 De Klerk, *Last Trek*, p 134.

123 Prinsloo, *Stem uit die Wildernis*, pp 390–419 for a verbatim record of the meeting.

124 Pottinger, *The Imperial Presidency*, p 451.

CHAPTER 8

1 Dippenaar, *The History of South African Police*, p 578.
2 SAIRR *Survey*, 1980, pp 279–80; Barrell, *MK*, p 46.
3 Barrell, *MK*, p 64.
4 Kasrils, *Armed and Dangerous*, p 125.
5 *Ibid*, p 189.
6 Dippenaar, *The History of South African Police*, p 6.
7 Lelyveld, *Move Your Shadow*, p 331.
8 Barrell, *MK*, p 60.
9 Kasrils, *Armed and Dangerous*, p 245.
10 Barrell, *MK*, p 60.
11 Johns and Davis, *Mandela, Tambo and the African National Congress*, pp 243–5.
12 Twala and Bernard, *Mbokodo*, pp 118–19.
13 TRC, vol 2, p 366.
14 Ellis and Sechaba, *Comrades against Apartheid*, pp 118–121.
15 Terry Bell, 'ANC Crisis Rooted in its History', *Cape Times*, September 30 2008.
16 Mark A Uhlig, 'The African National Congress', p 172.
17 TRC, vol 2, p 373.
18 ANC, Statement to the TRC, August 1996, pp 53, 57.
19 Dippenaar, *The History of South African Police*, p 779.
20 SAIRR *Survey*, 1987/8, p 555.
21 *Ibid*, 1988/9, p 522.
22 Indicator Project South Africa, *Political Conflict in South Africa*, pp 98–9.
23 Ellis and Sechaba, *Comrades against Apartheid*, p 200.
24 O'Malley, *Shades of Difference*, pp 282–3.
25 Mandela, *Long Walk*, pp 512–3.
26 Lodge and Nasson, *All, Here, and Now*, p 184.
27 André Pisani (analysis), *What Do We Think?* no 4.
28 Gerwel, 'The State of Civil Society', p 21.
29 Kane-Berman, *Political Violence in South Africa*, p 13.
30 This discussion first appeared in Welsh, *Whither South Africa?* pp 3–4.
31 Kane-Berman, *South Africa's Silent Revolution*, p 9.
32 O'Dowd, *Understanding South Africa*, p 10.
33 Hartshorne, *Crisis and Challenge*, p 204.
34 Hyslop, *The Classroom Struggle*, p 169.
35 Hartshorne, *Crisis and Challenge*, p 181.
36 SAIRR *Survey*, 1983, p 465.
37 Marks, *Young Warriors*, p 51.
38 Hartshorne, *Crisis and Challenge*, p 76.

39 SAIRR *Survey*, 1988/9, p 552.
40 Johnson, '"The Soldiers of Luthuli": Youth in the Politics of Resistance of South Africa', p 95.
41 Cited in Morris, *Soweto*, p 40.
42 Hartshorne, *Crisis and Challenge*, pp 80–1.
43 *Sowetan*, 5 October 2000.
44 Mathiane, *Beyond the Headlines*, p 2.
45 Mtshali, *Give Us a Break*, p 13.
46 Lodge and Nasson, *All, Here and Now*, p 98.
47 Mathiane, *Beyond the Headlines*, p 52.
48 Manona, 'The impact of political conflict and violence on the youth of Grahamstown', pp 358, 360.
49 Xaba, 'Masculinity and its Malcontents: The Confrontation between "Struggle Masculinity" and "Post-Struggle Masculinity" (1990 – 1997)', p 110.
50 Seekings, *Heroes or Villains? Youth Politics in the 1980s*, p 64.
51 Straker, *Faces in the Revolution*, p 85.
52 Marks, *Young Warriors*, p 52.
53 Mathiane, *Beyond the Headlines*, p 4.
54 Stadler, *The Other Side of the Story*, p 179. (The figure cannot be independently confirmed.)
55 Lodge and Nasson, *All, Here and Now*, pp 97, 189.
56 Quoted in Emma Gilbey, *The Lady: The Life and Times of Winnie Mandela*, p 145.
57 Quoted in Seekings, *Heroes or Villains?* p 18.
58 Johnson, '"The Soldiers of Luthuli": Youth in the Politics of Resistance of South Africa', pp 115–6.
59 Lodge and Nasson, *All, Here and Now*, p 35.
60 Karis and Gerhart, *From Protest to Challenge*, vol 5, pp 720, 723, 730.
61 Seekings, *The UDF*, pp 59, 91.
62 De Klerk, *Last Trek*, p 114.
63 Rantete, *The Third Day of September*.
64 Noonan, *They're Burning the Churches*, pp 51, 53.
65 *Ibid*, pp 269–271.
66 Baynham, 'Political Violence and the Security Response', pp 115–6.
67 *South African Catholic Bishops' Conference Report on Police Conduct during Township Protests*, p 5.
68 Dippenaar, *The History of South African Police*, p 747.
69 *Report of the Commission Appointed to Inquire Into the Incident which occurred on 21 March 1985 at Uitenhage*, paras 32, 38, 153, 164, 165–6.
70 Olivier, 'Causes of Ethnic Collective Action in the Pretoria – Witwatersrand – Vaal Triangle, 1970-1984', p 99.
71 Suzman, *In No Uncertain Terms*, p 246.
72 Brogden and Shearing, *Policing for a New South Africa*, p 36.
73 Wentzel, *Liberal Slideaway*, p 124.

74 Shubane, 'Politics in Soweto', pp 264–7.

75 Noonan, *They're Burning the Churches,* p 86.

76 Catholic Bishops' Conference Report, pp 26–7.

77 Kane-Berman, *Political Violence*, pp 61–70.

78 Mark Swilling, 'The United Democratic Front and Township Revolt', p 99.

79 Swilling, 'Stayaways, Urban Protest and the State', *passim.*

80 *Ibid*, pp 134–141.

81 Trevor Manuel, quoted in Karen Jochelson and Susan Brown, 'UDF and AZAPO: Evaluation and Expectations', pp 13–14.

82 Mosiuoa Lekota, quoted in *ibid.*

83 Lodge, 'Rebellion: The Turning of the Tide', p 129.

84 Seekings, *The UDF*, p 59.

85 SAIRR *Survey*, 1985, p 41.

86 *Ibid*, pp 41, 511, 514.

87 *Ibid*, 1986, pp 372–3.

88 *Ibid*, 1985, p 39. 'After today South Africa will never again be the same.'

89 Tambo, *Preparing for Power*, pp 151–163.

90 O'Malley, *Shades of Difference*, p 232.

91 Tambo, *Preparing for Power*, p 215.

92 Dippenaar, *The History of South African Police*, p 783.

93 Zwelakhe Sisulu, 'Forward to People's Power', p 338.

94 *Ibid.*

95 Johnson, '"The Soldiers of Luthuli": Youth in the Politics of Resistance in South Africa', p 119.

96 Naidoo, 'Internal Resistance in South Africa: The Political Movement', p 184.

97 SAIRR *Survey*, 1986, p 445.

98 Mathiane, *Beyond the Headlines*, p 49.

99 Zwelakhe Sisulu, in Lodge and Nasson (eds), *All, Here, and Now*, p 342.

100 Dippenaar, *The History of South African Police*, p 826.

101 SAIRR *Survey*, 1986, p 824.

102 'Law and Order: The Story of a Former Commissioner of Police', in Foster *et al*, *The Theatre of Violence*, p 116–7.

103 The United Democratic Front's Message to all South Africans on the Whites-only Election of 6 May 1987, Press release, 9 March 1987, p 6.

104 Adam and Moodley, *South Africa without Apartheid*, p 93.

105 Mandela, *Long Walk*, p 584.

106 Quoted in Sampson, *Mandela*, p 332.

107 SAIRR *Survey*, 1987/8, p 778.

108 Mandela, *Long Walk*, p 448.

109 Hanf *et al*, *South Africa: The Prospects of Peaceful Change*, pp 350, 337–8.

110 Seekings, *The UDF*, p 324.

111 Neuhaus, *Dispensations,* p 132.

112 Johnson in Johnson (ed), *South Africa: No Turning Back*, pp 120–1.

113 Wentzel, *Liberal Slideaway*, passim.

114 Quoted in *ibid*, p 152.

115 Quoted in *ibid*, p 253.

116 Labuschagne, *On South Africa's Secret Service*, pp 260 ff.

117 Malan, *My Traitor's Heart,* pp 323–4.

118 *Ibid*, pp 325–8; SAIRR *Survey*, 1986, p 683.

119 Niehaus *et al, Witchcraft, Power and Politics,* pp 190–1.

120 Cameron, 'The Crossroads: Sectarianism and the State', pp 57–8.

121 SAIRR *Survey*, 2000/1, p 88.

122 *Ibid*, 1973, p 284.

123 Institute for Industrial Education, *The Durban Strikes 1973*, p 52.

124 Godsell, 'The Regulation of Labour', p 213.

125 Quoted in Institute for Industrial Education, *The Durban Strikes 1973,z* p 111.

126 SAIRR *Survey*, 1984, p 249.

127 Wiehahn Report, para 1.16.4

128 LACOM, *Freedom from Below: The Struggle for Trade Unions in South Africa*, p 1987; Lewis, 'Overview: The Registration Debate and Industrial Councils', pp 170–5.

129 Morris, 'Unions and Industrial Councils: why do unions' policies change?', pp 148–52.

130 Hindson, 'Overview: Trade Unions and Politics', p 209.

131 Foster, 'The Workers' Struggle: Where does FOSATU stand?', p 228.

132 Hindson, 'Overview: Trade Unions and Politics', p 215.

133 Njikelana, 'The Unions and the Front: A Response to the General Workers' Union', p 257.

134 Adler and Webster, 'Challenging Transition Theory: The Labor Movement, Radical Reform and Transition to Democracy in South Africa', p 81.

135 SAIRR *Survey*, 1986, p 236.

136 Van Niekerk, 'The Trade Union Movement in the Politics of Resistance in South Africa', p 156.

137 SAIRR *Survey*, 1986, p 236.

138 *Ibid*, 1987–8, p 608.

139 *Ibid*, p 612.

140 *Ibid*, pp 626–33.

141 Webster, 'The Rise of Social-movement Unionism: The Two Faces of the Black Trade Union Movement in South Africa', pp 192–3.

142 Maree, 'The COSATU Participatory Democratic Tradition and South Africa's New Parliament: Are They Compatible?', p 35.

143 Lambert and Webster, 'The Re-emergence of Political Unionism in Contemporary South Africa?', p 24.

144 SAIRR *Survey*, 1988/9, p 494.

145 Van Niekerk, 'The Trade Union Movement in the Politics of Resistance in South Africa', p 166.

146 SAIRR *Survey*, 1987–8, pp 678–9.

147 *Ibid*, pp 652–3.

148 *Ibid*, 1988/9, pp 681–2.

149 *Ciskei Commission Report,* p 216.

150 The Buthelezi Commission , pp 266, 288.

151 Labuschagne, *On South Africa's Secret Service,* pp 252–6; Holomisa and Meyer, *A Better Future,* pp 36–7.

152 *Inyandza National Movement 1978-1990: A Collection of Speeches by Enos J Mabuza.*

153 Buthelezi, *White and Black Nationalism, Ethnicity and the Future of the Homelands.*

154 Buthelezi, *South Africa: My Vision for the Future,* p 102.

155 Hanf et al, *South Africa: The Prospects of Peaceful Change,* pp 352–6.

156 Callinicos, *Oliver Tambo: Beyond the Engeli Mountains,* p 397.

157 Quotations are from Inkatha Documents for Discussion at the 1979 Summit Meeting.

158 Temkin, *Buthelezi: A Biography,* p 205.

159 Pogrund, *Sobukwe and Apartheid,* p 375.

160 Tambo, *Preparing for Power: Oliver Tambo Speaks,* p 146–7.

161 Temkin, *Buthelezi,* p 207.

162 Quoted in *ibid,* p 247.

163 Waldmeir, *Anatomy of a Miracle,* p 172.

164 Mzala (pseudonym), *Gatsha Buthelezi: Chief with a Double Agenda.*

165 Cassidy, *A Witness for Ever: The Dawning of Democracy in South,* p 128.

166 Temkin, *Buthelezi,* p 208.

167 Colenso, *Ten Weeks in Natal,* pp xxxvi, 11.

168 Quoted in Colenso, *History of the Zulu War and Its Origin,* p 248.

169 Morris, *The Washing of the Spears: The Rise and Fall of the Zulu Nation,* p 308.

170 Welsh, *The Roots of Segregation,* p 310.

171 Temkin, *Buthelezi,* p 304.

172 Quoted in Maré and Hamilton, *An Appetite for Power: Buthelezi's Inkatha and the Politics of 'Loyal Resistance',* p 232.

173 Kentridge, *An Unofficial War: Inside the Conflict in Pietermaritzburg,* pp 24, 21.

174 Published by the South African Institute of Race Relations in 1997.

175 Booth, 'A Strategic Divide: Townships on Contested Terrain', p 78.

176 Minnaar, '"Undisputed Kings": Warlordism in Natal', p 61.

177 O'Malley, *Shades of Difference,* p 568.

178 Johnston, 'The Political World of KwaZulu-Natal', p 178.

179 Minnaar, 'Patterns of Violence', p 18.

180 TRC, vol 3, pp 220, 188.

181 De Klerk, *Last Trek,* p 197.

182 Mandela, *Long Walk,* p 565.

CHAPTER 9

1 *Concensus*, vol 3, no 4, November 2006, p 6.
2 *Die Burger*, 15 August 1989 (translation).
3 *Ibid*, 16 August 1989 (translation).
4 *Ibid*, 4 August 1989.
5 *House of Assembly Debates*, 2 February 1989, col 201.
6 *Ibid*, cols 201–2, 203.
7 South African Law Commission, *Group and Human Rights – Interim Report*, pp 11, 176.
8 Mandela, *Long Walk*, pp 554–5.
9 De Klerk, *Last Trek*, pp 157–8.
10 Geldenhuys, *What Do We Think? A survey of white opinion on foreign policy issues*, p 31.
11 Gagiano, 'Ruling Group Cohesion', p 196.
12 Schlemmer, 'Strategies for the Future', p 250.
13 Shubin, *ANC: A View from Moscow,* p 347.
14 De Klerk, *Last Trek*, p 161.
15 Mandela, *Long Walk*, p 534.
16 De Klerk, *Last Trek*, p 619.
17 Mandela, *Long Walk*, p 525.
18 *Die Burger*, 18 February 1992.
19 Mandela, *Long Walk*, p 526.
20 *Ibid*, p 527.
21 *Ibid*, pp 535–6.
22 *Ibid*, p 539.
23 Prinsloo, *Stem uit die Wildernis*, pp 285–7.
24 Sparks, *Tomorrow is Another Country,* pp 76–8; Waldmeir, *Anatomy of a Miracle*, pp 75–9.
25 Rosenthal, *Mission Improbable: A Piece of the South African Story*.
26 De Klerk, *Last Trek*, p 96.
27 Willem de Klerk, *FW de Klerk: The Man in his Time*, p 22.
28 *Ibid*, p 25.
29 Rosenthal, *Mission Improbable*, pp 262–3.
30 *Die Burger*, 6 March 1989 (translation).
31 Willem de Klerk, *FW de Klerk: The Man in his Time,* p 68.
32 *Die Burger*, 15 August 1989.
33 *Ibid*, 8 August 1989 (translation).
34 *Ibid*, 22 August 1989.
35 *Business Day*, 16 August 1989.
36 Quoted in Sampson, *Mandela: The Authorised Biography,* p 386.
37 De Klerk, *Last Trek*, pp 152–3.
38 Hamann, *Days of the Generals*, pp 182–3.
39 Speech to Andersen Consulting, London, 21 January 1997, p 5.
40 De Klerk, *Last Trek*, p 161.

41 Speech to Andersen Consulting, p 3.

42 *South African Communists Speak, 1915–1980*, pp 312–5.

43 Karis and Gerhart, *From Protest to Challenge*, vol 5, p 378.

44 Callinicos, *Oliver Tambo: Beyond the Engeli Mountains*, p 329.

45 Tambo (ed), *Preparing for Power*, pp 151, 161.

46 Mandela, *Long Walk*, pp 509–511.

47 *Ibid*, p 502; Buntman, *Robben Island and Prisoner Resistance to Apartheid*, p 230.

48 Mandela, *Long Walk*, p 514.

49 *Ibid*.

50 *Ibid*, p 523.

51 Ahmed Kathrada, *Memoirs*, pp 321–2.

52 Mandela, *Long Walk*, pp 517–18.

53 Ginwala, 'Into and Out of Codesa Negotiations: the view from the ANC', pp 7–8.

54 Rosenthal, *Mission Improbable*, p 22.

55 Tambo (ed), *Preparing for Power*, pp 267, 261.

56 Waldmeir, *Anatomy of a Miracle*, pp 82–3.

57 Cas Coovadia, 'Community Negotiations in South Africa', p 96.

58 Piroshaw Camay, 'Comments on the development of the negotiation process in the labour arena', p 92.

59 Rantete, *The African National Congress and the negotiated settlement in South Africa*, p 132.

60 Quoted in Rosenthal, *Mission Improbable*, p 109.

61 *Ibid*, p 214.

62 For Mbeki's background see Mark Gevisser, *Thabo Mbeki: The Dream Deferred*.

63 Hadland and Rantao, *The Life and Times of Thabo Mbeki*, p 86.

64 Callinicos, *Oliver Tambo: Beyond the Engeli Mountains*, pp 602–3.

65 Rosenthal, *Mission Improbable*, pp 213–4.

66 Shubin, *ANC: A View from Moscow*, pp 340–53.

67 *Ibid*, p 325.

68 Callinicos, *Oliver Tambo: Beyond the Engeli Mountains*, pp 604–5.

69 Waldmeir, *Anatomy of a Miracle*, p 83.

70 Shubin, *ANC: A View from Moscow*, p 328.

71 Sparks, *The Mind of South Africa: The Story of the Rise and Fall of Apartheid*, p 366.

72 Shubin, *ANC: A View from Moscow*, p 345.

73 *Ibid*, pp 352–3.

74 Rantete, *The African National Congress and the Negotiated Settlement in South Africa*, p 138.

75 The full text of the notes of Mandela's memorandum to Botha, dated 8 July 1989, is contained in Ebrahim, *The Soul of a Nation: constitution-making in South Africa*.

76 Filatova, 'The ANC's Soviet World'.

77 Ottaway, *Afrocommunism*.

78 Mandela, *Long Walk*, p 527.

79 For the (false) allegations against Mandela see: O'Malley, *Shades of Difference*, pp 302–3, Sampson, *Mandela: The Authorised Biography*, p 292 and Sparks, *Tomorrow is Another Country*, p 61.

80 The critical sections of the Harare Declaration are contained in Ebrahim, pp 451–5.

81 Mandela, *Long Walk*, p 545.

82 De Klerk, *Last Trek*, p 157.

83 Willem de Klerk, *FW de Klerk: The Man in his Time*, p 80.

84 Mandela, *Long Walk*, pp 544–5.

85 Quoted in O'Malley, pp 517–18.

CHAPTER 10

1. De Klerk, *Last Trek*, pp 159–60.

2   The full text of the speech, apart from Hansard, is reproduced in Willem de Klerk, *FW de Klerk: The Man in his Time*, pp 34–46.

3   *House of Assembly Debates*, vol 16, 1990, col 67.

4   Speech to Andersen Consulting, 1 January 1997.

5   Sparks, *Tomorrow is Another Country*, p 121.

6   Callinicos, *Oliver Tambo: Beyond the Engeli Mountains*, p 405.

7   *Weekly Mail*, 26 January–1 February 1990.

8   Temkin, *Buthelezi*, pp 254, 261, 263, 264.

9   W de Klerk, *FW de Klerk*, pp 104–5.

10 De Klerk, *Last Trek*, p 166.

11 Mandela, *Long Walk*, p 553.

12 The full text is in Clark (ed), *Mandela Speaks: Forging a Democratic Non-racial South Africa*, pp 23–8.

13 *Weekly Mail*, 26 January–1 February 1990.

14 Sampson, *Mandela*, p 410.

15 Moore, *Social Origins of Dictatorship and Democracy*, p 196.

16 Mandela, *Long Walk*, p 568.

17 De Klerk, *Last Trek*, p 180.

18 Quoted in Mkhondo, *Reporting South Africa*, p 36.

19 Ebrahim, *The Soul of a Nation*, pp 483–4.

20 Shubin, *ANC: A View from Moscow*, p 383.

21 De Klerk, *Last Trek*, p 182.

22 Stadler, *The Other Side of the Story*, p 90.

23 De Klerk, *Last Trek*, p 201.

24 Mandela, *Long Walk*, p 577.

25 Waldmeir, *Anatomy of a Miracle*, p 162.

26 Quoted in Braam, *Operation Vula*, p 3.

27 Callinicos, *Oliver Tambo: Beyond the Engeli Mountains*, p 600.

28 Quoted in Stadler, *The Other Side of the Story,* p 92.

29 Quoted in Waldmeir, *Anatomy of a Miracle,* p 162.

30 South African Institute of International Affairs, *What Do We Think? A survey of white opinion on foreign policy issues,* no 5. Analysed by André du Pisani, p 26; Institute for Black Research, *The People Speak: Negotiation and Change,* p 6.

31 Mandela, *Long Walk,* pp 577–8.

32 Waldmeir, *Anatomy of a Miracle,* p 166.

33 Mkhondo, *Reporting South Africa,* pp 42–3.

34 *Weekly Mail,* 19–25 October 1990.

35 Ebrahim, *The Soul of a Nation,* pp 485–7.

36 Mandela, *Long Walk,* p 561; SAIRR *Survey,* 1989/90, p 257.

37 Ebrahim, *The Soul of a Nation,* pp 293–7.

38 Jeffery, *Riot Policing in Perspective,* pp 33–5.

39 Jeffery (ed), *Forum on Mass Mobilisation,* pp 44, 47.

40 Welsh, 'Right-Wing Terror in South Africa', pp 239–64.

41 Stadler, *The Other Side of the Story,* pp 137–45.

42 De Klerk, *Last Trek,* p 215.

43 *Ibid,* p 203.

44 ANC National Consultative Conference, *Counter-Revolution in the Making,* pp 5, 6, 4.

45 Ottaway, *South Africa: The Struggle for a New Order,* p 44.

46 Waldmeir, *Anatomy of a Miracle,* p 175.

47 Temkin, *Buthelezi,* p 261.

48 SAIRR *Survey,* 1991/2, pp 519, 521.

49 Jeffery, *The Natal Story,* p 102; SAIRR *Survey,* 1992/3, p 449; 1993/4, p 653.

50 *Weekly Mail,* 23–9 November 1990.

51 Mallaby, *After Apartheid,* p 90.

52 Clark (ed), *Mandela Speaks,* pp 63–4.

53 Mandela, *Long Walk,* p 581.

54 Clark (ed), *Mandela Speaks,* pp 58–61.

55 *Weekly Mail,* 12 December 1990.

56 Clark (ed), *Mandela Speaks,* pp 69–70.

57 CA Norgaard, Advice to the United Nations Special Representative on the Entitlement of 16 persons to release as political prisoners under para 7 of the Namibian Settlement Proposal.

58 De Klerk, *Last Trek,* p 250.

59 Mandela, *Long Walk,* p 573.

60 SAIRR *Survey,* 1991/2, pp 65–6.

61 Temkin, *Buthelezi,* pp 274–5.

62 TRC, vol 3, p 188.

63 De Klerk, *Last Trek,* p 211.

64 Hamann, *Days of the Generals,* pp 145, 154.

65 De Klerk, *Last Trek,* p 194.

66 Frederickse, *They Fought for Freedom: David Webster,* pp 57–8.

67 Quoted in Mkhondo, *Reporting South Africa*, p 85.
68 SAIRR *Survey*, 1991/2, p 493.
69 Mandela, *Long Walk*, p 583.
70 De Klerk, *Last Trek*, p 188.
71 *Ibid*, p 209.
72 *Business Day*, 15 May 1989.
73 TRC, vol 6, p 252.
74 Hamann, *Days of the Generals*, pp 158–9.
75 Waldmeir, *Anatomy of a Miracle*, p 186.
76 Boraine, *A Country Unmasked: Inside South Africa's Truth and Reconciliation Commission*, pp 139–40.
77 Van Rooyen, *Hard Right*, pp 175–182.
78 SAIRR *Survey*, 1991/2, pp 200–1.
79 See Van Rooyen, *Hard Right*, pp 117–200 for a detailed account.
80 Mkhondo, *Reporting South Africa*, p 172.
81 *Mau-Mauing the Media: New Censorship for the New South Africa*, pp 11, 25.
82 Quoted in Brink *et al*, *Soweto: 16 June 1976*, p 175.
83 Mkhondo, *Reporting South Africa*, p 95.
84 Quoted in Haw, *Bearing Witness*, p 333.
85 Quoted in Mkhondo, *Reporting South Africa*, p 134.
86 De Klerk, *Last Trek*, pp 216–17.
87 Mandela, *Long Walk*, p 617.
88 Jeffery, *The Natal Story*; and *The Truth about the Truth Commission*.
89 Mandela, *Long Walk*, p 589.
90 SAIRR *Survey*, 1991–2, pp 522–556 for text of Accord.
91 'The National Peace Accord', Supplement to the *Financial Mail*, 9 April 1993, p 20.
92 De Klerk, *Last Trek*, p 213.
93 Richard J Goldstone, *For Humanity: Reflections of a War Crimes Investigator*, pp 3–13.
94 Zartman, 'Prenegotiation: phases and functions', p 240
95 *Ibid*, p 245.

CHAPTER 11

1 The text of the Guidelines is in *ANC Perspectives: Policy Documents and ANC Statements*, pp 18–21.
2 Sachs, *Perfectibility and Corruptibility: Preparing Ourselves for Power*. Sachs was a key ANC constitutional advisor.
3 *Grondwetlike Regering in 'n Deelnemende Demokrasie: Die Nasionale Party se raamwerk vir 'n nuwe demokrasie in Suid-Afrika*.
4 South African Law Commission, *Report on Constitutional Models*.
5 Horowitz, *A Democratic South Africa?* pp 28–9.

6 'Advance to National Democracy: Guidelines to strategy and tactics of the ANC', in Ebrahim, *The Soul of a Nation,* p 510.

7 Buthelezi, *South Africa: My Vision of the Future*, pp 33,139–141.

8 Ebrahim, *The Soul of a Nation,* p 453.

9 Clark, *Mandela Speaks*, p 108.

10 Buthelezi, *South Africa*, p 132.

11 Clark, *Mandela Speaks*, pp 103, 109.

12 Quoted in Sampson, *Mandela*, pp 429–430.

13 Waldmeir, *Anatomy of a Miracle*, p 196.

14 Holomisa and Meyer, *A Better Future*, p 14.

15 Meyer, 'From Parliamentary Sovereignty to Constitutionality: The Democratization of South Africa, 1990 to 1994', p 51.

16 Ebrahim, *The Soul of a Nation*, pp 529–31.

17 Mkhondo, *Reporting South Africa*, p 5; SAIRR *Survey*, 1991/2, p Li

18 SAIRR *Survey*, 1991/2, pp iL-L.

19 Mandela, *Long Walk*, p 604.

20 SAIRR *Survey*, 1991/2, p Lii.

21 De Klerk, *Last Trek*, p 219–20.

22 Clark, *Mandela Speaks*, pp 153–8.

23 Waldmeir, *Anatomy of a Miracle*, p 193.

24 Meyer, 'From Parliamentary Sovereignty to Constitutionality', p 50.

25 De Klerk, *Last Trek*, p 222.

26 *Ibid*, pp 231–2.

27 NP referendum pamphlet.

28 Van Rooyen, *Hard Right*, p 154.

29 Mandela, *Long Walk*, p 594.

30 Holomisa and Meyer, *A Better Future*, pp 16–17.

31 Rantete, *The African National Congress and the negotiated settlement in South Africa*, p 176.

32 Quoted in *ibid*, p 175.

33 Steven Friedman (ed), *The Long Journey: South Africa's Quest for a Negotiated Settlement*, p 64.

34 Waldmeir, *Anatomy of a Miracle*, p 202.

35 De Klerk, *Last Trek*, p 238.

36 Waldmeir, *Anatomy of a Miracle*, p 202.

37 Mkhondo, *Reporting South Africa*, p 147.

38 Mandela, *Long Walk*, p 595.

39 Meyer, 'From Parliamentary Sovereignty to Constitutionality', pp 55–6.

40 Mandela, *Long Walk*, p 595.

41 Eglin, 'Shake-out: Colin Eglin on Codesa and its aftermath', p 12.

42 Clark, *Mandela Speaks*, pp 175–7.

43 The correspondence between Mandela and De Klerk is published in Ebrahim, *The Soul of a Nation*, pp 532–87.

44 Malan and Beckett, 'Was it revenge for murders by ANC comrades?', *Guardian Weekly*, 3–9 July 1992, reprinted in Wentzel, *Liberal Slideaway*, pp 391–3.

45 TRC, vol 3, p 689.
46 Jeffery, *Truth about the Truth Commission*, pp 138–44.
47 Goldstone, *For Humanity*, p 31.
48 South African Institute of Race Relations, Website Comment by Anthea Jeffery, 30 November 2000.
49 Princeton N Lyman, *Partner to History: The US Role in South Africa's Transition to Democracy*, pp 61–3.
50 Rantete, *The African National Congress and the negotiated settlement in South Africa*, p 184.
51 Clark, *Mandela Speaks*, pp 191, 194.
52 Mkhondo, *Reporting South Africa*, p 145.
53 SAIRR *Survey*, 1992/3, pp 342–3.
54 Quoted in Mkhondo, *Reporting South Africa*, p 151.
55 Kasrils, *Armed and Dangerous*, pp 356–7.
56 *Ibid.*
57 Goldstone Commission, *Report on the Bisho incident on 7 September 1992*, pp 11–12.
58 Sampson, *Mandela*, p 463.
59 Clark, *Mandela Speaks*, p 209.
60 SAIRR *Survey*, 1992/3, p 567.
61 Waldmeir, *Anatomy of a Miracle*, p 257.
62 Personal communications to the author from Derek Keys and Trevor Manuel.
63 Holomisa and Meyer, *A Better Future*, p 18.
64 *Ibid*, p 19.
65 De Klerk, *Last Trek*, p 251.
66 Temkin, *Buthelezi*, p 282.
67 Waldmeir, *Anatomy of a Miracle*, p 216.
68 Quoted in Tom Lodge, *Mandela: A Critical Life*, p 178.
69 De Klerk, *Last Trek*, p 256.
70 Van Rooyen, *Hard Right*, pp 50–1.
71 Quoted in Mkhondo, *Reporting South Africa*, p 115.
72 *Ibid*, p 154.
73 Statement released by Office of the State President, 26 September 1992 (translation).
74 Joe Slovo, 'Negotiations: What room for compromise?', p 37.
75 Quoted in Waldmeir, *Anatomy of a Miracle*, pp 213–14.
76 Quoted in Mkhondo, *Reporting South Africa*, p 163.
77 Sampson, *Mandela*, p 467.
78 For text of the Record of Understanding see Ebrahim, *The Soul of a Nation*, pp 588–94.
79 Temkin, *Buthelezi*, pp 283–4.
80 Quoted in Mkhondo, *Reporting South Africa*, p 158.
81 Lyman, *Partner to History*, p 137.
82 Van Rooyen, *Hard Right*, p 110.

83 SAIRR *Survey*, 1992/3, pp 39–40.

84 De Klerk, *Last Trek*, p 270.

85 Waldmeir, *Anatomy of a Miracle,* p 216.

86 *Die Burger*, 20 February 1997.

87 'Negotiations: a strategic perspective', in Ebrahim, *The Soul of a Nation,* pp 595–603.

88 Hamann, *Days of the Generals*, p 197.

89 De Klerk, *Last Trek*, p 264.

90 TRC, vol 2, p 694.

91 De Klerk, *Last Trek*, p 316.

92 Adam and Moodley, *The Negotiated Revolution,* p 155.

93 Lyman, *Partner to History,* p 161.

94 Van Rooyen, *Hard Right*, pp 71–2.

95 Dave Steward, 'The Steyn Investigation', pp 10–12.

96 *Ibid*, p 11.

97 De Klerk, *Last Trek*, p 263.

98 *Ibid*, p 265.

99 Lyman, *Partner to History,* p 161.

100 *Rapport*, 5 August 2007; see the interview with Thirion in Foster, Haupt and De Beer, *The Theatre of Violence*, pp 151–75.

101 Malan, *My lewe saam met die SA weermag*, p 378.

102 De Klerk, Submission to the TRC, August 1997, p 16.

103 Goldstone, *For Humanity*, p 52.

104 Boraine, *A Country Unmasked,* pp 303–5.

105 *Ibid*, pp 21, 130.

106 *Die Burger*, 29 November 2008 (translation).

107 Temkin, *Buthelezi*, p 311.

108 *Rapport*, 29 July 2007 (translation).

109 *Mail and Guardian*, September 8–14 2006.

110 *Rapport*, 25 June 2006 (translation).

111 John Allen, *Rabble-Rouser for Peace: The Authorized Biography of Desmond Tutu*, pp 365–6.

112 *The Economist*, 29 February 1992.

113 Reynolds, 'The Results', p 193.

114 Allen, *Rabble-Rouser for Peace,* pp 364, 326.

115 Sampson, *Mandela*, p 467.

116 TRC, vol 2, pp 684, 710.

117 Allen, *Rabble-Rouser for Peace,* pp 367–8.

118 Cf. Temkin, *Buthelezi*, p 346.

119 TRC, vol 3, pp 174, 159, 160, 162.

120 De Klerk, *Last Trek*, p 379, 377.

CHAPTER 12

1 Quoted in Ebrahim, *The Soul of a Nation*, p 150.

2 *Ibid*, pp 150–2; Meyer 'From Parliamentary Sovereignty to Constitutionality', pp 62–8.

3 Waldmeir, *Anatomy of a Miracle*, p 241.

4 Mandela, *Long Walk*, p 599.

5 Quoted in Mkhondo, *Reporting South Africa*, p 165.

6 Dommisse, *Anton Rupert*, p 294.

7 De Klerk, *Last Trek*, p 276.

8 Clark, *Mandela Speaks*, pp 235–7.

9 *Ibid*, pp 238–46.

10 Mkhondo, *Reporting South Africa*, p 165.

11 *Ibid*, pp 164–5.

12 TRC, vol 2, p 685.

13 *Ibid*, p 692.

14 *Sunday Independent*, 5 August 2007.

15 De Klerk, *Last Trek*, p 286.

16 Stadler, *The Other Side of the Story*, p 124.

17 Giliomee, 'The National Party's Campaign for a Liberation Election', pp 49, 54.

18 Hamill, 'A Disguised Surrender? South Africa's Negotiated Settlement and the Politics of Conflict Resolution', p 19.

19 Based on Ebrahim, *The Soul of a Nation*, pp 606–8.

20 Slovo, 'The Negotiations Victory: a political overview', p 7.

21 *Monitor*, October 1991, pp 86–7.

22 Neuberger, 'Federalism and Political Integration in Africa', p 182.

23 Humphries *et al*, 'The Shape of the Country: Negotiating Regional Government', p 157.

24 Quoted in Welsh, 'Federalism and South Africa: the future is not yet written', p 59.

25 Welsh, 'Federalism and the problem of South Africa', p 254.

26 Sachs, *Perfectibility and Corruptibility*, p 12.

27 Meyer, 'From Parliamentary Sovereignty to Constitutionality', p 61.

28 Lyman, *Partner to History*, pp 131, 94.

29 Sachs, *Perfectibility and Corruptibility*, p 12.

30 Interview with Thozamile Botha, *Mayibuye*, April 1993, p 10.

31 ANC, *Ten proposed regions for South Africa* (Discussion document prepared by ANC Constitutional Committee, 1992) p 19.

32 Interview with Thozamile Botha, *Mayibuye*, April 1993, p 10.

33 Quoted in Welsh, 'Federalism and South Africa: The Future is Not Yet Written', p 68.

34 Humphries *et al*, 'The Shape of the Country: Negotiating Regional Government', p 157.

35 *Ibid*.

36 Slovo, *Negotiations Victory*, p 11.

37 Guelke, *South Africa in Transition: The Misunderstood Miracle*, pp 89–111.

38 Quoted in Mkhondo, *Reporting South Africa*, p 156.

39 *Ibid*, p 157.

40 Oomen, *Chiefs in South Africa: Law, Power and Culture in the Post-Apartheid Era*, p 95.

41 Horowitz, *A Democratic South Africa?*, pp 66, 71, 75.

42 Reynolds, 'The Results', p 211.

43 Lyman, *Partner to History*, p 136.

44 *Ibid*, p 137.

45 Temkin, *Buthelezi*, p 298.

46 De Klerk, *Last Trek*, p 308.

47 Vryheidsfront, Further Submissions to the TRC, May 1997, p 22.

48 Van Rooyen, *Hard Right*, p 111.

49 Jan Heunis, *The Inner Circle*, p 187.

50 Goldstone Commission, *Report on the Inquiry into Events at the World Trade Centre on 25 June 1993*, p 19.

51 Freedom Front, Further Submissions, p 23.

52 *Ibid*, p 22.

53 Freedom Front, Submission to the TRC, 19 August 1996, p 11.

54 *Ibid*, pp 32–3.

55 Sparks, *Tomorrow is Another Country*, p 200.

56 Lyman, *Partner to History*, pp 170–1.

57 Quoted in Giliomee, *The Afrikaners: Biography of a People*, p 646.

58 Hamann, *Days of the Generals*, p 210.

59 Hadland and Rantao, *Life and Times of Thabo Mbeki*, p 81.

60 Vryheidsfront, Further Submissions, p 26.

61 Vryheidsfront, Submission, pp 22–3.

62 De Klerk, *Last Trek*, p 310.

63 Sparks, *Tomorrow is Another Country*, p 204.

64 De Klerk, *Last Trek*, p 311.

65 Lyman, *Partner to History*, p 173.

66 Waldmeir, *Anatomy of a Miracle*, p 239.

67 Hadland and Rantao, *Life and Times of Thabo Mbeki*, p 80.

68 SAIRR *Survey*, 1993/4, pp 509–510.

69 Ebrahim, *The Soul of a Nation*, p 172.

70 Welsh, 'The Provincial Boundary Demarcation Process', pp 223–9.

71 Waldmeir, *Anatomy of a Miracle*, p 242.

72 *Business Day*, 21 May 1993.

73 *Sunday Times*, 14 November 1993.

74 Haysom, 'Federal Features of the Final Constitution', p 508.

75 Etienne Mureinik, quoted in Humphries *et al*, 'The Shape of the Country: Negotiating Regional Government', p 173.

76 Lyman, *Partner to History*, p 137.

77 Mandela, *Long Walk*, p 607.

78 Waldmeir, *Anatomy of a Miracle*, p 245.

79 *The Citizen*, 4 March 1994.

80 Goldstone Commission, *Interim Report on criminal violence by elements within the South African Police, the Kwazulu Police and the Inkatha Freedom Party*.

81 O'Malley, *Shades of Difference*, p 295.

82 SAIRR *Survey*, 1994/5, p 404.

83 *Pretoria News*, 8 June 1993.

84 *Business Day*, 28 April 1993.

85 For a full account see Sparks, *Tomorrow is Another Country*, pp 197–225; see also Viljoen's submission to the (Tebbutt) Commission of Inquiry, 17 October 1996.

86 Waldmeir, *Anatomy of a Miracle*, p 247.

87 Van Rooyen, 'The White Right', p 102.

88 Vryheidsfront, Further Submissions, pp 23, 25.

89 Hadland and Rantao, *Life and Times of Thabo Mbeki*, p 81.

90 Temkin, *Buthelezi*, p 303.

91 Lyman, *Partner to History*, p 207.

92 Quoted in Cassidy, *Witness For Ever*, p 168.

93 Jeffery, *Truth about the Truth Commission*, p 145.

94 De Klerk, *Last Trek*, pp 321–2.

95 Cassidy, *A Witness for Ever*, pp 170–89.

96 De Klerk, *Last Trek*, p 327.

97 *Weekly Mail*, 4–10 March 1994.

98 *Beeld*, 25 November 1993.

99 Waldmeir, *Anatomy of a Miracle*, p 228.

100 *Financial Times*, reprinted in *Weekly Mail*, 11–17 June 1993.

101 *Business Day*, 15 June 1993.

102 *Star*, 14 June 1993.

103 Meyer, 'From Parliamentary Sovereignty to Constitutionality', p 61.

104 Waldmeir, *Anatomy of a Miracle*, p 227.

105 De Klerk, *Last Trek*, p 237.

106 *Ibid*, p 290.

107 Waldmeir, *Anatomy of a Miracle*, p 252.

108 *Pretoria News*, 15 November 1993.

109 Mandela, *Long Walk*, p 604.

110 Waldmeir, *Anatomy of a Miracle*, p 231.

111 *Ibid*, p 232.

112 Hamann, *Days of the Generals*, p 227.

113 *Rapport*, 27 August 2006.

114 *ThisDay*, 2 November 2003.

115 SAIRR *Survey*, 1993/4, p 86.

116 ANC Constitutional Committee, *A Bill of Rights for a New South Africa*, p 11.

117 Giliomee, *The Afrikaners*, p 644.

118 Schlemmer, 'Liberalism in South Africa: the Challenges beyond Opposition', p 86.

119 Hirsch, *Season of Hope: Economic Reform under Mandela and Mbeki*, p 43.

120 Sachs, *Affirmative Action and the New Constitution*, p 1.

121 K Savage, 'Negotiating South Africa's New Constitution', pp 176–183; Spitz with Chaskalson, *The Politics of Transition*, pp 313–29.

122 Marais, *South Africa: Limits to Change*, p 154.

123 Leon, *On the Contrary: Leading the Opposition in a Democratic South Africa*, pp 223–8.

124 *House of Assembly Debates*, 1993–4, cols 13 794, 13 801.

125 De Klerk, *Last Trek*, p 291.

CHAPTER 13

1 SAIRR *Survey*, 1994/5, pp 439 ff.

2 Przeworski, *Democracy and the Market*, p 26.

3 All data are drawn from Independent Electoral Commission, *An End to Waiting: The Story of South Africa's Election 26 April to 6 May 1994*.

4 De Klerk, *Last Trek*, p 335.

5 IEC, *An End to Waiting*, p 55.

6 *Weekly Mail*, 11–17 March 1994.

7 *The Citizen*, 4 March 1994.

8 *Pretoria News*, 25 April 1994.

9 Quoted in Mattes, 'The Road to Democracy', p 14.

10 De Klerk, *Last Trek*, pp 328–9.

11 Lodge, 'The ANC and its Allies', pp 23, 32, 41.

12 Waldmeir, *Anatomy of a Miracle*, p 58.

13 Sampson, *Mandela*, p 479.

14 De Klerk, *Last Trek*, p 330.

15 Hirsch, *Season of Hope*, pp 59–60.

16 Sampson, *Mandela*, p 478.

17 *Pretoria News*, 25 April 1994.

18 De Klerk, *Last Trek*, p 330.

19 *Business Day*, 8 March 1994.

20 *Business Day*, 18 March 1994.

21 Giliomee, 'The National Party's Campaign for a Liberation Election', p 60.

22 *Pretoria News*, 25 April 1994.

23 *Pretoria News*, 24 April 1994.

24 Adam and Moodley, *Negotiated Revolution*, p 108.

25 Buthelezi Commission, vol 1, p 312.

26 Horowitz, *A Democratic South Africa?* pp 82–3.

27 Neuhaus, *Dispensations*, pp 212, 221.

28 Johnson and Schlemmer, 'National Issues and National Opinion', pp 78–9.
29 *The Citizen*, 25 March 1994.
30 Giliomee, 'The National Party's Campaign for a Liberation Election', p 65.
31 Quoted in Mattes, Giliomee and James, 'The Election in the Western Cape', p 114.
32 Seekings, *The UDF*, p 320.
33 *Ibid*, p 320.
34 Johnson and Schlemmer, 'National Issues and National Opinion', pp 79–80.
35 Mattes *et al*, 'The Election in the Western Cape', p 122.
36 *Ibid*, p 121.
37 *Ibid*, p 135.
38 Giliomee, 'The National Party's Campaign for a Liberation Election', pp 63–4.
39 Cooper, 'The PAC and AZAPO', p 118.
40 Reynolds, 'The Results', p 198.
41 Eglin, *Crossing the Borders of Power*, pp 308–9.
42 *Pretoria News*, 22 April 1994.
43 *Weekly Mail*, 31 March–6 April 1994.
44 *Sunday Times*, 24 April 1994.
45 Van Rooyen, 'The White Right', pp 100–1.
46 *Pretoria News*, 25 April 1994.
47 Reynolds, 'The Results', pp 195, 211.
48 Johnson, 'The Election, the Count and the Drama in Kwazulu-Natal', pp 274–300.
49 Mandela, *Long Walk*, p 611.
50 *Ibid*, p 609.
51 De Klerk, *Last Trek*, p 332.
52 IEC, *An End to Waiting*, p 44.
53 *Ibid*, pp 122–3.
54 Waldmeir, *Anatomy of a Miracle*, p 260.
55 De Klerk, *Last Trek*, pp 334–5.
56 *Ibid*, p 335.
57 Mandela, *Long Walk*, p 641.
58 Sampson, *Mandela*, p 491.
59 Mandela, *Long Walk*, p 612.
60 Reynolds, 'The Results', p 191.
61 *The Citizen*, 5 May 1994.
62 Eglin, *Crossing the Borders*, p 322.
63 IEC, *An End to Waiting*, p 27.
64 Brink (compiler), *SA 27 April 1994: An Author's Diary*, pp 73, 74, 94.
65 IEC, *An End to Waiting*, p 30.
66 *Business Day*, 2 May 1994.
67 Waldmeir, *Anatomy of a Miracle*, p 261.
68 IEC, *An End to Waiting*, p 124.
69 Mattes *et al*, 'The Election in the Western Cape', p 144.

70 IEC, *An End to Waiting*, p 70.
71 Johnson, 'How Free? How Fair?', p 332.

CONCLUSION

1 *Towards Democracy*, third quarter, 1992, p 12.
2 Clarke, *A Question of Leadership*, p 332.
3 Ash, *We the People: The Revolution of 1989*, p 14.
4 Steyn, *Penvegter*, p 331 (translation).
5 Figures compiled from SAIRR *Surveys*; Dippenaar, *History of South African Police*; and Jeffery, *The Natal Story*.
6 Commonwealth Group of Eminent Persons, *Mission to South Africa*, p 129.
7 For data see Smith, *The Atlas of War and Peace*.
8 Robertson, *Crimes Against Humanity*, p 40.
9 BBC News website, 7 November 2008.
10 FW de Klerk, Transcript of Submission to TRC, 21 August 1996.
11 TRC, vol 4, p 58.
12 Horwitz, *The Political Economy of Growth*, p 427; Blumer, 'Industrialisation and Growth', pp 238–9.
13 Lipton, *Capitalism and Apartheid*.
14 De Klerk, *Last Trek*, pp 72–3.
15 O'Dowd, *South Africa: The Growth Imperative*, p 72.
16 Acemoglu and Robinson, *The Economic Origins of Dictatorship and Democracy*, p 31.
17 Meredith, *Nelson Mandela*, p 107.
18 Lodge, *Mandela*, p 205.
19 Ottaway, 'Liberation movements and transitions to democracy: The case of the ANC', p 66.
20 *Die Burger*, 3 March 2006 (translation).
21 Quoted in Olivier (ed), *Praat met die ANC*, p 26.

Bibliography

Michael Abeldas and Alan Fischer (eds), *A Question of Survival: Conversations with Key South Africans* (Jonathan Ball, Johannesburg, 1987).

Daron Acemoglu and James Robinson, *The Economic Origins of Dictatorship and Democracy* (Cambridge University Press, Cambridge, 2006).

Raymond Ackerman, *Hearing Grasshoppers Jump: The Story of Raymond Ackerman as told to Denise Prichard* (David Philip, Cape Town, 2001).

Heribert Adam, 'The South African Power-Elite: A Survey of Ideological Commitment', in Heribert Adam (ed), *South Africa: Sociological Perspectives* (Oxford University Press, London, 1971).

Heribert Adam and Hermann Giliomee, *The Rise and Crisis of Afrikaner Power* (David Philip, Cape Town, 1979).

Heribert Adam and Kogila Moodley, *South Africa without Apartheid: Dismantling Racial Domination* (Maskew Miller Longman, Cape Town, 1986).

Heribert Adam and Kogila Moodley, *The Negotiated Revolution: Society and Politics in Post-Apartheid South Africa* (Jonathan Ball, Johannesburg, 1993).

Glenn Adler and Eddie Webster, 'Challenging Transition Theory: The Labor Movement, Radical Reform and Transition to Democracy in South Africa', *Politics and Society*, vol 23, no 1, 1995.

Afrikanerbond, *Bearer of an Ideal* (Afrikanerbond, Johannesburg, 1997).

Cornie Alant, 'Die Rol van die Kerk in die Moderne Afrikanersamelewing' in Hendrik W van der Merwe (ed), *Identiteit en Verandering: Sewe Opstelle oor die Afrikaner Vandag* (Tafelberg, Cape Town, 1975).

JR Albertyn, P du Toit and HS Theron, *Kerk en Stad* (Pro Ecclesia, Stellenbosch, 1947).

John Allen, *Rabble-Rouser for Peace: The Authorized Biography of Desmond Tutu* (Rider Books, London, 2006).

Amnesty International Report, *Political Imprisonment in South Africa* (London, 1978).

ANC, *ANC Perspectives: Policy Documents and ANC Statements* (Lusaka, 1990).

ANC Constitutional Committee, *A Bill of Rights for a New South Africa* (1990).

ANC Constitutional Committee, *Ten Proposed Regions for South Africa* (Discussion document, 1992).

ANC National Consultative Conference, *Counter-Revolution in the Making: Towards a Common Perception of Violence in the Transitional Period*, 1990.

Penelope Andrews and Stephen Ellmann (eds), *The Post-Apartheid Constitutions: Perspectives on South Africa's Basic Law* (Witwatersrand University Press, Johannesburg, 2009).

Seán Archer, 'Defence expenditure and arms procurement in South Africa' in Jacklyn Cock and Laurie Nathan (eds), *War and Society: The Militarisation of South Africa* (David Philip, Cape Town, 1989).

Millard Arnold (ed), *The Testimony of Steve Biko: Black Consciousness in South Africa* (Granada, London, 1979).

Millard W Arnold (ed), *Steve Biko: No Fears Expressed* (Skotaville Publishers, Johannesburg, 1987).

Timothy Garton Ash, *We the People: The Revolution of 1989* (Granta Books, Cambridge, 1990).

Howard Barrell, *MK: The ANC's Armed Struggle* (Penguin, London, 1990).

Simon Baynham, 'Political Violence and the Security Response' in Jesmond Blumenfeld (ed), *South Africa in Crisis* (Royal Institute of International Affairs, London, 1987) pp 115–16.

Anton Bekker, *Eben Dönges, Balansstraat – Historiese Perspektief* (Sun Press, Stellenbosch, 2005).

Terry Bell, 'ANC crisis rooted in its history', *Cape Times*, 30 September 2008.

Peter L Berger and Bobby Godsell (eds), *A Future South Africa: Visions, Strategies and Realities* (Human & Rousseau/Tafelberg, Pretoria, 1988).

Rusty Bernstein, *Memory Against Forgetting: Memoirs from a Life in South African Politics 1938–1964* (Viking, London, 1999).

Chris Beyers and Piet Kotzé, *Die Opmars van die AWB* (Oranjewerkers Promosies, Morgenzon, 1988).

WJ Bezuidenhout (compiler), *Dr Tinie Louw: 'n Kykie in die Ekonomiese Geskiedenis van die Afrikaner* (Afrikaanse Pers Boekhandel, Johannesburg, 1969).

Steve Biko (ed), *Black Viewpoint* (Spro-cas Black Community Programmes, Durban, 1972).

Steve Biko, 'White Racism and Black Consciousness', in Hendrik W van der Merwe and David Welsh (eds), *Student Perspectives on South Africa* (David Philip, Cape Town, 1972).

George Bizos, *Odyssey to Freedom* (Random House, Johannesburg, 2007).

Jesmond Blumenfeld (ed), *South Africa in Crisis* (Royal Institute of International Affairs, London, 1987).

Herbert Blumer, 'Industrialisation and Growth', in Guy Hunter (ed), *Industrialisation and Race Relations: A Symposium* (Oxford University Press, London, 1965) pp 238–9.

Philip Bonner and Lauren Segal, *Soweto: A History* (Maskew Miller Longman, Pinelands, 1998).

Douglas Booth, 'A Strategic Divide: Townships on Contested Terrain', *Political Conflict in South Africa – Data Trends 1984–1988* (Indicator Project SA, 1988) p 78.

Alex Boraine, *A Country Unmasked: Inside South Africa's Truth and Reconciliation Commission* (Oxford University Press, Cape Town, 2000).

DP Botha, *Die Opkoms van Ons Derde Stand* (Human & Rousseau, Cape Town, 1960).

MC Botha, *Die Swart Vryheidspaaie* (Perskor, Johannesburg, 1982).

Connie Braam, *Operation Vula* (Jacana, Bellevue, 2004).

Breyten Breytenbach, *The True Confessions of an Albino Terrorist* (Harcourt Brace, San Diego, 1983).

André Brink, 'Samisjdat, tamisjdat, lamisjdat', in Charles Malan and Bartho Smit (eds), *Skrywer en Gemeenskap: Tien Jaar Afrikaanse Skrywersgilde* (HAUM, Pretoria, 1985).

André Brink (compiler), *SA 27 April 1994: An Author's Diary* (Queillerie Publishers, Pretoria, 1994).

Elsabé Brink and Gandhi Malungane (compilers), *Soweto: 16 June 1976: Personal Accounts of the Uprising* (Kwela Books, Cape Town, 2001).

Mike Brogden and Clifford Shearing, *Policing for a New South Africa* (Routledge, London, 1993).

Edgar H Brookes (ed), *A Documentary Study of Modern South Africa* (Routledge & Kegan Paul, London, 1968).

Alan Brooks and Jeremy Brickhill, *Whirlwind Before the Storm* (International Defence and Aid Fund for Southern Africa, London, 1980).

Brian Bunting, *Moses Kotane: South African Revolutionary* (Inkululeko Publications, London, 1975).

Fran Buntman, *Robben Island and Prisoner Resistance to Apartheid* (Cambridge University Press, Cambridge, 2003).

Buro vir Ekonomiese Navorsing Insake Bantoe-Ontwikkeling, *Swart Ontwikkeling in Suid-Afrika* (Pretoria, 1976).

Chief M Gatsha Buthelezi, *White and Black Nationalism, Ethnicity and the Future of the Homelands* (South African Institute of Race Relations, Johannesburg, 1974).

MG Buthelezi, *South Africa: My Vision for the Future* (Weidenfeld & Nicolson, London, 1990).

Buthelezi Commission, *The Buthelezi Commission Report* (H&H Publications, Durban, 1982).

Luli Callinicos, *Oliver Tambo: Beyond the Engeli Mountains* (David Philip, Cape Town, 2004).

Piroshaw Camay, 'Comments on the Development of the Negotiation Process in the Labour Arena', in Louise Nieuwmeijer and Fanie Cloete (eds), *The Dynamics of Negotiation in South Africa* (HSRC, Pretoria, 1991) p 92.

Robert Cameron, 'The Crossroads: Sectarianism and the State', *Indicator South*

Africa Issue Focus: Political Conflict in South Africa – Data Trends 1984–1988, pp 57–8.

WJP Carr, *Soweto: Its Creation, Life and Decline* (SAIRR, Johannesburg, 1990).

Michael Cassidy, *A Witness for Ever: The Dawning of Democracy in South Africa* (Hodder & Stoughton, London, 1995).

PJ Cillié, *Tydgenote* (Tafelberg, Cape Town, 1980).

PJ Cillié, *Baanbrekers vir Vryheid* (Tafelberg, Cape Town, 1990).

Ciskei Commission Report (Conference Associates, Pretoria, 1979).

Ciskei Commission, *The Quail Report* (Conference Associates (Pty) Ltd, Silverton, 1980).

Steve Clark (ed), *Mandela Speaks: Forging a Democratic Non-racial South Africa* (Pathfinder, New York, 1993).

Liz Clarke, Karen MacGregor and William Saunderson-Meyer, *The Industrial Trade Union Guide* (Durban, 1989).

Peter Clarke, *A Question of Leadership: From Gladstone to Thatcher* (Penguin, London, 1991).

William Cobbett and Robin Cohen (eds), *Popular Struggles in South Africa* (James Currey, London, 1988).

Jacklyn Cock and Laurie Nathan (eds), *War and Society: The Militarisation of South Africa* (David Philip, Cape Town, 1989).

Frances E Colenso, *History of the Zulu War and Its Origin* (Chapman & Hall, London, 1880).

John W Colenso, *Ten Weeks in Natal* (Macmillan, Cambridge, 1855).

The Commonwealth Group of Eminent Persons, *Mission to South Africa: The Commonwealth Report* (Penguin, Harmondsworth, 1986).

Saths Cooper, 'The PAC and AZAPO' in Andrew Reynolds (ed), *Election '94 SA: The Campaign, Results and Future Prospects* (David Philip, Cape Town, 1994).

Cas Coovadia, 'Community Negotiations in South Africa', in Louise Nieuwmeijer and Fanie Cloete (eds), *The Dynamics of Negotiation in South Africa* (HSRC, Pretoria, 1991).

Hugh Corder, 'Crowbars or Cobwebs? Executive Autocracy and the Law in South Africa', Inaugural Lecture, University of Cape Town, 1988.

Chester A Crocker, *High Noon in Southern Africa: Making Peace in a Rough Neighbourhood* (Jonathan Ball, Johannesburg, 1992).

Stephen M Davis, *Apartheid's Rebels: Inside South Africa's Hidden War* (Yale University Press, New Haven, 1987).

Kevin Davie, 'How South Africa Gets Its Oil', *The Executive*, August 1991.

CW de Kiewiet, *A History of South Africa* (Oxford University Press, London, 1941).

FW de Klerk, *The Last Trek: A New Beginning* (Macmillan, London, 1998).

FW de Klerk, *Concensus*, vol 3, no 4, November 2006, p 6.

WA de Klerk, *The Puritans of Africa* (Rex Collings, London, 1975).

Willem de Klerk, *Politieke Gesprek* (Perskor, Johannesburg, 1980).

Willem de Klerk, *Die Tweede (R)evolusie: Afrikanerdom en die Identiteitskrisis* (Jonathan Ball, Johannesburg, 1984).

Willem de Klerk, *FW de Klerk: The Man in his Time* (Jonathan Ball, Johannesburg, 1991).

Willem de Klerk, 'Gerrit Viljoen se Leierskap van die Afrikaner Broederbond', in Bernhard Louw and Frans van Rensburg (eds), *Bestendige Binnevuur: Perspektiewe op Gerrit Viljoen* (Tafelberg, Cape Town, 1997).

Bertus de Villiers (ed), *The Birth of a Constitution* (Juta, Kenwyn, 1994).

Dirk and Johanna de Villiers, *Paul Sauer* (Tafelberg, Cape Town, 1977).

Dirk and Johanna de Villiers, *PW* (Tafelberg, Cape Town, 1984).

JC de Villiers, 'Evidence given to the (Cillié) Kommissie van Ondersoek in Soweto en Elders van 16 Junie 1976 tot 28 Februarie 1977' (unpublished transcript).

Les de Villiers, *Secret Information* (Tafelberg, Cape Town, 1980).

Riaan de Villiers, 'Blowing Hot, Catching Cold', *Sanctions* (*Leadership*, 1988/9).

Marius de Witt Dippenaar, *The History of South African Police – 1913–1988* (SA Police Commemorative Album, Silverton, 1988).

John D'Oliviera, *Vorster – The Man* (Ernest Stanton, Johannesburg, 1977).

Ebbe Dommisse, 'The Changing Role of the Afrikaans Press', in Edwin S Munger (ed), *The Afrikaners* (Tafelberg, Cape Town, 1979).

Ebbe Dommisse, *Anton Rupert: A Biography* (Tafelberg, Cape Town, 2005).

John Dugard, 'The Judicial Process, Positivism and Civil Liberty', *South African Law Journal*, vol 88, 1971.

Sheena Duncan, 'A Birthright Stolen', *The Black Sash Magazine*, vol 21, no 1, May 1979.

JA du Pisani, *John Vorster en die Verlig/Verkrampstryd* (Institute for Contemporary History, Bloemfontein, 1988).

Max du Preez, *Pale Native: Memories of a Renegade Reporter* (Zebra Press, Cape Town, 2003).

Pierre du Toit, 'Regional Services Councils: Control at Local Government Level', in C Heymans and G Tötemeyer (eds), *Government by the People?: The Politics of Local Government in South Africa* (Juta, Johannesburg, 1988).

Hassen Ebrahim, *The Soul of a Nation: constitution-making in South Africa* (Oxford University Press, Cape Town, 1998).

Melville Edelstein, *What Do Young Africans Think?* (SAIRR, Johannesburg, 1972).

Colin Eglin, 'Shake-out: Colin Eglin on Codesa and its Aftermath', *Towards Democracy*, third quarter, 1992.

Colin Eglin, *Crossing the Borders of Power* (Jonathan Ball, Johannesburg, 2007).

Daniel J Elazar (ed), *Federalism and Political Integration* (Turtledove Publishing, Ramat Gan, 1979).

Stephen Ellis and Tsepo Sechaba, *Comrades against Apartheid: The ANC and South African Communist Party in Exile* (James Currey, London, 1992).

Richard Elphick and Rodney Davenport (eds), *Christianity in South Africa – A Political, Social and Cultural History* (David Philip, Cape Town, 1997).

WP Esterhuyse, *Anton Rupert: Advocate of Hope* (Tafelberg, Cape Town, 1986).

WP Esterhuyse, *Broers Buite Hoorafstand: Skeiding van die Kerklike Weë* (Tafelberg, Cape Town, 1989).

Norman Etherington (ed), *Peace, Politics and Violence in the New South Africa* (Hans Zell Publishers, London, 1992).

Gavin Evans, *Dancing Shoes is Dead: A Tale of Fighting Men in South Africa* (Black Swan, London, 2003).

Irina Filatova, 'The ANC's Soviet World', *Times Literary Supplement*, 1 January 2000.

Robert Fine with Dennis Davis, *Beyond Apartheid: Labour and Liberation in South Africa* (Ravan Press, Johannesburg, 1991).

Murray Forsyth (ed), *Federalism and Nationalism* (Leicester University Press, Leicester, 1989).

Don Foster, Paul Haupt and Marésa de Beer (eds), *The Theatre of Violence: Narratives of Protagonists in the South African Conflict* (HSRC Press, Cape Town, 2005).

Joe Foster, 'The Workers' Struggle: Where does FOSATU stand?', in Johann Maree (ed), *The Independent Trade Unions – 1974–1984* (Ravan Press, Johannesburg, 1987).

Philip Frankel, *An Ordinary Atrocity: Sharpeville and its Massacre* (Witwatersrand University Press, Johannesburg, 2001).

Philip Frankel, Noam Pines and Mark Swilling (eds), *State, Resistance and Change in South Africa* (Southern Book Publishers, Johannesburg, 1988).

Julie Frederickse, *They Fought for Freedom: David Webster* (Maskew Miller Longman, Cape Town, 1998).

Bernard Friedman, *Smuts: A Reappraisal* (Hugh Keartland Publishers, Johannesburg, 1975).

Steven Friedman (ed), *The Long Journey: South Africa's Quest for a Negotiated Settlement* (Ravan Press, Johannesburg, 1993).

Steven Friedman and Doreen Atkinson (eds), *The Small Miracle: South Africa's Negotiated Settlement* (Ravan Press, Johannesburg, 1994).

Steven Friedman and Richard Humphries (eds), *Federalism and Its Foes* (Centre for Policy Studies, Johannesburg, 1993).

Jannie Gagiano, 'Ruling Group Cohesion', in Hermann Giliomee and Jannie Gagiano (eds), *The Elusive Search for Peace: South Africa – Israel – Northern Ireland* (Oxford University Press, Cape Town, 1990).

Deon Geldenhuys, *What Do We Think? A Survey of White Opinion on Foreign Policy Issues*, no 3, May (South African Institute of International Affairs, Johannesburg, 1986).

FE O'Brien Geldenhuys, *In die Stroomversnellings: Vyftig Jaar van die NG Kerk* (Tafelberg, Cape Town, 1982).

Gail M Gerhart, *Black Power in South Africa: The Evolution of an Ideology* (University of California Press, Berkeley, 1978).

Jakes Gerwel, 'The State of Civil Society', in P Graham and R Meyer (eds), *In Conversation: The Civil Society Conference* (IDASA, Cape Town, 2001).

Mark Gevisser, *Thabo Mbeki: The Dream Deferred* (Jonathan Ball, Johannesburg, 2007).

AS Geyser, BJ Marais, Hugo du Plessis, BB Keet, A van Selms *et al*, *Delayed Action* (published by the authors, Pretoria, 1960).

O Geyser (ed), *BJ Vorster: Select Speeches* (Institute for Contemporary History, Bloemfontein, 1977).

Emma Gilbey, *The Lady: The Life and Times of Winnie Mandela* (Vantage Books, London, 1994).

Hermann Giliomee, 'The National Party's Campaign for a Liberation Election', in Andrew Reynolds (ed), *Election '94 SA: The Campaign, Results and Future Prospects* (David Philip, Cape Town, 1994).

Hermann Giliomee, *The Afrikaners: Biography of a People* (Tafelberg, Cape Town, 2003).

Hermann Giliomee and Jannie Gagiano (eds), *The Elusive Search for Peace: South Africa – Israel – Northern Ireland* (Oxford University Press, Cape Town, 1990).

Frene Ginwala, 'Into and Out of Codesa Negotiations: The View from the ANC', in Norman Etherington (ed), *Peace, Politics and Violence in the New South Africa* (Hans Zell Publishers, London, 1992) pp 7–8.

RM Godsell, 'The Regulation of Labour', in Robert Schrire (ed), *South Africa: Public Policy Perspectives* (Juta, Cape Town, 1982).

Richard J Goldstone, *For Humanity: Reflections of a War Crimes Investigator* (University of the Witwatersrand Press, Johannesburg, 2000).

Goldstone Commision, Commission of Inquiry regarding the Prevention of Public Violence and Intimidation, *Report on the Bisho Incident on 7 September 1992* (Pretoria, 29 September 1992).

Goldstone Commission, *Report on the Inquiry into Events at the World Trade Centre on 25 June 1993* (Pretoria, 1993).

Goldstone Commission, *Interim Report on Criminal Violence by Elements within the South African Police, the Kwazulu Police and the Inkatha Freedom Party* (Pretoria, 18 March 1994).

P Graham and R Meyer (eds), *In Conversation: The Civil Society Conference* (IDASA, Cape Town, 2001).

Albert Grundlingh, '"Rocking the boat?" The "Voëlvry" music movement in South Africa: Anatomy of Afrikaans Anti-apartheid Social Protest in the Eighties', *International Journal of African Historical Studies*, vol 37, no 3, 2004.

Adrian Guelke, *South Africa in Transition: The Misunderstood Miracle* (IB Taurus, London, 1999).

Hilton Hamann, *Days of the Generals: The Untold Story of South Africa's Apartheid-era Military Generals* (Zebra Press, Cape Town, 2001).

James Hamill, 'A Disguised Surrender? South Africa's Negotiated Settlement and the Politics of Conflicts Resolution', *Diplomacy and Statecraft*, vol 14, no 3, 2003.

WK Hancock, *Smuts*, 2 vols (Cambridge University Press, Cambridge, 1962).

Theodor Hanf, Heribert Weiland and Gerda Vierdag, *South Africa: The Prospects of Peaceful Change* (Rex Collings, London, 1981).

Heinz Hartmann, *Enterprise and Politics in South Africa* (Princeton University Press, Princeton, 1962).

Ken Hartshorne, *Crisis and Challenge: Black Education 1910–1990* (Oxford University Press, Cape Town, 1992).

Simon Haw, *Bearing Witness* (Natal Witness, Pietermaritzburg, 1996).

Nicholas Haysom, 'Federal Features of the Final Constitution', in Penelope Andrews and Stephen Ellmann (eds), *The Post-Apartheid Constitutions: Perspectives on South Africa's Basic Law* (Witwatersrand University Press, Johannesburg, 2009).

Kenneth A Heard, *General Elections in South Africa 1943–1970* (Oxford University Press, London, 1974).

Denis Herbstein, *White Man, We Want To Talk To You* (André Deutsch, London, 1979).

Jan Heunis, *The Inner Circle: Reflections on the Last Days of White Rule* (Jonathan Ball, Cape Town, 2007).

Irving Hexham, *The Irony of Apartheid* (Edwin Mellon Press, New York, 1981).

C Heymans and G Tötemeyer (eds), *Government by the People?: The Politics of Local Government in South Africa* (Juta, Johannesburg, 1988).

Doug Hindson, 'Overview: Trade Unions and Politics', in Johann Maree (ed), *The Independent Trade Unions – 1974–1984* (Ravan Press, Johannesburg, 1987).

Alan Hirsch, *Season of Hope: Economic Reform under Mandela and Mbeki* (University of KwaZulu-Natal Press, Scottsville, 2005).

Janet Hodgson, 'A Battle for Sacred Power: Christian Beginnings Among the Xhosa', in Richard Elphick and Rodney Davenport (eds), *Christianity in South Africa – A Political, Social and Cultural History* (David Philip, Cape Town, 1997).

RFA Hoernlé, *South African Native Policy and the Liberal Spirit* (University of the Witwatersrand Press, Johannesburg, 1939).

Adrian Holland and Jovial Rantao, *The Life and Times of Thabo Mbeki* (Zebra Press, Rivonia, 1999).

JF (Hans) Holleman, 'The Great Purge', in Pierre Hugo (ed), *South African Perspectives: Essays in Honour of Nic Olivier* (Die Suid-Afrikaan, Cape Town, 1989).

Bantu Holomisa and Roelf Meyer, *A Better Future* (United Democratic Movement, Pretoria, 1999).

Pat Hopkins and Helen Grange, *The Rocky Rioter Teargas Show: The Inside Story of the 1976 Soweto Uprising* (Zebra Press, Cape Town, 2001).

Donald L Horowitz, *A Democratic South Africa? Constitutional Engineering in a Divided Society* (University of California Press, Berkeley, 1991).

Muriel Horrell (compiler), *Laws Affecting Race Relations in South Africa: 1948–1976* (SAIRR, Johannesburg, 1978).

Ralph Horwitz, *The Political Economy of Growth* (Weidenfeld & Nicolson, London, 1967).

D Hobart Houghton, *The South African Economy* (Oxford University Press, Cape Town, 1964).

D Hobart Houghton, 'Economic Development, 1865–1965', in Monica Wilson
    and Leonard Thompson (eds), *Oxford History of South Africa,* vol 2
    (Clarendon Press, Oxford, 1971).
Pierre Hugo, 'Frontier Farmers in South Africa', *African Affairs,* vol 8, no 4,
    1988.
Pierre Hugo (ed), *South African Perspectives: Essays in Honour of Nic Olivier*
    (Die Suid-Afrikaan, Cape Town, 1989).
Pierre Hugo, 'The Politics of "Untruth": Afrikaner Academics for Apartheid',
    Politikon, vol 25, no 1, 1998.
Koos Human, *'n Lewe met Boeke* (Human & Rousseau, Cape Town, 2006).
Richard Humphries *et al,* 'The Shape of the Country: Negotiating Regional
    Government', in Steven Friedman and Doreen Atkinson (eds), *The Small Miracle:
    South Africa's Negotiated Settlement* (Ravan Press, Johannesburg, 1994).
Guy Hunter (ed), *Industrialisation and Race Relations: A Symposium* (Oxford
    University Press, London, 1965).
Jonathan Hyslop, *The Classroom Struggle: Policy and Resistance in South
    Africa 1940–1990* (University of Natal Press, Pietermaritzburg, 1999).
Independent Electoral Commission, *An End to Waiting: The Story of South
    Africa's Election 26 April to 6 May 1994* (IEC, Johannesburg, 1994).
Indicator Project South Africa, *Political Conflict in South Africa: Data Trends
    1984–1988* (Durban, 1988).
Inkatha Documents for Discussion at the 1979 Summit Meeting (unpublished).
Institute for Black Research, *The People Speak: Negotiation and Change*
    (Madiba Publications, Durban, 1990).
Institute for Industrial Education, *The Durban Strikes 1973* (Ravan Press,
    Johannesburg, 1973).
Investor Responsibility Research Center, *The Impact of Sanctions on South
    Africa: Whites' Political Attitudes* (Washington DC, 1990).
Gideon Jacobs (ed), *South Africa: The Road Ahead* (Jonathan Ball,
    Johannesburg, 1986).
Anthea Jeffery (ed), *Forum on Mass Mobilisation* (South African Institute of
    Race Relations, Johannesburg, 1991).
Anthea Jeffery, *Riot Policing in Perspective* (South African Institute of Race
    Relations, Johannesburg, 1991).
Anthea Jeffery, *The Natal Story: 16 Years of Conflict* (South African Institute of
    Race Relations, Johannesburg, 1997).
Anthea Jeffery, *The Truth about the Truth Commission* (South African Institute
    of Race Relations, Johannesburg, 1999).
Carolyn Jenkins, 'Economic Implications of Capital Flight', in Liz Clarke,
    Karen MacGregor and William Saunderson-Meyer, *The Industrial Trade
    Union Guide* (Durban, 1989).
Simon Jenkins, 'Good morals, good business?', *Times Literary Supplement,* 3
    April 1987.
Karen Jochelson and Susan Brown, 'UDF and AZAPO: Evaluation and
    Expectations', *Work in Progress,* 35, February 1985.

Joel Joffe, *The Rivonia Story* (Mayibuye Books, Bellville, 1995).

Sheridan Johns and R Hunt Davis, *Mandela, Tambo and the African National Congress: The Struggle against Apartheid, 1948–1990* (Oxford University Press, New York, 1991).

RW Johnson, 'How Free? How Fair?' and 'The Election, the Count and the Drama in Kwazulu-Natal' in Johnson and Schlemmer (eds), *Launching Democracy in South Africa: The First Open Election, April 1994* (Yale University Press, New Haven, 1996).

RW Johnson and Lawrence Schlemmer (eds), *Launching Democracy in South Africa: The First Open Election, April 1994* (Yale University Press, New Haven, 1996).

RW Johnson and Lawrence Schlemmer, 'National Issues and National Opinion', in Johnson and Schlemmer (eds), *Launching Democracy in South Africa: The First Open Election, April 1994* (Yale University Press, New Haven, 1996).

Shaun Johnson (ed), *South Africa: No Turning Back* (Macmillan, Basingstoke, 1988).

Shaun Johnson, '"The Soldiers of Luthuli": Youth in the Politics of Resistance of South Africa' in Johnson (ed), *South Africa: No Turning Back* (Macmillan, Basingstoke, 1988).

Alexander Johnston, 'The Political World of KwaZulu-Natal', in RW Johnson and Lawrence Schlemmer (eds), *Launching Democracy in South Africa: The First Open Election, April 1994* (Yale University Press, New Haven, 1996).

Graham Jooste and Abrie Oosthuizen, *So Het Hulle Gesterf* (JP van der Walt, Pretoria, 1998).

John Kane-Berman, *Soweto: Black Revolt, White Reaction* (Ravan Press, Johannesburg, 1978).

John Kane-Berman, *South Africa's Silent Revolution* (South African Institute of Race Relations, Johannesburg, 1990).

John Kane-Berman, *Political Violence in South Africa* (South African Institute of Race Relations, Johannesburg, 1993).

Thomas Karis and Gwendolen M Carter (eds), *From Protest to Challenge: A Documentary History of African Politics in South Africa* (5 vols) (Hoover Institution Press, Stanford).

–Vol 1, Sheridan Johns, III (ed), *Protest and Hope – 1882–1934* (1972).

–Vol 2, Thomas Karis (ed), *Hope and Challenge – 1935–1952* (1973).

–Vol 3, Thomas Karis and Gail M Gerhart (eds) *Challenge and Violence – 1953–1964* (1977).

Thomas Karis and Gail M Gerhart (eds), *From Protest to Challenge: A Documentary History of African Politics, 1882–1990, vol 5, Nadir and Resurgence, 1964–1979* (UNISA Press, Pretoria, 1997).

Ronnie Kasrils, *Armed and Dangerous: From Undercover Struggle to Freedom* (Jonathan Ball, Johannesburg, 1998).

Ahmed Kathrada, *Memoirs* (Zebra Press, Cape Town, 2004).

Matthew Kentridge, *An Unofficial War: Inside the Conflict in Pietermaritzburg* (David Philip, Claremont, 1990).

Philip Ata Kgosana, *Lest We Forget: An Autobiography* (Skotaville Publishers, Johannesburg, 1988).

Bennie A Khoapa, 'The New Black', in BS Biko (ed), *Black Viewpoint* (Spro-cas Black Community Programmes, Durban, 1972).

Johann Kinghorn, 'Vormende Faktore', in J Kinghorn (ed.), *Die NG Kerk en Apartheid* (Macmillan South Africa, Johannesburg, 1986).

Koos Kombuis, *Seks en Drugs en Boeremusiek: Die Memoires van 'n Volksveraaier* (Human & Rousseau, Cape Town, 2000).

Leo Kuper, *Passive Resistance in South Africa* (Jonathan Cape, London, 1956).

Labour and Community Resources Project (LACOM), *Freedom from Below: The Struggle for Trade Unions in South Africa* (Skotaville Publishers, Braamfontein, 1989).

Riaan Labuschagne, *On South Africa's Secret Service: An Undercover Agent's Story* (Galago, Alberton, 2002).

Robert Lambert and Eddie Webster, 'The Re-emergence of Political Unionism in Contemporary South Africa?', in William Cobbett and Robin Cohen (eds), *Popular Struggles in South Africa* (James Currey, London, 1988).

JP Landman, Philip Nel and Anton van Niekerk (eds), *Wat Kom Na Apartheid?: Jong Afrikaners aan die Woord* (Southern Book Publishers, Johannesburg, 1988).

Patrick Laurence, *Death Squads: Apartheid's Secret Weapon* (Penguin, London, 1990).

Adrian Leftwich (ed), *South Africa: Economic Growth and Political Change* (Allison & Busby, London, 1974).

Mosiuoa Patrick (Terror) Lekota, *Prison Letters to a Daughter* (Taurus, Bramley, 1991).

Joseph Lelyveld, *Move Your Shadow: South Africa, Black and White* (Michael Joseph, London, 1986).

Anton Muziwakhe Lembede, *Freedom in Our Lifetime* (edited by Robert R Edgar and Luyanda ka Msumza) (Skotaville Publishers, Braamfontein, 1996).

Tony Leon, *On the Contrary: Leading the Opposition in a Democratic South Africa* (Jonathan Ball, Johannesburg, 2008).

Jon Lewis, 'Overview: The Registration Debate and Industrial Councils', in Johann Maree (ed), *The Independent Trade Unions – 1974–1984* (Ravan Press, Johannesburg, 1987).

Steven R Lewis, *The Economics of Apartheid* (Council on Foreign Relations Press, New York, 1990).

Merle Lipton, *Capitalism and Apartheid* (Gower, Aldershot, 1985).

Tom Lodge, 'The ANC and its Allies', in Andrew Reynolds (ed), *Election '94 SA: The Campaign, Results and Future Prospects* (David Philip, Cape Town, 1994).

Tom Lodge, *Mandela: A Critical Life* (Oxford University Press, Oxford, 2006).

Tom Lodge, 'Rebellion: The Turning of the Tide', in Tom Lodge and Bill Nasson, *All, Here, and Now: Black Politics in South Africa in the 1980s* (Ford Foundation/David Philip, Cape Town, 1991), p 129.

Tom Lodge and Bill Nasson, *All, Here, and Now: Black Politics in South Africa in the 1980s* (Ford Foundation/David Philip, Cape Town, 1991).

JA Loubser, *The Apartheid Bible: A Critical Review of Racial Theology in South Africa* (Maskew Miller Longman, Cape Town, 1987).

Bernhard Louw and Frans van Rensburg (eds), *Bestendige Binnevuur: Perspektiewe op Gerrit Viljoen* (Tafelberg, Cape Town, 1997).

AH Lückhoff, *Cottesloe* (Tafelberg, Cape Town, 1978).

Gerard Ludi, *Operation Q-018* (Nasionale Boekhandel, Cape Town, 1969).

Albert Luthuli, *Let My People Go: An Autobiography* (Collins, London, 1962).

Louis Luyt, *Walking Proud* (Don Nelson, Cape Town, 2003).

Princeton N Lyman, *Partner to History: The US Role in South Africa's Transition to Democracy* (United States Institute of Peace Press, Washington DC, 2002).

Enos J Mabuza, *Inyandza National Movement 1978–1990: A Collection of Speeches by Enos J Mabuza* (Barberton, 1990).

WM Macmillan, *Complex South Africa* (Faber & Faber, London, 1930).

Mac Maharaj (ed), *Reflections in Prison* (Zebra, Cape Town, 2000).

Charles Malan and Bartho Smit (eds), *Skrywer en Gemeenskap: Tien Jaar Afrikaanse Skrywersgilde* (HAUM, Pretoria, 1985).

DF Malan, *Afrikaner Volkseenheid en My Ervarings op die Pad Daarheen* (Nasionale Boekhandel, Cape Town, 1959).

Magnus Malan, *My Lewe Saam met die SA Weermag* (Protea Boekhuis, Pretoria, 2006).

Rian Malan, *My Traitor's Heart* (Viking, London, 1991).

Rian Malan and Denis Beckett, 'Was it revenge for murders by ANC comrades?', *Guardian Weekly*, 3–9 July 1992, reprinted in Jill Wentzel, *Liberal Slideaway* (South African Institute of Race Relations, Johannesburg, 1995).

EG Malherbe, *Never a Dull Moment* (Timmins Publishers, Cape Town, 1981).

Sebastian Mallaby, *After Apartheid* (Faber & Faber, London, 1992).

Nelson Mandela, *No Easy Walk to Freedom* (Heinemann, London, 1956).

Nelson Mandela, *Long Walk to Freedom: The Autobiography of Nelson Mandela* (Macdonald Purnell, Randburg, 1994).

Nelson Mandela, 'Clear the Obstacles and Confront the Enemy' and 'Whither the Black Consciousness Movement? An assessment', in Mac Maharaj (ed), *Reflections in Prison* (Zebra, Cape Town, 2000).

Nelson Mandela, 'Biko', in Kader Asmal, David Chidester and Wilmot James (eds), *Nelson Mandela: From Freedom to the Future – Tributes and Speeches* (Jonathan Ball, Johannesburg, 2003).

CW Manona, 'The impact of political conflict and violence on the youth of Grahamstown' in F van Zyl Slabbert *et al* (eds), *Youth in the New South Africa* (Human Sciences Research Council, Pretoria, 1994).

Hein Marais, *South Africa: Limits to Change: The Political Economy of Transformation* (University of Cape Town Press, Cape Town, 1998).

Gerhard Maré and Georgina Hamilton, *An Appetite for Power: Buthelezi's Inkatha and the Politics of 'Loyal Resistance'* (Ravan Press, Johannesburg, 1987).

Johann Maree (ed), *The Independent Trade Unions – 1974–1984* (Ravan Press, Johannesburg, 1987).

Johann Maree, 'The COSATU Participatory Democratic Tradition and South Africa's New Parliament: Are They Compatible?', *African Affairs*, vol 97, 1998.

Monique Marks, *Young Warriors: Youth Politics, Identity and Violence in South Africa* (University of the Witwatersrand Press, Johannesburg, 2001).

Harry Mashabela, *A People on the Boil: Reflections on Soweto* (Skotaville, Johannesburg, 1987).

AS Mathews, *Freedom, State Security and the Rule of Law: Dilemmas of the Apartheid Society* (Juta, Cape Town, 1986).

Nomavenda Mathiane, *Beyond the Headlines: Truths of Soweto Life* (Southern Book Publishers, Johannesburg, 1990).

R Mattes, 'The Road to Democracy', in Andrew Reynolds (ed), *Election '94: The Campaign, Results and Future Prospects* (David Philip, Claremont, 1994).

R Mattes, H Giliomee and W James, 'The Election in the Western Cape', in RW Johnson and Lawrence Schlemmer (eds), *Launching Democracy in South Africa: The First Open Election, April 1994* (Yale University Press, New Haven, 1996).

Frieda Matthews, *Remembrances* (Mayibuye Books, Bellville, 1995).

ZK Matthews, *Freedom for My People: The Autobiography of ZK Matthews* (Rex Collings, London, 1981).

Mau-Mauing the Media: New Censorship for the New South Africa (South African Institute of Race Relations, Johannesburg, 1991).

Philip Mayer, 'Class, Status, and Ethnicity as Perceived by Johannesburg Africans', in Leonard Thompson and Jeffrey Butler (eds), *Change in Contemporary South Africa* (University of California Press, Berkeley, 1975).

Thoko Mbanjwa (ed), *Apartheid: Hope or Despair for Blacks?* (Black Community Programmes, Durban, 1976).

Ismail Meer, *A Fortunate Man* (Zebra Press, Cape Town, 2002).

Kobus Meiring, *In Interesting Company* (privately published, Cape Town, 2004).

Albert Memmi, *The Colonizer and the Colonized* (Beacon Press, Boston, 1967).

Robert Menzies, *Afternoon Light: Some Memories of Men and Events* (Cassell, London, 1967).

Martin Meredith, *Nelson Mandela: A Biography* (Penguin, London, 1997).

Roelf Meyer, 'From Parliamentary Sovereignty to Constitutionality: The Democratization of South Africa, 1990 to 1994', in Penelope Andrews and Stephen Ellmann (eds), *The Post-Apartheid Constitutions: Perspectives on South Africa's Basic Law* (Witwatersrand University Press, Johannesburg, 2009).

Anthony Minnaar, ''Undisputed Kings': Warlordism in Natal', in Anthony Minnaar (ed), *Patterns of Violence: Case Studies of Conflict in Natal* (HSRC, Pretoria, 1992).

Rich Mkhondo, *Reporting South Africa* (James Currey, London, 1993).

Barrington Moore, *Social Origins of Dictatorship and Democracy: Lord and Peasant in the Making of the Modern World* (Allen Lane, London, 1969).

Robert Morrell (ed), *Changing Men in Southern Africa* (University of Natal Press, Pietermaritzburg, 2001).

Donald R Morris, *The Washing of the Spears: The Rise and Fall of the Zulu Nation* (Jonathan Cape, London, 1966).

Mike Morris, 'Unions and Industrial Councils: Why do Unions' Policies Change?', in Nicoli Nattrass and Elizabeth Ardington (eds), *The Political Economy of South Africa* (Oxford University Press, Cape Town, 1990).

Pauline Morris, *Soweto: A Review of Existing Conditions and Some Guidelines for Change* (Urban Foundation, Johannesburg, 1980).

A Mouton, *Voorloper: Die Lewe van Schalk Pienaar* (Tafelberg, Cape Town, 2002).

Es'kia Mphahlele, *Es'kia* (Kwela Books, Cape Town, 2002).

Mbuyiseni Oswald Mtshali (ed), *Give Us a Break: Diaries of a Group of Soweto Children* (Skotaville Press, Johannesburg, 1988).

Edwin S Munger (ed), *The Afrikaners* (Tafelberg, Cape Town, 1979).

Mzala (pseudonym), *Gatsha Buthelezi: Chief with a Double Agenda* (Zed Books, London, 1988).

Kumi Naidoo, 'Internal Resistance in South Africa: The Political Movement', in Shaun Johnson (ed.), *South Africa: No Turning Back* (Macmillan, Basingstoke, 1988).

Natives Land Commission: Minute addressed to the Hon. the Minister of Native Affairs by the Hon. Sir WH Beaumont (Government Printers, Cape Town, 1916).

Jill Nattrass and IG Duncan, *A Study of Employers' Attitudes Towards African Worker Representation* (Department of Economics, University of Natal, Durban, 1975).

Nicoli Nattrass and Elizabeth Ardington (eds), *The Political Economy of South Africa* (Oxford University Press, Cape Town, 1990).

Njabulo Ndebele, *Rediscovery of the Ordinary: Essays on South African Literature and Culture* (Congress of South African Writers, Johannesburg, 1991).

Sifiso Mxolisi Ndlovu, *The Soweto Uprisings: Counter-Memories of June 1976* (Ravan Press, Randburg, 1998).

National Party, *Grondwetlike Regering in 'n Deelnemende Demokrasie: Die Nasionale Party se Raamwerk vir 'n Nuwe Demokrasie in Suid-Afrika* (Federale Raad van die Nasionale Party, Pretoria, 1991).

Benyamin Neuberger, 'Federalism and Political Integration in Africa', in Daniel J Elazar (ed), *Federalism and Political Integration* (Turtledove Publishing, Ramat Gan, 1979) p 182.

Richard John Neuhaus, *Dispensations: The Future of South Africa as South Africans See it* (Eerdmans, Grand Rapids, 1986).

NGK, *Die verhaal van die Nederduitse Gereformeerde Kerk se Reis met Apartheid – 1960–1994* (Algemene Sinode, Wellington, 1997).

Isak Niehaus, with Eliazaar Mohala and Kathy Shokane, *Witchcraft, Power and Politics: Exploring the Occult in the South African Lowveld* (David Philip, Cape Town, 2001).

Louise Nieuwmeijer and Fanie Cloete (eds), *The Dynamics of Negotiation in South Africa* (HSRC, Pretoria, 1991).

Sisa Njikelana, 'The Unions and the Front: A Response to the General Workers' Union', in Johann Maree (ed), *The Independent Trade Unions – 1974–1984* (Ravan Press, Johannesburg, 1987).

Lewis Nkosi, *Home and Exile* (Longman, London, 1983).

Patrick Noonan, *They're Burning the Churches: The Final Dramatic Events that Scuttled Apartheid* (Jacana, Bellevue, 2003).

CA Norgaard, Advice to the United Nations Special Representative on the Entitlement of 16 persons to release as political prisoners under para 7 of the Namibian Settlement Proposal (1989) (unpublished).

André Odendaal, *Vukani Bantu: The Beginnings of Black Protest Politics in South Africa* (David Philip, Cape Town, 1984).

Michael O'Dowd, 'South Africa in the Light of the Stages of Economic Growth', in Adrian Leftwich (ed), *South Africa: Economic Growth and Political Change* (Allison and Busby, London, 1974).

Michael O'Dowd, *South Africa: The Growth Imperative* (Jonathan Ball, Johannesburg, 1991).

Michael O'Dowd, *Understanding South Africa* (British-South African Policy Trust, London, 1991).

Gerrit Olivier (ed), *Praat met die ANC* (Taurus, Johannesburg, 1985).

Johan Olivier, 'Causes of Ethnic Collective Action in the Pretoria-Witwatersrand-Vaal Triangle, 1970–1984', *South African Sociological Review*, vol 2, no 2, April 1990.

Padraig O'Malley, *Shades of Difference: Mac Maharaj and the Struggle for South Africa* (Viking Penguin, New York, 2007).

Barbara Oomen, *Chiefs in South Africa: Law, Power and Culture in the Post-Apartheid Era* (James Currey, Oxford, 2005).

Ope Brief, *Die Kerkbode*, 9 June 1984.

David and Marina Ottaway, *Afrocommunism* (Africana Publishing Co, New York, 1981).

Marina Ottaway, *South Africa: The Struggle for a New Order* (Brookings Institution, Washington DC, 1993).

Marina Ottaway, 'Liberation Movements and Transitions to Democracy: The Case of the ANC', *Journal of Modern African Studies*, vol 20, no 1, 1994.

Alan Paton, *Towards the Mountain: An Autobiography* (David Philip, Cape Town, 1980).

Alan Paton, *Journey Continued: An Autobiography* (David Philip, Cape Town, 1988).

Jacques Pauw, *Into the Heart of Darkness: Confessions of Apartheid's Assassins* (Jonathan Ball, Johannesburg, 1997).

AN Pelzer, *Die Afrikaner-Broederbond: Eerste Vyftig Jaar* (Tafelberg, Cape

Town, 1979).

AN Pelzer (ed), *Verwoerd Speaks: Speeches 1948–1966* (APB Publishers, Johannesburg, 1966).

SW Pienaar (ed), *Glo in u Volk: DF Malan as Redenaar* (Tafelberg, Cape Town, 1964).

SW Pienaar, *Getuie van groot tye* (Tafelberg, Cape Town, 1979).

André Pisani, *What Do We Think? A Survey of White Opinion on Foreign Policy Issues*, no 4 (South African Institute of International Affairs, Johannesburg, 1986).

N Barney Pityana, Mamphela Ramphele, Malusi Mpumlwana and Lindy Wilson (eds), *Bounds of Possibility: The Legacy of Steve Biko and Black Consciousness* (David Philip, Cape Town, 1991).

Sol Plaatje, *Native Life in South Africa,* second edition (King and Son, London, nd).

Laurine Platzky and Cheryl Walker, *The Surplus People: Forced Removals in South Africa* (Ravan Press, Johannesburg, 1985).

Benjamin Pogrund, *Sobukwe and Apartheid* (Jonathan Ball, Johannesburg, 1990).

Benjamin Pogrund, *War of Words: Memoir of a South African Journalist* (Seven Stories Press, New York, 2000).

Deborah Posel, *The Making of Apartheid – 1948–1961* (Clarendon Press, Oxford, 1991).

Brian Pottinger, *The Imperial Presidency: P.W. Botha – the first 10 years* (Southern Book Publishers, Johannesburg, 1988).

Daan Prinsloo, *Stem uit die Wildernis: 'n Biografie Oor Oud-pres PW Botha* (Vaandel-uitgewers, Mossel Bay, 1997).

Adam Przeworski, *Democracy and the Market: Political and Economic Reforms in Eastern Europe and Latin America* (Cambridge University Press, Cambridge, 1991).

Mamphela Ramphele, 'Government-Created Platforms' in Thoko Mbanjwa (ed), *Apartheid: Hope or Despair for Blacks?* (Black Community Programmes, Durban, 1976).

Mamphela Ramphele, 'Empowerment and Symbols of Hope: Black Consciousness and Community Development', in N Barney Pityana, Mamphela Ramphele, Malusi Mpumlwana and Lindy Wilson (eds), *Bounds of Possibility: The Legacy of Steve Biko and Black Consciousness* (David Philip, Cape Town, 1991).

Peter Randall (ed), *Anatomy of Apartheid* (Spro-cas publication no 1, Johannesburg, 1970).

Johannes Rantete, *The African National Congress and the Negotiated Settlement in South Africa* (JL van Schaik Publishers, Pretoria, 1998).

Johannes Rantete, *The Third Day of September: An Eyewitness Account of the Sebokeng Rebellion of 1984* (Ravan Press, Johannesburg, 1984).

Mervyn Rees and Chris Day, *Muldergate: The Story of the Info Scandal* (Macmillan, Johannesburg, 1980).

Gavin Relly, 'A Businessman's View', in Gideon Jacobs (ed), *South Africa: The Road Ahead* (Jonathan Ball, Johannesburg, 1986).

Robin Renwick, *Unconventional Diplomacy in Southern Africa* (Macmillan, London, 1997).

Report of the Carnegie Commission, 1932.

Report of the Commission Appointed to Inquire Into the Incident which occurred on 21 March 1985 at Uitenhage (Government Printer, Cape Town, RP74 – 1985).

Report of the Interdepartmental Committee on Social, Health and Economic Conditions of Urban Natives (Government Printer, Pretoria, 1942).

Report of the Native Economic Commission 1930–1932 (Government Printer, Pretoria, UG 22 – 1932).

Report of the Native Laws Commission 1946–48 (Government Printer, Pretoria, UG 28 – 1948).

Report of the South African Native Affairs Commission, 1903–5 (Government Printers, Cape Town, 1905).

Report of the Transvaal Labour Commission (Pretoria, 1903), evidence.

Report of the Transvaal Local Government Commission, 1921 (Stallard Commission) (Pretoria, 1922).

Report of the Truth and Reconciliation Commission, vol 3.

Andrew Reynolds (ed), *Election '94 SA: The Campaign, Results and Future Prospects* (David Philip, Cape Town, 1994).

Andrew Reynolds, 'The Results', in Andrew Reynolds (ed), *Election '94 SA: The Campaign, Results and Future Prospects* (David Philip, Cape Town, 1994).

Dirk Richard, *Moedswillig die Uwe* (Perskor, Johannesburg, 1985).

PJ Riekert, 'Black local government in the Republic of South Africa', in DJ van Vuuren, NE Wiehahn, JA Lombard and NJ Rhoodie (eds), *Change in South Africa* (Butterworths, Durban, 1983).

Alf Ries and Ebbe Dommisse, *Broedertwis: Die Verhaal van die 1982-skeuring in die Nasionale Party* (Tafelberg, Cape Town, 1982).

Geoffrey Robertson, *Crimes Against Humanity: The Struggle for Global Justice* (Penguin, London, 1999).

Howard Rogers, *Native Administration in the Union of South Africa*, second edition revised by PA Linington (Government Printer, Pretoria, 1949).

Richard Rosenthal, *Mission Improbable: A Piece of the South African Story* (David Philip, Cape Town, 1998).

Albie Sachs, *Perfectibility and Corruptibility: Preparing Ourselves for Power* (Inaugural Lecture, University of Cape Town, 1992).

Albie Sachs, *Affirmative Action and the New Constitution* (ANC, Johannesburg, nd).

JL Sadie, 'Was Professor Tomlinson Verwoerd se Slagoffer?', in *Rapport*, 3 March 1991.

JL Sadie, *The Fall and Rise of the Afrikaner in the South African Economy* (Stellenbosch University Annale, Stellenbosch, 2002/1).

Anthony Sampson, *Mandela: The Authorised Biography* (Jonathan Ball, Johannesburg, 1999).

Katharine Savage, 'Negotiating South Africa's New Constitution: An Overview of the Key Players in the Negotiation Process', in Penelope Andrews and Stephen Ellmann (eds), *The Post-Apartheid Constitutions: Perspectives on South Africa's Basic Law* (Witwatersrand University Press, Johannesburg, 2009).

Michael Savage, 'The Cost of Apartheid' (inaugural lecture, University of Cape Town, 1986).

Michael Savage, 'The Imposition of Pass Laws on the African Population in South Africa – 1916–1984', *African Affairs*, vol 85, 1986.

Lawrence Schlemmer, 'Factors Underlying Apartheid', in Peter Randall (ed), *Anatomy of Apartheid* (Spro-cas publication no 1, Johannesburg, 1970).

Lawrence Schlemmer, 'South Africa's National Party government', in Peter L Berger and Bobby Godsell (eds), *A Future South Africa: Visions, Strategies and Realities* (Human & Rousseau/Tafelberg, Pretoria, 1988).

Lawrence Schlemmer, 'Strategies for the Future', in Hermann Giliomee and Jannie Gagiano (eds), *The Elusive Search for Peace: South Africa – Israel – Northern Ireland* (Oxford University Press, Cape Town, 1990).

Lawrence Schlemmer, 'Liberalism in South Africa: the Challenges beyond Opposition', in Milton Shain (ed), *Opposing Voices: Liberalism and Opposition in South Africa Today* (Jonathan Ball, Johannesburg, 2006).

Lawrence Schlemmer and David Welsh, 'South Africa's Constitutional and Political Prospects', *Optima*, vol 30, no 4, 1982.

Ben Schoeman, *My Lewe in die Politiek* (Perskor, Johannesburg, 1978).

GD Scholtz, *Het die Afrikaanse Volk 'n Toekoms?* (Voortrekkerpers, Johannesburg, 1954).

GD Scholtz, *Dr Hendrick Frensch Verwoerd – 1901–1966*, 2 vols (Perskor, Johannesburg, 1974).

JJJ Scholtz (compiler), *Vegter en Hervormer: Grepe uit die Toesprake van PW Botha* (Tafelberg, Cape Town, 1988).

Leopold Scholtz, *Waarom die Boere die Oorlog Verloor Het* (Protea Boekhuis, Menlopark, 1999).

Robert Schrire (ed), *South Africa: Public Policy Perspectives* (Juta, Cape Town, 1982).

Lynda Schuster, *A Burning Hunger: One Family's Struggle Against Apartheid* (Jonathan Cape, London, 2004).

Jeremy Seekings, *Heroes or Villains? Youth Politics in the 1980s* (Ravan Press, Braamfontein, 1993).

Jeremy Seekings, *The UDF: A History of the United Democratic Front in South Africa, 1983–1991* (David Philip, Cape Town, 2000).

James Selfe, 'South Africa's National Management System', in Jacklyn Cock and Laurie Nathan (eds), *War and Society: The Militarisation of South Africa* (David Philip, Cape Town, 1989).

Milton Shain (ed), *Opposing Voices: Liberalism and Opposition in South Africa*

Today (Jonathan Ball, Johannesburg, 2006).

Khehla Shubane, 'Politics in Soweto' in Tom Lodge and Bill Nasson, *All, Here, and Now: Black Politics in South Africa in the 1980s* (Ford Foundation/David Philip, Cape Town, 1991).

Vladimir Shubin, *ANC: A View from Moscow* (Mayibuye Books, Bellville, 1997).

HJ and RE Simons, *Class and Colour in South Africa, 1850–1950* (Penguin, Harmondsworth, 1969).

Elinor Sisulu, *Walter and Albertina Sisulu: In Our Lifetime* (David Philip, Cape Town, 2002).

Walter Sisulu, 'We Shall Overcome!', in Mac Maharaj (ed), *Reflections in Prison* (Zebra, Cape Town, 2000).

F van Zyl Slabbert, 'Afrikaner Nationalism, White Politics, and Political Change in South Africa', in Leonard Thompson and Jeffrey Butler (eds), *Change in Contemporary South Africa* (University of California Press, Berkeley, 1975).

F van Zyl Slabbert, *The Last White Parliament* (Jonathan Ball, Johannesburg, 1985).

F van Zyl Slabbert, *The System and the Struggle: Reform, Revolt and Reaction in South Africa* (Jonathan Ball, Johannesburg, 1989).

F van Zyl Slabbert *et al* (eds), *Youth in the New South Africa* (Human Sciences Research Council, Pretoria, 1994).

Gillian Slovo, *Every Secret Thing: My Family, My Country* (Little Brown, London, 1997).

Joe Slovo, 'Negotiations: What room for compromise?', *African Communist*, third quarter, 1992.

Joe Slovo, 'The Negotiations Victory: A Political Overview', *African Communist*, fourth quarter, 1993.

Joe Slovo, *Slovo: The Unfinished Autobiography* (Ravan Press, Randburg, 1995).

Dan Smith, *The Atlas of War and Peace* (Earthscan Publications, London, 2003).

Ian Smith, *Bitter Harvest: The Great Betrayal* (Jonathan Ball, Johannesburg, 2001).

Nico J Smith, FE O'Brien Geldenhuys, Piet Meiring (compilers), *Storm-Kompas* (Tafelberg, Cape Town, 1981).

JC Smuts, *A Century of Wrong* (Review of Reviews, London, 1900).

JC Smuts, 'Problems in South Africa', *Journal of the African Society*, vol 16, 1917.

JC Smuts, *The Basis of Trusteeship* (South African Institute of Race Relations, Johannesburg, 1942).

South African Catholic Bishops' Conference Report on Police Conduct during Township Protests, August–November 1984 (Pretoria, 1984).

South African Communists Speak: Documents from the History of the South African Communist Party (Inkululeko Publications, London, 1981).

South African Institute of International Affairs, *What Do We Think? A Survey of White Opinion on Foreign Policy Issues* (South African Institute of

International Affairs, Johannesburg, 1988).

South African Institute of Race Relations, 'South Africa in Travail: The disturbances of 1976–7: Evidence presented by the SAIRR to the Cillié Commission' (SAIRR, Johannesburg, 1978).

South African Institute of Race Relations, *Survey of Race Relations 1968, 1970–72, 1975–78, 1980–86, 1987/88, 1988/89, 1991/92, 1992/93, 1993/94, 1994/95, 2000/01.*

South African Law Commission, Project 58, *Group and Human Rights – Interim Report* (Pretoria, 1991).

South African Law Commission, *Report on Constitutional Models* (Project 77, Pretoria, 1991).

Marion Sparg, Jenny Schreiner and Gwen Ansell (eds), *Comrade Jack: The Political Lectures and Diary of Jack Simons, Novo Catengue* (STC Publishers, New Doornfontein, 2001).

Allister Sparks, *The Mind of South Africa: The Story of the Rise and Fall of Apartheid* (William Heinemann, London, 1990).

Allister Sparks, *Tomorrow is Another Country: The Inside Story of South Africa's Negotiated Revolution* (Struik, Sandton, 1994).

Richard Spitz, with Matthew Chaskalson, *The Politics of Transition: A Hidden History of South Africa's Negotiated Settlement* (Witwatersrand University Press, Johannesburg, 2000).

HD Stadler (ed), *The Other Side of the Story: A True Perspective* (Contact Publishers, Pretoria, 1997).

Dave Steward, 'The Steyn Investigation', *Concensus*, second quarter, 2006.

Jan Steyn, *Managing Change in South Africa* (Tafelberg/Human & Rousseau, 1990).

JC Steyn, *Penvegter: Piet Cillié van Die Burger* (Tafelberg, Cape Town, 2002).

JC Steyn, *Trouwe Afrikaners* (Tafelberg, Cape Town, 1987).

JC Steyn, *Van Wyk Louw: 'n Lewensverhaal*, vol 2 (Tafelberg, Cape Town, 1998).

Gill Straker, *Faces in the Revolution: The Psychological Effects of Violence on Township Youth in South Africa* (David Philip, Cape Town, 1992).

Aelred Stubbs (ed), *Steve Biko: I Write What I Like* (Heinemann International, Oxford, 1987).

Newell M Stultz, *The Nationalists in Opposition 1934–1948* (Human & Rousseau, Cape Town, 1974).

Clem Sunter, *The World and South Africa in the 1990s* (Human & Rousseau, Cape Town, 1987).

Clem Sunter, *The High Road: Where Are We Now?* (Human & Rousseau, 1996).

Raymond Suttner, *The ANC Underground in South Africa to 1976* (Jacana, Johannesburg, 2008).

Helen Suzman, *In No Uncertain Terms: Memoirs* (Jonathan Ball, Johannesburg, 1993).

Mark Swilling, 'Stayaways, Urban Protest and the State' in *South African Review*, vol 3 (Ravan Press, Johannesburg, 1986).

Mark Swilling, 'The United Democratic Front and Township Revolt' in William Cobbett and Robin Cohen (eds), *Popular Struggles in South Africa* (James Currey, London, 1988).

Mark Swilling and Mark Phillips, 'State Power in the 1980s: From "Total Strategy" to "Counter-Revolutionary Warfare"', in Jacklyn Cock and Laurie Nathan (eds), *War and Society: The Militarisation of South Africa* (David Philip, Cape Town, 1989).

Adelaide Tambo (compiler), *Preparing for Power: Oliver Tambo Speaks* (Heinemann, London, 1987).

CM Tatz, *Shadow and Substance in South Africa: A Study in Land and Franchise Policies Affecting Africans, 1910–1960* (University of Natal Press, Pietermaritzburg 1962).

Ben Temkin, *Buthelezi: A Biography* (Frank Cass, London, 2003).

HB Thom, *Dr DF Malan en Koalisie* (Tafelberg, Cape Town, 1988).

Leonard Thompson, *The Cape Coloured Franchise* (South African Institute of Race Relations, Johannesburg, 1949).

Leonard Thompson and Jeffrey Butler (eds), *Change in Contemporary South Africa* (University of California Press, Berkeley, 1975).

AP Treurnicht, *Credo van 'n Afrikaner* (Tafelberg, Cape Town, 1975).

Ben Turok, *Nothing But the Truth: Behind the ANC's Struggle Politics* (Jonathan Ball, Johannesburg, 2003).

Mwezi Twala and Ed Bernard, *Mbokodo: Inside MK – Mwezi Twala: A Soldier's Story* (Jonathan Ball, Johannesburg, 1994).

Mark A Uhlig, 'The African National Congress' in Mark Uhlig (ed), *Apartheid in Crisis* (Penguin, Harmondsworth, 1986).

Pieter-Dirk Uys, *Elections and Erections: A Memoir of Fear and Fun* (Zebra Press, Cape Town, 2002).

CM van den Heever, *Generaal JBM Hertzog* (AP Boekhandel, Johannesburg, 1948).

CN van der Merwe, *Breaking Barriers: Stereotypes and the Changing of Values in Afrikaans Writing 1875–1990* (Editions Rodopi BV, Amsterdam, 1994).

Hendrik W van der Merwe (ed), *Identiteit en Verandering: Sewe Opstelle oor die Afrikaner Vandag* (Tafelberg, Cape Town, 1975).

Hendrik W van der Merwe and David Welsh (eds), *Student Perspectives on South Africa* (David Philip, Cape Town, 1972).

HW van der Merwe, *Peacemaking in South Africa: A Life in Conflict Resolution* (Tafelberg, Cape Town, 2000).

HW van der Merwe, MJ Ashley, NCJ Charton and BJ Huber, *White South African Elites: A Study of Incumbents of Top Positions in the Republic of South Africa* (Juta, Cape Town, 1974).

Johan van der Merwe, 'Law and Order: The Story of a Former Commissioner of Police', in Don Foster, Paul Haupt and Marésa de Beer (eds), *The Theatre of Violence: Narratives of Protagonists in the South African Conflict* (HSRC Press, Cape Town, 2005).

Stoffel van der Merwe, MP, *... And what about the Black People?* (Federal

Information Service of the National Party, 1985).

RE van der Ross, *The Rise and Decline of Apartheid: A Study of Political Movements among the Coloured People of South Africa, 1880–1985* (Tafelberg, Cape Town, 1986).

Hennie van Deventer, *Kroniek van 'n Koerantman* (Tarlehoet BK, Welgemoed, 1998).

Phillip van Niekerk, 'The Trade Union Movement in the Politics of Resistance in South Africa', in Shaun Johnson (ed), *South Africa: No Turning Back* (Macmillan, Basingstoke, 1988).

Rykie van Reenen, *Op die Randakker* (Tafelberg, Cape Town, 1980).

Johann van Rooyen, *Hard Right: The New White Power in South Africa* (IB Taurus, London, 1994).

Johann van Rooyen, 'The White Right' in Andrew Reynolds (ed), *Election '94 SA: The Campaign, Results and Future Prospects* (David Philip, Cape Town, 1994).

DJ van Vuuren, NE Wiehahn, JA Lombard and NJ Rhoodie (eds), *Change in South Africa* (Butterworths, Durban, 1983).

At van Wyk, *The Birth of a New Afrikaner* (Human & Rousseau, Cape Town, 1991).

NP van Wyk Louw, *Liberale Nasionalisme* (Nasionale Boekhandel, Johannesburg, 1958).

NP van Wyk Louw, *Gedagtes Vir Ons Tyd* (Tafelberg, Cape Town, 1988).

Verslag van die Kommissie van Ondersoek na Aangeleenthede rakende die Kleurlingbevolkingsgroep (Government Printer, Pretoria, 1976).

Verslag van die Kommissie van Ondersoek oor die Oproer in Soweto en Elders van 16 Junie 1976 tot 28 Februarie 1977 (Cillié Commission) (Government Printer, Pretoria, 1979) vol 1.

Randolph Vigne, *Liberals against Apartheid: A History of the Liberal Party of South Africa 1953–68*, (Macmillan, Basingstoke, 1997).

Absolom Vilakazi, *Zulu Transformations: A Study of the Dynamics of Social Change* (University of Natal Press, Pietermaritzburg, 1962).

Gerrit Viljoen, *Ideaal en Werklikheid: Rekenskap deur 'n Afrikaner* (Tafelberg, Cape Town, 1978).

Patti Waldmeir, *The Anatomy of a Miracle: The End of Apartheid and the Birth of the New South Africa* (Penguin, London, 1997).

Peter Walshe, *The Rise of African Nationalism in South Africa: The African National Congress 1912–1952* (C Hurst, London, 1972).

Andreas Wassenaar, *Assault on Private Enterprise: The Freeway to Communism* (Tafelberg, Cape Town, 1977).

Eddie Webster, 'The Rise of Social-movement Unionism: The Two Faces of the Black Trade Union Movement in South Africa' in Philip Frankel, Noam Pines and Mark Swilling (eds), *State, Resistance and Change in South Africa* (Southern Book Publishers, Johannesburg, 1988).

David Welsh, *The Roots of Segregation: Native Policy in Natal (1845–1910)* (Oxford University Press, Cape Town, 1971).

David Welsh, 'The Growth of Towns', in Monica Wilson and Leonard Thompson (eds), *Oxford History of South Africa*, vol 2 (Clarendon Press, Oxford, 1971).

David Welsh, 'The Policies of Control: Blacks in the Common Area', in Robert Schrire (ed), *South Africa: Public Policy Perspectives* (Juta, Cape Town, 1982).

David Welsh, 'Politics and Business', *Optima*, vol 36, no 3, 1988.

David Welsh, *Whither South Africa?* (University of Port Elizabeth, 1988).

David Welsh, 'Federalism and the Problem of South Africa', in Murray Forsyth (ed), *Federalism and Nationalism* (Leicester University Press, Leicester, 1989).

David Welsh, 'Federalism and South Africa: The Future is Not Yet Written', in Steven Friedman and Richard Humphries (eds), *Federalism and Its Foes* (Centre for Policy Studies, Johannesburg, 1993).

David Welsh, 'The Provincial Boundary Demarcation Process', in Bertus de Villiers (ed), *The Birth of a Constitution* (Juta, Kenwyn, 1994).

David Welsh, 'Right-Wing Terror in South Africa', *Terrorism and Political Violence*, vol 7, no 1, 1995.

Jill Wentzel, *Liberal Slideaway* (South African Institute of Race Relations, Johannesburg, 1995).

PL Wickens, *The Industrial and Commercial Workers' Union of South Africa* (Oxford University Press, Cape Town, 1978).

The (Wiehahn) Commission into Labour Legislation, *The Complete Wiehahn Report: Parts 1-6* (Lex Patria Publishers, Johannesburg, 1982).

NE Wiehahn, 'Industrial relations in South Africa – A Changing Scene', in DJ van Vuuren, NE Wiehahn, JA Lombard and NJ Rhoodie (eds), *Change in South Africa* (Butterworths, Durban, 1983).

Ivor Wilkins and Hans Strydom, *The Super Afrikaners: Inside the Afrikaner Broederbond* (Jonathan Ball, Johannesburg, 1978).

Brian Willan, *Sol Plaatje: A Biography* (Ravan Press, Johannesburg, 1984).

Thokozani Xaba, 'Masculinity and its Malcontents: The Confrontation between "Struggle Masculinity" and "Post-Struggle Masculinity" (1990–1997)' in Robert Morrell (ed), *Changing Men in Southern Africa* (University of Natal Press, Pietermaritzburg, 2001).

I William Zartman, 'Prenegotiation: Phases and Functions', *International Journal*, vol XLIV, 1989.

Index